GLEIM®

2017 CIA REVIEW

PART 3: INTERNAL AUDIT KNOWLEDGE ELEMENTS

by

Irvin N. Gleim, Ph.D., CPA, CIA, CMA, CFM

Gleim Publications, Inc.
P.O. Box 12848
University Station
Gainesville, Florida 32604
(800) 874-5346
(352) 375-0772
Fax: (352) 375-6940
Internet: www.gleim.com
Email: admin@gleim.com

For updates to the first printing of the 2017 edition of *CIA Review: Part 3*

Go To: www.gleim.com/updates

Or: Email update@gleim.com with **CIA 3 2017** in the subject line. You will receive our current update as a reply.

Updates are available until the next edition is published.

ISSN: 2332-0559

ISBN: 978-1-61854-040-9 *CIA Review: Part 1*
ISBN: 978-1-61854-041-6 *CIA Review: Part 2*
ISBN: 978-1-61854-042-3 *CIA Review: Part 3*
ISBN: 978-1-61854-047-8 *How to Pass the CIA Exam: A System for Success*

ACKNOWLEDGMENTS FOR PART 3

The author is grateful for permission to reproduce the following materials copyrighted by The Institute of Internal Auditors: Certified Internal Auditor Examination Questions and Suggested Solutions (copyright © 1980-2015), excerpts from *Sawyer's Internal Auditing* (5th and 6th editions), parts of the 2014 *Certification Candidate Handbook*, The IIA Code of Ethics, *International Standards for the Professional Practice of Internal Auditing*, Practice Advisories, and parts of Practice Guides.

CIA® is a Registered Trademark of The Institute of Internal Auditors, Inc. All rights reserved.

Environmental Statement -- This book is printed on recyclable, environmentally friendly groundwood paper, sourced from certified sustainable forests and produced either TCF (totally chlorine-free) or ECF (elementally chlorine-free).

ABOUT THE AUTHOR

Irvin N. Gleim is Professor Emeritus in the Fisher School of Accounting at the University of Florida and is a member of the American Accounting Association, Academy of Legal Studies in Business, American Institute of Certified Public Accountants, Association of Government Accountants, Florida Institute of Certified Public Accountants, The Institute of Internal Auditors, and the Institute of Management Accountants. He has had articles published in the *Journal of Accountancy*, *The Accounting Review*, and *The American Business Law Journal* and is author/coauthor of numerous accounting books, aviation books, and CPE courses.

REVIEWERS AND CONTRIBUTORS

Garrett W. Gleim, B.S., CPA (not in public practice), received a Bachelor of Science degree from The Wharton School at the University of Pennsylvania. Mr. Gleim coordinated the production staff, reviewed the manuscript, and provided production assistance throughout the project.

Grady M. Irwin, J.D., is a graduate of the University of Florida College of Law, and he has taught in the University of Florida College of Business. Mr. Irwin provided substantial editorial assistance throughout the project.

Michael Kustanovich, M.A., CPA, is a graduate of Ben-Gurion University of the Negev in Israel. He is a Lecturer of Accountancy in the Department of Accountancy at the University of Illinois at Urbana-Champaign. He has worked in the audit departments of KPMG and PWC and as a financial accounting lecturer in the Department of Economics of Ben-Gurion University of the Negev. Mr. Kustanovich provided substantial editorial assistance throughout the project.

Lawrence Lipp, J.D., CPA (Registered), is a graduate from the Levin College of Law and the Fisher School of Accounting at the University of Florida. Mr. Lipp provided substantial editorial assistance throughout the project.

Dr. Steven A. Solieri, CPA, CMA, CIA, CISA, CITP, CFF, CRISC, is an Assistant Professor at Queens College in Flushing, New York, and is a Founding Member in the Firm of Solieri & Solieri, CPAs, PLLC, New Hyde Park, NY, where he currently practices. Dr. Solieri earned his Ph.D. from Binghamton University and holds four Masters from the University of Michigan, Pace University, Kettering University, and Binghamton University. Dr. Solieri helped develop the instructor materials to be used in conjunction with this text.

A PERSONAL THANKS

This manual would not have been possible without the extraordinary effort and dedication of Julie Cutlip, Blaine Hatton, Kelsey Olson, Teresa Soard, Justin Stephenson, Joanne Strong, and Elmer Tucker, who typed the entire manuscript and all revisions and drafted and laid out the diagrams, illustrations, and cover for this book.

The authors also appreciate the production and editorial assistance of Jacob Bennett, Melody Dalton, Jessica Felkins, Jim Harvin, Kristen Hennen, Katie Larson, Diana León, Jake Pettifor, Shane Rapp, Drew Sheppard, and Martha Willis.

The authors also appreciate the critical reading assistance of Brett Babir, Brian Darby, Solomon Gonite, Josh Lehr, Melissa Leonard, Monica Metz, Sunny Shang, Daniel Sinclair, Tingwei Su, Diana Weng, Madison Willis, and Josie Zhao.

The authors also appreciate the video production expertise of Matthew Church, Rich Hibner, and Rebecca Pope, who helped produce and edit our Gleim Instruct Video Series.

Finally, we appreciate the encouragement, support, and tolerance of our families throughout this project.

TABLE OF CONTENTS

DETAILED TABLE OF CONTENTS

PREFACE

The purpose of this book is to help **you** prepare to pass Part 3 of the CIA exam. Our overriding consideration is to provide an inexpensive, effective, and easy-to-use study program. This book

1. Explains how to optimize your grade by focusing on Part 3 of the CIA exam.

2. Defines the subject matter tested on Part 3 of the CIA exam.

3. Outlines all of the subject matter tested on Part 3 in 20 easy-to-use-and-complete study units, including all relevant authoritative pronouncements.

4. Presents multiple-choice questions from past CIA examinations to prepare you for questions in future CIA exams. Our answer explanations are presented to the immediate right of each question for your convenience. Use a piece of paper to cover our explanations as you study the questions.

5. Suggests exam-taking and question-answering techniques to help you maximize your exam score.

The outline format, the spacing, and the question-and-answer formats in this book are designed to facilitate readability, learning, understanding, and success on the CIA exam. Our most successful candidates use the Gleim Premium CIA Review System*, which includes expertly authored books, the Gleim Access Until You Pass guarantee, and the Gleim Instruct Video Series. Students who prefer to study in a group setting may attend Gleim Professor-Led Reviews, which combine the Gleim Review System with the coordination and feedback of a professor.

To maximize the efficiency and effectiveness of your CIA review program, augment your studying with *How to Pass the CIA Exam: A System for Success*. This booklet has been carefully written and organized to provide important information to assist you in passing the CIA examination.

Thank you for your interest in our materials. We deeply appreciate the comments and suggestions we have received from thousands of CIA, CMA, CPA, and EA candidates and accounting students and faculty during the past 5 decades.

If you use Gleim materials, we want YOUR feedback immediately after the exam upon receipt of your exam scores. The CIA exam is NONDISCLOSED, and you must maintain the confidentiality and agree not to divulge the nature or content of any CIA question or answer under any circumstances. We ask only for information about our materials, i.e., the topics that need to be added, expanded, etc.

Please go to www.gleim.com/feedbackCIA3 to share your suggestions on how we can improve this edition.

Good Luck on the Exam,

Irvin N. Gleim

May 2016

PREPARING FOR AND TAKING THE CIA EXAM

READ *HOW TO PASS THE CIA EXAM: A SYSTEM FOR SUCCESS*

Scan the Gleim *How to Pass the CIA Exam: A System for Success* booklet and note where to revisit later in your studying process to obtain a deeper understanding of the CIA exam. This booklet is included with your package of shippable items or is available at www.gleim.com/PassCIA.

How to Pass the CIA Exam: A System for Success has six study units:

Study Unit 1: The CIA Examination: An Overview and Preparation Introduction
Study Unit 2: CIA Exam Syllabus
Study Unit 3: Content Preparation, Test Administration, and Performance Grading
Study Unit 4: Multiple-Choice Questions
Study Unit 5: Preparing to Pass the CIA Exam
Study Unit 6: How to Take the CIA Exam

OVERVIEW OF THE CIA EXAMINATION

The total exam is 6.5 hours of testing (including 5 minutes per part for a survey). It is divided into three parts, as follows:

CIA Exam (3-Part)			
Part	Title	Exam Length	Number of Questions
1	Internal Audit Basics	2.5 hrs	125 multiple-choice
2	Internal Audit Practice	2 hrs	100 multiple-choice
3	Internal Audit Knowledge Elements	2 hrs	100 multiple-choice

All CIA questions are multiple-choice. The exam is offered continually throughout the year. The CIA exam is computerized to facilitate easier and more convenient testing. Pearson VUE, the testing company that The IIA contracts to proctor the exams, has hundreds of testing centers worldwide. The online components of Gleim CIA Review provide exact exam emulations of the Pearson VUE computer screens and procedures to prepare you to pass.

SUBJECT MATTER FOR PART 3

Below, we have provided The IIA's abbreviated CIA Exam Syllabus for Part 3. The percentage coverage of each topic is indicated to its right. The IIA provides a range of % coverage, but for simplicity Gleim provides the average of that range. We adjust the content of our materials to any changes in The IIA's CIA Exam Syllabus.

Part 3: Internal Audit Knowledge Elements

I.	Governance / Business Ethics	10%
II.	Risk Management	15%
III.	Organizational Structure/Business Processes and Risks	20%
IV.	Communication	7.5%
V.	Management / Leadership Principles	15%
VI.	IT / Business Continuity	20%
VII.	Financial Management	20%
VIII.	Global Business Environment	5%

Appendix A contains the CIA Exam Syllabus in its entirety as well as cross-references to the subunits in our text where topics are covered. Remember that we have studied and restudied the syllabus in developing our CIA Review materials. Accordingly, you do not need to spend time with Appendix A. Rather, it should give you confidence that Gleim CIA Review is the best review source available to help you PASS the CIA exam.

NONDISCLOSED EXAM

As part of The IIA's nondisclosure policy and to prove each candidate's willingness to adhere to this policy, a confidentiality and nondisclosure statement must be accepted by each candidate before each part is taken. This statement is reproduced here to remind all CIA candidates about The IIA's strict policy of nondisclosure, which Gleim consistently supports and upholds.

> *This exam is confidential and is protected by law. It is made available to you, the examinee, solely for the purpose of becoming certified. You are expressly prohibited from disclosing, publishing, reproducing, or transmitting this exam, in whole or in part, in any form or by any means, verbal or written, electronic or mechanical, for any purpose, without the prior written permission of The Institute of Internal Auditors (IIA).*

> *In the event of any actual or anticipated breach by you of the above, you acknowledge that The IIA will incur significant and irreparable damage for each such breach that The IIA has no adequate remedy at law for such breach. You further acknowledge that such breach may result in your certification being revoked, disqualification as a candidate for future certification, and suspension or revocation of membership privileges at The IIA's discretion.*

> *If you do not accept the exam non-disclosure agreement, your exam will be terminated. If this occurs, your registration will be voided, you will forfeit your exam registration fee, and you will be required to register and pay for that exam again in order to sit for it in the future.*

THE IIA'S REQUIREMENTS FOR CIA DESIGNATIONS

The CIA designation is granted only by The IIA. Candidates must complete the following steps to become a CIA®:

1. Complete the appropriate certification application form online and register for the part(s) you are going to take. The *How to Pass the CIA Exam: A System for Success* booklet contains concise instructions on the application and registration process and a useful worksheet to help you keep track of your process and organize what you need for exam day.

2. Pass all three parts of the CIA exam within 4 years of application approval.

3. Fulfill or expect to fulfill the education and experience requirements (see *How to Pass the CIA Exam: A System for Success*).

4. Provide a character reference proving you are of good moral character.

5. Comply with The IIA's Code of Ethics.

ELIGIBILITY PERIOD

Credits for parts passed can be retained as long as the requirements are fulfilled. However, candidates must complete the program certification process within 4 years of application approval. Candidates should note that this time period begins with application approval and not when they pass the first part. If a candidate has not completed the certification process within 4 years, all fees and exam parts will be forfeited.

Candidates who have not successfully completed their exam(s), or who have been accepted into the program but have not taken their exam(s), have the opportunity to extend their program eligibility by 12 months. To take advantage of The IIA's one-time Certification Candidate Program Extension, candidates must pay a set fee per applicant and apply through the Candidate Management System.

MAINTAINING YOUR CIA DESIGNATION

After certification, CIAs are required to maintain and update their knowledge and skills. Practicing CIAs must complete and report 40 hours of Continuing Professional Education (CPE) every year. The reporting deadline is December 31. Complete your CPE Reporting Form through the online Certification Candidate Management System. Nonmembers must submit a US $100 processing fee with their report. Contact Gleim for all of your CPE needs at www.gleim.com/cpe.

HOW TO USE THE GLEIM REVIEW SYSTEM

To ensure that you are using your time effectively, we have formulated a three-step process that includes all components (book, CIA Test Prep, Audio Reviews, and Gleim Online) together and should be applied to each study unit.

Step 1: Diagnostic

a. Multiple-Choice Quiz #1 (20 minutes, plus 10 minutes for review) – Complete Multiple-Choice Quiz #1 in 20 minutes. This is a diagnostic quiz, so it is expected that your scores will be lower.

   1) Immediately following the quiz, review the questions you flagged and/or answered incorrectly. For each question, analyze and understand why you flagged it or answered it incorrectly. This step is essential to identifying your weak areas. "Learning from Your Mistakes" on page 7 has tips on how to determine why you missed the questions you missed.

Step 2: Comprehension

a. Audiovisual Presentation (30 minutes) – This presentation provides an overview of the study unit. The Gleim CIA Audio Lectures can be substituted when you are on the go!

b. Gleim Instruct CIA Video Series (30-90 minutes) – These videos are for candidates who prefer more of a live instruction model rather than the slide show style of the audio visual presentation.

c. Focus Questions (45 minutes) – Complete the Focus Questions and receive immediate feedback.

d. Knowledge Transfer Outline (60-80 minutes) – Study the Knowledge Transfer Outline, particularly the troublesome areas identified from your Multiple-Choice Quiz #1 in Step 1. The Knowledge Transfer Outlines can be studied either online or in the book.

e. Multiple-Choice Quiz #2 (20 minutes, plus 10 minutes for review) – Complete Multiple-Choice Quiz #2.

    1) Immediately following the quiz, review the questions you flagged and/or answered incorrectly. This step is an essential learning activity. "Learning from Your Mistakes" on page 7 has tips on how to determine why you missed the questions you missed.

Step 3: Application

a. CIA Test Prep (40 minutes, plus 20 minutes for review) – Complete two 20-question quizzes in the CIA Test Prep using the Practice Exam feature. Spend 20 minutes taking each quiz and then spend about 10 minutes reviewing each quiz as needed.

Additional Assistance

a. Gleim Instruct Supplemental Videos (watch as needed) – Gleim has made available to everyone a special Gleim Instruct video explaining how to best approach the types of multiple-choice questions candidates have said are the most difficult.

b. Core Concepts – These consolidated documents provide overviews of the key points that serve as a foundation for learning the material in each study unit.

Final Review

a. CIA Exam Rehearsal (2 hours/120 minutes) – Take the Exam Rehearsal at the beginning of your final review stage. It contains 100 multiple-choice questions, just like the CIA exam. This will help you identify where you should focus during the remainder of your final review.

b. CIA Test Prep (10-20 hours) – Use Test Prep to focus on your weak areas identified from your Exam Rehearsal. Also, be sure to do a cumulative review to refresh yourself with topics you learned at the beginning of your studies. View your performance chart to make sure you are scoring 75% or higher.

The times mentioned above are recommendations based on prior candidate feedback and how long you will have to answer questions on the actual exam. Each candidate's time spent in any area will vary depending on proficiency and familiarity with the subject matter. Remember to set up your customized study plan through the Gleim Study Planner found in Gleim CIA Review.

GLEIM KNOWLEDGE TRANSFER OUTLINES

This edition of the Gleim *CIA Review* books has the following features to make studying easier:

1. **Guidance Designations:** In an effort to help CIA candidates better grasp The IIA authoritative literature, we have come up with visual indicators to help candidates easily identify each type of guidance.

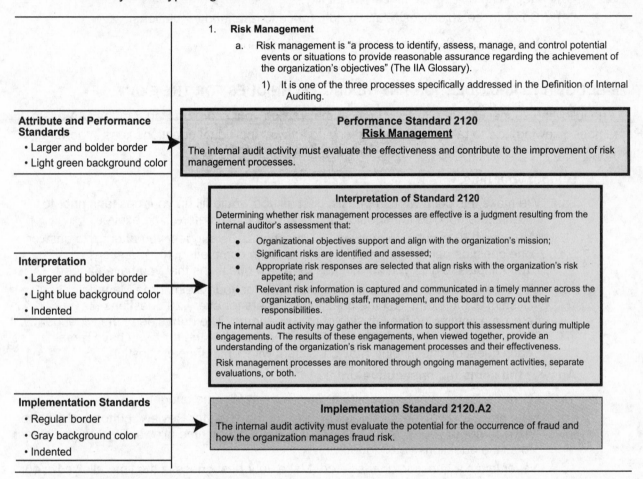

Attribute and Performance Standards
- Larger and bolder border
- Light green background color

Interpretation
- Larger and bolder border
- Light blue background color
- Indented

Implementation Standards
- Regular border
- Gray background color
- Indented

1. **Risk Management**
   a. Risk management is "a process to identify, assess, manage, and control potential events or situations to provide reasonable assurance regarding the achievement of the organization's objectives" (The IIA Glossary).
      1) It is one of the three processes specifically addressed in the Definition of Internal Auditing.

> **Performance Standard 2120**
> **Risk Management**
> The internal audit activity must evaluate the effectiveness and contribute to the improvement of risk management processes.

> **Interpretation of Standard 2120**
> Determining whether risk management processes are effective is a judgment resulting from the internal auditor's assessment that:
> - Organizational objectives support and align with the organization's mission;
> - Significant risks are identified and assessed;
> - Appropriate risk responses are selected that align risks with the organization's risk appetite; and
> - Relevant risk information is captured and communicated in a timely manner across the organization, enabling staff, management, and the board to carry out their responsibilities.
>
> The internal audit activity may gather the information to support this assessment during multiple engagements. The results of these engagements, when viewed together, provide an understanding of the organization's risk management processes and their effectiveness.
>
> Risk management processes are monitored through ongoing management activities, separate evaluations, or both.

> **Implementation Standard 2120.A2**
> The internal audit activity must evaluate the potential for the occurrence of fraud and how the organization manages fraud risk.

2. **Examples:** We use illustrative examples, set off in shaded, bordered boxes, to make the concepts more relatable.

> ### EXAMPLE of Depreciable Base Calculation
>
> At the beginning of Year 1, a manufacturer paid US $270,000 for a new machine.
>
> Depreciable base = US $270,000 − $20,000 = US $250,000
>
> The entity estimates that, at the end of the machine's 5-year useful life, it will be able to sell the machine for US $20,000.

3. **Gleim Success Tips:** These tips supplement the core exam material by suggesting how certain topics might be presented on the exam or how you should prepare for an issue.

 Candidates for the CIA exam should understand that an organization uses structural analysis to choose the industries in which it will compete and then determines what competitive strategies are appropriate in those industries.

4.   **Memory Aids:** We offer mnemonic devices to help you remember important concepts.

The following four categories of objectives apply to all entities:

1)   <u>S</u>trategic objectives are consistent with and support the entity's mission.
2)   <u>O</u>perations objectives address effectiveness and efficiency.
3)   <u>R</u>eporting objectives concern reliability.
4)   <u>C</u>ompliance objectives relate to adherence to laws and regulations.

Memory aid: <u>S</u>tudying <u>O</u>bsessively <u>R</u>eally <u>C</u>ounts

TIME-BUDGETING AND QUESTION-ANSWERING TECHNIQUES FOR THE EXAM

The following suggestions are to assist you in maximizing your score on Part 3 of the CIA exam. Remember, knowing how to take the exam and how to answer individual questions is as important as studying/reviewing the subject matter tested on the exam.

1.   **Budget your time.**

a.   We make this point with emphasis. Just as you would fill up your gas tank prior to reaching empty, so too should you finish your exam before time expires.

b.   You have 120 minutes to answer 100 questions. We suggest you attempt to answer one question per minute, which would result in completing 100 questions in 100 minutes to give you 20 minutes to review questions that you have flagged.

c.   Use the wipeboard provided by Pearson VUE for your Gleim Time Management System at the exam. List the question numbers for every 20 questions (i.e., 1, 21, 41, etc.) in a column on the left side of the wipeboard. The right side of the wipeboard will have your start time at the top and allows you to fill in the time you have remaining at each question checkpoint. Stay consistent with 1 minute per question.

2.   **Answer the items in consecutive order.**

a.   Do **not** agonize over any one item. Stay within your time budget.

b.   Note any items you are unsure of by clicking the "Flag for Review" button in the upper-right corner of your screen, and return to them later if time allows. Plan on going back to all the questions you flagged.

c.   Never leave a question unanswered. Make your best guess in the time allowed. Your score is based on the number of correct responses out of the total scored questions, and you will not be penalized for guessing incorrectly.

3.   **For each multiple-choice question,**

a.   **Try to ignore the answer choices.** Do not allow the answer choices to affect your reading of the question.

1)   If four answer choices are presented, three of them are incorrect. These incorrect answers are called **distractors** for good reason. Often, distractors are written to appear correct at first glance until further analysis.

2)   In computational items, distractors are carefully calculated such that they are the result of making common mistakes. Be careful and double-check your computations if time permits.

b.   **Read the question carefully** to determine the precise requirement.

1)   Focusing on what is required enables you to ignore extraneous information and to proceed directly to determining the correct answer.

a)   Be especially careful to note when the requirement is an **exception**; e.g., "Which of the following is **not** an indication of fraud?"

c. **Determine the correct answer** before looking at the answer choices.

　　1) However, some multiple-choice questions are structured so that the answer cannot be determined from the stem alone. See the stem in 3.b.1)a) on the previous page.

d. **Then, read the answer choices carefully.**

　　1) Even if the first answer appears to be the correct choice, do not skip the remaining answer choices. Questions often ask for the "best" of the choices provided. Thus, each choice requires your consideration.

　　2) Treat each answer choice as a true/false question as you analyze it.

e. **Click on the best answer.**

　　1) If you are uncertain, you have a 25% chance of answering the question correctly by blindly guessing. Improve your odds with educated guessing.

　　2) For many of the multiple-choice questions, two answer choices can be eliminated with minimal effort, thereby increasing your educated guess to a 50-50 proposition.

4. After you have answered all 100 questions, return to the questions that you flagged. Also, verify that all questions have been answered.

5. **If you don't know the answer:**

a. Again, guess but make it an educated guess, which means select the best possible answer. First, rule out answers that you think are incorrect. Second, speculate on what The IIA is looking for and/or the rationale behind the question. Third, select the best answer, or guess between equally appealing answers. Your first guess is usually the most intuitive. If you cannot make an educated guess, read the stem and each answer and pick the most intuitive answer. It's just a guess!

b. Make sure you accomplish this step within your predetermined time budget per checkpoint.

LEARNING FROM YOUR MISTAKES

Learning from questions you answer incorrectly is very important. Each question you answer incorrectly is an **opportunity** to avoid missing actual test questions on your CIA exam. Thus, you should carefully study the answer explanations provided until you understand why the original answer you chose is wrong, as well as why the correct answer indicated is correct. This study technique is clearly the difference between passing and failing for many CIA candidates.

Also, you **must** determine why you answered questions incorrectly and learn how to avoid the same error in the future. Reasons for missing questions include

1. Misreading the requirement (stem)
2. Not understanding what is required
3. Making a math error
4. Applying the wrong rule or concept
5. Being distracted by one or more of the answers
6. Incorrectly eliminating answers from consideration
7. Not having any knowledge of the topic tested
8. Employing bad intuition when guessing

It is also important to verify that you answered correctly for the right reasons. Otherwise, if the material is tested on the CIA exam in a different manner, you may not answer it correctly.

HOW TO BE IN CONTROL WHILE TAKING THE EXAM

You have to be in control to be successful during exam preparation and execution. Control can also contribute greatly to your personal and other professional goals. Control is a process whereby you

1. Develop expectations, standards, budgets, and plans
2. Undertake activity, production, study, and learning
3. Measure the activity, production, output, and knowledge
4. Compare actual activity with expected and budgeted activity
5. Modify the activity, behavior, or study to better achieve the desired outcome
6. Revise expectations and standards in light of actual experience
7. Continue the process or restart the process in the future

Exercising control will ultimately develop the confidence you need to outperform most other CIA candidates and PASS the CIA exam! Obtain our *How to Pass the CIA Exam: A System for Success* booklet for a more detailed discussion of control and other exam tactics.

IF YOU HAVE QUESTIONS ABOUT GLEIM MATERIALS

Gleim has an efficient and effective way for candidates who have purchased the Premium CIA Review System to submit an inquiry and receive a response regarding Gleim materials directly through their course. This system also allows you to view your Q&A session in your Gleim Personal Classroom.

Questions regarding the **information in this introduction and/or the *How to Pass the CIA Exam: A System for Success* booklet (study suggestions, studying plans, exam specifics)** should be emailed to personalcounselor@gleim.com.

Questions concerning **orders, prices, shipments, or payments** should be sent via email to customerservice@gleim.com and will be promptly handled by our competent and courteous customer service staff.

For **technical support**, you may use our automated technical support service at www.gleim.com/support, email us at support@gleim.com, or call us at (800) 874-5346.

FEEDBACK

Please fill out our online feedback form (www.gleim.com/feedbackCIA3) immediately after you take the CIA exam so we can adapt to changes in the exam. Our approach has been approved by The IIA.

STUDY UNIT ONE
GOVERNANCE

(15 pages of outline)

This study unit covers **Section I: Governance/Business Ethics** from The IIA's CIA Exam Syllabus. This section makes up 5% to 15% of Part 3 of the CIA exam and is tested at the **awareness level** (unless otherwise indicated below). The relevant portion of the syllabus is highlighted below. (The complete syllabus is in Appendix A.)

I. GOVERNANCE/BUSINESS ETHICS (5%–15%)

> **A. Corporate/Organizational Governance Principles** – *Proficiency Level (P)*
> **B. Environmental and Social Safeguards**
> **C. Corporate Social Responsibility**

The way in which an organization meets its responsibilities is its governance process. This process is closely related to risk management and control. The board and senior management are accountable for governance, and the assurance function of internal auditors includes evaluating and improving it. Because governance is external as well as internal, environmental and social safeguards also are addressed in this study unit. The organization's sensitivity to its corporate social responsibilities is a related subject.

 CIA candidates should understand the governance process, governance principles, and ethical culture. The IIA may ask questions that require candidates to apply knowledge to a set of facts.

1.1 GOVERNANCE PRINCIPLES

1. **Definition of Corporate Governance**

    a. **Governance** is the combination of people, policies, procedures, and processes (including internal control) that help ensure that an entity effectively and efficiently directs its activities toward meeting the objectives of its stakeholders.

    1) Stakeholders are persons or entities who are affected by the activities of the entity. Among others, these include shareholders, employees, suppliers, customers, neighbors of the entity's facilities, and government regulators.

    b. Corporate governance can be either internal or external.

    1) Corporate charters and bylaws, boards of directors, and internal audit functions are internal.

    2) Laws, regulations, and the government regulators who enforce them are external.

2. **Governance Principles**

    a. The following summary of principles is based on a publication of The IIA:

        1) An independent and objective board with sufficient expertise, experience, authority, and resources to conduct independent inquiries

        2) An understanding by senior management and the board of the operating structure, including structures that impede transparency

        3) An organizational strategy used to measure organizational and individual performance

        4) An organizational structure that supports accomplishing strategic objectives

        5) A governing policy for the operation of key activities

        6) Clear, enforced lines of responsibility and accountability

        7) Effective interaction among the board, management, and assurance providers

        8) Appropriate oversight by management, including strong controls

        9) Compensation policies–especially for senior management–that encourage appropriate behavior consistent with the organization's values, objectives, strategy, and internal control

        10) Reinforcement of an ethical culture, including employee feedback without fear of retaliation

        11) Effective use of internal and external auditors, ensuring their independence, the adequacy of their resources and scope of activities, and the effectiveness of operations

        12) Clear definition and implementation of risk management policies and processes

        13) Transparent disclosure of key information to stakeholders

        14) Comparison of governance processes with national codes or best practices

        15) Oversight of related party transactions and conflicts of interest

3. **Governance Process**

    a. Governance has two major components: strategic direction and oversight.

        1) Strategic direction determines

            a) The business model,
            b) Overall objectives,
            c) The approach to risk taking (including the risk appetite), and
            d) The limits of organizational conduct.

        2) Oversight is the governance component with which internal auditing is most concerned. It is also the component to which risk management and control activities are most likely to be applied. The elements of oversight are

            a) Risk management activities performed by senior management and risk owners and
            b) Internal and external assurance activities.

b.   The **board** is defined by The IIA as the highest governing body responsible for directing or overseeing the activities and management of the organization. It ordinarily includes an independent group of directors (e.g., a board of directors, a supervisory board, or a board of governors or trustees). If such a group does not exist, the board may be the head of the organization. The term also may refer to an audit committee to which the governing body has delegated certain functions. Thus, the board is the source of overall direction to, and the authority of, management. It also has the ultimate responsibility for oversight.

1)   Another responsibility is to identify stakeholders, whether directly involved with the business (employees, customers, and suppliers), indirectly involved (investors), or having influence over the business (regulators and competitors).

2)   The board must determine the expectations of stakeholders and the outcomes that are unacceptable.

3)   The board has the following duties:

a)   Selection and removal of officers

b)   Decisions about capital structure (mix of debt and equity, consideration to be received for shares, etc.)

c)   Adding, amending, or repealing bylaws (unless this authority is reserved to the shareholders)

d)   Initiation of fundamental changes (mergers, acquisitions, etc.)

e)   Decisions to declare and distribute dividends

f)   Setting of management compensation (sometimes performed by a subcommittee called the compensation committee)

g)   Coordinating audit activities (most often performed by a subcommittee called the audit committee)

h)   Evaluating and managing risk (sometimes performed by a subcommittee called the risk committee)

4)   A **risk committee** may be created that

a)   Identifies key risks,

b)   Connects them to risk management processes,

c)   Delegates them to risk owners, and

d)   Considers whether tolerance levels delegated to risk owners are consistent with the organization's risk appetite.

c.   **Management** performs day-to-day governance functions. Senior management carries out board directives (within specified tolerances for unacceptable outcomes) to achieve objectives.

1)   Senior management determines

a)   Where specific risks are to be managed,

b)   Who will be **risk owners** (managers responsible for specific day-to-day risks), and

c)   How specific risks will be managed.

2)   Senior management establishes reporting requirements for risk owners related to their risk management activities.

3)   Governance expectations, including tolerance levels, must be periodically reevaluated by the board and senior management. The result may be changes in risk management activities.

   d. Governance applies to all organizational activities. Thus, its processes provide overall direction for risk management activities.

   1) Internal control activities are in turn a key element of risk management. They implement the organization's risk management strategies.

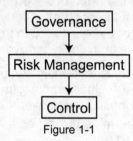

Figure 1-1

   2) The functions of risk owners include

   a) Evaluating the adequacy of the design of risk management activities and the organization's ability to carry them out as designed;

   b) Determining whether risk management activities are operating as designed;

   c) Establishing monitoring activities; and

   d) Ensuring that information to be reported to senior management and the board is accurate, timely, and available.

4. **Governance Practices**

   a. Governance practices reflect the organization's unique culture and largely depend on it for effectiveness.

   1) The organizational culture

   a) Sets values, objectives, and strategies;

   b) Defines roles and behaviors;

   c) Measures performance; and

   d) Specifies accountability.

   2) Thus, the culture determines the degree of sensitivity to social responsibility.

   b. Governance practices may use various legal forms, structures, strategies, and procedures. They ensure that the organization

   1) Complies with society's legal and regulatory rules;

   2) Satisfies the generally accepted business norms, ethical principles, and social expectations of society;

   3) Provides overall benefit to society and enhances the interests of the specific stakeholders in both the long and short term; and

   4) Reports fully and truthfully to its stakeholders, including the public, to ensure accountability for its decisions, actions, and performances.

5. **Ethical Culture**

   a. The ethical culture is an important component of the organizational culture and is crucial to the effectiveness of governance practices. Because decision making is complex and dispersed in most organizations, each person should be an ethics advocate, whether officially or informally.

   1) Codes of conduct and vision statements are issued to state

   a) The organization's values and objectives;

   b) The behavior expected; and

   c) The strategies for maintaining a culture consistent with legal, ethical, and societal responsibilities.

2)   Some organizations designate a chief ethics officer.

3)   **Internal auditors** may have an active role in support of the organization's ethical culture. Roles may include chief ethics officer, member of an ethics council, or assessor of the ethical climate.

   a)   In some circumstances, the role of chief ethics officer may conflict with the independence attribute of the internal audit activity.

      i)   The organizational independence of the internal audit activity is necessary because it performs internal assurance services.

         •   External assurance may be provided by external auditors, consultants, industry groups, or regulators.

   b)   The role of, and advice given by, the internal audit activity depend on the maturity of the governance system.

      i)   In a less mature system, the internal audit activity emphasizes compliance with policies, procedures, laws, etc. It also addresses the basic risks to the organization.

      ii) In a more mature governance system, the internal audit activity's emphasis is on optimizing structure and practices.

   c)   The responsibility of the internal audit activity in an assurance engagement for ethics-related matters is described in the following standard:

Implementation Standard 2110.A1

The internal audit activity must evaluate the design, implementation, and effectiveness of the organization's ethics-related objectives, programs, and activities.

---

4)   The internal audit activity periodically assesses the elements of the ethical climate of the organization and its effectiveness in achieving legal and ethical compliance. Internal auditors therefore evaluate the effectiveness of the following:

   a)   A formal code of conduct and related statements and policies (including procedures covering fraud and corruption)

   b)   Frequent demonstrations of ethical attitudes and behavior by influential leaders

   c)   Explicit strategies to support the ethical culture

   d)   Confidential reporting of alleged misconduct

   e)   Regular declarations by employees, suppliers, and customers about the requirements of ethical behavior

   f)   Clear delegation of responsibilities for providing counsel, investigation, and reporting

   g)   Easy access to learning opportunities

   h)   Personnel practices that encourage contributions by employees

   i)   Regular surveys of employees, suppliers, and customers to determine the state of the ethical climate

   j)   Regular reviews of the processes that undermine the ethical culture

   k)   Regular reference and background checks

Stop and review! You have completed the outline for this subunit. Study multiple-choice questions 1 through 6 beginning on page 24.

1.2 THE SARBANES-OXLEY ACT OF 2002 (SOX)

Background

In late 2001 and 2002, massive accounting scandals were reported in the media. They involved such large firms as Enron (hid debt of over US $1 billion in improper off-the-books partnerships), Global Crossing (inflated revenues; shredded accounting-related documents), and WorldCom (booked operating expenses as capital assets; made large off-the-books payments to founder). In response to these and many other fraudulent practices, Congress passed the Sarbanes-Oxley Act of 2002, named for its sponsors, Democratic Senator Paul Sarbanes of Maryland and Republican Representative Mike Oxley of Ohio.

---

1. **Applicability to Publicly Held Companies (Issuers) and Their Auditors**

   a. Each member of the issuer's audit committee must be an independent member of the board of directors.

      1) To be independent, a director must not be affiliated with, or receive any compensation (other than for service on the board) from, the issuer.

         a) At least one member of the audit committee must be a financial expert.

      2) The audit committee must be directly responsible for appointing, compensating, and overseeing the work of the independent auditor.

         a) The independent auditor must report directly to the audit committee, not to management.

   b. SOX established the **Public Company Accounting Oversight Board (PCAOB)** as a private-sector body to regulate the accounting profession.

      1) The PCAOB

         a) Issues auditing and related standards;

         b) Inspects and investigates accounting firms; and

         c) Enforces compliance with its rules, professional standards, the act, and relevant securities laws.

      2) Public accounting firms that act as independent auditors must register with the PCAOB.

   c. A public accounting firm is prohibited from performing consulting, legal, and internal auditing services (with some exceptions) for the audit client.

      1) But audit firms may provide conventional tax planning and certain other nonaudit services if preapproved by the audit committee.

2. **Section 302 -- Corporate Responsibility for Financial Reports**

   a. In every annual or quarterly filing with the SEC, the CEO and CFO must certify the following:

      1) To the best of their knowledge, the financial statements are free of material misstatements.

      2) They are responsible for the system of internal control and have evaluated its effectiveness.

      3) They have informed the audit committee and the independent auditors of all significant control deficiencies and any fraud, whether or not material.

      4) Significant changes were (or were not) made in internal controls, including corrective actions.

    b.   Intentional violations of this section of SOX can result in the forfeiture of

        1)   Any bonus or other incentive-based compensation received during the previous 12 months and

        2)   Any profits received from the sale of stock during the previous 12 months.

3.   **Section 404 -- Management Assessment of Internal Control**

    a.   Under current regulations, the annual report must contain a statement by the CEO and CFO that includes the following:

        1)   A statement that management has taken responsibility for establishing and maintaining an adequate system of internal control over financial reporting

        2)   The name of the internal control model, if any, used to design and assess the effectiveness of the internal control system (COSO's *Internal Control – Integrated Framework* is the most widely used model in the United States)

        3)   An assessment of whether internal control over financial reporting is effective

        4)   A statement that an independent public accounting firm that is registered with the PCAOB also has assessed the system

4.   **Section 407 -- Disclosure of Audit Committee Financial Expert**

    a.   An issuer must disclose whether its audit committee has at least one financial expert.

        1)   If the audit committee lacks a financial expert, the issuer must disclose the reason(s) why not.

    b.   To be considered a financial expert, the director must have

        1)   An understanding of generally accepted accounting principles and financial statements;

        2)   Experience in

            a)   The preparation or auditing of financial statements of generally comparable issuers and

            b)   The application of such principles in connection with the accounting for estimates, accruals, and reserves;

        3)   Experience with internal accounting controls; and

        4)   An understanding of audit committee functions.

5.   **Whistleblowers**

    a.   Under SOX and the Dodd-Frank Wall Street Reform Act, the SEC may compensate whistleblowers who provide information other than that from an audit or investigation.

        1)   Whistleblowers may sue retaliating employers.

        2)   Whistleblower claims may be asserted for up to 180 days.

        3)   Trial by jury is allowed.

        4)   Whistleblower rights and remedies may not be waived, for example, in an employment contract.

Stop and review! You have completed the outline for this subunit. Study multiple-choice questions 7 through 9 on page 26.

1.3 ROLES OF INTERNAL AUDITORS IN GOVERNANCE

1.   Governance is one of the three basic processes identified in the Definition of Internal Auditing.

    a.   The design and implementation of governance processes are the responsibility of the board and management.

Performance Standard 2110
Governance

The internal audit activity must assess and make appropriate recommendations for improving the governance process in its accomplishment of the following objectives:

- Promoting appropriate ethics and values within the organization;
- Ensuring effective organizational performance management and accountability;
- Communicating risk and control information to appropriate areas of the organization; and
- Coordinating the activities of and communicating information among the board, external and internal auditors, and management.

---

    b.   Understanding the role of the internal audit activity begins with understanding the nature of governance in a specific organization.

        1)   Governance has a range of definitions depending on the circumstances.

            a)   The chief audit executive (CAE) may use a different definition when the organization uses a different model.

        2)   Governance models generally treat governance as a process or system that is not static.

            a)   The approach in the *Standards* emphasizes the board and its governance activities.

        3)   Governance requirements vary by entity type and regulatory jurisdiction. Examples include publicly traded companies, not-for-profits, governments, private companies, and stock exchanges.

        4)   The design and practice of effective governance vary with

            a)   The size, complexity, and life-cycle maturity of the organization;
            b)   Its stakeholder structure; and
            c)   Legal and cultural requirements.

        5)   The CAE should work with the board and senior management to determine how governance should be defined for audit purposes.

        6)   The unique position of internal auditors in the organization enables them to observe and formally assess the governance structure while remaining independent.

c. Governance, risk management, and control are closely related.

1) Governance does not exist as distinct processes and structures but as relationships with risk management and control.

2) Effective governance considers risk when setting strategy, and risk management relies on effective governance (e.g., tone at the top, risk appetite and tolerance, risk culture, and the oversight of risk management).

3) Effective governance relies on controls, and communication to the board relies on their effectiveness.

4) Control and risk also are related.

5) The CAE should consider the following in planning assessments of governance:

    a) An audit should address controls in governance processes that are designed to prevent or detect events that could have a negative effect on the organization.

    b) Controls within governance processes often are significant in managing multiple risks. For example, controls related to the code of conduct may be relied upon to manage compliance and fraud risks.

    c) If other audits assess controls in governance processes, the auditor should consider relying on their results.

d. The internal audit activity's ultimate responsibility is to evaluate and improve governance.

1) Internal auditors assess the design and operating effectiveness of governance processes. They also provide advice on improving those processes.

    a) Internal auditors may facilitate board self-assessments of governance.

2) The definition of governance should be agreed upon with the board and senior management. The internal auditors should understand governance processes and the relationships among governance, risk, and control.

3) The audit plan should be based on an assessment of risks that considers governance processes. The plan should include the higher-risk governance processes.

    a) Moreover, inclusion of an assessment of processes or risk areas should be considered if the board or senior management has requested that work be performed.

    b) The plan should define (1) the nature of the work; (2) the governance processes; and (3) the nature of the assessments, e.g., consideration of specific risks, processes, or activities.

4) When control issues are known, or the governance process is not mature, the CAE may consider different methods for improving control or governance through consulting services.

5) Assessments of governance are likely to be based on numerous audits. The internal auditor should consider

    a) Audits of specific processes,

    b) Governance issues arising from audits not focused on governance,

    c) The results of other assurance providers' work, and

    d) Such other information as adverse incidents indicating an opportunity to improve governance.

6) During the planning, evaluating, and reporting phases, the internal auditor should be sensitive to the consequences of the results and ensure appropriate communications with the board and senior management.

    a) The internal auditor should consider consulting legal counsel both before the audit and before issuing the final report.

7) The board and senior management should be able to rely on the quality assurance and improvement program of the internal audit activity and external quality assessments based on the *Standards*.

e. Governance Roles of Internal Auditors

1) Obtain the board's approval of the internal audit charter.
2) Communicate the plan of engagements.
3) Report significant audit issues.
4) Communicate key performance indicators to the board on a regular basis.
5) Discuss areas of significant risk.
6) Support the board in enterprise-wide risk assessment.
7) Review the positioning of the internal audit activity within the risk management framework within the organization.
8) Monitor compliance with the corporate code of conduct/business practices.
9) Report on the effectiveness of the control framework.
10) Assess the ethical climate of the board and the organization.
11) Conduct follow-up and report on management's response to regulatory body reviews.
12) Conduct follow-up and report on management's response to external audit.
13) Assess the adequacy of the performance measurement system and achievement of organizational objectives.
14) Support a culture of fraud awareness and encourage the reporting of improprieties.

2. **Other Aspects of Corporate Governance**

a. Trusteeship

1) The board and senior management act as custodians of corporate assets in the pursuit of positive outcomes for stakeholders.

b. Empowerment and Control

1) Decision making should occur at appropriate levels of the organization, and freedom of management should be exercised within a framework of checks and balances.

c. Good Corporate Citizenship

1) Integrity and ethical values should be reflected by the tone at the top.

d. Transparency of Disclosures

1) Transparency may involve accepting a higher cost of capital.

3. The chart below depicts a typical U.S. corporate governance structure. (In the U.S., the Securities and Exchange Commission enforces the securities laws and the Public Company Accounting Oversight Board regulates the auditors of public companies.)

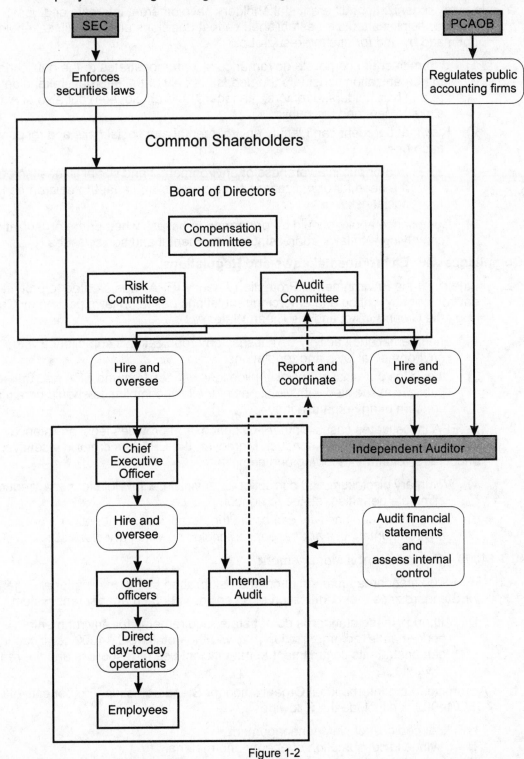

Figure 1-2

Stop and review! You have completed the outline for this subunit. Study multiple-choice questions 10 through 13 on page 27.

1.4 ENVIRONMENTAL AND SOCIAL SAFEGUARDS

1. **Corporate Governance and Society**

   a. In every organization, different stakeholders have different interests and goals. Thus, a set of principles should be established so that decisions affecting all stakeholders are not made by and for one interest group.

      1) Commitment to corporate governance also demonstrates to the public that the organization considers the needs not only of the internal stakeholders (e.g., shareholders, directors, managers, and employees) but also of external stakeholders and the public.

      2) Risk management can identify environmental and social risks and responses to each risk.

         a) Greater public awareness of environmental and social issues increases the need for organizations to prepare for and adapt to environmental and social risks.

      3) Compliance audits should be performed to assess whether the organization is complying with laws addressing environmental and social issues.

2. **Compliance with Environmental Laws and Regulations**

   a. In the U.S., the Environmental Protection Agency (EPA) was created to protect the environment by writing and enforcing regulations based on laws passed by Congress (e.g., the Clean Air Act and the Clean Water Act).

      1) The internal audit activity can assess an organization's compliance with environmental laws and regulations.

      2) Due to the potential financial implications of fines from the EPA and the negative publicity associated with violations of the law, compliance should be a major concern of any organization.

   b. The EPA investigates cases, gathers evidence, and provides legal assistance in the prosecution of criminal conduct. Moreover, the EPA has created incentives to encourage voluntary reporting and compliance.

      1) Voluntary disclosure and correction of environmental violations may reduce or eliminate penalties related to noncompliance.

      2) The internal audit activity can assist the organization in identifying potential environmental risks and responses (including voluntary disclosure).

3. **ISO 14000 – Environmental Management**

   a. ISO 14000 standards are a set of criteria established by the International Organization for Standardization for certification of an environmental management system.

      1) Although these standards do not state requirements for environmental performance, an organization may want to obtain ISO 14000 certification to demonstrate its commitment to the efficient use of resources and the reduction of waste.

   b. According to the International Organization for Standardization, the benefits of using ISO 14000 can include the following:

      1) Reduced cost of waste management
      2) Savings in consumption of energy and materials
      3) Lower distribution costs
      4) Improved corporate image among regulators, customers, and the public

    c. ISO 14000 standards have not been as widely accepted as the ISO 9000 standards (guidance for establishing and maintaining a quality management system). But ISO 14000 certification may become more necessary for conducting international business.

       1) Some European countries already have environmental systems standards in place, and the relationship of these single-country standards with ISO 14000 is not clear.

          a) The standards of individual countries are typically more strict.

4. Employment Regulation in the United States

    a. To address changing attitudes about the treatment of employees in the workplace, Congress passed laws designed to improve workplace conditions for all employees.

    b. The Occupational Safety and Health Act of 1970

       1) The purpose of this act is to develop safety standards, prevent injuries, and promote job safety.

       2) This act is administered by the Occupational Safety and Health Administration (OSHA).

          a) OSHA is authorized to develop detailed health and safety standards and to enforce them.

          b) It investigates complaints and conducts inspections and has developed procedures to encourage compliance.

       3) Under the act, employers are required to

          a) Provide employees with a workplace free from recognized hazards that are likely to cause death or serious physical harm,

          b) Keep detailed records of job-related injuries,

          c) Post annual summaries of the records, and

          d) Report serious accidents to OSHA.

5. Privacy Concerns

    a. As the threat of hacking and identity theft has become more prevalent, information reliability and integrity has become a major concern for many organizations.

       1) Allowing, or failing to prevent, access to sensitive customer information (e.g., bank account information) can reflect negatively on an organization and potentially leave it vulnerable to legal liability. Customers and other businesses also may be less willing to give sensitive information to an organization that fails to protect it.

       2) Some organizations also need to protect proprietary information (i.e., trade secrets). Failure to do so could affect the organization's ability to compete effectively or continue as a going concern.

    b. The following summarizes the provisions of Practice Advisory 2130.A1-1, *Information Reliability and Integrity*:

       1) Information reliability and integrity includes accuracy, completeness, and security. The internal audit activity determines whether senior management and the board clearly understand that it is a management responsibility for all critical information regardless of its form.

       2) The CAE determines whether the internal audit activity has competent audit resources for evaluating internal and external risks to information reliability and integrity.

       3) The CAE determines whether senior management, the board, and the internal audit activity will be promptly notified about breaches and conditions that might represent a threat.

4)   Internal auditors assess the effectiveness of preventive, detective, and mitigative measures against past and future attacks. They also determine whether the board has been appropriately informed.

5)   Internal auditors periodically assess reliability and integrity practices and recommend new or improved controls. Such assessments can be made as separate engagements or as multiple engagements integrated with other elements of the audit plan.

c.   Internal auditors also evaluate compliance with laws and regulations concerning privacy. Thus, they assess the adequacy of the identification of risks and the controls that reduce those risks.

Stop and review! You have completed the outline for this subunit. Study multiple-choice questions 14 through 17 on page 28.

1.5 CORPORATE SOCIAL RESPONSIBILITY (CSR)

1.   **Nature of CSR**

a.   According to CSR concepts, a corporation's purpose is not only to benefit shareholders but also to serve other groups in society beyond what the law requires.

b.   The following are examples of actions in accordance with CSR:

1)   An organization builds and maintains public parks in areas where it does business.

2)   An organization applies core competencies to assist people in need.

a)   For example, the United Parcel Service (a company in the U.S.) used its unique understanding of logistics to help get necessary supplies to Hurricane Katrina victims as quickly as possible.

3)   An organization helps increase awareness about important causes or issues.

a)   For example, many organizations, including professional sports teams, help the National Breast Cancer Foundation (a charity in the U.S.) to raise money for breast cancer research.

c.   Actions must be voluntary. If service to the community is required, it is more akin to punishment than CSR.

1)   Furthermore, CSR in response to corporate misdeeds does not have the same positive effect as voluntary CSR.

d.   CSR can be profitable. Serving the community involves certain costs (e.g., time, labor, and other resources). The benefits of CSR may exceed the costs. Examples are

1)   Positive public perception on a local, national, and international level;
2)   Retention of workers;
3)   Charity as a form of advertising (brand building); and
4)   Deductibility of charitable donations.

e.   However, an organization should avoid the perception that it is committed to CSR solely for profit. Questionable motives could negatively affect the organization's image.

2.   **Developing a Framework for CSR**

a.   **Identifying stakeholders.** Internal and external stakeholders should be identified so that an organization can balance its needs and desires in a mutually beneficial way.

1)   Internal stakeholders include the following:

a)   Shareholders
b)   Employees
c)   Management

2) External stakeholders include the following:

    a) Suppliers
    b) Customers
    c) Society

b. **Identifying goals.** An organization should determine how it wants to serve its stakeholders. Identifying goals communicates the organization's motives to its stakeholders.

    1) For example, Molson Coors Canada is committed to educating its consumers about drinking responsibly. When the Toronto Transit Authority canceled its free-ride program on New Year's Eve in 2008, Molson Coors launched a campaign to privately fund the program, starting with its own US $20,000 contribution.

3. **ISO Framework – ISO 26000**

a. ISO 26000 standards provide guidance on how businesses and other organizations can be socially responsible, i.e., act in an ethical and transparent way that contributes to the health and welfare of society.

    1) Although compliance with ISO 26000 is not required, compliance could improve relationships with suppliers, regulators, customers, and other stakeholders.

4. **CSR Auditing**

a. A CSR audit can facilitate a better understanding of an organization's

    1) Goals;
    2) Practices, policies, and culture; and
    3) Internal decision-making process in regard to CSR.

b. As in any compliance audit, a CSR audit program begins with identifying relevant risks. They include

    1) The effectiveness of implementation of large CSR projects,
    2) The reliability of performance measurements, and
    3) Risks associated with external factors (i.e., regulatory bodies).

c. Once these risks are identified, the audit function should review how management addresses these risks.

5. **CSR Reporting**

a. Once an organization has committed to CSR and effectively incorporated CSR into its operations, it should demonstrate its accomplishments to internal and external stakeholders.

    1) Showing employees how their actions contributed to society can help empower them through acknowledgment of their achievements.
    2) Showing shareholders how the actions of the organization contributed to a better image can demonstrate the value of CSR.
    3) Informing the public of the accomplishments of the organization can improve its brand and serve as a form of advertising.

Stop and review! You have completed the outline for this subunit. Study multiple-choice questions 18 through 20 on page 29.

QUESTIONS

1.1 Governance Principles

1. The internal audit activity has a role in an organization's governance process. The internal audit activity most directly contributes to this process by

- A. Identifying significant exposures to risk.
- B. Evaluating the effectiveness of internal control over financial reporting.
- C. Promoting continuous improvement of controls.
- D. Evaluating the design of ethics-related activities.

Answer (D) is correct.

REQUIRED: How the internal audit activity most directly contributes to an organization's governance process.

DISCUSSION: Perf. Std. 2110 states, "The internal audit activity must assess and make appropriate recommendations for improving the governance process in its accomplishment of the following objectives:

- Promoting appropriate ethics and values within the organization;
- Ensuring effective organizational performance management and accountability;
- Communicating risk and control information to appropriate areas of the organization; and
- Coordinating the activities of and communicating information among the board, external and internal auditors and management."

Thus, in an assurance engagement, the internal audit activity must evaluate the design, implementation, and effectiveness of the organization's ethics-related objectives, programs, and activities.

Answer (A) is incorrect. Identifying significant exposures to risk most directly relates to risk management rather than to governance. Answer (B) is incorrect. Evaluating the effectiveness of internal control over financial reporting more directly relates to risk management rather than to governance. Answer (C) is incorrect. Promoting continuous improvement of controls relates to controls rather than to governance.

2. The role of the internal audit activity in the ethical culture of an organization is to

- A. Avoid active support of the ethical culture because of possible loss of independence.
- B. Evaluate the effectiveness of the organization's formal code of conduct.
- C. Assume accountability for the effectiveness of the governance process.
- D. Become the chief ethics officer.

Answer (B) is correct.

REQUIRED: The minimum role of the internal audit activity in the ethical culture of an organization.

DISCUSSION: The internal audit activity periodically assesses the elements of the ethical climate of the organization and its effectiveness in achieving legal and ethical compliance. Internal auditors therefore evaluate the effectiveness of, among other things, a formal code of conduct and related statements and policies.

Answer (A) is incorrect. Internal auditors must be active ethics advocates. However, assuming the role of, for example, chief ethics officer may, in some circumstances, impair individual objectivity and the internal audit activity's independence. Answer (C) is incorrect. The organization's board and its senior management are responsible for the effectiveness of the governance process. Answer (D) is incorrect. The internal auditor's basic role is to be the assessor of the ethical culture. However, an internal auditor may become chief ethics officer or a member of an ethics council, although the first role may, in some circumstances, impair individual objectivity and the internal audit activity's independence.

3. Which of the following correctly classifies the corporate governance functions as internal or external?

	Internal	External
A.	Corporate charter	Bylaws
B.	Laws	Board of directors
C.	Internal audit function	Corporate charter
D.	Bylaws	Government regulation

Answer (D) is correct.

REQUIRED: The correct classification of the corporate governance functions.

DISCUSSION: Bylaws are an example of internal corporate governance, and laws, regulations, and the government regulators who enforce them are examples of external governance.

Answer (A) is incorrect. Bylaws are an example of internal corporate governance. Answer (B) is incorrect. Laws provide external corporate governance, and a board of directors provides internal corporate governance. Answer (C) is incorrect. A corporate charter is an example of internal corporate governance.

4. Which of the following is a **false** statement about the role of internal auditors in an organization's ethical culture?

A. Roles may include chief ethics officer.

B. The role of chief ethics officer sometimes conflicts with the independence of the internal audit activity.

C. In a more mature system, the internal audit activity emphasizes compliance.

D. In a more mature governance system, the internal audit activity's emphasis is on optimizing structure and practices.

Answer (C) is correct.
REQUIRED: The false statement about the role of internal auditors in an organization's ethical culture.
DISCUSSION: The role of the internal audit activity depends on the maturity of the governance system. In a less mature system, the internal audit activity emphasizes compliance with policies, procedures, laws, etc. It also addresses the basic risks to the organization.
Answer (A) is incorrect. Internal auditors' roles may include chief ethics officer. Answer (B) is incorrect. In some circumstances, the role of chief ethics officer may conflict with the independence attribute of the internal audit activity. Answer (D) is incorrect. In a more mature governance system, the internal audit activity's emphasis is on optimizing structure and practices.

5. Which of the following is most likely an internal audit role in a less structured governance process?

A. Designing specific governance processes.

B. Playing a consulting role in optimizing governance practices and structure.

C. Providing advice about basic risks to the organization.

D. Evaluating the effectiveness of specific governance processes.

Answer (C) is correct.
REQUIRED: The internal audit activity's likely role in a less structured governance process.
DISCUSSION: A less mature governance system will emphasize the requirements for compliance with policies, procedures, plans, laws, regulations, and contracts. It will also address the basic risks to the organization. Thus, the internal audit activity will provide advice about such matters. As the governance process becomes more structured, the internal audit activity's emphasis will shift to optimizing the governance structure and practices.
Answer (A) is incorrect. Internal auditors impair their objectivity by designing processes. However, evaluating the design and effectiveness of specific processes is a typical internal audit role. Answer (B) is incorrect. Playing a consulting role in optimizing governance practices and structure is typical of a more structured internal auditing governance maturity model. The emphasis shifts to considering best practices and adapting them to the specific organization. Answer (D) is incorrect. Evaluating the effectiveness of specific governance processes is typical of a more structured internal auditing governance maturity model.

6. Which of the following is a situation in which an internal auditor's role of chief ethics officer conflicts with the independence attribute of the internal audit activity?

A. The chief ethics officer requests that the internal auditors assess whether the organization as a whole is not complying with the organization's code of conduct.

B. The chief ethics officer informs the board of recommendations made by the internal audit activity regarding the organization's compliance with the code of conduct.

C. The chief ethics officer proposes and implements a new whistleblower program for the organization.

D. The internal audit activity informs the chief ethics officer that the organization is in compliance with all laws and regulations.

Answer (C) is correct.
REQUIRED: The situation in which the internal auditor's role is inconsistent with the independence attribute.
DISCUSSION: Proposing and implementing a new whistleblower program conflicts with the independence attribute of the internal audit activity. Implementation is a management function and is therefore inconsistent with the organizational independence of the internal audit activity.

1.2 The Sarbanes-Oxley Act of 2002 (SOX)

7. The Sarbanes-Oxley Act of 2002 has strengthened auditor independence by requiring that management

A. Engage auditors to report in accordance with the Foreign Corrupt Practices Act.

B. Report the nature of disagreements with former auditors.

C. Select auditors through audit committees.

D. Hire a different CPA firm from the one that performs the audit to perform the company's tax work.

Answer (C) is correct.
REQUIRED: The SOX requirement that strengthened auditor independence.
DISCUSSION: The Sarbanes-Oxley Act requires that the audit committee of a public company hire and pay the external auditors. Such affiliation inhibits management from changing auditors to gain acceptance of a questionable accounting method. Also, a potential successor auditor must inquire of the predecessor auditor before accepting an engagement.
Answer (A) is incorrect. The SEC does not require an audit report in accordance with the FCPA. Answer (B) is incorrect. Reporting the nature of disagreements with auditors has been a long-time SEC requirement. Answer (D) is incorrect. The Sarbanes-Oxley Act does not restrict who may perform a company's tax work. Other types of engagements, such as the outsourcing of the internal audit function and certain consulting services, are limited.

8. Under the Sarbanes-Oxley Act of 2002 (SOX),

A. An issuer must disclose whether at least one member of the audit committee is a financial expert.

B. The chairman of the board of directors must be a financial expert.

C. The audit committee must rotate at least one seat on an annual basis.

D. All members of the audit committee must be financial experts.

Answer (A) is correct.
REQUIRED: The SOX requirement relevant to the audit committee.
DISCUSSION: Under the terms of SOX, an issuer must disclose whether at least one member of the audit committee is a financial expert. If the audit committee lacks a financial expert, the issuer must disclose the reason(s).
Answer (B) is incorrect. The SOX requirement regarding a financial expert does not refer to the chairman of the board. Answer (C) is incorrect. SOX imposes no requirements regarding membership rotation of the audit committee. Answer (D) is incorrect. Under the terms of SOX, only one member of the audit committee need be a financial expert.

9. Under the reporting requirements of Section 404 of the Sarbanes-Oxley Act of 2002 (SOX), the CEO and CFO must include a statement in the annual report to the effect that

A. The system of internal control has been assessed by an independent public accounting firm that is registered with the PCAOB.

B. The system of internal control has been assessed by an independent public accounting firm that is not currently the subject of any PCAOB investigation.

C. The board of directors has taken responsibility for establishing and maintaining an adequate system of internal control over financial reporting.

D. The issuer has used the COSO model to design and assess the effectiveness of its system of internal control.

Answer (A) is correct.
REQUIRED: The statement required by Sarbanes-Oxley.
DISCUSSION: The CEO and CFO must include a statement in the annual report to the effect that the system of internal control has been assessed by an independent public accounting firm that is registered with the PCAOB.
Answer (B) is incorrect. Section 404 of SOX does not require that the independent auditor not be under investigation by the PCAOB. Answer (C) is incorrect. Section 404 of SOX requires the CEO and CFO to state that they, not the board, have taken responsibility for internal controls. Answer (D) is incorrect. Section 404 of SOX requires that if the issuer used an internal control model, it must be named; it does not have to be the COSO model.

1.3 Roles of Internal Auditors in Governance

10. Which of the following should be defined in the internal audit plan for an assessment of governance?

1. The nature of the work
2. The governance process
3. The nature of the assessments

    A. 1 and 2 only.

    B. 2 and 3 only.

    C. 1 and 3 only.

    D. 1, 2, and 3.

Answer (D) is correct.
    REQUIRED: The items that should be defined in the internal audit plan for an assessment of governance.
    DISCUSSION: The audit plan should include higher-risk governance processes. It should define (1) the nature of the work; (2) the governance processes; and (3) the nature of the assessments, e.g., consideration of specific risks, processes, or activities.

11. A basic principle of governance is

    A. Assessment of the governance process by an independent internal audit activity.

    B. Holding the board, senior management, and the internal audit activity accountable for its effectiveness.

    C. Exclusive use of external auditors to provide assurance about the governance process.

    D. Separation of the governance process from promoting an ethical culture in the organization.

Answer (A) is correct.
    REQUIRED: The basic principle of governance.
    DISCUSSION: The internal audit activity must assess and make appropriate recommendations for improving the governance process.
    Answer (B) is incorrect. The internal audit activity is an assessor of the governance process. It is not accountable for that process. Answer (C) is incorrect. External parties and internal auditors may provide assurance about the governance process. Answer (D) is incorrect. The internal audit activity must assess and make appropriate recommendations for improving the governance process in its promotion of appropriate ethics and values within the organization.

12. Which aspect of corporate governance requires checks and balances?

    A. Trusteeship.

    B. Empowerment and control.

    C. Good corporate citizenship.

    D. Transparency of public disclosures.

Answer (B) is correct.
    REQUIRED: The aspect of corporate governance that requires checks and balances.
    DISCUSSION: Empowerment and control mean that decision making should occur at appropriate levels of the organization, and freedom of management should be exercised within a framework of checks and balances.
    Answer (A) is incorrect. Trusteeship means that the board and senior management act as custodians of corporate assets in the pursuit of positive outcomes for stakeholders. Answer (C) is incorrect. Good corporate citizenship means that integrity and ethical values should be reflected by the tone at the top. Answer (D) is incorrect. Transparency of public disclosures means that pursuit of transparency may involve accepting a higher cost of capital.

13. Which of the following correctly depicts a typical U.S. corporate governance structure from top to bottom?

    A. Board of directors, common shareholders, chief executive officer, employees.

    B. Common shareholders, chief executive officer, board of directors, employees.

    C. Common shareholders, board of directors, chief executive officer, employees.

    D. Chief executive officer, common shareholders, board of directors, employees.

Answer (C) is correct.
    REQUIRED: The typical U.S. corporate governance structure.
    DISCUSSION: The common shareholders elect the board of directors, who appoint the chief executive officer, who hires the employees.
    Answer (A) is incorrect. The common shareholders elect the board of directors; therefore, the shareholders are "above" the board in the corporate governance structure. Answer (B) is incorrect. The board of directors appoints the chief executive officer; therefore, the board is "above" the CEO in the corporate governance structure. Answer (D) is incorrect. The common shareholders elect the board of directors, who appoint the chief executive officer; therefore, the correct order is common shareholders, board of directors, and then chief executive officer.

1.4 Environmental and Social Safeguards

14. Which of the following is most likely to result from an organization's voluntary disclosure of a violation of laws to a regulatory body?

- A. Harsher penalties due to the intentional nature of the violation.

- B. Harsher penalties due to the reduced cost incurred by the regulatory body.

- C. Lesser penalties due to incentives for voluntary compliance and disclosure.

- D. No difference in penalties because an infraction of the law requires penalties.

Answer (C) is correct.
REQUIRED: The most likely result of an organization's voluntary disclosure of a violation of laws.
DISCUSSION: Many regulatory bodies have systems that allow voluntary disclosure of infractions, often reducing or eliminating the associated penalties.
Answer (A) is incorrect. Voluntary disclosure of information regarding the infraction does not imply that the violation was intentional. Instead, it is likely that the regulatory body would believe the infraction was unintentional if the entity consistently discloses its status on such matters. Answer (B) is incorrect. Reducing the cost of the regulatory agency to monitor companies would likely reduce the penalties associated with infractions, not increase them. Answer (D) is incorrect. Laws often provide flexibility in their enforcement to encourage voluntary disclosure and compliance in exchange for reduced costs if infractions occur.

15. Which of the following is **not** a benefit of implementing ISO 14000?

- A. Increased cost of waste management.

- B. Savings in consumption of energy.

- C. Lower distribution costs.

- D. Improved corporate image.

Answer (A) is correct.
REQUIRED: The item that is not a benefit of implementing ISO 14000.
DISCUSSION: Using ISO 14000 can (1) decrease, not increase, the cost of waste management; (2) provide savings in consumption of energy and materials; (3) lower distribution costs; and (4) improve corporate image among regulators, customers, and the public.
Answer (B) is incorrect. Using ISO 14000 should result in savings in consumption of energy and materials. Answer (C) is incorrect. Using ISO 14000 should lower distribution costs. Answer (D) is incorrect. Using ISO 14000 should improve corporate image among regulators, customers, and the public.

16. Internal auditors perform risk assessment audits to identify environmental and social risks. When the safeguards against these risks become legally mandated, which of the following is added to the internal audit activity's duties?

- A. No additional tasks are required because the internal audit activity is already engaged in determining the risk level.

- B. Identifying environmental and social risks and responses for each risk.

- C. Performing risk assessments by using risk management techniques.

- D. Performing compliance audits to assess whether the organization is complying with the legal mandates.

Answer (D) is correct.
REQUIRED: The task added to an internal audit activity's duties when environmental and social safeguards become legally mandated.
DISCUSSION: Compliance audits are undertaken by the internal audit activity to ensure that the organization is compliant with all legal requirements to which it is subject.
Answer (A) is incorrect. An additional responsibility is created when the safeguards become legally mandated. Answer (B) is incorrect. This level of responsibility exists before the safeguards become legally required. Answer (C) is incorrect. This level of responsibility exists before the safeguards become legally required.

17. Which of the following failures in information protection is most likely to directly lead to an organization losing its ability to continue as a going concern?

- A. A gym membership list is discovered by a rival gym.

- B. A rival company discovers the secret recipe for a soft drink company's product.

- C. An airplane manufacturer discovers the supplier for its primary competitor.

- D. A computer repair store discovers that many of its customers have used competitors in the past.

Answer (B) is correct.
REQUIRED: The failure in information protection that is most likely to directly lead to an organization losing its ability to continue as a going concern.
DISCUSSION: Discovery of trade secrets, such as secret formulas, often threatens the company's ability to continue as a going concern. At the very least, such a discovery impairs the company's ability to compete effectively.
Answer (A) is incorrect. Though this discovery may lead to mistrust by the gym's membership, it is unlikely that it would directly result in the loss of the gym's ability to operate as a going concern. Answer (C) is incorrect. Though this information may have been intended as a secret, it is unlikely that the discovery of a supplier for a competitor would directly lead to the failure of the competitor to continue as a going concern. Answer (D) is incorrect. This type of information does not represent a breach of privacy or information security.

1.5 Corporate Social Responsibility (CSR)

18. Which of the following best describes the concept of corporate social responsibility (CSR)?

A. A corporation's purpose to serve only the interests of shareholders.

B. A well-defined codification of corporate responsibilities as determined by a panel of professional organizations.

C. A developing concept according to which a corporation has duties to parties other than society.

D. A corporation's duties to serve the interests of groups other than shareholders.

Answer (D) is correct.
 REQUIRED: The best description of CSR.
 DISCUSSION: According to CSR, a corporation has duties not only to its shareholders but also to other groups beyond what the law requires. These include customers and society.
 Answer (A) is incorrect. CSR is a not a well-defined concept, but its purpose is not to serve only the interests of shareholders. Answer (B) is incorrect. CSR is a not a well-defined system, and it has not been codified. Answer (C) is incorrect. CSR is a developing concept that states that corporations have duties to parties such as society.

19. Examples of CSR include all of the following **except**

A. A pharmaceutical company that produces potentially addictive pain medication donates to addiction treatment facilities.

B. A tobacco company donates money to stop-smoking initiatives as a result of the settlement to a lawsuit.

C. A professional services firm pays its employees a bonus each year for providing services as volunteers to local not-for-profit organizations.

D. A delivery company uses its distribution network to deliver supplies for free to areas affected by natural disasters.

Answer (B) is correct.
 REQUIRED: The item that is not an example of CSR.
 DISCUSSION: The donation is not an example of CSR because it is not voluntary. Socially responsible actions that are required in response to corporate misdeeds or in response to a lawsuit are more akin to punishment than to CSR.
 Answer (A) is incorrect. The donation is voluntary and intended to benefit groups other than shareholders. Answer (C) is incorrect. The bonus is voluntary and benefits groups other than shareholders. CSR does not only apply to corporate entities, despite its title. Answer (D) is incorrect. The delivery is voluntary and benefits groups other than shareholders.

20. Which of the following statements is correct regarding CSR?

A. Profitable actions for an organization cannot be considered CSR because this would reflect priority being given to the needs of shareholders.

B. CSR often results in high turnover of employees due to the inconsistent nature of the corporate profits.

C. The perception of profitability related to CSR can have a positive effect on the organization's image.

D. Charity as a form of advertising risks damaging the corporate image.

Answer (D) is correct.
 REQUIRED: The correct statement regarding CSR.
 DISCUSSION: CSR tends to be beneficial to an organization if it is perceived to have good motives. If these intentions are questionable, any positive effect of the charitable act may be outweighed by the perception that its motives are selfish.
 Answer (A) is incorrect. Although CSR should maintain its altruistic motivations, it can be a profitable venture for an organization. Answer (B) is incorrect. CSR efforts often help retain employees as they feel more connected to their employer and to the community in which it operates due to the positive impacts of the organization's efforts. Answer (C) is incorrect. While CSR can be profitable for the organization, it risks damaging the positive image of the organization in the community by appearing to be done for a profit motive versus an altruistic intent.

Access the **CIA Review System** from your Gleim Personal Classroom to continue your studies with exam-emulating multiple-choice questions!

STUDY UNIT TWO
RISK MANAGEMENT

(13 pages of outline)

This study unit covers **Section II: Risk Management** from The IIA's CIA Exam Syllabus. This section makes up 10% to 20% of Part 3 of the CIA exam and is tested at the **proficiency level**. The relevant portion of the syllabus is highlighted below. (The complete syllabus is in Appendix A.)

II. RISK MANAGEMENT (10%–20%)

A. Risk Management Techniques
B. Organizational Use of Risk Frameworks

2.1 RISK MANAGEMENT TECHNIQUES

 Audit professionals do not consider risk only in the context of an audit (e.g., the probability of not discovering a material financial statement misstatement). After extensive research and many scholarly publications, risk is recognized as something that must be examined and mitigated in every aspect of an organization's operations. Thus, CIA candidates should understand the distinct responsibilities of (1) the internal audit activity and (2) senior management and the board for enterprise-wide risk.

1. **Risk Management**

   a. Risk management is "a process to identify, assess, manage, and control potential events or situations to provide reasonable assurance regarding the achievement of the organization's objectives" (The IIA Glossary).

      1) It is one of the three processes specifically addressed in the Definition of Internal Auditing.

Performance Standard 2120
Risk Management

The internal audit activity must evaluate the effectiveness and contribute to the improvement of risk management processes.

 CIA candidates should understand risk management and how to apply this knowledge to assessing the adequacy of risk management processes. The IIA may ask candidates questions involving circumstances that require application of their knowledge.

2. **The Risk Management Process**

   a. Risk management processes include (1) risk identification, (2) risk assessment and prioritization, (3) risk response, and (4) risk monitoring. Management must focus on risks at all levels of the entity and take the necessary action to manage them.

      1) All risks that could affect achievement of objectives must be considered.

b. Step 1 – Risk identification

1) Risk identification must be performed for the entire entity.

a) Examples of external risk factors at the entity level include technological changes and changes in customer wants and expectations.

b) Examples of internal risk factors at the entity level include (1) interruptions in automated systems, (2) the quality of personnel hired, and (3) the level of training provided.

2) Some occurrences may be inconsequential at the entity level but disastrous for an individual unit.

3) Risk identification should consider past events (trends) and future possibilities. Methods used include the following:

a) Event inventories. Certain events are common to particular industries. Software is available that provides lists that can be used as a starting point for event identification.

b) Internal analysis. The entity can consider its own experience with similar risks when planning a response to future events.

c) Escalation or threshold triggers. A predetermined risk response may be made when a certain event occurs, such as when cash is below a given level or a competitor cuts prices.

d) Facilitated workshops and interviews. A facilitator leads a discussion group consisting of management, staff, and other stakeholders through a structured process of conversation and exploration about potential events.

e) Process flow analysis. A single business process, such as vendor authorization and payment, is studied in isolation to identify the events that affect its inputs, tasks, responsibilities, and outputs.

f) Leading event indicators. When a pattern that predicts an adverse event is identified, a predetermined response is made. An example is avoiding debtor default by acting when a late payment occurs.

g) Loss event data methodologies. The losses associated with adverse events in the past can be used to make predictions. An example is matching workers' compensation claims with the frequency of accidents.

4) Other methods for identifying risks are (a) brainstorming, (b) SWOT (Strengths, Weaknesses, Opportunities, Threats) analysis, and (c) scenario analysis (what-if analysis).

c. Step 2 – Risk assessment and prioritization

1) The results of assessing the probabilities and potential effects of the risk events identified are used to prioritize risks and produce decision-making information.

2) The risk assessment process may be formal or informal. It involves

a) Estimating the significance of an event,
b) Assessing the event's likelihood, and
c) Considering the means to manage the risk.

3) The seriousness of a risk and its likelihood are inversely related.

a) For example, the inherent risk that petty cash will be misappropriated is relatively high. However, the amount of the loss is relatively low. A fraud involving bonds is more likely to be material, but, given the accounting and legal scrutiny of a bond issue, the probability of such an event is low.

4) Risk assessment methods may be qualitative or quantitative.

    a) Qualitative methods include (1) lists of all risks, (2) risk rankings, and (3) risk maps.

    b) Quantitative methods include probabilistic models. For example, some organizations focus on earnings at risk by examining how variables influence earnings.

5) Risk modeling is a method of risk assessment and prioritization.

    a) Risk modeling ranks and validates risk priorities when setting the priorities of engagements in the audit plan.

    b) Risk is the possibility of an event that affects the achievement of objectives. Risk is measured in terms of impact and likelihood.

        i) Risk factors may be weighted based on professional judgments to determine their relative significance, but the weights need not be quantified.

        ii) This simple model and the resulting risk assessment process can be depicted as follows:

EXAMPLE

A chief audit executive is reviewing the following enterprise-wide **risk map**:

I M P A C T		LIKELIHOOD		
		Remote	Possible	Likely
	Critical	Risk A	Risk B	
	Major			Risk D
	Minor		Risk C	

To establish priorities for the use of limited internal audit resources, the CAE makes the following analysis:

- Risk D clearly takes precedence over Risk C because D has both a higher likelihood and a greater impact.
- Risk B also clearly has a higher priority than Risk A because B has a higher likelihood and the same impact.

Choosing the higher priority between Risk D and Risk B is a matter of professional judgment based on the organizational risk assessment and the stated priorities of senior management and the board.

- If the more likely threat is considered the greater risk, Risk D will rank higher in the internal audit work plan.
- Likewise, if the threat with the greater possible impact causes senior management and the board more concern, the internal audit activity will place a higher priority on Risk B.

---

    c) Open channels of communication with senior management and the board are necessary to ensure the audit plan is based on the appropriate risk assessments and audit priorities. The audit plan should be reevaluated as needed.

    d) Risk modeling in a consulting service is done by ranking the engagement's potential to (1) improve management of risks, (2) add value, and (3) improve the organization's operations (Implementation Standard 2010.C1). Senior management assigns a weight to each item based on organizational objectives. The engagements with the appropriate weighted values are included in the annual audit plan.

  d. Step 3 – Risk responses

1) Each organization must assess the relationship between likelihood and significance and design the appropriate controls.

2) Strategies for risk response include the following:

    a) Risk avoidance ends the activity from which the risk arises. For example, the risk of having a pipeline sabotaged can be avoided by selling the pipeline.

      b)   Risk retention accepts the risk of an activity. This term is synonymous with self-insurance.

      c)   Risk reduction (mitigation) lowers the level of risk associated with an activity. For example, the risk of systems penetration can be reduced by maintaining a robust information security function within the entity.

      d)   Risk sharing transfers some loss potential to another party. Examples are insurance, hedging, and entering into joint ventures.

      e)   Risk exploitation seeks risk to pursue a high return on investment.

3)   Some risks simply may be accepted, but others require the creation of elaborate control structures. For example, the total physical destruction of the data center may be highly unlikely. However, the ability of the entity to function effectively after its destruction may be questionable. Thus, a contingency plan for such an occurrence is a necessity.

4)   In large or complex entities, senior management may appoint a risk committee to (a) review the risks identified by the various operating units and (b) create a coherent response plan.

      a)   All personnel must be aware of the importance of the risk response appropriate to their levels of the entity.

   e.   Step 4 – Risk monitoring

1)   Risk monitoring (a) tracks identified risks, (b) evaluates current risk response plans, (c) monitors residual risks, and (d) identifies new risks.

2)   The two most important sources of information for ongoing assessments of the adequacy of risk responses (and the changing nature of the risks) are

      a)   Those closest to the activities themselves. The manager of an operating unit is in the best position to monitor the effects of the chosen risk response strategies.

      b)   The audit function. Operating managers may not always be objective about the risks facing their units, especially if they had a stake in designing a particular response strategy. Analyzing risks and responses are among the normal duties of internal auditors.

3.   **Responsibility for Aspects of Organizational Risk Management**

   a.   The division of responsibility is described in Practice Advisory 2120-1, *Assessing the Adequacy of Risk Management Processes.*

1)   Risk management is a key responsibility of senior management and the board.

      a)   Management ensures that sound risk management processes are functioning.

      b)   Boards have an oversight function. They determine that risk management processes are in place, adequate, and effective.

      c)   The internal audit activity may be directed to examine, evaluate, report, or recommend improvements.

         i)   It also has a consulting role in identifying, evaluating, and implementing risk management methods and controls.

2)   Senior management and the board determine the internal audit activity's role in risk management based on factors such as (a) organizational culture, (b) abilities of the internal audit activity staff, and (c) local conditions and customs.

      a)   That role may range from no role; to auditing the process as part of the audit plan; to active, continuous support and involvement in the process; to managing and coordinating the process.

i)   But assuming management responsibilities and the threat to internal audit activity independence must be fully discussed and board-approved.

3)   The CAE must understand management's and the board's expectations of the internal audit activity in risk management. The understanding is codified in the charters of the internal audit activity and the board.

   a)   If the organization has no formal risk management processes, the CAE has formal discussions with management and the board about their obligations for understanding, managing, and monitoring risks.

4)   Risk management processes may be formal or informal, quantitative or subjective, or embedded in business units or centralized. They are designed to fit the organization's culture, management style, and objectives. For example, a small entity may use an informal risk committee.

   a)   The internal audit activity determines that the methods chosen are comprehensive and appropriate for the organization.

4. **Internal Audit's Role in Risk Management**

   a.   The IIA issued the following Interpretation to clarify internal audit's role:

Interpretation of Standard 2120

Determining whether risk management processes are effective is a judgment resulting from the internal auditor's assessment that:

- Organizational objectives support and align with the organization's mission;
- Significant risks are identified and assessed;
- Appropriate risk responses are selected that align risks with the organization's risk appetite; and
- Relevant risk information is captured and communicated in a timely manner across the organization, enabling staff, management, and the board to carry out their responsibilities.

The internal audit activity may gather the information to support this assessment during multiple engagements. The results of these engagements, when viewed together, provide an understanding of the organization's risk management processes and their effectiveness.

Risk management processes are monitored through ongoing management activities, separate evaluations, or both.

---

   b.   Two Implementation Standards link the assessment of risk to specific risk areas.

Implementation Standard 2120.A1

The internal audit activity must evaluate risk exposures relating to the organization's governance, operations, and information systems regarding the:

- Achievement of the organization's strategic objectives;
- Reliability and integrity of financial and operational information;
- Effectiveness and efficiency of operations and programs;
- Safeguarding of assets; and
- Compliance with laws, regulations, policies, procedures, and contracts.

Implementation Standard 2120.A2

The internal audit activity must evaluate the potential for the occurrence of fraud and how the organization manages fraud risk.

---

1)   To form an opinion on the adequacy of the risk management processes, the internal auditor should obtain sufficient, appropriate evidence regarding achievement of key objectives. The internal auditor may consider the following:

   a)   Current developments, trends, and industry information to determine risks and exposures and related controls

   b)   Corporate policies and minutes of board meetings to determine strategies, philosophy, methods, appetite for risk, and acceptance of risks

   c)   Previous risk evaluation reports by management, auditors, and others

   d)   Interviews with line and senior management to determine objectives, related risks, and risk mitigation and control monitoring activities

   e)   Information to evaluate the effectiveness of risk mitigation, monitoring, and communication of risks and controls

   f)   Assessment of the appropriateness of reporting lines

   g)   Review of the adequacy and timeliness of reporting on results

   h)   Review of the completeness of management's risk analysis and actions taken to remedy problems

   i)   Suggesting improvements

   j)   Determining the effectiveness of management's self-assessment processes, e.g., through observation, direct tests of controls and monitoring, and testing information used in monitoring

   k)   Reviewing risk-related indications of weakness in risk management processes and, as appropriate, discussing them with management and the board

c.   PA 2120-3, *Internal Audit Coverage of Risks to Achieving Strategic Objectives*, further clarifies internal audit's role in risk management. It is summarized below:

   1)   Internal audit should understand (a) the organization's strategy, (b) how it is executed, (c) the associated risks, and (d) how these risks are being managed.

   2)   To permit focus on critical risks, the strategy should be a fundamental basis for a risk-based audit plan that (a) aligns internal audit with strategic priorities and (b) helps ensure its resources are allocated to areas of significant importance.

   3)   To develop the audit plan, internal audit should use the work of management and other assurance functions to help identify the risks that are the most significant threats to, and opportunities for, achievement of strategic objectives.

      a)   Internal audit should consider providing assurance services related to strategic initiatives. The purpose is to assess whether strategic risks are managed to an acceptable level by evaluating some or all of the mitigation efforts. Internal audit also might provide advisory services that directly affect the organization's evolution.

   4)   After determining the strategic risks to include in the audit plan, internal audit should assess whether it has the required skills and knowledge to perform the appropriate assurance or advisory engagements. Specialized skills and knowledge may need to be outsourced or insourced to obtain needed qualifications.

Stop and review! You have completed the outline for this subunit. Study multiple-choice questions 1 through 10 beginning on page 43.

2.2 ENTERPRISE RISK MANAGEMENT

1. **The COSO ERM Framework**

   a. *Enterprise Risk Management – Integrated Framework* describes a model that incorporates the earlier COSO control framework while extending it to the broader subject of ERM. The purpose is to provide a basis for coordinating and integrating all of the entity's risk management activities.

      1) ERM is based on key concepts applicable to many types of organizations. The emphasis is on (a) the objectives of a specific entity and (b) establishing a means for evaluating the effectiveness of ERM.

   b. The COSO Framework defines ERM as follows:

      Enterprise risk management is a process, effected by an entity's board of directors, management, and other personnel, applied in strategy setting and across the enterprise, designed to identify potential events that may affect the entity, and manage risk to be within its risk appetite, to provide reasonable assurance regarding the achievement of entity objectives.

2. **ERM Glossary**

   a. Risk is the possibility that an event will occur and negatively affect the achievement of objectives.

   b. Inherent risk is the risk in the absence of a risk response.

   c. Residual risk is the risk after a risk response.

   d. Risk appetite is the amount of risk an entity is willing to accept in pursuit of value. It reflects the entity's risk management philosophy and influences the entity's culture and operating style.

   e. An opportunity is the possibility that an event will occur and positively affect the achievement of objectives by creating or preserving value.

      1) Management plans to exploit opportunities, subject to the entity's objectives and strategies.

   f. Risk management, at any level, consists of (1) identifying potential events that may affect the entity and (2) managing the associated risk to be within the entity's risk appetite.

      1) Risk management should provide reasonable assurance that entity objectives are achieved.

3. **ERM Capabilities**

   a. ERM allows management to optimize stakeholder value by coping effectively with uncertainty and the risks and opportunities it presents. ERM helps management to

      1) Reach objectives,
      2) Prevent loss of reputation and resources,
      3) Report effectively, and
      4) Comply with laws and regulations.

   b. The following are the capabilities of ERM:

      1) Consideration of risk appetite and strategy

         a) Risk appetite should be considered in

            i) Evaluating strategies,
            ii) Setting objectives, and
            iii) Developing risk management methods.

2) Risk response decisions

    a) ERM permits identification and selection of such responses to risk as

        i) Avoidance,
        ii) Reduction,
        iii) Sharing, and
        iv) Acceptance.

3) Reduction of operational surprises and losses

    a) These are reduced by an improved ability to anticipate potential events and develop responses.

4) Multiple and cross-enterprise risks

    a) Risks may affect different parts of the entity. ERM allows

        i) Effective responses to interrelated effects and
        ii) Integrated responses to multiple risks.

5) Response to opportunities

    a) By facilitating the identification of potential events, ERM helps management to respond quickly to opportunities.

6) Use of capital

    a) The risk information provided by ERM permits

        i) Assessment of capital needs and
        ii) Better capital allocation.

4. **ERM Components**

  a. The components ordinarily are addressed in the order below:

    1) The **internal environment** reflects the entity's (a) risk management philosophy, (b) risk appetite, (c) integrity, (d) ethical values, and (e) overall environment. It sets the tone of the entity.

    2) **Objective setting** precedes event identification. ERM ensures that (a) a process is established and (b) objectives are consistent with the mission and the risk appetite. The following categories of objectives apply to all entities:

        a) S̲trategic objectives are consistent with and support the entity's mission.
        b) O̲perations objectives address effectiveness and efficiency.
        c) R̲eporting objectives concern reliability.
        d) C̲ompliance objectives relate to adherence to laws and regulations.

        Memory aid: S̲tudying O̲bsessively R̲eally C̲ounts

    3) **Event identification** relates to internal and external events affecting the organization that may create opportunities or risks. Impact factors are potential results of an event.

    4) **Risk assessment** considers likelihood and impact as a basis for risk management. The assessment considers inherent risk and residual risk.

    5) **Risk responses** reduce the impact or likelihood of adverse events. They include control activities. They should be consistent with the entity's risk tolerances and appetite.

    6) **Control activities** are policies and procedures to ensure the effectiveness of risk responses.

    7) The **information and communication** component identifies, captures, and communicates relevant and timely information.

    8) **Monitoring** involves ongoing management activities or separate evaluations. The full ERM process is monitored.

b. These distinct categories overlap. They apply to different needs, and different managers may be assigned responsibility for them.

1) **Safeguarding of resources** is another category that may be appropriate for some entities.

c. The achievement of strategic and operational matters is affected by external events that the entity may not control. Thus, ERM should provide reasonable assurance that management and the board receive timely information about whether those objectives are being achieved.

d. Reporting and compliance are within the entity's control. Accordingly, ERM should provide reasonable assurance of achieving those objectives.

5. **Responsibilities**

a. **Senior Management**

1) The CEO sets the tone at the top of the entity and has ultimate responsibility for ERM.

2) Senior management should ensure that sound risk management processes are functioning.

3) Senior management also determines the entity's risk management philosophy. For example, officers who issue definitive policy statements, insist on written procedures, and closely monitor performance indicators have one type of risk management philosophy. Officers who manage informally and take a relaxed approach to performance monitoring have a different philosophy.

a) Assurance about the effectiveness of risk management processes and the reduction of key risks to an acceptable level comes primarily from management.

b. **Board of Directors**

1) The board has an oversight role. It should determine that risk management processes are in place, adequate, and effective.

2) Directors' attitudes are a key component of the internal environment. They must possess certain qualities to be effective.

a) A majority of the board should be outside directors.

b) Directors generally should have years of experience either in the industry or in corporate governance.

c) Directors must be willing to challenge management's choices. Complacent directors increase the chances of adverse consequences.

c. **Risk Committee and Chief Risk Officer**

1) Larger entities may wish to establish a risk committee composed of directors that also includes managers, the individuals most familiar with entity processes.

a) A chief risk officer, who should **not** be from the internal audit function, may be appointed to coordinate the entity's risk management activities. (S)he is a member of, and reports to, the risk committee.

b) The chief risk officer is most effective when supported by a specific team with the necessary expertise and experience related to organization-wide risk.

6.   **ERM Matrix**

    a.   The matrix is a cube with rows, slices, and columns.

        1)   The rows are the eight components, the slices are the four categories of objectives, and the columns are the organizational units of the entity.

    b.   The entity should make the appropriate response at each intersection of the matrix, such as control activities for achieving reporting objectives at the division level.

COSO ERM Framework

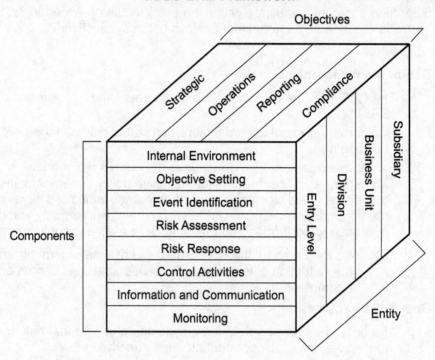

Figure 2-1

    c.   The **components** should be present and functioning effectively. Consequently, the components are criteria for the effectiveness of ERM.

        1)   No material weaknesses should exist, and risk should be within the risk appetite.

        2)   When ERM is effective regarding all **objectives**, the board and management have reasonable assurance that (a) reporting is reliable, (b) compliance is achieved, and (c) the extent of achievement of strategic and operations objectives is known.

        3)   The components operate differently in different organizations. For example, they may be applied in a less formal way in smaller organizations.

7.   **ERM Limitations**

    a.   Limitations of ERM arise from the possibility of

        1)   Faulty human judgment,
        2)   Cost-benefit considerations,
        3)   Simple errors or mistakes,
        4)   Collusion, and
        5)   Management override of ERM decisions.

8. **Internal Audit's Role in ERM**

   a. The IIA specifically addresses ERM in its Position Paper, *The Role of Internal Auditing in Enterprise-wide Risk Management*. This publication defines ERM as a structured, consistent, and continuous process across the whole organization. ERM identifies, assesses, decides on responses to, and reports on opportunities and threats that affect the achievement of objectives.

   b. **Assurance** is needed about the effectiveness of risk management processes and the reduction of key risks to an acceptable level.

      1) Objective assurance is provided by the internal audit activity, external auditors, and independent specialists. The internal audit activity usually provides assurance about the following:

         a) The design and effectiveness of risk management processes
         b) Management of key risks, including the effectiveness of response activities
         c) Risk assessment
         d) Reporting risk and control status

      2) The internal audit activity provides value to the organization primarily through giving objective assurance that (a) key risks are properly managed, and (b) the risk management and control framework is effective.

   c. The internal audit activity also may provide **consulting** services, depending on the availability of other resources and the organization's risk maturity.

      1) Risk maturity is the extent to which a robust risk management approach has been applied.

      2) As risk maturity increases, or if the organization has a risk management specialist or function, the internal audit activity's consulting role is reduced.

      3) The internal audit activity may provide ERM consulting services if it does not actually manage risks.

   d. Roles of the internal audit activity

      1) The following **core assurance roles** provide assurance:

         a) Giving assurance on risk management processes
         b) Giving assurance that risks are correctly evaluated
         c) Evaluating risk management processes
         d) Evaluating the reporting of key risks
         e) Reviewing the management of key risks

      2) The following **legitimate internal audit roles** may be performed as consulting engagements, given safeguards against loss of independence and objectivity:

         a) Facilitating identification and evaluation of risks
         b) Coaching management in responding to risks
         c) Coordinating ERM activities
         d) Consolidating the reporting on risks
         e) Maintaining and developing the ERM framework
         f) Championing establishment of ERM
         g) Developing a risk management strategy for board approval

      3) The internal audit activity should **not** undertake roles that threaten its independence and objectivity. The following are examples:

         a) Setting the risk appetite
         b) Imposing risk management processes
         c) Managing assurance on risks
         d) Making decisions on risk responses
         e) Implementing risk responses on management's behalf
         f) Being accountable for risk management

9.   **ISO 31000**

a.   In addition to the Position Paper outlined in the previous section, The IIA has issued related guidance based on ISO 31000, a publication of the International Organization for Standardization. The Practice Guide, *Assessing the Adequacy of Risk Management Using ISO 31000*, presents an alternative ERM framework with many similarities to the COSO model. That framework is depicted below.

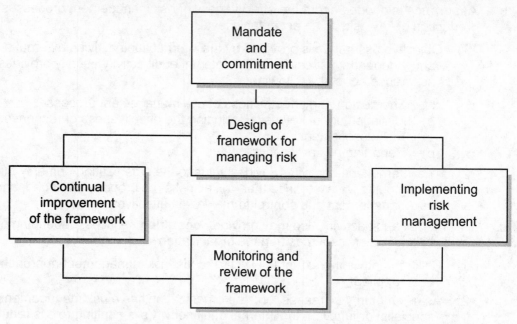

Figure 2-2

b.   The Practice Guide describes three approaches to providing assurance on the risk management process.

1)   The **process element** approach determines whether each element has been implemented. The following are the elements:

a)   Ongoing, structured communication with those affected by operations
b)   Understanding the external and internal environments
c)   Formal risk identification
d)   Formal risk analysis
e)   Risk evaluation (ranking risks)
f)   Risk treatment (avoiding, sharing, controlling, or accepting risks)
g)   Monitoring and reviewing treatment plans, controls, and the environment

2)   The **key principles** approach determines the extent to which risk management

a)   Creates and protects value. Risk management should be most rigorous when value is greatest.

b)   Is fully integrated with management at all levels.

c)   Is part of decision making, most explicitly for the most significant decisions.

d)   Directly addresses uncertainty in risk assessment.

e)   Is systematic, structured, and timely.

f)   Is based on the best available information, with guidance on what is sufficient.

g)   Is adapted to the specific entity.

h)   Considers human and cultural factors so that results are helpful to users of the process.

i)   Is transparent and inclusive of stakeholders.

j)   Remains relevant because it responds to change.

k)   Promotes continuous improvement.

3)   The **maturity model** approach is based on the principle that effective risk management processes develop as value is added at each stage of maturation. Accordingly, this approach determines where risk management is on the maturity curve and whether (a) it is progressing as expected, (b) adds value, and (c) meets organizational needs.

a)   Risk management performance and progress in executing the risk management plan should be linked with a performance measurement system.

10.   **Turnbull**

a.   This approach to ERM is named for the chair of the working group in the United Kingdom that developed the guidance. It is an internal control framework with an emphasis on internal control, the assessment of its effectiveness, and risk analysis.

Stop and review! You have completed the outline for this subunit. Study multiple-choice questions 11 through 20 beginning on page 46.

QUESTIONS

2.1 Risk Management Techniques

1. When the executive management of an organization decided to form a team to investigate the adoption of an activity-based costing (ABC) system, an internal auditor was assigned to the team. The best reason for including an internal auditor is the internal auditor's knowledge of

A.   Activities and cost drivers.

B.   Information processing procedures.

C.   Current product cost structures.

D.   Risk management processes.

Answer (D) is correct.
   REQUIRED: The best reason for including an internal auditor in a team investigating an ABC system.
   DISCUSSION: The internal audit activity's scope of work extends to evaluating the organization's risk management processes. The internal audit activity should assist the organization by identifying and evaluating significant exposures to risk and contributing to the improvement of risk management and control systems.
   Answer (A) is incorrect. An engineer has more knowledge than an internal auditor about activities and cost drivers. Answer (B) is incorrect. An information systems expert has more knowledge than an internal auditor about information needs and information processing procedures. Answer (C) is incorrect. A management accountant has more knowledge than an internal auditor about a company's current product cost.

2. Internal auditors should review the means of physically safeguarding assets from losses arising from

A.   Misapplication of accounting principles.

B.   Procedures that are not cost justified.

C.   Exposure to the elements.

D.   Underusage of physical facilities.

Answer (C) is correct.
   REQUIRED: The cause of losses giving rise to physical safeguards that should be reviewed by the auditor.
   DISCUSSION: The internal audit activity must evaluate risk exposures relating to governance, operations, and information systems regarding the safeguarding of assets (Impl. Std. 2120.A1). For example, internal auditors evaluate risk exposure arising from theft, fire, improper or illegal activities, and exposure to the elements.
   Answer (A) is incorrect. Misapplication of accounting principles relates to the reliability of information and not physical safeguards. Answer (B) is incorrect. Procedures that are not cost justified relate to efficiency, not effectiveness, of operations. Answer (D) is incorrect. Underusage of facilities relates to efficiency of operations.

3. Which of the following activities is outside the scope of internal auditing?

    A. Evaluating risk exposures regarding compliance with policies, procedures, and contracts.

    B. Safeguarding of assets.

    C. Evaluating risk exposures regarding compliance with laws and regulations.

    D. Ascertaining the extent to which management has established criteria to determine whether objectives have been accomplished.

Answer (B) is correct.
    REQUIRED: The activity outside the scope of internal auditing.
    DISCUSSION: Safeguarding assets is an operational activity and is therefore beyond the scope of the internal audit activity. However, the internal audit activity evaluates (1) risk exposures and (2) the adequacy and effectiveness of controls related to the organization's governance, operations, and information systems.
    Answer (A) is incorrect. Internal auditors must evaluate risk exposures relating to, among other things, the organization's compliance with laws, regulations, policies, procedures, and contracts. Answer (C) is incorrect. The internal audit activity must evaluate risk exposures relating to, among other things, the organization's compliance with laws, regulations, policies, procedures, and contracts. Answer (D) is incorrect. Ascertaining the extent to which management has established adequate criteria to determine whether objectives and goals have been accomplished is within the scope of internal auditing.

4. In the risk management process, management's view of the internal audit activity's role is likely to be determined by all of the following factors **except**

    A. Organizational culture.

    B. Preferences of the independent auditor.

    C. Ability of the internal audit staff.

    D. Local conditions and customs of the country.

Answer (B) is correct.
    REQUIRED: The factor not influencing management's view on the role of internal auditing.
    DISCUSSION: Ultimately, the role of internal auditing in the risk management process is determined by senior management and the board. Their view on internal auditing's role is likely to be determined by factors such as the culture of the organization, ability of the internal audit staff, and local conditions and customs (PA 2120-1, para. 5).
    Answer (A) is incorrect. Organizational culture is a factor that influences management's view of the role of internal auditing. Answer (C) is incorrect. The ability of the internal audit staff is a factor that influences management's view of the role of internal auditing. Answer (D) is incorrect. Local conditions and customs of the country influence management's view of the role of internal auditing.

5. Which of the following is the most accurate term for a process to identify, assess, manage, and control potential events or situations to provide reasonable assurance regarding the achievement of the organization's objectives?

    A. The internal audit activity.

    B. Control process.

    C. Risk management.

    D. Consulting service.

Answer (C) is correct.
    REQUIRED: The process to identify, assess, manage, and control potential events or situations.
    DISCUSSION: Risk management is "a process to identify, assess, manage, and control potential events or situations to provide reasonable assurance regarding the achievement of the organization's objectives" (The IIA Glossary).
    Answer (A) is incorrect. The internal audit activity assists in risk management; it is not the same thing as risk management. Answer (B) is incorrect. Control processes are "the policies, procedures, and activities that are part of a control framework designed to ensure that risks are contained within the risk tolerances established by the risk management process" (The IIA Glossary). Answer (D) is incorrect. Consulting services are "advisory and related client service activities, the nature and scope of which are agreed with the client" (The IIA Glossary).

6. The board's expectations of the internal audit activity regarding the risk management process are

    A. Noted in the work programs for formal consulting engagements.

    B. Included in the business continuity plan.

    C. Codified in the charters of the internal audit activity and the board.

    D. Reviewed by the internal auditors immediately following a disaster.

Answer (C) is correct.
    REQUIRED: The treatment of the board's expectations of the internal audit activity regarding the risk management process.
    DISCUSSION: The chief audit executive (CAE) is to obtain an understanding of senior management's and the board's expectations of the internal audit activity in the organization's risk management process. This understanding is then codified in the charters of the internal audit activity and the board (PA 2120-1, para. 4).
    Answer (A) is incorrect. A work program is a listing of specific procedures. Answer (B) is incorrect. Business continuity planning is just one element of risk management. Answer (D) is incorrect. The internal audit activity's role needs to be understood before a crisis.

7. The internal audit activity must evaluate the effectiveness and contribute to the improvement of risk management processes. With respect to evaluating the adequacy of risk management processes, internal auditors most likely should

    A. Recognize that organizations should use similar techniques for managing risk.

    B. Determine that the key objectives of risk management processes are being met.

    C. Determine the level of risks acceptable to the organization.

    D. Treat the evaluation of risk management processes in the same manner as the risk analysis used to plan engagements.

Answer (B) is correct.

    REQUIRED: The responsibility of internal auditors for assessing the adequacy of risk management processes.

    DISCUSSION: Internal auditors need to obtain sufficient and appropriate evidence to determine that key objectives of the risk management processes are being met to form an opinion on the adequacy of risk management processes (PA 2120-1, para. 8).

    Answer (A) is incorrect. Risk management processes vary with the size and complexity of an organization's business activities. Answer (C) is incorrect. Management and the board determine the level of acceptable organizational risks. Answer (D) is incorrect. Evaluating management's risk processes differs from the internal auditors' risk assessment used to plan an engagement, but information from a comprehensive risk management process is useful in such planning.

8. Quantitative risk management methods are most appropriate for

    A. Assessing personnel risks.

    B. Developing a risk matrix.

    C. The use of derivatives by the organization.

    D. Identifying risks from the COSO's enterprise risk management framework.

Answer (C) is correct.

    REQUIRED: The item most appropriate for quantitative RM methods.

    DISCUSSION: The organization designs risk management processes based on its culture, management style, and business objectives. For example, the use of derivatives or other sophisticated capital market products by the organization could require the use of quantitative risk management tools. But the internal auditor determines that the methodology chosen is sufficiently comprehensive and appropriate for the nature of the organization (PA 2120-1, para. 7).

    Answer (A) is incorrect. Matters addressed in the control environment, e.g., integrity and ethical values, human resources, and organizational structure are subject to soft controls and soft risk management approaches. Answer (B) is incorrect. A risk matrix links identified risks to, for example, controls or business processes. Answer (D) is incorrect. An ERM framework contains broad statements of classes of risks. They are not stated in the detail (quantitative or not) required by a specific organization.

9. Which of the following is a **false** statement about risk responses?

    A. Each organization must assess the relationship between the likelihood and significance of risks.

    B. Identified risks cannot simply be accepted.

    C. Some risks require the creation of elaborate control structures.

    D. There is no direct correlation between the severity of a risk and the cost of the response to that risk.

Answer (B) is correct.

    REQUIRED: The statement about risk responses that is false.

    DISCUSSION: While some risks require the creation of elaborate control structures, others may simply be accepted.

    Answer (A) is incorrect. Each organization must assess the relationship between the likelihood and significance of risks and must design the appropriate controls. Answer (C) is incorrect. This is a true statement about risk responses. For example, although the total physical destruction of a data center may be highly unlikely, if it were to occur, the ability of the entity to function may be questionable. Therefore, a contingency plan for such an occurrence is almost a necessity. Answer (D) is incorrect. There is no direct correlation between the severity of a risk and the cost of the response to that risk.

10. Which of the following is **not** an activity undertaken as part of risk management?

    A. Risk identification.

    B. Risk analysis.

    C. Risk exposure.

    D. Risk response.

Answer (C) is correct.

    REQUIRED: The activity that is not part of risk management.

    DISCUSSION: Risk exposure is a condition, not an activity.

    Answer (A) is incorrect. Risk management processes include risk identification, risk analysis, and appropriate risk response. Answer (B) is incorrect. Risk management processes include risk identification, risk analysis, and appropriate risk response. Answer (D) is incorrect. Risk management processes include risk identification, risk analysis, and appropriate risk response.

2.2 Enterprise Risk Management

11. Which of the following is a factor affecting risk?

A. New personnel.

B. New or revamped information systems.

C. Rapid growth.

D. All of the answers are correct.

Answer (D) is correct.
REQUIRED: The item that is a factor affecting risk.
DISCUSSION: New personnel, new or revamped information systems, and rapid growth are all factors that affect risk.

12. Management considers risk appetite for all of the following reasons **except**

A. Evaluating strategic options.

B. Setting objectives.

C. Developing risk management techniques.

D. Increasing the net present value of investments.

Answer (D) is correct.
REQUIRED: The item not a reason for considering risk appetite.
DISCUSSION: As described in the COSO ERM framework, risk appetite should be considered in

1. Evaluating strategies,
2. Setting related objectives, and
3. Developing risk management methods.

Increasing the net present value of investments is an operational objective. It would be determined after consideration of the entity's risk appetite and other strategic factors.

13. Limitations of enterprise risk management (ERM) may arise from

A. Faulty human judgment.

B. Cost-benefit considerations.

C. Collusion.

D. All of the answers are correct.

Answer (D) is correct.
REQUIRED: The limitations of ERM.
DISCUSSION: The limitations of ERM are the same as those for control in general. They arise from the possibility of (1) faulty human judgment, (2) cost-benefit considerations, (3) simple errors or mistakes, (4) collusion, and (5) management override.
    Answer (A) is incorrect. Limitations of ERM can also arise from cost-benefit considerations and collusion. Answer (B) is incorrect. Limitations of ERM can also arise from faulty human judgment and collusion. Answer (C) is incorrect. Limitations of ERM can also arise from faulty human judgment and cost-benefit considerations.

14. Components of enterprise risk management (ERM) are integrated with the management process. Which of the following correctly states four of the eight components of ERM according to the COSO's framework?

A. Event identification, risk assessment, control activities, and objective setting.

B. Internal environment, risk responses, monitoring, and risk minimization.

C. External environment, information and communication, monitoring, and event identification.

D. Objective setting, response to opportunities, risk assessment, and control activities.

Answer (A) is correct.
REQUIRED: The item identifying four components of ERM.
DISCUSSION: ERM ensures that (1) a process is established and (2) objectives align with the mission and the risk appetite. Event identification, risk assessment, control activities, and objective setting are components of ERM. Event identification relates to internal and external events affecting the organization. Risk assessment considers likelihood and impact (see the definitions of risk in The IIA Glossary) as a basis for risk management. Control activities are policies and procedures to ensure the effectiveness of risk responses. Objective setting precedes event identification.
    Answer (B) is incorrect. Risk assessment, not minimization, is a component of ERM. Answer (C) is incorrect. The internal, not external, environment is a component of ERM. Answer (D) is incorrect. Response to opportunities is a capability of ERM.

15. Which of the following control models is fully incorporated into the broader integrated framework of enterprise risk management (ERM)?

A. CoCo.

B. COSO.

C. *Electronic Systems Assurance and Control.*

D. COBIT.

Answer (B) is correct.
REQUIRED: The control model incorporated in the ERM framework.
DISCUSSION: The Committee of Sponsoring Organizations of the Treadway Commission published *Enterprise Risk Management – Integrated Framework.* This document describes a model that incorporates the earlier COSO internal control framework while extending it to the broader area of enterprise risk management.
    Answer (A) is incorrect. ERM extends the COSO, not the CoCo, model. Answer (C) is incorrect. ERM extends the COSO, not the eSAC, model. Answer (D) is incorrect. ERM extends the COSO, not the COBIT, model.

16. Which of the following is closely related to traditional risk management instead of enterprise risk management (ERM)?

    A. Rapid response to opportunities.

    B. Organization-level view of risk.

    C. Emphasis on specific functions.

    D. Achieving financial goals.

Answer (C) is correct.
    REQUIRED: The difference between traditional risk management and ERM.
    DISCUSSION: The enterprise risk management approach set forth by the Committee of Sponsoring Organizations of the Treadway Commission (COSO) attempts to approach an organization as a whole instead of focusing on any specific area or risk.
    Answer (A) is incorrect. Rapid response to opportunities is a characteristic of ERM, which tries to offset potential risks with opportunities. Answer (B) is incorrect. ERM tries to view risk as it affects every level of an organization. Answer (D) is incorrect. Financial goals are an example of the methods ERM uses to achieve objectives in one or more separate but overlapping categories.

17. Which of the following members of an organization has ultimate ownership responsibility of the enterprise risk management, provides leadership and direction to senior managers, and monitors the entity's overall risk activities in relation to its risk appetite?

    A. Chief risk officer.

    B. Chief executive officer.

    C. Internal auditors.

    D. Chief financial officer.

Answer (B) is correct.
    REQUIRED: The member of the organization with the stated responsibilities.
    DISCUSSION: The chief executive officer (CEO) sets the tone at the top of the organization and has ultimate responsibility for ownership of the ERM. The CEO will influence the composition and conduct of the board, provide leadership and direction to senior managers, and monitor the entity's overall risk activities in relation to its risk appetite. If any problems arise with the organization's risk appetite, the CEO will also take any measures to adjust the alignment to better suit the organization.
    Answer (A) is incorrect. The risk officer works in assigned areas of responsibility in a staff function. The work of a risk officer often extends beyond one specific area because the officer will have the necessary resources to work across many segments or divisions. Answer (C) is incorrect. The internal auditors evaluate the ERM and may provide recommendations. Answer (D) is incorrect. The CFO is subordinate to the CEO.

18. Which of the entity objectives address effectiveness and efficiency?

    A. Strategic objectives.

    B. Operations objectives.

    C. Reporting objectives.

    D. Compliance objectives.

Answer (B) is correct.
    REQUIRED: The entity objectives that address effectiveness and efficiency.
    DISCUSSION: Operations objectives address effectiveness and efficiency.
    Answer (A) is incorrect. Strategic objectives are consistent with and support the entity's mission. Answer (C) is incorrect. Reporting objectives concern reliability. Answer (D) is incorrect. Compliance objectives relate to adherence to laws and regulations.

19. When ERM is effective regarding all of the objectives, the board and management have reasonable assurance that

1. Reporting is reliable

2. Compliance is achieved

3. The extent of achievement of strategic and operations objectives is known

    A. 1 and 2 only.

    B. 2 and 3 only.

    C. 1 and 3 only.

    D. 1, 2, and 3.

Answer (D) is correct.
    REQUIRED: The reasonable assurance that management has when ERM is effective.
    DISCUSSION: When ERM is effective regarding all of the objectives, the board and management have reasonable assurance that (1) reporting is reliable, (2) compliance is achieved, and (3) the extent of achievement of strategic and operations objectives is known.
    Answer (A) is incorrect. The board and management also have reasonable assurance that the extent of achievement of strategic and operations objectives is known. Answer (B) is incorrect. The board and management also have reasonable assurance that reporting is reliable. Answer (C) is incorrect. The board and management also have reasonable assurance that compliance is achieved.

20. Which of the following statements regarding the chief risk officer is **false**?

- A. The creation of a separate risk management function may include the appointment of a chief risk officer.

- B. The chief risk officer is a member of management assigned primary responsibility for ERM processes.

- C. The chief risk officer is most effective when supported by a specific team with the necessary expertise.

- D. The chief risk officer should be employed in the internal audit function.

Answer (D) is correct.

REQUIRED: The false statement regarding the chief risk officer.

DISCUSSION: The chief risk officer should not be employed in the internal audit function.

Answer (A) is incorrect. A separate function may coordinate and manage ERM and apply special skills and knowledge. The creation of a separate risk management function may include the appointment of a chief risk officer. Answer (B) is incorrect. It is true that the chief risk officer is a member of management assigned primary responsibility for ERM processes. Answer (C) is incorrect. The chief risk officer is most effective when supported by a specific team with the necessary expertise and experience related to organization-wide risk.

Access the **CIA Review System** from your Gleim Personal Classroom to continue your studies with exam-emulating multiple-choice questions!

STUDY UNIT THREE
STRUCTURE AND PROCESSES

(23 pages of outline)

This study unit is the first of two covering **Section III: Organizational Structure / Business Processes and Risks** from The IIA's CIA Exam Syllabus. This section makes up 15% to 25% of Part 3 of the CIA exam and is tested at the **awareness level**. The relevant portion of the syllabus is highlighted below. (The complete syllabus is in Appendix A.)

III. **Organizational Structure/Business Processes and Risks (15%–25%)**

A. **Risk/Control Implications of Different Organizational Structures**
B. **Structure (e.g., centralized/decentralized)**
C. **Typical Schemes in Various Business Cycles (e.g., procurement, sales, knowledge, supply-chain management)**
D. **Business Process Analysis (e.g., workflow analysis and bottleneck management, theory of constraints)**

E. Inventory Management Techniques and Concepts
F. Electronic Funds Transfer (EFT) / Electronic Data Interchange (EDI) / E-commerce
G. Business Development Life Cycles
H. The International Organization for Standardization (ISO) Framework
I. Outsourcing Business Processes

3.1 RISK/CONTROL IMPLICATIONS OF ORGANIZATIONAL STRUCTURES

 CIA candidates can expect questions asking how organizational structure affects internal control. By understanding the concepts in Subunit 3.1, successful candidates will be able to apply their knowledge to the facts provided in questions.

1. **Basic Approaches to Organizational Design**

    a. The oldest approach to design, known as **traditional or classical approach**, emphasizes such factors as authority, responsibility, unity of command, tasks, hierarchy, and a narrow span of control.

    1) This approach prescribes (or dictates) relationships and then places people in them. Thus, the person is selected for the job.

    2) Management's primary goal is profit.

    b. The **behavioral approach** developed more recently. It emphasizes the limits, strengths, availability, and interests of the people available. The participants provide feedback in the role-definition process.

    1) This approach is less deterministic than the traditional approach because group dynamics and the feelings of subordinates are included in the process.

    2) The job is designed for the person.

    c.   The **contingency approach** is another relatively recent development. It designs the organization for its unique situation.

        1)   It combines traditional and behavioral principles of organization: The job and the person must fit each other.

        2)   Traditional theory assumed workers have only economic motives. The modern approaches assume they have multiple motives.

2.   **Unity of Objective**

    a.   Unity of objective is a basic principle of organizational design. Thus, the structure of every organization should facilitate the achievement of its objectives.

        1)   A structure is effective if it contributes to unity of objective.
        2)   A structure is efficient if it does so with a minimum of waste.

3.   **Span of Control**

    a.   Span of control also is a basic principle of structural design. It is the number of subordinates who report directly to the manager.

    b.   The optimal span of control tends to **widen** in the following situations:

        1)   Managers have frequent contact with subordinates.
        2)   Managers are willing to delegate authority and therefore have more time to devote to subordinates.
        3)   Managers are well trained and communicate effectively with subordinates.
        4)   Managers have subordinates whose jobs are similar and whose procedures are standardized.
        5)   Managers and subordinates are in the same physical location.

    c.   The optimal span of control narrows in the following situations:

        1)   The work done becomes more complex.
        2)   The frequency and intensity of required supervision increase.
        3)   The time needed for coordination with other supervisors increases.
        4)   The time needed for planning increases.

    d.   Behaviorists advocate expanding the span of control if possible. The following are advantages:

        1)   Increasing autonomy and morale of individual workers by reducing the time available to a manager to direct them (the more people per manager, the less time available per person)

        2)   Decreasing communication problems by reducing organizational levels (given a fixed number of employees, the narrower the span of control, the taller the organization, and the greater the number of levels)

    e.   The contingency approach suggests that the appropriate span of control varies widely. The following are the situational variables that determine the span of control:

        1)   The supervisor's training, interests, abilities, personality, time available, etc.
        2)   Workers' interests, drives, commitment to the job, training, attitudes, aptitudes, etc.
        3)   The work situation, including the technological process used (job shop, mass production, continuous process), frequency of change in job method, complexity of the task, dependence on the work of others, and supervision required
        4)   The organizational culture and established policies and procedures
        5)   The organization's environment, including how rapidly it is compelled to change by technological innovation or market pressure and the amount of uncertainty in the environment

f. The number of levels in an organization is influenced by the span of control.

    1) **Flat structures** have relatively few levels from top to bottom. They have wide spans of control.

        a) Flat structures provide fast information flow from top to bottom of the organization and increased employee satisfaction.

        b) Disadvantages of reduced supervision are poorer employee training, lack of coordination, and behavioral problems.

    2) **Tall structures** have many levels between top and bottom. They have relatively narrow spans of control.

        a) Tall structures are faster and more effective at problem resolution than flat structures. They increase frequency of interaction between superior and employee and impose greater order.

        b) Disadvantages are slow decision making; excessive supervision; greater administrative costs; and lack of initiative, resulting from too little delegation of authority.

    3) Studies do not indicate great advantages for either flat or tall structures.

4. **Size-Structure Relationship**

    a. As an organization increases in size, its structure tends to become more formal. More policies and procedures are necessary to coordinate the increased number of employees, and more managers must be hired.

        1) The relationship of size and structure, however, is linear only within a certain range. For example, adding 100 employees to a company with 100 employees is likely to cause significant structural change. Adding the same number to a workforce of 10,000 is likely to have little structural effect.

5. **Unity of Command**

    a. This principle is emphasized in traditional organizations, e.g., the military. Thus, the authority and responsibility of the parties should be clearly defined, and every subordinate should report only to one superior.

        1) A line-and-staff design helps to preserve unity of command. This type of design is described in the next section.

    b. As organizations grow, unity of command becomes more important.

6. **Line and Staff Design**

    a. The traditional approach views line activities as those directly responsible for the primary function, product, or service of the organization. Staff members provide supporting technical expertise.

    b. Production is a line activity. Moreover, sales (marketing) and finance may be line activities.

    c. Staff activities are advisory activities that are necessary to the organization but secondary to the line functions.

        1) **Personal staff** are individuals assigned to a given manager.

        2) **Specialized staff** are functions that serve the whole organization.

7. **Authority**

    a. The behavioral approach to line and staff relationships regards informal authority as a limit on formal chains of command.

        1) Advice offered by senior staff members may be similar to a command. They have access to senior management and can exercise more informal authority than a junior line manager.

b.   The difficult issue in a line-staff relationship is how to ensure adoption of specialized staff advice without undermining line authority. The resolution of this issue depends on whether a staff group's authority is advisory, concurrent, complete in a specialized area, or a form of control.

1)   Advisory. A staff group with advisory authority can offer only suggestions, prepare plans for consideration by line managers, and evaluate organizational performance.

   a)   A staff member often has an area of technical expertise, such as law, industrial labor relations, operations research, or personnel.

   b)   The staff member's goal is the approval (or rejection) of a complete recommended solution, but a line manager may want a quick fix to a problem rather than a complete solution.

   c)   Consultation with line personnel is essential.

   d)   The line manager is not required to use the staff's services.

2)   Concurrent. A staff group may have concurrent authority. Line management must persuade experts in specified areas to agree to an action or decision.

3)   Complete in an area. A staff group may be given complete authority in a specialized area, and its specialized activities are separated from line management.

   a)   The line manager must use the staff services.
   b)   Examples include information systems, purchasing, and personnel.

4)   Control. A staff group occasionally may be given control authority. Thus, line authority may be superseded by that of the specialist staff designated by higher levels of management to make certain decisions in the area of staff expertise.

   a)   Control staff authority appears to violate the principle of unity of command. However, no violation occurs when members of the control staff act as agents for the higher-level line manager who delegated authority.

   b)   For example, quality-control inspectors have the authority to reject marginal products. But, because this authority is exercised on behalf of the manufacturing manager, the chain of command actually remains intact.

8.   **Functional Authority**

a.   A hybrid of the control authority relationship of line and staff is functional authority. This kind of design is common in organic organizations.

b.   An individual is given functional authority outside the chain of command for certain specified activities. The individual may be either a line or a staff manager who is a specialist in a particular field.

1)   For example, the vice president in charge of sales may be given functional authority over manufacturing executives in scheduling customer orders, packaging, or making service parts available.

c.   Functional authority may be created for numerous reasons when a line manager is not the person best suited to oversee a given activity.

1)   For example, the vice president for industrial labor relations may have functional authority over the production manager for the purpose of negotiating a new labor contract, though no line relationship exists at other times.

d.   Functional specialists have the authority to determine the appropriate standards in their own field of specialization and to enforce those standards.

1)   For example, the chief engineer of an airline may have the authority to remove airplanes from service, overriding the vice president for operations.

9. **Line and Staff Conflicts**

    a.   Line and staff conflicts are inevitable given the differences in their backgrounds and activities. These individuals tend to have different training and education, perspectives on the organization, career and other objectives, and temperaments.

        1)   Operating executives with line authority often see a high potential for harm in staff activity. A staff member with vaguely defined authority from a chief executive may effectively undermine line managers.

        2)   Staff members normally are not responsible for the success of a line department. If an implemented suggestion fails, line managers tend to blame the suggestion and staff blame the implementation.

        3)   Setting staff members apart from line responsibilities gives them the time and environment in which to think. However, this separation also can lead to thinking in a vacuum and suggestions by staff that are inappropriate or not feasible.

        4)   Excessive staff activity may violate the principle of unity of command.

    b.   Line-staff conflicts may be minimized by

        1)   Clearly defining areas of activity and authority.

        2)   Sharply defining the nature and place of line managers and staff.

        3)   Stressing the systems approach to all employees, whether line or staff, to encourage them to work together toward organizational goals.

        4)   Reducing areas of possible conflict, e.g., keeping functional authority to a minimum and providing feedback to staff of line's reaction to proposals.

        5)   Using the concept of completed staff work when possible. Thus, recommendations should be complete enough to make yes-or-no responses from line managers possible. Advice should be clear and complete.

10. **System Theory**

    a.   Every position and task must contribute to achievement of organizational objectives.

        1)   Distinctions between producers and helpers are irrelevant.

    b.   The changing nature of work environments from predominantly production to predominantly service makes assignment of responsibility more difficult.

        1)   For example, at a hotel with the objective of customer satisfaction, who is line and who is staff?

11. **Matrix Structure**

    a.   In a matrix structure, the reporting relationships of an entity are in a grid or matrix. This structure allows authority to flow both vertically and horizontally. Thus, employees have dual reporting relationships, generally to a functional manager and a product manager.

    b.   The advantages of matrix structure include the following:

        1)   Resources can be used more efficiently.

        2)   Information flows better.

        3)   Employees' motivation and commitment are enhanced.

        4)   Management can respond to changing market and technical requirements rapidly.

    c.   The disadvantages of matrix structure include the following:

        1)   Confusion. People may not recognize which manager to report to.

        2)   Power struggles. Managers may seek greater authority.

        3)   Excessive overhead. Matrix structure incurs greater management costs because it has a dual chain of command.

12. **Mechanistic vs. Organic Structures**

    a.   A mechanistic structure has (1) tight controls, (2) extensive division of labor, (3) high formalization, and (4) centralization. The information network is limited, and employees rarely participate in decision making.

       1)   A mechanistic organization (an inflexible bureaucracy) is most likely to succeed in stable and certain environments. In such an entity,

          a)   Tasks are specifically defined and have little flexibility.

          b)   Knowledge tends to be task-specific.

          c)   Hierarchical authority is strong, with an emphasis on employee obedience.

          d)   Communication is mostly top-down.

          e)   Rights and obligations are clearly defined, but how individual efforts relate to achieving organizational objectives is not.

    b.   An organic structure is decentralized and has low complexity and formalization. It has an extensive information system, and employees participate in decision making. It tends to be flexible and adaptive.

       1)   An organic organization is most likely to succeed in unstable and uncertain environments because it is adaptive. In such an entity,

          a)   Tasks are broadly and flexibly defined.

          b)   The relationship of individual effort and organizational objectives is clear.

          c)   Knowledge tends to be professional.

          d)   Work methods, rights, and obligations are purposely left unclear.

          e)   Self-control is preferred to hierarchical control.

          f)   Superiors have an informational and advisory role.

          g)   Communication is participative and horizontal.

    c.   Structure is a function of the following:

       1)   **Size.** Larger organizations tend to be mechanistic because greater formalization is needed. Strategies also change as size changes. A growing organization often expands activities within its industry.

          a)   For example, manufacturers might be unit producers (units or small batches), mass producers (large batches), or process producers (continuous processing). Mass production is most effective if the organization has a mechanistic structure with moderate vertical differentiation, high horizontal differentiation, and high formalization.

              i)   Vertical differentiation is the depth of the hierarchy. More levels mean more complexity.

              ii)   Horizontal differentiation is the extent to which tasks require special skills and knowledge. Greater diversity makes communication and coordination more difficult.

       2)   **Technology.** An organic structure may be best for coping with nonroutine technology because formalization is low.

       3)   **Environment.** In general, the more stable the environment, the more mechanistic the organization. A mechanistic structure also is appropriate when the environment has little capacity for growth.

          a)   Dynamic environments require an organic structure because of their unpredictability. Moreover, a complex environment (e.g., one with numerous and constantly changing competitors) also requires the flexibility and adaptability of an organic structure.

        b)   Uncertainty is a general, not a specific, environmental factor. The uncertainty in the environment depends on its

            i)   Capacity (the degree of growth an environment can support),

            ii)   Volatility (the relative instability in the environment), and

            iii) Complexity (the amount of heterogeneity and concentration in the environment).

    4)   **Formalization**. The extent to which job performance is standardized by job descriptions and clear procedures that define how tasks are to be accomplished.

        a)   Low formalization enhances worker discretion.

  d.   The choice of structure is a function of the organization's fundamental strategy.

    1)   Innovation focuses on developing important new products or services. An organic structure provides the flexibility for this strategy.

    2)   Cost-minimization imposes tight controls over expenses and reduces product prices. The mechanistic structure is appropriate.

    3)   Imitation is adopted by organizations that enter new markets only after smaller competitors have demonstrated the potential for success. Imitation is best suited to a structure that combines mechanistic and organic components.

13. **Organizational Structures**

  a.   According to Henry Mintzberg, an organization has five basic parts. Depending on which is dominant, one of ~~five~~ structures will evolve.

    1)   The five parts of an organization are the following:

        a)   Operating core (workers who perform the basic tasks related to production)
        b)   Strategic apex (top managers)
        c)   Middle line (managers who connect the core to the apex)
        d)   Technostructure (analysts who achieve a certain standardization)
        e)   Support staff (indirect support services)

    2)   The following are the five structures:

        a)   A simple structure (entrepreneurial), such as that of a small retailer, has low complexity and formality, and authority is centralized. Its simplicity usually precludes significant inefficiency in the use of resources. The strategic apex is the dominant component.

        b)   A machine bureaucracy, such as the military, is a complex, formal, and centralized organization that (1) performs highly routine tasks, (2) groups activities into functional departments, (3) has a strict chain of command, and (4) distinguishes between line and staff relationships. The technostructure dominates.

        c)   A professional bureaucracy (e.g., a university or library) is a complex and formal but decentralized organization in which highly trained specialists have great autonomy. Duplication of functions is minimized. For example, a university has only one history department. The operating core dominates.

        d)   A divisional structure, such as an industrial conglomerate, is essentially a self-contained organization. Hence, it must perform all or most of the functions of the overall organization of which it is a part. It has substantial duplication of functions compared with more centralized structures. The middle line dominates.

e) An adhocracy (an organic structure) has low complexity, formality, and centralization. Vertical differentiation is low, and horizontal differentiation is high. The emphasis is on flexibility and response. Support staff dominates. Small software developers may be adhocracies.

14. **New Structures**

a. These emerging organizational structures tend to be flatter (fewer layers), make more use of teams, and create entrepreneurial units.

b. An **hourglass** organization has the following three layers:

1) The strategic layer determines the mission of the organization and ensures that it is successful.

2) A few middle managers coordinate a variety of lower-level, cross-functional activities. These managers are generalists, not specialists, and they do not simply transfer operating information. Computer systems can instantly transfer such information directly to the top layer.

3) Empowered technical specialists are most often self-supervised. They lack promotion possibilities but are motivated by (a) lateral transfers, (b) challenging work, (c) training in new skills, and (d) pay-for-performance plans.

c. A **cluster** organization is in essence a group of teams. Workers are multiskilled and move among teams as needed. Communication and group skills are vital, requiring special training and team-building exercises. Pay is for knowledge.

d. A **network** organization consists of relatively independent firms.

1) A network is based on coordination through adaptation. It is a long-term, strategic relationship based on implicit contracts. A network allows member firms to gain a competitive advantage against competitors outside the network.

a) A network is an ultimate expression of outsourcing, which involves obtaining goods or services from outside sources that could be acquired internally. For example, a firm may choose to outsource its computer processing or legal work, and a manufacturer may buy rather than make components.

2) A network may be viewed as a group of activities involving suppliers and customers that add value. Each activity may be performed internally at an internal cost or subcontracted at an external cost.

a) When an activity is subcontracted, a transaction cost is incurred.

b) A restriction on a network is that the sum of external costs and transaction costs must be less than internal costs.

c) The difference between a network and a normal market is that transaction costs in the market are low enough for any player.

e. **Virtual** organizations are flexible networks of value-adding subcontractors who communicate using the Internet and telecommunicating technology.

1) The emphasis is on speed and constant, if not too rapid, change.
2) Constant learning is essential.
3) Cross-functional teams are emphasized.
4) Stress is high.

Stop and review! You have completed the outline for this subunit. Study multiple-choice questions 1 through 4 beginning on page 71.

3.2 DEPARTMENTATION

1. **Division of Labor**

    a. Division of labor reduces complex processes to their simpler components to make task specialization possible. However, dividing labor creates a need for efficient coordination of those performing the separate tasks.

        1) One response to the need is departmentation, a structural format intended to promote coordination. It is the grouping of related activities into significant organizational subsystems (e.g., groups, divisions, units, departments).

2. **Types of Departmentation**

    a. Departmentation by **function** is found in almost every organization at some level. The most common departments are marketing, production, and finance (though other terms may be used). These often extend upward in the organizational chart to the level below the chief executive.

        1) Advantages include occupational specialization, simplified training, and representation of primary functions at the top level of the organization.

        2) Disadvantages include lack of coordination among primary functions and absence of profit centers within the organization.

    b. Departmentation by **territory** (geographic location) is used by national or multinational firms and government agencies with dispersed resources, offices, or plants.

        1) Advantages include

            a) Quicker reaction to local market changes,
            b) Greater familiarity with local problems or unique geographic concerns, and
            c) Reduced shipping costs and travel time.

        2) Disadvantages (which may be offset by telecommunications) include

            a) More delegation of authority to regional managers,
            b) Problems of control for headquarters, and
            c) Duplication of facilities and service functions (personnel, purchases, etc.).

    c. Departmentation by **product or service** is typical in multiline, large-scale enterprises. It often results from functional departmentation.

        1) Thus, product or service subunits may be treated as separate businesses with a high degree of autonomy. Managers must have a broad perspective, not merely a functional orientation.

        2) Advantages include

            a) Better use of specialized capital and skills,
            b) Ease of coordination,
            c) Simpler assignment of profit responsibility,
            d) Compatibility with a decentralization strategy, and
            e) A basis for allocating capital efficiently to products or services likely to achieve the best returns.

        3) Disadvantages include

            a) The requirement for a greater number of persons with managerial ability,
            b) Duplication of facilities and service functions, and
            c) Difficulty integrating operations.

    d.   Departmentation by **customer** allows for service to a particular customer to be provided under the management of a subunit.

        1)   This form of departmentation seldom appears at the top level of an organizational structure, but it is common at middle levels (e.g., the loan officer of a large bank who handles one account exclusively).

           a)   Customer departmentation is typical in the sales department of a firm organized by function.

        2)   Advantages include

           a)   Improved customer service as a result of greater expertise in a particular business and

           b)   Ease in identifying contributions to profit by different types and locations of customers.

        3)   Disadvantages include

           a)   Difficulties in coordination with other units in the organization,
           b)   Pressure to give preferential treatment to certain customers, and
           c)   Duplication of facilities and service functions.

    e.   Departmentation by **project** is appropriate for experimental or one-time activities, e.g., the construction of a ship or large building, or a major design project (such as the development of a new generation of large-scale passenger aircraft).

        1)   Advantages include specialization and ease of communication and coordination of efforts required for a particular project.

        2)   Disadvantages include the need for reorganization at the end of the project, problems of recruitment at the start of the project, and difficulty of maintaining control at the central office.

    f.   Departmentation by **work flow process** is used in reengineered organizations.

        1)   Reengineering involves starting anew to redesign an organization's core processes rather than attempting to improve the current system. Reengineering is not merely downsizing or continuous improvement, but a complete change in ways of doing business.

           a)   In the modern, highly competitive business environment, an organization needs to adapt quickly and radically to change. Thus, reengineering is usually a cross-functional process of innovation requiring substantial investment in information technology and retraining.

        2)   Organizations that use work flow process design are horizontal organizations. Their objective is an outward focus on customer satisfaction.

           a)   For this purpose, the horizontal work flow between identification of customer needs and satisfaction of those needs is to be managed quickly and efficiently.

Stop and review! You have completed the outline for this subunit. Study multiple-choice questions 5 through 8 beginning on page 72.

3.3 CENTRALIZATION AND DECENTRALIZATION

    1.   **Overview**

        a.   Centralization and decentralization are relative terms. Absolute centralization or decentralization is impossible.

        b.   Traditionalists view decentralization with distrust because they seek to avoid any dilution of control by senior managers.

        c.   Behaviorists view decentralization in the same way as delegation, that is, as a good way to improve motivation and morale of lower-level employees.

2. **Modern View**

   a. The contingency view is that neither centralization nor decentralization is good or bad in itself. The degree to which either is stressed depends upon a given situation.

   b. Decisions cannot be decentralized to those who do not have necessary information, e.g., knowledge of job objectives or measures for evaluation of performance.

   c. Decisions cannot be decentralized to people who do not have the training, experience, knowledge, or ability to make them.

   d. Decisions requiring a quick response should be decentralized to those near the activity.

   e. Decentralization should not occur below the organizational level at which coordination must be maintained (e.g., each supervisor on an assembly line cannot be allowed to decide the reporting time for employees).

   f. Decisions that are important to the survival of the organization should not be decentralized.

   g. Decentralization has a positive influence on morale.

3. **Degree of Decentralization**

   a. Decentralization is a philosophy of organizing and managing. Careful selection of which decisions to push down the hierarchy and which to make at the top is required. The degree of decentralization is greater if

      1) More decisions are made lower in the hierarchy.
      2) More of the important decisions are made lower in the hierarchy.
      3) More functions are affected by decisions made at lower levels.
      4) Fewer decisions made lower in the hierarchy are monitored by senior management.

4. **Organizational Design**

   a. Organizational design should achieve a balance between centralization and decentralization. The main benefits of centralization are more effective control and reduced costs through resource sharing.

      1) The main benefits of decentralization are flexibility and adaptability that permit a rapid response to changes in circumstances.

   b. The more centralized organization tends to be more successful in a relatively stable and certain environment.

   c. The more decentralized organization tends to be more successful in a relatively unstable and uncertain environment.

5. **Strategic Business Units**

   a. Establishment of strategic business units (SBUs) is a means of decentralization used by large corporations seeking to enjoy the entrepreneurial advantages of smaller entities.

   b. An SBU in principle is permitted by its parent to function as an independent business, including development of its own strategic plans. A true SBU

      1) Is not merely a supplier of the parent, but serves its own markets
      2) Encounters competition
      3) Is a profit center
      4) Makes all important decisions about its business although it may share resources with the parent

6.   **Delegation**

a.   Delegation is the formal process of assigning authority downward. Delegation is similar to decentralization in philosophy, process, and requirements.

1)   The traditional approach is to avoid delegation because the superior is deemed to be both responsible and knowledgeable. Under that view, delegation avoids responsibility.

2)   The behavioral view sees delegation as useful in every organization because no one has time to make every decision, and employees like to make decisions affecting their work.

3)   The contingency approach treats delegation as dependent on the situation and the people involved. Delegation requires the following:

a)   Skill, self-confidence, and knowledge of organizational objectives
b)   A feedback system to allow objective assessment of performance
c)   Faith in employees' abilities
d)   Clear recognition of the basic need to delegate
e)   Willingness to accept risk
f)   Desire to develop and train employees

b.   The delegation process involves the following:

1)   Determination of results expected
2)   Assignment of tasks and responsibilities
3)   Delegation of authority for accomplishing these tasks
4)   Recruitment of responsible people for the accomplishment of tasks
5)   Clear communication of what is expected in objective terms
6)   Follow-up, because the delegator still has ultimate responsibility

c.   The benefits of delegation are time savings for the delegator, training and development of lower-level managers, and improved morale.

d.   The following are obstacles to delegation:

1)   The delegator is a perfectionist, has low self-esteem, fears criticism or competition, lacks confidence in lower-level managers, or has low risk tolerance.

2)   Jobs are poorly defined.

3)   Controls are ineffective.

4)   Superiors are not role models for delegation.

e.   The following are degrees of delegation from low to high:

1)   Investigation and reporting back to the superior
2)   Investigation and recommendations of actions to the superior
3)   Investigation and advising the superior about plans
4)   Investigation and undertaking action, with reporting to the superior on what was done
5)   Investigation and undertaking action

Stop and review! You have completed the outline for this subunit. Study multiple-choice questions 9 through 12 beginning on page 73.

3.4 PRICING AND THE SUPPLY CHAIN

1. **Pricing**

   a. A seller uses pricing strategy to identify the optimal prices for its products.

   b. **Pricing objectives** direct the pricing process. They include the following:

      1) Profit maximization

      2) Quality leadership

         a) Sellers set prices to signal the market that their products are of high quality.

      3) Quantity maximization

         a) Sellers establish prices to maximize unit sales. These entities usually intend to take advantage of economies of scale.

      4) Survival

         a) Sellers need to set prices to cover essential costs.

   c. Pricing strategies

      1) **Nonprice competition** is a differentiation strategy used to attract customers. Price does not provide a competitive advantage for these entities.

      2) A **competitive pricing** strategy is used by a seller for which price is a competitive advantage. Prices are based on the prices in the market or the prices of major competitors.

   d. Pricing strategies for new products

      1) A **skimming** strategy sets an initial high price and then slowly lowers the price to make the product available to a wider market.

      2) A **penetration pricing** strategy sets a low price to increase sales and market share. This strategy generates greater sales and establishes the new product in the market more quickly.

   e. Alternative pricing strategies

      1) **Cost-oriented pricing** is widely used. It includes cost-plus pricing and markup pricing.

         a) Using **cost-plus pricing**, sellers add a projected gross margin to the costs of producing the product. A similar concept is **markup pricing**, which adds a projected percentage to the retailer's invoice price to determine the final selling price.

         b) Using **breakeven analysis**, sellers can determine the minimum price needed to recover costs at a certain level of production. This approach is commonly combined with a **target rate of return**. A detailed outline of breakeven analysis is in Study Unit 18.

      2) **Demand-oriented pricing** focuses on how customers' demand for a product changes at various price levels.

         a) **Price elasticity of demand** is used to measure the responsiveness of the quantity demanded of a product to a change in its price.

$$\text{Price elasticity of demand} = \frac{\text{Change in quantity} \div \text{Quantity}}{\text{Change in price} \div \text{Price}}$$

      3) **Value-based pricing** sets prices equal to the value of the benefits the products provide to customers.

2.   **The Supply Chain**

    a.   The supply chain consists of flows from sources of (1) raw materials, (2) components, (3) finished goods, (4) services, or (5) information through intermediaries to ultimate consumers.

        1)   These flows and the related activities may occur across the functions in an organization's value chain (R&D, design, production, marketing, distribution, and customer service). These flows and the related activities also may occur across separate organizations.

        2)   The activities in the supply chain, wherever they occur, should be integrated and coordinated for optimal cost management.

Example of a Supply Chain

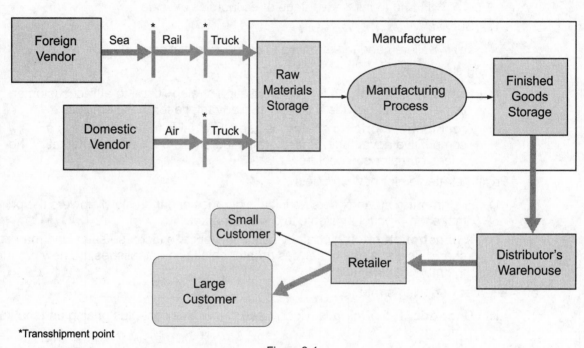

*Transshipment point

Figure 3-1

3.   **Supply Chain Coordination**

    a.   Sharing of information and coordination among the organizations in the supply chain can avoid the bullwhip, or whiplash, effect on inventories. This phenomenon begins when retailers face uncertain demand from consumers caused by randomness in buying habits.

        1)   However, the variability of retailers' orders to manufacturers is affected by factors in addition to consumer demand. In turn, manufacturers' orders to suppliers may reflect a still greater variability because those orders depend on factors in addition to retailer demand.

        2)   This cascade of demand variability throughout the supply chain may be caused by the following:

            a)   Difficulties of predicting demand and derived demand at each link in the supply chain

            b)   The need to purchase or manufacture goods in cost-efficient batches

            c)   Changes in price that may encourage purchases in anticipation of future increases

            d)   Shortages that may lead to rationing by suppliers or manufacturers and hoarding by manufacturers or retailers

b.   Sharing of information about sales, inventory, pricing, advertising campaigns, and sales forecasts by all functions and organizations in the supply chain moderates demand uncertainty for all parties. The following are desired results:

1)   Minimization of inventories held by suppliers, manufacturers, and retailers
2)   Avoidance of stockouts
3)   Fewer rush orders
4)   Production as needed by retailers

c.   The following are examples of difficulties in supply-chain inventory management:

1)   Incompatibility of the information systems of the parties
2)   Refusal of some parties to share information, possibly because of security concerns
3)   Devoting insufficient resources to the task
4)   Fear that others will not meet their obligations

4.   Distribution

a.   Distribution is the transfer of goods (and, in other contexts, services and information) from producers to customers or from distribution centers to merchandisers. Thus, distribution manages outflows, and purchasing manages inflows.

b.   Among the interrelated issues involved in distribution are selection of

1)   Distribution channels,
2)   Inventory placement,
3)   Means of transportation,
4)   Shipment schedules,
5)   Routes, and
6)   Carriers.

5.   Distribution Channel

a.   A distribution channel is a series of interdependent marketing institutions that facilitate the transfer of a product from producer to ultimate consumer or industrial user. A distribution channel creates place, time, and possession utility by bringing sellers and buyers together.

1)   For example, in Figure 3-1, the intermediaries in the distribution channel are the distributor's warehouse and retailer.

b.   The following are intermediaries (also called middlemen) between sellers and buyers:

1)   Merchant middlemen buy the goods outright and necessarily take title to them. They include merchant wholesalers (often called distributors or jobbers) and most retailers.

2)   An agent represents a principal in negotiating purchases, sales, or both, but does not take title to the goods.

3)   A broker serves as a go-between. Unlike an agent, a broker ordinarily does not maintain a relationship with a particular buyer or seller. A broker also does not assume title risks. An example is a travel agency.

4)   A consignee merely sells the consignor's goods for a fee. Title remains with the consignor until the goods are sold and title passes to the buyer.

5)   Facilitating intermediaries are persons or entities outside the channel that perform some services (inventory control, financial services, risk management, information services, promotions) more effectively and efficiently than the channel members.

    c.   The efficiencies gained by introducing intermediaries into a distribution channel can be calculated mathematically.

        1)   For instance, if a certain channel has three producers that serve the same three customers, the number of contacts is nine (three producers × three customers). If a distributor begins serving this channel, the number of contacts is reduced to six (three products + three customers).

6.   **Channel Structures**

    a.   The channel structure describes the relationship between the entities that make up the distribution system.

    b.   **Conventional distribution systems** consist of one or more independent producers, wholesalers, and retailers, each of which is a separate profit-maximizing business.

        1)   The profit objective of each independent channel member may result in actions that are not profit maximizing for the system as a whole.

        2)   The system offers no means for defining roles and controlling channel conflict.

    c.   In **vertical distribution systems**, producers, wholesalers, and retailers act as a unified system.

        1)   Channel conflict is managed through common ownership, contractual relationships, or administration by one or a few dominant channel members.

        2)   Conflict is between levels, e.g., when a manufacturer tries to enforce resale price agreements with dealers.

    d.   **Horizontal distribution systems** consist of two or more entities at one level of the channel working together to exploit new opportunities, such as the introduction of ATMs in supermarkets.

        1)   The joint nature of horizontal distribution efforts is the tool for managing channel conflict.

        2)   Conflict occurs at the same level, e.g., when service standards vary.

    e.   In a **multichannel system**, a single entity sets up two or more channels to reach one or more customer segments. Because such a system is managed by a single firm, channel conflicts can be evaluated and managed internally.

        1)   Conflict is between channels, e.g., when the manufacturer's stores compete with other retailers.

7.   **Inventory Placement**

    a.   Forward placement puts inventory close to final customers at a distribution center (warehouse), wholesaler, or retailer. This option minimizes transportation costs and delivery times.

        1)   Forward placement is typical for certain consumer goods and services that are usually low-priced and widely available. Consumers buy them often and with a minimum of comparison and effort. Examples are soap and newspapers. Producers of such goods ordinarily use intensive distribution to sell their products through a large number of retail or wholesale units, such as grocery stores.

    b.   Backward placement involves keeping inventory at the factory or, in the extreme case, maintaining no inventory at all (i.e., building to order). This option is indicated when products are customized or when regional demand fluctuates unpredictably.

    c.   Scheduling movements of freight balances purchasing, production, customer response times, shipping costs, and selection of routes and carriers.

Stop and review! You have completed the outline for this subunit. Study multiple-choice questions 13 through 16 beginning on page 74.

3.5 BUSINESS PROCESS ANALYSIS

1.　**Overview**

　　a.　Process analysis studies the means of producing a product or service for the purpose of lowering costs and increasing effectiveness (accomplishment of objectives) and efficiency (economical, timely, and accurate accomplishment of objectives) while producing items of appropriate quality.

　　　　1)　It differs from traditional product (or service) quality control, which involves inspection during production to eliminate unacceptable results.

2.　**Workflow Analysis**

　　a.　Workflow is the sequence of steps needed to accomplish a task, including consideration of any necessary physical objects.

　　b.　**Queuing theory** is a form of workflow analysis. An organization can improve throughput by carefully designing the way inputs arrive at workstations and how they are processed upon arrival.

　　　　1)　Manufacturing production lines are examples of queuing systems. Examples from other industries include the following:

　　　　　　a)　Bank teller windows
　　　　　　b)　Retail checkout counters
　　　　　　c)　Highway toll booths
　　　　　　d)　Airport holding patterns

　　　　2)　The most significant aspects of queuing theory are the number of lines and the service facility structure.

　　　　　　a)　Single channel, single phase. All users form a single line and are served at one point. An automated teller machine (ATM) is an example.

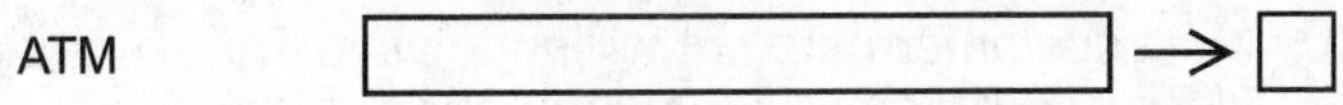

ATM

Figure 3-2

　　　　　　　　i)　A slight variation is an airline check-in counter or the teller line at a bank. All users form a single line, but multiple service points perform the single phase of the process. This structure is treated as having a higher capacity single service point.

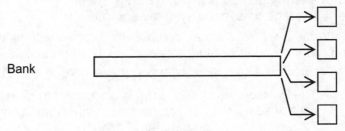

Bank

Figure 3-3

　　　　　　b)　Single channel, multiple phase. All users form a single line and must pass through more than one service point. A fast-food drive-through with sequential ordering microphone, payment station, and pickup window is an example.

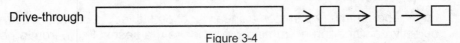

Drive-through

Figure 3-4

c)   Multiple channel, single phase. This structure has many service points, each with its own line. The checkout area in a large retail store is an example.

Large store

Figure 3-5

d)   Multiple channel, multiple phase. Users form many lines, and each line has multiple, sequential service points. A hospital is an example. Each department (inpatient surgery, outpatient surgery, clinical diagnostics, emergency, etc.) has its own admissions process and performs significantly different services for each patient.

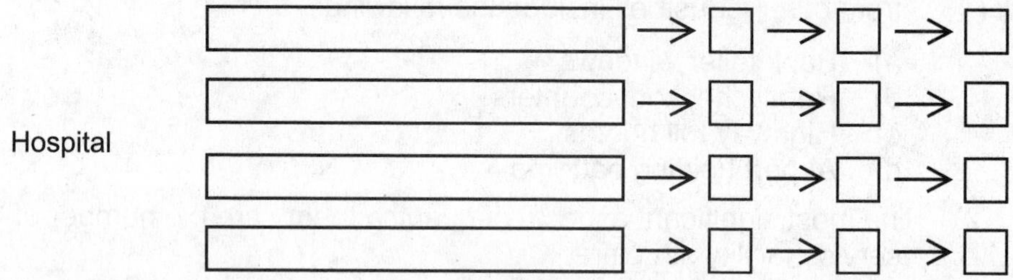

Hospital

Figure 3-6

3)   As capacity use increases, so does customer waiting time.

a)   Most customers are not willing to wait. Thus, management must balance loss of customers and overcapacity.

4)   Mathematical models can be applied to derive the following information:

a)   Average capacity use of the system
b)   Average number of units in the queue
c)   Average number of units in the system as a whole
d)   Average time spent waiting in the queue
e)   Average time in the system as a whole

5)   Mathematical solutions are available for simple systems having unscheduled random arrivals. For other systems, simulation must be used to find a solution.

6)   The arrivals in a queuing model occur in accordance with a Poisson process.

a)   The Poisson probability distribution is used to predict the probability of a specified number of occurrences of an event in a specified time interval, given the expected number of occurrences per time unit.

b)   The related exponential distribution is used to approximate service times. This distribution gives the probability of zero events in a given interval. Accordingly, it gives the probability that service time will not exceed a given length of time.

3.   **Linear Programming**

a.   Linear programming optimizes a linear function subject to certain constraints. The objective of linear programming is to choose the best solution from a potentially infinite number of possibilities.

1)   Applied to business, linear programming can be used to maximize revenue or profit or minimize cost, given limited resources.

b. The problem to be solved is the objective function.

1) After the objective function and its constraints have been stated in business terms, they are translated into mathematical terms. The functions can then be graphed and solved algebraically.

EXAMPLE

A company produces products Grimthon and Jonquin and is seeking the most profitable output levels. The profits per unit sold of Grimthon and Jonquin are US $5,000 and US $4,000, respectively. The objective function is therefore

Maximize 5,000G + 4,000J

In business terms, the constraints are stated as follows:

- At least 5 total units must be produced to justify the setup costs.
- A study of market demand shows that only 1 unit of Grimthon can be sold for every 3 of Jonquin.
- The production line can produce 2 units of Grimthon for every 3 of Jonquin, up to a maximum of 30 units combined.
- Partial units but not negative units can be produced.

The company translates the constraints into mathematical relations, which are then restated as equations.

1. Minimum production: $G + J \geq 5$ ===> $G + J = 5$
2. Market balance: $G \leq 3J$ ===> $G = 3J$ ===> $G - 3J = 0$
3. Production capacity: $2G + 3J \leq 30$ ===> $2G + 3J = 30$
4. Nonnegativity: $G, J \geq 0$ ===> $G, J = 0$

---

c. The graphical method plots the linear functions represented by the constraint formulas.

1) The area enclosed by the graphed functions is the feasible region. The optimal solution is at the intersection of two or more constraint equations.

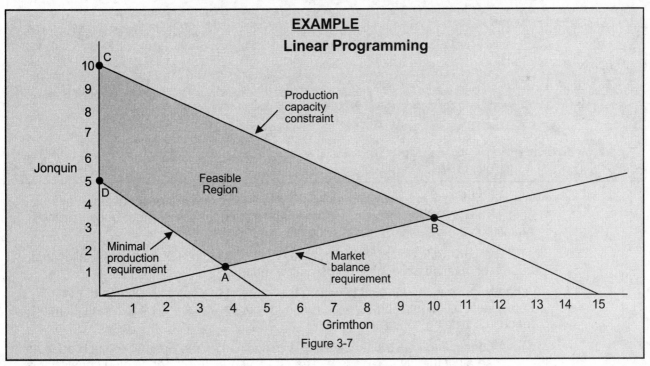

EXAMPLE
Linear Programming

Figure 3-7

d.   The algebraic method complements the graphical method. The combination of the two products that maximizes the objective function is at one of the corners of the feasible region.

1)   Thus, the coordinates of these intersections may be determined by simultaneously solving the relevant **pairs of equations**.

EXAMPLE

At point A:

$$\begin{array}{ll}\text{The minimal production requirement:} & G + J = 5 \\ \text{The market balance requirement:} & \underline{-G + 3J = 0} \\ & 4J = 5 \\ & J = 1.25\end{array}$$

Substituting 1.25 for J in the minimal production requirement formula gives a value for G of 3.75. Substituting both values in the objective function results in the level of profit at point A:

$$\text{Profit(A)} = \text{US } \$5{,}000(3.75) + \$4{,}000(1.25) = \underline{\textbf{US \$23,750}}$$

At point B:

$$\begin{array}{ll}\text{The market balance requirement:} & G - 3J = 0 \\ \text{The production capacity constraint:} & \underline{2G + 3J = 30} \\ & 3G = 30 \\ & G = 10\end{array}$$

Substituting 10 for G in the market balance requirement formula gives a value for J of 3.333. Substituting both values in the objective function results in the level of profit at point B:

$$\text{Profit(B)} = \text{US } \$5{,}000(10) + \$4{,}000(3.333) = \underline{\textbf{US \$63,333}}$$

At point C:

Point C is on the vertical axis, so the value of G is 0. Substituting this value in the production capacity constraint formula gives a value for J of 10. Substituting both values in the objective function results in the level of profit at point C:

$$\text{Profit(C)} = \text{US } \$5{,}000(0) + \$4{,}000(10) \quad = \underline{\textbf{US \$40,000}}$$

At point D:

Point D is on the vertical axis, so the value of G is 0. Substituting this value in the minimal production requirement formula gives a value for J of 5. Substituting both values in the objective function results in the level of profit at point D:

$$\text{Profit(D)} = \text{US } \$5{,}000(0) + \$4{,}000(5) \quad = \underline{\textbf{US \$20,000}}$$

The firm will maximize profits by producing at **point B**, that is, at an output level of 10 units of Grimthon and 3.333 units of Jonquin.

---

e.   When the number of constraint equations equals the number of variables, a unique solution exists. When the number of variables exceeds the number of constraint equations, the number of possible solutions is usually infinite.

1)   The constraint equations reflect the types of input (resources) being allocated, e.g., available machine hours or raw materials.

f.   A shadow price is the amount by which the value of the optimal solution of the objective function in a linear programming problem will change if a one-unit change is made in a binding constraint.

1)   A nonbinding constraint has excess capacity; i.e., the optimal solution does not use all of the given resource. The shadow price for a nonbinding constraint is zero because a one-unit change will not affect the optimal solution when excess capacity exists.

2)   The calculation of shadow prices is a simple example of sensitivity analysis, which is any procedure to test the responsiveness of the solution indicated by a model to changes in variables, alternative decisions, or errors.

g.   The advantage of linear programming is its applicability to many types of problems and its usefulness for sensitivity analysis. A major disadvantage is the restrictiveness of its linear assumptions, for example, that all costs are variable or fixed.

4.   **Theory of Constraints -- Overview**

a.   The theory of constraints (TOC) improves operating income when a manufacturing process has one or more bottleneck operations.

1)   The basic premise of TOC as applied to business is that improvement is best achieved not by trying to maximize efficiency in every part of the process but by focusing on the bottlenecks (constraints).

EXAMPLE

During the early days of the American Civil War, several units calling themselves legions were formed, consisting of combined infantry, artillery, and cavalry. This arrangement was abandoned because the entire unit could maneuver only as fast as the slowest part. The artillery was the constraint.

---

2)   Increasing the efficiency of processes that are not constraints merely creates backup in the system.

b.   The following are steps in a TOC analysis:

1)   Identify the constraint.
2)   Determine the most profitable product mix given the constraint.
3)   Maximize the flow through the constraint.
4)   Increase capacity at the constraint.
5)   Redesign the manufacturing process for greater flexibility and speed.

5.   **Detailed Steps in Performing a TOC Analysis**

a.   **Identify the constraint.**

1)   A constraint is a limited resource (e.g., number of machine hours available per month) that prevents the entity from producing the required amount of output.

2)   The bottleneck operation is the phase in the production process without enough resources to keep pace with input. The bottleneck operation is usually where production delays are longest.

b.   **Determine the most profitable product mix given the constraint.**

1)   A basic principle of TOC analysis is that short-term profit maximization requires maximizing the contribution margin through the constraint, called the **throughput margin** or throughput contribution.

a)   The throughput margin includes only direct materials costs as variable costs. All other manufacturing costs are ignored because they are considered fixed in the short run.

Throughput margin = Sales − Direct materials

b)   To determine the most profitable use of the bottleneck operation (or the limited resource), a manager next calculates the throughput margin per unit of time spent in the constraint.

i)   Profitability is maximized by keeping the bottleneck operation busy with the product with the highest throughput margin per unit of the constraint, not the highest contribution margin per unit of output.

c.   The intermediate step for improving the process and increasing the profitability in the short run is to maximize the flow through the constraint and increase the capacity of the constraint, e.g., by hiring more employees for the bottleneck operation.

EXAMPLE of TOC with a Limited Resource

A company produces products A, B and C. The sales price, direct materials, and amount of direct labor hours per product are provided below:

	Product A	Product B	Product C
Sale price	US $20	US $16	US $30
Direct materials	16	6	15
Direct labor hours	2	4	10

The company can sell 10,000 units of each product per month. However, the number of hours that the employees can work per month is limited to 50,000.

Due to the limited number of working hours per month, the company cannot produce 10,000 units of each product. Thus, the constraint (limited resource) is direct labor hours.

The company calculates the throughput margin for each product and then divides by the hours spent to produce it:

	A	B	C
Sales	US $20	US $ 16	US $ 30
Minus: direct materials	(16)	(6)	(15)
Throughout margin	US $ 4	US $ 10	US $ 15
Divided by: constraint time	÷ 2	÷ 4	÷ 10
Throughput margin per hour	US $ 2	US $2.5	US $1.5

According to the TOC, the company should produce the greatest possible number of the product with the highest throughput margin per hour (product B). Thus, 40,000 hours (10,000 units × 4 hours per unit) of direct labor should be used to produce 10,000 units of product B. The remaining available labor hours (50,000 − 40,000 = 10,000) should be used to produce the product with the second highest throughput margin per hour (product A). Thus, the company should produce 5,000 units (10,000 hours ÷ 2 hours per unit) of product A.

---

d.   **Redesign the manufacturing process for greater flexibility and speed.**

1)   The long-term solution is to reengineer the entire process. The firm should take advantage of new technology, drop product lines requiring too much effort, and redesign remaining products to ease the manufacturing process.

a)   Value engineering is useful for this purpose because it explicitly balances product cost and the needs of potential customers (product functions).

6.   **Reengineering Overview**

a.   One approach to business process analysis is business process reengineering. It involves process innovation and core process redesign. Instead of improving existing procedures, it finds new ways of doing things.

1)   The emphasis is on simplification and elimination of nonvalue-adding activities. Thus, reengineering is not continuous improvement or simply downsizing or modifying an existing system. It should be reserved for the most important processes.

2)   In the modern, highly competitive business environment, an organization may need to adapt quickly and radically to change. Accordingly, reengineering will usually be a cross-departmental process of innovation requiring substantial investment in information technology and retraining. Successful reengineering may bring dramatic improvements in customer service and the speed of new product introductions.

7. **Other Aspects**

a. A reengineered organization may use workflow process departmentation. Such a horizontal organization focuses on the flow of work between identifying and satisfying customer needs.

1) For example, sales, billing, and service might be combined in one account management process department.

b. Reengineering and TQM techniques eliminate many traditional controls. They exploit modern technology to improve productivity and decrease the number of clerical workers. Thus, controls should be automated and self-correcting and require minimal human intervention. Moreover, auditors must be prepared to encounter (and use) new technologies.

1) The emphasis therefore shifts to monitoring so management can determine when an operation may be out of control and corrective action is needed.

c. Monitoring is needed to assess the quality of internal control over time. Management considers whether internal control is properly designed and operating as intended and modifies it to reflect changing conditions. Monitoring may be in the form of separate, periodic evaluations or of ongoing monitoring.

1) Ongoing monitoring occurs as part of routine operations. It includes management and supervisory review, comparisons, reconciliations, and other actions by personnel as part of their regular activities.

d. Most reengineering and TQM methods also assume that humans will be motivated to work actively in improving operations when they are full participants in the process. However, these methods may be resisted by employees who are insecure because of lack of skills, fear of failure, breakup of work groups, and other factors.

Stop and review! You have completed the outline for this subunit. Study multiple-choice questions 17 through 20 beginning on page 75.

QUESTIONS

3.1 Risk/Control Implications of Organizational Structures

1. Which of the following factors is **least** likely to affect a manager's optimal span of control?

A. Frequency of supervisor-subordinate contact.

B. The manager's willingness to delegate authority.

C. The manager's training and communication skills.

D. Number of people in the organization.

Answer (D) is correct.
REQUIRED: The factor least likely to affect a manager's direct span of control.
DISCUSSION: The optimal span of control is the number of subordinates a manager can effectively supervise. It is a function of many situational factors. However, the total number of people in an organization has no bearing on the optimal span of control of a particular manager.
Answer (A) is incorrect. Managers who can contact subordinates frequently are able to control more people than those who have relatively infrequent contact with subordinates. Answer (B) is incorrect. Managers who delegate authority have more time to control the subordinates who report to them. These individuals can therefore supervise more people than managers who prefer not to delegate authority. Answer (C) is incorrect. Managers who have received effective training and are skillful communicators are equipped to control more individuals than managers who are untrained or have deficient communication skills.

2. Internal auditors frequently recommend that formal policies be written. However, the presence of certain conditions in an organization minimizes the need for written policies. One condition that minimizes the need for written policies is

    A. A high division of labor.

    B. A strong organizational culture.

    C. A large span of control.

    D. A strict unity of command.

Answer (B) is correct.
    REQUIRED: The condition minimizing the need for written policies.
    DISCUSSION: If the culture is strong, the organization's key values are intensely held and widely shared. Substantial training has been expended to achieve this high degree of acceptance, minimizing the need for formal, written policies.
    Answer (A) is incorrect. Specialization of labor increases the need for supervision and formal policies and procedures. Answer (C) is incorrect. Large spans of control minimize the ability of a manager to provide direct supervision. They increase the need for the indirect supervision provided by formalized policies and procedures. Answer (D) is incorrect. An organization exhibiting strict unity of command also most likely requires strict adherence to policies and procedures. Formalization of those policies and procedures promotes adherence.

3. When determining the appropriate span of control, the most important consideration is

    A. The set of policies and procedures currently in effect.

    B. The typical span of control used by other organizations.

    C. The preference of the organization's creditors.

    D. That all departments will be evaluated, whether or not they will be affected.

Answer (A) is correct.
    REQUIRED: The factor that is most important when choosing a span of control.
    DISCUSSION: The most important factors to consider are the employees' and manager's preferences and skills, the organization's culture, the tasks involved, physical location of the department, and established policies and procedures.
    Answer (B) is incorrect. Although examining similar entities may be useful, it is not one of the most important considerations. Answer (C) is incorrect. This consideration would only be necessary if required by an agreement with the creditors. Answer (D) is incorrect. Whether all departments will be evaluated is not normally considered in a span-of-control decision.

4. Which of the following is a disadvantage of a flat organizational structure?

    A. Employees are not encouraged to be creative.

    B. The input of fresh ideas from outside the organization is limited because employee turnover is low.

    C. Managers spend too much time training individuals and not enough time supervising.

    D. Employees may not be performing work tasks properly.

Answer (D) is correct.
    REQUIRED: The disadvantage of a flat organizational structure.
    DISCUSSION: A flat organizational structure concentrates decision-making authority at one level. Tasks and performance objectives may be unclear to employees because of a lack of supervision.
    Answer (A) is incorrect. The lack of supervision increases employee flexibility. Answer (B) is incorrect. The number of management levels limits the opportunity for advancement, which may cause high employee turnover. Answer (C) is incorrect. The lack of supervision decreases employee training.

3.2 Departmentation

5. Departmentation is the grouping of organizational subsystems. The greatest advantage of functional departmentation is that it

    A. Provides the benefits of specialization.

    B. Facilitates communication between primary functions.

    C. Helps to focus on achievement of organizational goals.

    D. Is appropriate for geographically dispersed companies.

Answer (A) is correct.
    REQUIRED: The greatest advantage of functional departmentation.
    DISCUSSION: Departmentation by function is the most widely used method and is found in almost every enterprise at some level. The most common departments are selling, production, and finance (though other terms may be used). These often extend upward in the organizational chart to the level below the chief executive. If persons within a department have similar knowledge, skills, and interests, they can specialize in the solution of particular problems. Thus, problem solving becomes more efficient.
    Answer (B) is incorrect. Departmentation by function facilitates communication and coordination within rather than between departments. Answer (C) is incorrect. The focus may tend to be on departmental, not organizational, goals. Answer (D) is incorrect. Territorial departmentation may be preferable for these companies.

6. Departmentation is a common form of business integration. Grouping together all related jobs, activities, and processes for a given business objective into a major organizational subunit is an example of

- A. Product-service departmentation.
- B. Functional departmentation.
- C. Geographic location departmentation.
- D. Customer classification departmentation.

Answer (A) is correct.
REQUIRED: The type of departmentation defined.
DISCUSSION: Departmentation by product or service is growing in importance for multiline, large-scale enterprises and is an outgrowth of functional departmentation. The result is that product-service subunits may be treated as separate businesses with a high degree of autonomy. Managers must therefore have a broad perspective, not a merely functional orientation.
Answer (B) is incorrect. Functional departmentation categorizes jobs according to the activity performed. Answer (C) is incorrect. Geographic location departmentation categorizes based upon the area in which a part of the business is located. Answer (D) is incorrect. Customer classification departmentation categorizes based upon the differing needs of discrete groups of customers.

7. The form of departmentation that most readily lends itself to use of profit centers is

- A. Project.
- B. Functional.
- C. Product.
- D. Matrix.

Answer (C) is correct.
REQUIRED: The form of departmentation most appropriate for use of profit centers.
DISCUSSION: Departmentation by product is growing in importance for multiline, large-scale enterprises. It is an outgrowth of functional departmentation and permits extensive authority for a division executive over a given product or product line. Its advantages include better use of specialized resources and skills, ease of coordination of the activities for a given product, and simpler assignment of profit responsibility. It is compatible with a decentralization strategy and provides, via product profit centers, a basis for allocating capital more efficiently.
Answer (A) is incorrect. A profit center is an organizational unit responsible for costs and revenues on an ongoing basis, not just for a one-time activity. Answer (B) is incorrect. The profitability of a single function is difficult to measure. Answer (D) is incorrect. Matrix is used for a specific project or for R&D.

8. Which of the following elements of an organization requires people to be accountable to superiors?

- A. Coordination of effort.
- B. Division of labor.
- C. Common goal or purpose.
- D. Hierarchy of authority.

Answer (D) is correct.
REQUIRED: The element requiring people to be accountable to their superiors.
DISCUSSION: A hierarchy of authority requires people to be accountable to their superiors in the hierarchy.
Answer (A) is incorrect. Coordination of effort involves cooperation in the social environment of the organization. Answer (B) is incorrect. Division of labor ensures efficient specialization of employees. Answer (C) is incorrect. A common goal or purpose is relevant to the employees and employer achieving a common objective.

3.3 Centralization and Decentralization

9. A claimed advantage of decentralizing is

- A. Concentration of authority.
- B. Manager development.
- C. Elimination of duplication of effort.
- D. Departmentation.

Answer (B) is correct.
REQUIRED: The advantage of decentralizing an organization.
DISCUSSION: When an organization changes from a centralized to a decentralized structure, top management is delegating more authority to middle and lower levels. Thus, managers at these lower levels are usually hired and developed more rigorously than under the centralized structure.
Answer (A) is incorrect. Authority is more concentrated in centralized management structures. Answer (C) is incorrect. Some effort will inevitably be duplicated under decentralization, of which departmentation is a moderate form. Answer (D) is incorrect. Departments are formed when one manager can no longer supervise the entire organization; departmentation is therefore a characteristic of centralized as well as decentralized organizations.

10. A network organizational structure is one in which

    A. An employee reports to two bosses.

    B. Authority and responsibility are concentrated at the top of the organization.

    C. Labor is specialized.

    D. Major business functions are subcontracted to third-party providers.

Answer (D) is correct.
    REQUIRED: The definition of a network organizational structure.
    DISCUSSION: The subcontracting of major business functions to others is a feature of network structures.
    Answer (A) is incorrect. An employee reporting to two bosses is a distinguishing feature of a matrix structure. Answer (B) is incorrect. Concentration of authority and responsibility at the top of the organization is a characteristic of centralization. Answer (C) is incorrect. Specialized labor is a characteristic of bureaucracy.

11. Which of the following is a reason that a manager may be reluctant to delegate?

    A. The manager fears being held accountable for the subordinate's performance.

    B. The manager fears failing because of some lack of knowledge.

    C. The manager did not monitor the subordinate's work.

    D. The manager fears unknown goals.

Answer (A) is correct.
    REQUIRED: The reason a manager is reluctant to delegate.
    DISCUSSION: Managers fear delegating because of insecurity, mistrust, insufficient planning, and/or aversion to the risk of being responsible for subordinates' actions.
    Answer (B) is incorrect. Fear of failing due to lack of knowledge is a fear that subordinates have about delegation. Answer (C) is incorrect. A manager not monitoring a subordinate's work is a potential implementation problem. Answer (D) is incorrect. Fear of unknown goals is a fear that subordinates have about delegation.

12. Which of the following is **not** a characteristic of decentralized organizations?

    A. Decentralized organizations are usually more flexible.

    B. Decentralized organizations have reduced costs through resource sharing.

    C. Decentralized organizations have fewer decisions made lower in the hierarchy that are monitored by senior management.

    D. Decentralization has a positive influence on morale.

Answer (B) is correct.
    REQUIRED: The characteristics of decentralized organizations.
    DISCUSSION: The main benefits of centralization are more effective control and reduced costs through resource sharing. In a centralized organization, senior management is able to direct control over subordinates and direct the flow of resources. Senior management is able to allocate costs most effectively because they are aware of where expenses can be reduced across departments within an organization.
    Answer (A) is incorrect. The main benefit to decentralized organizations is that they are more flexible and quickly adapt to changes. Therefore, decentralized organizations tend to thrive in relatively unstable or uncertain environments. Answer (C) is incorrect. A main feature of decentralization is for senior management to allow subordinates to make decisions without constant supervision or approval. Answer (D) is incorrect. Decentralization has been shown to improve employee morale by empowering employees to make decisions on their own.

3.4 Pricing and the Supply Chain

13. An organization must manage its flows of raw materials, components, finished goods, services, or information through intermediaries to ultimate consumers. These flows may occur across the functions in an organization's

    A. Supply chain.

    B. Value chain.

    C. Full-function chain.

    D. Integrated chain.

Answer (B) is correct.
    REQUIRED: The organizational arrangement in which flows of materials, components, goods, services, or information may occur.
    DISCUSSION: The supply chain consists of flows from sources of (1) raw materials, (2) components, (3) finished goods, (4) services, or (5) information through intermediaries to ultimate consumers. These flows and the related activities may occur across the functions in an organization's value chain (R&D, design, production, marketing, distribution, and customer service). These flows and the related activities also may occur across separate organizations.
    Answer (A) is incorrect. The supply chain consists of the flows that may occur across the functions in an organization's value chain or separate organizations. Answer (C) is incorrect. The phrase "full-function chain" is not a technical term. Answer (D) is incorrect. The phrase "integrated chain" is not a technical term.

14. A desired result of the sharing of information by all functions and organizations in the supply chain is

    A. Fewer rush orders.

    B. Maximization of inventories held by suppliers, manufacturers, and retailers.

    C. Stockouts.

    D. Incompatibility of the information systems of the parties.

Answer (A) is correct.
    REQUIRED: The desired result from sharing information by all functions and organizations in the supply chain.
    DISCUSSION: Sharing information about sales, inventory, pricing, advertising campaigns, and sales forecasts by all functions and organizations in the supply chain moderates demand uncertainty for all parties. The desired results are (1) minimization of inventories held by suppliers, manufacturers, and retailers; (2) avoidance of stockouts; (3) fewer rush orders; and (4) production as needed by retailers.
    Answer (B) is incorrect. Minimization of inventories held by all parties in the supply chain is a desired result of sharing information. Answer (C) is incorrect. Avoidance of stockouts is a desired result of sharing information. Answer (D) is incorrect. Incompatibility of the information systems of the parties is a difficulty faced by supply-chain management, not a desired result of sharing information.

15. The airlines have been leaders in the use of technology. Customers can make reservations either with an airline or through a travel agency. In this situation, a travel agency is classified as which type of distribution channel?

    A. An intermediary.

    B. A jobber.

    C. A distributor.

    D. A facilitating agent.

Answer (A) is correct.
    REQUIRED: The type of distribution channel of which a travel agency is an example.
    DISCUSSION: Marketing intermediaries assist companies in promoting, selling, and distributing their goods and services to ultimate consumers. For example, travel agents access an airline's computerized reservation system and make reservations for their customers without ever taking title to the ticket.
    Answer (B) is incorrect. Jobbers buy from manufacturers, then resell the products. Answer (C) is incorrect. Distributors, or wholesalers, usually have selective or exclusive distribution rights. Answer (D) is incorrect. Facilitating agents assist in functions other than buying, selling, or transferring title.

16. Which of the following is **not** a component of physical distribution?

    A. Transportation.

    B. Pricing.

    C. Location of retail outlets.

    D. Warehousing.

Answer (B) is correct.
    REQUIRED: The factor not a component of physical distribution.
    DISCUSSION: Physical distribution (market logistics) involves planning, implementing, and controlling the movement of materials and final goods to meet customer needs while earning a profit. Physical distribution systems coordinate suppliers, purchasing agents, marketers, channels, and customers. They include warehousing, transportation, and retail outlets.
    Answer (A) is incorrect. A physical distribution system includes transportation. Answer (C) is incorrect. A physical distribution system includes the location of retail outlets. Answer (D) is incorrect. A physical distribution system includes warehousing.

3.5 Business Process Analysis

17. Queuing models are concerned with balancing the cost of waiting in the queue with the

    A. Cost of providing service.

    B. Number of customers in the queue.

    C. Average waiting time in the queue.

    D. Usage rate for the service being rendered.

Answer (A) is correct.
    REQUIRED: The true statement about the objective of queuing models.
    DISCUSSION: Queuing (waiting-line) models minimize, for a given rate of arrivals, the sum of (1) the cost of providing service (including facility costs and operating costs) and (2) the cost of idle resources waiting in line. The latter may be a direct cost, if paid employees are waiting, or an opportunity cost in the case of waiting customers. This minimization occurs at the point where the cost of waiting is balanced by the cost of providing service.

18. A bank has changed from a system in which lines are formed in front of each teller to a one-line, multiple-server system. When a teller is free, the person at the head of the line goes to that teller. Implementing the new system will

A. Decrease the bank's wage expenses because the new system uses fewer tellers.

B. Decrease time customers spend in the line.

C. Increase accuracy in teller reconciliations at the end of the day because fewer customers are served by each teller.

D. Improve on-the-job training for tellers because each will perform different duties.

Answer (B) is correct.

REQUIRED: The effect of implementing the new queuing system.

DISCUSSION: When all customers must wait in a single queue, a decrease in waiting time is possible given multiple servers. An added effect is to increase customer satisfaction.

Answer (A) is incorrect. The number of employees is unlikely to change due to the new system. Answer (C) is incorrect. Assuming a Poisson process, the number of customers per teller will not change. Answer (D) is incorrect. Tellers' duties will not change, so on-the-job training will not improve.

19. The drive-through service at a fast-food restaurant consists of driving up to place an order, advancing to a window to pay for the order, and then advancing to another window to receive the items ordered. This type of waiting-line system is

A. Single channel, single phase.

B. Single channel, multiple phase.

C. Multiple channel, single phase.

D. Multiple channel, multiple phase.

Answer (B) is correct.

REQUIRED: The type of waiting-line system described.

DISCUSSION: The drive-through represents a single queue (channel). Because this waiting line has three services in series, it may be said to be multiple phase. Another example is the typical factory assembly line. This terminology (channel, phase), however, is not used by all writers on queuing theory.

Answer (A) is incorrect. Service by one ticket-seller at a movie theater is an example of a single-channel, single-phase system. Answer (C) is incorrect. Supermarket checkout lines are a common example of multiple single-phase servers servicing multiple lines. Answer (D) is incorrect. An example of a multiple-channel, multiple-phase system is a set of supermarket checkout lines, each of which is served in sequence by a cashier and a person who packs grocery bags.

20. Under throughput costing, the only cost considered to be truly variable in the short run is

A. Direct materials.

B. Direct labor.

C. Manufacturing overhead.

D. All manufacturing costs are considered variable.

Answer (A) is correct.

REQUIRED: The variable cost under throughput costing.

DISCUSSION: Throughput costing, also called supervariable costing, recognizes only direct materials costs as being truly variable and thus relevant to the calculation of throughput margin.

Answer (B) is incorrect. Under throughput costing, direct labor is considered fixed because of labor contracts and employment levels. Answer (C) is incorrect. Under throughput costing, overhead is considered fixed in the short run. Answer (D) is incorrect. Under throughput costing, only direct materials costs are considered variable in the short run.

Access the **CIA Review System** from your Gleim Personal Classroom to continue your studies with exam-emulating multiple-choice questions!

STUDY UNIT FOUR
BUSINESS PROCESSES AND RISKS

(15 pages of outline)

This study unit is the second of two covering **Section III: Organizational Structure/Business Processes and Risks** from The IIA's CIA Exam Syllabus. This section makes up 15% to 25% of Part 3 of the CIA exam and is tested at the **awareness level**. The relevant portion of the syllabus is highlighted below. (The complete syllabus is in Appendix A.)

III. ORGANIZATIONAL STRUCTURE/BUSINESS PROCESSES AND RISKS (15%–25%)

    A. Risk/Control Implications of Different Organizational Structures

    B. Structure (e.g., centralized/decentralized)

    C. Typical Schemes in Various Business Cycles (e.g., procurement, sales, knowledge, supply-chain management)

    D. Business Process Analysis (e.g., workflow analysis and bottleneck management, theory of constraints)

    E. Inventory Management Techniques and Concepts

    F. Electronic Funds Transfer (EFT)/Electronic Data Interchange (EDI)/E-commerce

    G. Business Development Life Cycles

    H. The International Organization for Standardization (ISO) Framework

    I. Outsourcing Business Processes

4.1 MANAGING INVENTORY COSTS AND QUANTITIES

    1. Costs of Inventory

        a.   An entity carries inventories because of the difficulty in predicting the amount, timing, and location of supply and demand.

            1)   Thus, one purpose of inventory control is to determine the optimal level of inventory necessary to minimize costs.

        b.   The **carrying costs** (also called **holding costs**) of inventory include rent, insurance, taxes, security, depreciation, and opportunity cost (i.e., the pretax return forgone by investing capital in inventory rather than the best alternative).

            1)   Carrying costs may also include a charge for shrinkage, e.g., from spoilage of perishable items, obsolescence, theft, or waste.

            2)   The annual opportunity cost of carrying inventory equals the average inventory level, times the per-unit purchase price, times the cost of capital.

            3)   Carrying costs are reduced by minimizing the amount of inventory. This practice risks stockouts, resulting in lost contribution margin on sales and customer ill will.

            4)   Safety stock is the extra inventory kept to guard against stockouts.

        c.   **Ordering costs** are the fixed costs of placing an order with a vendor and receiving the goods, independent of the number of units ordered.

            1)   Frequent ordering of small quantities thus may not be cost-beneficial compared with the relevant carrying costs.

d. Inventory management minimizes the total costs of inventory, i.e., the sum of carrying cost and ordering costs, as illustrated by this graph:

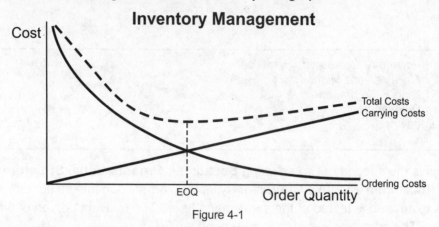

Figure 4-1

2. **Economic Order Quantity (EOQ) Model**

a. The EOQ results from using differential calculus to determine the minimum point on the total cost curve. It corresponds to the intersection of the carrying cost and ordering cost curves in Figure 4-1.

1) The basic formula is

$$EOQ = \sqrt{\frac{2aD}{k}}$$

If: a = variable cost per order (or production setup)
D = periodic demand in units
k = unit periodic carrying cost

EXAMPLE

If periodic demand is uniform at 1,000 units, the cost to place an order is US $4, and the cost to carry one unit in inventory for a period is US $2, the EOQ is calculated as follows:

$$EOQ = \sqrt{\frac{2(\text{US } \$4)(1,000)}{\text{US } \$2}} = 63.25 \text{ units per order}$$

---

2) The formula shows that the EOQ

a) Increases when demand or order costs increase
b) Decreases when demand or order costs decrease
c) Decreases when carrying costs increase
d) Increases when carrying costs decrease

3) The average level of inventory under this model is the safety stock plus one-half of the EOQ.

4) The EOQ is a periodic model. The number of orders (production runs) per period is given by the periodic demand divided by the EOQ.

EXAMPLE

Using the data from the previous example, the company has determined it also desires a safety stock of 15 units. Given that demand is constant and the EOQ is 63.25 units, the average inventory level without regard to safety stock is 31.625 (63.25 ÷ 2). Adding safety stock results in an average level of 46.625 (31.625 + 15). Given that carrying costs are US $2 per unit, the annual inventory holding costs are calculated as follows:

46.625 × US $2 = US $93.25 annual inventory holding costs

---

b. The limitations of the EOQ model are its restrictive assumptions.

1) The three variables in the formula (order placement or production setup cost, unit demand, per-unit carrying cost) remain constant throughout the period.

2) Full replenishment occurs instantly when the last item is used, stockout costs are zero, and no safety stock is held.

Stop and review! You have completed the outline for this subunit. Study multiple-choice questions 1 through 4 beginning on page 91.

4.2 INVENTORY MANAGEMENT METHODS

1. **ABC Inventory Management**

   a. The ABC system is a simple inventory management technique. It controls inventories by dividing items into three groups:

      1) Group A consists of high-monetary-value items, which account for a small portion (perhaps 10%) of the total inventory usage.

      2) Group B consists of medium-monetary-value items, which may account for perhaps 20% of the total inventory items.

      3) Group C consists of low-monetary-value items, which account for the remaining 70% of sales or usage.

   b. The ABC system permits managerial control over inventory to be exercised in the most cost-effective manner.

      1) The stocking levels and activity of group A items are reviewed on a regular basis.

      2) Group B items may not need review as often as group A items, but they may need review more often than group C items.

      3) For group C, extensive use of models and records is not cost effective. They are reviewed even less frequently.

2. **Just-in-Time (JIT)**

   a. Modern inventory control favors the just-in-time model. Companies have traditionally built parts and components for subsequent operations on a preset schedule.

      1) Such a schedule provides a cushion of inventory so that the next operation will always have parts to work with -- a just-in-case method.

   b. In contrast, JIT limits output to the amount required (the demand) by the next operation in the production process. Reductions in inventory result in less money invested in idle assets; reduction of storage space requirements; and lower inventory taxes, pilferage, and obsolescence risks.

      1) High inventory often conceals production problems because defective parts can be overlooked when plenty of good parts are available. If only enough parts are made for the subsequent operation, however, any defects will immediately halt production.

      2) The focus of quality control under JIT shifts from the discovery of defective parts to the prevention of quality problems, so zero machine breakdowns (achieved through preventive maintenance) and zero defects are ultimate goals. Higher quality and lower inventory go together.

c. The ultimate objectives of JIT methods are increased competitiveness and higher profits through

1) Higher productivity,
2) Reduced order costs as well as carrying costs,
3) Faster and cheaper setups,
4) Shorter manufacturing cycle times,
5) Better due date performance,
6) Improved quality, and
7) More flexible processes.

d. JIT systems are based on a manufacturing philosophy that combines purchasing, production, and inventory control. It also treats many inventory-related activities as nonvalue-added. Carrying inventory is regarded as indicating problems, such as poor quality, long cycle times, and lack of coordination with suppliers.

1) A JIT system **reduces carrying costs** by eliminating inventories and increasing supplier deliveries. Ideally, shipments are received just in time to be part of the manufacturing process. This system **increases the risk of stockout costs** because inventory is reduced or eliminated.

e. However, JIT also reorganizes the production process to eliminate waste of resources. JIT is a **pull system**. Items are pulled through production by current demand, not pushed through by anticipated demand. Thus, one operation produces only what is needed by the next operation, and components and raw materials arrive just in time to be used.

1) In a pull system, workers might often be idle if they were not multi-skilled. Hence, (a) central support departments are reduced or eliminated, (b) space is saved, (c) fewer and smaller factories may be required, and (d) materials and tools are brought close to the point of use. Manufacturing cycle time and setup time are also reduced. As a result, on-time delivery performance and response to changes in markets are enhanced, and production of customized goods in small lots becomes feasible.

f. The lower inventory in a JIT system eliminates the need for some internal controls.

1) Frequent receipt of deliveries from suppliers often means less need for a sophisticated inventory control system and for control personnel.

2) JIT also may eliminate central receiving areas, hard copy receiving reports, and storage areas. A central warehouse is not needed because deliveries are made by suppliers directly to the area of production.

3) The quality of parts provided by suppliers is verified by use of statistical controls rather than inspection of incoming goods. Storage, counting, and inspecting are eliminated in an effort to perform only value-adding work.

g. In a JIT system, the dependability of suppliers is crucial.

1) Organizations that adopt JIT systems therefore have strategic teaming agreements with a few carefully chosen suppliers who are extensively involved in the buyer's processes.

2) Long-term contracts are typically negotiated to reduce order costs.

3) Buyer-supplier relationships are further facilitated by electronic data interchange (EDI), a technology that allows the supplier access to the buyer's online inventory management system. Thus, electronic messages replace paper documents (purchase orders and sales invoices), and the production schedules and deliveries of the parties can be more readily coordinated.

3. **Materials Requirements Planning (MRP)**

    a. MRP is an integrated computer-based system designed to plan and control materials used in production.

        1) MRP is a push system, that is, the demand for raw materials is driven by the forecast demand for the final product, which can be programmed into the computer.

    b. The MRP system consults the **bill of materials (BOM)**, a record of which (and how many) subassemblies go into the finished product. The system then generates a complete list of every part and component needed.

EXAMPLE

A manufacturer has the following bill of materials for a car:

Subunit	Quantity
Engine	1
Suspension	4

The bill of materials for the component subunits is as follows:

Subunit	Contains	Quantity
Engine	Cylinder Head	2
	Pistons	6
Suspension	Shock Absorber	4

Current inventory quantities are as follows:

Subunit	On Hand
Engine	25
Suspension	35
Shock Absorber	50
Cylinder Head	30
Pistons	40

The company has 20 units of the finished product in inventory and wishes to maintain this level throughout the year. Production of 40 units is scheduled for the upcoming month. The quantities of the principal subunits that must be produced are calculated below:

Subunit	Quantity per Finished Product		Production Run		Quantity Needed		Quantity On Hand		To Be Built
Engine	1	×	40	=	40	−	25	=	15
Suspension	4	×	40	=	160	−	35	=	125

The parts that must be ordered from vendors can thus be calculated as follows:

Subunit	Components	Component Quantity		Subunits To Be Built		Quantity Needed		Quantity On Hand		To Be Purchased
Engine	Cylinder Head	2	×	15	=	30	−	30	=	0
	Pistons	6	×	15	=	90	−	40	=	50
Suspension	Shock Absorber	4	×	125	=	500	−	50	=	450

---

    c. MRP, in effect, creates schedules of when items of inventory will be needed in the production departments.

        1) If parts are not in stock, the system automatically generates a purchase order on the proper date (considering lead times) so that deliveries will arrive on time. The timing of deliveries is vital to avoid both production delays and excessive inventory of raw materials.

4.   **Manufacturing Resource Planning**

a.   Manufacturing resource planning (MRP-II) expands the scope of MRP to integrate all facets of a manufacturing business, including production, sales, inventories, schedules, and cash flows.

1)   The same system is used for both financial reporting and management of operations (both use the same transactions and numbers).

2)   MRP-II uses a master production schedule (MPS), which is a statement of the anticipated manufacturing schedule for selected items for selected periods.

3)   A further refinement in MRP-II is the inclusion of a feedback loop that makes possible the continuous revision of a production plan.

5.   **Computer-Integrated Manufacturing (CIM)**

a.   Computer technology has advanced beyond planning and controlling resource use to the automation of actual production process.

b.   A CIM system involves (1) designing products using computer-aided design (CAD), (2) testing the design using computer-aided engineering (CAE), (3) manufacturing products using computer-aided manufacturing (CAM), and (4) integrating all components with a computerized information system.

1)   CIM is a comprehensive approach to manufacturing in which design is translated into product by centralized processing and robotics. The concept also includes materials handling.

2)   The advantages of CIM include increased flexibility, productivity, integration, synergism, and cost minimization because of decreased waste, scrap, rework, and spoilage.

c.   Flexibility is a key advantage. A traditional manufacturing system might become disrupted from an emergency change, but CIM will reschedule everything in the plant when a priority requirement is inserted into the system. The areas of flexibility include the following:

1)   Varying production volumes during a period
2)   Handling new parts added to a product
3)   Changing the proportion of parts being produced
4)   Adjusting to engineering changes of a product
5)   Adapting the sequence in which parts come to the machinery
6)   Adapting to changes in materials

Stop and review! You have completed the outline for this subunit. Study multiple-choice questions 5 through 9 beginning on page 92.

4.3 EDI, EFT, AND E-COMMERCE

1.   **Electronic Data Interchange (EDI)**

a.   EDI is the communication of electronic documents directly from a computer in one organization to a computer in another organization, for example, to order goods from a supplier or to transfer funds. EDI was the first step in the evolution of e-business.

1)   EDI was developed to enhance JIT (just-in-time) inventory management.

b.   Advantages of EDI include reduction of clerical errors, speed of transactions, and elimination of repetitive clerical tasks. EDI also eliminates document preparation, processing, and mailing costs.

c.   A disadvantage of EDI is that it cannot handle a large volume of custom orders. The lack of standardization imposes unacceptable costs.

    d.   The following are risks of EDI:

        1)   Security of information

            a)   End-to-end data encryption is a security procedure that protects data during transmission.

        2)   Loss of data

    e.   An extension of EDI is computer-stored records, which can be less expensive than traditional physical file storage.

2.   **EDI Terms and Components**

    a.   Standards have been developed by national and international organizations for converting written documents into an electronic document-messaging format to facilitate EDI.

    b.   Conventions are the procedures for arranging data elements in specified formats for various accounting transactions, e.g., invoices, materials releases, and advance shipment notices.

    c.   A data dictionary prescribes the meaning of data elements, including specification of each transaction structure.

    d.   Transmission protocols are rules to determine how each electronic envelope is structured and processed by the communications devices.

        1)   Normally, a group of transactions is combined in an electronic envelope and transmitted into a communications network.

        2)   Rules are required for transmission and the separation of envelopes.

    e.   Because EDI formats and elements vary, trading partners must negotiate EDI standards. A large organization may gain a competitive advantage by forcing its trading partners to adopt its standards.

3.   **Methods of EDI Communication**

    a.   Originally, point-to-point connections were used in which both parties had fixed, dedicated computer connections.

    b.   Third-party value-added networks (VANs) are private mailbox-type services in which the sender's and receiver's computers are never directly connected to each other. Instead, the parties to an EDI arrangement subscribe to the third-party VAN provider.

        1)   Because of the third-party buffer, the VAN users are not required to conform to the same standards, conventions, and protocols. Also, VANs can store messages (in a mailbox), so the parties can batch outgoing and incoming messages.

        2)   Encryption, preferably by physically secure hardware rather than software, is a critical control.

    c.   Cost advantages are leading to increased use of the Internet as a means of conducting business directly with a trading partner. It can be used in a more open environment in which one firm transmits documents to another.

        1)   This approach is based on less formal agreements between the trading partners than in EDI and requires the sending firm to format the documents into the format of the receiving firm.

4.   **Implications for Internal Auditors**

    a.   EDI eliminates the paper documents, both internal and external, that are the traditional basis for many procedures performed in substantive testing and in tests of controls.

        1)   An organization that has reengineered its procedures and processes to take advantage of EDI may have eliminated even the electronic equivalents of paper documents.

b.   For example, the buyer's point-of-sale (POS) system may directly transmit information to the seller, which delivers on a JIT basis. Purchase orders, invoices, and receiving reports are eliminated and replaced with

1)   A long-term contract establishing quantities, prices, and delivery schedules;
2)   Production schedules;
3)   Advance ship notices;
4)   Evaluated receipts settlements (periodic payment authorizations transmitted to the trading partner with no need for matching purchase orders, invoices, and receiving reports); and
5)   Payments by EFT.

c.   Internal auditors must seek new forms of evidence to support assertions about EDI transactions, whether the evidence exists at the client organization, the trading partner, or a third party, such as a VAN. Examples of such evidence are

1)   The authorized paper purchase contract,
2)   An electronic completed production schedule image, and
3)   Internal and external evidence of evaluated receipts settlements sent to the trading partner.

d.   Internal auditors must evaluate digital signatures and reviews when testing controls.

e.   Internal auditors may need to consider other subsystems when testing a particular subsystem. For example, production cycle evidence may be needed to test the expenditure cycle.

5.   **EDI Controls**

a.   EDI controls vary with the organization's objectives and applications. Authorized users with independent access may include the following:

1)   The people initiating transactions
2)   The people authorizing transactions
3)   Other authorizing parties
4)   Senders for exceptional transactions

b.   Messages may be authenticated using smart cards and other hardware and software techniques. Protection of message integrity by authentication is especially important for such EDI applications as EFT and ordering.

c.   Messages also must be protected from interception or tampering while in transit. Controls include the following:

1)   Encryption
2)   Numerical sequencing to identify missing or false messages
3)   Nonrepudiation methods

a)   Digital certificates are used to prove origination and delivery so that parties cannot disclaim responsibility for sending or receiving a message.
b)   E-commerce sellers and buyers routinely provide acknowledgments and confirmations, respectively, in a website dialogue to avoid later disputes.
c)   In an EDI application, control over nonrepudiation is achieved by sequencing, encryption, and authentication.

6.   **Electronic Funds Transfer (EFT)**

a.   EFT is a service provided by financial institutions worldwide that is based on electronic data interchange (EDI) technology.

1)   EFT transaction costs are lower than for manual systems because documents and human intervention are eliminated from the transaction process. Moreover, transfer customarily requires less than a day.

        2) A typical consumer application of EFT is the direct deposit of payroll checks in employees' accounts or the automatic withdrawal of payments for cable and telephone bills, mortgages, etc.

   b. The most important application of EFT is check collection. To reduce the enormous volume of paper, the check-collection process has been computerized.

        1) The result has been to reduce the significance of paper checks because EFT provides means to make payments and deposit funds without manual transfer of negotiable instruments. Thus, wholesale EFTs among financial institutions and businesses (commercial transfers) are measured in trillions of U.S. dollars.

7. **E-Commerce**

   a. **Electronic commerce (e-commerce)** is the purchase and sale of goods and services by electronic means. **E-business** is a more comprehensive term defined as all methods of conducting business electronically.

   b. E-commerce may occur via online transactions on public networks, electronic data interchange (EDI), and email.

8. **Security Issues for E-commerce**

   a. The correct identification of the transacting parties (authentication)

   b. Determination of who may rightfully make decisions, such as entering into contracts or setting prices (authorization)

   c. Methods for protecting the confidentiality and integrity of information, providing evidence of the transmission and receipt of documents, and guarding against repudiation by the sender or recipient

   d. The trustworthiness of listed prices and the confidentiality of discounts

   e. The confidentiality and integrity of orders, payments, delivery addresses, and confirmations

   f. The proper extent of verification of payment data

   g. The best method of payment to avoid wrongdoing or disagreements

   h. Lost or duplicated transactions

   i. Determining who bears the risk of fraud

9. **Responses to Security Issues**

   a. Encryption and associated authentication methods

   b. Compliance with legal requirements, such as privacy statutes

   c. Documentation of trading agreements, especially the terms of trade and methods of authorization and authentication

   d. Agreements for end-to-end security and availability with providers of information services and VANs

   e. Disclosure by public trading systems of their terms of business

   f. The capacity of the host computer to avoid downtime and repel attacks

10. **Audit Considerations**

NOTE: The IIA's Practice Advisory 2100-6, *Control and Audit Implications of E-commerce Activities*, has been withdrawn. However, it contained much useful information about engagements to audit electronic commerce activities.

   a. E-commerce means "conducting commercial activities over the Internet."

        1) These activities can be business-to-business (B2B), business-to-consumer (B2C), and business-to-employee (B2E).

        2) Technology changes and the dramatic growth of e-commerce create significant control and management challenges.

b. In planning an e-commerce engagement, the auditor should understand the changes in business and information systems, the related risks, and how strategies relate to design and market requirements.

1) The auditor reviews

a) Strategic planning;
b) Risk assessment; and
c) Management's decisions about risks, controls, and monitoring.

c. The auditor also

1) Assesses control and whether reasonable assurance exists that objectives are achievable,
2) Determines risk acceptability,
3) Understands information flow,
4) Reviews interfaces, and
5) Evaluates disaster recovery plans.

d. The CAE's concerns are the competency and capacity of the internal audit activity, and deliverability of the expected audit plan.

e. The risk assessment considers

1) The existence of a business plan;
2) Its integration of the planning, design, and implementation of the e-commerce system with the entity's strategies;
3) The effects on the system;
4) Whether users' needs will be met;
5) Regulatory issues;
6) The security and effectiveness of hardware and software controls;
7) Transaction processing integrity and accuracy;
8) Completeness of the risk assessment;
9) Inherent risks associated with the Internet;
10) Whether a going concern evaluation of outside vendors has been made by a trusted, qualified third party;
11) Whether vendors that provide hosting services have a tested business contingency plan; and
12) Legal matters.

f. Risk is inherent. Beyond the risks assumed by management may be threats not clearly understood and fully evaluated.

1) Managing risk requires an understanding of risk elements and an awareness of new threats and changes in technology affecting information security. The following seven key questions identify organizational risk and possible ways of controlling the exposures:

a) What adverse events could happen (threat events)?
b) What will be the financial effect (single loss exposure value)?
c) How often will threats occur (frequency)?
d) How probable are the preceding answers (uncertainty)?
e) What risk management procedures are feasible (safeguards and controls)?
f) What is the cost (of safeguards and controls)?
g) How efficient is risk management?

    g.   Critical risk and control issues include

       1) General project management,
       2) Specific security threats,
       3) Transaction integrity in a complex network,
       4) Website content changes,
       5) Technology change,
       6) Legal issues and concerns, and
       7) Changes in business processes and structures.

    h.   The overall audit objective is effective control, and management of e-commerce should be documented in an approved strategic plan. The following are specific audit objectives for an e-commerce engagement:

       1) Evidence of transactions,
       2) Availability and reliability of security,
       3) Effective interface with financial systems,
       4) Security of monetary transactions,
       5) Effectiveness of customer authentication,
       6) Adequacy of business continuity processes,
       7) Compliance with security standards,
       8) Use and control of digital signatures,
       9) Adequacy of control of public key certificates,
       10) Adequacy and timeliness of operating data, and
       11) Documentation of effective control.

    i.   The following are the components of a general e-commerce audit of key areas:

       1) E-commerce organization,
       2) Fraud conditions (red flags),
       3) Authentication of transactions and evaluation of controls,
       4) Evaluation of controls over data integrity,
       5) Review of the continuity plan for business interruptions, and
       6) Evaluation of how well business units are managing e-commerce.

Stop and review! You have completed the outline for this subunit. Study multiple-choice questions 10 through 16 beginning on page 94.

4.4 BUSINESS DEVELOPMENT LIFE CYCLES

1.   The business life cycle interacts with product life cycles and the overall economic cycle. For example, successful new product introductions may increase sales and profits during a recession.

2.   In the **initial or formative stage**, the emerging entity most likely relies on the personal resources of its owners, assistance from governmental agencies, and trade credit for its financing needs.

3.   If the entity is successful and enters the **rapid growth stage**, internal financing becomes feasible, and trade credit continues to be used. Moreover, the entity's performance may enable it to secure bank credit to meet seasonal needs and intermediate-term loans. Such an entity also may attract equity financing from venture capitalists.

    a.   If the entity is extremely successful, it may be able to issue securities that are publicly traded. Thus, the entity may enter the formal capital and money markets. These markets provide financing at lower cost than venture capitalists.

4. The entity must consider the limitations of the product life cycle. Absent the development of new products, growth will not continue, and the entity will enter the **product maturity and decline stage**. The financing pattern at this stage usually includes internal financing, diversification, share repurchases, and mergers.

5. Another perspective on life cycles compares the entity's growth rate with the economy's.

   a. Thus, during the early stages of the cycle, the entity's rate is much greater than that of the economy. Later, the rates tend to be about the same. In the decline stage, the entity's growth rate is lower than the economy's.

   b. Accordingly, its earnings, dividends, and share price fall. Entities with growth rates that do not approximate the economy's growth rate are nonconstant growth entities. Calculations using the dividend growth model are more complicated for such entities.

Stop and review! You have completed the outline for this subunit. Study multiple-choice question 17 on page 95.

4.5 ISO FRAMEWORK

1. **The International Organization for Standardization (ISO)**

   a. In 1987, the ISO introduced **ISO 9000**, a group of 11 voluntary standards and technical reports that provide guidance for establishing and maintaining a quality management system (QMS).

      1) The ISO's rules specify that its standards be revised every 5 years to reflect technical and market developments. (NOTE: ISO is not an acronym. It means equal, suggesting that entities certified under ISO 9000 have equal quality.)

   b. The intent of the standards is to ensure the quality of the process, not the product. The marketplace determines whether a product is good or bad.

      1) For this reason, the ISO deems it unacceptable for phrases referring to ISO certification to appear on individual products or packaging.

   c. ISO 9001:2008 is a generic standard that states requirements for a QMS. It applies when an entity needs to demonstrate its ability to (1) sell a product that meets customer and regulatory requirements and (2) increase customer satisfaction through improving the QMS and ensuring conformity with requirements.

   d. ISO 9000:2015 expands on the concepts found in ISO 9001:2008 and makes them more accessible to all types of enterprises.

2. **Aspects of ISO Certification**

   a. Some entities are obtaining ISO certification because of concern that the European Union will require compliance with the standards in an attempt to restrict imports.

      1) The standards are not yet mandatory. However, they are required for certain regulated products (for which health and safety are concerns), such as medical devices, telecommunications equipment, and gas appliances.

      2) Some customers demand that suppliers register.

      3) ISO 9000 registration may be necessary to be competitive. It makes customers more comfortable with suppliers' products and services.

      4) Many entities implementing the standards make internal process and quality improvements as a result. ISO 9000 forces them to share information and understand who internal customers and users are.

    b.   A registrar, or external auditor, must be selected. Registrars are usually specialists within certain Standard Industrial Classification (SIC) codes. Certification by a registrar avoids the need for each customer to audit a supplier.

        1)   Following an onsite visit, the registrar, if convinced that a quality system conforms to the selected standard, issues a certificate describing the scope of the registration. Registration is usually granted for a 3-year period.

        2)   All employees are subject to being audited. They must have the ability to "say what they do" and to demonstrate that they "do what they say."

3.   **Basic Requirements of an ISO QMS**

    a.   **Key Process Identification**

        1)   Key processes affecting quality must be identified and included.

        2)   A process management approach must be used. It manages the entity as a set of linked processes that are controlled for continuous improvement.

    b.   **General Requirements**

        1)   The entity must have a quality policy and quality goals. It also must design a QMS to control process performance. Quality goals are measurable and specific.

        2)   The QMS is documented in the (a) quality policy, (b) quality manual, (c) procedures, (d) work instructions, and (e) records.

        3)   The entity also must demonstrate its ability to increase customer satisfaction through improving the QMS and ensuring conformity with requirements.

    c.   **Management Responsibility**

        1)   Management (a) reviews the quality policy, (b) analyzes data about QMS performance, and (c) assesses opportunities for improvement and the need for change.

        2)   Management ensures that systems exist to determine and satisfy customer requirements.

    d.   **Resource Management**

        1)   The resources needed to improve the QMS and satisfy customer requirements must be provided.

    e.   **Product Realization**

        1)   These processes result in products or services received by customers. They must be planned and controlled.

        2)   Issues are (a) means of control, (b) objectives, (c) documentation and records needed, and (d) acceptance criteria.

    f.   **Measurement, Analysis, and Improvement**

        1)   The entity must have processes for (a) inspection, (b) testing, (c) measurement, (d) analysis, and (e) improvement.

4.   **Other Areas of Standardization**

    a.   The ISO also has issued ISO 14000, a set of environmental standards. These standards are comparable in purpose to ISO 9000 but concern environmental quality systems.

        1)   Although they have not been as widely adopted as the ISO 9000 standards, they may become necessary for conducting international business. Some European countries already have environmental systems standards in place, and the relationship of these single-country standards with ISO 14000 is not clear. However, individual countries' standards are typically more strict.

b.   The scope of ISO 19011:2002 extends to (1) the principles of auditing, (2) managing audit programs, (3) conducting QMS audits and environmental management system (EMS) audits, and (4) the competence of QMS and EMS auditors.

1)   It applies to all entities that must perform internal or external audits of QMSs or environmental management systems or manage an audit program.

2)   ISO 19011 may apply to other types of audits if due consideration is given to identifying the competencies required of the auditors.

c.   ISO 10012:2003 is a generic standard. It addresses the management of measurement processes and confirmation of measuring equipment used to support compliance with required measures.

1)   It states quality management requirements of a measurement management system (MMS) that can be used as part of the overall management system.

2)   It is not to be used as a requirement for demonstrating conformance with other standards. Interested parties may agree to use ISO 10012:2003 as an input for satisfying MMS requirements in certification activities.

a)   However, other standards apply to specific elements affecting measurement results, e.g., details of measurement methods, competence of personnel, or comparisons among laboratories.

d.   ISO 14063:2006 states principles, policies, strategies, and activities for environmental communications, whether external or internal. It addresses the unique circumstances of environmental communications and applies to every entity regardless of whether it has an EMS.

e.   ISO Guide 64:2008 applies to environmental questions arising in the setting of product standards. Its purpose is to help standard setters to minimize negative environmental effects at each step in the product life cycle.

f.   ISO 14050:2009 is a glossary of environmental management vocabulary.

Author's Note: It is not necessary to commit the ISO numbers to memory. Simply having a general understanding of these concepts and their implications will be sufficient to help you pass the exam.

Stop and review! You have completed the outline for this subunit. Study multiple-choice questions 18 and 19 on page 96.

4.6 OUTSOURCING

1.   **Business Process Outsourcing**

a.   Business process outsourcing is the transfer of some of an organization's business processes to an outside provider to improve service quality while achieving

1)   Cost savings,
2)   Operating effectiveness, or
3)   Operating efficiency.

b.   Such processes as human resources, payroll, and information services may not be core competencies of some organizations. To streamline operations and reduce costs, they outsource processes.

1)   By contracting with outside service providers who specialize in these functions, the organization also may avoid the problem of knowledge drain when key employees leave.

2.   **Management Responsibilities**

a.   Management is still responsible for ensuring that an adequate system of internal control exists over processes performed by an external service provider.

b.   *Internal Auditing: Assurance & Consulting Services* (2nd edition) recommends the following practices for effective risk management and control of outsourced business processes:

1)   Document the outsourced process and indicate which key controls have been outsourced.

2)   Ensure that the effectiveness of the outsourced process is monitored.

3)   Obtain assurance that the internal controls embedded in the outsourced process are operating effectively, either through internal audits of such controls or an external review of these controls.

4)   Periodically reevaluate whether the business case for outsourcing the process remains valid.

3.   **Advantages and Disadvantages**

a.   **Advantages** of outsourcing include

1)   Access to expertise,
2)   Superior service quality,
3)   Avoidance of changes in the organization's infrastructure,
4)   Cost predictability,
5)   Use of human and financial capital, and
6)   Avoidance of fixed costs.

b.   The potential **disadvantages** include

1)   Inflexibility of the relationship,
2)   Loss of core knowledge,
3)   Loss of control over the outsourced function,
4)   Unexpected costs,
5)   Vulnerability of important information,
6)   Need for contract management, and
7)   Dependence on a single vendor.

Stop and review! You have completed the outline for this subunit. Study multiple-choice question 20 on page 96.

QUESTIONS

4.1 Managing Inventory Costs and Quantities

1. An entity sells 1,500 units of a particular item each year and orders the items in equal quantities of 500 units at a price of US $5 per unit. No safety stocks are held. If the entity has a cost of capital of 12%, its annual opportunity cost of carrying inventory is

A.   US $150
B.   US $180
C.   US $300
D.   US $900

Answer (A) is correct.
     REQUIRED: The annual cost of carrying inventory.
     DISCUSSION: The annual opportunity cost of carrying inventory equals the average inventory level, times the per-unit purchase price, times the cost of capital. The average inventory level is the order quantity divided by 2. Thus, the annual opportunity cost of carrying inventory is US $150 [(500 units ÷ 2) × $5 × .12].
     Answer (B) is incorrect. A US $180 cost is obtained by using the total annual quantity rather than the average inventory level and by not multiplying by the unit price. Answer (C) is incorrect. A US $300 cost is obtained by using the order size rather than the average inventory level. Answer (D) is incorrect. A US $900 cost is based on the total annual quantity rather than the average inventory level.

2. An organization sells a product for which demand is uncertain. Management would like to ensure that there is sufficient inventory on hand during periods of high demand so that it does not lose sales (and customers). To do so, the organization should

    A. Keep a safety stock.

    B. Use a just-in-time inventory system.

    C. Employ a materials requirements planning system.

    D. Keep a master production schedule.

Answer (A) is correct.
    REQUIRED: The means of ensuring that sufficient inventory is on hand.
    DISCUSSION: Safety stock is inventory maintained to reduce the number of stockouts resulting from higher-than-expected demand during lead time. Maintaining a safety stock avoids the costs of stockouts, e.g., lost sales and customer dissatisfaction.
    Answer (B) is incorrect. The goal of a just-in-time inventory system is to reduce, not increase, inventory on hand. Answer (C) is incorrect. Materials requirements planning is a system for scheduling production and controlling the level of inventory for components with dependent demand. Answer (D) is incorrect. A master production schedule is a statement of the timing and amounts of individual items to be produced.

3. Which of the following is used in determining the economic order quantity (EOQ)?

    A. Regression analysis.

    B. Calculus.

    C. Markov process.

    D. Queuing theory.

Answer (B) is correct.
    REQUIRED: The technique used in determining the EOQ.
    DISCUSSION: The primary business application of differential calculus is to identify the maxima or minima of curvilinear functions. In business and economics, these are the points of revenue or profit maximization (maxima) or cost minimization (minima). The EOQ results from differentiating the total cost with regard to order quantity.
    Answer (A) is incorrect. Regression analysis is used to fit a linear trend line to a dependent variable based on one or more independent variables. Answer (C) is incorrect. Markov process models are used to study the evolution of certain systems over repeated trials. Answer (D) is incorrect. Queuing theory is a waiting-line technique used to balance desirable service levels against the cost of providing more service.

4. One of the elements included in the economic order quantity (EOQ) formula is

    A. Safety stock.

    B. Yearly demand.

    C. Selling price of item.

    D. Lead time for delivery.

Answer (B) is correct.
    REQUIRED: The element to include in the EOQ calculation.
    DISCUSSION: The basic EOQ formula is used to minimize the total of inventory carrying and ordering costs. The basic EOQ equals the square root of a fraction consisting of a numerator equal to the product of twice the unit periodic demand and the variable cost per order and a denominator equal to the unit periodic carrying cost.
    Answer (A) is incorrect. The safety stock is not included in the basic EOQ formula. Answer (C) is incorrect. The selling price of the item is not included in the basic EOQ formula. Answer (D) is incorrect. The lead time for delivery is not included in the basic EOQ formula.

4.2 Inventory Management Methods

5. A company uses a planning system that focuses first on the amount and timing of finished goods demanded and then determines the derived demand for raw material, components, and subassemblies at each of the prior stages of production. This system is referred to as

    A. Economic order quantity.

    B. Materials requirements planning.

    C. Linear programming.

    D. Just-in-time purchasing.

Answer (B) is correct.
    REQUIRED: The planning system that calculates derived demand for inventories.
    DISCUSSION: Materials requirements planning (MRP) is usually a computer-based information system designed to plan and control raw materials used in a production setting. It assumes that estimated demand for materials is reasonably accurate and that suppliers can deliver based upon this accurate schedule. It is crucial that delivery delays be avoided because, under MRP, production delays are almost unavoidable if the materials are not on hand. An MRP system uses a parts list, often called a bill of materials, and lead times for each type of material to obtain materials just as they are needed for planned production.
    Answer (A) is incorrect. The economic order quantity is a decision model that focuses on the trade-off between carrying and ordering costs. Answer (C) is incorrect. Linear programming is a decision model concerned with allocating scarce resources to maximize profit or minimize costs. Answer (D) is incorrect. Just-in-time purchasing involves the purchase of goods such that delivery immediately precedes demand or use.

6. The effect of just-in-time production approaches

    A. Reduces the dependency on suppliers.

    B. Reduces the cost of implementing strategies.

    C. Decreases production facility flexibility.

    D. Decreases the need for a dependable workforce.

Answer (B) is correct.
    REQUIRED: The effect of just-in-time production approaches.
    DISCUSSION: A just-in-time (JIT) inventory system can reduce the cost of production by lowering or eliminating inventory costs.
    Answer (A) is incorrect. JIT production increases the need for reliable suppliers. When inventories are at low or nonexistent levels, supplier performance is critical. Answer (C) is incorrect. JIT production increases flexibility. Production is pulled by demand. Answer (D) is incorrect. JIT requires workers to be multi-skilled and independent. Thus, they need to be more dependable. Such traits are needed in a pull system.

7. Just-in-time (JIT) inventory systems have been adopted by large manufacturers to minimize the carrying costs of inventories. Identify the primary vulnerability of JIT systems.

    A. Computer resources.

    B. Materials supply contracts.

    C. Work stoppages.

    D. Implementation time.

Answer (C) is correct.
    REQUIRED: The primary vulnerability of JIT systems.
    DISCUSSION: JIT minimizes inventory by relying on coordination with suppliers to provide deliveries when they are needed for production. Consequently, work stoppages are more likely due to stockouts, because the inventory buffer is reduced or eliminated.
    Answer (A) is incorrect. JIT systems can require significant computer resources, but they can also be maintained manually. Answer (B) is incorrect. Contracts may have to be renegotiated with strict delivery and quality specifications, but these changes usually occur over extended periods. Answer (D) is incorrect. JIT can be implemented over an extended period or a shorter time frame depending on the manufacturer's immediate needs.

8. An inventory planning method that minimizes inventories by arranging to have raw materials and subcomponents arrive immediately preceding their use is called

    A. A safety stock planning system.

    B. An economic order quantity model.

    C. A just-in-time inventory system.

    D. A master budgeting system.

Answer (C) is correct.
    REQUIRED: The inventory planning method that minimizes inventories by arranging to have raw materials and subcomponents arrive immediately preceding their use.
    DISCUSSION: JIT is a manufacturing philosophy that combines purchasing, production, and inventory control. Minimization of inventory is a goal, but JIT also changes the production process itself. An emphasis on quality and the pull of materials related to demand are key characteristics of JIT. The factory is organized so as to bring materials and tools close to the point of use rather than keeping them in storage areas. A key element of the JIT system is reduction or elimination of waste of materials, labor, factory space, and machine usage. Minimizing inventory is the key to reducing waste. When a part is needed on the production line, it arrives just in time, not before.
    Answer (A) is incorrect. Safety stock is the inventory maintained in order to reduce the number of stockouts resulting from higher-than-expected demand during lead time. Answer (B) is incorrect. The economic order quantity is the order quantity that minimizes total inventory costs. Answer (D) is incorrect. The master budget is the detailed financial plan for the next period.

9. Companies that adopt just-in-time purchasing systems often experience

    A. An increase in carrying costs.

    B. A reduction in the number of suppliers.

    C. A greater need for inspection of goods as the goods arrive.

    D. Less need for linkage with a vendor's computerized order entry system.

Answer (B) is correct.
    REQUIRED: The true statement about companies that adopt just-in-time (JIT) purchasing systems.
    DISCUSSION: The objective of JIT is to reduce carrying costs by eliminating inventories and increasing the deliveries made by suppliers. Ideally, shipments of materials are received just in time to be used in the manufacturing process. The focus of quality control under JIT is the prevention of quality problems. Quality control is shifted to the supplier. Entities that adopt JIT typically do not inspect incoming goods. The assumption is that receipts are of perfect quality. Suppliers are limited to those who guarantee perfect quality and prompt delivery.
    Answer (A) is incorrect. Carrying costs typically decline in JIT companies. Less inventory is on hand. Answer (C) is incorrect. In a JIT system, materials are delivered directly to the production line ready for insertion in the finished product. Answer (D) is incorrect. The need for communication with the vendor is greater. Orders and deliveries must be made on short notice, sometimes several times a day.

4.3 EDI, EFT, and E-Commerce

10. Which of the following risks is **not** greater in an electronic funds transfer (EFT) environment than in a manual system using paper transactions?

    A. Unauthorized access and activity.

    B. Duplicate transaction processing.

    C. Higher cost per transaction.

    D. Inadequate backup and recovery capabilities.

Answer (C) is correct.
    REQUIRED: The risk not greater in an EFT environment than in a manual system using paper transactions.
    DISCUSSION: EFT is a service provided by financial institutions worldwide that is based on EDI technology. EFT transaction costs are lower than for manual systems because documents and human intervention are eliminated from the transactions process.
    Answer (A) is incorrect. Unauthorized access and activity is a risk specific to EFT. Answer (B) is incorrect. Inaccurate transaction processing (including duplication) is a risk specific to EFT. Answer (D) is incorrect. Inadequate backup and recovery capabilities is a risk specific to EFT.

11. Which of the following is usually a benefit of using electronic funds transfer (EFT) for international cash transactions?

    A. Improvement of the audit trail for cash receipts and disbursements.

    B. Creation of self-monitoring access controls.

    C. Reduction of the frequency of data entry errors.

    D. Off-site storage of source documents for cash transactions.

Answer (C) is correct.
    REQUIRED: The benefit of using EFT for international cash transactions.
    DISCUSSION: The processing and transmission of electronic transactions, such as EFTs, virtually eliminates human interaction. This process not only helps eliminate errors but also allows for the rapid detection and recovery from errors when they do occur.
    Answer (A) is incorrect. The audit trail is typically less apparent in an electronic environment than in a manual environment. Answer (B) is incorrect. A key control is management's establishment and monitoring of access controls. Answer (D) is incorrect. Source documents are often eliminated in EFT transactions.

12. Companies now can use electronic transfers to conduct regular business transactions. Which of the following terms best describes a system in which an agreement is made between two or more parties to electronically transfer purchase orders, sales orders, invoices, and/or other financial documents?

    A. Electronic mail (email).

    B. Electronic funds transfer (EFT).

    C. Electronic data interchange (EDI).

    D. Electronic data processing (EDP).

Answer (C) is correct.
    REQUIRED: The term best describing electronic transfer of documents.
    DISCUSSION: Electronic data interchange is the electronic transfer of documents between businesses. EDI was developed to enhance just-in-time (JIT) inventory management. Advantages include speed, reduction of clerical errors, and elimination of repetitive clerical tasks and their costs.
    Answer (A) is incorrect. Email can send text or document files, but the term encompasses a wide range of transfers. EDI specifically applies to the system described in the question. Answer (B) is incorrect. EFT refers to the transfer of money. Answer (D) is incorrect. EDP is a generic term for computerized processing of transaction data within organizations.

13. The emergence of electronic data interchange (EDI) as standard operating practice increases the risk of

    A. Unauthorized third-party access to systems.

    B. Systematic programming errors.

    C. Inadequate knowledge bases.

    D. Unsuccessful system use.

Answer (A) is correct.
    REQUIRED: The risk increased by the emergence of EDI as standard operating practice.
    DISCUSSION: EDI is the communication of electronic documents directly from a computer in one entity to a computer in another entity. EDI for business documents between unrelated parties has the potential to increase the risk of unauthorized third-party access to systems because more outsiders will have access to internal systems.
    Answer (B) is incorrect. Systematic programming errors are the result of misspecification of requirements or lack of correspondence between specifications and programs. Answer (C) is incorrect. Inadequate knowledge bases are a function of lack of care in building them. Answer (D) is incorrect. A benefit of EDI is to improve the efficiency and effectiveness of system use.

14. Which of the following is usually a benefit of transmitting transactions in an electronic data interchange (EDI) environment?

A. A compressed business cycle with lower year-end receivables balances.

B. A reduced need to test computer controls related to sales and collections transactions.

C. An increased opportunity to apply statistical sampling techniques to account balances.

D. No need to rely on third-party service providers to ensure security.

Answer (A) is correct.
REQUIRED: The benefit of EDI.
DISCUSSION: EDI transactions are typically transmitted and processed in real time. Thus, EDI compresses the business cycle by eliminating delays. The time required to receive and process an order, ship goods, and receive payment is greatly reduced compared with that of a typical manual system. Accordingly, more rapid receipt of payment minimizes receivables and improves cash flow.
Answer (B) is incorrect. Use of a sophisticated processing system would increase the need to test computer controls. Answer (C) is incorrect. Computer technology allows all transactions to be tested rather than just a sample. Answer (D) is incorrect. EDI often uses a VAN (value-added network) as a third-party service provider, and reliance on controls provided by the VAN may be critical.

15. Which type of risks assumed by management are often drivers of organizational activities?

A. Opportunity risks.

B. Inherent risks.

C. General project management risks.

D. Control risks.

Answer (A) is correct.
REQUIRED: The type of risks assumed by management that are often drivers of organizational activities.
DISCUSSION: Risk can be defined as the uncertainty of an event occurring that could have a negative impact on the achievement of objectives. Risk is inherent to every business or government entity. Opportunity risks assumed by management are often drivers of organizational activities. Beyond these opportunities may be threats and other dangers that are not clearly understood or fully evaluated and are too easily accepted as part of doing business.

16. What is the overall audit objective when auditing an e-commerce activity?

A. To ensure that all e-commerce processes have efficient internal controls.

B. To ensure that all e-commerce processes have effective internal controls.

C. To ensure that all e-commerce processes are adequate to fulfill their intended objectives.

D. To ensure that all e-commerce processes meet the functionality requirements of the end users.

Answer (B) is correct.
REQUIRED: The overall audit objective when auditing an e-commerce activity.
DISCUSSION: According to PA 2100-6 (now withdrawn), when auditing e-commerce activities, the overall audit objective should be to ensure that all e-commerce processes have effective internal controls.
Answer (A) is incorrect. The overall audit objective is not about ensuring the efficiency of internal controls. It is about ensuring the effectiveness of internal controls. Answer (C) is incorrect. Adequacy of processes should be considered during the internal auditor's risk assessment. Answer (D) is incorrect. Meeting functional requirements should be considered during the internal auditor's risk assessment.

4.4 Business Development Life Cycles

17. Faced with 3 years of steadily decreasing profits despite increased sales and a growing economy, which of the following is the healthiest course of action for a chief executive officer to take?

A. Set a turnaround goal of significantly increasing profits within 2 months. Set clear short-term objectives for each operating unit that, together, should produce the turnaround.

B. Reduce staff by 10% in every unit.

C. Classify all job functions as either (1) adding value in the eyes of the customer (such as production and sales) or (2) not adding value in the eyes of the customer (such as accounting and human resources). Reduce staff in the non-value-adding functions by 20%.

D. Implement a plan to encourage innovation at all levels. Use early retirement and reemployment programs to trim staff size.

Answer (D) is correct.
REQUIRED: The healthiest course of action given decreasing profits despite increasing sales.
DISCUSSION: Organizational decline has been found to have the following characteristics: greater centralization, lack of long-term planning, reduced innovation, scapegoating, resistance to change, high turnover of competent leaders, low morale, nonprioritized downsizing, and conflict. Reversing these characteristics is the key to reversing organizational decline, for example, by encouraging innovation in all aspects of the organization's activities and by redeploying personnel.
Answer (A) is incorrect. This response illustrates two of the characteristics of organizational decline: increased centralization of decision making and lack of long-term planning. The exclusive emphasis on short-term results is likely to be counterproductive. Answer (B) is incorrect. Another characteristic of organizational decline is nonprioritized downsizing. By itself, downsizing rarely turns an entity around. Answer (C) is incorrect. Reducing staff disproportionately in control functions could have disastrous consequences.

4.5 ISO Framework

18. Why have many European Union countries **not** adopted ISO 14000 environmental standards?

A. Following ISO 14000 standards will not reduce monitoring and inspection by regulatory agencies.

B. Individual European Union countries' standards are typically more strict than ISO 14000 standards.

C. Regulators are permitted to use voluntary audits as a basis for punitive action.

D. ISO 14000 standards will not make it easier to do business across borders.

Answer (B) is correct.
   REQUIRED: The reason many European Union countries have not adopted ISO 14000 standards.
   DISCUSSION: Some European countries already have environmental systems in place, and individual countries' standards are typically more strict than the ISO 14000 standards. Furthermore, the relationship of these single-country standards with ISO 14000 is unclear.
   Answer (A) is incorrect. Many believe following ISO 14000 standards will reduce monitoring or inspection by regulatory agencies. Answer (C) is incorrect. Many countries in the European Union have adopted measures similar to the ones in the US to prevent self-incrimination during voluntary ISO audits. Answer (D) is incorrect. ISO 14000 establishes internationally recognized standards that are intended to diminish trade barriers and make it easier to do business across borders.

19. Which of the following statements is **not** true regarding ISO 9000 standards?

A. Compliance with the standards is voluntary.

B. The ISO 9000 standards are revised every 5 years to account for technical and market developments.

C. The objective of ISO 9000 standards is to ensure high quality products and services.

D. ISO 9000 is a set of generic standards for establishing and maintaining a quality system within an entity.

Answer (C) is correct.
   REQUIRED: The false statement regarding ISO 9000 standards.
   DISCUSSION: The objective of ISO 9000 standards is to ensure consistent quality of the process even if the product quality is poor. The market determines the quality of the product.
   Answer (A) is incorrect. Compliance is voluntary, but many entities are adopting the standards for competitive reasons or because of concern that the standards will be required in foreign markets. Answer (B) is incorrect. The ISO rules specify that standards are periodically revised every 5 years to reflect technical and market developments. Answer (D) is incorrect. ISO 9000 standards are generic and only ensure consistent quality in the product being produced.

4.6 Outsourcing

20. In some organizations, internal audit functions are outsourced. Management in a large organization should recognize that the external auditor may have an advantage, compared with the internal auditor, because of the external auditor's

A. Familiarity with the organization. Its annual audits provide an in-depth knowledge of the organization.

B. Size. It can hire experienced, knowledgeable, and certified staff.

C. Size. It is able to offer continuous availability of staff unaffected by other priorities.

D. Structure. It may more easily accommodate engagement requirements in distant locations.

Answer (D) is correct.
   REQUIRED: The advantage of outsourcing internal audit functions.
   DISCUSSION: Large organizations that are geographically dispersed may find outsourcing internal audit functions to external auditors to be effective. A major public accounting firm ordinarily has operations that are national or worldwide in scope.
   Answer (A) is incorrect. The internal auditors are likely to be more familiar with the organization than the external auditors, given the continuous nature of their responsibilities. Answer (B) is incorrect. The internal auditor also can hire experienced, knowledgeable, and certified staff. Answer (C) is incorrect. The internal auditor is more likely to be continuously available. The external auditor has responsibilities to many other clients.

Access the **CIA Review System** from your Gleim Personal Classroom to continue your studies with exam-emulating multiple-choice questions!

STUDY UNIT FIVE
COMMUNICATION

(10 pages of outline)

This study unit covers **Section IV: Communication** from The IIA's CIA Exam Syllabus. This section makes up 5% to 10% of Part 3 of the CIA exam and is tested at the **awareness level**. The relevant portion of the syllabus is highlighted below. (The complete syllabus is in Appendix A.)

IV. Communication (5%–10%)

> **A. Communication (e.g., the process, organizational dynamics, impact of computerization)**
> **B. Stakeholder Relationships**

5.1 NATURE OF COMMUNICATION

 The word "communicate" appears several times in The IIA's CIA Exam Syllabus. The ability to communicate effectively with senior management and the board, as well as with other internal auditors and client personnel, is a critical skill for an internal auditor.

1. **Overview**

   a. Communication is the process of conveying and understanding information between one person and another. It affects all organizational activities and moves in many directions.

   b. The communication process has six elements:

      1) The sender originates the message.
      2) Encoding is the process of translating thoughts into a message the receiver can understand.
      3) The medium is the channel through which the message flows.
      4) Decoding is the act of understanding a message.
      5) The receiver is the person who decodes the message and interprets the sender's meaning.
      6) Feedback is acknowledging to the sender that the message was correctly understood.

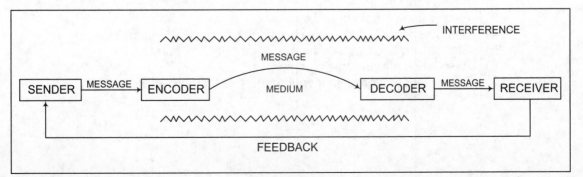

Figure 5-1

2.   **Types of Communication**

    a.   All managerial functions require communication. A manager's ability to understand other people and their ability to understand the manager are crucial to accomplishing organizational objectives. Communication ties an organization together and transforms a diverse group of people into a cohesive whole.

    b.   An organization's internal communications network should (1) facilitate decision making among managers, (2) promote goal congruence among employees, (3) integrate the efforts of all employees, and (4) build high morale and mutual trust.

        1)   Managers must spend most of their time communicating with subordinates, peers, and superiors. They communicate

            a)   Organizational goals and plans downward,

            b)   Lower-level results and problems upward, and

            c)   Coordinating information horizontally (among peers or across organizational channels).

    c.   Formal communication is conducted through the formal structure of the organization, e.g., budgets, bonus programs, memoranda, or technical manuals.

    d.   Informal communication (the grapevine) operates outside the formal organization.

        1)   The grapevine exists wherever people are.

        2)   The grapevine is usually accurate, but it can carry gossip and rumor, and it serves as an emotional outlet for employees. It also satisfies employees' desire to know what is actually happening.

            a)   The emergence of electronic media in the workplace has made the grapevine even more pervasive and important.

        3)   Managers can minimize the damage that a grapevine can cause by transmitting accurate and timely information and maintaining open media of communication. The effective manager monitors the grapevine and uses it constructively.

    e.   Written communication provides a permanent record of the message and tends to be accurate, but it can be time consuming to prepare.

        1)   An inherent weakness of written communication is that it inhibits feedback because the sender and the receiver are not in simultaneous communication.

    f.   Oral communication is less formal and less accurate than written communication but permits immediate feedback. It also permits messages to be transmitted rapidly.

        1)   Managers may spend more of their time in oral communication than in written communication.

    g.   Electronic communication. Modern technology (e.g., voicemail, fax, texting, social networking, and email) blurs the distinction between written and oral communications. The benefits of electronic communication include

        1)   Better control of information,
        2)   More timely information,
        3)   Elimination of tedious tasks,
        4)   Improvement of competitiveness due to improved technology,
        5)   Standardization of procedures by computer programs,
        6)   Assistance for strategic planning, and
        7)   Optimization of organizational resources to improve productivity.

3.   **Aspects of Communication**

    a.   Directions of Communication

        1)   Downward communication (from superior to subordinate) is vertical communication consisting of orders, instructions, notices, memos, bulletins, newsletters, handbooks, loudspeakers, and the chain of command.

        2)   Upward communication (from subordinate to superior) is vertical communication consisting of morale surveys, traditional grievance procedures, peer review of grievances, suggestion systems, informal meetings, Internet chat, exit interviews, and conferences.

            a)   Upward communication must overcome more barriers and is slower than downward communication.

        3)   Horizontal (lateral) communication is from one peer to another.

    b.   Media Richness

        1)   The fundamental concept of the contingency model for media selection is media richness, the ability to convey information and promote learning.

            a)   Media richness may be high, e.g., in a face-to-face meeting or in another interactive framework. A rich medium has many cues (content, tone of voice, body language, its personal emphasis, and immediate feedback).

            b)   Media richness may be lean (low), e.g., company memos or general email that may be viewed as impersonal static. A lean medium is essentially the opposite of a rich medium.

            c)   The management problem is to choose the appropriate medium with the degree of richness appropriate to the circumstances. For example, rich (lean) media should be used for nonroutine (routine) problems.

4.   **Interaction with Receiver**

    a.   The effectiveness of communication can be determined only when the sender seeks feedback and observes the effect on the receiver.

        1)   The sender must obtain feedback to ensure the communication process is complete.

        2)   The receiver must give feedback to the sender.

        3)   The importance of feedback to the effectiveness of the communication process indicates the limitations of one-way communications (e.g., memos).

        4)   The best indicator of effectiveness is the change in the receiver's behavior in the direction requested or required by the communication. The sender must obtain feedback (or observe results) to determine the communication's effectiveness.

            a)   A receiver who understands a message may change attitude but may not necessarily change behavior.

    b.   Managers must consider the nature of the message receiver. Receivers vary in their perception of messages because of language, education, culture, attitudes toward the sender and job, etc. This variance may result in communication distortion.

        1)   The following are some examples of this phenomenon:

            a)   In some cultures, to move toward a person while speaking is expected. In others, it is considered an act of aggression.

            b)   In some cultures, consistently being late to appointments means laxness, lack of concern, discourtesy, and disinterest. In others, it is normal, expected, and carries no particular meaning.

        2)   A speaker analyzes the audience to gather the right information. Understanding the other participants' opinions and needs enables the speaker to express his or her ideas in the way most likely to be persuasive.

   c.   Perception is the process through which someone gives meaning to the surrounding environment. It consists of the following elements:

       1)   Selectivity screens out certain stimuli to focus on details. Without selectivity, a person is overwhelmed by sensory overload.

       2)   Organization groups disorganized stimuli to give meaning to otherwise meaningless information.

       3)   Interpretation gives meaning to a set of stimuli based on the individual's experience.

5. Nonverbal Communication

   a.   Nonverbal signals occur in clusters, whether or not accompanied by verbal communication. The following are examples:

       1)   Vocal characteristics and tone of voice
       2)   Facial expressions and eye contact
       3)   Hand and body gestures and other movements
       4)   Breathing, sighs, and other noises that are not words
       5)   Physical distance between the sender and the receiver
       6)   Posture and other aspects of physical appearance
       7)   Touch
       8)   Mode of attire
       9)   Decoration and layout of rooms

   b.   Nonverbal communication is easily misunderstood because

       1)   Different cultures and languages employ different nonverbal signals, and
       2)   Clarifying the ambiguities inherent in nonverbal communication is difficult.

   c.   Interpreting nonverbal communication requires the establishment of the norms for a particular person.

       1)   For example, folded arms may indicate resistance or inflexibility or may simply be a habit.

       2)   People should not be judged solely on established or learned norms of nonverbal communication but instead on an individual basis.

   d.   For any communication to be effective, verbal and nonverbal messages should complement each other.

6. Organizational Aspects

   a.   Organizational structure determines how communication is transmitted.

   b.   Traditional management stresses one-way communications from senior management down to subordinates. This military model of organization (command and control) is autocratic or mechanistic and ignores feedback.

   c.   Participative management stresses multidirectional communication. All parts of the organization are expected to communicate with each other, not merely along lines of authority.

   d.   Systems theory stresses the importance of feedback in determining the effectiveness of communications. Without a channel from the receiver back to the sender, the sender does not know how or whether the information has affected the performance of the receiver.

Stop and review! You have completed the outline for this subunit. Study multiple-choice questions 1 through 8 beginning on page 106.

5.2 PROBLEMS IN COMMUNICATION

1. **Poorly Encoded/Decoded Messages**

    a. Encoding is the way that meaning is transmitted in communication. Decoding is the way a recipient of a message applies meaning to what is received. Poorly encoded messages result from the following:

    1) Inappropriate choice of words or phrases

        a) An example is using technical language (jargon) in speaking with a layperson. The knowledge of the sender and the recipient is relevant to the manner in which a message should be encoded.

    2) Careless omissions of key ideas

    3) Lack of coherence in forming the message

    4) Inconsistency between verbal and nonverbal messages

    5) Incomplete ideas or ideas out of the receiver's context

    6) Projection, the tendency of the sender to attribute his or her traits, values, and emotions to the receiver and vice versa

    7) Filtering the message so that it reflects more favorably on the sender, a typical problem in upward communication

2. **Faulty Medium Selection**

    a. Examples include the following:

    1) Trying to speak while a loud airplane flies overhead

    2) Gesturing to someone who cannot see the gesture

    3) Using a medium, e.g., a telephone, that creates no permanent record to send a purchase order with detailed specifications

3. **Noise**

    a. Noise in the communications medium is interference with the normal understanding of a message, for example,

    1) Random events that cause a breakdown in communication (e.g., loss of mail or cell phone service),

    2) Use of technical language by the sender that is unlikely to be understood by the receiver, or

    3) Poor hearing or eyesight.

4. **Perceptual Problems**

    a. Perceptual problems may arise from the following:

    1) The sender's dislike of the receiver or vice versa

    2) Distortion created by personal enthusiasm for overstating good news and understating bad news (or vice versa)

    3) Status differences among people that impede free and open communication

        a) Few people are secure enough to tell a superior that what was just said was not understood.

    4) Selective perception caused by the receiver's needs, motives, projections, experiences, and expectations

        a) People tend to interpret what they see and hear based on their own needs, etc., and to regard that interpretation as reality.

        b) Moreover, people necessarily must narrow their perception to avoid sensory overload. Such screening is required to organize and interpret experience.

5) Stereotyping or attributing to another person traits that are commonly associated with a category or group to which that person belongs

b. Perceptual problems can be minimized by

1) Feedback from the receiver about his or her perceptions and interpretations of the message,

2) Understanding of the sender's perspective by the receiver,

3) The sender's sensitivity to the receiver's problems, and

4) Implementation of an organization-wide training program to improve communication skills.

5. **Use of Communication Media for Enhancement of Personal Status**

a. Some lower-level employees who have access to management become influential among their peers. These individuals are, in effect, gatekeepers because they can determine which messages will be communicated.

1) For example, an editor of a newspaper is a gatekeeper. (S)he can control what is communicated through the newspaper.

b. Opinion leaders can be used to enhance the reception of a message. Celebrities may or may not be good opinion leaders.

1) For example, the opinion of a local mechanic about a new car might carry greater weight than would a celebrity endorsement of the same car.

c. A media liaison is an individual in an organization who has been formally charged with the job of facilitating communication. An example is a public relations director.

6. **Loss in Transmission and Poor Retention**

a. Much of the information in oral communication is lost in each transmission. Even written communications are subject to some loss. After passing through a chain of command, little of the message may have been received.

b. One study found that as little as 50% of communicated information was retained by employees.

7. **Nonreception**

a. The following are common reasons for a receiver not to receive any communication:

1) Inattention or disinterest in the message. Messages are sometimes screened, and those in which the recipient has no interest are ignored.

2) Information overload. The receiver is already receiving so many messages that (s)he cannot process what (s)he is hearing.

3) Confusing messages. The sender is not sending enough information to fully communicate thoughts, and the receiver must allocate too much time to interpreting what the sender is saying.

8. **Formal Breakdowns of Communications Media**

a. An example is omission from a mailing list.

9. **Problems in Listening**

a. Listening is the responsibility of both the speaker (sender) and the listener (receiver). Listening is one of the problems in communication that can be improved by the manager. The art of listening must be exercised effectively to

1) Gain more information about the work situation and

2) Have a positive effect on both superiors and subordinates through showing concern for their views.

b. People can listen several times faster than words can be spoken, which may result in inattention.

c. Evaluating, or prejudgment of the message, before or during the communication process may reduce the ability to listen objectively. In other words, the recipient could be biased and may fail to give the message adequate consideration.

d. A decoding problem occurs when concentration is focused on the words used to the exclusion of the ideas.

10. **Solutions to Communications Problems**

a. Effective communicators overcome problems in communication by adopting the following strategies:

1) The message should be in the context of the receiver's perceptions.

a) Explaining an accounting concept to a nonaccountant requires language different from that used in communicating with an accountant.

2) The sender must monitor media to ensure they are free from distortion or breakdown.

3) The sender must actively solicit feedback to ensure reception and understanding.

4) The organizational climate should encourage the elimination of interpersonal barriers to communication.

5) The sender should look for nonverbal cues or feedback (such as body language).

6) The sender must (a) deliver the communication with appropriate symbols through appropriate media and (b) never make assumptions about the receiver's reaction.

7) Two-way (interactive) communication should be used whenever possible to permit ease of feedback.

8) Communication can be improved through redundancy, that is, by repeating the message in several different formats and in several media.

9) Empathy is the process of mentally putting oneself in another person's position to better understand his or her feelings, attitudes, and thoughts. Empathy

a) Enables the sender and the receiver to consider each other's backgrounds, biases, beliefs, and values;

b) Aids in anticipating others' reactions to messages; and

c) Aids in effective communication by guiding the choice of

i) Words used and their meanings,
ii) Word inflection and emphasis, and
iii) Tone of voice and gestures.

10) Effective listening tools include

a) Paraphrasing what has been heard,
b) Being attentive physically and mentally,
c) Asking relevant questions,
d) Avoiding premature judgments, and
e) Summarizing after the speaker has finished.

Stop and review! You have completed the outline for this subunit. Study multiple-choice questions 9 through 16 beginning on page 108.

5.3 ELECTRONIC COMMUNICATION

1. **Electronic Communication**

   a. The following are five principal means of electronic communication:

      1) Telecommuting is working outside the office using computers and other telecommunications devices.

         a) Advantages are (1) savings of travel time and expenses, (2) reduced cost of office space, (3) access to a larger pool of employees, (4) avoidance of office distractions, and (5) potentially greater productivity.

         b) Problems associated with employees who telecommute include (1) a tendency to fall behind in their fields of specialization, (2) a lack of strong working relationships with other employees, (3) a loss of career opportunities, and (4) inadequate organizational socialization.

         c) The primary strength of telecommuters is their skill in communication.

         d) Many corporations have taken advantage of email, virtual private networks (VPNs), and various network configurations to make telecommuting more feasible and useful.

      2) Email is part of a global communications revolution. To avoid its excessive, inefficient, or offensive use, an organization should adopt an email policy.

         a) Employees should understand that the organization has the legal right to monitor their use of the email system.

         b) The policy should stress that the system is not for private use.

         c) Filters should be installed to protect against spam. If it eludes the filters, it should be promptly deleted.

         d) The principles of good writing apply to email messages, especially the need for concision.

         e) The policy should provide guidelines for transmission, receipt, and retention of email.

      3) Cell phones provide mobile communications at reasonable cost. Because they provide a means of performing work outside a traditional work place, business communications may be more timely, flexible, and convenient.

         a) The disadvantage of cell phones is the increased security risk. Thus, critical information might be revealed to eavesdroppers.

         b) Cell phone use should be consistent with the principles of good manners, including consideration for people nearby.

      4) Videoconferencing permits people at distant locations to meet without the cost and expenditure of time required for travel.

         a) Videoconferencing via live television or the Internet may enhance productivity. Its expense has decreased, and its availability (e.g., through rental of a videoconferencing facility) has increased.

      5) Social networks such as Facebook, Twitter, and LinkedIn are valuable communication tools. Organizations can receive feedback on these sites.

Stop and review! You have completed the outline for this subunit. Study multiple-choice question 17 on page 110.

5.4 COMMUNICATION AND STAKEHOLDER RELATIONSHIPS

1. Effective communication helps maintain good relationships between internal auditors and key stakeholders.

   a. Key stakeholders include the board of directors, audit committees, management, external auditors, and regulators.

2. **Stakeholder Relationships**

   a. For internal auditors to be effective, *Sawyer's Guide for Internal Auditors*, 6th edition, states that they must build and maintain strong constructive relationships with managers and other stakeholders within the organization.

   b. These relationships require conscious ongoing focus to ensure that risks are appropriately identified and evaluated to best meet the needs of the organization.

   c. Internal auditors have a responsibility to work together with external auditors and other stakeholders to facilitate work efforts and compliance with laws and regulations.

3. **The Board and the Audit Committee**

   a. For the internal audit activity to achieve organizational independence, the chief audit executive (CAE) must have direct and unrestricted access to senior management and the board.

      1) The IIA Glossary defines a board as an organization's governing body, such as a board of directors or other designated body of the organization, including the audit committee, to whom the CAE may functionally report.

   b. The audit committee is a subunit of the board of directors. However, not every member of the board is necessarily qualified to serve on the audit committee.

      1) Some statutes have imposed the following significant restrictions on the membership of the audit committee:

         a) No member may be an employee of the organization except in his or her capacity as a board member.

         b) At least one member must be a financial expert.

      2) Many stock exchanges require that all listed organizations have an audit committee.

4. **Role of the Audit Committee**

   a. The most important function of the audit committee is to promote the independence of the internal and external auditors by protecting them from management's influence.

   b. The following are other functions of the audit committee regarding the internal audit activity:

      1) Selecting or removing the CAE and setting his or her compensation

      2) Approving the internal audit charter

      3) Reviewing and approving the internal audit activity's work plan

      4) Ensuring that the internal audit activity is allocated sufficient resources

      5) Resolving disputes between the internal audit activity and management

      6) Communicating with the CAE, who attends all audit committee meetings

      7) Reviewing the internal audit activity's work product (e.g., interim and final engagement communications)

      8) Ensuring that engagement results are given due consideration

      9) Overseeing appropriate corrective action for deficiencies noted by the internal audit activity

      10) Making appropriate inquiries of management and the CAE to determine whether audit scope or budgetary limitations impede the ability of the internal audit activity to meet its responsibilities

5. Relationships with Management

   a.   According to *Sawyer's Guide for Internal Auditors*, 6th edition, internal auditors are responsible for performing their mission, maintaining their objectivity, and ensuring the internal audit activity's independence. Also, they also should develop and maintain good working relationships with management.

   b.   Good relationships are developed by communicating effectively, resolving conflicts constructively, and using participative auditing methods.

      1)   Participative auditing is a collaboration between the internal auditor and management during the auditing process. The objective is to minimize conflict and build a shared interest in the engagement. People are more likely to accept changes if they have participated in the decisions and in the methods used to implement changes.

      2)   However, internal auditors are ultimately responsible for guiding and directing the audit because the responsibility for the final audit opinion is theirs.

Stop and review! You have completed the outline for this subunit. Study multiple-choice questions 18 through 20 on page 111.

QUESTIONS

5.1 Nature of Communication

1. Which one of the following is **not** an example of formal internal communication?

   A.   Input for the yearly budget provided by the Purchasing Department to the director of budgeting.

   B.   Environmental impact statements.

   C.   Expense account reports.

   D.   Safety bulletins.

Answer (B) is correct.
   REQUIRED: The item not a formal internal communication.
   DISCUSSION: A formal communication is conducted through the formal structure of the organization. Informal communication operates outside of officially established channels. An internal communication is one that is both generated and received within the organization. An environmental impact statement is generated within the organization, but the recipient (a governmental body) is outside the organization.
   Answer (A) is incorrect. Input for the yearly budget is a form of communication that is both generated internally and received by a person within the organization. Answer (C) is incorrect. Expense reports are a form of communication that is both generated internally and received by a person within the organization. Answer (D) is incorrect. Safety bulletins are a form of communication that is both generated internally and received by a person within the organization.

2. Which of the following is **least** appropriate with regard to management's approach to informal group or grapevine communication? Management should

   A.   Use informal group information to supplement communication channels of the formal organization.

   B.   Try to suppress informal group information as a possible source of conflicting information.

   C.   Take advantage of informal group information as a device to correct misinformation.

   D.   Make use of informal group information as a means of transmitting information not appropriate for formal communication channels.

Answer (B) is correct.
   REQUIRED: The least appropriate management actions regarding the grapevine.
   DISCUSSION: The effective manager stays tuned in to the grapevine and uses it constructively.
   Answer (A) is incorrect. Management can use a grapevine or informal communication network to supplement the formal communication process. Answer (C) is incorrect. Management can use a grapevine or informal communication network to correct misinformation. Answer (D) is incorrect. Management can use a grapevine or informal communication network to transmit information not appropriate for formal communication channels.

3. The biggest advantage of oral communication over written communication is that oral communication

    A. Tends to be more accurate.

    B. Promotes feedback.

    C. Is less time-consuming.

    D. Does not provide a permanent record.

Answer (B) is correct.
    REQUIRED: The biggest advantage of oral communication over written communication.
    DISCUSSION: Oral communication promotes immediate feedback so that the sender knows that the message has been clearly received by the receiver.
    Answer (A) is incorrect. Written communication tends to be more accurate than oral communication. Answer (C) is incorrect. Although oral communication is less time-consuming than written communication, immediate feedback is a greater advantage. Answer (D) is incorrect. Providing a permanent record is advantageous.

4. When evaluating communication, the accountant should be aware that nonverbal communication

    A. Is independent of a person's cultural background.

    B. Is often imprecise.

    C. Always conveys a more truthful response.

    D. Always conveys less information than verbal communication.

Answer (B) is correct.
    REQUIRED: The true statement about nonverbal communication.
    DISCUSSION: Nonverbal communication (body language) consists of facial expressions, vocal intonations, posture, gestures, and appearance, and physical distance. Thus, by its nature, nonverbal communication is much less precise than verbal communication.
    Answer (A) is incorrect. Nonverbal communication is heavily influenced by culture. For example, a nod of the head may have opposite meanings in different cultures. Answer (C) is incorrect. Nonverbal communication is not necessarily more truthful. Answer (D) is incorrect. Nonverbal communication can sometimes convey more information.

5. Which of the following is an example of upward communication?

    A. Management's notices on bulletin boards.

    B. Grievance actions.

    C. Informational inserts in pay envelopes.

    D. Personnel policy manuals.

Answer (B) is correct.
    REQUIRED: The item that is an example of upward communication.
    DISCUSSION: Grievance actions are a formal means of bringing employee dissatisfaction to the attention of management, i.e., from the bottom upward.
    Answer (A) is incorrect. This is an example of downward communication. Official changes in procedures or benefits can be announced by notices on bulletin boards. Answer (C) is incorrect. This is an example of downward communication. Official changes in procedures or benefits can be announced by notices on bulletin boards. Answer (D) is incorrect. This is an example of downward communication. Official changes in procedures or benefits can be announced by notices on bulletin boards.

6. An advisable strategy for a participant in a meeting of the internal auditing staff is to

    A. Read the agenda and supporting materials for the meeting during the early part of the meeting to prepare for later discussion.

    B. Present strong opinions on one side of a proposal right away.

    C. Present views as trial balloons that can be researched later.

    D. Consider the opinions and information needs of other participants before speaking.

Answer (D) is correct.
    REQUIRED: The strategy for a participant in a meeting of the internal audit staff.
    DISCUSSION: Analyzing the audience assists a speaker to gather the right information for the meeting. Moreover, understanding the other participants' opinions and needs enables the speaker to express his or her ideas in the way best calculated to be persuasive.
    Answer (A) is incorrect. The most effective meeting participants come to meetings prepared. The agenda and other materials should be read in advance. Answer (B) is incorrect. Unless the speaker is certain of others' opinions (or is the most powerful person in the organization), (s)he should not commit to a position until the degree of support for that view can be estimated. Answer (C) is incorrect. Ideas should be researched in advance of the meeting so that the participant appears to be prepared and productive.

7. Because communication is vital to effective management, managers spend most of their time communicating. Consequently, managers

    A. Who are good communicators will be effective.

    B. Mostly engage in oral communication.

    C. Devote most of their time to formal, written communication.

    D. Are essentially senders of messages.

Answer (B) is correct.
    REQUIRED: The true statement about managerial communication.
    DISCUSSION: Because communication is the process of conveying meaning or understanding from one person to another, managers must spend most of their time communicating with subordinates, peers, and superiors. More of this communication is oral and informal than written and formal. Managers communicate lower-level results and problems upward, and coordinating information horizontally. Infrequently, communication may also be among peers or across organizational channels.
    Answer (A) is incorrect. Management involves more than communication skills. Answer (C) is incorrect. Most communication is oral and informal. Answer (D) is incorrect. Modern management theory stresses feedback and multi-channel communication, not the sending of one-way messages to subordinates.

8. Studies of managerial communications have indicated that

    A. Most managers are excellent communicators.

    B. Managers spend most of their time communicating.

    C. Written communication takes more of a manager's time than oral communication.

    D. Most effective communicators will be good managers.

Answer (B) is correct.
    REQUIRED: The true statement concerning managerial communications.
    DISCUSSION: Because communication is the process of conveying meaning or understanding from one person to another, managers must spend most of their time communicating with subordinates, peers, and superiors. They communicate organizational goals and plans downward, lower-level results and problems upward, and coordinating information horizontally (among peers or across organizational channels).
    Answer (A) is incorrect. One of the problems within management is the inability of many managers to clearly and concisely communicate ideas, concepts, directives, policies, results, etc. Answer (C) is incorrect. Managers spend more time in oral than in written communication. Answer (D) is incorrect. Good management requires more than just effective communication. If a manager cannot motivate subordinates, even clearly communicated information will be ineffective to achieve organizational objectives.

5.2 Problems in Communication

9. Which of the following terms does **not** apply to noise in communication?

    A. Encoding.

    B. Sending.

    C. Interpretation.

    D. Decoding.

Answer (C) is correct.
    REQUIRED: The term that does not apply to noise in communication.
    DISCUSSION: Interpretation is a subprocess of perception. Noise is a disruption that impedes the communication process.
    Answer (A) is incorrect. Encoding is part of the communication process that can be disrupted by noise. Answer (B) is incorrect. Sending is a part of the communication process that can be impeded by noise. Answer (D) is incorrect. Decoding is part of the communication process that can be impeded by noise.

10. Noise may disrupt communication during transmission. All of the following are examples of noise **except**

    A. Selective perception.

    B. Static on a telephone line.

    C. A letter lost because it was interspersed with junk mail.

    D. A participant in a conversation being called away for a meeting.

Answer (A) is correct.
    REQUIRED: The item that is not an example of noise.
    DISCUSSION: Noise in a communication channel is an outside disruption that impedes the flow of a message. It can vary from real noise, such as loud machines running and static on a phone line, to disruptions such as phone calls during a face-to-face conversation. Selective perception on the part of either the sender or the receiver of a message is not noise because it is not an outside disruption.
    Answer (B) is incorrect. Static on a phone line is noise that might affect the quality of a communication. Answer (C) is incorrect. A lost letter is a random event that can cause a disruption in communication. Answer (D) is incorrect. An interruption during a conversation disrupts the communication.

11. In a report, an internal auditor stated that communication in the auditee area was poor with employees deciding in advance which information should be given to management so as to present themselves in the best possible light. This is an example of

A. Filtering.

B. Selective perception.

C. Emotion.

D. Language.

Answer (A) is correct.
REQUIRED: The definition of filtering.
DISCUSSION: Filtering of a message is the sender's manipulation of information so that it will be viewed more favorably by the receiver. Filtering is a typical problem in upward communication, e.g., from employee to manager.
Answer (B) is incorrect. Selective perception involves the receiver selectively interpreting what they see or hear based on their interest, background, experience, and attitudes. Answer (C) is incorrect. Emotions affect the interpretation of the message, not the contents. Answer (D) is incorrect. Choice of language involves the personal selection of words to communicate the same message without distorting it.

12. Which of the following is an example of a badly encoded message?

A. Inattention or disinterest in the message.

B. Inconsistency between verbal and nonverbal messages.

C. Gesturing to someone who cannot see the gesture.

D. Sender's dislike of receiver.

Answer (B) is correct.
REQUIRED: The example of a badly encoded message.
DISCUSSION: If body language or tone of voice send a message different from the spoken words, the receiver will not be clear about the meaning of the message.
Answer (A) is incorrect. Inattention or disinterest in the message is an example of nonreception in which the receiver fails to receive any communication. Answer (C) is incorrect. Gesturing to someone who cannot see the gesture is an example of faulty channel selection. Answer (D) is incorrect. The sender's dislike of the receiver is an example of interpersonal problems.

13. Which of the following is unlikely to cause changes in attitudes?

A. Make sure that the message is credible.

B. Present many different issues in as short a time as possible.

C. Shape the argument to the listener.

D. Focus the presentation on the ultimate objective.

Answer (B) is correct.
REQUIRED: The communication technique unlikely to cause changes in attitudes.
DISCUSSION: Presenting many different issues in as short a time as possible will confuse the listener and cause the message to be lost or disregarded. To convey a persuasive message effectively, the communicator should make a clear presentation that focuses on the ultimate objective. The argument should be stated one idea at a time, and unrelated subjects and jumping from issue to issue should be avoided. The presentation should guide the recipient of the communication directly to the desired conclusion.
Answer (A) is incorrect. Trust, competence, objectivity, and high ethical standards are important in changing attitudes. Answer (C) is incorrect. Effective persuasion demands flexibility so that the arguments presented have a better chance of changing the person's attitudes. Answer (D) is incorrect. To convey a persuasive message effectively, the communicator should make a clear presentation that focuses on the ultimate objective.

14. A manager found that instructions given to a subordinate were not followed. A review of the cause of the failure revealed that the manager was interrupted by several telephone calls while issuing the instructions. In terms of problems in the communications chain, the interruptions are

A. Noise.

B. Nonverbal feedback.

C. Semantics.

D. Closure.

Answer (A) is correct.
REQUIRED: The interruptions encountered in the communications process.
DISCUSSION: Noise in the communication channel refers to any disruption that impedes the encoding, sending, or receipt of a message, such as being interrupted by several telephone calls while issuing instructions.
Answer (B) is incorrect. Nonverbal feedback, or body language, encompasses the facial expressions, gestures, and posture that send various messages. Answer (C) is incorrect. Semantics is the study of meanings, especially connotative nuances. Answer (D) is incorrect. Closure is the process of filling in the blanks of an incomplete message.

15. Which of the following actions is most likely to minimize the effect of perceptual errors?

    A. The sender should ensure that the receiver understands the message by allowing only one-way communication.

    B. The receiver should consider how the sender decodes the message.

    C. The sender alone should minimize noise in the flow of communication.

    D. The receiver should try to understand the sender's perspective.

Answer (D) is correct.
    REQUIRED: The action that should be taken to minimize perceptual errors.
    DISCUSSION: Perceptual errors can be minimized in several ways, including feedback from the receiver concerning his or her perceptions and interpretations of the message, understanding of the sender's perspective by the receiver, the sender's sensitivity to the receiver's problems, and implementation of a training program to improve communication skills throughout the company.
    Answer (A) is incorrect. The sender should encourage feedback from the receiver through two-way communication. Answer (B) is incorrect. The sender encodes the message; the receiver decodes the message. Answer (C) is incorrect. Both parties should make an effort to minimize noise.

16. An individual who has been formally assigned the task of facilitating communication through a variety of media is sometimes called a

    A. Gatekeeper.

    B. Liaison.

    C. Opinion leader.

    D. Channel selector.

Answer (B) is correct.
    REQUIRED: The term for a person who has been formally assigned the task of facilitating communication through a variety of media.
    DISCUSSION: A liaison, or media liaison, is an individual in an organization who has been formally assigned the job of facilitating communication. This is usually in the form of a public relations liaison, but in large organizations, internal communication could also be a part of the job.
    Answer (A) is incorrect. The gatekeeper is an often informal position held by individuals who have the power to determine whether a message is transmitted. Answer (C) is incorrect. An opinion leader is a person whose opinion would be widely accepted by a person receiving a message. Opinion leaders are used to enhance the receptivity of messages. Answer (D) is incorrect. It is a nonsense term.

5.3 Electronic Communication

17. Which of the following is **false** with regard to email policies?

    A. Employees may use informal writing because email is often informal in nature.

    B. Employees should understand that the organization has a legal right to monitor the employees' use of the email system.

    C. Filters should be used to protect against spam.

    D. Emails should be concisely written.

Answer (A) is correct.
    REQUIRED: The policies associated with email use in an organization.
    DISCUSSION: The principles of good writing still apply to emails. Thus, emails should be written with the same care as formal communications within the organization.
    Answer (B) is incorrect. Employers are legally permitted to keep track of employee activities while employees are at work, including monitoring emails. Answer (C) is incorrect. Filters should be used to prevent incoming spam. If spam eludes the filters, it should be deleted. Answer (D) is incorrect. Emails are still supposed to be written with good writing skills.

5.4 Communication and Stakeholder Relationships

18. The audit committee may serve several important purposes, some of which directly benefit the internal audit activity. The most significant benefit provided by the audit committee to the internal audit activity is

A. Protecting the independence of the internal audit activity from undue management influence.

B. Reviewing annual engagement work schedules and monitoring engagement results.

C. Approving engagement work schedules, scheduling, staffing, and meeting with the internal auditors as needed.

D. Reviewing copies of the procedures manuals for selected organizational operations and meeting with organizational officials to discuss them.

Answer (A) is correct.
   REQUIRED: The most significant benefit provided by the audit committee to the internal auditor.
   DISCUSSION: The audit committee is a subcommittee of the board of directors composed of outside directors who are independent of corporate management. Its purpose is to help keep external and internal auditors independent of management and to ensure that the directors are exercising due care. This committee often selects the external auditors, reviews their overall audit plan, and examines the results of external and internal audits.

19. Which of the following features of a large manufacturer's organizational structure is a control weakness?

A. The information systems department is headed by a vice president who reports directly to the president.

B. The chief financial officer is a vice president who reports to the chief executive officer.

C. The audit committee of the board consists of the chief executive officer, the chief financial officer, and a major shareholder.

D. The controller and treasurer report to the chief financial officer.

Answer (C) is correct.
   REQUIRED: The control weakness in a large manufacturer's organizational structure.
   DISCUSSION: The audit committee has a control function because of its oversight of internal as well as external auditing. It should be made up of directors who are independent of management. The authority and independence of the audit committee strengthen the position of the internal audit activity.
   Answer (A) is incorrect. This reporting relationship is a strength. It prevents the information systems operation from being dominated by a user. Answer (B) is incorrect. It is a normal and appropriate reporting relationship. Answer (D) is incorrect. It is a normal and appropriate reporting relationship.

20. An audit committee of the board of directors of an organization is being established. Which of the following is normally a responsibility of the committee with regard to the internal audit activity?

A. Approval of the selection and dismissal of the chief audit executive.

B. Development of the annual engagement work schedule.

C. Approval of engagement work programs.

D. Determination of engagement observations appropriate for specific engagement communications.

Answer (A) is correct.
   REQUIRED: The responsibility of an audit committee.
   DISCUSSION: Independence is enhanced when the board concurs in the appointment or removal of the CAE (PA 1110-1). The audit committee is a subcommittee of outside directors who are independent of management. The term "board" includes the audit committee.
   Answer (B) is incorrect. Development of the annual engagement work schedule is an operational function of the CAE and the internal audit activity staff. A summary of the (1) audit plan, (2) work schedule, (3) staffing plan, and (4) financial budget is submitted annually to senior management and the board. Answer (C) is incorrect. Approval of engagement work programs is a technical responsibility of the internal audit activity staff. Answer (D) is incorrect. The determination of engagement observations appropriate for specific engagement communications is a field operation of the internal audit activity staff.

Access the **CIA Review System** from your Gleim Personal Classroom
to continue your studies with exam-emulating multiple-choice questions!

STUDY UNIT SIX
STRUCTURAL ANALYSIS WITHIN AN INDUSTRY

(20 pages of outline)

This study unit is the first of five covering **Section V: Management/Leadership Principles** from The IIA's CIA Exam Syllabus. This section makes up 10% to 20% of Part 3 of the CIA exam and is tested at the **awareness level**. The relevant portion of the syllabus is highlighted below. (The complete syllabus is in Appendix A.)

V. **MANAGEMENT/LEADERSHIP PRINCIPLES (10%–20%)**

- A. **Strategic Management**
  1. Global analytical techniques
     a. Structural analysis of industries
     b. Competitive strategies (e.g., Porter's model)
     c. Competitive analysis
     d. Market signals
     e. Industry evolution
  2. Industry environments
  3. Strategic decisions
  4. Forecasting
  5. Quality management (e.g., TQM, Six Sigma)
  6. Decision analysis
- B. **Organizational Behavior**
- C. **Management Skills/Leadership Styles**
- D. **Conflict Management**
- E. **Project Management/Change Management**

6.1 STRATEGIC MANAGEMENT

Candidates for the CIA exam should understand that an organization uses structural analysis to choose the industries in which it will compete and then determines what competitive strategies are appropriate in those industries.

1. **Strategic Management**

   a. Strategic management has a long-term planning horizon. Thus, a strategic orientation is traditionally associated with senior management. However, all employees should have this orientation because it encourages foresight. Strategic thinking also helps employees understand and implement managerial decisions. Moreover, it is consistent with the modern trend toward cooperation and teamwork and away from authoritarian managerial styles.

b. Strategic management is dependent on forecasts of outcomes of events, their timing, and their future values.

c. Strategic management involves developing a grand strategy and strategic planning. These processes are aided by synergistic thinking and result in adoption of an operations strategy.

2. **Steps in the Strategic Management Process**

a. Strategic management is a five-stage process:

1) The board of directors drafts the organization's mission statement.

2) The organization performs a situational analysis, also called a SWOT analysis.

3) Based on the results of the situational analysis, upper management develops a group of strategies describing how the mission will be achieved.

4) Strategic plans are implemented through the execution of component plans at each level of the entity.

5) Strategic controls and feedback are used to monitor progress, isolate problems, and take corrective action. Over the long term, feedback is the basis for adjusting the original mission and objectives.

Strategic Management

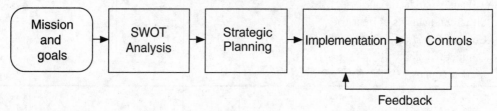

Figure 6-1

3. **SWOT Analysis**

a. A grand strategy describes how the organization's mission is to be achieved. This strategy is based on a situational analysis that considers organizational strengths and weaknesses (a capability profile) and their interactions with environmental opportunities and threats. Such an evaluation is also called a SWOT analysis.

1) Strengths and weaknesses (the internal environment) are usually identified by considering the firm's capabilities and resources. What the firm does particularly well or has in greater abundance are core competencies.

a) Core competencies are the source of competitive advantages that in turn are the basis for an overall strategy.

2) Opportunities and threats (the external environment) are identified by considering

a) Macroenvironmental factors (economic, demographic, political, legal, social, cultural, and technical factors) and

b) Microenvironmental factors (suppliers, customers, distributors, competitors, and other competitive factors in the industry).

3) For example, speed in reacting to environmental changes or introducing new products is an important competitive advantage. To achieve it, the organization may have to reengineer its processes.

4. **Strategic Planning**

    a. Strategic planning formulates specific and measurable objectives, plans, policies, and budgets.

        1) Thus, strategic planning involves

            a) Portfolio management of the organization's businesses,

            b) Determining the strength of each business with respect to the potential of markets and the position of businesses in their markets, and

            c) Creating a strategy for each business.

        2) At the highest level, a firm's strategic planning function involves (a) formulating its mission (ultimate firm purposes and directions), (b) determining its strategic business units (SBUs), (c) allocating resources to SBUs, (d) planning to start new businesses, and (e) downsizing or divesting old businesses.

            a) A mission statement should address reasonably limited objectives, define the firm's major policies and values, and state its primary competitive scopes. These scopes may extend to

                i) Industries,

                ii) Products and services,

                iii) Applications,

                iv) Core competencies,

                v) Market segments,

                vi) Degree of vertical integration, and

                vii) Geographic markets.

            b) Businesses should be defined in market terms, that is, in terms of needs and customer groups. Moreover, a distinction should be made between a target market definition and a strategic market definition.

                i) For example, a target market for a railroad might be freight hauling, but a strategic market might be transportation of any goods and people.

            c) A business also may be defined with respect to customer groups and their needs and the technology required to satisfy those needs.

            d) A large firm has multiple businesses. Thus, the concept of the strategic business unit is useful for strategic planning by large firms.

                i) An SBU is a business (or a group) for which separate planning is possible. It also has its own competitors and a manager who engages in strategic planning and is responsible for the major determinants of profit.

5. **Implementation**

    a. Strategic plans must be passed down the organizational structure through development of plans at each lower level. This process is most likely to succeed if

        1) The structure is compatible with strategic planning,

        2) Personnel have the necessary abilities,

        3) The organizational culture is favorable or can be changed, and

        4) Controls exist to facilitate implementation.

6. **Controls**

    a. Strategic controls should be established to monitor progress, isolate problems, identify invalid assumptions, and take prompt corrective action.

        1) As plans are executed at each organizational level, control measurements are made to determine whether objectives have been achieved. Thus, objectives flow down the organizational hierarchy, and control measures flow up.

2) One category of strategic control measures relates to external effectiveness.

    a) At the business-unit level, performance in the marketplace (market share, etc.) is measured.

    b) At the business-operating-system level, customer satisfaction and flexibility are measured.

    c) At the departmental or work-center level, quality and delivery are measured.

3) A second category of strategic control measures relates to internal efficiency.

    a) At the business-unit level, financial results are measured.

    b) At the business-operating-system level, flexibility (both an external effectiveness and internal efficiency issue) is measured.

    c) At the departmental or work-center level, cycle time (time to change raw materials into a finished product) and waste are measured.

7. **Synergies**

  a. Strategic management is facilitated when managers think synergistically. Synergy occurs when the combination of formerly separate elements has a greater effect than the sum of their individual effects. The following are types of synergy observed in business:

    1) Market synergy arises when products or services have positive complementary effects. Shopping malls reflect this type of synergy.

    2) Cost synergy results in cost reduction. It occurs in many ways, for example, in recycling of by-products or in the design, production, marketing, and sales of a line of products by the same enterprise.

    3) Technological synergy is the transfer of technology among applications. For example, technology developed for military purposes often has civilian uses.

    4) Management synergy also involves knowledge transfer. For example, a firm may hire a manager with skills that it lacks.

8. **Operations Strategies**

  a. An operations strategy is reflected in a long-term plan for using resources to reach strategic objectives. The following are five operations strategies:

    1) A cost strategy is successful when the enterprise is the low-cost producer. However,

      a) The product (e.g., a commodity) tends to be undifferentiated in these cases.

        i) A product is undifferentiated when competitors sell essentially the same thing, such as the same kind of grain.

      b) The market is often very large.

      c) The competition tends to be intense because of the possibility of high-volume sales.

    2) A quality strategy involves competition based on product quality or process quality.

      a) Product quality relates to design, for example, the difference between a luxury car and a subcompact car.

      b) Process quality is the degree of freedom from defects.

    3) A delivery strategy may permit an enterprise to charge a higher price when the product is consistently delivered rapidly and on time. An example firm is UPS.

4)   A flexibility strategy involves offering many different products or an ability to shift rapidly from one product line to another.

   a)   An example firm is a publisher that can write, edit, print, and distribute a book within days to exploit the public's short-term interest in a sensational event.

5)   A service strategy seeks to gain a competitive advantage and maximize customer value by providing services, especially post-purchase services, such as warranties on automobiles and home appliances.

Stop and review! You have completed the outline for this subunit. Study multiple-choice questions 1 through 5 beginning on page 132.

6.2 STRUCTURAL ANALYSIS OF INDUSTRIES

1.   **Overview**

   a.   An economy as a whole can be subdivided into sectors, industries, and segments.

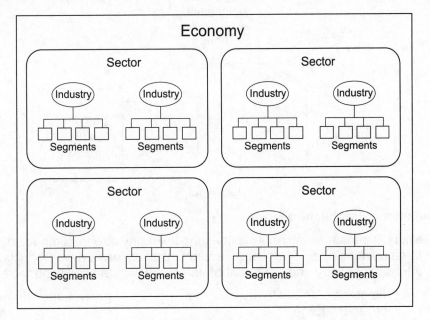

Figure 6-2

   b.   Examples of sectors are the healthcare sector or the transportation sector of the economy. Within each sector are multiple industries. An industry is a group of firms that provide products or services meeting the same fundamental customer needs.

   1)   Thus, the transportation sector has an automobile industry, an airline industry, and a passenger rail industry. Each provides its own way of moving people from one place to another.

   2)   A market segment is a set of customers with specific characteristics, needs, and wants.

   a)   Thus, the automobile industry serves one market segment with sedans, another with sport utility vehicles, another with minivans, etc.

   i)   Segments consist of customers, not firms.
   ii)   One firm in an industry may attempt to serve multiple segments.

   c.   Michael E. Porter has developed a model of the structure of industries and competition. It includes an analysis of the five competitive forces that determine long-term profitability as measured by long-term return on investment.

2.   **Porter's Five Competitive Forces**

   a.   The analysis of competitive forces evaluates the basic economic and technical characteristics that determine the strength of each force and the attractiveness of the industry. The competitive forces are depicted in the following diagram and discussed in detail below:

Porter's Five Competitive Forces

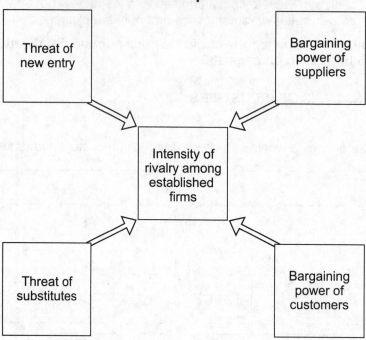

Figure 6-3

3.   **Rivalry among Established Firms**

   a.   Rivalry is intense when an industry contains many strong competitors. Price cutting, large advertising budgets, and frequent introduction of new products are typical. The intensity of rivalry and the threat of entry vary with the following factors:

   1)   The stage of the industry life cycle, e.g., rapid growth, growth, maturity, decline, or rapid decline

      a)   Growth is preferable to decline. In a declining or even a stable industry, a firm's growth must come from winning other firms' customers. Thus, rivalry is less intense during periods of growth and more intense during periods of decline.

   2)   The differences among products (product differentiation) and the costs of switching from one competitor's product to another

      a)   Less differentiation tends to heighten competition based on price, with price cutting leading to lower profits. But high costs of switching suppliers weaken competition.

   3)   Whether fixed costs are high in relation to variable costs

      a)   High fixed costs intensify rivalry. The greater the cost to generate a given amount of sales revenues, the greater the investment intensity and the greater the need to operate at or near capacity. Thus, price cutting to sustain demand is typical.

4) Capacity expansion

    a) If the size of the expansion must be large to achieve economies of scale, rivalry is more intense. The need for large-scale expansion to achieve production efficiency may result in an excess of industry capacity over demand.

        i) Economies of scale exist when the average cost of producing a product declines as a firm expands its output in the long run. The larger the scale of production needed to achieve profitability, the greater the barrier to entry into the industry.

5) Concentration and balance

    a) If an industry has many firms, rivalry will be intense.

    b) If an industry has a few equal competitors with no leader or leaders, the situation tends to be unstable and the rivalry intense.

6) The extent of exit barriers

    a) Low exit costs make an industry more attractive.

7) Competitors' incentives to remain in the industry

    a) When incentives are low, competitors are less likely to incur the costs and risks of intense rivalry.

4. Threats of New Entry

  a. The prospects of long-term profitability depend on the industry's exit and entry barriers.

    1) Entry barriers are lower and the threat of entry is higher in the following circumstances:

      a) Economies of scale (and learning curve effects) are not significant.

      b) Brand identity of existing products is weak.

      c) Costs of switching suppliers are low.

      d) Existing firms do not have the cost advantages of vertical integration.

      e) Product differences are few.

      f) Access to existing suppliers is not blocked, and distribution channels are willing to accept new products.

      g) Capital requirements are low.

      h) Existing firms are unlikely to retaliate against a new firm.

      i) The government's policy is to encourage new entrants.

    2) Exit barriers are reasons for a firm to remain in an industry despite poor (or negative) profits. They include the following:

      a) Assets with a low residual value because of obsolescence or specialization

      b) Legal or ethical duties to stakeholders such as employees, creditors, suppliers, or customers

      c) Governmental regulations

      d) Lack of favorable alternative investments

      e) Substantial vertical integration

      f) Emotional factors, such as history and tradition

3) The most favorable industry condition is one in which entry barriers are high and exit barriers are low. The following grid reflects Porter's view of the relationship of returns, entry barriers, and exit barriers:

		Exit Barriers	
		Low	High
Entry Barriers:	Low	Low, stable returns	Low, risky returns
	High	High, stable returns	High, risky returns

   a) When the threat of new entrants is minimal and exit is not difficult, returns are high, and risk is reduced in the event of poor performance.

   b) Low entry barriers keep long-term profitability low because new firms can enter the industry, increasing competition and lowering prices and the market shares of existing firms.

5. **Threat of Substitutes**

   a. The threat of substitute products limits price increases and profit margins. The greater the threat, the less attractive the industry is to potential entrants.

   1) Substitutes are types (not brands) of goods and services that have the same purposes, for example, plastic and metal or minivans and SUVs. Accordingly, a change in the price of one such product (service) causes a change in the demand for its substitutes.

      a) The market for generic pharmaceuticals is an example of the power of substitution. When a medication loses its patent protection, manufacturers of generic versions can enter the market. The price of a generic medication tends to be significantly lower because the seller need not incur most development costs.

   2) Structural considerations affecting the threat of substitutes are

      a) Relative prices,
      b) Costs of switching to a substitute, and
      c) Customers' inclination to use a substitute.

6. **Bargaining Power of Customers**

   a. As customers' bargaining power increases, the appeal of an industry to potential entrants decreases.

   1) Buyers seek lower prices, better quality, and more services. Moreover, they use their purchasing power to obtain better terms, possibly through a bidding process. Thus, buyers affect competition.

   2) Customers' bargaining power varies with the following factors:

      a) When purchasing power is concentrated in a few buyers or when buyers are well organized, their bargaining power is greater. This effect is reinforced when sellers are in a capital-intensive industry.

      b) High (low) switching costs decrease (increase) buyers' bargaining power.

      c) The threat of backward (upstream) vertical integration, that is, the acquisition of a supply capacity, increases buyers' bargaining power.

      d) Buyers are most likely to bargain aggressively when their profit margins are low and a supplier's product accounts for a substantial amount of their costs.

      e) Buyers are in a stronger position when the supplier's product is undifferentiated.

      f) The more important the supplier's product is to buyers, the less bargaining power they have.

3) A supplier may seek to limit buyers' power by choosing those with the least ability to bargain or switch to other suppliers. However, a preferable response is to make offers that are difficult to reject.

7. **Suppliers' Bargaining Power**

    a. As suppliers' bargaining power increases, the appeal of an industry to potential entrants decreases. Accordingly, suppliers affect competition through pricing and the manipulation of the quantity supplied.

        1) Suppliers' bargaining power is greater when

            a) Switching costs are substantial.

            b) Prices of substitutes are high.

            c) They can threaten forward (downstream) vertical integration.

            d) They provide something that is a significant input to the value added by the buyer.

            e) Their industry is concentrated, or they are organized.

        2) Buyers' best responses are to develop favorable, mutually beneficial relationships with suppliers or to diversify their sources of supply.

Stop and review! You have completed the outline for this subunit. Study multiple-choice questions 6 through 9 beginning on page 133.

6.3 COMPETITIVE STRATEGIES

1. **Overview**

    a. Although profitability is substantially determined by the industry in which the firm functions, its relative position in the industry is also important. That position is influenced by its choice of competitive strategy.

    b. Porter's generic strategies model is based on the concept that each of a firm's competitive advantages ultimately may be either a cost advantage (e.g., low cost) or a differentiation advantage (e.g., a unique product).

    c. The firm's advantages should be used within the firm's competitive (target) scope to achieve its objectives. This scope may be broad (e.g., industry-wide) or narrow (e.g., a market segment).

    d. Using the variables of competitive advantage (cost and differentiation) and competitive scope (broad and narrow), Porter described four generic strategies to be applied by business units.

	Competitive Advantage	
Competitive Scope	Low Cost	Unique Product
Broad (Industry-wide)	Cost Leadership Strategy	Differentiation Strategy
Narrow (Market segment)	Focused Strategy: Cost	Focused Strategy: Differentiation

Figure 6-4

2. **Cost Leadership**

  a. Cost leadership is the generic strategy of a firm that seeks competitive advantage through lower costs. It has a broad competitive scope. Such a firm can earn higher profits than its competitors at the industry average price or charge a lower price to increase market share.

    1) A firm acquires a cost advantage over its competitors by the following:

      a) Vertical integration (acquisition of suppliers, wholesalers, or retailers)
      b) Exclusive access to low-cost materials
      c) Economies of scale or other efficiencies resulting in low unit cost
      d) Outsourcing

    2) Strengths of cost leaders. The typical firm that follows a cost-leadership strategy has low profit margins, a high volume of sales, and a substantial market share. Such a firm

      a) Has efficient supply and distribution channels,

      b) Is capable of large capital investment,

      c) Has strengths in product design and process engineering if it is a manufacturer, and

      d) Closely supervises its labor force.

    3) The risks of this strategy include the possibility that advances in technology or successful imitation may eliminate the cost leader's advantage.

      a) Furthermore, multiple firms following a strategy with a narrow focus on cost may achieve advantages in their market segments.

      b) Still another risk is that the emphasis on cost may cause managers to overlook product and marketing changes. For example, the cost advantage must outweigh the differentiation advantages held by others.

    4) Organization. A cost leader is ordinarily highly structured to achieve close control of costs. Detailed reports are provided with great frequency, and benefits are tied to numerical goals.

3. **Differentiation**

  a. Differentiation is the generic strategy of a firm that seeks competitive advantage through providing a unique product or service. This strategy has a broad competitive scope. Such a firm may earn higher profits because consumers are willing to pay a price higher than that charged by competitors. However, that price difference must exceed the additional cost of the differentiated product or service.

    1) A successful differentiation strategy creates a buyer perception that few, if any, substitutes are available. Thus, the firm may have the additional advantage of being able to pass supplier cost increases to buyers.

      a) Uniqueness may be based on, for example, massive promotion, excellence of design, superior service, technical leadership, or brand identification.

      b) A differentiation strategy does not signify a disregard for cost control, but simply a greater emphasis on creating a perception of the uniqueness of the product or service.

    2) The following are typical strengths of successful broad-scope differentiators:

      a) An effective R&D function

      b) Creative product development

      c) A strong marketing function that communicates (or helps to create) the perceived uniqueness of the product or service

      d) A reputation for quality or technical leadership

        e)   A long tradition

        f)   Effective coordination with suppliers and distributors

        g)   An ability to apply the expertise of other enterprises

   3)   The risks of a differentiation strategy include the following:

        a)   The maturing of the industry produces successful imitation by competitors.

        b)   Consumer tastes change as they become more sophisticated buyers or as they have less need for the differentiating factor.

        c)   Multiple firms following a strategy with a narrow focus on differentiation can achieve advantages in their market segments.

        d)   The differentiating factor may no longer justify its premium price. Brand loyalty may decrease as lower-cost competitors improve the quality and image of their products or services.

   4)   An organization adopting a differentiation strategy usually has close cooperation among its R&D and marketing functions. Incentive compensation is often based on relatively subjective performance measures, and the firm must succeed in attracting highly skilled or creative individuals.

4. Cost Focus

   a.   Cost focus is the generic strategy of a firm that seeks competitive advantage through lower costs but with a narrow competitive scope (e.g., a regional market or a specialized product line). The reason for a cost-focus strategy is that the narrower market can be better served because the firm knows it well.

   1)   Firms that successfully adopt a cost-focus strategy achieve very strong customer loyalty, a disincentive to potential competitors.

   2)   The strengths of successful firms employing a cost-focus strategy are similar to those of broad-target firms.

   3)   The risks of a cost-focus strategy include the following:

        a)   A narrow focus means lower purchasing volume and a weaker position relative to suppliers.

        b)   The cost (or differentiation) advantage of serving a narrow target may be more than offset by the cost advantage achieved by broad-target competitors through economies of scale and other factors.

        c)   Even more narrowly focused competitors may serve their niches better.

        d)   A firm following a broad-target strategy may, by imitation or otherwise, change its product or service to compete more effectively in the narrower market.

        e)   The narrower market itself may change.

   4)   The organizational attributes of firms using a cost-focus strategy are similar to those of broad-target firms.

5. Focused Differentiation

   a.   Focused differentiation is the generic strategy of a firm that seeks competitive advantage through providing a unique product or service but with a narrow competitive scope, e.g., a regional market or a specialized product line.

   1)   The analysis of these firms is similar to that for cost-focus firms.

6.   **Combination Strategies**

a.   According to Porter, using a combination of generic strategies may leave the firm stuck in the middle, that is, unable to create or sustain a competitive advantage. The danger is that attempting to follow more than one generic strategy will prevent the firm from achieving a competitive advantage.

1)   Thus, pursuit of, for example, both cost leadership and differentiation may interfere with reaching either objective. Furthermore, even if the firm could succeed by following multiple generic strategies, the result might be an ambiguous public image.

2)   A firm that pursues multiple generic strategies may be more likely to succeed if it creates a separate strategic business unit to implement each strategy.

a)   However, some writers argue that following a single strategy may not serve the needs of customers who want the best combination of product attributes, e.g., price, service, and quality.

3)   A firm also may need to adapt as a result of the changes that occur as the firm, its products or services, and the industry proceed through their life cycles.

a)   For example, an appropriate and successful focus strategy may need to be changed to a cost-leadership strategy as the firm matures.

7.   **Competitive Strategies and Porter's Five Forces**

a.   Porter's generic strategies are responses to the following five competitive forces:

1)   **Rivalry among Existing Firms**

a)   Cost leadership permits a firm to compete by charging lower prices.

b)   Differentiation strengthens brand loyalty.

c)   Focus strategies provide superior attention to customer needs, whether for quality, price, or other product attributes.

2)   **Threats of, and Barriers to, Entry**

a)   Cost leadership permits a firm to reduce prices as a deterrent to potential entrants.

b)   Differentiation creates brand loyalty that a new entrant may not be able to overcome.

c)   Focus strategies develop core competencies in a narrow market that potential entrants may not be able to match.

3)   **Threat of Substitutes**

a)   Cost leadership may result in low prices that substitutes cannot match.

b)   Differentiation may create unique product (service) attributes not found in substitutes.

c)   Focus strategies are efforts to develop core competencies or unique product attributes that may protect against substitutes as well as potential entrants.

4)   **Buyers' Bargaining Power**

a)   Cost leadership may enable a firm to remain profitable while charging the lower prices required by strong buyers.

b)   Differentiation may reduce the power enjoyed by strong buyers because of the uniqueness of the product and the resulting lack of close substitutes.

c)   Focus strategies also may reduce buyers' ability to negotiate in a narrow market. Substitutes may not be able to compete on price, quality, etc.

    5) **Threat of Suppliers' Bargaining Power**

        a) Cost leadership provides protection from strong suppliers.

        b) Differentiation may permit a firm to increase its price in response to suppliers' price increases.

        c) Focus strategies must allow for the superior bargaining power of suppliers when sellers operate in a narrow, low-volume market. For example, focused differentiation may permit the firm to pass along suppliers' price increases.

8. **Market-Based Strategies**

  a. **Market Leader**

    1) The dominant firm in a market pursues a market-leader strategy.

        a) The leader should attempt to expand the total market because, as the market increases, so will demand. The market expands if the firm

            i) Attracts new users.

                • A market-penetration strategy focuses on customers who might use the product or service.

                • A new-market segment strategy pursues customers who have never used the product or service.

                • A geographical expansion strategy targets users in previously unserved localities.

            ii) Encourages new uses of the product or service.

            iii) Promotes increased use, for example, by planned obsolescence.

        b) Moreover, the leader must protect current market share against attacks by competitors.

            i) Constant innovation to improve products and services, control costs, and increase distribution effectiveness is the basis for a good offensive strategy. The leader must continuously improve the value offered to customers.

        c) The leader also may attempt to obtain a greater market share. In general, a firm that increases its market share in its served (target) market, as opposed to the total market, will increase profits if it adopts an appropriate strategy.

  b. **Market Challenger**

    1) Trailing (runner-up) firms may choose a market-challenger strategy.

        a) A challenger must determine its strategic objective (such as leadership or a larger market share) and specific targets.

            i) The challenger may attack the leader, for example, by across-the-board innovation or by better serving the market.

            ii) The attack may be directed at firms of similar size that are not serving the market, e.g., by failing to introduce new products or by overpricing.

            iii) The challenger may seek to grow by absorbing small firms.

        b) Kotler's *Principles of Marketing,* 14th edition, suggests that full frontal attacks make little sense. The challenger should make an indirect attack on the competitor's weaknesses or gaps in its market coverage.

    c)   The market challenger also must devise combinations of strategies that are more specific than the general strategies.

        i)   Price discounting tends to succeed if buyers are price sensitive, the product or service is similar to the market leader's, and the discounts are not matched.

        ii)   Lower-priced goods of average quality may substantially outsell higher quality goods if the price is much lower.

        iii)   Prestige goods are high-quality items sold at a high price.

        iv)   Product proliferation is a strategy based on better product variety.

        v)   Other specific strategies emphasize improved service, development of a new distribution channel, increased marketing expenditures, or manufacturing efficiencies.

c.   Market Follower

1)   Market-follower strategies are adopted by firms that do not wish to challenge the leader.

    a)   These firms believe that product imitation may be preferable to product innovation. Because the innovator has already incurred the expenses of bringing the new product to market, the imitator that introduces a similar product may be profitable without being the leader.

        i)   A counterfeiter operates illegally by selling copies on the black market.

        ii)   A cloner sells cheap variations of a product with sufficient differentiation to avoid liability for counterfeiting.

        iii)   An imitator sells a product that is significantly differentiated, e.g., with respect to price, promotion, location, and packaging.

        iv)   An adapter improves products and may operate in different markets or evolve into a market challenger.

    b)   Some industries are characterized by conscious parallelism. These industries (e.g., fertilizers and chemicals) tend to have high fixed costs and little product and image differentiation. Market followers tend to imitate the leader because competing for a greater market share provokes painful retaliation.

    c)   A market follower requires a strategy to (1) maintain its share of current and new customers, (2) fend off challengers, (3) protect its advantages (e.g., service or location), (4) lower its costs, and (5) improve the quality of its products and services.

    d)   Market followers ordinarily have lower percentage returns than market leaders.

d.   Market Nicher

1)   Market-nicher strategies are followed by small or mid-size firms that compete in small (niche) markets that may be overlooked by large firms.

    a)   The essence of niche marketing is specialization. However, success often depends on multiple niching. Creating new niches diversifies risk and increases the firm's probability of survival.

2)   Successful niche marketers often have higher rates of return than firms in large markets. They often sell high-quality products at premium prices and have low manufacturing costs.

    a)   Successful niche marketers have high profit margins. By contrast, mass marketers sell in high volume but have low profit margins.

3)   Niche marketers must create, expand, and protect their niches. The risk is that a niche may evaporate or be entered by a large firm.

e. **Firm Orientations**

1) Product-centered firms focus primarily on the product.
2) Competitor-centered firms mainly base moves on competitors' actions and reactions.
3) Customer-centered firms focus on customer developments and delivering value to customers.
4) Market-centered firms watch both customers and competitors.

    a) Finding the balance between customers and competitors is the most effective orientation in today's market.

Stop and review! You have completed the outline for this subunit. Study multiple-choice questions 10 through 14 beginning on page 134.

6.4 COMPETITIVE ANALYSIS

The internal audit activity is management's partner in improving risk management, control, and governance processes. To fulfill this role effectively, internal auditors must be familiar with the standard tools for analyzing the competitive environment in which the organization operates.

1. **Competitive Intelligence**

   a. A competitive intelligence system should be established to

      1) Identify competitor strategies,
      2) Monitor their new-product introductions,
      3) Analyze markets for the firm's own new-product introductions and acquisitions,
      4) Obtain information about nonpublic firms,
      5) Evaluate competitor R&D activity,
      6) Learn about competitors' senior executives, and
      7) Perform other necessary information-gathering tasks.

   b. Setting up the system involves determining the kinds of information to be collected, sources, and persons responsible.

   c. Data collection should be continuous. Field sources include the firm's own sales agents, distributors, and suppliers. Trade associations and market researchers are also useful sources.

      1) Other information may come from competitors' customers and suppliers and observation of competitors.
      2) An enormous amount of published information is publicly available from various services (Dun & Bradstreet, Moody's, Standard & Poor's, and others), newspapers, general business periodicals, special business publications, government data, reports submitted to government regulators, and much more.
      3) The Internet, e.g., websites of competitors, trade associations, and governments, is a fertile source of business intelligence. Patent applications, help wanted ads, licensing agreements, and many other activities may be revealing.

   d. Data analysis validates and processes the intelligence gathered.

   e. Information dissemination. The system should be able to transmit timely information to decision makers and respond to queries.

2. **Customer Value Analysis**

   a. Competitive intelligence permits a firm to create effective competitive strategies that target the appropriate competitors.

b.   A starting point is customer value analysis (CVA). The premise of CVA is that customers choose from competitors' products or services the brands that provide the greatest customer value.

    1)   Customer value equals customer benefits (product, service, personnel, and image benefits) minus customer costs (price and the costs of acquisition, use, maintenance, ownership, and disposal).

    2)   The steps in a CVA are as follows:

        a)   Determine what customers value.

        b)   Assign quantitative amounts to the elements of customer value and have customers rank their relative significance.

        c)   Evaluate how well the firm and its competitors perform relative to each element.

        d)   Focus on performance with respect to each element compared with an important competitor in a given market segment. For example, if the firm outperforms the competitor in every way, it may be able to raise its price.

        e)   Repeat the foregoing steps as circumstances change.

c.   Using the results of the CVA, the firm may then target a given class of competitors.

    1)   Targeting weak competitors may be the cheapest way to gain market share. However, targeting strong competitors also may be appropriate because this strategy forces the firm to improve. Moreover, a strong competitor may have an exploitable weakness.

    2)   Close competitors, that is, firms that are similar, are the usual targets. Nevertheless, distant competitors are also threats. For example, any beverage may be a competitor of soft drink makers.

    3)   Bad competitors should be targeted because they disturb the competitive equilibrium, e.g., by excessive expansion of capacity or overly risky behavior.

        a)   Good competitors make sound business decisions that promote the long-term health of the industry, e.g., about prices, entry into new segments, and pursuit of market share.

3.   **Integration and Diversification**

a.   Vertical integration occurs upstream (backward) by acquiring suppliers or downstream (forward) by acquiring wholesalers and retailers.

b.   Horizontal integration is the acquisition of competitors.

c.   Firms use diversification to grow, improve profitability, and manage risk.

d.   Concentric diversification results from developing or acquiring related businesses that do not have products, services, or customers in common with current businesses. However, they offer internal synergies, e.g., through common use of brands, R&D, plant facilities, or marketing expertise.

e.   Horizontal diversification is the acquisition of businesses making products unrelated to current offerings but that might be demanded by the firm's current customers.

f.   Conglomerate diversification is the acquisition of wholly unrelated businesses. The objectives of such an acquisition are financial, not operational, because of the absence of common products, customers, facilities, expertise, or other synergies.

4.   **The Growth-Share Matrix**

a.   A large firm may be viewed as a portfolio of investments in the form of strategic business units (SBUs). Hence, techniques of portfolio analysis have been developed to aid management in making decisions about resource allocation, new business startups and acquisitions, downsizing, and divestitures.

b.   One of the models most frequently used for competitive analysis was created by the Boston Consulting Group (BCG). This model, the growth-share matrix, has two variables. The market growth rate (MGR) is on the vertical axis, and the firm's relative market share (RMS) is on the horizontal axis.

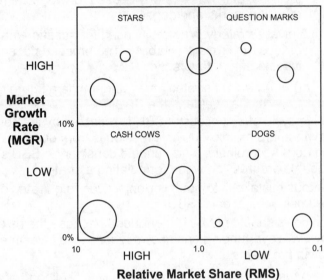

**Boston Consulting Group
(BCG)
Growth – Share Matrix**

Figure 6-5

1)   The annual MGR is stated in constant units of the currency used in the measurement. It reflects the maturity and attractiveness of the market and the relative need for cash to finance expansion.

2)   The RMS reflects the SBU's competitive position in the market segment. It equals the SBU's absolute market share divided by that of its leading competitor.

3)   The growth-share matrix has four quadrants. The firm's SBUs are commonly represented in their appropriate quadrants by circles. The size of a circle is directly proportional to the SBU's sales volume.

a)   Dogs (low RMS, low MGR) are weak competitors in low-growth markets. Their net cash flow (plus/minus) is modest.

b)   Question marks (low RMS, high MGR) are weak competitors and poor cash generators in high-growth markets. They need large amounts of cash not only to finance growth and compete in the market, but also to increase RMS. If RMS increases significantly, a question mark may become a star. If not, it becomes a dog.

c)   Cash cows (high RMS, low MGR) are strong competitors and cash generators. A cash cow ordinarily enjoys high profit margins and economies of scale. Financing for expansion is not needed, so the SBU's excess cash can be used for investments in other SBUs. However, marketing and R&D expenses should not necessarily be slashed excessively. Maximizing net cash inflow might precipitate a premature decline from cash cow to dog.

d)   Stars (high RMS, high MGR) are strong competitors in high growth markets. Such an SBU is profitable but needs large amounts of cash for expansion, R&D, and meeting competitors' attacks. Net cash flow (plus/minus) is modest.

e)   A portfolio of SBUs should not have too many dogs and question marks or too few cash cows and stars.

4)   Each SBU should have objectives, a strategy should be formulated to achieve those objectives, and a budget should be allocated.

    a)   A hold strategy is used for strong cash cows.

    b)   A build strategy is necessary for a question mark with potential to be a star.

    c)   A harvest strategy maximizes short-term net cash inflow. Harvesting means zero-budgeting R&D, reducing marketing costs, not replacing facilities, etc. This strategy is used for weak cash cows and possibly question marks and dogs.

    d)   A divest strategy is normally used for question marks and dogs that reduce the firm's profitability. The proceeds of sale or liquidation are then invested more favorably.

        i)   A harvest strategy may undermine a future divestiture by decreasing the fair value of the SBU.

5)   The life cycle of a successful SBU is reflected by its movement within the growth-share matrix. The progression is from question mark to star, cash cow, and dog. Accordingly, a firm should consider an SBU's current status and its probable progression when formulating a strategy.

6)   A serious mistake is to not tailor objectives (e.g., rates of return or growth) to the circumstances of each SBU.

7)   Cash cows should not be underfunded because the risk is premature decline. However, overfunding cash cows means less investment in SBUs with greater growth prospects.

    a)   A large investment in a dog with little likelihood of a turnaround is also a typical mistake.

    b)   A firm should not have too many question marks. Results are excess risk and underfunded SBUs.

5.   Problems with Matrix Approaches

    a.   According to Kotler, managers need to be aware of the limitations inherent in the use of a matrix (*Principles of Marketing*, 14th edition). Managers may find it difficult to measure market share and growth or even define SBUs. Thus, BCG's growth-share matrix may have limited strategic value.

Stop and review! You have completed the outline for this subunit. Study multiple-choice questions 15 though 18 beginning on page 135.

6.5 MARKET SIGNALS

1.   Overview

    a.   Porter defines a market signal as "any action by a competitor that provides a direct or indirect indication of its intentions, motives, goals, or internal situation." These indirect communications are helpful in competitive analysis and the design of competitive strategies.

    b.   However, signals may be sent to warn or mislead rather than to indicate a genuine intention to execute a planned action. Accordingly, the firm must understand competitors so as not to ignore, or be deceived by, their signals.

2.   Types of Signals

    a.   Market signals may be classified as true signals or bluffs. The types of signals vary with the nature of the competitor's signaling behavior and the media used.

    b.   Prior announcements of moves, that is, to do or not do something, have value as signals in part because an announced move need not actually occur. A competitive battle may be fought entirely with announcements, thus avoiding the negative effects of, for example, a price war.

      c.   A bluff is an announcement of an action not intended to be executed. For example, a firm may issue a threat in an effort to prevent a competitor action even though following through would not be beneficial. Bluffs may cause loss of credibility for future announcements.

      d.   Prior announcements may be in many media. Examples are interviews with journalists, news conferences, meetings with securities analysts, updates of website content, and regulatory disclosures.

      e.   The medium and the breadth of the audience chosen have signaling value. Thus, an announcement that is widely disseminated may represent a greater commitment.

3.   Announcements of results or actions after the fact, especially of information difficult to obtain or that is surprising, ensure competitor awareness. Misleading announcements of this kind may be intended to preempt action or affirm commitment.

      a.   However, a firm's discovery that an announcement is misleading (or wrong) may be a source of useful inferences about the competitor's purposes and strengths.

4.   Competitors' public discussions of the industry address such matters as cost increases and forecasts of demand, prices, and capacity. These discussions may signal, perhaps unintentionally, the firm's assumptions underlying its strategy. Thus, they may be sincere efforts to clarify motives, prevent conflict, and promote cooperation.

      a.   The discussions also may be ways for the firm to seek an advantage, for example, to portray competitors' prices as excessive. Hence, other firms must evaluate the firm's true intent by determining whether and how the firm's position may be improved by its interpretation of industry conditions.

      b.   Direct commentary on a competitor's moves likewise may be subject to different interpretations of its motives.

5.   Competitors' discussions of their own moves may be in public or private forums (e.g., with customers or suppliers) with the intent of signaling to competitors. One motive is to persuade others that a move is appropriate and not provocative. A second motive is preemption. A third motive is to express commitment.

6.   Competitors' tactics may have signaling content if they differ from the feasible alternative conduct. A conciliatory (aggressive) signal is conveyed by a move within the range of options that is the least (most) harmful to competitors.

7.   The manner of initially implementing a strategic change may signal aggressive intent or a cooperative attitude, or it may be a bluff. For example, initial price cutting on a competitor's key products rather than in secondary markets, introducing a new product targeted to a competitor's most important customers, or undertaking a move at an unusual time during the year may signal aggressive, if not punitive, intent.

8.   A firm's divergence from prior strategic objectives suggests that other firms should be alert to profound changes in its objectives and assumptions.

9.   A firm's divergence from industry precedent, e.g., discounting of never-before-discounted items, implies aggressive intent.

10.   A cross-parry is a response to a competitor's move in one area with a move in another. For example, firm X, which is well established in region A, may move to compete with firm Y in its stronghold in region B. Firm Y's cross-parry is to enter the market in region A.

      a.   A cross-parry is an indirect response by the defending firm that potentially avoids destructive conflict in the newly penetrated market. However, it also signals the possibility of retaliation, especially if it occurs in one of the initiating firm's key markets. For example, price cutting as a cross-parry may be very effective against a firm with a large share of the market where the parry is made. This firm has more to lose in a price war in that market. Consequently, maintenance of a presence in a cross-market deters the large-share firm from attacking elsewhere.

11. Introduction of a fighting brand by a firm threatened or potentially threatened by a competitor is a tactic similar to the cross-parry. The brand may threaten or deter the rival, or it may bear the burden of competition. Thus, a competitor's product that is gaining market share could be countered by introduction of a very similar product in the competitor's key markets.

12. A private antitrust suit, which can be dismissed by the plaintiff at any time, may simply indicate displeasure without incurring the risks of a more serious signal, e.g., a price cut. Suits also may be harassing or delaying tactics.

    a. A suit by a large firm against a small firm is a way to punish the defendant regardless of the outcome. The legal costs of the small firm may be high, and the suit may prove a distraction over a long period.

13. **Relationship between Signals and Actions**

    a. One aspect of competitor analysis is the study of the relationship between a firm's signals and later moves or other events. This study may reveal unconscious signals (what poker players call "tells") that help to interpret and react to the firm's actions.

        1) However, an effective competitor analysis should discover any economic and organizational factors that might cause a firm to behave in a manner inconsistent with its prior patterns.

Stop and review! You have completed the outline for this subunit. Study multiple-choice questions 19 and 20 on page 137.

QUESTIONS

6.1 Strategic Management

1. Which of the following is **least** likely to be an example of synergy?

A. A shopping mall with several businesses providing different products and performing different services.

B. A car dealership providing warranties on automobile parts to maximize customer value.

C. A manufacturing company hiring a new manager with technological experience lacking in the company.

D. Military Humvees being converted into sports utility vehicles for sale to civilians.

Answer (B) is correct.
   REQUIRED: The least likely example of synergy.
   DISCUSSION: Synergy occurs when the combination of formerly separate elements has a greater effect than the sum of their individual effects. However, a car dealership's provision of warranties reflects an operational strategy designed to provide post-purchase services to gain a competitive advantage and maximize customer value. It does not reflect the complementary sharing of resources, technology, or competencies. In contrast, synergy arises from selling a line of cars that share some components or a brand identification.
   Answer (A) is incorrect. A shopping mall with several businesses providing different products and performing different services is an example of market synergy. Answer (C) is incorrect. Hiring a manager with needed skills is an example of management synergy. Answer (D) is incorrect. Conversion of Humvees to SUVs is an example of technological synergy.

2. Which of the following best describes a market synergy?

A. Technology transfer from one product to another.

B. Bundling of products distributed through the same channels.

C. Production of multiple products at one facility.

D. Use of complementary management skills to achieve entry into a new market.

Answer (B) is correct.
   REQUIRED: The best description of market synergy.
   DISCUSSION: Market synergy arises when products or services have positive complementary effects. Shopping malls reflect this type of synergy. Also, bundling of products, distribution through the same distribution channels, and use of the same sales force are other examples of market synergies.
   Answer (A) is incorrect. Technology transfer constitutes technology synergy. Answer (C) is incorrect. The production of multiple products at one production facility is an example of cost synergy. Answer (D) is incorrect. Using complementary management skills is an example of management synergy.

3. Which of the following is a market-oriented definition of a business versus a product-oriented definition of a business?

   A. Making air conditioners and furnaces.

   B. Supplying energy.

   C. Producing movies.

   D. Selling men's shirts and pants.

Answer (B) is correct.
   REQUIRED: The market-oriented business definition.
   DISCUSSION: Businesses should be defined in market terms, that is, in terms of needs and customer groups. Moreover, a distinction should be made between a target market definition and a strategic market definition. For example, a target market for a railroad might be freight hauling, but a strategic market might be transportation of any goods and people. Accordingly, stating that a business supplies energy is a market-oriented definition as opposed to the product-oriented definition. Moreover, it is also a strategic market definition.

4. Which one of the following is a social trend affecting the organization?

   A. Changes in labor markets.

   B. Tougher legislation to protect the environment.

   C. Rising inflation.

   D. Replacements for steel in cars and appliances.

Answer (A) is correct.
   REQUIRED: The social trend that affects organizations.
   DISCUSSION: Social trends, such as changes in labor markets, reflect social, cultural, and demographic factors in the organization's macroenvironment that may constitute opportunities or threats (identified in a SWOT analysis). The attributes of people (age, education, income, ethnicity, family status, etc.) and their beliefs, attitudes, and values shape and are shaped by social trends that in turn affect the organization. Thus, changes in the characteristics, sources, locations, and costs of labor resources supplied (a basic factor of production) have great effects on an organization's strategic position.
   Answer (B) is incorrect. Tougher legislation to protect the environment is a political trend. Answer (C) is incorrect. Rising inflation is an economic trend. Answer (D) is incorrect. Replacements for steel in cars and appliances represent a technological trend.

5. Which of the following best describes a cost synergy?

   A. Recycling of by-products.

   B. Selling one product strengthens sales of another product.

   C. Transferring knowledge to new uses.

   D. Acquiring new management skills.

Answer (A) is correct.
   REQUIRED: The best description of a cost synergy.
   DISCUSSION: Cost synergy results in cost reduction. It occurs in many ways, for example, in recycling of by-products or in the design, production, marketing, and sales of a line of products by the same enterprise.
   Answer (B) is incorrect. Selling one product strengthens sales of another product is an example of market synergy. Answer (C) is incorrect. Transferring knowledge to new uses is an example of technological synergy. Answer (D) is incorrect. Acquiring new management skills is an example of management synergy.

6.2 Structural Analysis of Industries

6. Which of the following factors is **least** typical of an industry that faces intense competitive rivalry?

   A. Price cutting.

   B. Large advertising budgets.

   C. Frequent introduction of new products.

   D. A high threat of substitutes.

Answer (D) is correct.
   REQUIRED: The situation least typical of an industry facing intense rivalry.
   DISCUSSION: A high threat of substitutes reduces the attractiveness of an industry. It tends to increase the price elasticity of demand and therefore limits price increases and profit margins. If other factors are constant, fewer entrants result in less intense competition.

7. A firm is performing research to determine the feasibility of entering the truck rental industry. Entry is **least** likely if

   A. Buyer switching costs are low.

   B. Buyers view the product as differentiated.

   C. The market consists of many small buyers.

   D. Buyers enjoy large profit margins.

Answer (A) is correct.
   REQUIRED: The deterrent to market entry.
   DISCUSSION: Low switching costs increase buyers' bargaining power.
   Answer (B) is incorrect. Buyers are in a weaker position when the supplier's product is differentiated. Answer (C) is incorrect. When a market has many small buyers, buyers have less bargaining power. Answer (D) is incorrect. Buyers are most likely to bargain aggressively when their profit margins are low, especially if the supplier's product accounts for a substantial amount of their costs.

8. Which industry factor does **not** contribute to competitive rivalry?

A. Minimal product differentiation.

B. A firm's growth must come from winning other firms' customers.

C. High costs of customers switching suppliers.

D. High fixed costs relative to variable costs.

Answer (C) is correct.

REQUIRED: The industry factor that does not contribute to competitive rivalry.

DISCUSSION: If it is expensive to switch suppliers, customers will be less motivated to respond to competitor advances.

Answer (A) is incorrect. Less differentiation tends to increase competition based on price. Answer (B) is incorrect. The need to win other firms' customers to grow strengthens competition. Answer (D) is incorrect. The greater the fixed costs needed to generate a given amount of sales revenues, the greater the incentive to compete on price, service, etc., to maintain and increase sales levels.

9. Which factor most likely encourages entry into an existing market?

A. Governmental subsidies for new investors.

B. High product differentiation, principally produced by trademarks.

C. Knowledge of the industry, with high investments in development.

D. Low fixed exit costs.

Answer (A) is correct.

REQUIRED: The factor likely to encourage market entry.

DISCUSSION: Subsidies for new firms lower entry barriers. Thus, new firms may enter the industry and intensify competition. Government policy also may affect competition by means of regulations that encourage or discourage substitutes or affect costs, that govern competitive behavior, or that limit growth. Government also may be a buyer or supplier.

Answer (B) is incorrect. Product differentiation is an entry barrier. New firms may be incapable of offering a comparable product, so the industry's profitability is protected. Answer (C) is incorrect. Knowledge of the industry is an asset that new firms must acquire. This cost in some cases becomes extremely high and may discourage new firms from entering the industry. Answer (D) is incorrect. Low fixed exit costs facilitate exit when firms decide to leave the industry. They mildly encourage entry because they make investment less risky.

6.3 Competitive Strategies

10. A manufacturing company produces plastic utensils for a particular segment at the lowest possible cost. The company is pursuing a cost

A. Leadership strategy.

B. Focus strategy.

C. Differentiation strategy.

D. Containment strategy.

Answer (B) is correct.

REQUIRED: The cost strategy pursued by the manufacturing company.

DISCUSSION: Cost focus is the generic strategy that seeks competitive advantage through lower costs but with a narrow competitive scope (e.g., a regional market or a specialized product line). The reason for a cost-focus strategy is that the narrower market can be better served because the firm knows it well.

Answer (A) is incorrect. A cost leader is the lowest cost producer in the industry as a whole. Answer (C) is incorrect. Cost differentiation aims at providing a product at different costs in different market segments. Answer (D) is incorrect. Cost containment aims at controlling costs related to a particular product/market but not necessarily producing at the lowest possible cost.

11. According to Michael E. Porter's generic strategies model, a firm that successfully adopts a differentiation strategy is most likely to

A. Tend to disregard cost control.

B. Risk overlooking product changes.

C. Closely supervise its labor force.

D. Be able to pass supplier cost increases on to its customers.

Answer (D) is correct.

REQUIRED: The true statement about a firm that successfully adopts a differentiation strategy.

DISCUSSION: Differentiation is the generic strategy of a firm that seeks competitive advantage through providing a unique product or service. This strategy has a broad competitive scope. A successful differentiation strategy creates a consumer perception that few, if any, substitutes are available. Thus, a firm that adopts this strategy may have the additional advantage of being able to pass supplier cost increases to buyers.

Answer (A) is incorrect. A differentiation strategy does not signify a disregard for cost control, but simply a greater emphasis on creating a perception of the uniqueness of the product or service. Answer (B) is incorrect. A firm with a cost leadership strategy risks overlooking product changes. Answer (C) is incorrect. A firm with a cost leadership strategy is more likely to closely supervise its labor force.

12. According to Michael E. Porter's generic strategies model, a firm that successfully adopts a cost focus strategy is most likely to

    A. Have weak customer loyalty.

    B. Have a strong R&D function.

    C. Know its market well.

    D. Enjoy economies of scale.

Answer (C) is correct.
    REQUIRED: The true statement about a firm that successfully adopts a cost-focus strategy.
    DISCUSSION: Cost focus is the generic strategy of a firm that seeks competitive advantage through lower costs but with a narrow competitive scope (e.g., a regional market or a specialized product line). The reason for a cost focus strategy is that the narrower market can be better served because the firm knows it well.
    Answer (A) is incorrect. Firms that successfully adopt a cost focus strategy achieve very strong customer loyalty, a disincentive to potential competitors. Answer (B) is incorrect. A firm adopting a differentiation strategy is more likely to have a strong R&D function. A firm that successfully adopts a cost focus strategy is more likely to have the strengths of a cost leadership firm. Answer (D) is incorrect. The cost (or differentiation) advantage of servicing a narrow target may be more than offset by the cost advantage achieved by broad-target competitors through economies of scale and other factors.

13. Which factor is most likely to discourage a firm's entry into a new capital-intensive industry?

    A. Buyer switching costs are high.

    B. Buyers view the product as differentiated.

    C. The market is dominated by a small consortium of buyers.

    D. Buyers enjoy large profit margins.

Answer (C) is correct.
    REQUIRED: The factor that discourages market entry.
    DISCUSSION: When purchasing power is concentrated in a few buyers, or buyers are well organized, their bargaining power is greater. This effect is reinforced when sellers are in a capital-intensive industry.
    Answer (A) is incorrect. High switching costs decrease buyers' bargaining power. Answer (B) is incorrect. Buyers are in a weaker position when the supplier's product is differentiated. Answer (D) is incorrect. Buyers are most likely to bargain aggressively when their profit margins are low, especially if the supplier's product accounts for a substantial amount of their costs.

14. What strategy seeks to gain a larger share of a current market for a current product?

    A. Market penetration.

    B. Market development.

    C. Product development.

    D. Diversification.

Answer (A) is correct.
    REQUIRED: The strategy to gain market share for a current product in current market.
    DISCUSSION: Market penetration is the percentage of potential users of a product in a current market who buy the product. A firm's market penetration strategy may be to (1) convince its current customers to increase their usage frequency, (2) convince other firms' customers to switch, or (3) convert nonusers in the target market.
    Answer (B) is incorrect. Market development seeks new markets for current products. Answer (C) is incorrect. Product development is launching new products in existing markets. Answer (D) is incorrect. Diversification is launching new products for new markets.

6.4 Competitive Analysis

15. Which of the following is **not** a step in the establishment of a competitive intelligence system?

    A. Data analysis.

    B. Data collection.

    C. Information dissemination.

    D. Classification of competitors.

Answer (D) is correct.
    REQUIRED: The choice not a step in the establishment of a competitive intelligence system.
    DISCUSSION: A competitive intelligence system is established to identify competitor strategies, monitor their new-product introductions, analyze markets for the firm's own new-product introductions and acquisitions, obtain information about nonpublic firms, evaluate competitor R&D activity, learn about competitors' senior executives, and perform other necessary information gathering tasks. Its establishment consists of setting up the system, collecting data, analyzing the data, and disseminating the information. Classification of competitors, however, is not a step in this process. Competitors are classified and targeted by a firm based on that classification following the results of a customer value analysis (CVA).

16. A starting point for developing competitive strategies is customer value analysis (CVA). According to the CVA approach,

    A. Customer value equals customer benefits.

    B. Bad competitors rather than good competitors should be targeted.

    C. Strong competitors should be avoided even when they have exploitable weaknesses.

    D. Distant competitors are the usual threats.

Answer (B) is correct.
    REQUIRED: The true statement regarding the CVA approach.
    DISCUSSION: Bad competitors should be targeted because they disturb the competitive equilibrium, e.g., by excessive expansion of capacity or overly risky behavior. Good competitors make sound business decisions that promote the long-term health of the industry, e.g., about prices, entry into new segments, and pursuit of market share.
    Answer (A) is incorrect. Customer value equals all customer benefits minus all customer costs. Answer (C) is incorrect. Targeting weak competitors may be the cheapest way to gain market share. However, targeting strong competitors also may be appropriate because this strategy forces the firm to improve. Moreover, a strong competitor may have an exploitable weakness. Answer (D) is incorrect. Close competitors, that is, firms that are similar, are the usual targets. Nevertheless, distant competitors are also threats. For example, any beverage may be a competitor of soft drink makers.

17. A company sells a diverse line of cookies. Its acquisition of another company, a maker of cake mixes, is most likely an example of

    A. Vertical integration.

    B. Horizontal diversification.

    C. Concentric diversification.

    D. Conglomerate diversification.

Answer (B) is correct.
    REQUIRED: The nature of the acquisition.
    DISCUSSION: Horizontal diversification is the acquisition of businesses making products unrelated to current offerings but that might appeal to the firm's current customers. Cookies and cake mixes are based on different technologies but may be demanded by the same customers.
    Answer (A) is incorrect. Vertical integration occurs when suppliers, wholesalers, or retailers are acquired. Answer (C) is incorrect. Concentric diversification results from developing or acquiring related businesses that do not have products, services, or customers in common with current businesses but that offer internal synergies. Thus, the new products or services may be demanded by customers different from those currently served by the company. Answer (D) is incorrect. Conglomerate diversification is the acquisition of wholly unrelated businesses.

18. A strategic business unit (SBU) has a high relative market share (RMS) and a low market growth rate (MGR). According to the growth-share matrix for competitive analysis created by the Boston Consulting Group, such an SBU is considered a

    A. Star.

    B. Question mark.

    C. Cash cow.

    D. Dog.

Answer (C) is correct.
    REQUIRED: The characterization by the growth-share matrix of an SBU.
    DISCUSSION: The annual MGR reflects the maturity and attractiveness of the market and the relative need for cash to finance expansion. The RMS reflects an SBU's competitive position in the market segment. A high RMS signifies that the SBU has a strong competitive position. Cash cows have high RMS and low MGR. They are strong competitors and cash generators in low-growth markets.
    Answer (A) is incorrect. Stars have both high RMS and high MGR because they are strong competitors in high growth markets. Answer (B) is incorrect. Question marks are weak competitors in high-growth markets, meaning they have a low RMS and a high MGR. Answer (D) is incorrect. Dogs have both low RMS and low MGR, meaning they are weak competitors in low-growth markets.

6.5 Market Signals

19. When firms compete in different geographical locations or have multiple product lines that do not necessarily overlap, the most effective way of responding to an aggressive move by a competitor without directly triggering destructive moves and countermoves is to

A. Mislead the competitor into taking or not taking an action.

B. Make a prior announcement of intended moves.

C. Initiate a move in the market where the competitor is strong.

D. Initiate direct aggressive moves.

Answer (C) is correct.
   REQUIRED: The most effective response to an aggressive move by a competitor.
   DISCUSSION: Initiating a move in the market where the competitor is strong is a cross-parry. A cross-parry is an effective way to signal displeasure and raise the threat of more serious retribution without directly triggering destructive moves and countermoves.
   Answer (A) is incorrect. Misleading other firms into taking or not taking an action to benefit the firm is a bluff. A bluff is a form of market signal that is not intended to be carried out. Answer (B) is incorrect. A market signal by a competitor that provides a direct or indirect indication of its intentions, motives, goals, or internal situation is a means of communicating in the market place and an essential input in competitor analysis. A prior announcement may therefore incite countermoves. Answer (D) is incorrect. Direct aggressive moves are aimed at reducing the performance of significant competitors or threatening their goals. They are likely to cause a countermove.

20. A firm discounts never-before-discounted items. This action is an example of a

A. Divergence from industry precedent.

B. Cross-parry.

C. Divergence from prior strategic objectives.

D. Bluff.

Answer (A) is correct.
   REQUIRED: The nature of a firm's discounting of never-before-discounted items.
   DISCUSSION: The discounting of never-before-discounted items implies aggressive intent. It is an example of a divergence from industry precedent.
   Answer (B) is incorrect. A cross-parry is a response to a competitor's move in one area with a move in another. Answer (C) is incorrect. A firm's divergence from prior strategic objectives suggests that other firms should be alert to profound changes in its objectives and assumptions. Answer (D) is incorrect. A bluff is an announcement of an action not intended to be executed. The discounts have already been executed; thus, they are considered true signals, not bluffs.

Access the **CIA Review System** from your Gleim Personal Classroom
to continue your studies with exam-emulating multiple-choice questions!

STUDY UNIT SEVEN
INDUSTRY EVOLUTION AND ENVIRONMENTS

(18 pages of outline)

This study unit is the second of five covering **Section V: Management/Leadership Principles** from The IIA's CIA Exam Syllabus. This section makes up 10% to 20% of Part 3 of the CIA exam and is tested at the **awareness level**. The relevant portion of the syllabus is highlighted below. (The complete syllabus is in Appendix A.)

V. **MANAGEMENT/LEADERSHIP PRINCIPLES (10%–20%)**

    A. **Strategic Management**

        1. Global analytical techniques

            a. Structural analysis of industries

            b. Competitive strategies (e.g., Porter's model)

            c. Competitive analysis

            d. Market signals

            e. Industry evolution

        2. Industry environments

            a. Competitive strategies related to:

                1) Fragmented industries

                2) Emerging industries

                3) Declining industries

            b. Competition in global industries

                1) Sources/impediments

                2) Evolution of global markets

                3) Strategic alternatives

                4) Trends affecting competition

        3. Strategic decisions

        4. Forecasting

        5. Quality management (e.g., TQM, Six Sigma)

        6. Decision analysis

    B. **Organizational Behavior**

    C. **Management Skills/Leadership Styles**

    D. **Conflict Management**

    E. **Project Management/Change Management**

7.1 INDUSTRY EVOLUTION

1. **Basis for Analysis**

   a. An industry consists of firms selling products or services that are substitutes.

   b. One way to describe an industry considers the number of sellers and the extent of differentiation of products and services.

   c. Another way to describe an industry considers its entry, exit, or mobility barriers.

      1) Entry barriers may be high or low. Industries vary as to the necessary capital investment, economies of scale, intellectual property, materials, locations, distribution channels, and other factors.

      2) Exit barriers may consist of legal and moral obligations, regulatory requirements, lack of alternative investments, vertical integration, low residual value of assets, and tradition.

      3) Mobility barriers restrict movement within an industry's segments. They are similar to industry entry barriers.

      4) In general, high entry and mobility barriers and low exit barriers promote profitability.

   d. Porter's five competitive forces (fully discussed in Study Unit 6, Subunit 2) within an industry or market are a basis for analyzing its structure. However, that structure and the firm's competitive strategies will evolve. Early recognition of change and prompt adjustment of strategies are essential to maintaining a competitive advantage. The costs of adjustments will be lower and their benefits greater the sooner they are made.

2. **Product Life Cycle Stages**

   a. The strategy in the precommercialization (product development) stage is to innovate by conducting R&D, marketing research, and production tests. During product development, the entity has no sales, but it has high investment costs.

   b. The **introduction stage** is characterized by slow sales growth and lack of profits because of the high expenses of promotion and selective distribution to generate awareness of the product and encourage customers to try it. Thus, the per-customer cost is high.

      1) Competitors are few, basic versions of the product are produced, and higher-income customers (innovators) are usually targeted. Cost-plus prices are charged. They may initially be high to permit cost recovery when unit sales are low.

      2) The strategy is to infiltrate the market, plan for financing to cope with losses, build supplier relations, increase production and marketing efforts, and plan for competition.

   c. In the **growth stage**, sales and profits increase rapidly, cost per customer decreases, customers are early adopters, new competitors enter an expanding market, new product models and features are introduced, and promotion spending declines or remains stable.

      1) The entity enters new market segments and distribution channels and attempts to build brand loyalty and achieve the maximum share of the market. Thus, prices are set to penetrate the market, distribution channels are extended, and the mass market is targeted through advertising.

      2) During the growth stage, the opportunity for cost reductions is at its maximum because production volume is increasing at a high rate. Thus, fixed costs are being spread over more units of production, and the benefits of the learning curve are being realized.

d.   In the **maturity stage**, sales peak but growth declines, competitors are most numerous but may begin to decline in number, and per-customer cost is low.

1)   Profits are high for large market-share entities. For others, profits may fall because of competitive price cutting and increased R&D spending to develop improved versions of the product.

2)   The strategy is to defend market share and maximize profits through diversification of brands and models to enter new market segments; still more intensive distribution, cost cutting, advertising and promotions to encourage brand switching; and emphasizing customer service.

3)   This stage usually has some of the lowest prices during a product's life cycle.

e.   During the **decline stage**, sales and profits drop, and some entities leave the market. Customers include late adopters (laggards), and per-customer cost is low.

1)   Weak products and unprofitable distribution media are eliminated, and advertising budgets are pared to the level needed to retain the most loyal customers. The strategy is to withdraw by reducing production, promotion, and inventory.

f.   **Trends of Sales and Profits**

Product Life Cycle

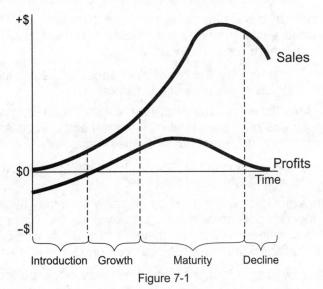

Figure 7-1

3.   **Industry Evolution**

a.   Evolutionary processes are the incentives or pressures that cause structural change. These processes operate to move an industry from its initial structure (technology, entry and exit barriers, power of suppliers and buyers, product traits, beginning size constraints, etc.) to its potential structure. The nature of that structure and the speed of change are not known.

1)   They depend on factors that are hard to predict, such as

a)   Innovations in technology and marketing,

b)   Resources and skills of firms,

c)   Favorable or unfavorable random events, and

d)   Judgments about investments.

4.   **Major Evolutionary Processes**

   a.   The 14 major evolutionary processes are interacting factors common to all industries. Their speed and direction vary.

   1)   Long-run changes in the industry growth rate affect rivalry, entry, expansion, etc.

   a)   These changes occur because of changes in five external factors:

   i)   Demographic traits (such as consumer ages and income levels),

   ii)   Trends in needs of buyers (caused by changes in regulation, tastes, and lifestyles),

   iii)   Relative positions of substitute products,

   iv)   Relative positions of complementary products, and

   v)   Sales to new customers (market penetration).

   b)   Product innovation, an internal factor, alters the industry's position regarding the external factors.

   2)   Changes in buyer segments served occur when new segments are created (e.g., sale of computers to scientists, then business, and finally consumers), existing segments are subdivided, and old segments are no longer served.

   a)   Industry structure evolves to meet the requirements of new customers.

   3)   Learning by buyers decreases product differentiation. Buyers increasingly demand similar product traits (quality, service, etc.). Thus, products may become more like commodities.

   a)   This effect may be offset by changes in the product or its marketing and by attracting inexperienced customers.

   4)   Experimentation reduces uncertainty about such factors as market size, solution of technical problems, buyers, and marketing. Successful strategies are imitated and unsuccessful strategies discarded.

   a)   The reduction in risk attracts new and often larger competitors, especially if the potential market is large.

   5)   Proprietary knowledge (held by only one firm) may become more available to new competitors as the industry evolves, for example, because of (a) competitive intelligence (discussed in Study Unit 6, Subunit 4), (b) expiration of patents, (c) purchase, and (d) loss of personnel to new firms.

   a)   However, if further technological advances are feasible, economies of scale in R&D may create an entry barrier.

   6)   Accumulation of experience permits unit costs of manufacturers to decrease. This lead may not be sustainable because of the spread of proprietary knowledge.

   7)   Expansion of industry scale and firm scale permits more strategies to be used. Entry barriers are higher if economies of scale, capital needs, feasibility of vertical integration, and bargaining power of suppliers and customers are greater.

   a)   But large firms may enter if the scale justifies the investment.

   8)   Changes in input costs (labor, materials, capital, communication, and transport) directly affect the cost and price of a product and the demand for it.

   a)   These changes affect economies of scale, inputs, reorganization of production, and marketing media.

   b)   Distribution channels and geographic market boundaries may be altered.

   c)   Exchange rate changes have similar effects on competition.

9) Product innovation may broaden markets or increase product differentiation.

    a) Barriers are raised because innovation may involve high costs. Other changes are to marketing, distribution, manufacturing, and economies of scale.

    b) Innovation cancels buyer experience and changes purchasing behavior.

    c) Innovation may come from external sources, suppliers, and buyers.

10) Marketing innovation (e.g., in media, channels, or themes) may increase demand by differentiating the product, appealing to new buyers, or lowering costs.

11) Process innovation in manufacturing may affect (a) the degree to which it is more or less capital intensive, (b) economies of scale, (c) vertical integration, (d) the proportions of fixed and variable costs, and (e) the ways of gaining experience, among other things.

    a) Technology changes may occur outside the industry.

12) Structural changes in suppliers' and customers' industries affect their bargaining power. For example, as concentration of customers' industries increases, sellers' industries may become more concentrated.

13) Government policies regulate entry, competitive practices, licensing, and pricing. Moreover, strong regulation affects foreign trade and global competition. Product quality and safety, worker safety and compensation, environmental quality, and investor protection also are regulated.

    a) The social benefits must be weighed against the costs of regulation.

14) Entry changes structure, especially when strong outsiders with special skills are the entrants. Entry occurs when firms believe that potential profits justify the costs.

    a) Exit is motivated by diminished returns on investment. It is impeded by exit barriers. Exit strengthens and exit barriers weaken the remaining firms.

b. Firms should consider how each evolutionary process may affect industry structure, their strategic position, and the ways of coping with the resulting change.

1) Thus, firms must monitor the environment for the strategic signals relative to each evolutionary process.

2) Moreover, firms must be aware that some processes (e.g., learning) may be operating without the occurrence of obvious external events.

Although internal auditors cannot make management decisions, they can form expectations about the financial condition and competitive outlook for the organization's lines of business given the development stage of the particular industry.

Stop and review! You have completed the outline for this subunit. Study multiple-choice questions 1 through 4 beginning on page 157.

7.2 INDUSTRY ENVIRONMENTS -- FRAGMENTED

1. **Fragmented Industries**

   a. Individual firms in a fragmented industry have insignificant market shares and little influence on industry outcomes.

   b. The industry has no market leader, products may or may not be significantly differentiated, and the technology may or may not be sophisticated.

   c. Examples are agriculture, grocery retailing, and fitness clubs.

2. **Economic Causes of Fragmentation**

   a. Although industries may be fragmented for purely historical reasons, economic causes for fragmentation exist in other situations.

   b. Low entry barriers are a necessary but not a sufficient condition for fragmentation.

   c. Economies of scale and a learning curve (experience) effect usually do not exist in fragmented industries. For example, operations may be simple or labor-intensive.

   d. High transportation costs may outweigh economies of scale, for example, when customers must come to a service provider or vice versa.

   e. High inventory carrying costs or sharp and unpredictable changes in sales may affect a large firm's advantage in economies of scale. A small firm's flexibility in adapting to demand changes may be a competitive advantage.

   f. Buyers or suppliers may have such strong bargaining power that size offers little additional advantage in dealing with them.

   g. Important diseconomies of scale may favor fragmentation. For example, small, flexible firms have an advantage when the following needs are important:

      1) Quick responses to style changes,
      2) The maintenance of low overhead,
      3) Customization of a product line to the needs of specific customers,
      4) Substantial creative content in the product,
      5) Individualized personal service, and
      6) Local contacts and image.

   h. Diverse market needs resulting from fragmentation of buyers' tastes may prevent the product standardization needed to prevent fragmentation.

   i. High product differentiation based on an image of exclusivity also promotes fragmentation. Buyers may wish to have their own brands, and suppliers (e.g., performing artists) may wish to deal with firms that create a unique image.

   j. Exit barriers keep firms in the industry and minimize concentration.

   k. Local regulations that vary from community to community impede concentration even when other conditions are not present.

   l. Government antitrust laws may prohibit significant concentration.

   m. Newness is a reason for fragmentation. New firms may not yet have the resources and abilities to achieve concentration.

3. **Overcoming Fragmentation**

   a. Overcoming fragmentation has significant strategic payoffs given that entry is not costly and competitors are weak. If the factor(s) preventing consolidation can be eliminated, industry structure will change.

   b. One method is to use technology to create economies of scale in production, marketing, distribution, service, etc. For example, television marketing has led to consolidation of many industries.

    c.   Standardizing diverse market needs may result from introducing a new product, e.g., one that appeals to most buyers in a market.

        1)   Another possibility is a new product design, e.g., to facilitate mass production of modularized components that may be assembled in different ways.

        2)   Standardizing products means maintaining the same product or standardizing the production, operations, and facilities in different locations or markets. Franchises all use standardized products to reduce costs.

    d.   Strategies such as franchising and horizontal mergers are commonly used in fragmented industries.

        1)   The franchisor provides national advertising, centralized purchasing, and other services, which result in economies of scale and industry consolidation. In effect, the service or production function is separated from the rest of the business.

        2)   Another approach when diverse market needs exist is for a firm to use multiple brands to appeal to the tastes of different customers.

    e.   Early recognition of trends may permit a firm to exploit them. For example, if the industry is new, the firm may recognize the early signs of industry evolution.

        1)   Early awareness of external factors, such as technology changes, that negate fragmentation also provide an opportunity for the firm.

    f.   Industries may be stuck in a fragmented state for reasons other than underlying economic factors.

        1)   Firms in the industry lack the resources, skills, awareness, or ambition to make the strategic moves needed for consolidation.

        2)   Outside firms do not recognize the opportunity offered by an industry stuck in a fragmented state, for example, because it is new, small, or obscure.

4. **Coping with Fragmentation**

    a.   Coping with fragmentation requires strategic positioning.

    b.   When local management, close control, and personal service are critical success factors, tightly managed decentralization may be the appropriate strategy. Local operations remain small scale and autonomous, but managers are held to high standards with performance-based compensation.

    c.   Developing formula facilities for use in numerous localities reduces construction and operating costs via standardization.

    d.   When products or services cannot be significantly differentiated, the best strategy may be to increase the value added, for example, by adding services or by forward integration.

    e.   Specialization by product type or segment is a focus strategy. This focus may enhance bargaining power with suppliers. It also may increase differentiation because of the perceived expertise and image. The downside is reduced growth opportunities.

    f.   Specialization by customer type (e.g., small customers or those who are not price sensitive), type of order (e.g., small orders for quick delivery or custom orders), or geographic areas are other focus strategies.

    g.   A cost strategy is to adopt a bare-bones, no-frills approach by emphasizing tight control of costs, low overhead, and low payroll.

    h.   Backward integration is the selective acquisition of suppliers to reduce costs.

5.   **Strategic Traps**

   a.   The following are strategic traps in a fragmented industry:

   1)   Barring basic change in the industry's structure, seeking dominance is usually a losing strategy.

   2)   Lack of strategic discipline means not focusing on an appropriate strategy for a fragmented industry (if the structure cannot be altered).

   3)   Overcentralization of the organizational structure is often a mistake. In the intense competition of a fragmented industry, quick response times, local contacts, personal service, and tight operating control are essential.

   4)   Assuming that competitors have similar costs and objectives is frequently wrong. Small, privately held firms in the industry may be content with much lower rates of return, use family members in the business, and avoid some costs of regulation.

   5)   Overreaction to new products results when investments are made to respond to new product demand that are inconsistent with the industry structure. As the product enters maturity, price competition from many rivals will become intense, and the profit margins needed to pay for the investments will vanish.

6.   **Competitive Strategy in a Fragmented Industry**

   a.   The following is a framework for developing a competitive strategy:

   1)   Determine the industry's structure and the circumstances of major competitors.

   2)   Create a full list of the reasons for fragmentation, if any, and their connection with the industry's economics.

   3)   Analyze whether the causes of fragmentation can be overcome by innovation, strategic changes, additional resources, or a new perspective.

   a)   Determine the effects of trends.

   4)   If fragmentation can be overcome, evaluate whether the new structure will yield acceptable returns and the position needed to earn those returns. This step requires repeating the first step above.

   5)   If fragmentation cannot be overcome, select the best strategy for operating in a fragmented environment.

Stop and review! You have completed the outline for this subunit. Study multiple-choice questions 5 through 8 beginning on page 158.

7.3 INDUSTRY ENVIRONMENTS -- EMERGING

1.   **Emerging Industries**

   a.   An emerging industry is new or newly formed and is small initially. It results from innovation, changes in cost structures, new customer needs, or another factor that creates an opportunity for selling a product or service.

   1)   Established firms also must cope with these changes.

   b.   No rules exist for an emerging industry, creating risks and opportunities.

   c.   Examples include electronic calculators in the 1970s, long-distance telephone service in the 1980s, cell phone service in the 1990s, and Web-based retailing in the 2000s.

2.   **Structural Characteristics of Emerging Industries**

   a.   Technological uncertainty regarding products and production methods is one characteristic.

    b.   Strategic uncertainty arises because effective strategies have not yet been identified. Firms experiment with product features, production methods, marketing approaches, etc.

        1)   Competitive intelligence is poor because competitors have not been identified and industry data are not available.

    c.   Initial costs are high, but the learning curve is steep. When the efficiency gains from experience combine with economies of scale achieved by growth, cost decreases are dramatic.

    d.   Embryonic companies (firms newly formed) are numerous because entry is not discouraged by the presence of economies of scale or strategic certainty.

        1)   Spin-offs from existing firms are common. Given the uncertainties and the lure of equity interests, employees have incentives to create new firms. They may want to exploit ideas rejected by their former employers.

    e.   Customers are first-time buyers. The marketing problem is to convince them that the benefits of substituting the product or service for something else exceed the risks.

    f.   The short time horizon for product and customer development means that policies may evolve for reasons other than well-researched decision making.

    g.   Subsidy of early entrants by government or others may occur when the technology is radically new or societal concern is strong. Subsidies create instability because they result from political decisions.

    h.   Early mobility barriers tend to consist of willingness to accept risk, proprietary technology, access to resource supplies, and the lower costs of more experienced firms.

        1)   Barriers tend not to be branding, economies of scale, or capital intensity.

3. **Limits on Development**

    a.   Limits on emerging industry development arise because it is new, depends on external entities for growth, and must change customer buying habits.

    b.   Raw materials and components may be scarce because new suppliers must be found or existing suppliers must expand or modify their output.

    c.   Raw materials prices may increase rapidly as suppliers struggle to keep pace with demand during the early phase of industry development.

        1)   Initially high unit costs may require below-cost pricing or slow industry growth.

    d.   Infrastructure (e.g., distribution channels, service centers, skilled labor, and complementary products or services) may not be available.

    e.   Standardization lags because of product and technology uncertainty.

    f.   Customers' belief that product obsolescence will occur rapidly may cause slow growth.

    g.   Customer confusion and increased risk of purchase are caused by technological uncertainty, lack of standardization, and the proliferation of products.

    h.   Product quality may be uneven because of the presence of many new firms and technological uncertainty (and the lack of technical standards).

    i.   Due to the limits described above, the industry's image and financial credibility may suffer. Thus, lenders may be unwilling to provide debt capital at favorable rates, and customers may have difficulty in securing credit.

    j.   Regulatory approval may be hard to obtain, especially if customer needs are already served by an established regulated industry.

        1)   However, favorable government policy may jump-start an industry, for example, when use of a safety product becomes mandatory. But further growth may be slowed by first-time regulation.

k.   Threatened entities (e.g., makers of substitutes or unions) may respond.

1)   The responses may be political pressure, lobbying of regulators, collective bargaining, lower prices, or reduction of costs.

2)   Entities threatened by substitution are more likely to adopt a price or investment strategy when exit barriers are high.

4.   **Forecasting Markets**

a.   Forecasting early and late markets is necessary to guide product development and marketing efforts and to predict structural evolution. Markets, market segments, and customers within a segment may vary in how quickly they accept a new industry's product or service. The following are factors affecting acceptance:

1)   The nature of the benefit is the most significant factor. At one extreme, the benefit may consist of a performance advantage unattainable by other methods. At the other extreme, the benefit may be a pure cost advantage. Ordinarily, early markets purchase a product because it offers a performance advantage. Early markets tend to be suspicious of a product offering a cost advantage.

2)   Early adoption depends on the technical performance buyers require. Different buyers may require different levels of product development.

3)   A higher cost of product failure for a buyer leads to later adoption. For example, a buyer that will use the product as part of an integrated system or pay a high price for interrupted service has a high cost of failure.

4)   Buyers vary in the switching costs they face, e.g., (a) retraining, (b) additional equipment purchases, (c) disposal of old equipment, (d) requirements for support services, (e) capital needs, and (f) modification of related processes or business elements.

5)   The cost of obsolescence is less for emerging technology if an initial version will meet later buyer needs even though upgrades appear periodically.

6)   Different buyers face different regulatory, governmental, or union constraints.

7)   Buyer resource availability affects the decision to change.

8)   The perception of technological change is less daunting to a sophisticated buyer. Change may be a threat to some but an opportunity to others.

9)   Early adoption is less likely the greater the personal risk to the decision maker.

5.   **Strategic Choices**

a.   The following are strategic choices in emerging industries:

1)   The firm is best able to shape the structure of an emerging industry. It is best able to influence approaches on such matters as pricing, marketing, and product policy.

2)   A firm in an emerging industry needs to consider externalities in industry development. It should balance its self-interest with the need to promote the industry.

a)   Thus, to appeal to first-time buyers and encourage substitution, the firm's enlightened self-interest ordinarily requires industry cooperation, improved quality, and standardization.

b)   An initial industry orientation also may require the firm to follow a strategy and enter market segments on a temporary basis.

3)   A firm benefits by early awareness of the changing role of suppliers and distribution channels, which may be more cooperative as the industry strengthens.

4) Early mobility barriers may disappear as the industry grows and technology improves. Thus, the firm may no longer be able to rely on early advantages, such as proprietary technology. The response may be a large investment.

5) The nature of entrants may change to include larger firms attracted by the proven and less risky industry. Firms must predict when such entry is likely given existing and probable future barriers and the costs of surmounting them.

    a) Firms need to predict how new entrants will compete, e.g., on the basis of marketing power or economies of scale. Furthermore, new entrants may emerge through vertical integration.

6) Timing of entry is critical. Risk and returns may be high, but barriers are low.

    a) Factors favoring early entry: (1) improvement of the firm's reputation, (2) persistence of an important experience advantage, (3) high customer loyalty, and (4) cost advantages (through early commitment to suppliers or distributors).

    b) Factors not favoring early entry: (1) significant change in the bases of competition and market segments, (2) high costs of opening the market without retention of the benefits, (3) expensive early competition and later emergence of larger and stronger competitors, and (4) early obsolescence of products and processes.

    c) Beneficial tactical moves may include early commitment to suppliers and taking advantage of lower capital costs if investors are attracted.

7) Early response to competitors is often a poor strategic choice. A firm is frequently best served by reinforcing its strengths and by developing the industry, perhaps by encouraging new entrants (e.g., by licensing) who will sell the industry's products and expedite its technological evolution.

Stop and review! You have completed the outline for this subunit. Study multiple-choice questions 9 through 12 beginning on page 159.

7.4 INDUSTRY ENVIRONMENTS -- DECLINING

1. **Declining Industries**

    a. A declining industry has sustained a permanent decrease in unit sales over the long run. However, this phase of the industry life cycle does not correspond exactly to the decline stage in the product life cycle.

    b. The nature of the competition and the range of strategic choices are diverse and vary widely from industry to industry. Thus, some industries may avoid intense rivalry, long-term overcapacity, and ruinous losses during the decline phase.

    c. Social and technological changes can affect industry decline. Examples include tobacco, passenger rail service, and film developing.

2. **Structural Characteristics**

    a. Structure and competition in the decline phase are determined by the decreased profits resulting from lower unit sales and more intense competition. However, various factors affect the degree of the damage suffered.

    b. The conditions of demand and the nature of market segments determine competition.

        1) Perceived uncertainty about demand by competitors is a major influence on the competitive intensity. Rivalry is strong if demand is expected to increase. But if all firms expect demand to decrease, the weaker firms may withdraw early and reduce capacity.

            a) The stronger the firm and the higher its exit barriers, the more likely that its demand perception will be optimistic.

2) The rate and pattern of decline affect uncertainty, which stimulates competitive volatility. Thus, a slow decline creates uncertainty, but a rapid decline tends to reduce uncertainty and unjustified optimism. Moreover, the rapid decline makes wholesale decreases in capacity more probable.

   a) The rate of decline in demand is influenced by the pattern of withdrawal. For example, the departure of some suppliers may encourage customers to switch to substitutes so as to guarantee the availability of inputs.

   b) The rate of decline also tends to increase as withdrawals decrease sales volume and increase costs and prices.

3) The structure of the remaining pockets of demand determines whether the surviving firms can be profitable. Prospects are favorable if the pockets include price-insensitive buyers of highly differentiated products.

   a) Prospects also are favorable if buyers have little bargaining power because of high switching costs or other factors, such as the need to replace the equipment of the suppliers that have withdrawn from the industry.

   b) Furthermore, firms operating in remaining pockets may thrive if mobility barriers are high (preventing firms in other segments from competing) and if substitute products or strong suppliers are not threats.

4) The causes of decline in industry demand include innovation or shifts in costs or quality that make attractive substitutes available.

   a) Other causes are a reduction in the size of a demographic customer group and changes in the needs or tastes of customers.

   b) A firm should consider these causes when evaluating the uncertainty of future demand and potential profits from remaining in particular market segments.

c. High exit barriers may restrain firms from leaving the industry.

   1) Specialized assets and inventory in a declining industry may have a low liquidation value. Few purchasers may be available.

      a) Durable assets may have a carrying amount far greater than the liquidation value. Thus, liquidation may result in a large loss.

      b) A low liquidation value means that the discounted cash flows from remaining in the industry may exceed the opportunity cost of capital.

   2) Net liquidation value is reduced when the fixed costs of exit are high, e.g., the costs of (a) labor settlements, (b) payments to CPAs and attorneys, (c) cancelation of contracts, and (d) resettlement or retraining.

      a) Announcement of exit may result in reduced productivity, loss of customers, and a decline in supplier reliability.

      b) But some required investments, such as in environmental safeguards, may be avoided.

   3) One type of strategic exit barrier exists when a business is part of a group executing an overall strategy. Divesting the business may undermine the strategy. For example, it may be important to the parent's image, relations with distributors, or bargaining power with suppliers.

      a) Exit may harm the financial standing of a firm. For example, the firm's share price may decrease and its cost of capital increase. Also, a single large loss may be worse than a succession of small operating losses.

      b) Vertical integration of a business may require exit of the entire chain. But when only one part is in a declining industry, integration is an argument for exit of the affected part.

4) Information barriers exist when one business is closely related to others in the firm. Its actual performance may be unclear in these circumstances.

5) Management and emotional barriers arise because managers may have personal involvement in the business, not wish to admit failure, or be concerned about future employment.

6) Government and social barriers reflect opposition to the negative effects of exit: unemployment and harm to local communities.

7) High exit barriers tend to keep capacity in a declining industry, intensifying rivalry and harming even healthy firms.

d. Asset disposition affects the health of the declining industry. For example, sale within the industry but at a discount gives the buyer a lower investment base. Thus, the buyer may be able to take financially rational actions (e.g., prices) that damage other firms.

1) Discounted sales of assets to employee groups and government subsidies to failing firms have similar negative effects.

e. Price wars are more likely in the decline phase.

1) Rivalry is more volatile (intense) when

a) The product is viewed as a commodity,

b) Fixed costs or exit barriers are high,

c) Firms have strategic reasons for remaining and the resources to do so,

d) Firms are relatively equally strong, and

e) Firms are tempted to take ill-advised competitive actions because of uncertainty about their positions.

2) The greater power of suppliers and distributors in the decline phase means higher prices and worse service for industry firms and more intense rivalry.

3. Strategic Choices

a. The following are strategic choices in declining industries:

1) A leadership strategy is adopted by a firm that believes it can achieve market share gains to become the dominant firm. One assumption is that additional investment can be recovered. A second assumption is that success will allow the firm to maintain its position or subsequently to follow a harvest strategy.

a) This strategy may involve

i) Aggressive pricing, marketing, or other investments;

ii) Reducing competitors' exit barriers, e.g., by acquiring their capacity or products;

iii) Demonstrations of strength and resolve to remain in the industry; and

iv) Publicizing accurate data to dispel competitors' uncertainty.

2) A niche strategy seeks a market segment (pocket of demand) with stable or slowly decreasing demand with the potential for above-average returns. Some of the moves undertaken when following a leadership strategy may be appropriate.

a) The firm may eventually change to a harvest or divest strategy.

3) A harvest strategy is in effect a controlled, gradual liquidation. It maximizes cash flow by reducing costs and using the firm's remaining strengths (e.g., goodwill) to increase prices or maintain sales.

a) To be successful, the strategy assumes no intense competition.

i) Thus, other firms are less likely to gain market share or lower prices.

ii) However, cost reductions must not cause immediate failure.

      b)   A harvest strategy may be visible to customers (less advertising or higher prices) or invisible. A firm without strength may be limited to invisible actions.

      4)   A quick divestment strategy assumes that the highest net recovery is obtained by sale early in the decline phase. It is then that uncertainty about the industry's future is greatest and other markets for the assets are most favorable.

         a)   Divestiture may be indicated during the maturity phase prior to decline.

4.   **Choosing a Strategy**

   a.   One factor in the choice is whether the declining industry is likely to yield profits to the firm, that is, whether industry structure is favorable (e.g., with regard to uncertainty, competitor exit barriers, and conditions of demand).

   b.   A second factor is the firm's relative position, or strengths and weaknesses.

   c.   Given a favorable industry structure, a firm with strengths in the remaining pockets of demand is most likely to follow a leadership or niche strategy. Lacking such strengths, it will most likely adopt a harvest or quick divestment strategy.

   d.   Given an unfavorable industry structure, a firm with strengths in the remaining pockets of demand is most likely to follow a niche or harvest strategy. Lacking such strengths, it will most likely adopt a quick divestment strategy.

   e.   However, the firm's strategic needs may affect the choice. For example, a need for cash flow may override other considerations and prompt an early sale.

   f.   A crucial element of a strategy in the decline phase is to discover methods for influencing competitors to exit.

   g.   Potential mistakes made by firms in a declining industry are (1) not recognizing the onset of decline, (2) engaging in wars of attrition with competitors having high exit barriers, and (3) adopting a harvest strategy in the absence of strengths.

   h.   Preparing for decline during the maturity phase may be possible given accurate forecasts, e.g., by (1) avoidance of actions creating exit barriers, (2) focusing on market segments that will be profitable in the decline phase, and (3) increasing the customers' costs of switching in those segments.

Stop and review! You have completed the outline for this subunit. Study multiple-choice questions 13 through 16 beginning on page 160.

7.5 COMPETITION IN GLOBAL INDUSTRIES

1.   **Global Competition**

   a.   Analysis of competition considers the economics of the industry and the characteristics of competitors. However, in a global industry, the analysis is not limited to one market, but extends to all markets.

   b.   In a global industry, the strategic positions of competitors in major geographic or national markets are fundamentally affected by their overall global positions. Competitive analysis must address issues of global competition.

   c.   A true global industry requires a firm to compete internationally. Accordingly, an industry is not global simply because some or all competitors are multinational.

   d.   Global competition obviously differs in important ways from national competition. For example, costs, market characteristics, and the roles of governments vary among countries. Available resources, competitive monitoring, and objectives also vary.

      1)   But the five competitive forces and the structural factors are the same.

         a)   The structural analysis of the forces and factors must still address

            i)   Foreign competitors,

            ii)   A larger group of possible entrants,

    iii) A wider range of substitute products, and

    iv) An even higher probability that firms will vary in their strategic objectives and corporate cultures.

  b) Competitiveness of firms is greatest, and the competitive environment is most intense, when the benefits of global integration and coordination and the benefits of localization (flexibility, proximity, and quick response time) are achieved.

 e. The primary issues are whether a firm should compete and the extent of the threat to the firm from global competition.

2. **Sources of Global Competitive Advantage**

 a. An industry becomes global because it perceives a net strategic advantage to competing in many national markets. Thus, the sources of competitive advantage must have greater weight than the impediments.

 b. A firm should consider the materiality of the source of advantage to total cost. Moreover, it also should consider the element of the business where the firm has a global competitive advantage.

  1) Still another consideration is that the sources of advantage reflect the implied presence of mobility barriers.

 c. Participation in foreign markets is usually by licensing; export; or, after the firm has obtained experience, direct investment. A genuinely global industry will have significant export activity or direct investment.

  1) Nevertheless, direct investment does not necessarily signal the existence of global competition.

 d. The competitive advantage of a nation regarding the cost or quality of a product means that it will produce and export the product. Consequently, a global firm's position in that nation is vital.

 e. Economies of scale in centralized production may yield a cost advantage achievable only when output exceeds the demand in one country and exports are feasible. Vertical integration may provide the necessary scale.

 f. Global experience may result in more rapid movement along the learning curve when similar products are sold in multiple national markets. Thus, the global firm may be first to achieve the maximum cost advantage from experience. Its cumulative production volume grows more rapidly than that of a purely national firm.

 g. Logistical economies of scale may be attained by a global firm that spreads its fixed costs by supplying multiple national markets. A logistical cost advantage also may result because a global firm uses specialized logistical systems.

 h. Marketing economies of scale may exceed the volume achievable in a national market even though much marketing is necessarily local. For example, one sales force may be employed globally when buyers are few and technical considerations are complex. Furthermore, some brands require no incremental investment to have international strength. Also, some advertising campaigns may be effective across national borders.

 i. Purchasing economies of scale may confer a cost advantage. A global firm will make larger purchases than a purely national firm. One result may be longer and therefore more economical production runs. Another result may be greater bargaining power versus suppliers.

 j. Product differentiation through enhanced image and reputation may be achieved in national markets by operating globally.

k.   Proprietary technology may be applicable in multiple national markets, thereby creating a global competitive advantage. Furthermore, achieving such an advantage may be only feasible in a global industry. Economies of scale for R&D may be attainable only when the market is global. Also, global operation may help a firm to stay in touch with new developments.

l.   Mobility of production allows a global firm to more readily achieve economies of scale and share proprietary technology among operating activities in multiple markets.

   1)   For example, a construction firm may have a larger organization than would be feasible in a national market. The fixed costs of that organization and of developing its technology will be lower relative to revenues because the global market is greater. Global operation is more likely to be profitable when construction crews and equipment are mobile.

3.   **Impediments to Global Competition**

a.   Impediments to global competition may (1) increase direct costs, (2) make management more difficult, (3) be imposed by governments or institutions, or (4) consist of perceptual or resource limitations. Impediments that do not block global competition may still create niches for national firms.

b.   High transportation and storage costs may require construction of plants in each market.

c.   Product needs may differ from country to country because of culture, climate, degree of economic development, income, legal requirements, and technical standards.

   1)   This barrier limits global procurement and achievement of economies of scale and experience. The height of the barrier depends on the costs of product modifications.

   2)   Complex segmentation within geographic markets has similar effects.

d.   Access to established distribution channels may be difficult, especially when large volumes of low-cost items are sold. Concessions required to persuade a channel to substitute the product for a domestic producer's may be too great. Chances are better if channels are not established or are few and high-volume.

e.   The need for a direct sales force creates a barrier based on a diseconomy of scale, especially if local competitors' sales agents market wide product lines. The need for local repair is similar.

f.   Sensitivity to lead times means that global firms may not respond quickly to changes in fashion, technology, etc., in a national market. Centralized functions may be at too great a distance from that market to meet quickly evolving customer needs, especially when local needs vary.

   1)   The relevant lead times include those for physical transportation at an economically acceptable cost.

g.   Lack of world demand may derive from the product's lack of appeal except in a few markets or its early position in the product life cycle of world trade.

   1)   Initial introduction of the product is in a few markets where the product has the greatest appeal. Demand then builds elsewhere by product imitation and technology diffusion, resulting in exports and foreign investment.

   2)   Greater demand and diffusion also may result in production in other markets by foreign firms.

   3)   During the maturity stage, the product is standardized, price competition increases, and local firms enter the market.

   4)   Thus, global competition may require some industry maturity, but the level of maturity is lower when experienced global competitors can rapidly spread the product to new markets.

h. Differing marketing tasks are required in different national markets. Hence, local firms with superior marketing experience in their countries may have the advantage. A possible solution is to have a local marketing function.

i. Local firms tend to be more responsive than global firms when intensive local services or other customer contacts are necessary. Accordingly, the local firm's advantages in marketing and other services could outweigh the global firm's advantages.

j. Rapid changes in technology that require product and process modifications for a local market also favor the local firm.

k. Governmental impediments to global competition are generally imposed to protect local firms and jobs and developing industries. These impediments are most likely when industries are viewed as crucial.

    1) They may raise revenue in the short run, but tax revenues ultimately will decline because of reduced trade.

    2) Examples of governmental impediments are

        a) Tariffs;

        b) Duties;

        c) Quotas;

        d) Domestic content rules;

        e) Preferences for local firms regarding procurement, taxes, R&D, labor regulations, and other operating rules; and

        f) Laws (e.g., antibribery or tax) enacted by a national government that impede national firms from competing globally.

l. Perceptual impediments arise because the complexities of global competition may impair the firm's ability to identify global opportunities.

m. Resource impediments consist of information and search costs, the costs of large-scale facilities construction, and the investments needed to penetrate new markets.

4. **Evolution of Global Markets**

a. The triggers of global market evolution establish or exploit the sources of global competitive advantage. They also may negate the impediments.

    1) However, negating impediments will not result in globalization unless the firm has sufficient strategic advantages. Moreover, a strategic innovation is always necessary for the industry to become global.

        a) Access to the largest markets also may be critical to successful globalization of an industry.

b. Environmental triggers include

    1) An increase in any of the types of economies of scale,
    2) Lower transportation or storage costs,
    3) Changes in distribution channels that facilitate access by foreign firms,
    4) Changes in the costs of the factors of production,
    5) Increased similarity of economic and social conditions in other nations, and
    6) Reduction of governmental limitations.

c. Strategic innovations may begin globalization even if environmental triggers are not present.

    1) Product redefinition may reduce national product differences resulting from industry maturity and product standardization. However, a marketing innovation that redefines the product's concept or image may make it more acceptable in global markets.

    2) Identification of common market segments among countries that are badly served by national firms is possible even if national product differences persist.

       3)   Despite national product differences, reducing the costs of adapting the product, for example, by modularization or increasing the product's range of compatibility, may permit global competition. Design changes may have the same effect when they result in standardization of components.

       4)   Combining centralized production with local assembly (deintegration of production) may satisfy governmental requirements while creating sufficient economies of scale to trigger global competition.

       5)   Elimination of resource or perceptual constraints may result from entry of new firms with greater resources or with a fresher perspective that is helpful in developing new strategies and identifying new opportunities.

5.   **Strategic Choices**

   a.   The following are strategic choices in global industries:

       1)   Broad line global competition is competition over the full product line of the firm based on differentiation or low cost. The firm needs large resources for this long-term strategy.

           a)   Governmental relations should emphasize impediment reduction.

       2)   A global focus strategy is limited to an industry segment with low impediments where the firm can compete effectively on a global basis against broad line firms.

           a)   The focus of competition is low cost or product differentiation.

       3)   A national focus strategy is limited to a national market or the segments with the greatest economic impediments to global competitors.

           a)   Low cost or product differentiation is the focus of competition.

       4)   A protected niche strategy is applied in nations where global competitors are discouraged by governmental impediments, such as domestic content rules or tariffs.

           a)   The strategy is designed to be effective in markets with governmental constraints and requires close attention to the national government.

       5)   Transnational coalitions may be created to help the firms overcome impediments to executing the broader strategies, for example, market access or technology barriers.

6.   **Trends in Global Competition**

   a.   Economic differences among developed and newly developed countries have narrowed.

   b.   Some countries are pursuing more aggressive industrial policies by providing resources to stimulate industries to achieve global status.

   c.   Governmental protection of distinctive national assets, such as natural assets, is reflected in direct ownership or joint ventures with private firms. A large labor pool is another asset increasingly recognized by some governments.

   d.   The freer flow of technology allows many firms, including those in newly developed countries, to invest in world-class facilities.

   e.   New large scale markets have emerged, e.g., China, Russia, and India.

   f.   Newly developed countries, e.g., Brazil, Taiwan, and South Korea, have emerged as global competitors because of their greater ability to make large investments, acquire new technology, and accept high risks.

Stop and review! You have completed the outline for this subunit. Study multiple-choice questions 17 through 20 beginning on page 161.

QUESTIONS

7.1 Industry Evolution

1. Of the major processes affecting the evolution of an industry, which one affects rivalry, entry, expansion, and supply?

A. Long-run changes in the industry growth rate.

B. Changes in input costs.

C. Structural changes in suppliers' and customers' industries.

D. Government policies.

Answer (A) is correct.
    REQUIRED: The evolutionary process that affects rivalry, entry, expansion, and supply.
    DISCUSSION: Long-run changes in the industry growth rate affect rivalry, entry, expansion, and supply. These changes occur because of changes in five external factors: demographic traits (such as consumer ages and income levels), trends in needs of buyers (caused by changes in regulation, tastes, and lifestyles), relative positions of substitute products, relative positions of complementary products, and sales to new customers (market penetration). Product innovation, an internal factor, alters the industry's position regarding the external factors.
    Answer (B) is incorrect. Changes in input costs most directly affect the cost and price of the product and the demand for it. Answer (C) is incorrect. Structural changes in suppliers' and customers' industries affect their bargaining power. Answer (D) is incorrect. Government policies affect industry evolution by explicit regulation of entry, competitive practices, licensing, and pricing.

2. During the growth stage of a product's life cycle,

A. The quality of products is poor.

B. New product models and features are introduced.

C. There is little difference between competing products.

D. The quality of the products becomes more variable and products are less differentiated.

Answer (B) is correct.
    REQUIRED: The true statement regarding the growth stage of a product's life cycle.
    DISCUSSION: In the growth stage, sales and profits increase rapidly, cost per customer decreases, customers are early adopters, new competitors enter an expanding market, new product models and features are introduced, and promotion spending declines or remains stable. The firm enters new market segments and distribution channels and attempts to build brand loyalty and achieve the maximum share of the market. Thus, prices are set to penetrate the market, distribution channels are extended, and the mass market is targeted through advertising. The strategy is to advance by these means and by achieving economies of productive scale.
    Answer (A) is incorrect. Poor product quality is evident during the introduction stage of the product life cycle. Answer (C) is incorrect. Competitors are most numerous, and products become less differentiated, during the maturity stage of the product life cycle. In this stage, imitators have entered the market and competitors have learned which technologies and features are successful. Answer (D) is incorrect. The quality of the products becomes more variable, and products are less differentiated, during the decline stage of the product life cycle.

3. In a product's life cycle, the first symptom of the decline stage is a decline in the

A. Firm's inventory levels.

B. Product's sales.

C. Product's production cost.

D. Product's prices.

Answer (B) is correct.
    REQUIRED: The initial symptom of the decline stage in a product's life cycle.
    DISCUSSION: The sales of most product types and brands eventually decrease permanently. This decline may be slow or rapid. This first symptom of the decline stage of a product's life cycle triggers such other effects as price cutting, narrowing of the product line, and reduction in promotion budgets.
    Answer (A) is incorrect. A decline in the firm's purchases, resulting in a decline in the firm's inventory levels, is not the first symptom. It will occur only when production declines as a result of a drop in sales. Answer (C) is incorrect. A decline in production costs may be due to many factors, e.g., new plant technology or the increased availability of raw materials. Moreover, production costs may decrease in any stage of a product's life cycle and not specifically in the decline stage. Answer (D) is incorrect. A change in prices is a marketing decision. It is an action that may be taken in the maturity stage to compete in the market. Moreover, a decrease in the product's prices is a response to a permanent decline in sales.

4. Patents are granted to encourage firms to invest in the research and development of new products. Patents are an example of

    A. Vertical integration.

    B. Market concentration.

    C. Entry barriers.

    D. Collusion.

Answer (C) is correct.

    REQUIRED: The true statement about patents.

    DISCUSSION: Entry barriers exist in all market structures other than perfect competition. The fewer the firms in an industry, the greater the barriers tend to be. Entry barriers include the existence of substantial economies of scale (low unit costs can be achieved only by large producers). They also include barriers created by existing firms. For example, large advertising expenditures may be necessary to compete. Control of raw materials or technology is another barrier. Consequently, patents held by existing firms may serve as an entry barrier because they prevent potential competitors from using certain technology. Patents are rights granted by the federal government to inventors to allow them the exclusive use of their inventions for a specific period.

    Answer (A) is incorrect. Vertical integration is the combination of a company with a supplier or a customer. Answer (B) is incorrect. Market concentration is the degree to which a few producers dominate an industry. Answer (D) is incorrect. A patent is a contract between the government and an inventor. There is no collusion.

7.2 Industry Environments -- Fragmented

5. A firm in a fragmented industry must position itself by adopting a competitive strategy appropriate to the industry. Which of the following is most clearly a focus strategy?

    A. Specialization by product type.

    B. Backward integration.

    C. An emphasis on low overhead and low payroll.

    D. Development of formula facilities.

Answer (A) is correct.

    REQUIRED: The focus strategy.

    DISCUSSION: A focus strategy is directed at a buyer group, segment of the product line, or geographic area. Thus, the strategic target is narrow compared with an industry wide strategy designed to achieve cost leadership or product differentiation. Specialization by product type or segment is a focus strategy. This focus may enhance bargaining power with suppliers. It may also increase differentiation because of the perceived expertise and image. The downside is reduced growth opportunities.

    Answer (B) is incorrect. Backward integration is the selective acquisition of suppliers to reduce costs. Answer (C) is incorrect. A cost strategy is to adopt a bare-bones, no-frills approach by emphasizing tight control of costs, low overhead, and low payroll. Answer (D) is incorrect. Developing formula facilities for use in numerous localities reduces construction and operating costs via standardization.

6. A fragmented industry is most likely to

    A. Have substantial economies of scale.

    B. Have low transportation costs.

    C. Be characterized by suppliers with little bargaining power.

    D. Approximate pure competition.

Answer (D) is correct.

    REQUIRED: The most likely characteristic of a fragmented industry.

    DISCUSSION: According to Michael E. Porter, individual firms in a fragmented industry have insignificant market shares and little influence on industry outcomes. Examples are retailing, agriculture, and creative enterprises. Thus, the situation approximates what economists call pure competition. Moreover, the industry has many small- or medium-sized firms with no market leader, products may or may not be significantly differentiated, and the technology may or may not be sophisticated.

    Answer (A) is incorrect. Economies of scale and a learning curve (experience) effect usually do not exist in fragmented industries. For example, operations may be simple or labor-intensive. Answer (B) is incorrect. High transportation costs are an economic cause of fragmentation. Answer (C) is incorrect. An economic cause of fragmentation is that buyers or suppliers may have such strong bargaining power that size offers little additional advantage in dealing with them.

7. What is the last step in Porter's framework for developing a competitive strategy in a fragmented industry?

    A. Create a full list of reasons for fragmentation.

    B. Select the best strategy for operating in a fragmented environment.

    C. Evaluate whether a new structure will yield acceptable returns and what position the firm should occupy.

    D. Determine the industry's structure.

Answer (B) is correct.
    REQUIRED: The last step in developing a competitive strategy.
    DISCUSSION: The framework's initial steps determine the causes of fragmentation, analyze whether the causes can be overcome, and determine the best strategy if fragmentation can be overcome. The last step is determining the best strategy if fragmentation cannot be overcome.

8. The opportunity for franchising comes from the ability to

    A. Develop products.

    B. Differentiate products.

    C. Standardize products.

    D. Diversify products.

Answer (C) is correct.
    REQUIRED: The opportunity for franchising.
    DISCUSSION: Standardizing products means to maintain the same product or to standardize the production, operations, and facilities in different locations or markets. Franchises all use standardized products to reduce costs.
    Answer (A) is incorrect. Developing products means adding more value or features to the existing product. Answer (B) is incorrect. Differentiating products implies that the products are to be different in different markets. Answer (D) is incorrect. Diversifying products means to deal in different products, although they may be related (part of the same line).

7.3 Industry Environments -- Emerging

9. An emerging industry is new or newly formed and is small in size initially. An emerging industry results from innovation, changes in cost structures, new customer needs, or another factor that creates an attractive opportunity for selling a product or service. Which of the following is a structural characteristic of an emerging industry?

    A. A long time horizon for product development.

    B. Low initial costs and a shallow learning curve.

    C. Mobility barriers include economies of scale and brand identification.

    D. The presence of embryonic companies and spin-offs.

Answer (D) is correct.
    REQUIRED: The characteristic of an emerging industry.
    DISCUSSION: Embryonic companies (firms newly formed and not new units of established entities) are numerous in the emerging phase of industry evolution. Entry is not discouraged by the presence of economies of scale or strategic certainty. Spin-offs from existing firms also are common. Given the strategic uncertainties and the lure of equity interests, employees of these firms may have the incentive, and be well-placed, to create new firms. Their motive is to exploit ideas that may not have received a favorable reception by their former employers.
    Answer (A) is incorrect. The time horizon for product and customer development is short. Thus, policies may evolve for reasons other than well-researched decision making. Answer (B) is incorrect. Initial costs are high, but the learning curve is steep. When the efficiency gains from experience combine with economies of scale achieved by growth, cost decreases are dramatic. Answer (C) is incorrect. Early mobility barriers tend to consist of willingness to accept risk, proprietary technology, access to resource supplies, and the lower costs of experienced firms. Branding, economies of scale, and the need for capital tend not to be barriers.

10. Which of the following is **not** a limit on emerging industry development?

    A. Raw materials and components.

    B. Subsidies.

    C. Product quality.

    D. Regulatory approval.

Answer (B) is correct.
    REQUIRED: The item that is not a limit on emerging industry development.
    DISCUSSION: Subsidies are a structural characteristic of an emerging market. If a subsidy is given by the government or other party, it usually assists the growth of the new industry instead of hindering it. Subsidies tend to focus on radically new technology or technology in which societal concern is strong.
    Answer (A) is incorrect. Raw materials and components may be scarce. New suppliers must be found or existing suppliers must expand or modify their output. Answer (C) is incorrect. Product quality limits development of emerging industries. Quality may be uneven because of the presence of many firms, technological uncertainty, and lack of standards. Answer (D) is incorrect. The difficulty of obtaining regulatory approval may limit development, especially if customers already are served by a regulated industry.

11. A structural characteristic of an emerging industry is

    A. Strategic uncertainty.

    B. Customers are sophisticated.

    C. Technological uncertainty has been overcome.

    D. Industry development is unlimited.

Answer (A) is correct.
    REQUIRED: The structural characteristic of an emerging industry.
    DISCUSSION: Strategic uncertainty arises because effective strategies have not yet been identified. Hence, firms are experimenting with product features, production methods, marketing approaches, etc. Moreover, competitive intelligence is necessarily poor because competitors have not been identified and industry sales and other data are not available.
    Answer (B) is incorrect. By definition, customers are first-time buyers. The marketing problem is to convince these customers that the benefits of substituting the product or service for something else exceed the risks. Answer (C) is incorrect. An emerging industry is characterized by technological uncertainty regarding products and production methods. Answer (D) is incorrect. Limits on industry development arise because it is new, depends on external entities for growth, and must persuade customers to substitute its product or service for another.

12. A firm considering entry into an emerging industry must be aware of many strategic factors. Thus, the firm must anticipate that

    A. Early mobility barriers are likely to persist.

    B. Early commitment to suppliers is a strategic trap.

    C. The high cost of opening the market favors early entry.

    D. The nature of entrants may change.

Answer (D) is correct.
    REQUIRED: The strategic factor to be considered by a firm considering entry into an emerging industry.
    DISCUSSION: The nature of entrants may change to include larger firms attracted by the proven and less risky industry. Firms must predict when such entry is likely given existing and probable future barriers and the costs of surmounting them. Firms also need to predict how new entrants will compete, e.g., on the basis of marketing power or economies of scale. Furthermore, new entrants may emerge through vertical integration.
    Answer (A) is incorrect. Early mobility barriers may disappear as the industry grows and technology improves. Hence, the firm may no longer be able to rely on early advantages, such as proprietary technology. The necessary response may be a large capital investment. Answer (B) is incorrect. A firm benefits by early awareness and exploitation of the changing role of suppliers and distribution channels, which may become more cooperative as the industry strengthens. Answer (C) is incorrect. The high cost of opening the market is a reason not to enter early.

7.4 Industry Environments -- Declining

13. Which of the following is a reason for a firm to remain in an industry despite poor profits?

    A. Lack of vertical integration.

    B. Economies of scale are not significant.

    C. The firm's assets have a low liquidation value.

    D. Distribution channels are willing to accept new products.

Answer (C) is correct.
    REQUIRED: A reason for a firm to remain in an industry despite poor profits.
    DISCUSSION: Specialized assets and inventory in a declining industry may have a low liquidation value. Few purchasers who wish to operate in the same industry may be available. Durable assets may have a carrying amount far greater than the liquidation value. Hence, liquidation may result in a loss that the firm may not wish to recognize. Furthermore, a low liquidation value means that the future discounted cash flows from remaining in the industry may exceed the opportunity cost of the capital invested in the declining industry. Thus, the returns from the proceeds of liquidation may be less than the returns from keeping those assets in the business.
    Answer (A) is incorrect. Substantial vertical integration increases exit costs when the business to be divested is closely interrelated with others that may be formed by exit. Answer (B) is incorrect. When economies of scale are not significant, entry by new competition is greater. Answer (D) is incorrect. When distribution channels are willing to accept new products, the threat of entry by new competitors is greater.

14. Which of the following is **not** characteristic of a mature industry environment?

    A. Consolidation.

    B. Competitive interdependence.

    C. Falling demand.

    D. Strategic focus on deterring entry of new competitors into the marketplace.

Answer (C) is correct.
    REQUIRED: The characteristic of a mature industry environment.
    DISCUSSION: Falling demand is characteristic of declining industries. These industries have sustained a permanent decrease in unit sales over the long run.

15. A firm in a declining industry that adopts a harvest strategy assumes that

    A. Intense competition is absent.

    B. It can achieve market share gains to become the dominant firm.

    C. The highest recovery is attainable by early sale.

    D. Aggressive marketing will drive out competition.

Answer (A) is correct.
    REQUIRED: The assumption made by a firm in a declining industry that adopts a harvest strategy.
    DISCUSSION: A harvest strategy is in effect a controlled, gradual liquidation. It maximizes cash flow by minimizing new investment, R&D, advertising service, maintenance, etc., and by exploiting the firm's remaining strengths (e.g., goodwill) to increase prices or maintain sales volume. To be successful, the strategy assumes that the firm has certain strengths and intense competition is absent. The strengths permit the firm to maintain sales for a time in the face of price increases, reduced advertising, etc. Absence of intense competition means that other firms will be less likely to seize market share or lower prices. Moreover, a firm must be capable of cost reductions that do not cause immediate failure.
    Answer (B) is incorrect. A leadership strategy is adopted by a firm that believes it can achieve market share gains to become the dominant firm. Answer (C) is incorrect. A quick divestment strategy assumes that the highest net recovery is obtained by sale early in the decline phase. Answer (D) is incorrect. A leadership strategy may entail aggressive marketing.

16. In a declining industry with a favorable structure, a firm may have the ability to recover additional investment or to earn above-average returns in the remaining pockets of demand. Such a firm is most likely to follow a

    A. Quick divestment strategy.

    B. Harvest strategy or quick divestment strategy.

    C. Leadership strategy or harvest strategy.

    D. Leadership strategy or niche strategy.

Answer (D) is correct.
    REQUIRED: The best strategy to follow in a declining market.
    DISCUSSION: A leadership strategy is pursued by a firm that believes it can achieve market share gains to become the dominant firm. An assumption is that additional investment can be recovered. A second assumption is that success will put the firm in a better position to hold its ground or subsequently to follow a harvest strategy. A niche strategy seeks a market segment (pocket of demand) with stable or slowly decreasing demand with the potential for above-average returns. Some of the moves undertaken when following a leadership strategy may be appropriate. The firm may eventually change to a harvest or divest strategy.
    Answer (A) is incorrect. Quick divestment is indicated when the highest net recovery is obtained by a sale of assets early in the decline phase. Answer (B) is incorrect. A harvest strategy is a controlled, gradual liquidation, and quick divestment is a sale of assets early in the decline phase. Answer (C) is incorrect. A harvest strategy is a controlled, gradual liquidation of assets.

7.5 Competition in Global Industries

17. Globalization and localization are shaping the competitive structure of industries. The scenario contributing to the most competitive environment is when

    A. Global forces dominate.

    B. Local forces dominate.

    C. A mix of global and local forces dominate.

    D. Neither global nor local forces dominate.

Answer (C) is correct.
    REQUIRED: The circumstances creating the most competitive environment.
    DISCUSSION: Competitiveness of firms is greatest, and the competitive environment is most intense, when the benefits of global integration and coordination and the benefits of localization (flexibility, proximity, and quick response time) are achieved.
    Answer (A) is incorrect. When global forces dominate, local adaptation and responsiveness are less significant. Answer (B) is incorrect. When local forces dominate, such global forces as efficiency, speed, arbitrage, and learning are less significant. Answer (D) is incorrect. When neither global nor local forces dominate, competition will not be as intense as when both global and local forces confer competitive advantages.

18. Which strategy in a global industry is most likely to be facilitated by a transnational coalition?

    A. A protected niche strategy.

    B. A national focus strategy.

    C. A national segment strategy.

    D. Broad line global competition.

Answer (D) is correct.
    REQUIRED: The strategy in a global industry most likely to be facilitated by a transnational coalition.
    DISCUSSION: Broad line global competition is competition over the full product line of the firm based on differentiation or low cost. The firm needs large resources for this long-term strategy. Governmental relations should emphasize impediment reduction. Transnational coalitions may be created to help the firms overcome impediments to executing the broader strategies, for example, market access or technology barriers.
    Answer (A) is incorrect. A protected niche strategy is applied in nations where global competitors are discouraged by governmental impediments. The strategy is designed to be effective in markets with governmental constraints and requires close attention to the national government. Answer (B) is incorrect. A national focus strategy is limited to a national market or the segments with the greatest economic impediments to global competitors. Low cost or differentiation is sought. Answer (C) is incorrect. A national focus strategy may be limited to national segments with the greatest economic impediments to global competitors. Low cost or differentiation is sought.

19. Which of the following is a source of global competitive advantage?

    A. Low fixed costs.

    B. Production economies of scale.

    C. Weak copyright protection.

    D. Intensive local service requirements.

Answer (B) is correct.
    REQUIRED: The source of global competitive advantage.
    DISCUSSION: Production economies of scale exist when a firm can produce and sell the output at which the average total cost of production is minimized. (The archetypal example is oil refining.) In other words, economies of scale in centralized production may yield a cost advantage achievable only when output exceeds the demand in one country, and exports are feasible.
    Answer (A) is incorrect. Low fixed costs generally imply weak barriers to entry and the consequent ability of local firms to compete effectively against a larger global firm. Answer (C) is incorrect. Weak intellectual property rights enforcement enables small local competitors to produce efficiently, if illicitly, in the short term. Answer (D) is incorrect. Intensive local service requirements dilute the advantage of a large and efficient global competitor.

20. Which strategy in a global industry is most likely to rely on domestic content rules or high tariffs?

    A. A protected niche strategy.

    B. A national focus strategy.

    C. A national segment strategy.

    D. A global focus strategy.

Answer (A) is correct.
    REQUIRED: The strategy most likely to rely on domestic content rules or high tariffs.
    DISCUSSION: A protected niche strategy is applied in nations where global competitors are discouraged by governmental impediments, such as domestic content rules or tariffs. The strategy is designed to be effective in markets with governmental constraints and requires close attention to the national government.
    Answer (B) is incorrect. A national focus strategy is limited to a national market or the segments with the greatest economic impediments to global competitors. Low cost or differentiation is sought. Answer (C) is incorrect. A national focus strategy may be limited to national segments with the greatest economic impediments to global competitors. Low cost or differentiation is sought. Answer (D) is incorrect. A global focus strategy is limited to an industry segment with low impediments where the firm can compete effectively on a global basis against the broad line firms. The focus of competition is low cost or product differentiation.

Access the **CIA Review System** from your Gleim Personal Classroom to continue your studies with exam-emulating multiple-choice questions!

STUDY UNIT EIGHT
STRATEGIC DECISIONS

(31 pages of outline)

This study unit is the third of five covering **Section V: Management/Leadership Principles** from The IIA's CIA Exam Syllabus. This section makes up 10% to 20% of Part 3 of the CIA exam and is tested at the **awareness level**. The relevant portion of the syllabus is highlighted below. (The complete syllabus is in Appendix A.)

V. MANAGEMENT/LEADERSHIP PRINCIPLES (10%–20%)

A. Strategic Management

1. Global analytical techniques
2. Industry environments

3. Strategic decisions
   a. Analysis of integration strategies
   b. Capacity expansion
   c. Entry into new businesses
4. Forecasting
5. Quality management (e.g., TQM, Six Sigma)
6. Decision analysis

B. Organizational Behavior
C. Management Skills/Leadership Styles
D. Conflict Management
E. Project Management/Change Management

The objectivity of an internal auditor is impaired if (s)he makes management decisions. However, as part of their role in improving governance processes, internal auditors must be able to assess strategic decisions made by management.

8.1 INTEGRATION STRATEGIES

1. **Vertical Integration**

   a. Vertical integration combines within a single firm production, distribution, selling, or other separate economic processes needed to deliver a product or service to a customer. All such processes could in principle be performed through market transactions with outside firms.

      1) However, vertical integration uses internal or administrative transactions for these purposes in the expectation they will increase efficiency or decrease costs and risks.

   b. The decision to integrate should consider direct economic issues (needed investment and effects on costs), broader strategic issues, and the potential difficulties of administering a vertically integrated firm. Thus, the extent of integration depends on the balance of economic and administrative benefits and costs.

      1) This balance varies with the industry, the firm's position, and whether the firm engages in

         a) Full integration,

         b) Tapered (partial) integration, or

         c) Quasi-integration (use of alliances, not ownership, to achieve the effects of integration).

   c. Whether integration should occur depends on

      1) The firm's volume of transactions with the external parties (throughput) and

      2) The magnitude of the capability required to achieve necessary economies of scale.

         a) If the integrating firm's need is for a capability less than the efficient scale, one option is to acquire a capability with a cost-inefficient scale.

         b) The other option is to acquire an efficient capability that provides excess output (in the upstream case) or creates excess demand (from, for example, a distribution capability in the downstream case).

            i) This option will require the integrated firm to sell or buy in the open market. Thus, the second option carries the risk of having to deal with competitors.

2. **Strategic Benefits of Vertical Integration**

   a. The following are generic strategic benefits of vertical integration:

      1) **Upstream (backward) integration** is acquisition of a capability that otherwise would be performed by external parties that are suppliers of the firm.

         a) For example, a car manufacturer acquires a company that supplies tires for automobiles.

      2) **Downstream (forward) integration** is acquisition of a capability performed by customers.

         a) For example, a car manufacturer acquires car dealerships that sell and lease the company's cars.

   b. **Economies of vertical integration** occur when throughput is great enough to achieve economies of scale. For example, economies of integration are available when the firm builds a supply facility that is large enough to be cost efficient, and the firm can use all of its output.

      1) Economies of combined operations may reduce production steps, handling and transportation, and slack time. For example, facilities for technologically different processes might be located near each other, or the same machines may be used for different steps.

2) Economies of control and coordination result from

    a) Better delivery scheduling,

    b) Common oversight of functions,

    c) Increased reliability of supply by a related entity,

    d) Internal redesign or new product introductions, and

    e) A leaner control structure.

3) Economies of information are achieved by an integrated firm because

    a) Some information may no longer be needed,

    b) The fixed costs of competitive intelligence and forecasting are borne by additional subunits of the firm, and

    c) Information may flow more rapidly between related than unrelated entities.

4) Economies result from avoiding some market transactions. Transaction costs of dealing with outside parties are greater than those of dealing with inside parties.

5) Stable relationships between internal sellers and buyers create economies because

    a) They need not fear loss of the related buyers and sellers or undue economic pressure from each other.

    b) They may more fully adapt to each other's needs than they would or could in dealings with outsiders.

    c) The relationship is locked in, so more efficient procedures for their relationship (e.g., dedicated controls and records) may be implemented.

c. A tap into technology of upstream or downstream firms is an integration benefit that is a vital economy of information. However, integration to obtain a better understanding of technology is usually tapered so as to manage risk.

d. Providing assurance of supply or demand is an integration benefit because it reduces some of the uncertainty caused by market fluctuations. Thus, the firm has less risk of interruptions, changes in customers and suppliers, or payment of excessive prices in emergencies.

1) However, demand in the absolute sense is not affected. For example, when a downstream subunit faces lower external demand, its internal supplier also faces lower demand.

2) To promote overall firm efficiency, transfer prices most likely should be market-based.

e. Integration benefits include offsetting the bargaining power of strong suppliers and customers.

1) If such parties have returns greater than the firm's opportunity cost of capital, the firm benefits even if no other advantages result from integration.

    a) Thus, upstream integration eliminates input cost distortion caused by the supplier's power, and downstream integration eliminates the customer's power to obtain an unjustifiably low price.

        i) Moreover, the special costs of dealing with powerful parties also are eliminated.

    b) Upstream integration also has the advantage of disclosing the true cost of the input provided by the powerful supplier. This information helps the firm to adjust its input mix and prices.

f. An integrated firm may have a better ability to differentiate itself because it has greater opportunities to offer value to customers, such as by improved service through integrated distribution channels.

g.   Integration that generates any of the benefits described on the previous page also raises entry and mobility barriers. Integration may provide a competitive advantage not matched by a nonintegrated firm, especially if it requires large capital investment or economies of scale.

h.   Integration may increase the firm's overall return on investment after considering any costs of overcoming barriers to integration.

i.   Integration may be a defense against foreclosure of access to suppliers or customers. It is a response to integration by competitors who threaten to secure the low-cost or high-quality suppliers, favorable distribution channels, or largest customers.

   1)   Defensive integration also increases mobility when investment or economies of scale are large.

3.   **Strategic Costs of Vertical Integration**

   a.   The following are generic strategic costs of vertical integration:

      1)   Integration is a special case of entry into a new business. The firm must incur costs to overcome mobility barriers to enter the adjacent business, such as economies of scale, proprietary technology, capital investment, and sources of materials.

      2)   Integration increases fixed costs and operating leverage, which is in itself a cause of increased business risk.

         a)   Thus, an integrated firm is exposed to fluctuations affecting any of its components. For example, sales of an upstream component depend on sales of downstream components.

      3)   Integration reduces the flexibility to change business partners because it increases the costs of switching to different suppliers or customers.

      4)   Integration may increase any exit barriers.

      5)   Integration requires investment capital. The return must at least equal the firm's opportunity cost of capital (after considering all strategic analytical factors).

         a)   Furthermore, the integration decision is in part dependent on the appetite for capital of the adjacent business to be entered. The danger is that it may continually require capital that could be more profitably invested elsewhere in the firm.

            i)   This loss of flexibility of capital allocation may prevent profitable diversification.

      6)   Integration may foreclose access to supplier or customer technology. The integrated firm may have to create its own technology rather than taking advantage of supplier/customer expertise.

      7)   Integration requires maintaining a balance among the operations of the firm's subunits. Excess output or demand of a subunit may require selling to, or buying from, competitors unless the needs can be satisfied by sales or purchases on the open market.

         a)   Imbalance may result because of unequal changes in capacity caused by technological change or alterations in the product mix or quality.

      8)   Integration may reduce incentives. For example, a buyer may not bargain as aggressively with an in-house seller, and a seller may not compete as aggressively because it is ensured of a customer.

         a)   Accordingly, internal projects may not be as carefully considered as external transactions. The response is for management to require that internal relationships be treated as if they are genuinely at arm's length.

         b)   Furthermore, subunit managers must resist the natural temptation to assist a failing subunit, thereby damaging the successful subunits.

9) A significant cost and risk of integration is that subunits have differing managerial requirements. It is a mistake to apply the same methods used in the core business to other parts of the integrated firm.

4. **Forward Integration**

   a. Enhanced product differentiation may follow forward integration because of better control of production, marketing, retailing, or service that adds value.

   b. Forward integration may secure access to distribution channels.

   c. Access to market information is improved. A forward subunit (the demand leading stage) controls the amount and mix of demand to be satisfied upstream.

      1) At the very least, forward integration improves

         a) The timeliness of demand information,
         b) Production planning,
         c) Inventory control, and
         d) The costs of being under- or overstocked.

      2) It also may provide information about changing tastes, competitors' moves, and the ideal mix of products.

      3) Whether forward integration is a suitable strategy depends on the relative instability of demand and the effect on information reliability of the number of customers.

   d. Forward integration may permit higher price realization, for example, by moving into businesses in which the price elasticity of demand is relatively high and lower prices must be set.

      1) When demand is elastic, raising prices decreases revenue. Thus, the firm may benefit by acquiring customers with high elasticities while selling to customers with low elasticities.

5. **Backward Integration**

   a. Backward integration allows the firm to protect its proprietary knowledge from suppliers.

   b. Controlling inputs may permit the firm to differentiate its product more effectively, or at least to argue persuasively that it does so.

6. **Contracts and Economies of Integration**

   a. Some of the economies of integration may be secured by contracts (long- or short-term) with independent parties, for example, through a long-term agreement with a supplier to provide all of the firm's needs for an input. However, such arrangements may be difficult to create because of the parties' dissimilar interests and the risks involved.

   b. Tapered (partial) integration implies that the firm can fully support an efficient subunit but has additional needs to be met in the market. If the in-house subunit will not be efficient, that inefficiency must be weighed against the benefits of tapering.

      1) Tapering results in lower fixed costs than full integration. Furthermore, the strategy may allow the firm's subunit(s) to maintain constant production rates while external parties bear the risk of fluctuations.

         a) Another use of tapering is to protect against operational imbalances (excesses of output or demand) among the subunits.

2) Risks of tapering include greater coordination cost and selling to, or buying from, competitors.

3) Advantages of tapering are

   a) Avoidance of locked-in relationships,

   b) Some access to external expertise,

   c) Increased managerial incentives,

   d) Offering a credible threat of full integration to suppliers or customers, and

   e) Obtaining knowledge of the adjacent business and an emergency supply source.

c. Quasi-integration is something more than a long-term contract and less than full ownership. It may be achieved by a minority common stock interest, debt guarantees, cooperation in R&D, an exclusive dealing arrangement, etc.

   1) Buyer and seller may, as a result, have a common interest leading to lower costs, smoothing of supply/demand fluctuations, or mitigating against bargaining power.

   2) Quasi-integration may avoid commitment to an adjacent business with its investment and management requirements. But many benefits of full integration may not be achievable in this way.

7. **Common Illusions of Integration**

   a. Strength in one part of the chain necessarily carries over to the other parts.
   b. Doing something internally is less expensive.
   c. Integrating into a highly competitive business is often wise.
   d. Integration may save a strategically sick firm.
   e. Experience in one part of the chain always carries over to other parts.

Stop and review! You have completed the outline for this subunit. Study multiple-choice questions 1 and 2 beginning on page 193.

8.2 CAPACITY EXPANSION

1. **Overview**

   a. Whether to expand capacity is a major strategic decision because of (1) the capital required, (2) the difficulty of forecasting, (3) the long lead times, and (4) the commitment. The key forecasts are long-term demand and behavior of competitors.

   1) The key strategic issue is avoidance of industry overcapacity.

   2) Undercapacity in a profitable industry tends to be a short-term issue. Profits ordinarily attract more investors. Overcapacity tends to be a long-term problem because firms are more likely to compete intensely rather than reverse their expansion.

   b. Formal capital budgeting involves predicting cash flows related to the expansion, discounting them at an appropriate interest rate, and determining whether the net present value is positive. This process permits comparison with other uses of the firm's resources.

   1) The apparent simplicity of this process is deceptive. It depends upon, among many other things, which expansion method is chosen, developments in technology, and profitability. Profitability in turn depends on such uncertainties as total long-term demand and the expansion plans of rival firms.

2. **The Decision to Expand Capacity**

    a. Porter's model of the decision process for capacity expansion has the following interrelated steps:

        1) The firm must identify the options in relation to their size, type, degree of vertical integration (if any), and possible response by competitors.

        2) The second step is to forecast demand, input costs, and technology developments. The firm must be aware that its technology may become obsolete or that future design changes to allow expansion may or may not be possible.

            a) Moreover, the expansion itself may put upward pressure on input prices.

        3) The next step is analysis of competitors to determine when each will expand. The difficulty is that forecasting their behavior depends on knowing their expectations.

            a) Another difficulty is that each competitor's actions potentially affect all other competitors' actions, with the industry leader being most influential.

        4) Using the information from the first three steps, the firm predicts total industry capacity and firms' market shares. These estimates, together with the expected demand, permit the firm to predict prices and cash flows.

        5) The final step is testing for inconsistencies.

    b. The extent of uncertainty about future demand is a crucial variable in industry expansion. For example, if uncertainty is great, firms willing to take greater risks because of their large cash resources or strategic stake in the industry will act first. Other firms will await events.

    c. When demand uncertainty is low, firms will tend to adopt a strategy of preemption, usually with strong market signals, to deter expansion by competitors.

        1) Excess preemption leads to excess industry capacity because firms

            a) Overestimate their competitive strengths,
            b) Misunderstand market signals, or
            c) Fail to accurately assess competitors' intentions.

3. **Causes of Overexpansion**

    a. Overbuilding occurs when existing firms **overexpand** production capabilities to take advantage of current undercapacity in an industry.

        1) Causes of overbuilding extend beyond poorly played games of preemption.

    b. Overbuilding is most frequent in firms that produce commodities.

        1) One reason is that such firms are usually cyclical so that capacity is always excessive at low points in the cycle. Moreover, many tend to overestimate the strength of upturns.

        2) A second reason is that commodities tend to be undifferentiated. Thus, competition is based on price, cost efficiency is crucial, and sales depend on capacity.

    c. The following are **technological** factors that may lead to overbuilding:

        1) Capacity may need to be added in large increments.

        2) The presence of economies of scale or the learning curve effect encourages preemption (discussed in more detail on page 171).

        3) Long lead times for adding capacity increase the risk of competitive inferiority if a firm does not act quickly to begin raising its capacity.

4) When the minimum efficient scale increases, large plants are becoming more efficient. Unless demand is growing, the number of plants must decline to avoid overbuilding.

5) Changes in production technology result in new construction while old plants remain in operation, particularly when exit barriers are high.

d. The following are **structural** factors that may lead to overbuilding:

1) When exit barriers are high, the period of overcapacity is extended.

2) Competitive pressures on suppliers of capital, equipment, materials, etc., may promote expansion by customer industries. Examples of competitive pressures include (a) lower supply prices, (b) government subsidies, (c) favorable interest rates, and (d) similar incentives.

3) Credibility of new products is promoted by capacity expansion that gives assurance to large buyers. Such customers need to know that capacity will exist to meet their long-term needs and that a few suppliers will not have excessive bargaining power.

4) When competitors are integrated, the pressure to build despite uncertain demand intensifies. Each firm wants to ensure that it can supply its downstream operations.

5) Capacity leadership is important in some industries as a means of increasing market share. Customers may be more likely to buy from the capacity leader.

   a) The age and type of capacity also may be competitive advantages.

e. The following are **competitive** factors that may lead to overbuilding:

1) Many firms with the ability to add capacity want to improve market share.

2) The lack of a credible market leader makes for a less orderly expansion. A stronger leader can retaliate effectively against inappropriate expansion by others.

3) New entrants, possibly encouraged by low entry barriers and favorable economic conditions, may cause or intensify overcapacity.

4) First mover advantages may be significant. Thus, shorter lead times for ordering equipment, lower costs, and the ability to exploit an excess of demand over supply may encourage too many firms to expand.

f. The following are **information flow** factors that may lead to overbuilding:

1) Future expectations may be inflated because of industry buzz.

2) Firms' assumptions or perceptions about competitors' strengths, weaknesses, and plans may be inaccurate.

3) Market signaling may be ineffective because it is no longer regarded as credible. Firms' signals may no longer be trusted as indicators of planned moves, such as expansion, because of new entrants, a period of bitter rivalry, or other reasons.

4) Changes in industry structure may lead directly to new investment or create uncertainties leading to faulty decisions.

5) The financial community encourages overbuilding when analysts criticize firms that have not expanded. Also, management's optimistic comments to the financial community may be taken as aggressive signals by competitors.

g. The following are **managerial** factors that may lead to overbuilding:

1) Management that is production-oriented may be more likely to overbuild than marketing- or finance-oriented management.

2) A manager's career risk is asymmetric when the consequences of overcapacity appear to be less serious than those of undercapacity.

h. The following are governmental factors that may lead to overbuilding:

1) Tax incentives may promote excess capacity, for example, by permitting foreign subsidiaries to pay no tax on earnings retained in the business.

2) A nation may wish to create a local industry. When the minimum efficient scale is great in relation to worldwide demand, the excess production in the country may contribute to global overcapacity.

3) Governmental employment pressures may result in overbuilding to create jobs or avoid job loss.

i. The following are limits on capacity expansion:

1) Most firms have great uncertainty about future conditions.

2) The firm faces financial limitations.

3) The firm is diversified. As a result, the opportunity cost of capital is greater, and management's perspective is broader.

4) Senior managers have finance backgrounds.

5) Expansion is costly, e.g., because of environmental regulations.

6) The firm experienced distress during a prior period of overbuilding.

7) A firm's behavior sends signals to competitors that building is unwise. For example, it may announce an expansion project or indicate in some way that forecasts of demand are unfavorable or that current technology will soon be obsolete.

4. **Preemptive Strategies**

a. Preemption requires investments in plant facilities and the ability to accept short-term unfavorable results. The strategy is risky because it anticipates demand and often sets prices in the expectation of future cost efficiencies. Moreover, a failed preemption strategy may provoke intense, industry-damaging conflict. The following conditions must be met for the strategy to succeed:

1) The expansion must be large relative to the market, and competitors must believe that the move is preemptive. Hence, the firm should know competitors' expectations about the market or be able to influence them favorably. A move that is too small is by definition not preemptive.

2) Economies of scale should be large in relation to demand, or the learning-curve effect will give an initial large investor a permanent cost advantage.

a) For example, the preemptive firm may be able to secure too much of the market to allow a subsequent firm to invest at the efficient scale. That is, the residual demand available to be met by the later firm is less than the efficient scale of production. The later firm therefore must choose between intense competition at the efficient scale or a cost disadvantage.

3) The preempting firm must have credibility to support its statements and moves, such as resources, technology, and a history of credibility.

4) The firm must provide credible signals before action by competitors.

5) The competitors of the firm should be willing not to act. This condition may not be met if competitors have noneconomic objectives, the business is strategically vital to them, or they have greater ability or willingness to compete.

Stop and review! You have completed the outline for this subunit. Study multiple-choice questions 3 and 4 on page 194.

8.3 ENTRY INTO NEW BUSINESSES

1. **Entry through Internal Development**

    a. Entry through internal development ordinarily involves creation of a new business entity. This internal entrant must cope with structural barriers and retaliation by existing firms.

    b. Thus, costs include

        1) Initial investments to overcome entry barriers (facilities, inventory, branding, technology, distribution channels, sources of materials, etc.),

        2) Operating losses in the start-up phase,

        3) The effects of retaliation (e.g., higher marketing costs, capacity expansion, or lower prices), and

        4) Price increases for factors of production that may result because of the new entry.

    c. Also, the capacity added to the industry by the entrant may affect the equilibrium level of supply and demand.

        1) The result may be additional competitive costs as firms with excess capacity cut prices.

    d. An internal entrant is most likely to cause industry disruption and retaliation, with a consequent negative effect on future results, in the following industries:

        1) In a slow-growth industry, existing firms cannot compensate for the loss in market share, and the added capacity will depress prices.

        2) If the product is a commodity or is commodity-like, brand identification and market segmentation do not exist to protect existing firms. Price cuts are probable.

        3) High fixed costs indicate that existing firms will retaliate if their capacity usage decreases materially.

        4) In a highly concentrated industry, the internal entrant is more likely to have a significant and noticeable effect on particular firms with the ability to retaliate.

            a) In a fragmented industry, many firms might be affected but not significantly. These firms also might have no ability to retaliate.

        5) Existing firms view the industry as strategically important, e.g., as a source of cash flow or growth or because of integration.

        6) Management attitudes of well-established firms, especially if engaged in a single business, may provide a psychological basis for retaliation. An internal entrant should consider the prior reactions of such firms to new entrants or to existing firms that attempted to move to a new strategic group.

    e. The internal entrant should undertake a structural analysis, including consideration of profitability as a function of the five competitive forces, to identify target industries.

        1) If the industry is in equilibrium, the internal entrant should expect normal (average) profits even if established firms earn above-average profits. The reason is that the internal entrant's costs exceed those of existing firms. It must pay the costs of overcoming entry barriers and coping with retaliation.

            a) If the entry costs did not negate above-average profits, other firms would previously have entered the industry and lowered the available profits.

            b) Consequently, unless the firm has special advantages, it should most likely not target an industry in equilibrium.

2) However, a firm may be able to achieve above-average profits by choosing appropriate targets, such as an industry in disequilibrium.

    a) An industry may be in disequilibrium.

        i) In a new industry, (a) the structure is not established, (b) entry barriers are low, (c) retaliation is unlikely, (d) resource supplies are not yet controlled by existing firms, and (e) brands are not well developed.

            • However, initial firms may have greater costs than later entrants if entry barriers are low.

        ii) Rising entry barriers favor an early entrant whose subsequent competitors will incur higher costs. The early entrant also may have an advantage in product differentiation.

        iii) Poor information may perpetuate disequilibrium because firms that might enter the industry may not be aware of its potential.

        iv) An internal entrant must understand that the indicators of disequilibrium may be apparent to other firms.

            • Hence, the firm's decision to enter should be based on some advantage that will enable it to earn above-average profits.

    b) The balance of expected profits and entry costs may be favorable when existing firms do not or cannot retaliate against the internal entrant swiftly and effectively. Industries of this kind do not have the attributes discussed earlier in item 1.d. The following are other relevant factors:

        i) The costs to existing firms of retaliation may exceed the benefits. The new firm also may be able to persuade existing firms that the costs are excessive.

        ii) The industry may have a dominant firm or a long-time leadership group that acts to protect the industry rather than maximize its own standing, e.g., by retaliating against a new entrant.

        iii) Existing firms' costs of retaliation are high in relation to the need to protect their business. For example, a response might alienate distributors, reduce sales of key products, or be inconsistent with the retaliating firm's image.

        iv) Conventional wisdom about industry operating practices may impair the ability of existing firms to retaliate. A new firm may perceive circumstances in which the conventional wisdom does not apply.

    c) Lower industry entry costs may be incurred by a firm with special advantages, such as a well-known brand, proprietary technology, or a strong distribution network.

        i) Moreover, the respect for such a powerful competitor may deter retaliation.

    d) A distinctive ability to influence industry structure is another basis for earning above-average profits. Thus, an ability to raise mobility barriers after the firm has entered the industry is a reason to target that industry. Furthermore, a firm may be able to recognize that entering a fragmented industry will start a process of consolidation and increased entry barriers.

    e) Internal entry having a positive effect on the firm's existing businesses is justified even if above-average profits cannot be earned in the new industry.

f.   The following basic entry strategies are methods of inexpensively overcoming entry barriers:

1)   Product costs may be reduced by use of new process technology, economies of scale, a modern plant, or sharing functions with existing businesses.

2)   A low initial price that sacrifices profits for market share may succeed if competitors do not retaliate.

3)   A better product or service overcomes the product differentiation barrier.

4)   Barriers can be overcome by finding an unserved niche market.

5)   A marketing innovation overcomes product differentiation and distribution barriers.

6)   Use of an established distribution network is another way to overcome entry barriers.

2.   **Entry by Acquisition**

a.   The analysis of entry by acquisition differs from that for entry by internal development. A key point is that prices are set in the market for acquisitions. In the industrialized countries, this market is active and well organized, indicating that it is also efficient and therefore tends to eliminate above-average profits.

b.   One factor contributing to efficiency (and the elimination of above-average profits for a buyer) is that a seller normally can choose to continue running the business.

1)   Accordingly, a bidder ordinarily must pay the seller a premium in excess of the expected present value to the seller of continuing operations. The price minus that floor value equals the premium.

c.   Acquisitions are most likely to earn above-average profits when

1)   The floor is low, e.g., because the seller perceives that it needs funds, has management weaknesses, or cannot grow or compete because of capital limits.

2)   The market for acquisitions is imperfect.

a)   The buyer may have better information.
b)   There are few bidders.
c)   The economy is weak.
d)   The seller is weak.
e)   The seller has reasons to sell other than profit maximization.

3)   The buyer may have a unique ability to operate the seller.

a)   The buyer may be uniquely able to improve operations.
b)   The buyer purchases a firm in an industry that meets one of the conditions for an internal entrant to earn above-average profits.
c)   The purchase may improve the buyer's position in its current businesses.

4)   A pitfall to avoid is competition from irrational bidders. An acquisition may be a genuine or perceived value to the irrational bidder, which exceeds the value to the firm.

d.   Sequential entry may be the best entry strategy. It involves entering one strategic group in the industry with subsequent mobility to another group.

Stop and review! You have completed the outline for this subunit. Study multiple-choice questions 5 and 6 beginning on page 194.

8.4 FORECASTING -- TIME-SERIES MODELS

1. **Overview**

   a. Forecasts attempt to answer questions about the outcomes of events (e.g., the effect of a war involving a producer of oil on the oil market) or the timing of events (e.g., when will unemployment fall). Forecasts are the basis for business plans.

   b. Examples of forecasts include sales projections, inventory demand, cash flow, and future capital needs.

2. **Forecasting Methods**

   a. Qualitative (judgment) methods rely on experience and human intuition.

      1) The Delphi method summarizes the opinions of experts regarding a given problem. These summaries are then fed back to the experts without revealing the identities of the other participants. The process is repeated until the opinions converge on an optimal solution.

   b. Quantitative methods use mathematical models and graphs.

      1) Causal relationship forecasting quantifies the link between some factor in the organization's environment (the independent variable, plotted on the horizontal axis) and an outcome at a moment in time (the dependent variable, plotted on the vertical axis).

         a) The most common of these techniques is linear regression, discussed in Subunit 8.6.

      2) Time series analysis relies on past experience to project future outcomes. The time dimension is plotted on the horizontal axis.

         a) Time series analysis includes trend projection, moving average, exponential smoothing, and learning curves.

3. **Trend Analysis**

   a. Trend analysis fits a trend line to the data and extrapolates it.

      1) The dependent variable (sales, profits, etc.) is regressed (i.e., plotted on the y axis) on time (the independent variable, plotted on the x axis).

   b. Changes in business activity over time may have several possible components:

      1) The secular trend is the long-term change that occurs despite variability.

      2) Seasonal variations are common in many businesses, most obviously retail, which experiences a large increase in activity during the winter holidays.

         a) To remove the effect of seasonal variation from a time series, the original data are divided by the seasonal factor.

      3) Cyclical fluctuations are variations related to the level of aggregate economic activity.

      4) Irregular or random variables are the random happenings that affect business (weather, strikes, fires, etc.).

4. **Moving Average**

   a.   A moving average is appropriate when the demand for a product is relatively stable and not subject to seasonal variations.

   b.   Each period's average includes the newest observation and discards the oldest one, illustrated in the table below:

				Moving Average			
Month	Sales	January Forecast	February Forecast	March Forecast	April Forecast	May Forecast	June Forecast
September	US $6,200	US $ 6,200					
October	6,000	6,000	US $ 6,000				
November	5,800	5,800	5,800	US $ 5,800			
December	5,600	5,600	5,600	5,600	US $ 5,600		
January	5,400	US $23,600	5,400	5,400	5,400	US $ 5,400	
February	5,500	÷ 4	US $22,800	5,500	5,500	5,500	US $ 5,500
March	5,700	US $ 5,900	÷ 4	US $22,300	5,700	5,700	5,700
April	5,800		US $ 5,700	÷ 4	US $22,200	5,800	5,800
May	5,900			US $ 5,575	÷ 4	US $22,400	5,900
					US $ 5,550	÷ 4	US $22,900
						US $ 5,600	÷ 4
							US $ 5,725

5. **Exponential Smoothing**

   a.   Exponential smoothing is useful when large amounts of data cannot be retained.

      1)   Exponential means that greater weight is placed on the most recent data, with the weight assigned to older data falling off exponentially.

   b.   The selection of the smoothing factor, called alpha (α), is important because a high alpha places more weight on recent data.

      1)   The forecast for a period is the result for the previous period times the smoothing factor, plus the forecast for the previous period times 1 minus the smoothing factor.

6. **Learning Curves**

   a.   A learning curve reflects the increased rate at which people perform tasks as they gain experience. The result is a decrease in labor hours (and costs) for a given quantity of output.

   b.   The time required to perform a given task becomes progressively shorter during the early stages of production (see the following figure).

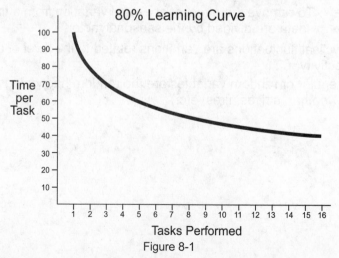

Figure 8-1

c. The following are the two best known learning curve **models**:

1) In the **cumulative average-time learning model**, the assumption is that the cumulative average time **per task** (e.g., a unit of production) decreases by a constant percentage each time the cumulative quantity of tasks doubles. For example, if (a) unit output in a production process doubles from 10 to 20 and (b) the learning curve is estimated to be 80%, the cumulative average time for 20 units is projected to be 80% of the cumulative average time for 10 units.

2) In the **incremental unit-time learning model**, the assumption is that the incremental (additional) time to perform the **last task** (e.g., a unit of production) decreases by a constant percentage each time the cumulative quantity of tasks doubles. For example, if (a) unit output in a production process doubles from 10 to 20 and (b) the learning curve is estimated to be 80%, the time needed to produce the 20th unit is 80% of the time needed to produce the 10th unit.

EXAMPLE

A firm determines that 100 minutes of labor are required to complete one unit of product. Assuming an 80% learning curve, the following table illustrates the difference between the two methods.

Learning Curve 80% at Each Doubling		Cumulative Average-Time Model		Incremental Unit-Time Model	
(A) Unit Produced	(B) Time per Unit	(A) × (B) Cumulative Total Time	Time Spent on Last Unit	Σ(B) Cumulative Total Time	Σ (B) ÷ (A) Cumulative Average Time per Unit
1	100.00	100.00	100.00	100.00	100.00
2	80.00 (100 × 80%)	160.00 (80 × 2)	60.00 (160 – 100)	180.00 (100 + 80)	90.00 (180 ÷ 2)
3	70.21	210.63	50.63	250.21	83.40
4	64.00 (80 × 80%)	256.00 (64 × 4)	45.37 (256 – 210.63)	314.21 (250.21 + 64)	78.55 (314.21 ÷ 4)

---

d. The cumulative average-time model is the most common.

e. The limitation of the learning curve in practice is the difficulty in knowing the shape of the learning curve.

1) The learning curve effect undoubtedly exists, but firms typically do not know what percentage to use in calculations until after it is too late to use the information effectively. As a result, many firms simply assume an 80% learning curve and make decisions based on those results.

f. The curve is usually expressed as a percentage of reduced time to complete a task for each doubling of cumulative production. The most common percentage used in practice is 80%.

1) An 80% learning curve indicates that a doubling of production will reduce the cumulative average unit completion time by 20%.

g. The following table assumes an 80% learning curve for a product whose first unit takes 100 minutes to produce:

Cumulative Units Produced	Total Time	Cumulative Average Time per Unit	The Learning Rate %
1	100	100	–
2	160	80 = (160 ÷ 2) = (100 × 80%)	[160 ÷ (100 × 2)] = 80%
4	256	64 = (256 ÷ 4) = (80 × 80%)	[256 ÷ (160 × 2)] = 80%
8	409.6	51.2 = (409.6 ÷ 8) = (64 × 80%)	[409.6 ÷ (256 × 2)] = 80%
16	655.36	40.96 = (655.36 ÷ 16) = (51.2 × 80%)	[655.36 ÷ (409.6 × 2)] = 80%

1) With more sophisticated quantitative techniques, a more accurate average can be calculated of the units within each "batch."

a) With the completion of the final batch (units 9 through 16), the average had come down to 40.96 minutes.

b) For it to reach this level from the 51.2 minutes it had reached at the end of the fourth batch (units 5 through 8), the average of the units in the fifth batch alone must have been 30.72 minutes [(40.96 minutes × 2) − 51.2 minutes], or [(655.36 minutes − 409.6 minutes) ÷ (16 units − 8 units)].

Stop and review! You have completed the outline for this subunit. Study multiple-choice question 7 on page 195.

8.5 FORECASTING -- PROBABILISTIC MODELS

1. **Simulation**

    a. Simulation experiments with logical and mathematical models using a computer. Because of the behavior of the many variables involved and the complexity of their interactions, many problems cannot be solved by using simple algebraic formulas.

        1) The availability of computer spreadsheets makes the construction of simulation models a practical alternative for all sizes of entities.

    b. The first step is to define the objectives. Examples include

        1) Increasing the understanding of an existing system (e.g., an inventory system with rising costs);

        2) Exploring alternatives (e.g., the effect of investments on the firm's financial structure); and

        3) Estimating the behavior of a new system, such as a production line.

    c. The second step is to define the variables, their individual behavior, and their interrelationships in precise logical-mathematical terms. The variables then must be included in a coherent model.

    d. The third step is to obtain some assurance that the model will adequately predict the desired results.

        1) This can be accomplished by entering historical data into the model and comparing the output with actual results.

    e. The fourth step is to design the experiment. (Experimentation is sampling the operation of a system.) For example, if a change in a cost-flow assumption is simulated on an inventory model for 2 years, the results are a single sample.

        1) With replication, the sample size and the confidence level can be increased. The number of runs to be made, length of each run, measurements to be made, and methods for analyzing the results are part of the design of the experiment.

    f. The fifth and final step is to perform the simulation and analyze the results using appropriate statistical methods.

2. **Monte Carlo Simulation**

    a. Monte Carlo simulation uses a random number generator to produce individual values for a random variable.

        1) These numbers have a uniform probability distribution (equal likelihoods of occurrence). They are then transformed into values consistent with the desired distribution.

    b. The performance of a quantitative model may be investigated by randomly selecting values for each of the variables in the model (based on the probability distribution of each variable) and then calculating the value of the solution.

        1) If this process is performed many times, the distribution of results from the model will be obtained.

    c.   For example, a new marketing model includes a factor for a competitor's introduction of a similar product any month within the next 3 years. The earlier the competitor releases this product, the sooner the firm's revenues will begin to decrease. Each month has an equal chance of being the month the competitor releases its product. A Monte Carlo simulation will allow the firm to gauge the effects on future revenues without knowing for certain the competitor's launch date.

        1)   The marketing department generates 1,000 random numbers between 1 and 36 to represent each of the months in the next 3 years. Thus, each month has an equal chance of being the launch month.

            a)   The Monte Carlo simulation could choose any number of random simulations, but in this example, the marketing department chooses 1,000. They could have chosen 2,000, 10,000, or 100,000.

        2)   The simulation model, which has the unknown variable for the competitor's launch date, is then run 1,000 times, each time using one of the generated random numbers to indicate which month the competitor's product will launch. The results help the firm estimate its revenues over the next 3 years.

3. Sensitivity Analysis

    a.   After a problem has been formulated into any mathematical model, it may be subjected to sensitivity analysis, which examines how the model's outcomes change as the parameters change. Examples include the following:

        1)   Cost-volume-profit analysis can be used to determine how changes in the amounts of fixed costs and level of production will affect profitability.

        2)   Capital budgeting can be used to determine how changes in assumptions about interest rates affect a project's profitability.

4. Markov Process

    a.   A Markov process quantifies the likelihood of a future event based on the current state of the process.

        1)   For example, a machine tool may be in one of two states, in adjustment or out of adjustment. Over time, the manufacturer can predict how likely the machine is to be in (out of) adjustment tomorrow based on its being in (out of) adjustment today.

    b.   Another application is the aging of accounts receivable. An entity can predict how likely a 60-day-old receivable is to become a 90-day-old receivable, and how likely a 90-day-old receivable is to become delinquent.

        1)   Such a series of successive probabilities is termed Markov chain analysis.

        2)   Markov chain analysis also can be used to estimate the allowance for doubtful accounts.

    NOTE: Probabilistic models also are called stochastic, meaning that they contain both determinable and random elements.

5. Game Theory

    a.   Game theory is a mathematical approach to decision making when confronted with an enemy or competitor. Games are classified according to the number of players and the algebraic sum of the payoffs.

        1)   In a two-player game, if the payoff is given by the loser to the winner, the algebraic sum is zero, and the game is a **zero-sum game**. If it is possible for both players to profit, the game is a **positive-sum game**.

            a)   A decision that results in neither player improving his or her position is a no-win strategy.

2) In a **cooperative game**, the players are permitted to negotiate and form binding agreements prior to the selection of strategies. In these games, the sums of certain payoff combinations do not equal zero.

3) The prisoner's dilemma is a special outcome of a partly competitive game in which each player has a strategy that dominates all other strategies. However, when each player chooses his or her dominant strategy, the outcome for both is less favorable than if one or both chooses some other strategy.

4) Games against nature are formulations of problems in which only one player chooses a strategy, and the set of outcomes and payoffs is not influenced by the selection.

6. **Decision Making under Uncertainty**

   a. Various decision rules based on the level of risk accepted by the decision maker have been developed.

   1) In this example, a small business wishes to open a new store in one of five locations. Market research provides the following payoff table:

Location:		A	B	C	D	E
	High	US $18	US $20	US $16	US $28	US $25
Traffic Level	Medium	15	11	5	13	9
	Low	(2)	5	2	(4)	(7)

   2) The **maximax** criterion is applied by risk-seeking, optimistic decision makers. They select the option with the highest potential payoff regardless of the state of nature. In the example, it is location D (US $28).

   3) The **maximin** criterion is applied by conservative (risk-averse) decision makers. They select the option with the lowest potential loss (or the highest potential payoff) from the set of worst possible outcomes (low traffic level in this example) for each alternative, i.e., "the best of the worst." In the example, it is location B (US $5).

   4) The **minimax** regret criterion is applied by decision makers with moderate appetites for risk. This strategy seeks to minimize the effect of a bad decision in either direction (minimize opportunity loss).

   a) To determine the location meeting this criterion, an opportunity loss table must be prepared for each state of nature:

Opportunity Loss Tables

High traffic:	A	B	C	D	E
Highest profit of other locations	US $ 28	US $ 28	US $ 28		US $ 28
Profit	(18)	(20)	(16)		(25)
Opportunity loss	US $ 10	US $ 8	US $ 12		US $ 3

Medium traffic:	A	B	C	D	E
Highest profit of other locations		US $ 15	US $15	US $ 15	US $15
Profit		(11)	(5)	(13)	(9)
Opportunity loss		US $ 4	US $10	US $ 2	US $ 6

Low traffic:	A	B	C	D	E
Highest profit of other locations	US $5		US $ 5	US $5	US $ 5
Loss (profit)	2		(2)	4	7
Opportunity loss	US $7		US $ 3	US $9	US $12

   b) The decision maker next identifies the maximum regret (highest potential profit forgone) for each location:

Location:	A	B	C	D	E
Maximum regret	US $10	US $8	US $12	US $9	US $12

   c) The location with the lowest maximum regret is B (US $8).

5) The **insufficient reason** (Laplace) criterion may be used by a risk-neutral player when probabilities cannot be assigned.

    a) The assumption is that, with no probability distribution, the probabilities must be equal, and the payoffs for the states of nature are simply added. The decision with the highest total is chosen.

6) An **expected value** criterion may be used by a risk-neutral player, that is, one for whom the utility of a gain is the same as the disutility of an equal loss.

7. **Expected Value**

    a. When risk is quantifiable, expected value is a rational means of making the best decision (a choice among options).

        1) The expected value of a decision is found by multiplying the probability of each state of nature by its payoff and adding the products. The best choice has the highest expected value.

EXAMPLE

An investor is considering the purchase of two identically priced pieces of property. The value of the properties will change if a road currently planned by the state is built.

The following are estimates that road construction will occur:

Future State of Nature (SN)	Event	Probability
SN 1	No road is ever built.	.1
SN 2	A road is built this year.	.2
SN 3	A road is built more than 1 year from now.	.7

The following are estimates of the values of the properties under each of the three possible events:

Property	SN 1	SN 2	SN 3
Bivens Tract	US $10,000	US $40,000	US $35,000
Newnan Tract	US $20,000	US $50,000	US $30,000

The expected value of each property is determined by multiplying the probability of each state of nature by the value under that state of nature and adding all of the products.

		Expected Value
Bivens Tract:	.1(US $10,000) + .2($40,000) + .7($35,000) =	**US $33,500**
Newnan Tract:	.1(US $20,000) + .2($50,000) + .7($30,000) =	**US $33,000**

Thus, the Bivens Tract is the better investment.

Stop and review! You have completed the outline for this subunit. Study multiple-choice questions 8 and 9 on page 195.

8.6 REGRESSION AND CORRELATION

1. **Simple Regression**

    a. Regression analysis is the process of deriving the linear equation that describes the relationship between two variables.

        1) Simple regression is used when exactly one independent variable is involved, and multiple regression is used when there is more than one.

    b. The simple regression equation is the algebraic formula for a straight line.

$$y = a + bx$$

Where: y = the dependent variable
a = the y intercept
b = the slope of the regression line
x = the independent variable

        1) The best straight line that fits a set of data points is derived using calculus.

    c.   Regression analysis is particularly valuable for budgeting and cost accounting purposes.

        1)   One extremely common application of simple regression in a business setting is the estimation of a mixed cost function, i.e., one with a fixed component and a variable component.

        2)   The y-axis intercept is the fixed portion, and the slope of the regression line is the variable portion.

EXAMPLE

A firm has performed a linear regression analysis and determined that total manufacturing costs (y) consist of fixed costs of US $420,000 and variable costs of US $32 per unit of output. This relationship can be stated mathematically as follows:

$$y = \text{US } \$420{,}000 + \$32x$$

If the firm is planning to produce 12,000 units of output, its forecast for total manufacturing costs is US $804,000 = US $420,000 + $32 × 12,000.

The firm has collected the following observations on units of output (independent variable) and total manufacturing costs (dependent variable) to support its linear regression analysis:

Units of Output (000s)	Total Manufacturing Costs (US $000s)
5	US $ 620
8	640
14	850
17	1,010

The observations are graphed as follows:

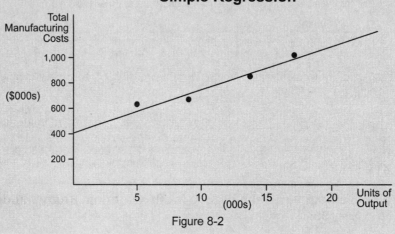

Simple Regression

Figure 8-2

---

2. **Multiple Regression**

    a.   Multiple regression is used when there is more than one independent variable.

        1)   Multiple regression allows a firm to identify many factors (independent variables) and to weight each one according to its influence on the overall outcome.

$$y = a + b_1x_1 + b_2x_2 + b_3x_3 + b_4x_4 + etc.$$

3. **Aspects of Regression Analysis**

    a.   The linear relationship established for x and y is only valid across the relevant range. The user must identify the relevant range and ensure that (s)he does not project the relationship beyond it.

    b.   Regression analysis assumes that past relationships can be validly projected into the future.

    c.   Regression does not determine causality.

        1)   Although *x* and *y* move together, the apparent relationship may be caused by some other factor. For instance, car wash sales volume and sunny weather are strongly correlated, but car wash sales do not cause sunny weather.

4.   High-Low Method

    a.   The high-low method is used to generate a regression line by basing the equation on only the highest and lowest of a series of observations.

EXAMPLE

A regression equation covering electricity costs could be developed by using only the high-cost month and the low-cost month. If the lowest costs were US $400 in April when production was 800 machine hours and the highest costs were US $600 in September when production was 1,300 hours, the equation would be determined as follows:

High month	US $600	for	1,300 hours
Low month	400	for	800 hours
Increase	US $200		500 hours

Because costs increased US $200 for 500 additional hours, the variable cost is US $.40 per machine hour (US $200 ÷ 500 hours). For the low month, the total variable portion of that monthly cost is US $320 ($.40 × 800 hours). Given that the total cost is US $400 and US $320 is variable, the remaining US $80 must be a fixed cost.

The regression equation is y = 80 + .4x.

---

        1)   The major criticism of the high-low method is that the high and low points may be abnormalities not representative of normal events.

5.   Correlation Analysis

    a.   Correlation is the strength of the linear (straight-line) relationship between two variables, expressed mathematically in terms of the coefficient of correlation, *r* (often called the correlation coefficient).

        1)   The coefficient *r* can be graphically depicted by plotting the values for the variables on a graph in the form of a scatter diagram.

    b.   The value of *r* ranges from 1 (perfect direct relationship) to −1 (perfect inverse relationship). The more the scatter pattern resembles a straight line, the greater the absolute value of *r*.

        1)   Perfect direct relationship (*r* = 1)

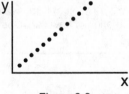

Figure 8-3

        2)   Perfect inverse relationship (*r* = −1)

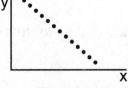

Figure 8-4

3)   Strong direct relationship (*r* = 0.7)

Figure 8-5

    a)   The data points in Figure 8-5 show a very strong direct relationship, reflected in an *r* value close to 0.7.

4)   No linear relationship (*r* = 0)

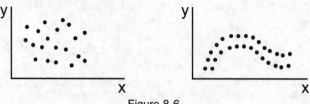

Figure 8-6

    a)   Note from the right-hand graph of the pair above that a coefficient of correlation of zero does not mean there is no relationship at all between the two variables, only that what relationship they may have cannot be expressed as a linear equation.

6.   **Determination**

    a.   The coefficient of determination (r^2), or the coefficient of correlation squared, is a measure of how good the fit between the independent and dependent variables is.

        1)   Mathematically, the coefficient of determination is the proportion of the total variation in the dependent variable that is accounted for by the independent variable.

        2)   The value of r^2 ranges from 0 to 1. The closer the value of r^2 is to 1, the more useful the independent variable (*x*) is in explaining or predicting the variation in the dependent variable (*y*).

EXAMPLE

A car dealership determines that new car sales are a function of disposable income with a coefficient of correlation of .8. This is equivalent to stating that 64% ($.8^2$) of the variation of new car sales from the average can be explained by changes in disposable income.

---

7.   **Standard Error**

    a.   Standard error measures how well the linear equation represents the data. It is the vertical distance between the data points in a scatter diagram and the regression line.

        1)   The closer the data points are to the regression line, the lower the standard error.

Stop and review! You have completed the outline for this subunit. Study multiple-choice questions 10 and 11 on page 196.

8.7 OVERVIEW OF QUALITY

1. **Perspectives on Quality**

   a. The traditional quality control process consisted of the mass inspection of goods as they came off the assembly line.

      1) Those defective items that could be modified cost-effectively to reach salable condition were reworked and then placed in finished goods inventory.

      2) Items whose defective condition could not be cured by rework were scrapped and written off.

   b. The focus of modern quality management is on preventing defects, not detecting them after production is finished.

      1) Quality management improves every phase of an entity's operations.

   c. Process quality is the effectiveness and efficiency of the entity's internal operations. Product quality is the conformance of the entity's output with customer expectations.

      1) Although improving the quality of processes increases efficiency, the most important component of a quality control system is ensuring the quality of the product.

      2) Quality guru Joseph Juran defined quality as **fitness for use**, meaning that products or services meet customer needs.

2. **Measures**

   a. The ultimate goal of any for-profit entity is to increase the value of owners' interests. Improved quality is simply a means to this end.

      1) Most measures of quality are nonfinancial. They do not directly measure revenues or costs but rather productivity.

   b. The following are examples of nonfinancial quality measures in manufacturing:

      1) The percentage of shipments returned by customers because of poor quality
      2) Number of defective products per thousand
      3) Defective output as a percentage of total output

   c. The following are examples of nonfinancial quality measures in service industries:

      1) Customer time spent waiting to be served
      2) Percentage of customers needing repeat service calls
      3) Customer perceptions of employee courtesy

3. **Benchmarking**

   a. Benchmarking is the comparison of some aspect of an organization's performance with best-in-class performance.

      1) The process should be continuous, and whether an operation is best-in-class should be constantly re-evaluated.

   b. Benchmarking can be either internal (comparison with the performance of another area within the organization) or external (comparison with the performance of another entity).

   c. The following are examples of quality benchmarks:

      1) Internal

         a) Average time from initiation of customer service request to final resolution of problem for division that reports highest overall customer satisfaction.

      2) External

         a) Biggest competitor's customer satisfaction as reported in a third-party consumer comparison survey.

    d.   Benchmarking can be carried out as a continuous process together with the plan-do-check-act (PDCA) cycle. PDCA is a "management by fact," or scientific-method, approach to continuous improvement.

        1)   PDCA creates a process-centered environment. It involves (a) studying the current process, (b) collecting and analyzing data to identify causes of problems, (c) planning for improvement, and (d) deciding how to measure improvement ("plan").

        2)   The plan is then implemented on a small scale, if possible ("do").

        3)   The next step is to determine what happened ("check").

        4)   If the experiment was successful, the plan is fully implemented ("act").

        5)   The cycle is then repeated using what was learned from the preceding cycle.

4.   **Kaizen**

    a.   Kaizen is the Japanese word for the continuous pursuit of improvement in every aspect of organizational operations.

        1)   For example, a kaizen budget projects costs based on future improvements. The possibility of such improvements must be determined, and the cost of implementation and the savings must be estimated.

5.   **Quality Circles**

    a.   Often, those closest to a process know best how to improve it.

        1)   Quality circles are a means of obtaining ideas for improving quality. They tend to be unstructured gatherings meant to encourage brainstorming and candid discussion.

6.   **Six Sigma**

    a.   Six Sigma is a quality improvement methodology devised by Motorola. Six Sigma is meant to reduce the number of defects per million opportunities (DPMO) in a mass-production process to 3.4, a level of good output of 99.99966%.

        1)   The name Six Sigma (sometimes written 6σ) is derived from statistics. In a normal distribution (a bell curve), 99.99966% of the items are within six standard deviations.

        2)   Statistical analysis has a major role in any Six Sigma program. Accurate, verifiable data are a necessity.

    b.   Specific individuals in the organization have the following roles:

        1)   The executive level must demonstrate commitment to the Six Sigma program and empower those in the other roles with enough authority and resources to implement the program successfully.

        2)   Champions are responsible for overseeing the implementation of the Six Sigma program across the organization.

        3)   Master black belts assist the champions in implementing the program across the organization.

        4)   Black belts, like champions and master black belts, devote all of their time to the Six Sigma program. They oversee particular Six Sigma projects.

        5)   Green belts and yellow belts do Six Sigma work in addition to their regular duties. They are closest to the production processes being improved.

Stop and review! You have completed the outline for this subunit. Study multiple-choice questions 12 and 13 on page 196.

8.8 COSTS OF QUALITY

1. **Four Costs of Quality**

   a. **Prevention costs** are incurred to prevent defects. Prevention is ordinarily less costly than the combined costs of appraisal, internal failure, and external failure. The following are examples:

      1) Design and implementation of a quality control system
      2) Costs of high-quality raw materials
      3) Preventive maintenance expense
      4) Training

   b. **Appraisal costs** are incurred to detect defective output during and after production. The following are examples:

      1) Inspection of raw materials
      2) Testing of products or equipment

   c. **Internal failure costs** are those associated with defective output discovered before shipping. The following are examples:

      1) Costs of rework
      2) Losses to scrap
      3) Write-offs of bad raw materials
      4) Production line downtime

   d. **External failure costs** are associated with defective output discovered after it has reached the customer. The following are examples:

      1) Storage of returned goods
      2) Repair costs
      3) Legal costs

   e. These costs may be summarized in a cost-of-quality report. An example is presented below:

Cost-of-Quality Report	
Prevention costs	US $10,000
Appraisal costs	6,000
Internal failure costs	5,000
External failure costs	3,000
Total costs of quality	US $24,000

2. **Quality Cost Index**

   a. These amounts may be used to calculate quality cost indices. These state costs of quality as a ratio to some other cost, such as total direct labor.

   $$Quality\ cost\ index = \frac{Total\ costs\ of\ quality}{Total\ direct\ labor\ costs} \times 100$$

      1) If direct labor costs for the period were US $110,000, the quality cost index was 21.8 [(US $24,000 ÷ $110,000) × 100].

Stop and review! You have completed the outline for this subunit. Study multiple-choice questions 14 and 15 on page 197.

8.9 TOOLS FOR ASSESSING QUALITY

1. **Statistical Control Charts**

   a. Statistical control charts are graphic aids for monitoring the variability of any process subject to random variations.

   1) The chart consists of three horizontal lines with a time scale from left to right. The center line represents the target value for the process being controlled. The upper line is the upper control limit (UCL), and the lower line is the lower control limit (LCL).

   2) The process is measured periodically, and results are plotted on the chart. If a result is outside the limits, the process is considered out of control and corrective action is taken.

   3) Statistical control charts make trends and cycles visible.

   b. Below is a chart depicting 2 weeks of production by a manufacturer that produces one precision part each day. To be salable, the part can vary from the standard by no more than +/– 0.1 millimeter.

Statistical Control Chart

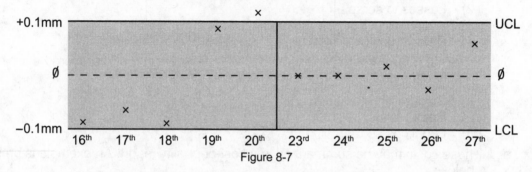

Figure 8-7

   1) The part produced on the 20th had to be scrapped, and the equipment was adjusted to return the process to the controlled state for the following week's production.

2. **Pareto Diagrams**

   a. A Pareto diagram is a bar chart that assists managers in what is commonly called 80:20 analysis.

   1) The 80:20 rule states that 80% of all effects are the result of only 20% of all causes. In the context of quality control, managers optimize their time by focusing their effort on the sources of most problems.

   b. The independent variable, plotted on the x axis, is the factor selected by the manager as the area of interest: department, time period, geographical location, etc. The frequency of occurrence of the defect (dependent variable) is plotted on the y axis.

   1) The occurrences of the independent variable are ranked from highest to lowest, allowing the manager to see at a glance which areas are of most concern.

c.   Following is a Pareto diagram used by a chief administrative officer who wants to know which departments are generating the most travel vouchers that have been rejected because of incomplete documentation.

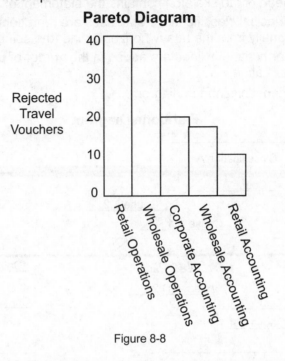

Figure 8-8

3.   **Histogram**

a.   A histogram displays a continuous frequency distribution of the independent variable.

b.   Below is a histogram showing the CAO the amount of travel reimbursement delayed by a typical returned travel voucher.

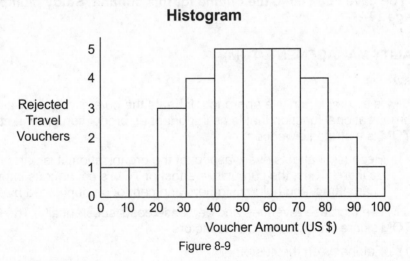

Figure 8-9

4.   **Fishbone Diagram**

a.   A fishbone diagram (also called a cause-and-effect diagram or an Ishikawa diagram) is a total quality management process improvement technique.

1)   It is useful in studying causation (why the actual and desired situations differ).

    b.   This format organizes the analysis of causation and helps to identify possible interactions among causes.

        1)   The head of the skeleton contains the statement of the problem.

        2)   The principal classifications of causes are represented by lines (bones) drawn diagonally from the heavy horizontal line (the spine).

        3)   Smaller horizontal lines are added in their order of probability in each classification.

    c.   Below is a generic fishbone diagram.

Fishbone Diagram

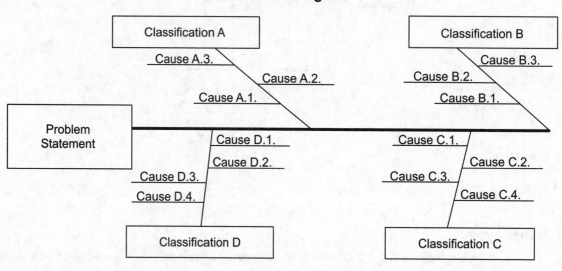

Figure 8-10

Stop and review! You have completed the outline for this subunit. Study multiple-choice question 16 on page 197.

8.10 TOTAL QUALITY MANAGEMENT (TQM)

1.   **Overview**

    a.   TQM is a comprehensive approach. It treats the pursuit of quality as a basic organizational function that is as important as production or marketing. Accordingly, TQM is a strategic weapon.

        1)   Because it affects every aspect of the organization, it is part of the organizational culture. Thus, the cumulative effect of TQM's continuous improvement process can attract and hold customers and cannot be duplicated by competitors.

    b.   TQM can increase revenues and decrease costs substantially. The following are TQM's core principles or critical factors:

        1)   Emphasis on the customer

            a)   Satisfaction of external customers
            b)   Satisfaction of internal customers
            c)   Requirements for external suppliers
            d)   Requirements for internal suppliers

        2)   Continuous improvement as a never-ending process, not a destination

        3)   Engaging every employee in the pursuit of total quality

            a)   Avoidance of defects in products or services and satisfaction of external customers requires that all internal customers be satisfied.

2. **Definition**

   a.   TQM is the continuous pursuit of quality in every aspect of organizational activities through

        1)   A philosophy of doing it right the first time,
        2)   Employee training and empowerment,
        3)   Promotion of teamwork,
        4)   Improvement of processes, and
        5)   Attention to the satisfaction of internal and external customers.

             a)   TQM emphasizes the supplier's relationship with the customer and identifies customer needs. It recognizes that everyone in a process is at some time a customer or supplier of someone else, either inside or outside of the organization.

             b)   Thus, TQM begins with external customer requirements, identifies internal customer-supplier relationships and requirements, and establishes requirements for external suppliers.

   b.   Organizations tend to be vertically organized, but TQM requires strong horizontal linkages.

3. **Implementation**

   a.   Implementation of TQM cannot be accomplished by application of a formula, and the process is lengthy and difficult. The following phases are typical:

        1)   Establishing an executive-level quality council of senior managers with strong involvement by the CEO
        2)   Providing quality training programs for senior managers
        3)   Conducting a quality audit to identify improvement opportunities and identify strengths and weaknesses compared with competitors
        4)   Preparing a gap analysis to determine what is necessary to close the gap between the organization and the quality leaders in its industry and to establish a database for the development of the strategic quality improvement plan
        5)   Developing strategic quality improvement plans for the short and long term
        6)   Conducting employee communication and training programs
        7)   Establishing quality teams to ensure that goods and services conform to specifications

             a)   Hierarchical structure is replaced with teams of people from different specialties. This change follows from an emphasis on empowering employees and teamwork. Employees should

                  i)   Have proper training, necessary information, and the best tools;
                  ii)   Be fully engaged in the decision process; and
                  iii) Receive fair compensation.

             b)   If empowered employees with the required skills are assembled in teams, they will be more effective than if they work separately in a rigid structure.

                  i)   Moreover, a team is a way to share ideas, which results in process improvement.

        8)   Creating a measurement system and setting goals
        9)   Revising compensation, appraisal, and recognition systems
        10) Reviewing and revising the entire effort periodically

Stop and review! You have completed the outline for this subunit. Study multiple-choice questions 17 and 18 beginning on page 197.

8.11 THE BALANCED SCORECARD

1. **Key Performance Indicators and SWOT Analysis**

    a. The trend in managing implementation of the entity's strategy is the balanced scorecard approach. A balanced scorecard connects key performance indicators (KPIs) with measures of performance.

    b. KPIs are financial and nonfinancial measures of the elements of performance vital to competitive advantage. SWOT analysis (strengths, weaknesses, opportunities, and threats) is used to identify KPIs.

2. **Four Categories of Measures**

    a. **Financial**

        1) The KPIs may be sales, fair value of the entity's shares, profits, and liquidity.

        2) Measures may include (a) sales, (b) projected sales, (c) accuracy of sales projections, (d) new product sales, (e) share prices, (f) operating earnings, (g) earnings trend, (h) revenue growth, (i) gross margin percentage, (j) cost reductions, (k) economic value added (EVA), (l) return on investment (or any of its variants), (m) cash flow coverage and trends, (n) turnover (assets, receivables, and inventory), and (o) interest coverage.

    b. **Customer**

        1) The KPIs may be (a) customer satisfaction, (b) customer retention rate, (c) dealer and distributor relationships, (d) marketing and selling performance, (e) prompt delivery, and (f) quality.

        2) Measures may include (a) returns, (b) complaints, (c) survey results, (d) coverage and strength of distribution channels, (e) market research results, (f) training of marketing people, (g) sales trends, (h) market share and its trend, (i) on-time delivery rate, (j) service response time and effectiveness, and (k) warranty expense.

    c. **Internal Business Processes**

        1) The KPIs may be (a) quality, (b) productivity (an input-output relationship), (c) flexibility of response to changing conditions, (d) operating readiness, and (e) safety.

        2) Measures may include (a) rate of defects, (b) amounts of scrap and rework, (c) returns, (d) survey results, (e) field service reports, (f) warranty costs, (g) vendor defect rate, (h) cycle (lead) time, (i) labor and machine efficiency, (j) setup time, (k) scheduling effectiveness, (l) downtime, (m) capacity usage, (n) maintenance, and (o) accidents and their results.

    d. **Learning, Growth, and Innovation**

        1) The KPIs may be (a) development of new products, (b) promptness of their introduction, (c) human resource development, (d) morale, and (e) competence of the workforce.

        2) Measures may include (a) new products marketed, (b) amount of design changes, (c) patents and copyrights registered, (d) R&D personnel qualifications, (e) actual versus planned shipping dates, (f) hours of training, (g) skill set levels attained, (h) personnel turnover, (i) personnel complaints and survey results, (j) financial and operating results, (k) technological capabilities, (l) organizational learning, and (m) industry leadership.

EXAMPLE

Each **objective** is associated with one or more **measures** that permit the organization to estimate progress toward the objective. Achievement of the objectives in each **perspective** makes it possible to achieve the organization's objectives.

Balanced Scorecard

Financial Perspective

    Objective: Increase shareholder value   **Measures:** Increase in ordinary (common) share price
                                                                 Reliability of dividend payment

Customer Perspective

    Objective: Increase customer satisfaction   **Measures:** Greater market share
                                                                Higher customer retention rate
                                                                Positive responses to surveys

Internal Business Process Perspective

    Objective: Improve product quality   **Measures:** Achievement of zero defects

    Objective: Improve internal processes   **Measures:** Reduction in delivery cycle time
                                                                    Smaller cost variances

Learning, Growth, and Innovation Perspective

    Objective: Increase employee confidence   **Measures:** Number of suggestions to improve processes
                                                                 Positive responses to surveys

    Objective: Increase employee competence   **Measures:** Attendance at internal and external training
                                                                         seminars

---

3. **Problems in Implementation**

    a. Using too many measures, with a consequent loss of focus on KPIs

    b. Failing to evaluate personnel on nonfinancial as well as financial measures

    c. Including measures that will not have long-term financial benefits

    d. Not understanding that subjective measures (such as customer satisfaction) are imprecise

    e. Trying to achieve improvements in all areas at all times

    f. Not observing when current nonfinancial measures no longer relate to ultimate financial success

NOTE: According to The IIA's four-part to three-part content map, this topic was removed from the CIA exam. However, we have received feedback from candidates that it is still being tested.

Stop and review! You have completed the outline for this subunit. Study multiple-choice questions 19 and 20 on page 198.

QUESTIONS

8.1 Integration Strategies

1. A milk producer company acquires its own dairy farms to supply milk. The growth strategy adopted by the company is

A. Horizontal integration.

B. Vertical integration.

C. Concentric diversification.

D. Conglomerate diversification.

Answer (B) is correct.

    REQUIRED: The correct type of growth strategy.

    DISCUSSION: Vertical integration occurs when a company becomes its own supplier or distributor. It combines within a firm production, distribution, selling, or other separate economic processes needed to deliver a product or service to a customer.

    Answer (A) is incorrect. Horizontal integration is the acquisition of competitors. Answer (C) is incorrect. Concentric diversification results from developing or acquiring related businesses that do not have products, services, or customers in common with current businesses, but that offer internal synergies, e.g., through common use of brands, R&D, plant facilities, or marketing expertise. Answer (D) is incorrect. Conglomerate diversification is the acquisition of wholly unrelated businesses. The objectives of such an acquisition are financial, not operational, because of the absence of common products, customers, facilities, expertise, or other synergies.

2. A vertically integrated organization is best described as one that

    A. Owns all of its production facilities.

    B. Manufactures the component parts used in its product.

    C. Is departmentalized by product or service.

    D. Fosters very narrow span of control.

Answer (B) is correct.
    REQUIRED: The characteristic of a vertically integrated company.
    DISCUSSION: An organization is vertically integrated if it unites sources of supply, the production of finished goods, and the marketing of the product. In other words, complete vertical integration combines all phases of the production and delivery of products or services.
    Answer (A) is incorrect. An organization that owns its production facilities may still depend on suppliers for component parts. Answer (C) is incorrect. Departmentation by product or service is a grouping of organizational subsystems that gives extensive authority to a division executive over a given product or product line or over a service or group of services. Answer (D) is incorrect. A narrow span of control signifies that the number of subordinates supervised is relatively small.

8.2 Capacity Expansion

3. A firm is performing an analysis of a capacity expansion decision. The simplest element of the analysis is

    A. Choosing the expansion method.

    B. Determining the expansion plans of rival firms.

    C. Calculating the net present value.

    D. Estimating total long-term demand.

Answer (C) is correct.
    REQUIRED: The simplest element in an analysis of capacity expansion.
    DISCUSSION: Formal capital budgeting involves predicting future cash flows related to the expansion, discounting them at an appropriate interest rate, and determining whether the net present value (NPV) is positive. This process permits comparison with other uses of the firm's resources. The apparent simplicity of this process is deceptive because it depends upon, among many other things, which expansion method is chosen, developments in technology, and profitability. Profitability in turn depends on such uncertainties as total long-term demand and the expansion plans of rival firms.
    Answer (A) is incorrect. Choosing the expansion method requires a complex analysis based on significant uncertainties. Answer (B) is incorrect. The expansion plans of rival firms are significant uncertainties. Answer (D) is incorrect. Total long-term demand is a significant uncertainty.

4. Which of the following is **not** a technological factor that may lead to overexpansion?

    A. Long lead times for adding capacity.

    B. Changes in production technology.

    C. The presence of economies of scale.

    D. High exit barriers.

Answer (D) is correct.
    REQUIRED: The item not a technological factor that may lead to overexpansion.
    DISCUSSION: The following are technological factors that may lead to overexpansion: (1) capacity may need to be added in large increments; (2) the presence of economies of scale or a steep learning curve encourages preemption; (3) long lead times for adding capacity increase the risk of competitive inferiority if a firm does not act quickly to raise capacity; (4) when the minimum efficient scale increases, large plants are becoming more efficient even though demand is not growing; and (5) changes in production technology result in new construction while old plants remain in operation. High exit barriers are a structural factor that may lead to overbuilding. The effect of high exit barriers is to extend the period of overcapacity.

8.3 Entry into New Businesses

5. Lower industry entry costs may be incurred by a firm with special advantages, such as

    A. Proprietary technology.

    B. An unfamiliar brand.

    C. A weak distribution network.

    D. High labor costs.

Answer (A) is correct.
    REQUIRED: A cause of lower industry entry costs.
    DISCUSSION: Lower industry entry costs may be incurred by a firm with special advantages, such as proprietary technology.
    Answer (B) is incorrect. Lower industry entry costs may be incurred by a firm with special advantages, such as a well-known brand, not an unfamiliar one. Answer (C) is incorrect. Lower industry entry costs may be incurred by a firm with special advantages, such as a strong distribution network, not a weak distribution network. Answer (D) is incorrect. High labor costs are not a special advantage.

6. Entry into a new business through internal development ordinarily entails

    A. The expansion of an existing business entity.

    B. The creation of a new business entity.

    C. The spin-off of an existing business entity.

    D. The sale of an existing business entity.

Answer (B) is correct.
    REQUIRED: The method of entry into a new business.
    DISCUSSION: Entry into a new business through internal development ordinarily entails the creation of a new business entity.

8.4 Forecasting -- Time-Series Models

7. The moving-average method of forecasting

    A. Is a cross-sectional forecasting method.

    B. Regresses the variable of interest on a related variable to develop a forecast.

    C. Derives final forecasts by adjusting the initial forecast based on the smoothing constant.

    D. Includes each new observation in the average as it becomes available and discards the oldest observation.

Answer (D) is correct.
    REQUIRED: The item that best describes the moving-average method of forecasting.
    DISCUSSION: The simple moving-average method is a smoothing technique that uses the experience of the past N periods (through time period t) to forecast a value for the next period. Thus, the average includes each new observation and discards the oldest observation. The forecast formula for the next period (for time period $t + 1$) is the sum of the last N observations divided by N.
    Answer (A) is incorrect. Cross-sectional regression analysis examines relationships among large amounts of data (e.g., many or different production methods or locations) at a particular moment in time. Answer (B) is incorrect. Regression analysis relates the forecast to changes in particular variables. Answer (C) is incorrect. Under exponential smoothing, each forecast equals the sum of the last observation times the smoothing constant, plus the last forecast times one minus the constant.

8.5 Forecasting -- Probabilistic Models

8. An account executive has just designed a Monte Carlo model to estimate the costs of a particular type of project. Validating the model could include all **except**

    A. Checking for errors in the computer programming.

    B. Checking that assumed probability distributions are reasonable.

    C. Comparing test results with previously validated models.

    D. Applying the model.

Answer (D) is correct.
    REQUIRED: The step not involved in validating a Monte Carlo model.
    DISCUSSION: The Monte Carlo technique is used in a simulation to generate the individual values for a random variable. An essential step in the simulation procedure is to validate the mathematical model used. This process involves not only searching for errors but also verifying the assumptions. It also should provide some assurance that the results of the experiment will be realistic. This assurance is often obtained using historical data. If the model gives results equivalent to what actually happened, the model is historically valid. There is still some risk, however, that changes could make the model invalid for the future. The model should not be implemented until this validation process is complete.

9. The decision rule that selects the strategy with the highest utility payoff if the worst state of nature occurs is the

    A. Minimize regret rule.

    B. Maximize utility rule.

    C. Maximin rule.

    D. Maximax rule.

Answer (C) is correct.
    REQUIRED: The rule that selects the strategy with the highest utility payoff if the worst state of nature occurs.
    DISCUSSION: The maximin rule determines the minimum payoff for each decision and then chooses the decision with the maximum minimum payoff. It is a conservative criterion adopted by risk-averse players, that is, those for whom the disutility of a loss exceeds the utility of an equal gain.
    Answer (A) is incorrect. The minimize regret rule selects the action that minimizes the maximum opportunity cost. Answer (B) is incorrect. The maximize utility rule is not a decision rule. Answer (D) is incorrect. The maximax rule selects the choice that provides the greatest payoff if the most favorable state of nature occurs.

8.6   Regression and Correlation

10. Quality control programs employ many tools for problem definition and analysis. A scatter diagram is one of these tools. The objective of a scatter diagram is to

A. Display a population of items for analysis.

B. Show frequency distribution in graphic form.

C. Divide a universe of data into homogeneous groups.

D. Show the vital trend and separate trivial items.

Answer (A) is correct.
REQUIRED: The objective of a scatter diagram.
DISCUSSION: The objective of a scatter diagram is to depict degrees of correlation. Each observation is represented by a dot on a graph corresponding to specific values of x (the independent variable) and y (the dependent variable).
Answer (B) is incorrect. The objective of a histogram is to present a frequency distribution in graphic form. Answer (C) is incorrect. The objective of stratification is to divide a universe of data into homogeneous groups. Answer (D) is incorrect. Regression analysis is used to find trend lines.

11. In regression analysis, which of the following correlation coefficients represents the strongest relationship between the independent and dependent variables?

A. 1.03

B. −.02

C. −.89

D. .75

Answer (C) is correct.
REQUIRED: The correlation coefficient with the strongest relationship between independent and dependent variables.
DISCUSSION: Because the range of values is between −1 and 1, −.89 suggests a very strong inverse relationship between the independent and dependent variables. A value of −1 signifies a perfect inverse relationship, and a value of 1 signifies a perfect direct relationship.
Answer (A) is incorrect. A correlation coefficient of 1.03 is impossible. Answer (B) is incorrect. A value of −.02 is a very weak correlation coefficient. Answer (D) is incorrect. A correlation coefficient of .75 is .25 from the maximum value, but −.89 is only .11 from the minimum value.

8.7   Overview of Quality

12. A traditional quality control process in manufacturing consists of mass inspection of goods only at the end of a production process. A major deficiency of the traditional control process is that

A. It is expensive to do the inspections at the end of the process.

B. It is not possible to rework defective items.

C. It is not 100% effective.

D. It does not focus on improving the entire production process.

Answer (D) is correct.
REQUIRED: The major deficiency of a traditional quality control process.
DISCUSSION: The process used to produce the goods is not thoroughly reviewed and evaluated for efficiency and effectiveness. Preventing defects and increasing efficiency by improving the production process raises quality standards and decreases costs.
Answer (A) is incorrect. Other quality control processes can also be expensive. Answer (B) is incorrect. Reworking defective items may be possible although costly. Answer (C) is incorrect. No quality control system will be 100% effective.

13. Which of the following criteria would be most useful to a sales department manager in evaluating the performance of the manager's customer-service group?

A. The customer is always right.

B. Customer complaints should be processed promptly.

C. Employees should maintain a positive attitude when dealing with customers.

D. All customer inquiries should be answered within 7 days of receipt.

Answer (D) is correct.
REQUIRED: The criterion most useful for evaluating a customer-service group.
DISCUSSION: A criterion that requires all customer inquiries to be answered within 7 days of receipt permits accurate measurement of performance. The quantitative and specific nature of the appraisal using this standard avoids the vagueness, subjectivity, and personal bias that may afflict other forms of personnel evaluations.
Answer (A) is incorrect. Customer orientation is difficult to quantify. Answer (B) is incorrect. The standard specified is vague. Answer (C) is incorrect. No measure of a positive attitude has been specified for the employee.

8.8 Costs of Quality

14. The management and employees of a large household goods moving company believe that if it became nationally known as adhering to total quality management and continuous improvement, one result would be an increase in the company's profits and market share. What should the company focus on to achieve quality more economically?

    A. Appraisal costs.

    B. Prevention costs.

    C. Internal failure costs.

    D. External failure costs.

Answer (B) is correct.
    REQUIRED: The necessary focus for achieving quality more economically.
    DISCUSSION: Prevention costs are incurred to prevent defects. Prevention is ordinarily less costly than the combined costs of appraisal, internal failure, and external failure.

15. The four categories of costs associated with product quality costs are

    A. External failure, internal failure, prevention, and carrying.

    B. External failure, internal failure, prevention, and appraisal.

    C. External failure, internal failure, training, and appraisal.

    D. Warranty, product liability, training, and appraisal.

Answer (B) is correct.
    REQUIRED: The categories of product quality costs.
    DISCUSSION: Prevention costs are incurred to prevent defects. Appraisal costs are incurred to detect defective output during and after the production process. Internal failure costs are associated with defective output discovered before shipping. External failure costs are associated with defective output discovered after it has reached the customer.
    Answer (A) is incorrect. Carrying cost is not one of the elements of quality costs. Answer (C) is incorrect. Training cost is a component of prevention costs. Answer (D) is incorrect. Warranty and product liability are external failure costs. Training cost is a component of prevention costs.

8.9 Tools for Assessing Quality

16. Statistical quality control often involves the use of control charts whose basic purpose is to

    A. Determine when accounting control procedures are not working.

    B. Control labor costs in production operations.

    C. Detect performance trends away from normal operations.

    D. Monitor internal control applications of information technology.

Answer (C) is correct.
    REQUIRED: The purpose of statistical quality control charts.
    DISCUSSION: Statistical control charts are graphic aids for monitoring the status of any process subject to random variations. The chart consists of three horizontal lines plotted on a horizontal time scale. The vertical scale represents the appropriate quantitative measure. The center line represents the average range or overall mean for the process being controlled. The other two lines are the upper control limit and the lower control limit. The processes are measured periodically, and the values are plotted on the chart. If the value falls within the control limits, no action is taken. If the value falls outside the limits, the process is considered "out of control," and an investigation is made for possible corrective action. Another advantage of the chart is that it makes trends visible.
    Answer (A) is incorrect. Quality control concerns product quality, not controls over accounting procedures. Answer (B) is incorrect. Quality control concerns product quality, not costs. Answer (D) is incorrect. Quality control concerns product quality, not information technology.

8.10 Total Quality Management (TQM)

17. Which of the following is a characteristic of total quality management (TQM)?

    A. Management by objectives.

    B. On-the-job training by other workers.

    C. Quality by final inspection.

    D. Education and self-improvement.

Answer (D) is correct.
    REQUIRED: The characteristic of TQM.
    DISCUSSION: TQM is the continuous pursuit of quality in every aspect of organizational activities. One of the means of achieving this is through employee training and empowerment.
    Answer (A) is incorrect. MBO involves the aggressive pursuit of numerical quotas; any such mechanistic requirement runs counter to the pursuit of TQM. Answer (B) is incorrect. Informal learning from coworkers serves to entrench bad work habits. Answer (C) is incorrect. A goal of TQM is to prevent the generation of defective output.

18. In which of the following organizational structures does total quality management (TQM) work best?

    A. Hierarchal.

    B. Teams of people from the same specialty.

    C. Teams of people from different specialties.

    D. Specialists working individually.

Answer (C) is correct.

    REQUIRED: The structure in which TQM works best.

    DISCUSSION: TQM advocates replacement of the traditional hierarchal structure with teams of people from different specialties. This change follows from TQM's emphasis on empowering employees and teamwork. Employees should (1) have proper training, necessary information, and the best tools; (2) be fully engaged in the decision process; and (3) receive fair compensation. If such empowered employees are assembled in teams of individuals with the required skills, TQM theorists believe they will be more effective than people performing their tasks separately in a rigid structure.

    Answer (A) is incorrect. Hierarchal organization stifles TQM. Answer (B) is incorrect. TQM works best with teams of people from different specialties. Answer (D) is incorrect. Teamwork is essential for TQM.

8.11 The Balanced Scorecard

19. Using the balanced scorecard approach, an organization evaluates managerial performance based on

    A. A single ultimate measure of operating results, such as residual income.

    B. Multiple financial and nonfinancial measures.

    C. Multiple nonfinancial measures only.

    D. Multiple financial measures only.

Answer (B) is correct.

    REQUIRED: The nature of the balanced scorecard approach.

    DISCUSSION: The trend in managerial performance evaluation is the balanced scorecard approach. Multiple measures of performance permit a determination as to whether a manager is achieving certain objectives at the expense of others that may be equally or more important. These measures may be financial or nonfinancial and usually include items in four categories: (1) financial; (2) customer; (3) internal business processes; and (4) learning, growth, and innovation.

    Answer (A) is incorrect. The balanced scorecard approach uses multiple measures. Answer (C) is incorrect. The balanced scorecard approach includes financial measures. Answer (D) is incorrect. The balanced scorecard approach includes nonfinancial measures.

20. Under the balanced scorecard concept, employee satisfaction and retention are measures used under which of the following perspectives?

    A. Customer.

    B. Internal business.

    C. Learning and growth.

    D. Financial.

Answer (C) is correct.

    REQUIRED: The perspective under which employee satisfaction and retention are measured on a balanced scorecard.

    DISCUSSION: The balanced scorecard is an accounting report that connects the firm's key performance indicators (KPIs) determined in a strategic analysis to measures of its performance. KPIs are financial and nonfinancial measures. For the learning, growth, and innovation perspective, the KPIs may be development of new products, promptness of their introduction, human resource development, morale, and competence of the workforce. Measures of employee satisfaction, retention, and competence may include R&D personnel qualifications, hours of training, skill set levels attained, personnel turnover, and personnel complaints and survey results.

    Answer (A) is incorrect. For the customer perspective, the KPIs may be customer satisfaction and retention rate, dealer and distributor relationships, marketing and selling performance, prompt delivery, and quality. Answer (B) is incorrect. For the internal business perspective, the KPIs may be quality, productivity, flexibility of response to changing conditions, operating readiness, and safety. Answer (D) is incorrect. For the financial perspective, the KPIs may be sales, fair value of the firm's equity, profits, and liquidity.

Access the **CIA Review System** from your Gleim Personal Classroom to continue your studies with exam-emulating multiple-choice questions!

STUDY UNIT NINE
ORGANIZATIONAL BEHAVIOR

(21 pages of outline)

This study unit is the fourth of five covering **Section V: Management/Leadership Principles** from The IIA's CIA Exam Syllabus. This section makes up 10% to 20% of Part 3 of the CIA exam and is tested at the **awareness level**. The relevant portion of the syllabus is highlighted below. (The complete syllabus is in Appendix A.)

V. MANAGEMENT/LEADERSHIP PRINCIPLES (10%–20%)

   A. Strategic Management

   B. Organizational Behavior
1. Organizational theory (structures and configurations)
2. Organizational behavior (e.g., motivation, impact of job design, rewards, schedules)
3. Group dynamics (e.g., traits, development stages, organizational politics, effectiveness)
4. Knowledge of human resource processes (e.g., individual performance management, supervision, personnel sourcing/staffing, staff development)

5. Risk/control implications of different leadership styles
6. Performance (productivity, effectiveness, etc.)

   C. Management Skills/Leadership Styles

   D. Conflict Management

   E. Project Management/Change Management

9.1 ORGANIZATIONAL THEORY

1. **Overview**

   a. The four elements of an organization have been defined as follows:

      1) Coordination of effort in a cooperative social arrangement
      2) A common objective or purpose
      3) Division of labor (efficient specialization)
      4) A hierarchy of authority

         a) Authority is the right to direct, and to expect performance from, other people. Those people are accountable to their superiors in the hierarchy.

   b. **Organizational charts** represent the formal organizational structure in two dimensions: vertical hierarchy and horizontal specialization. They often resemble a pyramid, with the chief executive on top and the operating workforce on the bottom.

      1) Recent trends in management, including increased span of control and decreased hierarchy, have resulted in flatter organizational charts.

2)   The typical organizational chart can be designed to do the following:

   a)   Reflect formal vertical authority channels (chain of command)
   b)   Show reporting relationships and task groupings (departmentation)
   c)   Describe communication channels
   d)   Identify sources of organizational expertise
   e)   Show promotional or career tracks
   f)   Depict the span of control and number of organizational levels
   g)   Show major functions and their respective relationships (horizontal specialization)

3)   The following are weaknesses of organizational charts:

   a)   Limited presentation of information, which may be overcome by supplementing the chart with a detailed manual
   b)   Tendency to become obsolete due to rapid change
   c)   Failure to show informal communication, influence, power, or friendships
   d)   Tendency to ignore informal job tradeoffs among titles on the chart
   e)   Possibility of misleading management by giving an appearance of structure and order that might not exist
   f)   Possibility that position titles do not reflect actual functions

2.   **Theories of Organizing**

   a.   Theories of organizing may be categorized as follows:

   1)   Traditional, closed-system theories and
   2)   Modern, open-system theories.

   b.   The **closed-system** approach treats the organization as focused on economic efficiency in a reasonably predictable environment. Planning and control processes can substantially eliminate uncertainty.

   1)   Closed systems are closed to the external environment. Few systems are truly closed, but boundaries may be artificially drawn to facilitate analysis by treating a system as if it were closed.

      a)   Early writers on management ignored most things external to the organization. Such a policy is unsound because effective management of a social system is not deterministic or mechanistic.

   2)   One of the first closed-system approaches was the scientific school of management. It emphasized the production process and ways to make it more efficient. It was a systematic, quantitative approach based on individual job design. The following are the principles of scientific management:

      a)   Scientific analysis of work
      b)   Scientific selection, training, and development of workers
      c)   Cooperation among work planners and operators
      d)   Equal sharing of responsibility by labor and management, who perform the tasks for which they are best suited

3) Another approach separated administration from technical, commercial, financial, and accounting operations. The following functions of management are the basis for the modern functional or process classification of a manager's activities:

    a) Planning
    b) Organizing
    c) Commanding
    d) Coordinating
    e) Controlling

4) The traditional closed-system approach resulted in **authoritarian** organizations with narrow spans of control, close supervision, and the top-down flow of authority. The following principles applied in these organizations:

    a) The hierarchy of authority should be precisely determined to achieve common objectives (unity of objective).

    b) The principle of unity of command should be followed. Each subordinate should have only one superior (though a superior may have as many subordinates as allowed by the superior's span of control).

        i) Violation of this principle leads to confusion and frustration for the subordinate.

    c) Authority should be proportionate to responsibility. Thus, a person should not be accountable for performance unless (s)he has the power to perform.

    d) Authority but not responsibility may be delegated.

5) A **bureaucracy** is the ultimate traditional organization. It is founded on efficient military principles, including merit-based personnel decisions.

    a) A bureaucracy is characterized by (1) division of labor, (2) a hierarchy of authority, (3) a framework of rules, and (4) impersonality.

    b) Despite its bad reputation, bureaucracy is a feature of every large organization. Accordingly, managers should be aware of the symptoms of an inefficient and otherwise dysfunctional bureaucracy, such as ignoring the needs of customers and employees, pointless rules, and boring jobs.

c. The **open-system** approach treats the organization as focused on survival in an uncertain environment. The organization itself and the environment contain variables that may not be controllable.

1) An organization may be treated as a cooperative system with a bottom-up flow of authority. According to this system, a manager's leadership depends on employees' acceptance.

    a) Thus, compliance with a message from a superior is dependent on employees'

        i) Understanding of the message,
        ii) Belief that it serves an organizational objective,
        iii) Belief that it serves their objectives, and
        iv) Ability to comply.

2) A successful organization must adapt rapidly to changes in such factors as

    a) Technology progress,
    b) Product evolution,
    c) Market conditions,
    d) Competitive challenges, and
    e) Globalization.

3)   An organizational system is a group of subsystems that are interrelated and form parts of a larger whole. According to the open-systems approach, an organization must consider the larger system of which it is a part.

    a)   It also considers human relations and structural issues.

    b)   Open systems are not self-sufficient. They must interact with an external environment. The system boundaries reflect external inputs and system outputs.

       i)   A closed system suffers entropy, or progressive degradation and disorganization. An open system seeks replenishment through its boundaries with the larger system (environment). Accordingly, an open system is in dynamic equilibrium. For example, a business may obtain external financing to modernize its plant.

    c)   An open system is synergistic. Its parts interact so that the total effect exceeds the sum of the effects of the separate parts.

    d)   Another attribute of open systems is equifinality, or the ability to achieve desired results by using different methods.

       i)   For example, a manufacturer may vary such inputs into the production process as labor and materials.

    e)   A business or other open system obtains inputs (information, capital, labor, materials, etc.) and produces outputs (goods, services, earnings, nonrecycled scrap, etc.).

    f)   An open system consists of the following:

       i)   The technical subsystem (the production function)

      ii)   The boundary-spanning subsystem, which interacts with the environment (sales, purchasing, public relations, planning, etc.)

      iii)   The management subsystem, which coordinates the other subsystems

    g)   An open-systems organization also should be a learning organization. It should effectively create, acquire, and transfer knowledge. Moreover, it must change its behavior in response.

       i)   Organizational learning proceeds by cognition (acquiring new knowledge), behavior (acquiring new skills), and performance.

      ii)   The following are skills required for an organization to prosper as it copes with inevitable change:

         •   Problem solving

         •   Learning by systematic experimentation

         •   Learning from its experience

         •   Learning from customers, competitors, and others

         •   Transferring and implementing what has been learned, e.g., through training and communication

d.   The **contingency approach** is derived from open-systems concepts. Organizational design depends on contingencies that can be discovered and studied. No one design format fits all organizations.

    1)   Because solutions are situationally determined, the key is finding the relevant factors in the organization's environment.

    2)   Moreover, the greater the environmental uncertainty, the more adaptive the organization must be. It should

      a)   Monitor problems and watch for the symptoms of decline.

      b)   Restate and clarify its objectives on a timely basis.

        c)   Identify the best markets and customers and the most threatening competitors.

        d)   Promote experimentation, communication, and participation.

        e)   Recognize that it may be the most vulnerable when it is the most successful. Overconfidence tends to be greatest then.

    3)   Contingency design determines the structure that suits the environmental (state) uncertainty faced by the organization. Environmental uncertainty is a function of, among other things,

        a)   Stability of demand for the organization's goods or services,
        b)   Reliability of supply,
        c)   Rate of technological change, and
        d)   Socioeconomic and political pressures.

3. **Organizational Performance**

    a.   The test of how well an entity is organized is its performance, for example, its effectiveness and productivity.

    b.   In the narrowest sense, **effectiveness** is achievement of objectives. It is contrasted with efficiency, the ratio of output to input. In the broadest sense, an organization must achieve its objectives efficiently to be considered effective.

        1)   Economists define **productivity** as the ratio of real output to a unit of input. Increased productivity is the goal of every organization because it improves the measures of performance, such as profit.

        2)   For example, in a retail store, a critical output is revenue per square foot. The floor space in the store is a limited resource whose productivity should be analyzed.

    c.   Continued profitability and growth are the obvious effectiveness criteria for businesses. However, society's expectations expressed through laws and regulations (e.g., antitrust, securities regulation, labor law, worker safety, environmental protection, pension security, antidiscrimination, consumer protection) provide many other criteria.

        1)   The weighting of these criteria is difficult for all businesses.

    d.   The definition of organizational effectiveness includes a time dimension. Thus, an organization needs to be effective beyond the near future. It should be effective and efficient, grow, be profitable, satisfy society's and its stakeholders' expectations, learn, adapt, develop, and survive over a period of years.

        1)   The organization needs to meet expectations of society, owners, employees, customers, and creditors in the near term (about 1 year).

        2)   It must adapt to change and develop its capacities in the intermediate term (about 2-4 years).

        3)   It must survive in an uncertain environment full of threats and opportunities in the long term (about 5 years or more).

    e.   Organizational decline (inflexibility and loss of effectiveness and efficiency) may lead to downsizing, merger, reorganization, or liquidation. It results from decreased demand, resource limitations, or mismanagement.

        1)   Management complacency is one of the main causes of organizational decline. The following are its characteristics:

            a)   A lack of innovation
            b)   Faulty perception of markets and competition
            c)   Failure to observe or properly appraise the initial warnings of decline
            d)   Not focusing on daily objectives

2) Downsizing results from organizational decline, changes in the business cycle, or business combinations. The objectives are cost reduction, improved efficiency, and higher profits.

    a) These purposes often are not achieved. Many organizations follow cycles of hiring, firing, and rehiring that do not yield the expected benefits to offset the harm to terminated employees, the loss of morale of the survivors, and the damage to communities.

    b) Downsizing also tends to have a disproportionate effect on women and members of minorities, who tend to be the last hired and first fired.

    c) The more enlightened view is that employees are not readily disposable commodities but valuable resources who should be terminated only as a last resort. This view seeks alternatives to involuntary termination.

Stop and review! You have completed the outline for this subunit. Study multiple-choice questions 1 through 4 beginning on page 219.

9.2 MOTIVATION

1. This subunit presents the major theories of motivation and describes how job design and rewards affect motivation.

2. **Overview**

    a. Motivation describes an entire class of drives, desires, needs, fears, and similar forces that cause behavior.

    b. The ideal management action motivates subordinates by structuring situations and requiring behaviors that satisfy the needs of subordinates and the organization.

    c. The organization's needs and those of the individual need not conflict.

    d. Motivation is determined by individuals' opportunity to satisfy their needs within the organizational setting. The greater the ability to satisfy these needs, the greater the motivation.

    e. The inducements that an organization offers an individual should be matched with the contributions expected from that individual. Thus, each side should be willing to give up something to receive a desired benefit.

    f. The task of a leader is to make available the kinds and amounts of rewards an individual requires in exchange for the kinds and amounts of contributions the organization requires.

3. **Maslow's Hierarchy of Needs**

    a. According to Abraham Maslow, human needs are a hierarchy, from lowest to highest. Lower-level needs must be satisfied before higher-level needs can influence (motivate) the individual.

    b. Maslow's **hierarchy of needs** is listed below, from lowest to highest:

        1) **Physiological needs** are the basic requirements for sustaining human life, such as water, food, shelter, and sleep. Until these needs are satisfied to the degree needed to maintain life, higher-level needs will not be motivators.

        2) **Security or safety needs** include protection from physical or emotional harm, the loss of a job, and other threats.

        3) **Affiliation or acceptance needs** are the needs of people as social beings for love, affection, friendship, and belonging.

        4) **Esteem** is the need to be valued by both one's self and others. These needs are satisfied by power, prestige, status, and self-confidence.

5) **Self-actualization** is the highest need in the hierarchy. It is the need to realize one's own potential for growth and continued development.

   a) Thus, the job itself is an intrinsic motivation; no extrinsic motivation (such as rewards or reinforcements) is needed. Intrinsic motivation provides the worker with psychological utility.

c. Research supports the proposition that biological needs must be satisfied before other needs become motivators. However, the strict order of the hierarchy may not always apply in other cases.

   1) Physiological and safety needs tend to decrease in importance for fully employed people. Needs for acceptance, esteem, and self-actualization tend to increase.

   2) Higher-level needs, esteem and self-actualization, are variable in their motivational effects, depending upon the individual.

d. Maslow's hierarchy does not apply equally to all situations. It is dependent on the social, cultural, and psychological backgrounds of the people involved.

   1) People of different cultures respond differently.

   2) Professional workers, skilled workers, and unskilled workers react differently.

   3) Other social, ethnic, and cultural factors make people react differently.

   4) The hierarchy is not a smooth, step-by-step path. It is a complicated and interdependent set of relationships.

      a) However, the tendency to move upward as lower needs are satisfied does exist.

4. **Classical Views**

a. Classical views stress fear and economics as motivators.

b. The following are examples:

   1) Economic incentive programs and bonuses are economic rewards.
   2) Loss of employment and demotion are feared by employees.

c. Motivation in the business organization simply consists of monetary incentives.

   1) Because money is the common ground between workers and management, prosperity for the company must be accompanied by prosperity for the worker and vice versa.

5. **Behaviorism**

a. Behaviorists believe that economic motivation is effective only for the short run or for people who do not have job alternatives. This approach focuses on participation and personal involvement in the work situation as motivational factors.

b. For a participative management approach to succeed,

   1) The parties must have sufficient time,
   2) The issues must be relevant to employees' interests,
   3) Employees must have the abilities (training and communication skills) to participate, and
   4) The organizational culture should support participation.

c. Accordingly, a limitation of the participative approach is that it is unlikely that all employees are willing and able to be involved in decision making.

6. **Theory X and Theory Y**

a. Douglas McGregor's Theory X and Theory Y are simplified models that define the extremes of managers' opinions on employee conduct. They permit a manager to evaluate his or her own tendencies.

b.   Theory X is the perspective of the autocratic manager.

  1)   Most people dislike work.

  2)   Most people must be controlled and threatened to induce them to make an adequate effort to achieve organizational objectives.

  3)   Most people want to be directed, lack ambition, and primarily seek security.

c.   Theory Y is the extreme opposite of Theory X. The permissive manager assumes the following:

  1)   Physical and mental effort in work is as natural as recreation or rest.

  2)   Control and threats are not the only means of motivating individuals to make an adequate effort to achieve organizational objectives. Employees will be self-directed and self-controlled if they believe the objectives are worthy.

  3)   Commitment to objectives is proportional to the rewards of accomplishment.

  4)   Most people can learn to seek responsibility.

  5)   The human ability to use imagination and creativity to solve problems is common.

  6)   In modern industrial life, the intellectual ability of most people is not fully realized.

d.   McGregor did not suggest that Theory Y was the only correct managerial behavior. He suggested these theories as starting points from which a manager can examine his or her own views about human nature.

7.   **Two-Factor Theory of Motivation**

a.   Frederick Herzberg's two-factor theory is based on satisfaction. The following two classes of motivational factors exist in the job situation:

  1)   Dissatisfiers (maintenance or hygiene factors) are found in the job context.

    a)   Their presence will not especially motivate people, but their absence will lead to diminished performance. They include

      i)   Organizational policy and administration,
      ii)   Supervision,
      iii)   Working conditions,
      iv)   Interpersonal relations,
      v)   Salary and status, and
      vi)   Job security.

  2)   Satisfiers (motivational factors) relate to job content.

    a)   Their absence will not diminish performance, but their addition or availability will motivate employees. They include

      i)   Achievement,
      ii)   Recognition,
      iii)   Challenging work,
      iv)   Advancement,
      v)   Growth in the job, and
      vi)   Responsibility.

b.   Satisfaction and dissatisfaction are on a continuum. In the middle is the point at which an employee experiences neither job satisfaction nor dissatisfaction.

  1)   At this point, (s)he is not dissatisfied with the job context but also is not positively motivated.

  2)   If Herzberg is correct, job content should be improved through the use of job enrichment strategies.

3) Some jobs obviously do not contain many motivators, but others have more than are being fully used by management. For example,

    a) Routine, low-status work such as mail sorting has few motivators.

    b) A company that may be paying above the industry average (maintenance factor) also could increase satisfaction by openly acknowledging sales or other efforts by initiating a salesperson of the week recognition program.

8. Expectancy Theory

a. Victor Vroom's expectancy theory is based on the common-sense idea that people have (1) subjective expectations of rewards, (2) beliefs as to what is valuable, and (3) expectations of receiving these rewards if they exert effort.

b. Thus, expectancy theory addresses individualized (1) motivations and (2) perceptions of the probability of success.

c. High effort expended, ability, and accurate role assessment will lead to a high performance level. That is, putting appropriate effort into the right task and having the right amount of ability to do it will lead to high performance.

    1) Insufficient ability will impede performance despite effort.

    2) Executing a task that is not desired or is improperly performed according to role definition will impede performance despite effort or ability.

d. Expectancy theory is based on individual perception of

    1) The value of rewards,

    2) The probability the required effort will result in the required performance, and

    3) The probability that the required performance will result in receipt of the desired rewards.

e. Expectancy results from past experiences and measures the strength of belief (the probability assessments) that a particular act will be followed by a specific outcome.

    1) Management is more able to control the expectancy factor than the individual perception of the value of rewards because expectations are based on past experiences.

        a) A consistent management policy will reinforce employee expectations.

f. Performance leads to rewards.

    1) Individuals evaluate rewards on the basis of the fairness of their treatment compared with others in similar jobs.

    2) If unfairness exists, individuals react, usually negatively.

g. Perception of the equity of rewards leads to satisfaction.

    1) The level of satisfaction or dissatisfaction feeds back into the next cycle's estimates of reward values, individual abilities, and role perceptions.

9. Goal-Setting Theory

a. According to Edwin Locke's goal-setting theory, specific, difficult goals to which the employee is committed provide the best motivation tool.

b. Performance improves when goals are specific rather than general, difficult rather than easy, and participative (self-set) rather than imposed by others.

c. Furthermore, specific feedback, especially self-generated feedback, also improves performance compared with lack of feedback.

d. Goals serve as motivators because they

    1) Focus attention on specific results,

    2) Require effort to achieve,

    3) Necessitate continued actions (persistence), and

    4) Create an incentive for developing strategies and action plans.

10. **Job Design**

    a.   Job design links tasks to particular jobs in a way consistent with the organization's strategies, structure, and resources (including technology).

    b.   One approach is to adapt people to the jobs. The following are methods of avoiding job dissatisfaction when this approach is used:

        1)   A **realistic job preview** is a full explanation of what the job involves, including its negative aspects. The purpose is to reduce or eliminate false expectations.

        2)   **Job rotation** is change in boring, highly specialized jobs. It also may have such benefits as cross-functional training.

        3)   **Contingent time off** is an award earned by early completion of a fair performance quota for a day's work without loss of pay.

    c.   Another approach to job design is to adapt the jobs to the people performing them. The following are common methods:

        1)   **Job enlargement** is primarily intended to reduce boredom in repetitive or fast-paced jobs through the assignment of a variety of simple tasks as part of one job. Such jobs are horizontally loaded.

        2)   **Job enrichment** structures the job so that each worker participates in planning and controlling. The purpose is satisfaction of social and ego needs and avoidance of routine work.

            a)   Job enrichment should improve motivation by vertically loading the job, that is, increasing its complexity and challenge.

            b)   According to the core job characteristics described by Hackman and Oldham, jobs are enriched by improving the following basic aspects:

                i)   Skill variety, or the diversity of talents required

                ii)   Task identity, or completion of an entire work product

                iii)   Task significance, or the effect on other people

                iv)   Autonomy, or greater discretion over how work is done

                v)   Feedback, or receipt of information about performance

            c)   Enrichment should produce three critical psychological states:

                i)   Meaningfulness (first three core job characteristics)

                ii)   Responsibility for work outcomes (autonomy)

                iii)   Knowledge of actual work outcomes (feedback)

            d)   The critical psychological states should produce high motivation, performance, and satisfaction; low turnover; and low absenteeism.

                i)   However, worker satisfaction does not necessarily lead to improved performance. It is more likely that a productive worker is a happy worker.

11. **Rewards**

    a.   **Equity theory** states that employee motivation is affected significantly by relative as well as absolute rewards. An employee compares the ratio of what (s)he receives from a job (outcomes such as pay or recognition) to what (s)he gives to the job (inputs such as effort, experience, ability, or education) with the ratios of relevant others.

        1)   If the ratios are equal, equity exists, but if they are unequal, equity tension exists, and the employee will be motivated to eliminate the tension.

        2)   The **referent** chosen (the employee's experience inside or outside the organization or the experiences of others inside or outside the organization) tends to be affected by the employee's job tenure, education, and salary level.

            a)   For example, better-educated employees are more likely to make comparisons with outsiders, and longer-tenured employees may rely on coworkers.

3) Equity tension leads to changes in inputs or outcomes, distorted perceptions of one's effort or of the referent, choice of a different referent, or abandonment of the job.

b. **Cognitive evaluation theory** states that intrinsic rewards (such as competence, responsibility, and achievement) tend to be reduced when extrinsic rewards (such as higher pay, promotion, and better working conditions) are provided for superior performance.

1) The individual may perceive a loss of control over his or her behavior. However, the negative effects of extrinsic rewards on motivation may not apply when a job provides either a very high or a very low level of intrinsic rewards.

a) In the second case, extrinsic rewards may actually increase intrinsic motivation.

c. Rewards are the benefits, psychological and otherwise, of work to employees. Proper management of reward systems should improve job satisfaction and performance.

d. Managers should strive for a high level of employee job satisfaction for the following reasons:

1) Satisfaction is negatively correlated with turnover, which means high job satisfaction usually results in lower turnover;

2) Job satisfaction is directly correlated with good health, which means dissatisfied workers are often less healthy; and

3) Many people feel that job satisfaction is as important as remuneration (salary).

a) Thus, dissatisfied workers may be less productive or be more likely to quit.

e. Extrinsic rewards are received from others. They range from pay to praise.

1) Social rewards normally include acknowledgment of employee achievement through actions, such as solicitation of advice.

2) Token rewards are normally nonrecurring. They show appreciation for the role of the employee. Examples are stock options, early time off with pay, or a paid vacation trip.

3) Examples of visual or auditory awards include a private office, book-club discussions, or redecoration of the work environment.

4) Examples of manipulatables are gifts, such as desk accessories, watches, trophies, clothing, or jewelry.

f. Intrinsic rewards are the internal psychological payoffs that an employee gives to himself or herself. The higher levels of Maslow's hierarchy consist of such rewards.

g. Employee compensation accounts for a high proportion of the organization's total costs. It also involves many complex legal and taxation questions.

1) Nonincentive plans include payment of hourly wages or annual salaries.

2) Incentive plans include piece rate (a fixed amount for each unit of physical output) and sales commission compensation. Merit pay provides bonuses for excellent performance. Sharing of profits, productivity gains, or cost savings gives employees a vested interest in the organization's success.

3) A cafeteria plan provides choices that suit an employee's personal circumstances, for example, health insurance, pension benefits, or family leave.

4) A compensation plan should be perceived by employees as fair. It meets the personal equity test if rewards are proportional to effort. It meets the social equity test if an employee believes that his or her effort-to-reward ratio is proportionate to that of others in similar circumstances.

5) A plan also should provide additional rewards for excellent performance. Hourly and annual compensation plans may not be effective in this respect.

6)   Other types of employee compensation may include (a) flexible working hours, (b) job-sharing, (c) compressed work weeks (e.g., 40 hours over 4 days), or (d) family support (e.g., paid or unpaid parental leave, family sickness leave, on-site daycare, emergency childcare, and eldercare).

Stop and review! You have completed the outline for this subunit. Study multiple-choice questions 5 through 9 beginning on page 220.

9.3 ORGANIZATIONAL POLITICS

1.   **Overview**

    a.   Organizational politics, or impression management, is acting in one's self-interest given actual or perceived opposition in the workplace.

    b.   Managers must understand (1) organizational politics as a matter of self-interest and (2) its negative effects on morale, the effectiveness of needed change, and ethical behavior.

2.   **Behaviors**

    a.   Self-interested behaviors are those not based solely on competence and diligence or resulting from good fortune.

    b.   Positive political behaviors include coalition building, networking, and seeking mentors.

    c.   Negative political behaviors include whistleblowing, sabotage, threats, taking credit for others' work or ideas, and building revolutionary coalitions.

        1)   Negative political behavior is considered by some managers to include whistleblowing. It is the reporting to internal or external parties (e.g., internal auditors, a compliance officer, government bodies, the media, or private watchdog groups) of entity conduct asserted to be wrongful.

            a)   Some managers believe whistleblowing to be an act of revenge that is disloyal to the organization. Moreover, some whistleblowers may have personal financial motives.

            b)   However, the prevailing view is that whistleblowing is a net social good. Revealing unethical behavior may be the only way to end misconduct that has substantial negative effects on the public interest.

            c)   Thus, many governments have enacted whistleblower protection statutes. These laws prohibit retaliation against insiders who appropriately disclose wrongdoing.

            d)   Some statutes even provide financial incentives. For example, in the U.S., a statute may allow employees of the government or of contractors to receive a percentage of any recovery of fraudulent payments made under defense contracts, provision of healthcare, etc.

3.   **Organizational Culture**

    a.   The organizational culture may encourage politics by creating unreasonable obstacles to group and individual advancement.

    b.   The following perceptions about organizational politics are widely held:

        1)   Political behavior increases as managers rise in the hierarchy.

        2)   The frequency of political behavior increases as the organization grows.

        3)   Line managers are less political than staff managers.

        4)   Marketing managers are the most political, and production managers are the least.

        5)   Reorganization results in more political behavior than other changes.

        6)   Political behavior helps career advancement.

7) Political behavior may be beneficial to the organization by promoting ideas, building teams, enhancing communication, and improving morale.

8) Political behavior may have a negative effect on the organization by distracting managers from focusing on entity objectives.

4. **Political Tactics**

   a. The following are common political tactics:

      1) **Posturing** is an attempt to make a good impression, for example, by taking credit for others' work or seeking to stay ahead of a rival (one-upmanship).

      2) **Empire building** is an attempt to control greater resources. Thus, a manager with a larger budget may believe that (s)he is in a safer position and is more influential.

      3) **Making the supervisor look good** is an effort to impress the person who controls one's career path.

      4) **Collecting and using social favors** is a tactic used by someone who views favors as the currency of advancement, not as unselfish acts. Such a manager may help another to look good or not to look bad, for example, by concealing a mistake.

      5) **Creating power and loyalty cliques** is a tactic based on the premise that a cohesive group has more power than an individual.

      6) **Engaging in destructive competition** includes such behaviors as gossip, lying, and sabotage.

5. **Limiting Politics**

   a. Organizational politics may reduce productivity. To avoid this result, the organization should

      1) Create an open, trusting environment;

      2) Focus on performance;

      3) Discourage senior managers from modeling political behavior for other managers;

      4) Use work and career planning to make individual objectives consistent with organizational objectives; and

      5) Rotate jobs to develop a broader perspective and understanding of the problems of others.

Stop and review! You have completed the outline for this subunit. Study multiple-choice question 10 on page 222.

 Internal auditors encounter many situations in which group dynamics should be considered. Group dynamics also affect the management of the internal audit activity. An understanding of this subdiscipline can help internal auditors fulfill their responsibilities.

9.4 GROUP DYNAMICS

1. **Overview**

   a. Management should improve the social capital of the organization by enhancing the relationships of the groups within its structure. A group consists of at least two individuals who interact freely, recognize themselves as group members (common identity), and agree on the reason for the group (common purpose).

2. **Formal Groups**

   a. Formal groups are work groups (designated as committees, teams, etc.) within the organization assembled to perform a productive activity.

      1) Individuals are assigned to formal groups based on their qualifications and the organization's purposes.

      2) Formal groups have explicitly designated leaders.

      3) Membership in formal groups is relatively more permanent than in informal groups.

      4) Formal groups are more structured than informal groups.

3. **Informal Groups**

   a. People seek association and group acceptance and tend to form informal as well as formal groups. Effective managers accept and take advantage of the informal organization.

      1) Informal groups are created within organizations because of the following:

         a) Authority relationships not definable on an organizational chart
         b) Unwritten rules of conduct
         c) Group preferences

      2) The following are characteristics of informal groups:

         a) Development primarily to satisfy esteem needs (friendship).
         b) Membership of most employees, including managers.
         c) Conformity of most members to group pressures.
         d) Small and often very complex. They develop their own leaders, satisfy the needs of members, and usually result from the frequent work interaction among individuals.

      3) Favorable effects of informal groups include the following:

         a) Reducing tension and encouraging production
         b) Improving coordination and reducing supervision required
         c) Assistance in problem solving
         d) Providing another (often faster) channel of communication

            i) The grapevine is the informal communication system in every organization. Computer networks have strengthened the grapevine.

         e) Providing social satisfactions that supplement job satisfaction

      4) The following are examples of potentially unfavorable effects:

         a) Circumventing managerial actions
         b) Reducing production (slowdowns caused by social interactions)
         c) Dissension in the formal organization
         d) Spreading rumors and distorting information
         e) Adding to the cost of doing business
         f) Forming subgroups that hinder group cohesiveness
         g) Adoption of group norms contrary to the objectives of the organization
         h) Developing dominant members

4. **Group Commitment**

   a. Commitment to a group depends on its attractiveness and cohesiveness.

   b. **Attractiveness** is a favorable view from the outside.

   c. **Cohesiveness** is the tendency of members to adhere to the group and unite against outside pressures.

    d.   Group attractiveness and cohesiveness are increased by

        1)   Its prestige and status,
        2)   Cooperation among the members,
        3)   Substantial member interaction,
        4)   Small size of the group,
        5)   Similarity of members,
        6)   Good public image, and
        7)   Common external threat.

    e.   Group attractiveness and cohesiveness are decreased by

        1)   Its unpleasant demands on members,
        2)   Disagreements about activities and procedures,
        3)   Bad experiences with the group,
        4)   Conflict between the group's demands and those of other activities,
        5)   Its bad public image, and
        6)   The possibility of joining other groups.

5. **Roles and Norms**

    a.   A role is the behavior expected of a person in a specific position. Everyone is expected to have different roles.

        1)   The term also refers to actual behavior.
        2)   Different people in the same position should behave similarly.
        3)   Role conflict occurs when a person has two or more conflicting roles.

            a)   Role models may help individuals resolve role conflicts.

        4)   Roles may be formally defined in job descriptions and procedures manuals.

    b.   Norms are general standards of conduct and have a broader effect than roles. Groups are guided by self-set norms of performance and behavior.

        1)   Norms vary from culture to culture and most often are unwritten.
        2)   The following are the functions of norms:

            a)   Protect the group (survival)
            b)   Better define role behavior and expectations
            c)   Safeguard members from embarrassment (self-image)
            d)   Reinforce the group's values and common identity

        3)   Enforcement of norms in the positive sense follows from attention, recognition, and acceptance (social reinforcement).

            a)   Enforcement of norms in the negative sense may be by ridicule or criticism. The ultimate punishment is rejection.

6. **Conformity**

    a.   Conformity is compliance with roles and norms.
    b.   The benefit of conformity is predictability of behavior, e.g., performance of assigned tasks. The cost may be illegal, unethical, or incompetent conduct.
    c.   One danger of cohesive groups is **groupthink**. It is the tendency of individuals committed to the group to ignore input that varies from the group opinion.

        1)   The following are symptoms of groupthink:

            a)   Over-optimism
            b)   Assumed morality of the preferred action
            c)   Intolerance of dissent
            d)   An urgent search for unanimity

2) The following are ways of avoiding groupthink:

   a) Being aware of its dangers
   b) Encouraging members to think critically
   c) Seeking outside opinions
   d) Expressly assigning a member of the group to advocate contrary positions
   e) Expressly considering the consequences of different actions
   f) Not using a group to approve a decision without discussion or dissent

3) Cooperative (constructive) conflict is a means of avoiding groupthink.

4) Formal groups (i.e., committees) can fall victim to groupthink, which can inhibit creative thinking and innovative viewpoints among the group members.

7. **Group-Aided Decision Making**

   a. Group-aided decision making and problem solving have the following advantages:

      1) The group has greater knowledge and experience than an individual.
      2) Lateral thinking allows the group to explore diverse views.
      3) Participants have a better understanding of the reasons for actions.
      4) Active participants tend to accept the result.
      5) Group involvement provides training for the less experienced members.

   b. The following are the disadvantages of group-aided decision making:

      1) The social pressure to conform may inhibit creativity.
      2) The group may be dominated by a few aggressive members.
      3) The decision or solution may be a product of political dealing (logrolling).
      4) Secondary concerns, e.g., competing with a rival, may distract the group.
      5) The process may suffer from groupthink.
      6) Groups tend to take longer than individuals.

   c. Group decision making differs from group-aided decision making.

      1) Groups submerge individual identity and responsibility and conceal the link between individual effort and outcome. Thus, greater acceptance of risk results because accountability is dispersed.

   d. The following are methods that may be applied to improve creativity:

      1) **Attribute listing** is applied primarily to improve a tangible object. It lists the parts and essential features of the object and systematically analyzes modifications.

      2) **Brainstorming** is an unstructured, nonjudgmental group approach that relies on spontaneous contribution of ideas. It breaks down broad problems into their essentials.

         a) Brainstorming generates a large number of ideas and overcomes the pressure to conform while the group is identifying options.

         b) Brainstorming has no predictable effect on the group's commitment to the solution.

      3) **Creative leap** formulates an ideal solution and then works back to a feasible one.

      4) The **scientific method** systematically (a) states a problem, (b) collects data by observation and experimentation, and (c) formulates and tests hypotheses.

      5) The **Edisonian** approach is a trial-and-error method. It should usually not be applied unless other approaches have been unsuccessful.

      6) **Free association** generates ideas by reporting the first thought to come to mind in response to a stimulus, for example, a symbol or analogy pertaining to a product for which an advertising slogan is sought. The objective is to express the content of consciousness without censorship or control.

Stop and review! You have completed the outline for this subunit. Study multiple-choice questions 11 through 15 beginning on page 222.

9.5 STAGES OF GROUP DEVELOPMENT

1. **Overview**

   a. Group development proceeds through stages in which conflicts over power, authority, and interpersonal relationships must be overcome.

   b. Mutual understanding, trust, and commitment tend to be absent in the beginning.

   c. Group objectives, members' roles, and leadership are initially uncertain.

2. **Stages of Development**

   a. The principal issue in the early stages is uncertainty about power and authority relationships. The principal issue in the later stages is uncertainty about interpersonal relationships.

   b. In its **orientation** stage, the group is the least mature, effective, and efficient. Uncertainties are high and temporary leaders emerge.

   c. During the **conflict and challenge** stage, leaders are opposed by people or subgroups with differing agendas. Redistribution of power and authority may occur.

   1) It also may be the final stage if conflicts cannot be resolved.

   d. In the **cohesion** stage, power shifts begun in the prior stage are completed. The members agree about authority, structure, and procedures. They also begin to identify with the group.

   1) If progress is to continue, the stage should be brief.

   e. In the **delusion** stage, members must overcome a false sense that all issues have been resolved. Harmony is emphasized.

   f. In the **disillusion** stage, cohesiveness diminishes as the members realize that their expectations are not being met. Absenteeism increases. Some members risk urging the group to do better.

   g. In the **acceptance** stage, members tend to be effective and efficient. Trust produces cohesiveness and a free exchange of information among group members. This stage is characterized by

   1) Personal and mutual understanding,
   2) Tolerance of differences,
   3) Constructive conflict about substantive matters,
   4) Realistic expectations, and
   5) Acceptance of the authority structure.

   h. The **maturity** stage is the end stage of group development. A mature group tends to be effective and productive compared with groups in earlier stages. A mature group has the following traits:

   1) Awareness of members' strengths and weaknesses related to the group's function
   2) Acceptance of members' differences
   3) Acceptance of group authority and interpersonal relationships
   4) Rational discussion of decisions with tolerance of dissent
   5) Limitation of conflict to substantive rather than emotional issues, e.g., group objectives and the means of reaching them
   6) Members' awareness of their roles in group processes

Stop and review! You have completed the outline for this subunit. Study multiple-choice question 16 on page 223.

9.6 MANAGING HUMAN RESOURCES

1. **Overview**

    a. Managing human resources means acquiring, retaining, and developing employees in accordance with the strategy and structure of the organization.

        1) The human resource strategy is a systems approach that treats employees as human capital, that is, as intangible assets whose full potential should be developed.

        2) The human resources function is responsible for (a) recruitment and selection, (b) evaluation of performance, and (c) training and development.

    b. A people-centered human resource strategy improves employee retention and profits by adopting the following practices:

        1) A job security policy
        2) Stringent hiring procedures
        3) Employee empowerment (e.g., use of self-managed teams)
        4) Basing compensation on performance
        5) Comprehensive training
        6) Reduction of status differences
        7) Information sharing

    c. Human resource planning forecasts future employment requirements. It includes the hiring, training, and monitoring of employees.

        1) Planning includes scanning the external environment to understand the area's labor supply, workforce composition, and work patterns.

        2) Companies must forecast future employee needs to ensure adequate resources when needed. Labor resources are not always as mobile as raw materials.

        3) A human resource audit evaluates compliance with laws and regulations, determines whether operations are efficient, and considers the company's recruitment and salary and benefit programs.

        4) Human resource or human asset accounting attempts to measure the value, and the changes in value, of the organization's investment in human capital.

2. **Designing the Job**

    a. Job analysis involves (1) interviewing superior employees about the way they accomplish their tasks, (2) analyzing work flows, and (3) studying the methods used to achieve work-unit objectives.

    b. A **job description**, based on job analysis, should list basic duties. For higher-level positions, reporting relationships also may be included.

        1) For example, for an accounting clerk, the job description may include

            a) Preparing payroll checks,
            b) Maintaining inventory ledgers, and
            c) Preparing invoices.

    c. **Job specifications**, based on the job description, should list the abilities needed for a job, e.g., education, experience, physical characteristics, and personal characteristics.

3. **Recruitment**

    a. Many countries prohibit employment discrimination with regard to any employment action, for example, hiring, training, compensation, retention, or promotion. Prohibited bases of discrimination may be race, color, religion, sex, national origin, age, or disability.

    b. Using temporary or part-time workers gives management the flexibility to adjust quickly to changing market conditions.

4. **Selection**

   a. The criteria for employee selection are the job specifications developed from each job description.

      1) All requirements, including selection tests, must be based on their relationship to the ability to perform successfully in a specific job.
      2) Employee information preferably should be verified.

   b. The selection process includes the following:

      1) Preparation by developing job descriptions and job specifications
      2) Writing and reviewing interview questions for fairness and legality
      3) Organizing by defining the roles and methods of interviewers
      4) Collecting information from applicants
      5) Evaluating
      6) Meeting to discuss information about applicants
      7) Deciding whether to offer employment

   c. Interviewing is the usual selection method. Interviews range from unstructured to structured.

      1) In an **unstructured interview**, questions are not prearranged. They are asked spontaneously and vary among candidates. Also, the responses are not evaluated in any consistent manner. Accordingly, the unstructured interview is subject to cultural and other biases.
      2) In a **structured interview**, all candidates are asked the same questions, and their responses are assessed based on job-specific criteria using a predetermined scorecard. Bias is minimized, so the structured interview is more effective.

   d. Testing applicants for jobs with quantifiable output (e.g., jobs requiring clerical skills or manual dexterity) is easier than testing for positions with a less tangible work product (e.g., public relations director or human resource manager).

      1) All tests must be validated in each organization and for minority and nonminority groups before they can be predictive of successful performance.
      2) Tests must be given to all applicants for the same job category.

5. **Training and Development**

   a. Training consists of organizational programs to prepare employees to perform currently assigned tasks.

      1) On-the-job training, for example, by job rotation, apprenticeships, and mentoring arrangements, is usually less costly than off-the-job training. However, it may disrupt the workplace and result in increased errors. It is suited to acquisition of technical skills.
      2) Off-the-job training is provided, for example, in classroom lectures, film study, and simulations. It develops problem solving and interpersonal abilities and teaches complex skills.
      3) Computer-based training is expected to become more common.

   b. Development programs prepare people to perform future tasks and learn new skills.

      1) The focus is mostly on development of human relations skills. Management coaching and mentoring enhance development.

   c. Training and development programs succeed when the greatest retention (learning) of skills and knowledge is transferred to the job. The following is a model for learning:

      1) Establishing objectives (goal setting)
      2) Modeling the skills or making a meaningful presentation of facts
      3) Practicing the skills
      4) Obtaining feedback

d.   Evaluation and appraisal help identify individual strengths and weaknesses. Also, jobs and markets change, leading to a need for workers with different skills. Organizations thrive when workers value lifelong learning.

1)   Viewing performance evaluation as a training and developmental process can foster a culture in which evaluation is sought.

2)   A training-needs assessment should determine (a) what training is relevant to employees' jobs, (b) what training will improve performance, and (c) whether training will make a difference. It also should (a) distinguish training needs from organizational problems and (b) link improved job performance with the organization's objectives.

3)   Self-assessment normally yields shorter-term training benefits and may relate more to personal career goals than strategic business needs. Thus, self-assessment often is only a supplement to other approaches.

6.   **Performance Evaluation**

a.   Reasons

1)   Evaluations are important to employees, the employer, and the organization.

2)   Evaluations provide an opportunity for growth and may prevent disputes.

3)   Evaluations tend to focus on who did the job, how it was done, or what was done.

b.   Types

1)   Behavior-oriented evaluation rewards the behavior desired by management. Behavior control examines work processes rather than work output.

2)   Goal-oriented evaluation measures how well the employee attained objectives.

3)   Trait-oriented evaluation tends to reward what the supervisor thinks of the employee.

4)   Employee-oriented evaluation focuses on who did the job.

c.   Purposes

1)   Performance criteria identify job-related abilities.

2)   Performance objectives direct employees toward achieving objectives without constant supervision.

3)   Performance outcomes promote employee satisfaction by acknowledging when jobs are completed and done well.

4)   Evaluation distinguishes effective from ineffective job performance.

5)   The organization develops employee strengths and identifies weaknesses.

6)   Evaluation sets compensation.

a)   But separating performance evaluations from compensation decisions may be beneficial. An advantage is that more emphasis is on long-term objectives and other rewards, such as feelings of achievement and the recognition of superiors.

b)   Another advantage is that the employee's good performance can be separated from the bad performance.

c)   A disadvantage is that the employee may not be motivated immediately by a good appraisal because of the delay of any monetary reward. The evaluation also may not be taken seriously by the employee if compensation is not correlated with performance.

7)   Evaluation identifies promotable employees.

a)   Internal promotions motivate employees and are less difficult and expensive than external hiring.

b)   Many firms hire external candidates because they have a different perspective on the organization's problems and may have more up-to-date training or education.

7. **Major Types of Appraisals**

   a. Management by Objectives (MBO)

     1) Supervisors and subordinates mutually establish objectives. A rating is based on achievement of the objectives.

   b. Behaviorally Anchored Rating Scales (BARS)

     1) BARS describe good and bad performance. They are developed through job analysis for a number of specific job-related behaviors.

   c. Check-the-Box

     1) This method provides a list of categories for rating performance for the supervisor to check off. The following are examples:

       a) Graphic scale, consisting of a list of job duties and a scale to grade them, e.g., 1 = Excellent, etc.

       b) A checklist of statements relating to job performance.

   d. Comparative Methods

     1) These involve comparing an employee's performance with the work of others. Comparative methods include

       a) Ranking all employees from highest to lowest. This method can lend itself to bias on the part of the evaluator.

       b) Ranking an employee against other employee(s) (paired comparison).

   e. Narrative Method

     1) This approach includes essays and critical incidents (specific inferior or superior performance). Both require large amounts of time.

     2) Field reviews require human resources personnel to prepare the evaluation for each employee based on the supervisor's input.

   f. 360° Performance Appraisal

     1) This method uses a multirater model for employee assessment. It provides anonymous feedback by peers, customers, supervisors, and subordinates.

     2) Appraisal is subjective and may be affected by popularity.

     3) Evaluations do not include copies of job descriptions or performance goals.

Stop and review! You have completed the outline for this subunit. Study multiple-choice questions 17 through 20 on page 224.

QUESTIONS

9.1 Organizational Theory

1. The organizational chart

A. Is used only in centralized organizations.

B. Is applicable only to profit-oriented companies.

C. Depicts only line functions.

D. Depicts the lines of authority linking various positions.

Answer (D) is correct.

   REQUIRED: The true statement about an organizational chart.

   DISCUSSION: An organizational chart is used to represent the organizational structure of an entity in two dimensions, vertical hierarchy and horizontal specialization. It often resembles a pyramid, with the chief executive on top and the operating work force on the bottom. Lines show reporting relationships, lines of authority, and task groupings. An organizational chart depicts promotional or career tracks and illustrates the span of control and the number of organizational levels.

   Answer (A) is incorrect. An organizational chart can be used in decentralized as well as centralized organizations. Answer (B) is incorrect. Not-for-profit agencies use organizational charts for the same reasons as profit-oriented companies. Answer (C) is incorrect. Both staff and line functions are depicted on organizational charts.

2. Organizational charts often represent the formal structure of an organization. Often the organizational chart represents a pyramid with the chief executive on the top and the operating workforce on the bottom. Which of the following would **not** be included in a typical organizational chart?

    A. The span of control and the number of organizational levels.

    B. Communication channels.

    C. Promotional or career tracks.

    D. Informal influence or friendships.

Answer (D) is correct.
    REQUIRED: The limitations of organizational charts.
    DISCUSSION: Organizational charts often show the formal relationships between employers and employees. However, a shortcoming of organizational charts is that they do not show informal relationships between the upper and lower levels of the corporate hierarchy.
    Answer (A) is incorrect. The span of control and the number of organizational levels is demonstrated by the pyramid. The chief executive at the top has the greatest control over the organization and then the levels of the pyramid show the number of organizational levels. Answer (B) is incorrect. The communication channels are often up the pyramid and are shown on the organizational chart. Answer (C) is incorrect. The higher levels of the pyramid are the levels that employees can be promoted to.

3. Which of the following concepts is **not** consistent with a successful authoritarian organization?

    A. Each subordinate should only have one superior.

    B. Superiors may have as many subordinates as possible within the superior's span of control.

    C. Responsibility may be delegated.

    D. The hierarchy of authority should be precisely defined.

Answer (C) is correct.
    REQUIRED: The characteristics of a successful authoritarian organization.
    DISCUSSION: Taylor, Fayol, and other traditionalists advocated the creation of authoritarian organizations. One of the criteria for success was the ability to delegate authority but not responsibility. Responsibility should always remain with the person who made the decision.
    Answer (A) is incorrect. The unity of command principle states that each subordinate should only have one superior in order to prevent confusion and frustration. Answer (B) is incorrect. The unity of command principle states that a superior can have as many subordinates as he or she can reasonably manage. Answer (D) is incorrect. The unity of objective principle requires that the hierarchy of authority be precisely defined to pursue common objectives.

4. Although bureaucracy is often perceived negatively by the public, bureaucracy is a feature of nearly every large company. Which of the following is a sign that a bureaucracy is dysfunctional?

    A. A diversity of jobs.

    B. Rules that obscure responsibility.

    C. A large number of rules necessary for day to day operations.

    D. Obedience to authority.

Answer (B) is correct.
    REQUIRED: The symptoms of a dysfunctional bureaucracy.
    DISCUSSION: A sign that a bureaucracy is dysfunctional is the development of rules that are meaningless or that obscure accountability. A lack of accountability shows that the bureaucracy is ineffective at identifying the source problems and creating solutions to solve the problems.
    Answer (A) is incorrect. A diversity of jobs prevents employees from becoming bored with routine and unchallenging tasks. Answer (C) is incorrect. Many bureaucracies have rules to guide day-to-day operations. As long as the rules have a purpose and are not meaningless, the rules do not create a dysfunctional environment. Answer (D) is incorrect. Obedience to authority is required for a corporation's operations to run smoothly. However, obedience at all costs is a sign that the bureaucracy is dysfunctional.

9.2 Motivation

5. Motivation is

    A. The extent to which goal-specific performance is recognized by supervisors.

    B. The extent to which individuals have the authority to make decisions.

    C. The extent of the attempt to accomplish a specific goal.

    D. The desire and the commitment to achieve a specific goal.

Answer (D) is correct.
    REQUIRED: The definition of motivation.
    DISCUSSION: Motivation is the desire to attain a specific goal (goal congruence) and the commitment to accomplish the goal (managerial effort). Managerial motivation is therefore a combination of managerial effort and goal congruence.
    Answer (A) is incorrect. Recognition of goal-specific performance is characteristic of a reward system. Answer (B) is incorrect. Autonomy is the extent to which individuals have the authority to make decisions. Answer (C) is incorrect. Goal congruence is the sharing of goals by supervisors and subordinates.

6. Frederick Herzberg postulated a two-factor theory of human behavior that included satisfiers and dissatisfiers. Which of the following is a dissatisfier?

A. Promotion to another position.

B. Salary.

C. Challenging work.

D. Responsibility.

Answer (B) is correct.

    REQUIRED: The item that is a dissatisfier.

    DISCUSSION: Frederick Herzberg's two-factor theory of human behavior postulates that there are two classes of factors in the job situation. Maintenance of hygiene factors (dissatisfiers) are those the presence of which will not especially motivate people but the absence of which will diminish performance. These factors are extrinsic to the work itself. They include supervision, working conditions, interpersonal relations, salary, and status. Motivational factors (satisfiers) are those the absence of which will not diminish performance but the addition or availability of which will motivate employees. Intrinsic to the work itself, these include achievement, recognition, challenging work, advancement, growth in the job, and responsibility.

    Answer (A) is incorrect. Recognition and achievement are satisfiers. Answer (C) is incorrect. Challenging work is a satisfier. Answer (D) is incorrect. Responsibility is a satisfier.

7. An employee's self-actualization need would be met by

A. Attractive pension provisions.

B. Challenging new job assignments.

C. Good working conditions.

D. Regular positive feedback.

Answer (B) is correct.

    REQUIRED: The item that meets an employee's self-actualization need.

    DISCUSSION: Self-actualization is the highest level need in Maslow's hierarchy. It is the desire to become what one is capable of becoming, to realize one's potential and accomplish to the limit of one's ability. In other words, the job itself is an intrinsic motivation; no extrinsic motivation (such as rewards or reinforcements) is needed. Intrinsic motivation provides the worker with psychological income. Thus, challenging new job assignments meet an employee's self-actualization needs.

    Answer (A) is incorrect. Attractive pension provisions meet an employee's physiological needs. Answer (C) is incorrect. Good working conditions meet an employee's physiological needs. Answer (D) is incorrect. Regular positive feedback meets an employee's esteem needs.

8. Some behavioral models stress employee participation as a key to motivation. A limitation of the participative approach is

A. Workers are intrinsically lazy and must be driven.

B. A number of dissatisfiers must be present in order for the approach to work.

C. It is difficult to elicit the participation of all employees.

D. Unresolvable conflicts arise when a mature, capable, creative person joins a structured, demanding, and limiting organization.

Answer (C) is correct.

    REQUIRED: The limitation of the participative approach.

    DISCUSSION: For a participative management approach to succeed, the parties must have sufficient time, the issues must be relevant to employees' interests, employees must have the abilities (training and communication skills) to participate, and the organizational culture should support participation. Accordingly, a limitation of the participative approach is that it is unlikely that all employees are willing to participate in decision making.

    Answer (A) is incorrect. The participative approach assumes that workers are positively motivated. Answer (B) is incorrect. The presence of dissatisfiers is not consistent with the participative approach. Answer (D) is incorrect. Such conflicts arise when the needs of individuals are not integrated with the needs of the organization.

9. According to the behavioral theory of management,

A. Employees are motivated to fulfill needs.

B. Morale problems are not goal related.

C. Compensation is a universal motivator.

D. Productivity is not correlated with job satisfaction.

Answer (A) is correct.

    REQUIRED: The behavioral theory of management.

    DISCUSSION: The behavioral theory of management holds that all people (including employees) have complex needs, desires, and attitudes. The fulfillment of needs is the goal toward which employees are motivated. Effective leadership matches need-fulfillment rewards with desired behavior (tasks) that accomplishes organizational goals.

    Answer (B) is incorrect. Management's role in the directing process is to motivate people to contribute toward accomplishment of organizational goals. Answer (C) is incorrect. Although management theories differ as to the motivational value of wages, compensation is not a motivator for all persons at all times. Answer (D) is incorrect. While research has indicated that satisfaction and productivity are not directly related, behavioral theorists believe that they must have some relationship.

9.3 Organizational Politics

10. Which of the following tactics may employees use when feeling that employees' individual power is insignificant?

    A. Employees may engage in posturing by taking credit for the work of a coworker.

    B. Employees may engage in destructive competition by spreading false rumors.

    C. Employees may engage in creating power and loyalty cliques with other coworkers.

    D. Employees may attempt to conceal errors made by a supervisor in order to aid the employees' own future advancement within the corporation.

Answer (C) is correct.

    REQUIRED: The tactics employees engage in when they feel a cohesive group has more power than an individual.

    DISCUSSION: Employees will often form groups when they feel their collective bargaining power is greater than the power of an individual.

    Answer (A) is incorrect. Posturing is the attempt to make a good impression and is often used when an individual feels his or her power is adequate. Answer (B) is incorrect. Engaging in destructive competition does not reveal that an individual feels his or her power is insignificant. Answer (D) is incorrect. Concealing errors by an employee demonstrates that (s)he feels his or her power is great enough to hide errors and not get caught.

9.4 Group Dynamics

11. Which one of the following is generally **not** beneficial to group decision making in an organization?

    A. More information.

    B. Acceptance.

    C. More knowledge.

    D. Dominant members.

Answer (D) is correct.

    REQUIRED: The item that is not beneficial to group decision making in an organization.

    DISCUSSION: Group decision making, such as by committee, works better when the committee is small and the members accept each other as contributing parts of the group. A dominant member is not desirable. The chair should act as a moderator and not be considered threatening or overbearing by the other members.

    Answer (A) is incorrect. A group decision, like an individual decision, is better when based on sufficient information. Answer (B) is incorrect. Acceptance of each member of the committee and the goals of the committee is essential. Answer (C) is incorrect. The more knowledge that group members possess, the better the decision is likely to be.

12. Which of the following is **not** an advantage of group decision making as compared to individual decision making?

    A. Groups obtain an increased degree of acceptance of a solution so that it may be more easily implemented.

    B. Group decision making is consistent with democratic methods.

    C. Group members bring more complete information and knowledge into the decision process.

    D. Group members avoid expressing opinions that deviate from what appears to be the group consensus.

Answer (D) is correct.

    REQUIRED: The item that is not an advantage of group decision making.

    DISCUSSION: The groupthink phenomenon is undesirable, whether a group makes the decision or aids the decision maker. Groupthink occurs when group members accept what appears to be the group consensus rather than giving their honest input. The result may be decisions with which some members of the group are not happy.

    Answer (A) is incorrect. If members of the group are responsible for the decision making, their participation in the implementation process will increase the ease with which the decisions are carried out. Answer (B) is incorrect. Group decision making adds legitimacy to the solution by following democratic methods. Answer (C) is incorrect. A group possesses greater resources than an individual.

13. Which of the following is **not** an advantage of group effort compared with work performed by individuals?

    A. Groups provide support to members.

    B. Groups make decisions that are more easily accepted.

    C. Groups provide a clear link between effort and outcome.

    D. Groups control and discipline members.

Answer (C) is correct.
    REQUIRED: The item not an advantage of group effort.
    DISCUSSION: In a culture that strongly emphasizes individual identity and competition, the preference tends to be for a clear link between effort and outcome. However, groups tend to submerge individual identity and responsibility and therefore to blur the link between individual effort and its results.
    Answer (A) is incorrect. Providing support and meeting other needs of members is an advantage. Answer (B) is incorrect. Members who participate in a group decision-making process tend to understand and accept the result. Answer (D) is incorrect. Groups develop and enforce behavioral norms that (1) protect the group, (2) define roles and expectations, (3) safeguard members from loss of face, and (4) reinforce group values and identity.

14. Which of the following statements about group decision making is most likely **false**?

    A. There is a lack of responsibility for group decisions.

    B. Group decision making is almost always less efficient than individual decision making.

    C. The desire by individual members to be accepted by the group often restrains open disagreement.

    D. Group decision making tends to be less creative than individual decision making.

Answer (D) is correct.
    REQUIRED: The false statement about group decision making.
    DISCUSSION: Groups tend to be more creative than individuals because diversity of member views generally results in the consideration of more alternatives for solving a problem (but the social pressure to conform also may inhibit creativity).
    Answer (A) is incorrect. Individuals do not accept responsibility for group decisions. Answer (B) is incorrect. Group decision making almost always takes more time than individual decision making, except when the need for diverse views is so great that an individual decision maker needs to consult many people or perform research. Answer (C) is incorrect. Group members generally have diverse views, but their common need to be accepted and respected by the group often restrains the full, open expression of their views when they fear strong disagreement.

15. Which of the following is **not** true with regard to informal groups?

    A. Members of the group are susceptible to group pressure.

    B. The groups develop primarily to satisfy esteem needs.

    C. Almost all employees and managers are members of an informal group.

    D. Informal groups tend to be small and have simple relationships.

Answer (D) is correct.
    REQUIRED: The false statement regarding informal groups.
    DISCUSSION: Informal groups tend to be small and are often very complex. They develop their own leaders and usually result from the frequent interaction among individuals in the course of their work.
    Answer (A) is incorrect. Group pressure is often a major characteristic of informal groups, and the pressure is often hard to resist because members seek acceptance from the group. Answer (B) is incorrect. Informal groups often form to establish friendships, which satisfy esteem needs. Answer (C) is incorrect. Almost everyone in an organization forms some type of friendship or other informal relationship with others in the organization.

9.5 Stages of Group Development

16. Which of the following characteristics is common with a mature group?

    A. Harmony is emphasized at the expense of addressing the problems.

    B. There is no attempt to force unanimity.

    C. Members begin to identify with the group.

    D. Redistributions of power and authority may occur.

Answer (B) is correct.
    REQUIRED: The characteristics of a mature group.
    DISCUSSION: A mature group is in the end stage of group development and tends to be more effective and productive compared to groups in earlier stages. A mature group engages in rational discussion of decisions with tolerance of dissent and no attempt to force unanimity.
    Answer (A) is incorrect. Harmony is emphasized at the expense of addressing problems during the delusion stage when members have the false sense that all emotional issues have been resolved. Answer (C) is incorrect. Members begin to identify with the group during the cohesion stage. In a mature group, members already identify with the group. Answer (D) is incorrect. Redistributions of power and authority occur during the conflict and challenge stage when leaders are opposed by members of the group with differing agendas.

9.6 Managing Human Resources

17. A manager discovers by chance that a newly hired employee has strong beliefs that are very different from the manager's and from those of most of the other employees. The manager's best course of action would be to

    A. Facilitate the reassignment of the new hire as quickly as possible before this situation becomes disruptive.

    B. Ask the rest of the team for their reaction and act according to the group consensus.

    C. Take no action unless the new hire's behavior is likely to cause harm to the organization.

    D. Try to counsel the new hire into more reasonable beliefs.

Answer (C) is correct.
    REQUIRED: The manager's best course of action when a new employee has strong beliefs that are very different from the manager's beliefs.
    DISCUSSION: The only legitimate grounds on which the supervisor may take action is the employee's behavior. Personal beliefs, such as those on religious and political matters, cannot be the basis of personnel actions. Discrimination on the basis of personal beliefs could expose the organization to legal action.

18. When faced with the problem of filling a newly created or recently vacated executive position, organizations must decide whether to promote from within or hire an outsider. One of the disadvantages of promoting from within is that

    A. Internal promotions can have a negative motivational effect on the employees of the firm.

    B. Internal promotions are more expensive to the organization than hiring an outsider.

    C. It is difficult to identify proven performers among internal candidates.

    D. Hiring an insider leads to the possibility of social inbreeding within the firm.

Answer (D) is correct.
    REQUIRED: The disadvantage of promoting from within.
    DISCUSSION: Hiring an internal candidate can lead to social inbreeding. Many firms look to external candidates for certain jobs because they bring a fresh perspective to the organization's problems and may have more up-to-date training or education.
    Answer (A) is incorrect. Internal promotions usually lead to increased motivation among employees. Answer (B) is incorrect. Internal promotions are less expensive. The firm can avoid the expenses associated with an executive search and certain training costs. Answer (C) is incorrect. It is more difficult to identify proven performers from among outside candidates than internal candidates.

19. Performance appraisal systems might use any of three different approaches: (1) who did the job, (2) how the job was done, or (3) what was accomplished. Which approach is used by a system that places the focus on how the job was done?

    A. Behavior-oriented.

    B. Goal-oriented.

    C. Trait-oriented.

    D. Employee-oriented.

Answer (A) is correct.
    REQUIRED: The approach used in a performance appraisal system that emphasizes how the job was done.
    DISCUSSION: Behavior-oriented performance evaluation rewards the behavior that is desired by management. Behavior control involves examining work processes rather than work output.
    Answer (B) is incorrect. The goal-oriented approach measures how well the employee attained the objectives or goals set by management. Answer (C) is incorrect. A trait-oriented approach tends to reward what the supervisor thinks of the employee rather than the job the employee did. Answer (D) is incorrect. An employee-oriented approach would focus on who did the job.

20. Evaluating performance is **not** done to

    A. Determine the amount of nondiscriminatory benefits that each employee deserves.

    B. Assess the available human resources of the firm.

    C. Motivate the employees.

    D. Determine which employees deserve salary increases.

Answer (A) is correct.
    REQUIRED: The statement that is not a purpose of performance evaluations.
    DISCUSSION: Evaluations reinforce accomplishments, help in assessing employee strengths and weaknesses, provide motivation, assist in employee development, permit the organization to assess its human resource needs, and serve as a basis for wage increases. Nondiscriminatory benefits are given to everyone in the organization in equal amounts, regardless of title, pay, or achievement of objectives.
    Answer (B) is incorrect. Performance evaluation is done to assess the available human resources of the firm. Answer (C) is incorrect. Performance evaluation is done to motivate the employees. Answer (D) is incorrect. Performance evaluation is done to determine which employees deserve salary increases.

STUDY UNIT TEN
LEADERSHIP AND CONFLICT MANAGEMENT

(24 pages of outline)

This study unit is the fifth of five covering **Section V: Management/Leadership Principles** from The IIA's CIA Exam Syllabus. This section makes up 10% to 20% of Part 3 of the CIA exam and is tested at the **awareness level**. The relevant portion of the syllabus is highlighted below. (The complete syllabus is in Appendix A.)

V. **MANAGEMENT/LEADERSHIP PRINCIPLES (10%–20%)**

   A. **Strategic Management**

   B. **Organizational Behavior**

      1. Organizational theory (structures and configurations)

      2. Organizational behavior (e.g., motivation, impact of job design, rewards, schedules)

      3. Group dynamics (e.g., traits, development stages, organizational politics, effectiveness)

      4. Knowledge of human resource processes (e.g., individual performance management, supervision, personnel sourcing/staffing, staff development)

      5. Risk/control implications of different leadership styles

      6. Performance (productivity, effectiveness, etc.)

   C. **Management Skills/Leadership Styles**

      1. Lead, inspire, mentor, and guide people, building organizational commitment and entrepreneurial orientation

      2. Create group synergy in pursuing collective goals

      3. Team-building and assessing team performance

   D. **Conflict Management**

      1. Conflict resolution (e.g., competitive, cooperative, and compromise)

      2. Negotiation skills

      3. Conflict management

      4. Added-value negotiating

   E. **Project Management/Change Management**

      1. Change management

      2. Project management techniques

Influence tactics, the exercise of power, and leadership are, like group dynamics, intangible qualities that substantially (if not decisively) affect organizational success. An internal auditor therefore must be alert to their effects on governance, risk management, and control processes.

10.1 LEADERSHIP STYLES

1. **Management, Leadership, and Power**

    a. Management is arranging the work of others to achieve organizational objectives.

    b. Leadership is a special type of management. It influences, inspires, and guides people to strive willingly to achieve group objectives through common effort.

2. **Influence**

    a. Influence in the work environment is an attempt to change the behavior of superiors, peers, or lower-level employees. Influence may be exerted in many ways, including the use of power and the exercise of leadership.

    b. Management literature describes generic influence tactics.

        1) They may be directed upward to influence superiors, laterally to influence peers, and downward to influence lower-level employees.

        2) The following are the generic influence tactics noted by researchers:

            a) Consultation permits the other person(s) to participate in the decision or change.

            b) Rational persuasion tries to convince others by reliance on a detailed plan, supporting evidence, and reason. This is used most often by employees of participative managers.

            c) Inspirational appeals are based on emotions, values, or ideals.

            d) Ingratiating tactics attempt to raise the other person's self-esteem prior to a request.

            e) Coalition tactics seek the aid of others to persuade someone to agree.

            f) Pressure tactics involve intimidation, threats, and demands.

            g) Upward appeals are based on the formal or informal support of higher management.

            h) Exchange tactics may involve an exchange of favors, a reminder of a past favor, or an offer of a personal sacrifice.

        3) The most commonly used influence tactics are consultation, rational persuasion, and inspirational appeals. The least commonly used are pressure tactics, upward appeals, and exchange tactics.

3. **Power**

    a. Power is the ability to influence employees to do what they would not ordinarily do. It also has been defined as the ability to use people, information, and material resources to accomplish something. Power and influence may be used formally or informally.

        1) The dimensions of power include the ability to control others, act freely, or resist control by others.

        2) **Authority** is the right to manage others. It differs from power, which is the ability to accomplish something.

            a) A manager may have one without the other.

    b.   The following are power sources:

        1) **Legitimate or position power** (closely associated with formal authority)

           a) Employees tend not to obey completely someone who relies solely on legitimate authority. Moreover, managers may not have the right to direct (exert formal authority over) some people whom they need to influence.

        2) **Expertise**

           a) A notable example is the power exerted by IT professionals.

        3) **Referent power** (derived from the leader's charisma or employees' identification with the leader)

           a) The negative aspect of referent power is that the individuals who have it often abuse it.

        4) **Coercive power**

           a) This power is based on the fear or threat of punishment.

        5) **Control of rewards**

           a) Performance may determine pay raises and promotions.

    c.   The greater the sources of a manager's power, the more likely an employee will accept his or her authority.

        1) Thus, a manager who has multiple sources of power, either formal or informal, will be more influential than one with a single source.

    d.   Modern management theory emphasizes employee empowerment. The question is not whether employees should be empowered but the circumstances in which it should occur.

        1) Individuals need to be honest, trustworthy, unselfish, and skilled.

        2) Empowerment is not the same as lack of control. Appropriate oversight is necessary.

        3) Employees should have adequate training, relevant information, and other necessary tools.

        4) Employees should participate fully in making important decisions.

        5) Employees should be fairly compensated.

        6) Managers who appropriately surrender power by empowering employees actually gain power. They have an increased ability to achieve desired results.

4. **Traitist Approach**

    a.   According to this approach, authority, decision making, and responsibility all may be decentralized to some extent. But leadership is a characteristic of the individual's personality and cannot be subdivided.

    b.   A few traits have a significant correlation with a leader's effectiveness:

        1) Intelligence
        2) Scholarship
        3) Dependability
        4) Social participation and interest
        5) Socioeconomic status (in comparison with nonleaders)

c.   The emotional intelligence of leaders (i.e., their social skills and judgment, maturity, and emotional control) also can contribute to a leader's effectiveness.

   1)   These abilities can be learned, especially when a person understands that immaturity, erratic behavior, and uncontrolled negative emotions have a bad effect on the workplace.

   2)   A leader can acquire social capital through exhibiting the following leadership traits:

      a)   Self-awareness is knowing oneself.

      b)   Self-management is the ability to prevent changes in one's mood from interfering with positive relationships.

      c)   Social awareness is understanding the actions and emotions of others. This ability helps a person to adapt in a productive way.

      d)   Relationship management is an ability possessed by a person who communicates and resolves conflict effectively. Humor and a benign approach are characteristics of people who develop good relationships.

d.   People often assert that men and women have different leadership traits. However, research indicates that male and female managers do not match the stereotypes.

5.   **Leader Behavior**

a.   Behavior-oriented researchers have examined leader behavior to determine whether leaders conduct themselves in certain ways.

b.   Styles of leadership are emphasized in behavioral approaches. The following are the traditional styles:

   1)   Authoritarian or autocratic

      a)   The manager does not share authority and responsibility. (S)he dictates all decisions to employees, so communication is downward with little employee input.

      b)   Tasks are clearly defined.

      c)   Authoritarian leaders rely on threats and punishment and do not trust employees.

      d)   Such leadership can sometimes be the most effective, such as when the time to make a decision is limited or when employees do not respond to any other leadership style.

   2)   Democratic

      a)   The leader delegates substantial authority.

      b)   Employees participate in defining and assigning tasks, and communication is actively upward as well as downward. Thus, employees are more committed.

   3)   Laissez faire

      a)   Employees in a group are given the authority and responsibility to make their own decisions.

      b)   Communication is mostly horizontal.

      c)   This style works best when employees show personal initiative, but the group also may be ineffective without the leader's guidance.

c. According to a model developed at Ohio State University, the initiation of structure and consideration by the leader are two behavior patterns that are consistently found in the study of leadership.

1) This model is a grid model where the x axis is called **structure**. It measures how well one is at accomplishing tasks. In other words, it assesses production.

2) The y axis is called **consideration** and it measures the personal relationship (warmth, respect, helpfulness, etc.) between the leader and the subordinate. Thus, it assesses how employee-centered the leader is.

3) The following are the four leadership styles in the Ohio State model based on the quadrants of the grid:

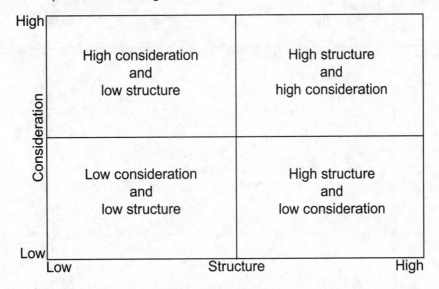

Figure 10-1

a) High consideration and low structure result from an emphasis on satisfying employee needs.

b) High structure and high consideration reflect a strong emphasis on both task accomplishment and satisfying employee needs.

c) Low consideration and low structure indicate a passive leader.

d) High structure and low consideration result from a primary focus on task accomplishment.

d.   The leadership grid developed by Robert Blake and Jane Mouton is a trademarked classification scheme. Concern for production is on the horizontal (x) axis, and concern for people is on the vertical (y) axis.

1)   Concern for production emphasizes output, cost control, and profit.

2)   Concern for people emphasizes friendship, aiding employees in accomplishing tasks, and addressing employee issues (e.g., compensation).

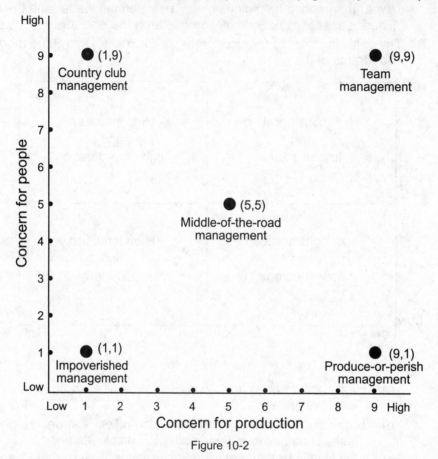

Figure 10-2

3)   Each axis has a scale of 1 to 9. Thus, the primary styles are the following:

a)   **Impoverished management** has little concern for production or people. The manager's main concern is not to be held responsible for mistakes.

b)   **Country club management** has a primary concern for people but little concern for production.

c)   **Produce-or-perish management** has a primary concern for production but little concern for people.

d)   **Middle-of-the-road management** has a moderate concern for production and people to maintain status quo.

e)   **Team management** has a great concern for production and people, trust, teamwork, and commitment.

i)   Blake, Mouton, and their associates assert that this management style is the best because it produces the best operating results, health outcomes, and conflict resolutions.

6. **Situational Theories**

    a. The assumption of situational theories of leadership is that the appropriate leadership style depends on the situation. The emphasis is on flexibility because no one style is best in every situation.

    b. According to Fred E. Fiedler's **contingency theory**, people become leaders because of personality attributes, various situational factors, and the interaction between the leaders and the situation.

        1) Thus, the right person at the right time may rise to a position of leadership if his or her personality and the needs of the situation complement each other.

            a) The same person might not become a leader in different circumstances because of failure to interact successfully with that situation.

        2) The contingency theory model has three dimensions:

            a) **Position power** is based on the formal authority structure. It is the degree to which the position held enables a leader to evaluate, reward, punish, or promote group members. It is independent of other sources of power, such as personality or expertise.

            b) **Task structure** is how clearly and carefully members' responsibilities for various tasks are defined. Quality of performance is more easily controlled when tasks are clearly defined.

            c) **Leader-member relations** reflect the extent to which group members like, trust, and are willing to follow a leader.

        3) Leaders tend to be task-motivated or relationship-motivated.

            a) The task-motivated style is most effective when the situation is very favorable or very unfavorable.

                i) The situation is very favorable when the leader's position of power is high, tasks are well defined, and leader-member relations are good. The situation is very unfavorable when the reverse is true.

                ii) In the favorable situation, a leader has little need to address relationship issues and should therefore concentrate on the work. In the unfavorable situation, the leader must emphasize close supervision.

            b) The relationship-motivated style is most effective in moderately favorable situations that have a combination of favorable and unfavorable factors.

        4) The most effective leadership style depends upon the degree to which the three dimensions are present in a situation.

        5) Leadership is therefore as much a responsibility of the organization's placement of leaders as it is of the leaders themselves.

            a) Thus, an organization should identify leadership situations and its managers' leadership styles and design the job to suit the manager if necessary.

    c. According to Hersey and Blanchard's **situational leadership theory**, the appropriate leadership style depends on the followers' maturity, which is their degree of willingness to be responsible for directing their behavior. The dimensions of the four styles of leadership described in the model are task and relationship behaviors.

        1) **Selling.** A selling leadership style explains decisions and provides opportunity for clarification (high task and high relationship).

        2) **Telling.** A telling leadership style provides specific instructions and closely supervises performance (high task and low relationship).

3) **Participating.** A participating leadership style encourages the sharing of ideas and facilitates decision making (low task and high relationship).

4) **Delegating.** A delegating leadership style turns over responsibility for decisions and implementation (low task and low relationship).

d. **Path-goal theory** emphasizes motivation. It combines the research on initiating structure and consideration with expectancy theory.

1) Leaders should motivate employees by clarifying employees' understanding of work goals, the relationship of achievement of those goals with rewards that matter to employees, and how the goals may be achieved.

2) A leadership style should be chosen that complements but does not duplicate the factors in the environment and is consistent with employees' characteristics.

a) The **directive** leader lets employees know what is expected of them, schedules work to be done, and gives specific guidance on how to accomplish tasks.

i) A directive style is most effective when the employees are externally controlled (i.e., not directly managed), tasks are ambiguous or stressful, and substantial conflict exists in the work group.

ii) Unknowledgeable or incompetent employees are best led using the directive style.

b) The **supportive** leader is friendly and shows concern for the needs of the employees.

i) The supportive style is best when tasks are highly structured and the authority relationships are clear and bureaucratic.

ii) This approach depends on people who want to work, grow, and achieve.

iii) The supportive style may be best when tasks are unsatisfying.

c) The **participative** leader consults with employees and considers their suggestions before making a decision.

i) The participative style is most useful when employees believe they control their own destinies, that is, when they have an internal locus of control. Such individuals may be resentful if they are not consulted.

d) The **achievement-oriented** leader is a facilitator who sets challenging goals and expects employees to perform at their highest level. Achievement-oriented leadership is appropriate when tasks are nonrepetitive and ambiguous and employee competence is high.

3) In contrast with Fiedler's approach, path-goal theorists believe that managers are able to adapt their styles to the situation.

7. **Transformational Leadership**

a. A transformational leader is an agent of change who combines initiating structure and consideration with such other behaviors as charisma. The transformational leader is able to inspire the members of the organization to aspire to and achieve more than they thought was possible.

1) Transformational leadership emphasizes

a) Vision,
b) Development of the individual,
c) Empowerment of the worker, and
d) The challenging of traditional assumptions.

2) The transformational leader normally has charisma, is inspirational, provides intellectual stimulation to workers, and gives individualized consideration.

8. **Transactional Leadership**

   a. A transactional leader emphasizes monitoring of employees so that they adhere to existing rules. Transactional leaders use both rewards and punishments to ensure high performance.

   b. Unlike transformational leaders, transactional leaders are looking not to change the future but to maintain the normal flow of operations.

9. **Behavior Modification**

   a. Behavior modification is the management of environmental factors to encourage desirable behavior and to discourage undesirable behavior. Environmental factors include antecedents and consequences of behavior.

   b. Consequences include the following:

      1) Positive reinforcement provides rewards for certain responses. It emphasizes desirable rather than undesirable behavior.

         a) Theorists regard positive reinforcement as the most effective approach.

         b) Examples are merit-based salary bonuses and payment based on the level of output.

         c) Continuous reinforcement rewards every occurrence of a desirable new behavior.

         d) Intermittent reinforcement provides occasional rewards for an established behavior.

            i) Variable-interval schedules of intermittent reinforcement lead to better performance. Employees are more alert because of the uncertainty involved, and performance and reward are connected.

            ii) Fixed-interval schedules of reinforcement do not clearly link performance and reward.

      2) Negative reinforcement is the withdrawal of an existing unpleasant condition (such as a threat) when the desired behavior occurs.

      3) Extinction discourages a behavior by ignoring it (not reinforcing it).

      4) Punishment discourages a behavior by following it with a negative consequence. Punishment is most effective when it immediately follows an undesirable behavior.

10. **Mentoring**

    a. Mentoring is systematic development of leadership by providing career counseling and social nurturing. It requires intensive tutoring, coaching, and guidance.

    b. Some organizations have formal mentoring programs that assign mentors to junior employees. However, some research indicates that a mentoring arrangement that occurs informally and voluntarily may have better results.

    c. Mentoring serves career and psychosocial functions.

       1) Career functions include sponsorship, visibility, coaching, protection, and assigning challenges.

       2) Psychosocial functions include role modeling, acceptance, confirmation, counseling, and friendship.

       3) Mentoring can be helpful in any working environment, even a negative one.

Stop and review! You have completed the outline for this subunit. Study multiple-choice questions 1 through 4 beginning on page 248.

10.2 TEAM BUILDING

1. **Participative Management**

   a. Participative management is a Theory Y approach (discussed in Study Unit 9). It gives employees greater control of the workplace when they can establish objectives, be involved in decision making, solve problems, or effect organizational change.

   b. Employees are more highly motivated and productive and turnover is lower when effective participative management programs are in place.

   c. Quality control circles, self-managed teams, and open-book management reflect the participative principle.

   1) **Quality circles (QCs)** are groups, usually of up to ten employees (management or subordinates) who do similar work and volunteer to meet at a specified time to discuss and solve problems associated with their work.

      a) The objectives of QCs are to use employee capabilities more fully, build a more congenial workplace, and contribute to the improvement and development of both the organization and individual employees.

      b) Introduction of QCs is evolutionary through training, support, and team building. They are not imposed by management directive.

      c) The following are advantages of quality circles:

         i) Easy implementation without major organizational change
         ii) More efficient and effective operation of the organization
         iii) Better-quality products
         iv) Improved employee morale and better cohesion among coworkers

      d) The following are disadvantages of quality circles:

         i) Objections from unions
         ii) Reduced morale if suggestions are not accepted by management and management fails to explain nonacceptance adequately
         iii) Potential loss of management control

   2) **Self-managed teams** are a facet of total quality management (TQM). They are autonomous groups that go beyond quality circles because they represent a major organizational change.

      a) Team members are not volunteers but have been assigned to the teams.

      b) Teams are assembled to produce a complete product or service. Accordingly, they are empowered to perform traditional management tasks, such as scheduling, ordering materials, and even hiring.

      c) Members' jobs are enriched or vertically loaded not only by performing some management functions but also by cross-training and job rotation.

      d) The benefits of teams flow from the principle that employee self-management (and self-organization) is best.

         i) Motivation is improved because decision making is decentralized. The increased authority of autonomous work groups is intended to create a sense of ownership in the work product. Better decision making, productivity, quality, and goal congruence should be the results.

         ii) An advantage of cross-functional teams is improved communication because all members have a better understanding of all team activities.

         iii) If teams are staffed appropriately and have the necessary resources and support from management, they should be able to improve the processes of production. The individuals who perform the work have the power to make decisions about the way it is done.

3) Open-book management (OBM) involves sharing important financial information with trained and empowered employees. This approach is founded on trusting employees, commitment to their training, and waiting patiently for results (usually at least 2 years). The STEP (share, teach, empower, pay) model for OBM is described below.

    a) Step one is to share important financial information (sales, expenses, profits, stock prices). It should be displayed prominently, e.g., on an internal website or in hallways.

    b) Step two is to teach employees how to understand this information and the organization's operations. Simulations and board games are possible methods.

    c) Step three is to empower employees to make needed changes.

    d) Step four is to pay employees fairly as recognition of their accomplishments. Profit sharing, stock options, and bonuses are among the methods of compensation.

d. The success of participative management rests upon employee support. This support is most likely when four conditions are present:

    1) Profit sharing
    2) Job security (a long-term relationship)
    3) Strong efforts to sustain group cohesiveness
    4) Protection of employee rights

2. Teams

a. A team is a group whose members work intensively with each other to achieve a specific common goal. A group consists of two or more people who interact to accomplish a goal. All teams are groups, but not all groups are teams. A team differs from a group because team leadership often rotates, and team members are accountable to each other.

    1) Teams can improve organizational performance, but they are often difficult to form because it takes time for members to learn to work together. Normally, the smaller the team, the better. A maximum of nine members is recommended.

    2) Members of a team are empowered when they are properly trained and equipped, have the relevant information they need, are fully involved in decision making, and receive fair compensation for their work.

        a) Teams can be empowered by monitoring their progress and offering timely feedback on performance.

        b) Performance feedback also counteracts social loafing, the situation in which a team member puts forth less effort in a group than (s)he would individually. Thus, individual efforts should be identifiable and subject to evaluation.

    3) Roles of team members include the following:

        a) A **contributor** is a task-oriented team member who provides the team with good technical information and pushes the team to set high performance goals.

        b) A **collaborator** binds the whole team and is open to new ideas. (S)he is willing to work outside the defined role and to share the recognition and credit with other team members.

        c) A **communicator** is a people-oriented member. (S)he is process-driven and an effective listener. Thus, a communicator plays the role of a facilitator and a consensus builder who focuses on the overall perspective and reminds others of the vision, mission, or goal of the team.

        d) A **challenger** is candid and open, questions the team goals, is willing to disagree with the team leader, and encourages well-conceived risk taking.

b. The following are types of teams:

1) A **cross-functional team** includes members who have different areas of expertise. A research-and-development team is an example of a team that is typically cross functional in that many skills are needed to identify and create a new product.

2) A **virtual team** uses computer and telecommunications technology (email, voicemail, fax, Internet-based project software, video conferencing, etc.) so that geographically distant members can work together on projects and reach common goals.

a) Such a team may be able to work faster than a traditional team. Nevertheless, experience indicates that occasional in-person interaction and trust- and team-building procedures are still vital.

b) Roles, expectations, performance standards, objectives, and deadlines must be clearly communicated.

3) A **problem-solving team** focuses on specific issues to develop and implement solutions.

c. The following are the stages in team development:

1) During the **forming** stage, the team starts to come together, and members behave cautiously. Conflict, controversy, and personal opinions are avoided even though members are beginning to form impressions of each other and gain an understanding of what the group will do together. The team needs authority for direction during this stage.

2) During the **storming** stage, team members start to feel comfortable expressing disagreement and challenging others' opinions. Conflict and competition are at their greatest.

3) During the **norming** stage, the team reaches consensus about roles and responsibilities. Big decisions are made by group agreement. Morale is high as group members actively acknowledge the talents, skills, and experience that each member brings to the group.

4) During the **performing** stage, the team becomes highly productive. Group members are unified, loyal, and supportive. Other characteristics of this stage are harmony and effective problem solving.

5) During the **adjourning** stage, the team has completed its task and is disbanded.

d. Team effectiveness is reflected in achievement of objectives, innovation, adaptability, commitment, and favorable evaluations by senior management.

1) Team effectiveness is determined by three sets of interdependent factors. Team effectiveness requires that all factors be addressed continually. A high performance team is committed to the personal growth of its team members.

a) People -- Job satisfaction, trust and team spirit, effective communication, successful conflict resolution, and job security

b) Organization -- Stability, job security, supportive management, a fair compensation system, and stable objectives and priorities

c) Tasks -- Clear objectives, direction, and planning; capable technical management; leadership; stimulating work; employee independence; experienced employees; team involvement; and visibility of the task

e. Trust is a key factor in any participative management approach. Management should take action to build trust from the time that teams or other work groups are formed.

      1)   The following are 10 methods to build trust:

          a)   A commitment to trust means that managers strive to improve personal interaction by being open, honest, and willing to change.

          b)   Managers' commitment to trust includes disclosure of information, emotions, and opinions.

          c)   The commitment to trust also extends to receptiveness to influence by others.

          d)   When mutual trust is achieved, control will be self-imposed. Direct supervision will not be necessary when all persons involved know that others will perform.

          e)   Timely and accurate communication.

          f)   Supportive behavior.

          g)   Showing respect, e.g., by delegation and effective listening.

          h)   Fairness of evaluations.

          i)   Predictability of behavior and promise keeping.

          j)   Competence exemplified by sound judgment and technical proficiency.

3.   **Synergy**

    a.   Synergy occurs when the combination of formerly separate elements has a greater effect than the sum of their individual effects. When teams are comprised of individuals with complementary, rather than identical, skills, they are able to create synergy in pursuing collective goals.

Stop and review! You have completed the outline for this subunit. Study multiple-choice questions 5 through 7 beginning on page 249.

10.3 CONFLICT MANAGEMENT

 An internal auditor is a highly visible component of the organization's governance process. The ability to deal with the inevitable conflicts that arise in the course of their work is a critical skill for individual internal auditors.

1.   **Good Conflict and Bad Conflict**

    a.   Conflict results in the perceptions of two parties that they are working in opposition to each other in ways that result in feelings of discomfort or animosity.

        1)   This definition is useful because it describes conflict in terms of the feelings of the parties rather than organizational goals. Thus, constructive (cooperative) conflict may be distinguished from destructive conflict.

    b.   Conflict may be beneficial because it encourages self-criticism, creativity, and necessary change.

        1)   Managers may stimulate controlled conflict. Methods include

            a)   Ambiguous or threatening communications;

            b)   Hiring outsiders with different values, managerial styles, attitudes, and backgrounds;

            c)   Designating an individual to argue against the majority opinions of the group; and

            d)   Restructuring the organization to disrupt the status quo.

        2)   Thus, bringing in outside managers may stimulate conflict but also eliminate complacency and improve creativity.

2. **Nature of Conflict**

    a. Effective interpersonal relationships and organizational change are closely tied to conflict management.

    b. **Cooperative conflict** is constructive. The existence of cooperative (shared) goals is the basis for treating the conflict as a mutual problem.

        1) In this context, the parties may be able to trust each other's motives and believe what the other says.

        2) Discussions are productive, the attitude (and the result) is win-win, and the parties move ahead together.

        3) Cooperative conflict is a means of avoiding groupthink.

    c. **Competitive conflict** is destructive. Opposite goals are pursued, and neither side trusts or believes the other.

        1) The parties avoid genuine dialogue, and the attitude is win-lose.
        2) Ultimately, the parties take separate paths.

3. **Conflict Triggers**

    a. Conflict triggers raise the probability of conflict between groups or individuals. They should be allowed to exist if they cause cooperative conflict. Otherwise, they should be eliminated.

    b. Conflict may be triggered by the following:

        1) **Badly defined job descriptions** (jurisdictional boundaries)

            a) Reorganization may be the solution.

        2) **Scarcity** of people, funds, or other resources

            a) Increasing resources may be the solution.

        3) **Failure of communication**

            a) Removing obstacles that hinder effective two-way communication is essential, but the problem is perennial.

        4) **Deadlines**

            a) Time pressure may induce better performance (constructive) or anger and frustration (destructive).

        5) Policies, procedures, rules, or other standards viewed by employees as **unfair**

            a) If very unpopular, they should be changed to avoid competitive conflict.

        6) Individual **personality differences**

            a) Reassignment or termination of employees may be the solution.

        7) **Differences in status**, an issue in any hierarchical entity

            a) The remedy is respect for the ideas, values, and concerns of lower-level employees.

        8) **Not meeting expectations**

            a) The problem can be avoided through clarifying in advance the expectations employees have about their jobs.

        9) **Role incompatibility**

            a) Better coordination is the solution.

b) For example, a sales manager may make delivery promises to customers that are incompatible with the low inventory levels maintained by the production managers.

i) The sales manager's role is to maximize sales, but one of the production manager's roles is to achieve production efficiencies, such as by maintaining low inventories.

ii) Thus, individual and intergroup conflict has occurred because functional responsibilities of these parties are independent in an interfunctional organization.

4. **Responses to Conflict**

a. **Problem solving** resolves the conflict by confronting it and removing its causes. The emphasis is on facts and solutions, not personalities and assignment of blame.

1) For the long run, this is the only effective technique. The disadvantage is that problem solving is time consuming.

b. **Withdrawing (diffusion/smoothing)** is a short-term avoidance approach. The parties are asked by management to suspend their conflict temporarily, e.g., until a project is completed. It does not resolve the conflict.

c. **Forcing** occurs when a superior uses his or her formal authority to order a particular outcome. It does not resolve the conflict. Indeed, forcing may intensify it and damage the relationship.

d. **Superordinate goals** are the overriding goals of the organization to which subunit and personal goals are subordinate. An appeal to these goals is another short-term solution that does not resolve the conflict.

1) An appeal to superordinate goals may promote collaboration. This response occurs when interaction is very important to achieving goals and they are compatible (but not necessarily identical). The result may be creative solutions.

e. **Compromise** is a style that highly values goals and relationships. Conflicts are viewed as problems to be solved, and negotiators seek a solution that both achieves goals and improves relationships.

1) However, if the negotiators on both sides are not skillful, the conflict is suppressed, not resolved.

2) The disadvantage of fully negotiating a compromise is that the process is time consuming.

f. **Competition** results when the parties' goals are incompatible and interactions are important to achieving goals. Thus, if only one party can reach its goal, competition exists.

g. **Expanding resources** resolves conflicts that result from scarcity.

h. **Avoidance** is inaction. It involves withdrawal from and suppression of the conflict but does not solve the underlying problem.

i. **Accommodation** is the willingness of one party to the conflict to place another's needs and concerns above his or her own.

j. In **interest-based bargaining**, the parties realize that the conflict is between interests, not their opposed positions. The interests underlying the positions may be both conflicting and compatible.

1) The strongest of these interests are basic human needs. By acknowledging and understanding the others' interests, the parties may be able to address the problem by bypassing their positions and finding a new option that serves their interests.

Stop and review! You have completed the outline for this subunit. Study multiple-choice questions 8 through 10 beginning on page 250.

10.4 NEGOTIATION SKILLS

1. **Overview**

   a. **Negotiation** is a decision-making process. The parties are interdependent and do not have the same preferred outcomes. The parties must decide through bargaining what values will be exchanged (given and taken) by each side.

      1) Two-party and three-party negotiations are common.

         a) An example of a **two-party negotiation** is a person's sale of a car to a used car dealer.

         b) An example of a **three-party negotiation** is a person's sale of stock through a broker to a third party.

2. **Effective Negotiation**

   a. Effective negotiation allows the parties to meet their needs and to establish the **trust** necessary for future bargaining. It emphasizes a **win-win attitude**.

   b. In some cultures, the dominant approach is **competitive**. Rewards are given for winning, and punishment is given for losing.

      1) This **win-lose attitude** views negotiation as a zero-sum game.
      2) The win-win attitude is to treat negotiation as a positive-sum game.

   c. The win-win attitude is **cooperative**, seeking mutual benefit and satisfaction.

      1) It is founded on the principle that resources are sufficient for all and that the **third alternative** (not one side's way or the other side's way) is preferable.

      2) An advantage of win-win negotiation is that it promotes support of, and commitment to, the agreement.

      3) For example, the benefits of effective negotiation of employee-supervisor differences include

         a) Communicating both sides of an issue without litigation,

         b) Recognizing employee concerns to indicate that management values each subordinate's needs and rights, and

         c) Impartially managing tensions in the work environment while finding compromise solutions.

   d. For a successful negotiation, the negotiator should understand the implications for both sides if the negotiation fails.

      1) **Precedents** (previous demands, concessions, and settlements) help to determine what can be achieved. The history of past practices and interactions tends to define current standards of fairness in negotiations.

3. **Best Alternative to a Negotiated Agreement (BATNA)**

   a. Effective negotiators understand their **best alternative to a negotiated agreement (BATNA)**, an idea developed by Harvard University researchers.

   b. The BATNA is the acceptable minimum outcome if a negotiator cannot obtain the desired result.

   c. Understanding the BATNA helps a negotiator to avoid the following two mistakes:

      1) Accepting an unfavorable agreement
      2) Rejecting a favorable agreement

   d. A reasonable BATNA protects against bad decisions caused by the following:

      1) **Framing error** is a perceptual problem. The presentation or context of information may bias its interpretation and the resulting decision.

a) Accordingly, favorably (unfavorably) presented information may be viewed more (less) favorably than is justified.

    i) For example, a job seeker may hope that the attractive appearance of a résumé will sway the judgment of a potential employer.

    ii) Purely semantic effects also may result in framing error. For example, a glass still holds 50% of its capacity whether it is described as half full or half empty. However, the first (second) characterization may lead to a more (less) favorable opinion.

2) **Escalation of commitment** is adherence to a failing course of action when a purely objective decision maker would abandon it. This irrational tendency to persist in error is based on a variety of organizational, social, and psychological factors.

3) **Overconfidence** is the common tendency to overestimate the chances of success. It tends, paradoxically, to be directly related to the difficulty of the undertaking.

4) A primary disadvantage of forcing another party to accept terms in a negotiation is that it damages the relationship between the negotiators.

e. The BATNA also helps to define the **bargaining zone**. It is the difference between the BATNAs belonging to each side, i.e., the set of outcomes acceptable to both.

1) For example, a parent wishes to sell a subsidiary for US $1.5 billion, with a BATNA of US $1.2 billion. A buyer wishes to acquire the subsidiary for US $1 billion, with a BATNA of US $1.3 billion. Hence, negotiation is feasible because a bargaining zone (buyer's BATNA of US $1.3 billion – seller's BATNA of US $1.2 billion) exists.

2) Negotiation is **not feasible** in the absence of a bargaining zone. In the example above, if the seller's BATNA were US $1.4 billion, negotiation would be fruitless.

3) Negotiation is **not necessary** if the parties do not disagree. For example, they may have contracted to accept the result of a formal appraisal of the value of something to be bought and sold.

4) Determining the other side's BATNA may be the most difficult aspect of a negotiation. Each side has an incentive to keep its BATNA confidential.

    a) Thus, the other side's BATNA must be estimated so that, in turn, the negotiating zone may be estimated.

4. **Steps to Overcome Resistance**

a. The steps to overcoming unexpected resistance from another party are as follows:

1) Attempt to determine the reason behind the resistance.
2) Stop the meeting and address the other party's concerns privately.
3) Restate the negotiator's position regarding the issue.
4) Research the other party to determine its views and requirements.

5. **Other Negotiation Concepts**

a. **Added-value negotiating** was developed by Karl and Steve Albrecht. It is applied when something more than the elements of negotiation described in this subunit is necessary. Its basic concept is that the two sides make **multiple deals** to add value to the process.

1) Step one is for the parties mutually to **clarify interests**.

    a) These interests may be subjective as well as objective. The purpose is to isolate commonalities.

   2)   Step two is to **identify options**.

      a)   The purpose is to establish a **marketplace of value**, i.e., the range of values each side can give the other.

   3)   Step three is to **design alternative deal packages**.

      a)   The distinctive feature of added-value negotiation is that it provides for multiple win-win offers. Each consists of groups of the values identified in step two.

   4)   Step four is to **select a deal** after the parties have considered the deal packages designed in step three.

      a)   They evaluate each possible deal's **value, balance, and fit**. The mutually acceptable deal is then chosen.

   5)   Step five is to **perfect the deal**.

      a)   Details are negotiated, and the deal is put in written form.

      b)   The process creates **relationships** that will benefit later negotiations.

      c)   The keys are openness, flexibility, and mutuality in the quest for a successful exchange of value.

b.   The **principled negotiation method** focuses on basic interests, mutually satisfying options, and fair standards. The following are basic principles:

   1)   Separating the people from the problem
   2)   Focusing on interests, not positions
   3)   Inventing options for mutual gain
   4)   Insisting on using objective criteria

c.   **Distributive bargaining** is a negotiation in zero-sum conditions (i.e., when a negotiation gain by one party is offset by a loss by the other party).

   1)   The negotiator operates with a maximum desired result (target point) and a minimum acceptable result (resistance point) in mind. If the ranges of feasible outcomes (aspiration ranges) overlap, an agreement is possible.

   2)   In **integrative bargaining**, both parties may gain.

d.   Various types of third-party negotiations are available to parties facing disagreement.

   1)   A **mediator** is a neutral third party who facilitates a negotiated solution by using persuasion and offering solutions. However, the mediator has no authority to make a decision.

   2)   An **arbitrator** has the authority to impose an agreement. Arbitration may be requested by the parties or may be imposed by law or by the terms of a contract.

   3)   A **consultant** is skilled in facilitation and communication skills but does not have authority to make a decision. A consultant helps improve relations between the two disagreeing parties but does not offer specific solutions.

   4)   A **conciliator** provides an informal communication link between the two parties but does not have authority to make a decision.

Stop and review! You have completed the outline for this subunit. Study multiple-choice questions 11 through 14 beginning on page 251.

10.5 CHANGE MANAGEMENT

1.   **Overview**

a.   Change management is important to all organizations. An appropriate balance between change and stability is necessary for an organization to thrive.

   1)   Organizational change is conducted through change agents, who may include managers, employees, and consultants hired for the purpose.

2. **Types of Change**

    a. **Cultural change** is a change in attitudes and mindset, for example, when a total quality management approach is adopted.

    b. A **product change** is a change in a product's physical attributes and usefulness to customers.

    c. A **structural change** is a change in an organization's systems or structures.

3. **Resistance**

    a. Organizational and procedural changes often are resisted by the individuals and groups affected. This response may be caused by simple surprise, inertia, or fear of failure. But it also may arise from the following:

        1) Misunderstandings or lack of needed skills
        2) Lack of trust of, or conflicts with, management
        3) Emotional reactions when change is forced
        4) Bad timing
        5) Insensitivity to employees' needs
        6) Perceived threats to employees' status or job security
        7) Dissolution of tightly knit work groups
        8) Interference with achievement of other objectives

    b. Methods of coping with employee resistance include the following:

        1) Prevention through education and communication
        2) Participation in designing and implementing a change
        3) Facilitation and support through training and counseling
        4) Negotiation by providing a benefit in exchange for cooperation
        5) Manipulation of information or events
        6) Co-optation through allowing some participation but without meaningful input
        7) Coercion

4. **Organizational Development (OD)**

    a. OD provides a framework for managing change using the findings of the behavioral sciences.

        1) True OD has three distinctive characteristics:

            a) The change must be planned and deliberate.
            b) The change must actually improve the organization. Changes forced by regulatory requirements or changes that merely attempt to follow management trends and fads are not included.
            c) The change must be implemented using the findings of the behavioral sciences, such as organizational behavior and group psychology.

        2) The following are the objectives of OD:

            a) Deepen the sense of organizational purpose and align individuals with it
            b) Promote interpersonal trust, communication, cooperation, and support
            c) Encourage a problem-solving approach
            d) Develop a satisfying work experience
            e) Supplement formal authority with authority based on expertise
            f) Increase personal responsibility
            g) Encourage willingness to change

Stop and review! You have completed the outline for this subunit. Study multiple-choice questions 15 through 17 beginning on page 252.

10.6 PROJECT MANAGEMENT

1. **Overview**

   a. A project is a temporary undertaking with specified objectives that often involves a cross-functional team and working outside customary organizational lines. Thus, interpersonal skills are important in project management. A manager may not have line authority over some team members.

      1) Examples include building construction, R&D projects, new product planning, feasibility studies, audit studies, movie production, and conversion to a new computer information system.

      2) Project management methods are designed to aid the planning and control of large-scale projects having many interrelated activities.

   b. A project life cycle generally includes the following phases:

      1) The **initiation phase** begins by defining the scope, purpose, objectives, resources, deliverables, timescales, and structure of the project.

      2) The **planning phase** includes creating a detailed project plan. Resources are assigned in this phase.

      3) In the **execution phase**, the project team produces the deliverables, and the project manager monitors and controls project delivery.

      4) The **closure phase** includes all the activities necessary for the project team to conclude the project.

   c. The risk of an unsuccessful project can be analyzed in terms of four components:

      1) Ensuring that resources are adequate

      2) Maintaining scope by avoiding the temptation to continue adding functions to a new system or process

      3) Controlling cost

      4) Providing deliverables

   d. Project management is the process of managing the tradeoff between the two major inputs (time and cost) and the major output (quality). The project management triangle graphically depicts this relationship.

Project Management Triangle

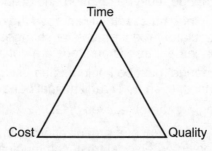

Figure 10-3

      1) The implication is that a high-quality deliverable can only be achieved either by devoting a large number of employee hours to a project or by spending a lot of money.

EXAMPLE

In the days before widespread computer use, old-fashioned job-order print shops used to display signs saying, "You Want It Fast -- Cheap -- Correct. Pick Two."

Designers of submarines often speak of their classic tradeoff of depth, speed, and stealth. A vessel with sufficient shielding to be silent and to survive at great depths is too heavy to go very fast.

e. Project management software is available and is used by most firms today.

f. Common techniques for project management include Gantt charts, PERT, and CPM. They are suitable for any project having a target completion date and single start.

2. Gantt Charts

a. Gantt charts are simple to construct and use. To develop a Gantt chart,

1) Divide the project into logical subprojects called activities or tasks,

2) Estimate the start and completion times for each activity, and

3) Prepare a bar chart showing each activity as a horizontal bar along a time scale.

b. Below is an example of a Gantt chart:

Gantt Chart

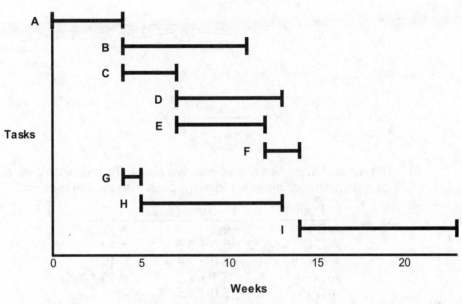

Figure 10-4

c. Gantt charts show the projected start and finish times for each task as well as for the project as a whole.

1) They also show, in a limited way, the interdependencies among tasks, i.e., which tasks can be performed simultaneously and which must be completed before other tasks can begin.

2) In the example, tasks B, C, and G can begin as soon as task A is complete, but task I cannot begin until all others are complete.

d. The major advantage of the Gantt chart is its simplicity: It requires no special tools or mathematics. It forces the planner to think ahead and define logical activities.

e. The major disadvantage of the Gantt chart is that it is unsuitable for a very large-scale project. The interdependencies among tasks become unmanageable.

3. Program Evaluation and Review Technique (PERT)

a. PERT was developed to control large-scale, complex projects. PERT diagrams are free-form networks showing each activity as a line between events. A sequence of lines shows interrelationships among activities.

1) PERT diagrams are more complex than Gantt charts, but they have the advantages of incorporating probabilistic time estimates and identifying the critical path.

b.   A PERT network consists of two components:

1)   Events are moments in time representing the start or finish of an activity. They consume no resources and are depicted on a network diagram with circles (called nodes).

2)   Activities are tasks to be accomplished. They consume resources (including time) and have a duration over time. They are depicted as lines connecting nodes.

PERT Network

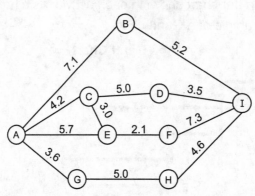

Figure 10-5

3)   The network depicted above has five paths. To calculate their durations, the project manager makes a forward pass through the network.

Path	Time (days)	
A-B-I	7.1 + 5.2	= 12.3
A-C-D-I	4.2 + 5.0 + 3.5	= 12.7
A-C-E-F-I	4.2 + 3.0 + 2.1 + 7.3	= 16.6
A-E-F-I	5.7 + 2.1 + 7.3	= 15.1
A-G-H-I	3.6 + 5.0 + 4.6	= 13.2

c.   Some processes contain activities that are performed simultaneously because they have the same start node and end node. Concurrent activities cannot be depicted graphically on a PERT network. Every path between nodes must be unique. Thus, two paths cannot both be designated B-I in Figure 10-5.

4.   **Calculating the Length of the Critical Paths**

a.   The critical path is the **longest** path in time through the network. It is critical because, if any activity on the critical path takes longer than expected, the entire project will be delayed.

1)   Every network has at least one critical path. In Figure 10-5, path A-C-E-F-I is the critical path because it has the longest time (16.6 days).

2)   The critical path is the **shortest** amount of time in which a project can be completed if all paths are begun simultaneously.

b.   Any activity that does not lie on the critical path has **slack time**, i.e., unused resources that can be diverted to the critical path.

5. **Expected Duration**

    a. A major advantage of PERT is that activity times can be expressed probabilistically.

        1) Three estimates are made: optimistic, most likely, and pessimistic. The usual weighting of the three estimates is 1:4:1. (The most likely time for the duration of a task is the one indicated on the PERT diagram.)

        2) In Figure 10-5 on the previous page, the most likely duration of task B-I is 5.2 days. The organization estimates the optimistic time at 5.0 and the pessimistic time at 5.8. The expected duration of task B-I is calculated as follows:

	Estimates		Weights		
Optimistic	5.0	×	1	=	5.0
Most likely	5.2	×	4	=	20.8
Pessimistic	5.8	×	1	=	5.8
Totals			6		31.6

Expected duration: 31.6 ÷ 6 = 5.27 days

6. **Critical Path Method (CPM)**

    a. CPM was developed independently of PERT and is widely used in the construction industry. Like PERT, CPM is a network technique, but it has two distinct differences:

        1) PERT uses probabilistic time estimates, but CPM is a deterministic method.

        2) PERT considers only the time required to complete a project. CPM incorporates cost amounts.

    b. Two estimates are made for each time and cost combination: a normal estimate and a crash estimate. A crash estimate consists of the time and cost required to complete an activity if all available resources are applied to it.

        1) Crashing a project applies all available resources to activities on the critical path (crashing a noncritical-path activity is not cost-effective).

EXAMPLE

Figure 10-5 can be converted to a CPM network with the addition of the following time and cost data for the critical path:

Critical Path Activity	Normal Time & Cost		Crash Time & Cost	
A-C	4.2	US $20,000	4.0	US $35,000
C-E	3.0	10,000	2.0	20,000
E-F	2.1	18,000	2.0	21,000
F-I	7.3	60,000	6.5	90,000

These amounts can be used to determine the costs and gains of crashing a given activity:

Critical Path Activity	Crash Cost Minus Normal Cost			Incremental Cost of Crashing	Normal Time Minus Crash Time		Time Gained
A-C	US $35,000 –	US $20,000	=	US $15,000	4.2 – 4.0	=	0.2
C-E	20,000 –	10,000	=	10,000	3.0 – 2.0	=	1.0
E-F	21,000 –	18,000	=	3,000	2.1 – 2.0	=	0.1
F-I	90,000 –	60,000	=	30,000	7.3 – 6.5	=	0.8

---

        2) The most cost-effective activity to crash is determined with the following formula:

$$\text{Time-cost tradeoff} = \frac{\text{Crash cost} - \text{Normal cost}}{\text{Normal time} - \text{Crash time}}$$

EXAMPLE

The ratio of crash cost to time gained reveals the best activity for crashing:

Critical Path Activity	Incremental Cost of Crashing		Time Gained		Cost per Day to Crash
A-C	US $15,000	÷	0.2	=	US $75,000
C-E	10,000	÷	1.0	=	10,000
E-F	3,000	÷	0.1	=	30,000
F-I	30,000	÷	0.8	=	37,500

The most cost-effective activity to crash is C-E. Assuming this activity will be crashed, the network is recalculated to determine whether a new critical path will result. If so, the time-cost tradeoff of the activities on the new critical path are calculated and the process is repeated.

---

7. **Network Models**

   a. Network models are used to solve managerial problems pertaining to project scheduling, information systems design, and transportation systems design.

      1) Networks consisting of nodes and arcs may be created to represent in graphic form problems related to transportation, assignment, and transshipment.

   b. A shortest-route algorithm minimizes total travel time from one site to each of the other sites in a transportation system.

   c. The maximal flow algorithm maximizes throughput in networks with distinct entry (source node) and exit (sink node) points. Examples of applications are highway transportation systems and oil pipelines. Flows are limited by capacities.

   d. The minimal spanning tree algorithm identifies the set of connecting branches having the shortest combined length. A spanning tree is a group of branches (arcs) that connects each node in the network to every other node. An example problem is the determination of the shortest telecommunications linkage among users at remote sites and a central computer.

Stop and review! You have completed the outline for this subunit. Study multiple-choice questions 18 through 20 beginning on page 253.

QUESTIONS

10.1 Leadership Styles

1. A manager can use power and authority to accomplish objectives. The relationship between these two important concepts is best explained as follows:

    A. Power is the right to do things, while authority is the ability to do things.

    B. Authority is the right to do things, while power is the ability to do things.

    C. Power and authority are both required to accomplish a task.

    D. Power and authority are simply two words that describe the same concept -- how to get things done in organizations.

Answer (B) is correct.
    REQUIRED: The relationship between power and authority.
    DISCUSSION: Authority is the officially sanctioned privilege to direct others. A clear hierarchy of authority enhances coordination and accountability. Power is the ability to marshal organizational resources to obtain results. A manager may have both authority and power or have one without the other.
    Answer (A) is incorrect. Authority is the right to do things, and power is the ability to do things. Answer (C) is incorrect. A manager may accomplish a task without having formal authority. Answer (D) is incorrect. Authority is the right to do things, and power is the ability to do things.

2. A company's decisions are made solely by one person, who is the CEO and major shareholder. Which of the following powers is this person **least** likely to have?

A. Coercive power.

B. Legitimate power.

C. Referent power.

D. Reward power.

Answer (C) is correct.
REQUIRED: The power that the sole decision maker is least likely to have.
DISCUSSION: A person who is the head of a company may exert influence through five types of power. Referent power is the capacity of the individual's personality and style to cause others to identify with or like him or her. Thus, it is the one type of power not necessarily held by a CEO and major shareholder. This person has the ability to reward others and apply pressure. (S)he also has the right to expect cooperation.
Answer (A) is incorrect. Coercive power is the ability of the individual to make others cooperate by applying pressure. Answer (B) is incorrect. Legitimate power is the leader's right to expect cooperation from others. Answer (D) is incorrect. Reward power is the individual's ability to influence others through their expectation that good behavior will be rewarded.

3. Which of the following is true concerning generic influence tactics?

A. Consultation involves appealing to emotions, values, or ordeals.

B. Ingratiating tactics attempt to raise the other person's self-esteem prior to a request.

C. Coalition tactics try to convince others by reliance on a detailed plan, supporting evidence, and reason.

D. Pressure tactics are based on the formal or informal support of higher management.

Answer (B) is correct.
REQUIRED: The true statement concerning generic influence tactics.
DISCUSSION: Management literature describes generic influence tactics that may be upward, lateral, or downward. As noted by researchers, ingratiating tactics attempt to raise the other person's self-esteem prior to a request.
Answer (A) is incorrect. Consultation permits the other person to participate in the decision or change. Answer (C) is incorrect. Coalition tactics seek the aid of others to persuade someone to agree. Answer (D) is incorrect. Pressure tactics involve intimidation, threats, and demands.

4. Which of the following is **not** an example of positive reinforcement of behavior?

A. Paying a bonus to employees who had no absences for any 4-week period.

B. Giving written warnings to employees after only every other absence.

C. Assigning a mentor to each employee who exhibits a desire to develop leadership skills.

D. Having a lottery every month where 10% of the employees with no absences receive a US $200 bonus.

Answer (B) is correct.
REQUIRED: The action not an example of positive reinforcement.
DISCUSSION: Positive reinforcement encourages a desired behavior by following it with the presentation of a reward. Punishment, on the other hand, discourages an undesired behavior by following it with a negative consequence. While punishment ideally should follow every occurrence of an undesirable behavior, this is not always possible. Thus, even though written warnings are given to employees only after every other absence, the action is considered punishment, not positive reinforcement.
Answer (A) is incorrect. Paying a bonus is a positive reinforcement. Answer (C) is incorrect. Assigning a mentor is a positive reinforcement. Answer (D) is incorrect. Holding a lottery is an intermittent positive reinforcement.

10.2 Team Building

5. Which of the following is **not** one of the advantages of self-managed teams?

A. Motivation is improved because decision making is decentralized.

B. Improved processes of production if the teams are supported properly.

C. Managerial acceptance by tradition-oriented managers.

D. Improved communication because all members understand the team's activities better.

Answer (C) is correct.
REQUIRED: The characteristic that is not an advantage of self-managed teams.
DISCUSSION: Managerial resistance is often the primary obstacle of self-managed teams. Organizational change is difficult, and tradition-oriented managers tend to regard self-managed teams as a threat to their status.
Answer (A) is incorrect. The increased authority of autonomous work groups creates a sense of ownership of the final product. Answer (B) is incorrect. Teams are often able to improve production processes if the team is properly supported by management. Answer (D) is incorrect. Cross-functional teams result in improved communication because all the members have a better understanding of the team activities.

6. Which of the following is **false** with regard to quality circles and self-managed teams?

- A. Managerial acceptance by tradition-oriented managers.

- B. Self-managed teams are assigned by management, and quality circle teams are voluntary.

- C. Self-managed teams and quality circles often have better cohesion among members.

- D. Self-managed teams and quality circles are often able to help the organization operate more efficiently and effectively.

Answer (A) is correct.

REQUIRED: The false statement regarding quality circles and self-managed teams.

DISCUSSION: Managerial acceptance is the primary obstacle to adoption of self-managed teams. Tradition-oriented managers often perceive the loss of authority to a self-managed team as a threat to their status.

Answer (B) is incorrect. Self-managed teams are assigned, while quality circles often include employees who meet at specified times to discuss and solve problems. Answer (C) is incorrect. Teams in general tend to have better cohesion among members than employees who are not part of teams. Answer (D) is incorrect. Both types of teams function to improve the organization overall. Quality circles often try to improve the quality of products and operations, while self-managed teams are assembled to accomplish a specified task or group of tasks.

7. Which of the following is key to any plan to empower teams?

- A. Give structure to team members.

- B. Monitor progress and offer timely feedback on performance.

- C. Reduce authority of the team when mistakes are made.

- D. Avoid tension and conflict within the team.

Answer (B) is correct.

REQUIRED: The key item to any plan to empower teams.

DISCUSSION: Members of a team are empowered when they are properly trained and equipped, have the relevant information they need, are fully involved in decision making, and receive fair compensation for their work. Monitoring and feedback are keys to maintaining empowerment because they are necessary to team effectiveness. Team effectiveness is reflected in achievement of objectives, innovation, adaptability, commitment, and favorable evaluations by senior management.

Answer (A) is incorrect. Empowered team members may determine their own structure. Answer (C) is incorrect. A tolerance for problems and mistakes is part of empowerment. Answer (D) is incorrect. Tension and conflict are a normal part of team development.

10.3 Conflict Management

8. One division of a large manufacturing company has traditionally performed much better than any of the other divisions. The management team of this division has risen through the ranks together and exhibits no signs of conflict. Recently, earnings of the division have begun to decline, and market share has eroded. Senior management of the parent company has asked the director of internal audit whether the introduction of conflict by bringing in outside managers might help resolve the deteriorating situation. The most appropriate response would be that

- A. Conflict is dysfunctional and should not be risked under these circumstances.

- B. All conflict can be beneficially controlled and should be encouraged in this situation.

- C. The management team has been together for a long time and should be allowed to work through its problems.

- D. Varying the management team could introduce new ideas and be beneficial to the division, and some conflict is not a problem.

Answer (D) is correct.

REQUIRED: The response to a suggestion that conflict be introduced by hiring outside managers.

DISCUSSION: Conflict may be constructive as well as destructive because it encourages self-criticism, creativity, and necessary change. Accordingly, managers may decide to stimulate controlled conflict. Techniques for this purpose may include (1) ambiguous or threatening communications; (2) hiring outsiders with different values, managerial styles, attitudes, and backgrounds; (3) designating an individual to argue against the majority opinions of the group; and (4) restructuring the organization to disrupt the status quo. Thus, bringing in outside managers may stimulate conflict but also may eliminate complacency and improve creativity.

Answer (A) is incorrect. Not all conflict is dysfunctional. Answer (B) is incorrect. Some conflict is dysfunctional. Answer (C) is incorrect. Ignoring the problem does not solve it.

9. Which of the following conflict resolution techniques has the goal of maintaining harmonious relationships by placing another's needs and concerns above your own?

    A. Accommodation.

    B. Compromise.

    C. Collaboration.

    D. Avoidance.

Answer (A) is correct.

    REQUIRED: The conflict resolution technique with a goal of maintaining harmonious relationships.

    DISCUSSION: The goal of accommodation is maintaining harmonious relationships by placing an emphasis on another's needs and concerns.

    Answer (B) is incorrect. Compromise resolves conflict through a process in which each side makes concessions. Answer (C) is incorrect. Collaboration resolves conflict. The parties work together to obtain a solution. Answer (D) is incorrect. Avoidance does not resolve conflict. It is inaction.

10. Time consumption is a disadvantage when managers address conflict by

    A. Smoothing.

    B. Forcing.

    C. Problem solving.

    D. None of the answers are correct.

Answer (C) is correct.

    REQUIRED: The way in which managers address conflict that uses excessive time.

    DISCUSSION: Problem solving is a way managers address conflicts, but it requires a large amount of time to resolve.

    Answer (A) is incorrect. Smoothing is a short-term avoidance approach. Answer (B) is incorrect. Forcing occurs when a superior uses his or her formal authority to order a particular outcome. Answer (D) is incorrect. Problem solving takes managers a long time to resolve conflicts.

10.4 Negotiation Skills

11. Which of the following is an example of a two-party negotiation?

    A. A person sells a car to a used car dealer.

    B. A person requests a financial institution to pay another person.

    C. A person sells stock through a broker.

    D. A person sells a house through a real estate agent.

Answer (A) is correct.

    REQUIRED: The true example of a two-party negotiation.

    DISCUSSION: A person's sale of a car to a used car dealer is an example of a two-party negotiation. Only the seller and dealer are involved in the negotiations.

    Answer (B) is incorrect. A person who requests a financial institution to pay another person is engaged in a three-party negotiation. The three parties involved are the person requesting the financial institution to use funds from his or her account to pay another individual, the financial institution responsible for paying the payee, and the person receiving the funds from the financial institution. Answer (C) is incorrect. A person who sells stock through a broker is engaged in a three-party negotiation. The seller, broker, and buyer are involved. Answer (D) is incorrect. Sale of a house through a real estate agent is a three-party negotiation.

12. A reasonable BATNA (best alternative to a negotiated agreement) protects against bad decisions caused by the following:

1. Framing error
2. Escalation of commitment
3. Overconfidence

    A. 1 and 3 only.

    B. 1, 2, and 3.

    C. 1 only.

    D. 2 and 3 only.

Answer (B) is correct.

    REQUIRED: The problems avoided by a reasonable BATNA.

    DISCUSSION: A reasonable BATNA protects against bad decisions caused by the following: framing error, escalation of commitment, and overconfidence. Framing error is a perceptual problem. The presentation or context of information may bias its interpretation and the resulting decision. Escalation of commitment is adherence to a failing course of action when a purely objective decision maker would abandon it. Overconfidence is the common tendency to overestimate the chances of success.

    Answer (A) is incorrect. A reasonable BATNA also protects against escalation of commitment. Answer (C) is incorrect. A reasonable BATNA also protects against escalation of commitment and overconfidence. Answer (D) is incorrect. A reasonable BATNA also protects against framing errors.

13. In effective negotiation, a win-win attitude is characterized by

    A. Seeking mutual benefit and satisfaction.

    B. Cooperation.

    C. It promotes support of, and commitment to, the agreement.

    D. All of the answers are correct.

Answer (D) is correct.
    REQUIRED: The characteristic(s) of a win-win attitude.
    DISCUSSION: In effective negotiation, a win-win attitude is characterized by seeking mutual benefit and satisfaction, being cooperative, and promoting support of, and commitment to, the agreement. In contrast to a win-win attitude, a win-lose attitude is competitive and is a zero-sum game instead of a positive-sum game.
    Answer (A) is incorrect. Cooperation and promoting support and commitment to the agreement are additional characteristics of a win-win attitude. Answer (B) is incorrect. Seeking mutual benefit and satisfaction and supporting and committing to the agreement are characteristics of a win-win attitude. Answer (C) is incorrect. Two additional characteristics of a win-win attitude are seeking mutual benefit and satisfaction and being cooperative.

14. When planning for successful negotiations, the negotiator should

    A. Understand the implications for both sides if the negotiation fails.

    B. Concentrate solely on the issues in the negotiation at hand.

    C. Not deviate from stated positions.

    D. Depend on the initial research prepared for the negotiation.

Answer (A) is correct.
    REQUIRED: The necessary action when planning for successful negotiations.
    DISCUSSION: Negotiators should assess the best alternatives for both themselves and the other parties to determine their relative strengths in the negotiation process. If alternatives are not readily available or are unattractive, a party is under additional pressure to make the negotiation work.
    Answer (B) is incorrect. The negotiator should evaluate all alternatives to avoid placing undue pressure on the success of the negotiation. Answer (C) is incorrect. An objective perspective may assist the negotiator in identifying alternatives. Answer (D) is incorrect. Additional research may be required to fully understand the other party's alternatives to negotiation.

10.5 Change Management

15. Organizational change must be considered in the light of potential employee resistance. Resistance

    A. May occur even though employees will benefit from the change.

    B. Will be greatest when informal groups are weakest.

    C. Will be insignificant if no economic loss by employees is expected.

    D. Is centered mostly on perceived threats to psychological needs.

Answer (A) is correct.
    REQUIRED: The true statement about resistance to organizational change.
    DISCUSSION: Resistance to change may be caused by fear of the personal adjustments that may be required. Employees may have a genuine concern about the usefulness of the change, perceive a lack of concern for workers' feelings, fear the outcome, worry about downgrading of job status, and resent deviations from past procedures for implementing change (especially if new procedures are less participative than the old). Social adjustments also may be required that violate the behavioral norms of informal groups or disrupt the social status quo within groups. Economic adjustments may involve potential economic loss or insecurity based on perceived threats to jobs. In general, any perceived deterioration in the work situation that is seen as a threat to economic, social, and/or psychological needs will produce resistance. The various adjustments required are most likely to be resisted when imposed unilaterally by higher authority. However, employees who share in finding solutions to the problems requiring change are less likely to resist because they will have some responsibility for the change.
    Answer (B) is incorrect. Strong informal groups are likely to offer more resistance. Answer (C) is incorrect. Resistance arises from threats to a complex pattern of economic, social, and psychological needs. Answer (D) is incorrect. Resistance arises from threats to a complex pattern of economic, social, and psychological needs.

16. An organization's management perceives the need to make significant changes. Which of the following factors is management **least** likely to be able to change?

    A. The organization's members.

    B. The organization's structure.

    C. The organization's environment.

    D. The organization's technology.

Answer (C) is correct.
    REQUIRED: The factor management is least likely to be able to change.
    DISCUSSION: The environment of an organization consists of external forces outside its direct control that may affect its performance. These forces include competitors, suppliers, customers, regulators, climate, culture, politics, technological change, and many other factors. The organization's members are a factor that managers are clearly able to change.

17. Co-optation is a

    A. Method of coping with employee resistance.

    B. Cause of resistance to change.

    C. Model for categorizing organizational changes.

    D. Way of allowing meaningful input by resistant employees.

Answer (A) is correct.
    REQUIRED: The definition of co-optation.
    DISCUSSION: Methods of coping with employee resistance include co-optation through allowing some participation but without meaningful input.
    Answer (B) is incorrect. Co-optation is a method of coping with employee resistance. Answer (C) is incorrect. Co-optation is a method of coping with employee resistance. Answer (D) is incorrect. Co-optation is a way of allowing some participation but without meaningful input.

10.6 Project Management

18. A Gantt chart

    A. Shows the critical path for a project.

    B. Is used for determining an optimal product mix.

    C. Shows only the activities along the critical path of a network.

    D. Does not necessarily show the critical path through a network.

Answer (D) is correct.
    REQUIRED: The true statement about a Gantt chart.
    DISCUSSION: The major advantage of a Gantt chart is its simplicity: It requires no special tools or mathematics. However, it depicts only the interrelationships between tasks in a limited way. Thus, trying to identify a project's critical path from a Gantt chart may not be feasible.
    Answer (A) is incorrect. The critical path is not shown on a Gantt chart. Answer (B) is incorrect. Linear programming is used to determine an optimal product mix. Answer (C) is incorrect. A Gantt chart shows all activities, not just those along the critical path.

19. When making a cost-time tradeoff in CPM analysis, the first activity that should be crashed is the activity

    A. With the largest amount of slack.

    B. With the lowest unit crash cost.

    C. On the critical path with the maximum possible time reduction.

    D. On the critical path with the lowest unit crash cost.

Answer (D) is correct.
    REQUIRED: The first activity that should be crashed when making a cost-time tradeoff in PERT analysis.
    DISCUSSION: When making a cost-time tradeoff, the first activity to be crashed (have its completion time accelerated) is one on the critical path. To select an activity on another path would not reduce the total time of completion. The initial activity chosen should be the one with the completion time that can be accelerated at the lowest possible cost per unit of time saved.
    Answer (A) is incorrect. Eliminating an activity with slack will not reduce the total time of the project. Answer (B) is incorrect. The activity with the lowest unit crash cost may not be on the critical path. Answer (C) is incorrect. The time reduction should be related to its cost. The maximum time reduction may not be cost effective.

20. In a critical path analysis, if slack time in an activity exists, the activity

    A. Is not essential to the overall project.

    B. Is a backup activity to replace a main activity should it fail.

    C. Could be delayed without delaying the overall project.

    D. Involves essentially no time to complete.

Answer (C) is correct.

    REQUIRED: The implication of the existence of slack time.

    DISCUSSION: Slack is the free time associated with activities not on the critical path. Slack represents unused resources that can be diverted to the critical path.

    Answer (A) is incorrect. An activity with slack may nevertheless be essential to the overall project. Answer (B) is incorrect. An activity with slack time is not a backup activity. Answer (D) is incorrect. Time is involved in a slack activity.

Access the **CIA Review System** from your Gleim Personal Classroom to continue your studies with exam-emulating multiple-choice questions!

STUDY UNIT ELEVEN
IT SECURITY AND APPLICATION DEVELOPMENT

(20 pages of outline)

This study unit is the first of three covering **Section VI: IT/Business Continuity** from The IIA's CIA Exam Syllabus. This section makes up 15% to 25% of Part 3 of the CIA exam and is tested at the **awareness level** (unless otherwise indicated below). The relevant portion of the syllabus is highlighted below. (The complete syllabus is in Appendix A.)

VI. IT/BUSINESS CONTINUITY (15%–25%)

A. Security

1. Physical/system security (e.g., firewalls, access control)
2. Information protection (e.g., viruses, privacy)
3. Application authentication
4. Encryption

B. Application Development

1. End-user computing
2. Change control – *Proficiency Level (P)*
3. Systems development methodology – *Proficiency Level (P)*
4. Application development – *Proficiency Level (P)*
5. Information systems development

C. System Infrastructure
D. Business Continuity

11.1 PHYSICAL AND SYSTEMS SECURITY

Broadly conceived, "security" can extend to almost any aspect of automated systems. An internal auditor's awareness of information security should encompass three general types: logical, physical, and communication.

1. **Data Integrity**

   a. The difficulty of maintaining the integrity of the data is the most significant limitation of computer-based audit tools.

   1) Electronic evidence is difficult to authenticate and easy to fabricate.

   2) Internal auditors must be careful not to treat computer printouts as traditional paper evidence. The data security factors pertaining to electronic evidence must be considered.

    3) The degree of reliance on electronic evidence by the auditor depends on the effectiveness of the controls over the system from which such evidence is taken.

    4) When making recommendations regarding the costs and benefits of computer security, the auditor should focus on

        a) Potential loss if security is not implemented,

        b) The probability of the occurrences, and

        c) The cost and effectiveness of the implementation and operation of computer security.

    5) The most important control is to enact an organization-wide network security policy. This policy should promote the following objectives:

        a) **Availability.** The intended and authorized users should be able to access data to meet organizational goals.

        b) **Security, privacy, and confidentiality.** The secrecy of information that could adversely affect the organization if revealed to the public or competitors should be ensured.

        c) **Integrity.** Unauthorized or accidental modification of data should be prevented.

  b. Many controls once performed by separate individuals may be concentrated in computer systems. Hence, an individual who has access to the computer may perform incompatible functions. As a result, other control procedures may be necessary to achieve the control objectives ordinarily accomplished by segregation of functions.

    1) These controls can be classified as one of two broad types, physical controls and logical controls. Physical controls are further divided into two subcategories, physical access controls and environmental controls.

2. **Physical Security Controls**

  a. **Physical access controls** limit who can physically enter the data center.

    1) Keypad devices allow entry of a password or code to gain entry to a physical location or computer system.

    2) Card reader controls are based on reading information from a magnetic strip on a credit, debit, or other access card. Controls can then be applied to information about the cardholder contained on the magnetic strip.

    3) Biometric technologies are automated methods of establishing an individual's identity using physiological or behavioral traits. These characteristics include fingerprints, retina patterns, hand geometry, signature dynamics, speech, and keystroke dynamics.

  b. **Environmental controls** are also designed to protect the organization's physical information assets. The most important are

    1) Temperature and humidity control
    2) Gaseous fire-suppression system (not water)
    3) Data center not located on an outside wall
    4) Building housing data center not located in a flood plain

3. **Logical Controls**

  a. Logical security controls are needed because of the use of communications networks and connections to external systems. User identification and authentication, restriction of access, and the generation of audit trails are required in this environment. Thus, access controls have been developed to prevent improper use or manipulation of data files and programs. They ensure that only those persons with a bona fide purpose and authorization have access to computer systems.

1) Access control software (a) protects files, programs, data dictionaries, processing, etc., from unauthorized access; (b) restricts use of certain devices (e.g., terminals); and (c) may provide an audit trail for both successful and unsuccessful access attempts. For example, a firewall separates internal from external networks.

2) Passwords and ID numbers. The use of passwords and identification numbers is an effective control in an online system to prevent unauthorized access to computer files. Lists of authorized persons are maintained in the computer. The entry of passwords or identification numbers; a prearranged set of personal questions; and the use of badges, magnetic cards, or optically scanned cards may be combined to avoid unauthorized access.

   a) A security card may be used with a personal computer so that users must sign on with an ID and a password. The card controls the machine's operating system and records access data (date, time, duration, etc.).

   b) Proper user authentication by means of a password requires password-generating procedures to ensure that valid passwords are known only by the proper individuals. Thus, a password should not be displayed when entered at a keyboard.

   c) Password security may also be compromised in other ways. For example, log-on procedures may be cumbersome and tedious. Thus, users often store log-on sequences on their personal computers and invoke them when they want to use mainframe facilities. A risk of this practice is that anyone with access to the personal computers could log on to the mainframe.

   d) To be more effective, passwords should consist of random letters, symbols, and numbers. They should not contain words or phrases.

3) File attributes can be assigned to control access to and the use of files. Examples are read/write, read only, archive, and hidden.

4) A device authorization table restricts file access to those physical devices that should logically need access. For example, because it is illogical for anyone to access the accounts receivable file from a manufacturing terminal, the device authorization table will deny access even when a valid password is used.

   a) Such tests are often called compatibility tests because they ascertain whether a code number is compatible with the use to be made of the information. Thus, a user may be authorized to enter only certain kinds of data, have access only to certain information, have access but not updating authority, or use the system only at certain times. The lists or tables of authorized users or devices are sometimes called access control matrices.

5) A system access log records all attempts to use the system. The date and time, codes used, mode of access, data involved, and operator interventions are recorded.

6) Encryption involves using a fixed algorithm to manipulate plaintext.

7) Controlled disposal of documents. One method of enforcing access restrictions is to destroy data when they are no longer in use. Thus, paper documents may be shredded and magnetic media may be erased.

8) Automatic log-off (disconnection) of inactive data terminals may prevent the viewing of sensitive data on an unattended data terminal.

9) Security personnel. An organization may need to hire security specialists. For example, developing an information security policy for the organization, commenting on security controls in new applications, and monitoring and investigating unsuccessful access attempts are appropriate duties of the information security officer.

4. **Internet Security**

    a.   Connection to the Internet presents security issues.

        1)   Thus, the organization-wide network security policy should at the very least include

            a)   A user account management system

            b)   Installation of an Internet firewall

            c)   Methods such as encryption to ensure that only the intended user receives the information and that the information is complete and accurate

        2)   User account management involves installing a system to ensure that

            a)   New accounts are added correctly and assigned only to authorized users

            b)   Old and unused accounts are removed promptly

            c)   Passwords are changed periodically, and employees are educated on how to choose a password that cannot be easily guessed (e.g., a password of at least six diverse characters that do not form a word)

        3)   A firewall separates an internal network from an external network (e.g., the Internet) and prevents passage of specific types of traffic. It identifies names, Internet Protocol (IP) addresses, applications, etc., and compares them with programmed access rules.

            a)   A firewall may have any of the following features:

                i)   A packet filtering system examines each incoming network packet and drops (does not pass on) unauthorized packets.

                ii)   A proxy server maintains copies of web pages to be accessed by specified users. Outsiders are directed there, and more important information is not available from this access point.

                iii)   An application gateway limits traffic to specific applications.

                iv)   A circuit-level gateway connects an internal device, e.g., a network printer, with an outside TCP/IP port. It can identify a valid TCP session.

                v)   Stateful inspection stores information about the state of a transmission and uses it as background for evaluating messages from similar sources.

            b)   Firewall systems ordinarily produce reports on organization-wide Internet use, unusual usage patterns, and system penetration attempts. These reports are very helpful to the internal auditor as a method of continuous monitoring, or logging, of the system.

                i)   Firewalls do not provide adequate protection against computer viruses. Thus, an organization should include one or more antivirus measures in its network security policy.

        4)   Data traveling across the network can be encoded so that it is indecipherable to anyone except the intended recipient.

        5)   Other Controls

            a)   Authentication measures verify the identity of the user, thus ensuring that only the intended and authorized users gain access to the system.

                i)   Most firewall systems provide authentication procedures.

                ii)   Access controls are the most common authentication procedures.

            b)   Checksums help ensure the integrity of data by checking whether the file has been changed. The system computes a value for a file and then proceeds to check whether this value equals the last known value for this file. If the numbers are the same, the file has likely remained unchanged.

5. **Data Storage**

    a. Storing all related data on one storage device creates security problems.

        1) If hardware or software malfunctions occur, or unauthorized access is achieved, the results could be disastrous.

        2) Greater emphasis on security is required to provide backup and restrict access to the database.

            a) For example, the system may employ dual logging, that is, use of two transaction logs written simultaneously on separate storage media. It may also use a snapshot technique to capture data values before and after transaction processing. The files that store these values can be used to reconstruct the database in the event of data loss or corruption.

        3) The responsibility for creating, maintaining, securing, and restricting access to the database belongs to the database administrator (DBA).

        4) A database management system (DBMS) includes security features. Thus, a specified user's access may be limited to certain data fields or logical views depending on the individual's assigned duties.

Stop and review! You have completed the outline for this subunit. Study multiple-choice questions 1 through 5 beginning on page 274.

11.2 INFORMATION PROTECTION

1. **Business Objective**

    a. According to a publication of The IIA, the following five categories are IT Business Assurance Objectives:

        1) **Availability.** The organization must ensure that information, processes, and services are available at all times.

        2) **Capability.** The organization must ensure reliable and timely completion of transactions.

        3) **Functionality.** The organization must ensure that systems are designed to user specifications to fulfill business requirements.

        4) **Protectability.** The organization must ensure that a combination of physical and logical controls prevents unauthorized access to system data.

        5) **Accountability.** The organization must ensure that transactions are processed under firm principles of data ownership, identification, and authentication.

    b. One of the primary concerns of protectability relates to malicious software (malware). IT should have safeguards in place to prevent unauthorized access, use, or harm.

        1) Controls over access and change management processes should be in place to achieve the objective of protectability.

        2) Moreover, security awareness by all concerned should be heightened. Consequently, the business assurance objective of accountability is also pertinent. The roles, actions, and responsibilities for security should be defined.

2. **Malicious Software (Malware)**

    a. Malicious software may exploit a known hole or weakness in an application or operating system program to evade security measures.

        1) Such a vulnerability may have been caused by a programming error. It also may have been intentionally (but not maliciously) created to permit a programmer simple access (a back door) for correcting the code.

        2) Having bypassed security controls, the intruder can do immediate damage to the system or install malicious software. In some cases, malware infection may have few or no effects noticeable by users.

b.   A **Trojan horse** is an apparently innocent program (e.g., a spreadsheet) that includes a hidden function that may do damage when activated.

   1)   For example, it may contain a virus, which is a program code that copies itself from file to file. The virus may destroy data or programs. A common way of spreading a virus is by email attachments and downloads.

   2)   A trojan horse may act as a back door to bypass normal authentication and provide unauthorized, remote access to data, computers, and networks.

c.   A **worm** copies itself not from file to file but from computer to computer, often very rapidly. Repeated replication overloads a system by depleting memory or disk space.

d.   A **logic bomb** is much like a Trojan horse, except it activates only upon some occurrence, e.g., on a certain date.

e.   Malware may create a **denial of service** by overwhelming a system or website with more traffic than it can handle.

3.   **Controls Against Malware**

a.   Controls to prevent or detect infection by malware are particularly significant for file servers in large networks. The following are broad control objectives:

   1)   A policy should require use only of authorized software.

   2)   A policy should require adherence to licensing agreements.

   3)   A policy should create accountability for the persons authorized to maintain software.

   4)   A policy should require safeguards when data or programs are obtained by means of external media.

   5)   Antivirus software should continuously monitor the system for viruses (or worms) and eradicate them. It should also be immediately upgraded as soon as information about new threats becomes available.

   6)   Software and data for critical systems should be regularly reviewed.

   7)   Investigation of unauthorized files or amendments should be routine.

   8)   Email attachments and downloads (and files on unauthorized media or from networks that are not secure) should be checked.

   9)   Procedures should be established and responsibility assigned for coping with malware.

      a)   Procedures should reflect an understanding that another organization that has transmitted malware-infected material may have done so unwittingly and may need assistance. If such events occur repeatedly, however, termination of agreements or contracts may be indicated.

      b)   Procedures and policies should be documented, and employees must understand the reasons for them.

   10) Business continuity (recovery) plans should be drafted, e.g., data and software backup.

   11) Information about malware should be verified and appropriate alerts given.

   12) Responsible personnel should be aware of the possibility of hoaxes, which are false messages intending to create fear of a malware attack. For example, a spurious email message may be received instructing users to delete supposedly compromised files.

   13) Qualified personnel should be relied upon to distinguish hoaxes from malware.

b.   The following are specific controls to prevent or detect infection by malware:

   1)   All computer media (incoming or outgoing) may be scanned by sheep dip (dedicated) computers.

   2)   Nonscreened media should not be allowed on the organization's computers.

3) Scanning may be done of standalone computers or those on networks as another line of defense if media control fails.

4) Software may reside in memory to scan for malware communicated through a network.

5) Email gateways may have software to scan attachments.

6) Network servers may have software to detect and erase or store malware.

7) Scanning software on a standalone device should be upgraded when it is networked.

c. Use of external rather than internal expertise for coping with malware problems may be more costly and time consuming but less risky.

1) External service providers should be subject to the terms of a contract, and access and other controls should be in place.

d. Off-site computers and media of employees should be subject to malware controls, such as screening.

e. Response to threats via covert channels and Trojan horse programs includes the following:

1) Purchases should be of evaluated products from trusted suppliers.

2) Purchases should be in source code so that they are verifiable. This code should be inspected and tested prior to use.

3) Access to and changes in code should be restricted after it is put in use.

4) The availability of security patches for bugs in programs should be monitored constantly, especially regarding such items as network operating systems, email servers, routers, and firewalls. Patches should be tested and installed promptly.

5) Trusted employees should be assigned to key systems.

6) Known Trojan horses can be detected by scanning.

7) Reviewing data outflows, for example, through the firewall, may detect suspicious activity meriting investigation.

f. Hosts are the most common targets in a network because they furnish services to other requesting hosts.

1) Protective measures include promptly installing the most recent patches, fixes, and updates.

a) How they affect other elements of the system should be considered.

b) Updates should be tested before installation.

4. **Types of Attacks**

a. **Password Attacks**

1) A number of methods may be used.

a) A brute-force attack uses password-cracking software to try large numbers of letter and number combinations to access a network.

i) A simple variation is the use of password-cracking software that tries all the words in a dictionary.

b) Passwords (and user accounts) also may be discovered by Trojan horses, IP spoofing, and packet sniffers.

i) Phishing (spoofing) is identity misrepresentation in cyberspace, for example, by using a false website to obtain information about visitors.

ii) Sniffing is the use of software to eavesdrop on information sent by a user to the host computer of a website.

2) Once an attacker has access, (s)he may do anything the rightful user could have done.

    a) If that user has privileged access, the attacker may create a back door to facilitate future entry despite password and status changes.

    b) The attacker also may be able to leverage the initial access to obtain greater privileges than the rightful user.

3) If a user has the same password for multiple hosts, cracking that password for one compromises all.

4) Expressive methods of thwarting password attacks are one-time password and cryptographic authentication.

5) Optimal passwords are randomly generated, eight-character or longer combinations of numbers, uppercase and lowercase letters, and special symbols.

    a) A disadvantage is that users often write down passwords that are hard to remember. However, software has been developed that encrypts passwords to be kept on a handheld computer. Thus, the user only needs to know one password.

b. A **man-in-the-middle attack** takes advantage of networking, packet sniffing, and routing and transport protocols.

1) These attacks may be used to

    a) Steal data
    b) Obtain access to the network during a rightful user's active session
    c) Analyze the traffic on the network to learn about its operations and users
    d) Insert new data or modify the data being transmitted
    e) Deny service

2) Encryption is the effective response to man-in-the-middle attacks. The encrypted data will be useless to the attacker unless it can be decrypted.

c. A **denial-of-service (DOS)** attack is an attempt to overload a system (e.g., a network or Web server) with false messages so that it cannot function (a system crash).

1) A distributed DOS (DDOS) attack comes from multiple sources, for example, the machines of innocent parties infected by Trojan horses. When activated, these programs send messages to the target and leave the connection open.

2) A DOS may establish as many network connections as possible to exclude other users, overloading primary memory, or corrupting file systems.

3) Responses

    a) Firewalls should not permit use of Internet relay chat channels or other TCP/IP ports unless for business purposes. Thus, the organization should determine what relay kits have been installed, e.g., by employees connected to virtual private networks via cable or DSL.

        i) These methods, intrusion detection systems, and penetration testing may prevent a system from being used to make a DOS attack.

    b) The best protection by the target is the Internet service provider (ISP). The ISP can establish rate limits on transmissions to the target's website.

        i) Thus, only a defined amount of message packets with certain characteristics are allowed to reach the site.

5. **Countermeasures -- Intrusion Detection Systems (IDS)**

   a. If an organization's computer system has external connections, an IDS is needed to respond to security breaches.

      1) The IDS complements the computer system's firewalls. It responds to attacks on

         a) The network infrastructure (protected by the network IDS component)

            i) Routers
            ii) Switches
            iii) Bandwidth

         b) Servers (protected by the host IDS component)

            i) Operating systems
            ii) Applications

      2) An IDS responds to an attack by

         a) Taking action itself
         b) Alerting the management system

   b. A host IDS provides maximum protection only when the software is installed on each computer. It may operate in the following ways:

      1) The aggressive response is to monitor every call on the operating system and application as it occurs.

      2) A less effective method of preventing attacks is analysis of access log files.

      3) A host IDS may also identify questionable processes and verify the security of system files.

   c. A network IDS works by using sensors to examine packets traveling on the network. Each sensor monitors only the segment of the network to which it is attached. A packet is examined if it matches a signature.

      1) String signatures (certain strings of text) are potential signs of an attack.

      2) Port signatures alert the IDS that a point subject to frequent intrusion attempts may be under attack.

         a) A port in this sense (as opposed to the physical serial and parallel ports on a personal computer) is a logical connection to the system.

            i) A port number included in the message header stipulates how the message will be handled. Because many port numbers are widely known, an attacker may be able to send messages to determine whether ports are open and therefore vulnerable.

      3) A header signature is a suspicious combination in a packet header.

   d. The preferable IDS combines host IDS and network IDS components.

      1) A host IDS has greater potential for preventing a specific attack, but the network IDS provides a necessary overall perspective. Thus, a host IDS should be in place for each host, with a network IDS for the whole system.

   e. Knowledge-based detection is based on information about the system's weaknesses and searches for intrusions that take advantage of them.

      1) This type of IDS depends on frequent and costly updating of information about intrusion methods. It is also specialized with respect to those methods and operating system methods.

         a) Problems are compounded when different versions of the operating system (or different operating systems) are in place.

f.   Behavior-based detection presumes that an attack will cause an observable anomaly. Actual and normal system behavior (a model of expected operations) are compared. A discrepancy results in an alert.

1)   This approach is more complete than the knowledge-based approach because every attack should be detected. However, the level of accuracy is lower. False alarms may be generated, so the model must be updated whenever operational changes are made.

2)   The advantages of behavior-based detection are that

a)   Knowledge of specific new intrusion techniques is not necessary.
b)   It is less specific to particular operating systems.

g.   Responses to detection of an intrusion normally include an automatic component. Continuous monitoring and response by individuals may not be feasible or sufficiently rapid.

1)   An automatically acting IDS provides continuous security. It responds without the presence of humans. Responses may include

a)   Disconnecting the entire network from outside access
b)   Locking access to all or part of the system
c)   Slowing the system's activity to reduce injury
d)   Validating the external user
e)   Sending console, email, pager, or phone messages to appropriate personnel

2)   Alarmed systems resources are dummy files or accounts, for example, a default administrator account with a default password set. They are traps for an intruder.

a)   Access to a dummy resource results in automatic action or notice to appropriate employees.
b)   The advantage of this method is that it is uncomplicated and inexpensive.
c)   The disadvantage is that authorized persons may inadvertently cause an alarm.

6.   **Information Integrity and Reliability**

a.   Internal auditors often assess the organization's information integrity and reliability practices.

b.   The IIA provides guidance on this topic in Practice Advisory 2130.A1-1, *Information Reliability and Integrity*:

1)   "Internal auditors determine whether senior management and the board have a clear understanding that information reliability and integrity is a management responsibility. This responsibility includes all critical information of the organization regardless of how the information is stored. Information reliability and integrity includes accuracy, completeness, and security" (para. 1).

2)   "The chief audit executive (CAE) determines whether the internal audit activity possesses, or has access to, competent audit resources to evaluate information reliability and integrity and associated risk exposures. This includes both internal and external risk exposures, and exposures relating to the organization's relationships with outside entities" (para. 2).

3)   "Internal auditors assess the effectiveness of preventive, detective, and mitigation measures against past attacks, as appropriate, and future attempts or incidents deemed likely to occur. Internal auditors determine whether the board has been appropriately informed of threats, incidents, vulnerabilities exploited, and corrective measures" (para. 4).

4) "Internal auditors periodically assess the organization's information reliability and integrity practices and recommend, as appropriate, enhancements to, or implementation of, new controls and safeguards. Such assessments can either be conducted as separate stand-alone engagements or integrated into other audits or engagements conducted as part of the internal audit plan" (para. 5).

7. **Privacy**

a. Management is responsible for ensuring that an organization's privacy framework is in place. Internal auditors' primary role is to ensure that relevant privacy laws and other regulations are being properly communicated to the responsible parties.

b. The IIA provides guidance on this topic in Practice Advisory 2130.A1-2, *Evaluating an Organization's Privacy Framework*:

1) "Risks associated with the privacy of information encompass personal privacy (physical and psychological); privacy of space (freedom from surveillance); privacy of communication (freedom from monitoring); and privacy of information (collection, use, and disclosure of personal information by others)" (para. 2).

a) Personal information is information associated with a specific individual.

2) "Effective control over the protection of personal information is an essential component of the governance, risk management, and control processes of an organization. The board is ultimately accountable for identifying the principal risks to the organization and implementing appropriate control processes to mitigate those risks. This includes establishing the necessary privacy framework for the organization and monitoring its implementation" (para. 3).

3) "In conducting such an evaluation of the management of the organization's privacy framework, the internal auditor:

a) Considers the laws, regulations, and policies relating to privacy in the jurisdictions where the organization operates;

b) Liaisons with in-house legal counsel to determine the exact nature of laws, regulations, and other standards and practices applicable to the organization and the country/countries in which it operates;

c) Liaisons with information technology specialists to determine that information security and data protection controls are in place and regularly reviewed and assessed for appropriateness;

d) Considers the level or maturity of the organization's privacy practices. Depending upon the level, the internal auditor may have differing roles" (para. 7).

Stop and review! You have completed the outline for this subunit. Study multiple-choice questions 6 through 9 on page 276.

11.3 AUTHENTICATION AND ENCRYPTION

1. **Application Authentication**

a. Application authentication is a means of taking a user's identity from the operating system on which the user is working and passing it to an authentication server for verification. This can be designed into an application from its inception.

b. There are three classes of authentication information.

1) Remembered information: name, birthdate, account number, password, PIN
2) Possessed objects: badge, plastic card, key, finger ring
3) Personal characteristics: fingerprint, voiceprint, hand size, signature, retinal pattern

2.   **Encryption Overview**

a.   Encryption technology converts data into a code. A program codes data prior to transmission. Another program decodes it after transmission. Unauthorized users still may be able to access the data, but without the encryption key, they cannot decode the information.

b.   Encryption software uses a fixed algorithm (a step-by-step, usually mathematical, procedure) to manipulate plaintext (the understandable form of the encrypted text) and an encryption key to introduce variation. The information is sent in its manipulated form (cyphertext), and the receiver translates the information back into plaintext. Although data may be accessed by tapping into the transmission line, the encryption key is necessary to understand the data being sent.

1)   The machine instructions necessary to code and decode data can constitute a 20-to-30% increase in system overhead.

c.   Encryption technology may be either hardware- or software-based. Two major types of encryption software exist.

3.   **Public-Key (Asymmetric) Encryption**

a.   Public-key (asymmetric) encryption requires two keys, one public and one private. These pairs of keys are issued by a trusted third party called a certificate authority (e.g., VeriSign, Thawte, GoDaddy).

1)   Every recipient's public key is available in the certificate authority's directory, but the associated private key is known only to the recipient.

2)   Any party who wishes to send a secure message encrypts it using the intended recipient's public key. The recipient then decrypts the message using the private key. The two keys are mathematically related so that a message encrypted with one key can be decrypted only with the other key.

b.   This arrangement is more secure than a single-key system, in which the parties must agree on and transmit a single key that could be intercepted.

1)   RSA, named for its developers (Rivest, Shamir, and Adelman), is the most commonly used public-key method.

c.   A **digital signature** is a means of authentication of an electronic document, for example, of the validity of a purchase order, acceptance of a contract, or financial information.

1)   The sender uses its private key to encode all or part of the message, and the recipient uses the sender's public key to decode it. Hence, if that key decodes the message, the sender must have written it.

2)   One variation is to send the message in both plaintext and cyphertext. If the decoded version matches the plaintext version, no alteration has occurred.

d.   A **digital certificate** is another means of authentication used in e-business. The certificate authority issues a coded electronic certificate that contains (1) the holder's name, (2) a copy of its public key, (3) a serial number, and (4) an expiration date. The certificate verifies the holder's identity.

1)   The recipient of a coded message sent by the holder uses the certificate authority's public key (available on the Internet) to decode the certificate included in the message. The recipient then determines that the certificate was issued by the certificate authority. Moreover, the recipient can use the sender's public key and identification data to send a coded response.

a)   Such methods may be used for transactions between sellers and buyers using credit cards.

2)   A certificate also may be used to provide assurance to customers that a website is genuine.

e. The public key infrastructure permits secure monetary and information exchange over the Internet. Thus, it facilitates e-business.

   1) The two main cryptographic protocols for secure communications over the Internet are SSL (Secure Sockets Layer) and TLS (Transport Layer Security).

      a) When HTTP (Hypertext Transfer Protocol, a higher-level protocol that makes the graphics-intensive World Wide Web possible) is used in conjunction with SSL or TLS, it is called HTTPS (HTTP Secure).

      b) The URLs of secure Web pages where shoppers enter their credit card numbers most often change from http:// to https://.

   2) Digital time stamping services verify the time (and possibly the place) of a transaction. For example, a document may be sent to a service, which applies its digital stamp and then forwards the document.

4. **Private-Key (Symmetric) Encryption**

   a. Private-key, or symmetric, encryption is less secure than the public-key method because it requires only a single (secret) key for each pair of parties that want to send each other coded messages.

      1) Data Encryption Standard (DES), a shared private-key method developed by the U.S. government, is the most prevalent secret-key method. It is based on numbers with 56 binary digits.

      2) The Advanced Encryption Standard (AES) is a cryptographic algorithm for use by U.S. government organizations to protect sensitive information. The AES will be widely used on a voluntary basis by organizations, institutions, and individuals, as well as by the U.S. government.

Stop and review! You have completed the outline for this subunit. Study multiple-choice questions 10 and 11 on page 277.

11.4 END-USER COMPUTING (EUC)

1. **End-User vs. Centralized Computing**

   a. EUC involves user-created or user-acquired systems that are maintained and operated outside of traditional information systems controls.

      1) Certain environmental control risks are more likely in EUC. They include copyright violations that occur when unauthorized copies of software are made or when software is installed on multiple computers.

      2) Unauthorized access to application programs and related data is another concern. EUC lacks physical access controls, application-level controls, and other controls found in mainframe or networked environments.

      3) Moreover, EUC may not have adequate backup, recovery, and contingency planning. The result may be an inability to re-create the system or its data.

   b. Program development, documentation, and maintenance also may lack the centralized control found in larger systems.

      1) The risk of allowing end users to develop their own applications is decentralization of control. These applications may not be reviewed by independent outside systems analysts and are not created using a formal development methodology. They also may not be subject to appropriate standards, controls, and quality assurance procedures.

      2) When end users create their own applications and files, private information systems may proliferate in which data are largely uncontrolled. Systems may contain the same information, but EUC applications may update and define the data in different ways. Thus, determining the location of data and ensuring data consistency become more difficult.

3) The auditors should determine that EUC applications contain controls that allow users to rely on the information produced. Identification of applications is more difficult than in a traditional centralized computing environment because few people know about and use them.

    a) The auditor's first concern is to discover their existence and their intended functions. One approach is to take an organization-wide inventory of major EUC applications. An alternative is for the auditors and the primary user (a function or department) to review major EUC applications.

    b) The next step is risk assessment. EUC applications that represent high-risk exposures are chosen for audit, for example, because they support critical decisions or are used to control cash or physical assets.

    c) The third step is to review the controls included in the applications chosen in the risk assessment.

c. In a personal computer setting, the user is often the programmer and operator. Thus, the protections provided by segregation of duties are eliminated.

d. The audit trail is diminished because of the lack of history files, incomplete printed output, etc.

e. In general, available security features for stand-alone machines are limited compared with those in a network.

2. **Three Basic Architectures for Desktop Computing**

a. **Client-server model.** A client-server system divides processing of an application between a client machine on a network and a server. This division depends on which tasks each is best suited to perform.

    1) However, user interaction is ordinarily restricted to the client part of the application. This portion normally consists of the user interface, data entry, queries, and receipt of reports.

    2) The server customarily manages peripheral hardware and controls access to shared databases. Thus, a client-server application must be designed as separate software components that run on different machines but appear to be one application.

    3) Security for client-server systems may be more difficult than in a mainframe-based system because of the numerous access points. They also use distributed processing methods that result in heightened risk of unauthorized access to data and processing. New methods of accessing data and processing, such as remote procedure calls, are also available.

b. **Dummy terminal model.** In this architecture, desktop machines that lack stand-alone processing power have access to remote computers in a network.

    1) Applications run on the remote network computers. The terminal simply displays output from the application and sends input from the user back to the application.

    2) These machines are relatively inexpensive because they have no disk drives.

c. The **application server model** involves a three-tiered or distributed network application. The middle (application) tier translates data between the database (back-end) server and the user's (front-end) server. The application server also performs business logic functions, transaction management, and load balancing.

    1) Business logic functions interpret transactions and determine how they will be processed, e.g., applicable discounts or shipping methods. These are primarily performed by the application server. The user's front-end server performs presentation logic functions.

    2) Transaction management tracks all of the steps in transaction processing to ensure completion, editing, or deletion.

      3) Load balancing distributes data and data processing among available servers, e.g., evenly to all servers or to the next available server.

Stop and review! You have completed the outline for this subunit. Study multiple-choice questions 12 and 13 on page 277.

11.5 PROGRAM CHANGE CONTROL

1. **Overview**

   a. Over the life of an application, users are constantly asking for changes. The process of managing these changes is referred to as systems maintenance, and the relevant controls are called program change controls.

   b. One of the key controls related to program changes is the power to update access for production data and for production programs.

      1) Users should have the power to update access for production data. Users need to update data through application programs but do **not** need access to change production programs.

      2) Application programmers should not have the power to update access for production data or for production programs.

2. **Program Change Control Process**

   a. The program change control process generally includes the following steps: (1) request, (2) assess, (3) plan, (4) build and test, (5) implement, and (6) gain acceptance.

   b. **Request.** The process starts when a user makes a formal request for something to be changed. The request is categorized based on its importance, impact, and complexity.

   c. **Assess.** The requested change is then assessed for risk.

   d. **Plan.** The change request is assigned to the programmer team, which will then plan the change in detail.

   e. **Build and test.** Once a plan is made, the programmers can begin.

      1) Once a change to a system has been approved, the programmer should save a copy of the production program in a test area of the computer, sometimes called a "sandbox."

         a) Except in emergencies, and then only under close supervision, should a change be made directly to the production version of a computer program.

         b) The IT function must be able to revert immediately to the prior version of the program if unexpected results are encountered during an emergency change.

      2) The programmer makes the necessary changes to this copy of the program.

         a) The program appears on the programmer's screen, not as digital bits and bytes, but as English-like statements and commands. A computer program in this form, i.e., readable by humans, is called source code.

      3) The programmer transforms the changed program into a form that the computer can execute. The resulting production-ready program is referred to as executable code.

         a) Programming languages that are transformed from source code into executable code at run time by a specialized converter program are said to be interpreted.

         b) Programming languages that are transformed in one step, before run time, and then executed directly on the computer are said to be compiled.

4)   Once the executable version of the changed program is ready, the programmer tests it to see if it performs the new task as expected.

a)   This testing process must absolutely not be run against production data. A special set of test data must be available for running test programs against.

5)   The programmer demonstrates the new functionality for the user who made the request.

a)   The user either accepts the new program, or the programmer can go back and make further changes.

6)   Once the program is in a form acceptable to the user, the programmer moves it to a holding area.

a)   Programmers (except in emergencies) should never be able to put programs directly into production.

f.   **Implement.** The programmer's supervisor reviews the new program, approves it, and authorizes its move into production, generally carried out by operations personnel.

1)   The compensating control is that operators generally lack the programming knowledge to put fraudulent code into production.

g.   **Gain acceptance.** Once the change is implemented, the rest of the users and the organization can be trained on and informed of the new change.

Stop and review! You have completed the outline for this subunit. Study multiple-choice questions 14 and 15 on page 278.

11.6 APPLICATION DEVELOPMENT

The development of new systems is another IT area that has undergone profound change from its early days. New, high-productivity software tools have dissolved the lines separating the old rigid steps in the process. Internal auditors must remain focused on the ultimate goal of implementing stable, maintainable systems.

1.   **Build or Buy**

a.   When an organization purchases a new system from an outside vendor, contract management personnel oversee the process. The future end users of the system, as well as IT personnel, are also involved, drawing up specifications and requirements.

1)   However, when a new system is to be created in-house, planning and managing the development process is one of the IT function's most important tasks.

a)   The needs of the end users must be balanced with budget and time constraints; the decision to use existing hardware vs. the purchase of new platforms must be weighed.

2)   Because so much time and so many resources are devoted to the creation of a new application (and because, generally, the more important the business function being automated, the more complex the application is), having a well-governed methodology for overseeing the development process is vital.

3)   Both the end users who specified the new system's functionality and IT management who are overseeing the development process must approve progress toward the completion of the system at the end of each of the stages described on the following pages. This requirement for ongoing review and approval of the project is a type of implementation control.

2. **Systems Development Life Cycle (SDLC)**

   a.   The systems development life cycle approach is the traditional methodology applied to the development of large, highly structured application systems.

      1)   A major advantage of the life cycle approach is enhanced management and control of the development process.

      2)   Once the need for a new system has been recognized, the five phases (each with multiple steps) of the SDLC proceed as depicted in the diagram below (portions of the phases can overlap).

Systems Development Life Cycle

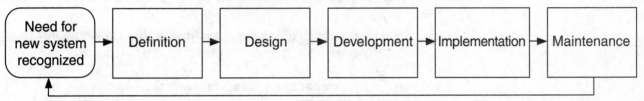

Figure 11-1

      3)   The feedback gathered during the maintenance of a system provides information for developing the next generation of systems, hence the name "life cycle."

   b.   The phases and component steps of the traditional SDLC can be described as follows:

      1)   **Definition (Systems Planning and Analysis)**

         a)   A proposal for a new system is submitted to the IT steering committee describing the need for the application and the business function(s) that it will affect.

         b)   Feasibility studies are conducted to determine

            i)   What technology the new system will require
            ii)   What economic resources must be committed to the new system
            iii)   How the new system will affect current operations

         c)   The steering committee gives its go-ahead for the project.

      2)   **Design**

         a)   Logical design consists of mapping the flow and storage of the data elements that will be used by the new system and the new program modules that will constitute the new system.

            i)   Data flow diagrams (DFDs) and structured flowcharts are commonly used in this step.
            ii)   Some data elements may already be stored in existing databases. Good logical design ensures that they are not duplicated.

         b)   Physical design involves planning the specific interactions of the new program code and data elements with the hardware platform (existing or planned for purchase) on which the new system will operate.

            i)   Systems analysts are heavily involved in these two steps.

      3)   **Development**

         a)   The actual program code and database structures that will be used in the new system are written.

    b) **Testing** is the most crucial step of the process.

        i) The programmers thoroughly test each new program module of the system, both alone and in concert with other modules.

- The data used in testing new programs is never the organization's actual production data; such testing would be far too risky to the organization's business.
- Instead, a carefully designed test database is filled with both good and bad data to test how well the new system deals with bad input.

    c) User acceptance testing is the final step before placing the system in live operation.

        i) IT must demonstrate to the user department that submitted the original request that the system performs the functionality that was desired.

        ii) Once the user department is satisfied with the new system, it acknowledges formal acceptance, and implementation begins.

4) **Implementation**

    a) Four strategies for converting to the new system can be used:

        i) With parallel operation, the old and new systems both are run at full capacity for a given period.

- This strategy is the safest since the old system is still producing output (in case there are major problems with the new system), but it is also the most expensive and time-consuming.

        ii) With cutover conversion, the old system is shut down, and the new one takes over processing at once.

- This is the least expensive and least time-consuming strategy, but it is also the riskiest.

        iii) Under pilot conversion, one branch, department, or division at a time is fully converted to the new system.

- Experience gained from each installation is used to benefit the next one. One disadvantage of this strategy is the extension of the conversion time.

        iv) In some cases, phased conversion is possible. Under this strategy, one function of the new system at a time is placed in operation.

- For instance, if the new system is an integrated accounting application, accounts receivable could be installed, then accounts payable, cash management, materials handling, etc.
- The advantage of this strategy is allowing the users to learn one part of the system at a time.

    b) Training and documentation are critical.

        i) The users must be made to feel comfortable with the new system and have plenty of guidance available, either as a hard copy or online.

        ii) Documentation consists of more than just operations manuals for the users. Layouts of the program code and database structures must also be available for the programmers who must modify and maintain the system.

        c)   Systems follow-up or post-audit evaluation is a subsequent review of the efficiency and effectiveness of the system after it has operated for a substantial time (e.g., 1 year).

    5) **Maintenance** is the final phase of the SDLC.

        a)   The system is assessed to ensure it does not become obsolete.

        b)   This stage also includes continuous evaluation of the system's performance.

           i)   Necessary changes are made to the initial software.

3. Prototyping

    a.   Prototyping is an alternative approach to application development that involves creating a working model of the system requested, demonstrating it for the user, obtaining feedback, and making changes to the underlying code.

        1)   This process repeats through several iterations until the user is satisfied with the system's functionality.

    b.   Formerly, this approach was derided as being wasteful of resources and tending to produce unstable systems, but with vastly increased processing power and high-productivity development tools, prototyping can, in some cases, be an efficient means of systems development.

4. Application Development Tools

    a.   **Computer-aided software engineering (CASE)** applies the computer to software design and development.

        1)   It provides the capacity to maintain on the computer all of the system documentation, e.g., data flow diagrams, data dictionaries, and pseudocode (structured English); to develop executable input and output screens; and to generate program code in at least skeletal form.

        2)   Thus, CASE facilitates the creation, organization, and maintenance of documentation and permits some automation of the coding process.

    b.   **Object-oriented programming (OOP)** combines data and the related procedures into an object. Thus, an object's data can be operated on only within the object.

        1)   If the procedures (called methods) for manipulating the data in an object are changed, no other parts of the program are affected. The idea of limiting code that operates on an object to its own source code unit is called encapsulation.

           a)   The basic concepts of OOP are class and inheritance. Programs are written by describing the creation and interaction of objects. One class of objects can inherit the characteristics of a more general class. Thus, a basic advantage of OOP is that the code is reusable.

           b)   In OOP, every object has attached to it two sets of characteristics, called attributes and methods.

EXAMPLE

A company's programmers have created an object named "order."

"order" has the following attributes: order_number, order_date, customer_number, part_number, qty_ordered, unit_price, bin_number.

"order" is given the following methods:

- extended_price (qty_ordered × unit_price)
- three_month_history (every order with the same customer_number and order_date less than 3 months old is retrieved)
- quantity_remaining (uses bin_number to determine current quantity on hand and subtracts qty_ordered)

The object "order" can now be reused by the programmers without all of its attributes and methods having to be recreated in every application that uses it.

   c. **Rapid application development (RAD)** is a software development process involving iterative development, the construction of prototypes, and the use of CASE tools.

      1) The RAD process usually involves compromises in usability, features, or execution speed. Increased speed of development occurs through rapid prototyping, virtualization of system related routines, and other techniques. However, end-user utility is usually decreased.

      2) Code-generation tools. RAD was designed in large part to take advantage of CASE technology, which involves aspects of requirements gathering and data modeling, but most especially of code generation.

         a) Code generation involves taking some input and transforming it to the source code that a developer might otherwise have to write according to templates.

      3) RAD involves four phases:

         a) In the **requirements planning phase**, users, managers, and IT staff determine the needs of the business, the system's requirements, and the project's scope and constraints.

         b) In the **user design phase**, users and systems analysts develop prototypes that represent the entire system, including all processes, inputs, and outputs.

            i) These prototypes are used to improve the original design and eventually approve a final working model.

         c) In the **construction phase**, programs and applications are developed and users continue to participate. By staying involved, users can suggest changes or improvements as each stage, or module, is developed.

            i) The system is then developed module by module, with input from the users, until completed.

         d) In the **testing and transition phase**, the application is tested and the staff begins transitioning over to the new application.

            i) All the new components and interfaces are tested.

Stop and review! You have completed the outline for this subunit. Study multiple-choice questions 16 through 20 beginning on page 278.

QUESTIONS

11.1 Physical and Systems Security

1. An Internet firewall is designed to provide adequate protection against which of the following?

   A. A computer virus.

   B. Unauthenticated logins from outside users.

   C. Insider leaking of confidential information.

   D. A Trojan horse application.

Answer (B) is correct.

    REQUIRED: The protection provided by an Internet firewall.

    DISCUSSION: A firewall is a combination of hardware and software that separates two networks and prevents passage of specific types of network traffic while maintaining a connection between the networks. Generally, an Internet firewall is designed to protect a system from unauthenticated logins from outside users, although it may provide several other features as well.

    Answer (A) is incorrect. A firewall cannot adequately protect a system against computer viruses. Answer (C) is incorrect. Industrial spies need not leak information through the firewall. A telephone or flash drive are much more common means of sharing confidential information. Answer (D) is incorrect. A firewall cannot adequately protect against a Trojan horse (a program, such as a game, that appears friendly but that actually contains applications destructive to the computer system) or any other program that can be executed in the system by an internal user.

2. Authentication is the process by which the

    A. System verifies that the user is entitled to enter the transaction requested.

    B. System verifies the identity of the user.

    C. User identifies himself or herself to the system.

    D. User indicates to the system that the transaction was processed correctly.

Answer (B) is correct.
    REQUIRED: The definition of authentication.
    DISCUSSION: Identification is the process of uniquely distinguishing one user from all others. Authentication is the process of determining that individuals are who they say they are. For example, a password may identify but not authenticate its user if it is known by more than one individual.
    Answer (A) is incorrect. Authentication involves verifying the identity of the user. This process does not necessarily confirm the functions the user is authorized to perform. Answer (C) is incorrect. User identification to the system does not imply that the system has verified the identity of the user. Answer (D) is incorrect. This procedure is an application control for accuracy of the transaction.

3. Which of the following issues would be of most concern to an auditor relating to an organization's Internet security policy?

    A. Auditor documentation.

    B. System efficiency.

    C. Data integrity.

    D. Rejected and suspense item controls.

Answer (C) is correct.
    REQUIRED: The item of most concern to the auditor relating to Internet security.
    DISCUSSION: Controls are intended to ensure the integrity, confidentiality, and availability of information. An auditor relies on the integrity of the system's data and programs in making critical decisions throughout the audit process.
    Answer (A) is incorrect. Auditor documentation is not as crucial as data integrity. Answer (B) is incorrect. Efficiency does not affect the basis for critical auditor decisions using information provided by the system. Answer (D) is incorrect. Rejected and suspense item controls represent a portion of the techniques used to ensure data integrity.

4. Passwords for personal computer software programs are designed to prevent

    A. Inaccurate processing of data.

    B. Unauthorized access to the computer.

    C. Incomplete updating of data files.

    D. Unauthorized use of the software.

Answer (D) is correct.
    REQUIRED: The function of passwords.
    DISCUSSION: The use of passwords is an effective control in an online system to prevent unauthorized access to computer files. Lists of authorized users are maintained in the computer. The entry of passwords or ID numbers; a prearranged act of personal questions; and use of badges, magnetic cards, or optically scanned cards may be combined to avoid unauthorized access.
    Answer (A) is incorrect. Passwords concern authorization, not accuracy of data. Answer (B) is incorrect. Passwords do not prevent physical access to the computer. Answer (C) is incorrect. Passwords concern authorization, not completeness of data.

5. A client installed sophisticated controls using the biometric attributes of employees to authenticate user access to the computer system. This technology most likely replaced which of the following controls?

    A. Use of security specialists.

    B. Reasonableness tests.

    C. Passwords.

    D. Virus protection software.

Answer (C) is correct.
    REQUIRED: The control most likely replaced by biometric technologies.
    DISCUSSION: The use of passwords is an effective control in an online system to prevent unauthorized access to computer systems. However, biometric technologies are more sophisticated and difficult to compromise.
    Answer (A) is incorrect. Biometric technologies do not eliminate the need for specialists who evaluate and monitor security needs. Answer (B) is incorrect. Reasonableness tests are related to input controls, not access controls. Answer (D) is incorrect. Virus protection software prevents damage to data in a system, not access to a system.

11.2 Information Protection

6. Which of the following is a computer program that appears to be legitimate but performs some illicit activity when it is run?

    A. Hoax virus.

    B. Web crawler.

    C. Trojan horse.

    D. Killer application.

Answer (C) is correct.

    REQUIRED: The apparently legitimate computer program that performs an illicit activity.

    DISCUSSION: A Trojan horse is a computer program that appears friendly, for example, a game, but that actually contains an application destructive to the computer system.

    Answer (A) is incorrect. A hoax virus is a false notice about the existence of a computer virus. It is usually disseminated through use of distribution lists and is sent by email or via an internal network. Answer (B) is incorrect. A web crawler (a spider or bot) is a computer program created to access and read information on websites. The results are included as entries in the index of a search engine. Answer (D) is incorrect. A killer application is one that is so useful that it may justify widespread adoption of a new technology.

7. The best preventive measure against a computer virus is to

    A. Compare software in use with authorized versions of the software.

    B. Execute virus exterminator programs periodically on the system.

    C. Allow only authorized software from known sources to be used on the system.

    D. Prepare and test a plan for recovering from the incidence of a virus.

Answer (C) is correct.

    REQUIRED: The best preventive measure against a computer virus.

    DISCUSSION: Preventive controls are designed to prevent errors before they occur. Detective and corrective controls attempt to identify and correct errors. Preventive controls are usually more cost beneficial than detective or corrective controls. Allowing only authorized software from known sources to be used on the system is a preventive measure. The authorized software from known sources is expected to be free of viruses.

    Answer (A) is incorrect. Comparing software with authorized versions is a detective control used to determine whether only authorized versions of the software are being used on the system. Answer (B) is incorrect. Executing virus exterminator programs is a corrective control against a computer virus. Answer (D) is incorrect. Preparing and testing a plan for virus recovery is a corrective control against a computer virus.

8. Which of the following is an indication that a computer virus is present?

    A. Frequent power surges that harm computer equipment.

    B. Unexplainable losses of or changes to data.

    C. Inadequate backup, recovery, and contingency plans.

    D. Numerous copyright violations due to unauthorized use of purchased software.

Answer (B) is correct.

    REQUIRED: The indicator of a computer virus.

    DISCUSSION: The effects of computer viruses range from harmless messages to complete destruction of all data within the system. A symptom of a virus would be the unexplained loss of or change to data.

    Answer (A) is incorrect. Power surges are caused by hardware or power supply problems. Answer (C) is incorrect. Inadequate backup, recovery, and contingency plans are operating policy weaknesses. Answer (D) is incorrect. Copyright violations represent policy or compliance problems.

9. The reliability and integrity of all critical information of an organization, regardless of the media in which the information is stored, is the responsibility of

    A. Shareholders.

    B. IT department.

    C. Management.

    D. All employees.

Answer (C) is correct.

    REQUIRED: The responsibility for information reliability and integrity.

    DISCUSSION: Internal auditors determine whether senior management and the board have a clear understanding that information reliability and integrity is a management responsibility (PA 2130.A1-1, para. 1). Information reliability and integrity includes accuracy, completeness, and security.

11.3 Authentication and Encryption

10. A client communicates sensitive data across the Internet. Which of the following controls would be most effective to prevent the use of the information if it were intercepted by an unauthorized party?

    A. A firewall.

    B. An access log.

    C. Passwords.

    D. Encryption.

Answer (D) is correct.

    REQUIRED: The most effective control for preventing the use of intercepted information.

    DISCUSSION: Encryption technology converts data into a code. Encoding data before transmission over communications lines makes it more difficult for someone with access to the transmission to understand or modify its contents.

    Answer (A) is incorrect. A firewall tries to prevent access from specific types of traffic to an internal network. After someone has obtained information from the site, a firewall cannot prevent its use. Answer (B) is incorrect. An access log only records attempted usage of a system. Answer (C) is incorrect. Passwords prevent unauthorized users from accessing the system. If information has already been obtained, a password cannot prevent its use.

11. To ensure privacy in a public-key encryption system, knowledge of which of the following keys would be required to decode the received message?

1. Private
2. Public

    A. 1.

    B. 2.

    C. Both 1 and 2.

    D. Neither 1 nor 2.

Answer (A) is correct.

    REQUIRED: The key(s) required to decode messages in a public-key system to ensure privacy.

    DISCUSSION: In a public-key system, the public key is used to encrypt the message prior to transmission, and the private key is needed to decrypt (decode) the message.

11.4 End-User Computing (EUC)

12. Responsibility for the control of end-user computing (EUC) exists at the organizational, departmental, and individual user level. Which of the following should be a direct responsibility of the individual users?

    A. Acquisition of hardware and software.

    B. Taking equipment inventories.

    C. Strategic planning of end-user computing.

    D. Physical security of equipment.

Answer (D) is correct.

    REQUIRED: The direct responsibility of an individual user.

    DISCUSSION: EUC involves user-created or user-acquired systems that are maintained and operated outside of traditional information systems controls. In this environment, an individual user is ordinarily responsible for the physical security of the equipment (s)he uses.

    Answer (A) is incorrect. The acquisition of hardware and software is an organizational- and departmental-level responsibility. Answer (B) is incorrect. Taking equipment inventories is an organizational-level responsibility. Answer (C) is incorrect. Strategic planning is an organizational- and departmental-level responsibility.

13. Which of the following risks is more likely to be encountered in an end-user computing (EUC) environment as compared with a centralized environment?

    A. Inability to afford adequate uninterruptible power supply systems.

    B. User input screens without a graphical user interface (GUI).

    C. Applications that are difficult to integrate with other information systems.

    D. Lack of adequate utility programs.

Answer (C) is correct.

    REQUIRED: The risk more likely to be encountered in an EUC environment.

    DISCUSSION: The risks arising from allowing end users to develop their own applications are the risks associated with decentralization of control. These applications may lack appropriate standards, controls, and quality assurance procedures.

    Answer (A) is incorrect. Inability to afford adequate uninterruptible power supply systems is a risk in all computing environments. Answer (B) is incorrect. Almost all EUC environments have some form of GUI. Answer (D) is incorrect. Lack of adequate utility programs is a risk in all computing environments.

11.5 Program Change Control

14. The process of monitoring, evaluating, and modifying a system as needed is referred to as systems

- A. Analysis.
- B. Feasibility study.
- C. Maintenance.
- D. Implementation.

Answer (C) is correct.

REQUIRED: The term for the process of monitoring, evaluating, and modifying a system.

DISCUSSION: Systems maintenance must be undertaken by systems analysts and applications programmers continually throughout the life of a system. Maintenance is the redesign of the system and programs to meet new needs or to correct design flaws. These changes should be part of a regular program of preventive maintenance.

Answer (A) is incorrect. Systems analysis is the process of determining user problems and needs, surveying the organization's present system, and analyzing the facts. Answer (B) is incorrect. A feasibility study determines whether a proposed system is technically, operationally, and economically feasible. Answer (D) is incorrect. Implementation involves training and educating users, testing, conversion, and follow-up.

15. A company often revises its production processes. The changes may entail revisions to processing programs. Ensuring that changes have a minimal impact on processing and result in minimal risk to the system is a function of

- A. Security administration.
- B. Change control.
- C. Problem tracking.
- D. Problem-escalation procedures.

Answer (B) is correct.

REQUIRED: The approach to ensure changes have a minimal impact on processing.

DISCUSSION: Change control is the process of authorizing, developing, testing, and installing coded changes so as to minimize the impact on processing and the risk to the system.

Answer (A) is incorrect. Security administration is concerned with access to data. Answer (C) is incorrect. Problem tracking is concerned with collecting data to be analyzed for corrective action. Answer (D) is incorrect. Problem escalation-procedures are a means of categorizing problems so that the least-skilled person can address them.

11.6 Application Development

16. Rejection of unauthorized modifications to application systems could be accomplished through the use of

- A. Programmed checks.
- B. Batch controls.
- C. Implementation controls.
- D. One-for-one checking.

Answer (C) is correct.

REQUIRED: The controls that reject unauthorized modifications to application systems.

DISCUSSION: General controls include organizational controls, such as a policy (an implementation control) that requires new programs and changes in programs (after adequate testing) to be formally approved before being put into operation (implemented). This policy is reflected in the maintenance of approval and change sheets with appropriate authorizations.

Answer (A) is incorrect. Programmed checks determine potential accuracy of input data (e.g., a range check). Answer (B) is incorrect. Batch control is used to ensure the completeness and accuracy of input and updating. Answer (D) is incorrect. One-for-one checking is a technique used to check individual documents for accuracy and completeness of data input or update.

17. The **least** risky strategy for converting from a manual to a computerized accounts receivable system would be a

- A. Direct conversion.
- B. Parallel conversion.
- C. Pilot conversion.
- D. Database conversion.

Answer (B) is correct.

REQUIRED: The least risky strategy for converting from a manual to a computerized accounts receivable system.

DISCUSSION: The least risky strategy for converting from a manual to a computerized system is a parallel conversion in which the old and new systems are operated simultaneously until satisfaction is obtained that the new system is operating as expected. Slightly more risky is a pilot conversion in which the new system is introduced by module or segment.

Answer (A) is incorrect. A direct conversion is more risky than a parallel conversion. Answer (C) is incorrect. A pilot conversion is more risky than a parallel conversion. Answer (D) is incorrect. A database conversion is more risky than a parallel conversion.

18. A systems development approach used to quickly produce a model of user interfaces, user interactions with the system, and process logic is called

    A. Neural networking.

    B. Prototyping.

    C. Reengineering.

    D. Application generation.

Answer (B) is correct.
    REQUIRED: The approach used to produce a model of user interfaces, user interactions with the system, and process logic.
    DISCUSSION: Prototyping produces the first model(s) of a new system. This technique usually employs a software tool for quick development of a model of the user interface (such as by report or screen), interaction of users with the system (for example, a menu-screen approach or data entry), and processing logic (the executable module). Prototyping stimulates user participation because the model allows quick exploration of concepts and development of solutions with quick results.
    Answer (A) is incorrect. Neural networking involves hardware or software that imitates the processing activities of the human brain. Answer (C) is incorrect. Reengineering salvages reusable components of existing systems and restructures them to develop new systems or to improve the old systems. Answer (D) is incorrect. An application generator is software that can be used to develop an application simply by describing its requirements to the computer rather than by writing a procedural program.

19. A benefit of using computer-aided software engineering (CASE) technology is that it can ensure that

    A. No obsolete data fields occur in files.

    B. Users become committed to new systems.

    C. All programs are optimized for efficiency.

    D. Data integrity rules are applied consistently.

Answer (D) is correct.
    REQUIRED: The benefit of CASE.
    DISCUSSION: CASE is an automated technology (at least in part) for developing and maintaining software and managing projects. A benefit of using CASE technology is that it can ensure that data integrity rules, including those for validation and access, are applied consistently across all files.
    Answer (A) is incorrect. Obsolete data fields must be recognized by developers or users. Once recognized, obsolete data fields can be treated consistently in CASE procedures. Answer (B) is incorrect. Using CASE will not ensure user commitment to new systems if they are poorly designed or otherwise do not meet users' needs. Answer (C) is incorrect. Although it has the potential to accelerate system development, CASE cannot ensure that all programs are optimized for efficiency. In fact, some CASE-developed modules may need to be optimized by hand to achieve acceptable performance.

20. Errors are most costly to correct during

    A. Programming.

    B. Conceptual design.

    C. Analysis.

    D. Implementation.

Answer (D) is correct.
    REQUIRED: The time when errors are most costly to correct.
    DISCUSSION: Errors can be corrected most easily and clearly when they are found at an early stage of systems development. Their correction becomes more costly as the life cycle progresses. Because implementation is the last stage of the process listed, errors are most costly to correct when discovered at the implementation stage.
    Answer (A) is incorrect. Error correction at the programming level would be less costly than at the implementation stage. Answer (B) is incorrect. Error correction at the conceptual design level would be less costly than at the implementation stage. Answer (C) is incorrect. Error correction at the analysis level would be less costly than at the implementation stage.

Access the **CIA Review System** from your Gleim Personal Classroom to continue your studies with exam-emulating multiple-choice questions!

STUDY UNIT TWELVE
IT SYSTEMS

(16 pages of outline)

This study unit is the second of three covering **Section VI: IT/Business Continuity** from The IIA's CIA Exam Syllabus. This section makes up 15% to 25% of Part 3 of the CIA exam and is tested at the **awareness level**. The relevant portion of the syllabus is highlighted below. (The complete syllabus is in Appendix A.)

VI. IT/BUSINESS CONTINUITY (15%–25%)

  A.   Security

  B.   Application Development

  C.   System Infrastructure
     1.   Workstations
     2.   Databases
     3.   IT control frameworks (e.g., eSAC, COBIT)

     4.   Functional areas of IT operations (e.g., data center operations)
     5.   Enterprise-wide resource planning (ERP) software (e.g., SAP R/3)
     6.   Data, voice, and network communications/connections (e.g., LAN, VAN, and WAN)
     7.   Server
     8.   Software licensing
     9.   Mainframe
     10.   Operating systems
     11.   Web infrastructure

  D.   Business Continuity

12.1 WORKSTATIONS AND DATABASES

1. **Workstations**

    a.   A workstation is any combination of input, output, and computing hardware that can be used for work. It may take the form of a personal computer (PC) or a powerful microcomputer, which is used for scientific or engineering work.

       1)   Workstations belong to the hardware component of the IT system infrastructure. Thus, they may be included in the audit of hardware controls.

          a)   Auditors can evaluate hardware controls in different ways. Examples include (1) interviewing users, (2) comparing actual downtime with normal expectations, and (3) reviewing failure logs.

2. **Data, Databases, and Database Management System (DBMS)**

    a.   A database is an organized collection of data in a computer system.

b.   Data in the database are integrated to eliminate redundancy of data items. A single integrated system allows for improved data accessibility.

1)   When systems within the organization are not integrated, they not only may contain different data but also may define and update data in inconsistent ways. Thus, determining the location of data and ensuring their consistency are more difficult.

c.   A DBMS is an integrated set of computer programs that (1) create the database, (2) maintain the elements, (3) safeguard the data from loss or destruction, and (4) make the data available to applications programs and inquiries.

1)   The DBMS allows programmers and designers to work independently of the technical structure of the database.

a)   Before the development of DBMSs, designing and coding programs that used databases was extremely time-consuming (and therefore expensive) because programmers had to know the exact contents and characteristics of the data in every database.

b)   DBMSs provide a common language for referring to databases, easing the design and coding of application programs.

c)   A DBMS includes security features. Thus, a specified user's access may be limited to certain data fields or logical views depending on the individual's assigned duties.

d.   The term database often includes the DBMS.

EXAMPLE

Data Redundancy

The various files related to human resources in the conventional record systems of most organizations include payroll, work history, and permanent personnel data.

An employee's name must appear in each of these files when they are stored and processed separately. The result is redundancy. When data are combined in a database, each data item is usually stored only once.

---

e.   The data are stored physically on direct-access storage devices (e.g., magnetic disks). They are also stored for efficient access.

1)   The most frequently accessed items are placed in the physical locations permitting the fastest access.

2)   When these items were stored in separate files under older file-oriented systems, the physical locations were usually similar to the logical structure of the data. Items that logically belonged together were stored in physical proximity to one another.

3)   A logical data model is a user view. It is the way a user describes the data and defines their interrelationships based on the user's needs, without regard to how the data are physically stored.

4)   A fundamental characteristic of databases is that applications are independent of the database structure; when writing programs or designing applications to use the database, only the name of the desired item is necessary.

5)   A data item is identified using the data manipulation language, after which the DBMS locates and retrieves the desired item(s).

a)   The data manipulation language is used to add, delete, retrieve, or modify data or relationships.

6)   The physical structure of the database can be completely altered without having to change any of the programs using the data items. Thus, different users may define different views of the data (subschemas).

7) Databases and the associated DBMS permit efficient storage and retrieval of data for formal system applications.

   a) They also permit increased ad hoc accessing of data (e.g., to answer inquiries for data not contained in formal system outputs) as well as updating of files by transaction processing.

   b) These increased capabilities, however, result in increased cost because they require

      i) The use of sophisticated hardware (direct-access devices)
      ii) Sophisticated software (the DBMS)
      iii) Highly trained technical personnel (database administrator, staff)
      iv) Increased security controls

3. **Two Early Database Structures**

   a. Storing all related data on one storage device creates security problems.

      1) Should hardware or software malfunctions occur, or unauthorized access be achieved, the results could be disastrous.

      2) Greater emphasis on security is required to provide backup and restrict access to the database.

         a) For example, the system may employ dual logging, that is, use of two transaction logs written simultaneously on separate storage media.

         b) It may also use a snapshot technique to capture data values before and after transaction processing.

         c) The files that store these values can be used to reconstruct the database in the event of data loss or corruption.

   b. To understand the vast improvement in performance brought about by database technology, it is helpful to review the development of file structures.

      1) The early mainframe computers used flat files, meaning that all the records and all the data elements within each record followed one behind the other. Much of the early mainframe storage was on magnetic tape, which naturally stored data in this fashion.

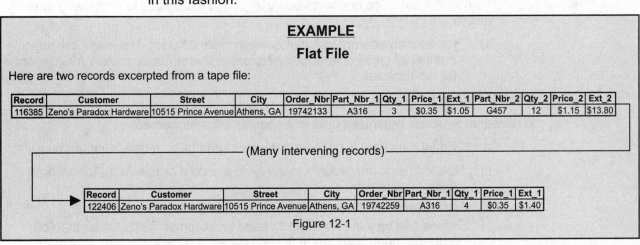

EXAMPLE

Flat File

Here are two records excerpted from a tape file:

Record	Customer	Street	City	Order_Nbr	Part_Nbr_1	Qty_1	Price_1	Ext_1	Part_Nbr_2	Qty_2	Price_2	Ext_2
116385	Zeno's Paradox Hardware	10515 Prince Avenue	Athens, GA	19742133	A316	3	$0.35	$1.05	G457	12	$1.15	$13.80

———————————————— (Many intervening records) ————————————————

Record	Customer	Street	City	Order_Nbr	Part_Nbr_1	Qty_1	Price_1	Ext_1
122406	Zeno's Paradox Hardware	10515 Prince Avenue	Athens, GA	19742259	A316	4	$0.35	$1.40

Figure 12-1

2) Two inefficiencies are apparent at once in this method of accessing data:

   a) The customer's address has to be stored with every order the customer places, taking up much unnecessary storage.

   b) All intervening records must be read and skipped over in order to find both records pertaining to this customer.

c.   Database technology overcame these two difficulties. The three main ways to organize a database are tree or hierarchical, network, and relational.

1)   A tree or hierarchical structure arranges data in a one-to-many relationship in which each record has one antecedent but may have an unlimited number of subsequent records.

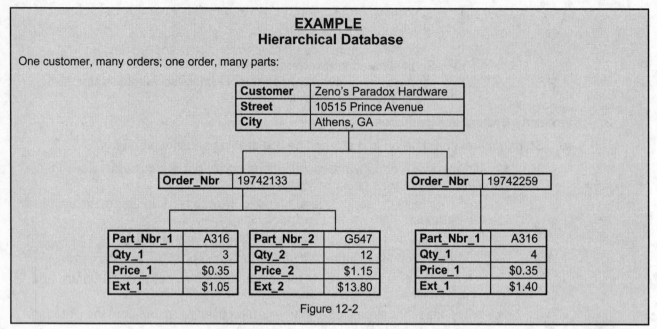

EXAMPLE
Hierarchical Database

One customer, many orders; one order, many parts:

Customer	Zeno's Paradox Hardware
Street	10515 Prince Avenue
City	Athens, GA

Order_Nbr	19742133

Order_Nbr	19742259

Part_Nbr_1	A316
Qty_1	3
Price_1	$0.35
Ext_1	$1.05

Part_Nbr_2	G547
Qty_2	12
Price_2	$1.15
Ext_2	$13.80

Part_Nbr_1	A316
Qty_1	4
Price_1	$0.35
Ext_1	$1.40

Figure 12-2

a)   Because the records are not stored one after the other, a tree database structure stores a pointer with each record. The pointer is the storage address of the next record.

b)   The tree structure cuts down on data redundancy but retains the necessity of searching every record to fulfill a query. Thus, like the flat file, adding new records is awkward and ad hoc queries are inefficient.

2)   The network structure connects every record in the database with every other record.

a)   This was an attempt to make queries more efficient. However, the huge number of cross-references inherent in this structure makes maintenance far too complex.

4.   **Relational Database Structure**

a.   A relational structure organizes data in a conceptual arrangement.

1)   An individual data item is called a field or column (e.g., name, date, amount).

a)   Related fields are brought together in a record or row (e.g., for a single sales transaction).

b)   Multiple records make up a file or table (e.g., sales).

c)   Tables can be joined or linked based on common fields rather than on high-overhead pointers or linked lists as in other database structures.

d)   Every record in a table has a field (or group of fields) designated as the key. The value (or combination of values) in the key uniquely identifies each record.

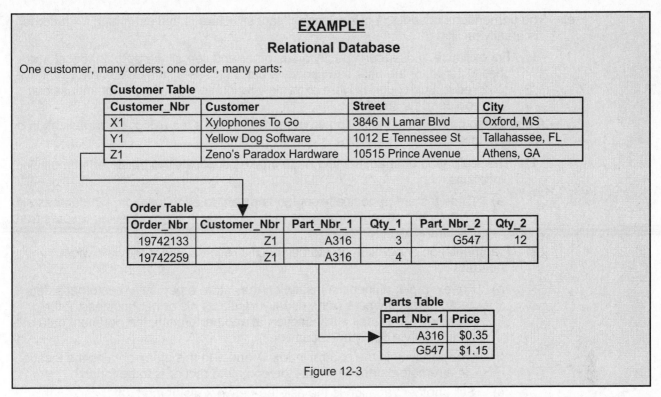

EXAMPLE

Relational Database

One customer, many orders; one order, many parts:

Customer Table

Customer_Nbr	Customer	Street	City
X1	Xylophones To Go	3846 N Lamar Blvd	Oxford, MS
Y1	Yellow Dog Software	1012 E Tennessee St	Tallahassee, FL
Z1	Zeno's Paradox Hardware	10515 Prince Avenue	Athens, GA

Order Table

Order_Nbr	Customer_Nbr	Part_Nbr_1	Qty_1	Part_Nbr_2	Qty_2
19742133	Z1	A316	3	G547	12
19742259	Z1	A316	4		

Parts Table

Part_Nbr_1	Price
A316	$0.35
G547	$1.15

Figure 12-3

b.   Note that in a relational structure, each data element is stored as few times as necessary. This is accomplished through the process of normalization. Normalization prevents inconsistent deletion, insertion, and updating of data items.

1)   The relational structure requires careful planning, but it is easy to maintain and processes queries efficiently.

c.   The three basic operations in the relational model are selecting, joining, and projecting.

1)   Selecting creates a subset of records that meet certain criteria.

2)   Joining is the combining of relational tables based on a common field or combination of fields.

3)   Projecting results in the requested subset of columns from the table. This operation creates a new table containing only the required information.

d.   Two features that make the relational data structure stand out are cardinality and referential integrity.

1)   Cardinality refers to how close a given data element is to being unique.

a)   A data element that can only exist once in a given table has high cardinality. In Figure 12-3, Customer_Nbr has high cardinality in the Customer Table.

b)   A data element that is not unique in a given table but that has a restricted range of possible values is said to have normal cardinality. Order_Nbr in the Order Table is an example.

c)   A data element that has a very small range of values is said to have low cardinality. A field that can contain only male/female or true/false is an example.

2)   Referential integrity means that for a record to be entered in a given table, there must already be a record in some other table(s).

a)   For example, the Order Table in Figure 12-3 cannot contain a record where the part number is not already present in the Parts Table.

e. The tremendous advantage of a relational data structure is that searching for records is greatly facilitated.

   1) For example, a user can specify a customer and see all the parts that customer has ordered, or the user can specify a part and see all the customers who have ordered it. Such queries were extremely resource-intensive, if not impossible, under older data structures.

f. A distributed database is stored in two or more physical sites using either replication or partitioning.

   1) The replication or snapshot technique makes duplicates to be stored at multiple locations.

      a) Changes are periodically copied and sent to each location. If a database is small, storing multiple copies may be cheaper than retrieving records from a central site.

   2) Fragmentation or partitioning stores specific records where they are most needed.

      a) For example, a financial institution may store a particular customer's data at the branch where (s)he usually transacts his or her business. If the customer executes a transaction at another branch, the pertinent data are retrieved via communication lines.

      b) One variation is the central index. A query to this index obtains the location in a remote database where the complete record is to be found.

      c) Still another variation is the ask-the-network distributed database. In this system, no central index exists. Instead, the remote databases are polled to locate the desired record.

   3) Updating data in a distributed system may require special protocols.

      a) Thus, a two-phase commit disk-writing protocol is used. If data are to be updated in two places, databases in both locations are cleared for updating before either one performs (commits) the update.

      b) In the first phase, both locations agree to the update. In the second phase, both perform the update.

   4) A deadly embrace (deadlock) occurs when each of two transactions has a lock on a single data resource.

      a) When deadly embraces occur, the database management system (DBMS) must have an algorithm for undoing the effects of one of the transactions and releasing the data resources it controls so that the other transaction can run to completion. Then, the other transaction is restarted and permitted to run to completion.

      b) If deadly embraces are not resolved, response time worsens or the system eventually fails.

5. **Additional Terminology**

a. The **database administrator (DBA)** is the individual who has overall responsibility for developing and maintaining the database and for establishing controls to protect its integrity.

   1) Thus, only the DBA should be able to update data dictionaries. In small systems, the DBA may perform some functions of a DBMS. In larger applications, the DBA uses a DBMS as a primary tool.

   2) The responsibility for creating, maintaining, securing, restricting access to, and redefining and restructuring the database belongs to the database administrator.

   3) The **data control language** specifies the privileges and security rules governing database users.

b. The **data dictionary** is a file that describes both the physical and logical characteristics of every data element in a database.

    1) The data dictionary includes, for example, the name of the data element (e.g., employee name, part number), the amount of disk space required to store the data element (in bytes), and what kind of data is allowed in the data element (e.g., alphabetic, numeric).

    2) Thus, the data dictionary contains the size, format, usage, meaning, and ownership of every data element. This greatly simplifies the programming process.

c. Data from a relational database can be displayed in graphs and reports, changed, and otherwise controlled using a program called **Query Management Facility (QMF)**.

d. The **schema** is a description of the overall logical structure of the database using data-definition language, which is the connection between the logical and physical structures of the database.

    1) A subschema describes a particular user's (application's) view of a part of the database using data definition language.

e. The **database mapping facility** is software that is used to evaluate and document the structure of the database.

f. **Data command interpreter languages** are symbolic character strings used to control the current state of DBMS operations.

g. An **object-oriented database** is a response to the need to store not only numbers and characters but also graphics and multimedia applications.

    1) Translating these data into tables and rows is difficult. However, in an object-oriented database, they can be stored, along with the procedures acting on them, within an object.

h. In a **hypermedia database**, blocks of data are organized into nodes that are linked in a pattern determined by the user so that an information search need not be restricted to the predefined organizational scheme. A node may contain text, graphics, audio, video, or programs.

    1) Hybrid systems containing object-oriented and relational database capabilities have also been developed.

i. Advanced database systems provide for **online analytical processing (OLAP)**, also called multidimensional data analysis, which is the ability to analyze large amounts of data from numerous perspectives.

    1) OLAP is an integral part of the data warehouse concept.

    2) Using OLAP, users can compare data in many dimensions, such as sales by product, sales by geography, and sales by salesperson.

j. A **data warehouse** contains not only current operating data but also historical information from throughout the organization. Thus, data from all operational systems are integrated, consolidated, and standardized in an organization-wide database into which data are copied periodically. These data are maintained on one platform and can be read but not changed.

    1) **Data cleansing** cleans up data in a database that is incorrect, incomplete, or duplicated before loading it into the database. It improves the quality of data. The need for data cleansing increases when multiple data sources are integrated.

2)   Data mining is facilitated by a data warehouse. **Data mining** is the process of analyzing data from different perspectives and summarizing it into useful information. Data mining software ordinarily is used.

a)   For example, data mining software can help to find abnormal patterns and unforeseen correlations among the data.

b)   Internal auditors can use data mining techniques to detect fraud.

3)   A **data mart** is a subset of a data warehouse.

Stop and review! You have completed the outline for this subunit. Study multiple-choice questions 1 through 6 beginning on page 297.

12.2 IT CONTROL FRAMEWORKS

The increasing integration of controls over automated systems with the organization's overall system of internal control is most clearly displayed in the eSAC and COBIT frameworks. These documents discuss at some length the role played by automated systems in pursuing the organization's mission, safeguarding assets, etc. Candidates for the CIA exam must be aware not just of detailed controls such as field checks, but also of the role that control over IT plays in the organization's strategy implementation.

1.   **Control Framework**

a.   A control framework is a model for establishing a system of internal control.

1)   The framework does not prescribe the actual controls themselves, but it does force management to focus on risk areas and design controls accordingly.

2)   Often, a control framework describes "families" of controls, that is, conceptual groupings of controls that attempt to address a particular type of risk exposure.

2.   **COSO**

a.   Probably the most well-known control framework in the U.S. is *Internal Control – Integrated Framework*, published in 1992 by the Committee of Sponsoring Organizations of the Treadway Commission (COSO). The document is commonly referred to as "the COSO Framework."

b.   The COSO Framework defines internal control as

A process, effected by an organization's board of directors, management, and other personnel, designed to provide reasonable assurance regarding the achievement of objectives in the following categories:

- *Effectiveness and efficiency of operations*
- *Reliability of financial reporting*
- *Compliance with applicable laws and regulations*

1)   COSO's simple and straightforward definition has proved extremely useful. Also, these principles are as applicable to an organization's IT function as they are to any other.

c.   COSO further describes five components of an internal control system:

1)   Control environment
2)   Risk assessment
3)   Control activities
4)   Information and communication
5)   Monitoring

a)   This part of the model also can easily be used in an IT context.

d.   The importance and durability of the COSO Framework was reinforced when the U.S. Securities and Exchange Commission acknowledged it as an appropriate model for designing internal controls under the requirements of the Sarbanes-Oxley Act of 2002.

3. **eSAC**

    a. *Electronic Systems Assurance and Control (eSAC)* is a publication of The IIA. In the eSAC model, the organization's internal processes accept inputs and produce outputs.

        1) Inputs: Mission, values, strategies, and objectives
        2) Outputs: Results, reputation, and learning

    b. The eSAC model's broad control objectives are influenced by those in the COSO Framework:

        1) Operating effectiveness and efficiency
        2) Reporting of financial and other management information
        3) Compliance with laws and regulations
        4) Safeguarding of assets

    c. eSAC's IT business assurance objectives fall into five categories:

        1) Availability. The organization must assure that information, processes, and services are available at all times.

        2) Capability. The organization must assure reliable and timely completion of transactions.

        3) Functionality. The organization must assure that systems are designed to user specifications to fulfill business requirements.

        4) Protectability. The organization must assure that a combination of physical and logical controls prevents unauthorized access to system data.

        5) Accountability. The organization must assure that transactions are processed under firm principles of data ownership, identification, and authentication.

4. **COBIT 4.1**

    a. Specifically for IT controls, the best-known framework is *Control Objectives for Information and Related Technology (COBIT)*. Version 4.1 of this document was published in 2007 by the IT Governance Institute.

        1) ISACA released COBIT 5 in April 2012 (described in item 5. beginning on the next page). However, version 4.1, described here, has been very successful and is not necessarily superseded by COBIT 5.

    b. Automated information systems have been woven into every function of the modern organization, making IT governance an integral part of overall organizational governance. The COBIT model for IT governance contains five focus areas:

        1) Strategic alignment
        2) Value delivery
        3) Resource management
        4) Risk management
        5) Performance measurement

    c. The COBIT framework embodies four characteristics:

        1) Business-focused
        2) Process-oriented
        3) Controls-based
        4) Measurement-driven

d.   Each characteristic contains multiple components.

1)   Business-focused

a)   This characteristic lists seven distinct but overlapping information criteria: effectiveness, efficiency, confidentiality, integrity, availability, compliance, and reliability.

b)   Business goals must feed IT goals, which in turn allow the organization to design the appropriate enterprise architecture for IT.

c)   IT resources include applications, information, infrastructure, and people.

2)   Process-oriented. This part of the model contains four domains:

a)   Plan and organize
b)   Acquire and implement
c)   Deliver and support
d)   Monitor and evaluate

3)   Controls-based. "An IT control objective is a statement of the desired result or purpose to be achieved by implementing control procedures in a particular IT activity." COBIT describes controls in three areas:

a)   Process controls. "Operational management uses processes to organize and manage ongoing IT activities."

b)   Business controls. These affect IT at three levels: the executive management level, the business process level, and the IT support level.

c)   IT general controls and application controls. This distinction for IT controls is of very long standing.

i)   "General controls are those controls embedded in IT processes and services . . . . Controls embedded in business process applications are commonly referred to as application controls."

4)   Measurement-driven

a)   The centerpiece of the COBIT framework in this area is the maturity model.

i)   "The organization must rate how well managed its IT processes are. The suggested scale employs the rankings of non-existent, initial, repeatable, defined, managed, and optimized."

b)   Performance measurement

Goals and metrics are defined in COBIT at three levels:

- *IT goals and metrics that define what the business expects from IT*
- *Process goals and metrics that define what the IT processes must deliver to support IT's objectives*
- *Process performance metrics*

5.   **COBIT 5 -- A Framework for IT Governance and Management**

a.   COBIT 4.1 and COBIT 5 constitute the best-known control and governance framework that addresses information technology.

1)   In its earliest versions, COBIT was focused on controls for specific IT processes.

2)   Over the years, information technology has gradually come to pervade every facet of the organization's operations. IT can no longer be viewed as a function distinct from other aspects of the organization.

a)   The evolution of this document has reflected this change in the nature of IT within the organization.

b.   COBIT 5 -- Five Key Principles

1)   Principle 1: Meeting Stakeholder Needs

a)   COBIT 5 asserts that value creation is the most basic stakeholder need. Thus, the creation of stakeholder value is the fundamental goal of any enterprise, commercial or not.

i)   Value creation in this model is achieved by balancing three components:

- Realization of benefits
- Optimization (not minimization) of risk
- Optimal use of resources

ii)   COBIT 5 also recognizes that stakeholder needs are not fixed. They evolve under the influence of both internal factors (e.g., changes in organizational culture) and external factors (e.g., disruptive technologies).

- These factors are collectively referred to as stakeholder drivers.

2)   Principle 2: Covering the Enterprise End-to-End

a)   COBIT 5 takes a comprehensive view of all of the enterprise's functions and processes. Information technology pervades them all; it cannot be viewed as a function distinct from other enterprise activities.

i)   Thus, IT governance must be integrated with enterprise governance.

b)   IT must be considered enterprise-wide and end-to-end, i.e., all functions and processes that govern and manage information "wherever that information may be processed."

3)   Principle 3: Applying a Single, Integrated Framework

a)   In acknowledgment of the availability of multiple IT-related standards and best practices, COBIT 5 provides an overall framework for enterprise IT within which other standards can be consistently applied.

b)   COBIT 5 was developed to be an overarching framework that does not address specific technical issues; i.e., its principles can be applied regardless of the particular hardware and software in use.

4)   Principle 4: Enabling a Holistic Approach

a)   COBIT 5 describes seven categories of enablers that support comprehensive IT governance and management:

i)   Principles, policies, and frameworks
ii)   Processes
iii)   Organizational structures
iv)   Culture, ethics, and behavior
v)   Information
vi)   Services, infrastructure, and applications
vii)   People, skills, and competencies

5)   Principle 5: Separating Governance from Management

a)   The complexity of the modern enterprise requires governance and management to be treated as distinct activities.

i)   In general, governance is the setting of overall objectives and monitoring progress toward those objectives. COBIT 5 associates governance with the board of directors.

- Within any governance process, three practices must be addressed: evaluate, direct, and monitor.

6.   **GTAG**

a.   Beginning in 2005, The IIA replaced its Practice Advisories on IT topics with an extremely detailed series of documents known collectively as the *Global Technology Audit Guide (GTAG)*.

b.   GTAG 1 recognizes three "families" of controls:

1)   General and application controls, described in Subunit 12.4.

2)   Preventive, detective, and corrective controls

a)   Preventive controls "prevent errors, omissions, or security incidents from occurring."

b)   Detective controls "detect errors or incidents that elude preventive controls."

c)   Corrective controls "correct errors, omissions, or incidents once they have been detected."

3)   Governance, management, and technical controls

a)   "Governance controls . . . are linked with the concepts of corporate governance, which are driven both by organizational goals and strategies and by outside bodies such as regulators."

b)   Management controls "are deployed as a result of deliberate actions by management to recognize risks to the organization, its processes, and assets; and enact mechanisms and processes to mitigate and manage risks."

c)   Technical controls "are specific to the technologies in use within the organization's IT infrastructures."

c.   GTAG1 recommends that each organization use the applicable components of existing frameworks to categorize and assess IT controls and to provide and document its own framework for

1)   Compliance with applicable regulations and legislation.

2)   Consistency with the organization's objectives.

3)   Reliable evidence (reasonable assurance) that activities comply with management's governance policies and are consistent with the organization's risk appetite.

Stop and review! You have completed the outline for this subunit. Study multiple-choice questions 7 through 9 beginning on page 298.

12.3 ASPECTS OF AUTOMATED INFORMATION PROCESSING

1.   **Characteristics of Automated Processing**

a.   The use of computers in business information systems has fundamental effects on the nature of business transacted, the procedures followed, the risks incurred, and the methods of mitigating those risks. These effects flow from the characteristics that distinguish computer-based from manual processing.

b.   **Transaction Trails**

1)   A complete trail useful for audit and other purposes might exist for only a short time or only in computer-readable form. The nature of the trail is often dependent on the transaction processing mode, for example, whether transactions are batched prior to processing or whether they are processed immediately as they happen.

c. **Uniform Processing of Transactions**

1) Computer processing uniformly subjects similar transactions to the same processing instructions and thus virtually eliminates clerical error, but programming errors (or other similar systematic errors in either the hardware or software) will result in all similar transactions being processed incorrectly when they are processed under the same conditions.

d. **Segregation of Functions**

1) Many controls once performed by separate individuals may be concentrated in computer systems. Hence, an individual who has access to the computer may perform incompatible functions. As a result, other controls may be necessary to achieve the control objectives ordinarily accomplished by segregation of functions.

e. **Potential for Errors and Fraud**

1) The potential for individuals, including those performing control procedures, to gain unauthorized access to data, to alter data without visible evidence, or to gain access (direct or indirect) to assets may be greater in computer systems. Decreased human involvement in handling transactions can reduce the potential for observing errors and fraud. Errors or fraud in the design or changing of application programs can remain undetected for a long time.

f. **Potential for Increased Management Supervision**

1) Computer systems offer management many analytical tools for review and supervision of operations. These additional controls may enhance internal control. For example, traditional comparisons of actual and budgeted operating ratios and reconciliations of accounts are often available for review on a more timely basis. Furthermore, some programmed applications provide statistics regarding computer operations that may be used to monitor actual processing.

g. **Initiation or Subsequent Execution of Transactions by Computer**

1) Certain transactions may be automatically initiated or certain procedures required to execute a transaction may be automatically performed by a computer system. The authorization of these transactions or procedures may not be documented in the same way as those in a manual system, and management's authorization may be implicit in its acceptance of the design of the system.

h. **Dependence of Controls in Other Areas on Controls over Computer Processing**

1) Computer processing may produce reports and other output that are used in performing manual control procedures. The effectiveness of these controls can be dependent on the effectiveness of controls over the completeness and accuracy of computer processing. For example, the effectiveness of a manual review of a computer-produced exception listing is dependent on the controls over the production of the listing.

2.   **Two Basic Processing Modes**

   a.   **Batch Processing**

   1)   In this mode, transactions are accumulated and submitted to the computer as a single batch. In the early days of computers, this was the only way a job could be processed.

   2)   In batch processing, the user cannot influence the process once the job has begun (except to ask that it be aborted completely). (S)he must wait until the job is finished running to see if any transactions in the batch were rejected and failed to post.

   3)   Despite huge advances in computer technology, this accumulation of transactions for processing on a delayed basis is still widely used. It is very efficient for such applications as payroll because large numbers of routine transactions must be processed on a regular schedule.

   4)   **Memo posting** is used by banks for financial transactions when batch processing is used. It posts temporary credit or debit transactions to an account if the complete posting to update the balance will be done as part of the end-of-day batch processing. Information can be viewed immediately after updating.

   a)   Memo posting is an intermediate step between batch processing and real-time processing.

   b.   **Online, Real-Time Processing**

   1)   In some systems, having the latest information available at all times is crucial to the proper functioning of the system. An airline reservation system is a common example.

   2)   In an online, real-time system, the database is updated immediately upon entry of the transaction by the operator. Such systems are referred to as **online transaction processing (OLTP)** systems.

Stop and review! You have completed the outline for this subunit. Study multiple-choice questions 10 through 14 beginning on page 299.

12.4 IT CONTROLS

1.   **Classification of Controls**

   a.   Version 4.1 of *Control Objectives for Information and Related Technology* (COBIT) has achieved widespread acceptance. It provides a model for the impact of an organization's internal controls on IT:

   *At the **executive management level**, business objectives are set, policies are established and decisions are made on how to deploy and manage the resources of the enterprise to execute the enterprise strategy.*

   *At the **business process level**, controls are applied to specific business activities. Most business processes are automated and integrated with IT application systems, resulting in many of the controls at this level being automated as well. These controls are known as application controls.*

   *To **support the business processes**, IT provides IT services, usually in a shared service to many business processes, as many of the development and operational IT processes are provided to the whole enterprise, and much of the IT infrastructure is provided as a common service (e.g., networks, databases, operating systems and storage). The controls applied to all IT service activities are known as IT general controls.*

    b.   The organization must implement appropriate controls at each of the three levels described in the COBIT 4.1 model.

        1)   For example, at the executive level, an IT steering committee should be established, composed of senior managers from both the IT function and the end-user functions. The committee approves development projects, assigns resources, and reviews their progress.

        2)   The steering committee also ensures that requests for new systems are aligned with the overall strategic plan of the organization.

    c.   The interaction between general and application controls is crucial for an audit. According to COBIT 4.1,

> *The reliable operation of these general controls is necessary for reliance to be placed on application controls.*

        1)   Because general controls affect the organization's entire processing environment, the auditor must become satisfied about their proper operation before relying on application controls.

    d.   The following are the categories of **general controls**: systems development, change management, security, and computer operations. (General controls are discussed in more detail in Study Unit 11, Subunits 1 and 5.)

        1)   Effective IT general controls are measured by the number of

            a)   Incidents that damage public reputation,
            b)   Systems that do not meet security criteria, and
            c)   Violations in segregation of duties.

    e.   The following are examples of types of **application controls**: completeness, accuracy, validity, authorization, and segregation of duties.

        1)   This classification reflects that a computer application is the automation of a business process and has the same control objectives.

2. **Application Controls**

    a.   Application controls relate to the business tasks performed by a particular system. They should provide reasonable assurance that the recording, processing, and reporting of data are properly performed.

        1)   The most economical point for correcting input errors in an application is the time at which the data are entered into the system.

        2)   For these reasons, input controls are the focus of an internal auditor's activity. Each of the two major types of processing modes has its own controls.

    b.   **Batch Input Controls**

        1)   **Financial totals** summarize monetary amounts in an information field in a group of records. The total produced by the system after the batch has been processed is compared to the total produced manually beforehand.

        2)   **Record counts** track the number of records processed by the system for comparison to the number that the user expected to be processed.

3) **Hash totals** are control totals without a defined meaning, such as the total of vendor numbers or invoice numbers, that are used to verify the completeness of the data.

EXAMPLE

A company has the following invoices in a batch:

Invoice Number	Product	Quantity	Unit Price
303	G7	100	US $15
305	A48	200	5
353	L30	125	10
359	Z26	150	20

The hash total is a control total without a defined meaning, such as the total of employee numbers or invoice totals, that is used to verify the completeness of data. Using invoice numbers, the hash total would be 1320.

---

c. **Online Input Controls**

1) **Preformatting** of data entry screens, i.e., to make them imitate the layout of a printed form, can aid the operator in keying to the correct fields.

2) **Field checks** are tests of the characters in a field to verify that they are of an appropriate type for that field. For example, the system is programmed to reject alphabetic characters entered in the field for Social Security number.

3) **Validity checks** compare the data entered in a given field with a table of valid values for that field. For example, the vendor number on a request to cut a check must match the table of current vendors, and the invoice number must match the approved invoice table.

4) **Limit (reasonableness) and range checks** are based on known limits for given information. For example, hours worked per week must be between 0 and 100, with anything above that range requiring management authorization.

5) **Self-checking digits** are used to detect incorrect identification numbers. The digit is generated by applying an algorithm to the ID number. During the input process, the check digit is recomputed by applying the same algorithm to the code actually entered.

6) **Sequence checks** are based on the logic that processing efficiency is greatly increased when files are sorted on some designated field, called the "key," before operations such as matching. If the system discovers a record out of order, it may indicate that the files were not properly prepared for processing.

7) **Zero balance checks** will reject any transaction or batch thereof in which the sum of all debits and credits does not equal zero.

d. **Processing controls** ensure that data are complete and accurate during updating.

1) **Concurrency controls** manage situations where two or more users attempt to access or update a file or database simultaneously. These controls ensure the correct results are generated while getting those results as quickly as possible.

e. **Output controls** ensure that processing results are complete, accurate, and properly distributed. An important output control is user review. Users should be able to determine when output is incomplete or not reasonable, particularly when the user prepared the input. Thus, users as well as computer personnel have a quality assurance function.

Stop and review! You have completed the outline for this subunit. Study multiple-choice questions 15 through 20 beginning on page 301.

QUESTIONS

12.1 Workstations and Databases

1. Of the following, the greatest advantage of a database (server) architecture is

   A. Data redundancy can be reduced.

   B. Conversion to a database system is inexpensive and can be accomplished quickly.

   C. Multiple occurrences of data items are useful for consistency checking.

   D. Backup and recovery procedures are minimized.

Answer (A) is correct.
   REQUIRED: The greatest advantage of a database architecture.
   DISCUSSION: In a database system, storage structures are created that render the applications programs independent of the physical or logical arrangement of the data. Because separate files for different applications programs are unnecessary, data redundancy can be substantially reduced.
   Answer (B) is incorrect. Conversion to a database is often costly and time consuming. Answer (C) is incorrect. A traditional flat-file system, not a database, has multiple occurrences of data items. Answer (D) is incorrect. Given the absence of data redundancy and the quick propagation of data errors throughout applications, backup and recovery procedures are just as critical in a database as in a flat-file system.

2. A file-oriented approach to data storage requires a primary record key for each file. Which of the following is a primary record key?

   A. The vendor number in an accounts payable master file.

   B. The vendor number in a closed purchase order transaction file.

   C. The vendor number in an open purchase order master file.

   D. All of the answers are correct.

Answer (A) is correct.
   REQUIRED: The item(s) used as a primary record key.
   DISCUSSION: The primary record key uniquely identifies each record in a file. Because there is only one record for each vendor in an accounts payable master file, the vendor number would be the appropriate key.
   Answer (B) is incorrect. Purchase order files can have multiple purchase orders made out to the same vendor. The primary key in purchase order files would be the purchase order number because it is the only unique identifier for the record. Answer (C) is incorrect. Purchase order files can have multiple purchase orders made out to the same vendor. The primary key in purchase order files would be the purchase order number because it is the only unique identifier for the record. Answer (D) is incorrect. Not all of the answer choices are correct.

3. In a database system, locking of data helps preserve data integrity by permitting transactions to have control of all the data needed to complete the transactions. However, implementing a locking procedure could lead to

   A. Inconsistent processing.

   B. Rollback failures.

   C. Unrecoverable transactions.

   D. Deadly embraces (retrieval contention).

Answer (D) is correct.
   REQUIRED: The potential problem of a locking procedure.
   DISCUSSION: In a distributed processing system, the data and resources a transaction may update or use should be held in their current status until the transaction is complete. A deadly embrace occurs when two transactions need the same resource at the same time.
   Answer (A) is incorrect. Inconsistent processing occurs when a transaction has different effects depending on when it is processed. Data locking ensures consistent processing. Answer (B) is incorrect. Rollback failure is the inability of the software to undo the effects of a transaction that could not be run to completion. A rollback failure is not caused by data locking. However, data locking may lead to situations in which rollback is required. Answer (C) is incorrect. Unrecoverable transactions are not a typical symptom of locking procedures.

4. Which of the following should **not** be the responsibility of a database administrator?

   A. Design the content and organization of the database.

   B. Develop applications to access the database.

   C. Protect the database and its software.

   D. Monitor and improve the efficiency of the database.

Answer (B) is correct.
   REQUIRED: The item not the responsibility of a database administrator.
   DISCUSSION: The database administrator (DBA) is the person who has overall responsibility for developing and maintaining the database. One primary responsibility is designing the content of the database. Another responsibility of the DBA is to protect and control the database. A third responsibility is to monitor and improve the efficiency of the database. The responsibility of developing applications to access the database belongs to systems analysts and programmers.
   Answer (A) is incorrect. Designing the content and organization of the database is a responsibility of the database administrator. Answer (C) is incorrect. Protecting the database and its software is a responsibility of the database administrator. Answer (D) is incorrect. Monitoring and improving the efficiency of the database is a responsibility of the database administrator.

5. Which of the following is a primary function of a database management system (DBMS)?

    A. Report customization.

    B. Capability to create and modify the database.

    C. Financial transactions input.

    D. Database access authorizations.

Answer (B) is correct.
    REQUIRED: The primary function of a database management system.
    DISCUSSION: A database management system (DBMS) is an integrated set of software tools superimposed on the data files that helps maintain the integrity of the underlying database. It allows programmers and designers to work independently of the physical and logical structure of the database. With a DBMS, the physical structure of the database can be completely altered without having to change any of the programs using the data items.
    Answer (A) is incorrect. Although report customization may be an aspect of a DBMS, it is not the primary function. Answer (C) is incorrect. Financial transactions input would be accomplished through the transaction processing system. Answer (D) is incorrect. The database administrator, not the database management system, is responsible for providing database access authorizations.

6. In an inventory system on a database management system (DBMS), one stored record contains part number, part name, part color, and part weight. These individual items are called

    A. Fields.

    B. Stored files.

    C. Bytes.

    D. Occurrences.

Answer (A) is correct.
    REQUIRED: The term for the data elements in a record.
    DISCUSSION: A record is a collection of related data items (fields). A field (data item) is a group of characters representing one unit of information.
    Answer (B) is incorrect. A file is a group or set of related records ordered to facilitate processing. Answer (C) is incorrect. A byte is a group of bits (binary digits). It represents one character. Answer (D) is incorrect. Occurrences is not a meaningful term in this context.

12.2 IT Control Frameworks

7. Which of the following types of controls is **not** described in the IT Governance Institute's *Control Objectives for Information and Related Technology* (COBIT)?

    A. General controls.

    B. Exchange controls.

    C. Business controls.

    D. Process controls.

Answer (B) is correct.
    REQUIRED: The type of control not described in COBIT.
    DISCUSSION: COBIT describes controls in three areas: process controls, business controls, and IT general and application controls.
    Answer (A) is incorrect. COBIT describes controls in three areas: process controls, business controls, and IT general and application controls. Answer (C) is incorrect. COBIT describes controls in three areas: process controls, business controls, and IT general and application controls. Answer (D) is incorrect. COBIT describes controls in three areas: process controls, business controls, and IT general and application controls.

8. Control objectives regarding effectiveness and efficiency, reliability, and compliance are the basis of which control framework?

    A. GTAG.

    B. eSAC.

    C. COBIT.

    D. COSO.

Answer (D) is correct.
    REQUIRED: The appropriate control framework.
    DISCUSSION: Probably the most well-known control framework in the U.S. is *Internal Control – Integrated Framework*, published in 1992 by the Committee of Sponsoring Organizations of the Treadway Commission (COSO). The document is commonly referred to as "the COSO Framework." The COSO Framework defines internal control as

A process, effected by an organization's board of directors, management, and other personnel, designed to provide reasonable assurance regarding the achievement of objectives in the following categories:

- *Effectiveness and efficiency of operations*
- *Reliability of financial reporting*
- *Compliance with applicable laws and regulations*

    Answer (A) is incorrect. GTAG, The IIA's *Global Technology Audit Guide*, is not the source of these three control objectives. Answer (B) is incorrect. The IIA's *Electronic Systems Assurance and Control*, eSAC, is not the source of these three control objectives. Answer (C) is incorrect. COBIT, the ITGI's *Control Objectives for Information and Related Technology*, is not the source of these three control objectives.

9. According to eSAC, accountability is

A. Usually an issue with regard to trade secrets and other intellectual property.

B. The control attribute that identifies the source of a transaction.

C. The restriction of access to processing and storage devices.

D. Most often applicable to personal information about employees and customers.

Answer (B) is correct.
 REQUIRED: The definition of accountability according to eSAC.
 DISCUSSION: Accountability is the control attribute that identifies the source of a transaction. It specifies employees' roles, actions, and responsibilities. Thus, the person who caused a transaction is identifiable. Fundamental concepts of accountability are data ownership, identification, and authentication.
 Answer (A) is incorrect. Confidentiality is usually an issue with regard to trade secrets and other intellectual property. Answer (C) is incorrect. Physical security is the restriction of access to processing and storage devices. Answer (D) is incorrect. Privacy is the attribute most often applicable to personal information about employees and customers.

12.3 Aspects of Automated Information Processing

10. Which of the following statements accurately describes the impact that automation has on the controls normally present in a manual system?

A. Transaction trails are more extensive in a computer-based system than in a manual system because there is always a one-for-one correspondence between data entry and output.

B. Responsibility for custody of information assets is more concentrated in user departments in a computer-based system than it is in a manual system.

C. Controls must be more explicit in a computer-based system because many processing points that present opportunities for human judgment in a manual system are eliminated.

D. The quality of documentation becomes less critical in a computer-based system than it is in a manual system because data records are stored in machine-readable files.

Answer (C) is correct.
 REQUIRED: The impact that automation has on the controls normally present in a manual system.
 DISCUSSION: Using a computer does not change the basic concepts and objectives of control. However, the use of computers may modify the control techniques used. The processing of transactions may be combined with control activities previously performed separately, or control function may be combined within the information system activity.
 Answer (A) is incorrect. The "paper trail" is less extensive in an automated system. Combining processing and controls within the system reduces documentary evidence. Answer (B) is incorrect. Information assets are more likely to be under the control of the information system function. Answer (D) is incorrect. Documentation is more important in an information system. This is because information is more likely to be stored in machine-readable form than in hard copy, requiring specialized knowledge for retrieval.

11. A small client recently put its cash disbursements system on a server. About which of the following internal control features would an auditor most likely be concerned?

A. Programming of the applications are in Visual Basic rather than Java.

B. The server is operated by employees who have cash custody responsibilities.

C. Only one employee has the password to gain access to the cash disbursement system.

D. There are restrictions on the amount of data that can be stored and on the length of time that data can be stored.

Answer (B) is correct.
 REQUIRED: The control feature of most concern to an auditor.
 DISCUSSION: Segregation of duties is a basic category of control activities. Functions are incompatible if a person is in a position both to perpetrate and conceal fraud or errors. Hence, the duties of authorizing transactions, recording transactions, and custody of assets should be assigned to different people. Those employees that operate the server may be able to override the controls to change records to conceal a theft of cash.
 Answer (A) is incorrect. The choice of language would have little effect on internal control. Answer (C) is incorrect. The limitation on access would be considered a strength. Answer (D) is incorrect. Restrictions on the amount of data that can be stored and on the length of time that data can be stored do not constitute a control weakness.

12. Which of the following statements most likely represents a disadvantage for an entity that keeps data files on a server rather than on a manual system?

A. Attention is focused on the accuracy of the programming process rather than errors in individual transactions.

B. It is usually easier for unauthorized persons to access and alter the files.

C. Random error associated with processing similar transactions in different ways is usually greater.

D. It is usually more difficult to compare recorded accountability with the physical count of assets.

Answer (B) is correct.
REQUIRED: The disadvantage of server-based data files.
DISCUSSION: In a manual system, one individual is usually assigned responsibility for maintaining and safeguarding the records. However, in a server environment, the data files may be subject to change by others without documentation or an indication of who made the changes.
Answer (A) is incorrect. The focus on programming is an advantage of using a server. A software program allows transactions to be processed uniformly. Answer (C) is incorrect. It describes a disadvantage of a manual system. Answer (D) is incorrect. The method of maintaining the files is independent of the ability to compare this information in the file with the physical count of assets.

13. A small company has changed from a system of recording time worked on clock cards to a computerized payroll system in which employees record time in and out with magnetic cards. The computer system automatically updates all payroll records. Because of this change,

A. A generalized computer audit program must be used.

B. Part of the audit trail is altered.

C. The potential for payroll-related fraud is diminished.

D. Transactions must be processed in batches.

Answer (B) is correct.
REQUIRED: The effect of computerization of a payroll system.
DISCUSSION: In a manual payroll system, a paper trail of documents is created to provide audit evidence that controls over each step in processing are in place and functioning. One element of a computer system that differentiates it from a manual system is that a transaction trail useful for auditing purposes might exist only for a brief time or only in computer-readable form.
Answer (A) is incorrect. Use of generalized audit software is only one of many ways of auditing a computer-based system. Answer (C) is incorrect. Conversion to a computer system may actually increase the chance of fraud by eliminating segregation of incompatible functions and other controls. Answer (D) is incorrect. Automatic updating indicates that processing is not in batch mode.

14. Batch processing

A. Is not used by most businesses because it reduces the audit trail.

B. Allows users to inquire about groups of information contained in the system.

C. Accumulates transaction records into groups for processing against the master file on a delayed basis.

D. Can only be performed on a centralized basis.

Answer (C) is correct.
REQUIRED: The true statement about batch processing.
DISCUSSION: Batch processing is the accumulation and grouping of transactions for processing on a delayed basis. The batch approach is suitable for applications that can be processed against the master file at intervals and involve large volumes of similar items, such as payroll, sales, inventory, and billing.
Answer (A) is incorrect. Batch processing provides as much of an audit trail as any computerized operation. Answer (B) is incorrect. Batch processing refers to the input of data, not inquiry. Answer (D) is incorrect. Batch processing can also be performed on a decentralized basis.

12.4 IT Controls

15. When assessing application controls, which one of the following input controls or edit checks is most likely to be used to detect a data input error in the customer account number field?

A. Limit check.

B. Validity check.

C. Control total.

D. Hash total.

Answer (B) is correct.
REQUIRED: The input control or edit check most likely to be used to detect a data input error in the customer account number field.
DISCUSSION: Validity checks are tests of identification numbers or transaction codes for validity by comparison with items already known to be correct or authorized. For example, Social Security numbers on payroll input records can be compared with Social Security numbers authorized by the personnel department.
Answer (A) is incorrect. Reasonableness, limit, and range checks are based upon known limits for given information. For example, the hours worked per week is not likely to be greater than 45. Answer (C) is incorrect. A record count is a control total of the number of records processed during the operation of a program. Financial totals summarize dollar amounts in an information field in a group of records. Answer (D) is incorrect. A hash total is the number obtained from totaling the same field value for each transaction in a batch. The total has no meaning or value other than as a comparison with another hash total.

16. If a control total were to be computed on each of the following data items, which would best be identified as a hash total for a payroll computer application?

A. Hours worked.

B. Total debits and total credits.

C. Net pay.

D. Department numbers.

Answer (D) is correct.
REQUIRED: The example of a hash total.
DISCUSSION: The three types of control totals are record counts, financial totals, and hash totals. Record counts establish the number of source documents and reconcile it to the number of output records. Financial totals compute dollar totals from source documents (e.g., the total dollar amount of invoices processed) and reconcile them with the output records. Hash totals add numbers on input documents that are not normally added (e.g., department numbers), resulting in a total that is "meaningless" for any purpose other than this control.
Answer (A) is incorrect. Hours worked is an example of a financial total. Answer (B) is incorrect. Total debits and total credits is a financial total. Answer (C) is incorrect. Net pay is a financial total.

17. A catalog company has been experiencing an increasing incidence of problems in which the wrong products have been shipped to the customer. Most of the customer orders come in over the telephone, and an operator enters the data into the order system immediately. Which of the following control procedures, if properly implemented, would address the problem?

1. Have the computer automatically assign a sequential order number to each customer order.

2. Implement a self-checking digit algorithm for each product number and request entries by product number.

3. Request entries by product number, have the computer program identify the product and price, and require the operator to orally verify the product description with the customer.

A. 2 only.

B. 1, 2, and 3.

C. 2 and 3 only.

D. 1 and 2 only.

Answer (C) is correct.
REQUIRED: The procedure(s) to prevent incorrect shipments.
DISCUSSION: A self-checking digit detects incorrect codes. The digit is generated by applying an algorithm to the code. During input, the digit is recomputed by applying the algorithm to the code actually entered. Oral verification also addresses the problem of incorrectly identifying the product number. Assigning a sequential number to the customer's order helps build an audit trail but does not address the product identification issue.
Answer (A) is incorrect. Oral verification also would address the problem. Answer (B) is incorrect. Assigning a sequential number to the customer's order helps build an audit trail but does not address the product identification issue. Answer (D) is incorrect. Assigning a sequential number to the customer's order helps build an audit trail but does not address the product identification issue.

18. The two broad groupings of information systems control activities are general controls and application controls. General controls include controls

    A. Relating to the correction and resubmission of faulty data.

    B. For developing, modifying, and maintaining computer programs.

    C. Designed to ensure that only authorized users receive output from processing.

    D. Designed to ensure that all data submitted for processing have been properly authorized.

Answer (B) is correct.
    REQUIRED: The characteristics of general controls in relation to information systems control activities.
    DISCUSSION: General controls are policies and procedures that relate to many information systems applications and support the effective functioning of application controls by helping to ensure the continued proper operation of information systems. General controls include controls over (1) data center and network operations; (2) systems software acquisition and maintenance; (3) access security; and (4) application systems acquisition, development, and maintenance.
    Answer (A) is incorrect. Control over report distribution (output), correction of input errors, and authorization of input are application controls. Answer (C) is incorrect. Control over report distribution (output), correction of input errors, and authorization of input are application controls. Answer (D) is incorrect. Control over report distribution (output), correction of input errors, and authorization of input are application controls.

19. An accounts payable program posted a payable to a vendor not included in the online vendor master file. A control that would prevent this error is a

    A. Validity check.

    B. Range check.

    C. Reasonableness test.

    D. Parity check.

Answer (A) is correct.
    REQUIRED: The control that would prevent the posting of a payable to a vendor not included in the online vendor master file.
    DISCUSSION: Validity checks are tests of identification numbers or transaction codes for validity by comparison with items already known to be correct or authorized. For example, Social Security numbers on payroll input records can be compared with Social Security numbers authorized by the personnel department.
    Answer (B) is incorrect. A range check is based on known limits for given information. Answer (C) is incorrect. A reasonableness test is based on known limits for given information. Answer (D) is incorrect. A parity check adds the bits in a character or message and checks the sum to determine if it is odd or even, depending on whether the computer has odd or even parity.

20. The purpose of check digit verification of an account number on an update transaction is to

    A. Verify that the account number corresponds to an existing account in the master file.

    B. Detect a transposition of an account number entered into the system.

    C. Ensure that supporting documentation exists for the update transaction.

    D. Require the account number to have the correct logical relationship with other fields.

Answer (B) is correct.
    REQUIRED: The purpose of check digit verification of an account number on an update transaction.
    DISCUSSION: A major control used to guard against errors made in transcribing or keying data is a check digit. A check digit is a detective control designed to establish the validity and appropriateness of numerical data elements, such as account numbers. The check digit within the code is a mathematical function of the other digits. Recalculation of the digit tests the accuracy of the other characters in the code. Check digit verification prevents single-digit errors from leading to erroneous updates.
    Answer (A) is incorrect. Verifying that the account number corresponds to an existing account in the master file is a master file reference check. Answer (C) is incorrect. Ensuring that supporting documentation exists for update transactions is a document reconciliation control. Answer (D) is incorrect. Requiring a field to have the correct logical relationship with other fields is a dependency check.

Access the **CIA Review System** from your Gleim Personal Classroom to continue your studies with exam-emulating multiple-choice questions!

STUDY UNIT THIRTEEN
IT SYSTEMS AND BUSINESS CONTINUITY

(20 pages of outline)

This study unit is the third of three covering **Section VI: IT/Business Continuity** from The IIA's CIA Exam Syllabus. This section makes up 15% to 25% of Part 3 of the CIA exam and is tested at the **awareness level**. The relevant portion of the syllabus is highlighted below. (The complete syllabus is in Appendix A.)

VI. IT/BUSINESS CONTINUITY (15%–25%)

    A. Security

    B. Application Development

    C. System Infrastructure

        1. Workstations

        2. Databases

        3. IT control frameworks (e.g., eSAC, COBIT)

        4. Functional areas of IT operations (e.g., data center operations)

        5. Enterprise-wide resource planning (ERP) software (e.g., SAP R/3)

        6. Data, voice, and network communications/connections (e.g., LAN, VAN, and WAN)

        7. Server

        8. Software licensing

        9. Mainframe

        10. Operating systems

        11. Web infrastructure

    D. Business Continuity

        1. IT contingency planning

13.1 FUNCTIONAL AREAS OF IT OPERATIONS

In the early days of computing, maintaining a rigid segregation of duties was a simple matter because the roles surrounding a mainframe computer were so specialized. As IT became more and more decentralized over the years, clear lines that once separated jobs such as systems analyst and programmer became blurred and then disappeared. Candidates for the CIA exam must be aware of the evolving roles of IT personnel.

1. **Segregation of Duties**

    a. Organizational controls concern the proper segregation of duties and responsibilities within the information systems department.

    b. Controls should ensure the efficiency and effectiveness of IT operations. They include proper segregation of the duties within the IT environment. Thus, the responsibilities of systems analysts, programmers, operators, file librarians, the control group, and others should be assigned to different individuals, and proper supervision should be provided.

c.   Segregation of duties is vital because a traditional segregation of responsibilities for authorization, recording, and access to assets may not be feasible in an IT environment.

   1)   For example, a computer may print checks, record disbursements, and generate information for reconciling the account balance, which are activities customarily segregated in a manual system.

      a)   If the same person provides the input and receives the output for this process, a significant control weakness exists. Accordingly, certain tasks should not be combined.

      b)   Thus, compensating controls may be necessary, such as library controls, effective supervision, and rotation of personnel. Segregating test programs makes concealment of unauthorized changes in production programs more difficult.

2.   **Responsibilities of IT Personnel**

   a.   **Systems analysts** are specifically qualified to analyze and design computer information systems. They survey the existing system, analyze the organization's information requirements, and design new systems to meet those needs. The design specifications will guide the preparation of specific programs by computer programmers.

      1)   Systems analysts should not have access to data center operations, production programs, or data files.

   b.   The **database administrator (DBA)** is the individual who has overall responsibility for developing and maintaining the database and for establishing controls to protect its integrity.

      1)   Thus, only the DBA should be able to update data dictionaries.

      2)   In small systems, the DBA may perform some functions of a database management system (DBMS). In larger applications, the DBA uses a DBMS as a primary tool.

   c.   **Programmers** design, write, test, and document the specific programs according to specifications developed by the analysts.

      1)   Programmers as well as analysts may be able to modify programs, data files, and controls. Thus, they should have no access to the data center operations or to production programs or data.

   d.   The **webmaster** is responsible for the content of the organization's website. (S)he works closely with programmers and network technicians to ensure that the appropriate content is displayed and that the site is reliably available to users.

   e.   **Operators** are responsible for the day-to-day functioning of the data center, whether the organization runs a mainframe, servers, or anything in between.

      1)   Operators load data, mount storage devices, and operate the equipment. Operators should not be assigned programming duties or responsibility for systems design. Accordingly, they also should have no opportunity to make changes in programs and systems as they operate the equipment.

      a)   Ideally, computer operators should not have programming knowledge or access to documentation not strictly necessary for their work.

   f.   **Help desks** are usually a responsibility of computer operations because of the operational nature of their functions. Help desk personnel log reported problems, resolve minor problems, and forward more difficult problems to the appropriate information systems resources, such as a technical support unit or vendor assistance.

g. **Information security officers** are typically in charge of developing information security policies, commenting on security controls in new applications, and monitoring and investigating unsuccessful login attempts.

h. **Network technicians** maintain the bridges, hubs, routers, switches, cabling, and other devices that interconnect the organization's computers. They are also responsible for maintaining the organization's connection to other networks, such as the Internet.

i. **End users** must be able to change production data but not programs.

Stop and review! You have completed the outline for this subunit. Study multiple-choice questions 1 through 3 on page 323.

13.2 ENTERPRISE-WIDE RESOURCE PLANNING (ERP)

1. **Materials Requirements Planning (MRP)**

   a. MRP was an early attempt to create an integrated computer-based information system. It was designed to plan and control materials used in a production setting.

      1) MRP is a push system. It assumes that the demand for materials is typically dependent upon some other factor, which can be programmed. Thus, the timing of deliveries is vital to avoid production delays.

      2) For example, an auto manufacturer need only tell the system how many autos of each type are to be manufactured. The MRP system then generates a complete list of every part and component needed. MRP, in effect, creates schedules of when items on inventory will be needed in the production departments.

         a) If parts are not in stock, the system will automatically generate a purchase order on the proper date (considering lead times) so that deliveries will arrive on time. Thus, effective application of MRP necessitates the generation of accurate data about costs and amounts of inventory, setup costs, and costs of downtime.

   b. Manufacturing resource planning (MRP II) continued the evolution begun with MRP. It is a closed-loop manufacturing system that integrates all facets of a manufacturing business, including production, sales, inventories, schedules, and cash flows. The same system is used for the accounting, finance, and directing functions, which use the same transactions and numbers.

      1) MRP II includes forecasting and planning capacities for generating cash and other budgets.

      2) MRP II uses an MPS (master production schedule), which is a statement of the anticipated manufacturing schedule for selected items for selected periods. MRP also uses the MPS. Thus, MRP is a component of an MRP II system.

2. **Traditional ERP**

   a. The traditional ERP system is one in which subsystems share data and coordinate their activities. ERP is intended to integrate enterprise-wide information systems across the organization by creating one database linked to all of the entity's applications.

      1) Thus, if marketing receives an order, it can quickly verify that inventory is sufficient to notify shipping to process the order.

         a) Otherwise, production is notified to manufacture more of the product, with a consequent automatic adjustment of output schedules.

         b) If materials are inadequate for this purpose, the system will issue a purchase order.

         c)   If more labor is needed, human resources will be instructed to reassign or hire employees.

         d)   The foregoing business processes (and others) should interact seamlessly in an ERP system. Moreover, the current generation of ERP software also provides the capability for smooth (and instant) interaction with the business processes of external parties.

    2)   The subsystems in a traditional ERP system are internal to the organization. Thus, they often are called back-office functions. The information produced is principally (but not exclusively) intended for internal use by the organization's managers.

    3)   Because ERP software is costly and complex, it is usually installed only by the largest enterprises. However, mid-size organizations are increasingly likely to buy ERP software.

    4)   The leading products in the field are R/3, distributed by SAP, and JD Edwards EnterpriseOne and PeopleSoft Enterprise, both distributed by Oracle.

  b.   ERP connects all functional subsystems (human resources, the financial accounting system, production, marketing, distribution, purchasing, receiving, order processing, shipping, etc.) and also connects the organization with its suppliers and customers.

    1)   Thus, ERP facilitates demand analysis and materials requirements planning.

    2)   By decreasing lead times, it improves just-in-time inventory management.

    3)   Even more importantly, ERP's coordination of all operating activities permits flexible responses to shifts in supply and demand.

  c.   The advantages of developing an ERP system are similar to those derived from business process reengineering.

    1)   Using ERP software that reflects the best practices forces the linked subunits in the organization not only to redesign and improve their processes but also to conform to one standard.

    2)   An organization may wish to undertake a reengineering project before choosing ERP software. The project should indicate what best practices already exist in the organization's processes. This approach may be preferable for a unique enterprise in a highly differentiated industry.

         a)   Carrying out a reengineering project before installing an ERP system defines what process changes are needed and which vendor software should be used.

         b)   If the organization is not especially unique, vendor software probably is already based on industry best practices. In these circumstances, a preliminary reengineering project may not be needed. Thus, the organization should simply conform its processes to the software.

    3)   The processes reflected in the ERP software may differ from the organization's. In this case, the better policy is usually to change the organization's processes. Customizing the ERP software is expensive and difficult, and it may result in bugs and awkwardness when adopting upgrades.

         a)   Implementing an ERP system is likely to encounter significant resistance because of its comprehensiveness. Most employees will have to change ingrained habits and learn to use new technology. Thus, successful implementation requires effective change management.

  d.   The disadvantages of ERP are its extent and complexity, which make customization of the software difficult and costly.

3. **Current Generation of ERP**

   a. The current generation of ERP software (ERP II) has added front-office functions. These connect the organization with customers, suppliers, shareholders or other owners, creditors, and strategic allies (e.g., the members of a trading community or other business association). Accordingly, an ERP II system has the following interfaces with its back-office functions:

      1) Supply-chain management applications for an organization focus on relationships extending from its suppliers to its final customers. Issues addressed include distribution channels, warehousing and other logistical matters, routing of shipments, and sales forecasting.

         a) In turn, one organization's supply chain is part of a linked chain of multiple organizations. This chain stretches from the producers of raw materials, to processors of those materials, to entities that make intermediate goods, to assemblers of final products, to wholesalers, to retailers, and lastly, to ultimate consumers.

         b) Supply chain management involves a two-way exchange of information. For example, a customer may be able to track the progress of its order, and the supplier may be able to monitor the customer's inventory. Thus, the customer has better information about order availability, and the supplier knows when the customer's inventory needs replenishment.

         c) An advanced planning and scheduling system may be an element of a supply chain management application for a manufacturer. It controls the flow of material and components within the chain. Schedules are created given projected costs, lead times, and inventories.

      2) Customer relationship management applications extend to customer service, finance-related matters, sales, and database creation and maintenance.

         a) Integrated data is helpful in better understanding customer needs, such as product preference or location of retail outlets. Thus, the organization may be able to optimize its sales forecasts, product line, and inventory levels.

            i) Business intelligence software is used to analyze customer data.

      3) Partner relationship management applications connect the organization not only with such partners as customers and suppliers but also with owners, creditors, and strategic allies (for example, other members of a joint venture).

         a) Collaborative business partnerships may arise between competitors or arise between different types of organizations, such as a manufacturer partnering with an environmental group. Special software may be helpful to the partners in sharing information, developing a common strategy, and measuring performance.

4. **Configuration**

   a. The following are the main elements of the architecture of an ERP:

      1) Current ERP systems have a client-server configuration with possibly scores or hundreds of client (user) computers.

         a) So-called thin clients have little processing ability, but fat clients may have substantial processing power.

         b) The system may have multiple servers to run applications and contain databases.

         c) The network architecture may be in the form of a local area network or wide-area network, or users may connect with the server(s) via the Internet.

         d) An ERP system may use almost any of the available operating systems and database management systems.

    b.   An advantage of an ERP system is the elimination of data redundancy through the use of a central database. In principle, information about an item of data is stored once, and all functions have access to it.

        1)   Thus, when the item (such as a price) is updated, the change is effectively made for all functions. The result is reliability (data integrity).

            a)   If an organization has separate systems for its different functions, the item would have to be updated whenever it was stored. Failure of even one function to update the item would cause loss of data integrity. For example, considerable inefficiency may arise when different organizational subunits (IT, production, marketing, accounting, etc.) have different data about prices and inventory availability.

    c.   An organization may not have the resources, desire, or need for an ERP system with the greatest degree of integration.

        1)   An alternative to a comprehensive system is a best-of-breed approach. Thus, an organization might install a traditional ERP system from one vendor and add e-commerce and other extended applications from separate niche vendors.

            a)   An organization that adopts this approach needs to use middleware, that is, software that permits different applications to communicate and exchange data. This type of middleware is called an extended application interface.

    d.   An ERP system that extends to customers, suppliers, and others uses Internet portals. In this case, a portal is a website through which authorized external users may gain access to the organization's ERP.

        1)   Portals provide links to related websites and services (e.g., newsletters, email, and e-commerce capabilities).

5.   **Implementation**

    a.   Implementation of ERP may take years and cost millions. Moreover, a poor implementation may cause the project to fail regardless of the quality of the software.

        1)   However, more rapid and less costly implementation may be possible if no customization is done.

    b.   The initial step is to do strategic planning and to organize a project team that is representative of affected employee groups.

    c.   The second step is to choose ERP software and a consulting firm.

        1)   One possibility is to choose the software before the consultants because the first decision may affect the second.

        2)   Another option is to hire consultants to help with the selection of the software.

            a)   The organization may then hire other consultants to help with implementation.

    d.   The third and longest step is preimplementation.

        1)   The length of the process design phase is a function of the extent of

            a)   Reengineering
            b)   Customization of the software

        2)   Data conversion may be delayed because all departments must agree on the meaning of every data field, i.e., what values will be considered valid for that field.

        3)   The ERP system and its interfaces must be tested.

     e.   Implementation ("going live") is not the final step. Follow-up is necessary to monitor the activities of the numerous employees who have had to change their routines. For example, a mistake caused by reverting to the old method of entering a sales order may have pervasive consequences in a new integrated system: a credit check, rescheduling of production, and ordering of materials.

     f.   Training should be provided during implementation not only regarding technical matters but also to help employees understand the reasons for process changes. For example, the employees who enter sales orders should know what the effects will be throughout the system.

        1)   Other change management techniques include effective communication to allay employee fears and the creation of user-friendly documents and interfaces.

6. Costs

     a.   The costs of an ERP system include

        1)   Losses from an unsuccessful implementation, e.g., sales declines
        2)   Purchasing hardware, software, and services
        3)   Data conversion from legacy systems to the new integrated system (but conversion software may help)
        4)   Training
        5)   Design of interfaces and customization
        6)   Software maintenance and upgrades
        7)   Salaries of employees working on the implementation

7. Benefits

     a.   The benefits of an ERP system may be hard to quantify. They include

        1)   Lower inventory costs
        2)   Better management of liquid assets
        3)   Reduced labor costs and greater productivity
        4)   Enhanced decision making
        5)   Elimination of data redundancy and protection of data integrity
        6)   Avoidance of the costs of other means of addressing needed IT changes
        7)   Increased customer satisfaction
        8)   More rapid and flexible responses to changed circumstances
        9)   More effective supply chain management
       10) Integration of global operations

Stop and review! You have completed the outline for this subunit. Study multiple-choice questions 4 through 6 on page 324.

13.3 WEB INFRASTRUCTURE

1. Overview

     a.   The Internet is a network of networks all over the world. The Internet is descended from the original ARPANet, a product of the Defense Department's Advanced Research Projects Agency (ARPA), introduced in 1969.

        1)   The idea was to have a network that could not be brought down during an enemy attack by bombing a single central location. ARPANet connected computers at universities, corporations, and government. In view of the growing success of the Internet, ARPANet was retired in 1990.

b. The Internet facilitates inexpensive communication and information transfer among computers, with gateways allowing mainframe computers to interface with personal computers.

1) Very high-speed Internet backbones carry signals around the world and meet at network access points.

c. Most Internet users obtain connections through Internet service providers (ISPs) that in turn connect either directly to a backbone or to a larger ISP with a connection to a backbone.

1) The topology of the backbone and its interconnections may once have resembled a spine with ribs connected along its length but is now almost certainly more like a fishing net wrapped around the world with many circular paths.

d. The three main parts of the Internet are the servers that hold information, the clients that view the information, and the Transmission Control Protocol/Internet Protocol (TCP/IP) suite of protocols that connect the two.

e. A gateway makes connections between dissimilar networks possible by translating between two or more different protocol families.

f. A bridge joins two similar networks so that they look like one network.

2. Servers

a. A server is generally a dedicated computer or device that manages specific resources.

1) A file server is a computer in a network that operates as a librarian.

2) A web server hosts a website.

3) An enterprise server manages computer programs that collectively serve the needs of an organization.

b. One of the risks associated with having data centrally located is that data files may be subject to change by unauthorized users without proper documentation or any indication of who made the changes.

3. Languages and Protocols

a. The Internet was initially restricted to email and text-only documents.

1) In the 1980s, English computer scientist Tim Berners-Lee conceived the idea of allowing users to click on a word or phrase (a hyperlink) on their screens and having another document automatically be displayed.

2) Berners-Lee created a simple coding mechanism called Hypertext Markup Language (HTML) to perform this function. He also created a set of rules called Hypertext Transfer Protocol (HTTP) to allow hyperlinking across the Internet rather than on just a single computer. He then created a piece of software, called a browser, that allowed users to read HTML from any brand of computer. The result was the World Wide Web (often simply called the Web).

3) As the use of HTML and its successor languages spread, it became possible to display rich graphics and stream audio and video in addition to displaying text.

b. Extensible Markup Language (XML) was developed by an international consortium and released in 1998 as an open standard usable with many programs and platforms. XML is a variation of HTML (hypertext markup language), which uses fixed codes (tags) to describe how web pages and other hypermedia documents should be presented.

1) XML codes all information in such a way that a user can determine not only how it should be presented but also what it is; i.e., all computerized data may be tagged with identifiers.

       2)   Unlike HTML, XML uses codes that are extensible, not fixed. Thus, if an industry can agree on a set of codes, software for that industry can be written that incorporates those codes.

       3)   For example, XML allows the user to label the Uniform Product Code (UPC), price, color, size, etc., of goods so that other systems will know exactly what the tag references mean. In contrast, HTML tags would only describe how items are placed on a page and provide links to other pages and objects.

       4)   Standards setters and other entities are attempting to find ways to incorporate XML with EDI.

   c.   Extensible Business Reporting Language (XBRL) for financial statements is the specification developed by an AICPA-led consortium for commercial and industrial entities that report in accordance with U.S. GAAP. It is a variation of XML that is expected to decrease the costs of generating financial reports, reformulating information for different uses, and sharing business information using electronic media.

4.   **Uses**

   a.   With the explosive growth of the World Wide Web in the 1990s, whole new distribution channels opened up for businesses. Consumers could browse a vendor's catalog using the rich graphics of the Web, initiate an order, and remit payment, all from the comfort of their homes.

       1)   An organization's presence on the Web is constituted in its website. The website consists of a home page, which is the first screen encountered by users, and subsidiary web pages (screens constructed using HTML or a similar language).

       2)   Every page on the World Wide Web has a unique address, recognizable by any web-enabled device, called a Uniform Resource Locator (URL). However, just because the address is recognizable does not mean it is accessible to every user; security is a major feature of any organization's website.

   b.   An intranet permits sharing of information throughout an organization by applying Internet connectivity standards and web software (e.g., browsers) to the organization's internal network.

       1)   An intranet addresses the connectivity problems of an organization with many types of computers. It is ordinarily restricted to those within the organization and to outsiders after appropriate identification.

       2)   An extranet consists of the linked intranets of two or more organizations, for example, of a supplier and its customers. It typically uses the public Internet as its transmission medium but requires a password for access.

Stop and review! You have completed the outline for this subunit. Study multiple-choice questions 7 and 8 on page 325.

13.4 IT SYSTEM COMMUNICATIONS

1.   **Systems Software**

   a.   Systems software performs the fundamental tasks needed to manage computer resources. The most basic piece of systems software is the operating system.

   b.   An **operating system** is an interface among users, application software, and the computer's hardware (CPU, disk drives, printers, communications devices, etc.).

       1)   z/OS is the most recent operating system for the IBM mainframe.

       2)   Server operating systems include Unix, Linux, Microsoft Windows Server, and Apple MacOS X Server. Inherent networking capabilities are an important part of server operating systems.

       3)   Microsoft Windows, Apple MacOS, and Linux are operating systems for desktop computers.

c. Controls over operating systems are essential because they may affect the entire database.

    1) Those controls include

        a) Segregation of duties.

            i) System programmers should not be allowed to perform applications programming.

        b) Testing before use.

        c) Making back-out plans and implementing changes in off-hours.

        d) Keeping detailed logs of all changes.

    2) Other controls include error notification for failed hardware and detection of abnormalities.

d. Internal auditors should review the controls over operating systems. They should monitor change procedures and determine whether

    1) System programmers have sufficient training.
    2) The operating system is up to date.
    3) An error tracking system exists.

e. **Utility programs** are sometimes called privileged software.

    1) Utilities perform basic data maintenance tasks, such as

        a) Sorting, e.g., arranging all the records in a file by invoice number;
        b) Merging, meaning combining the data from two files into one; and
        c) Copying and deleting entire files.

    2) Utilities are extremely powerful.

        a) For instance, a utility program could be used to read a file that contains all user access codes for the network. A control feature to negate this vulnerability is to encrypt passwords before storing them in the file.

        b) In any case, the use of utility programs should be restricted to appropriate personnel, and each occurrence should be logged.

2. **Network Equipment**

a. Networks consist of (1) the hardware devices being connected and (2) the medium through which the connection is made.

b. **Client devices.** Devices of all sizes and functions (mainframes, laptop computers, personal digital assistants, MP3 players, printers, scanners, cash registers, ATMs, etc.) can be connected to networks.

    1) Connecting a device to a network requires a network interface card (NIC). The NIC allows the device to speak that particular network's "language," that is, its protocol.

    2) A development in the late 1990s called the thin client explicitly mimics the old mainframe-and-terminal model.

        a) A typical thin client consists merely of a monitor, a keyboard, and a small amount of embedded memory. The key is that it has no local hard drive.

        b) Essentially all processing and data storage is done on the servers. Just enough of an application is downloaded to the client to run it.

        c) An advantage of this architecture is the large amount of IT staff time and effort saved that formerly went to configuring and troubleshooting desktop machines. A disadvantage is that there must be 100% server availability for any work to be done by users.

        d) The thin client architecture has not met with widespread use because the cost of hard drives has continued to steadily decrease, defying predictions.

3. **Data and Network Communication**

    a. A protocol is a set of formal rules or conventions governing communication between a sending and receiving device. It prescribes the manner by which data is transmitted between these communication devices. In essence, a protocol is the envelope within which each message is transmitted throughout a data communications network.

    b. A network consists of multiple connected computers at multiple locations. Computers that are electronically linked permit an organization to assemble and share transaction and other information among different physical locations.

    c. A **local area network (LAN)** connects devices within a single office or home or among buildings in an office park. The LAN is owned entirely by a single organization.

        1) The LAN is the network familiar to office workers all over the world. In its simplest form, it can consist of a few desktop computers and a printer.

        2) A peer-to-peer network operates without a mainframe or file server, but does processing within a series of personal computers.

        3) This need led to the development of the LAN. A LAN is any interconnection between devices in a single office or building.

            a) Very small networks with few devices can be connected using a peer-to-peer arrangement, where every device is directly connected to every other.

            b) Peer-to-peer networks become increasingly difficult to administer with each added device.

        4) The most cost-effective and easy-to-administer arrangement for LANs uses the client-server model.

            a) Client-server networks differ from peer-to-peer networks in that the devices play more specialized roles. Client processes (initiated by the individual user) request services from server processes (maintained centrally).

            b) In a client-server arrangement, servers are centrally located and devoted to the functions that are needed by all network users.

                i) Examples include mail servers (to handle electronic mail), application servers (to run application programs), file servers (to store databases and make user inquiries more efficient), Internet servers (to manage access to the Internet), and web servers (to host websites).

                ii) Whether a device is classified as a server is not determined by its hardware configuration but rather by the function it performs. A simple desktop computer can be a server.

            c) Technically, a client is any object that uses the resources of another object. Thus, a client can be either a device or a software program.

                i) In common usage, however, "client" refers to a device that requests services from a server. This understanding of the term encompasses anything from a powerful graphics workstation to a smartphone.

                ii) A client device normally displays the user interface and enables data entry, queries, and the receipt of reports. Moreover, many applications, e.g., word processing and spreadsheet software, run on the client computer.

            d) The key to the client-server model is that it runs processes on the platform most appropriate to that process while attempting to minimize traffic over the network.

            e) Security for client-server systems may be more difficult than in a highly centralized system because of the numerous access points.

      d.   A **metropolitan area network (MAN)** connects devices across an urban area, for instance, two or more office parks.

         1)   This concept had limited success as a wire-based network, but it may be more widely used as a microwave network.

      e.   A **wide area network (WAN)** consists of a group of LANs operating over widely separated locations. A WAN can be either publicly or privately owned.

         1)   WANs come in many configurations. The simplest consists of one desktop computer using a slow dialup line to connect to an Internet service provider.

         2)   Publicly owned WANs, such as the public telephone system and the Internet, are available to any user with a compatible device. The assets of these networks are paid for by means other than individually imposed user fees.

            a)   **Public-switched networks** use public telephone lines to carry data. This arrangement is economical, but the quality of data transmission cannot be guaranteed, and security is questionable.

         3)   Privately owned WANs are profit-making enterprises. They offer fast, secure data communication services to organizations that do not wish to make their own large investments in the necessary infrastructure.

            a)   **Value-added networks (VANs)** are private networks that provide their customers with reliable, high-speed secure transmission of data.

               i)   To compete with the Internet, these third-party networks add value by providing their customers with (a) error detection and correction services, (b) electronic mailbox facilities for EDI purposes, (c) EDI translation, and (d) security for email and data transmissions.

            b)   **Virtual private networks (VPNs)** are a relatively inexpensive way to solve the problem of the high cost of leased lines.

               i)   A company connects each office or LAN to a local Internet service provider and routes data through the shared, low-cost public Internet.

               ii)   The success of VPNs depends on the development of secure encryption products that protect data while in transit.

            c)   A **private branch exchange (PBX)** is a specialized computer used for both voice and data traffic.

               i)   A PBX can switch digital data among computers and office equipment, e.g., printers, copiers, and fax machines. A PBX uses telephone lines, so its data transmission capacity is limited.

   4.   **Classifying Networks by Protocol**

      a.   A protocol is a set of standards for message transmission among the devices on the network.

      b.   LAN Protocols

         1)   Ethernet has been the most successful protocol for LAN transmission. The Ethernet design breaks up the flow of data between devices into discrete groups of data bits called "frames."

            a)   Ethernet is described as following the "polite conversation" method of communicating.

               i)   Each device "listens" to the network to determine whether another conversation is taking place, that is, whether the network is busy moving another device's message.

               ii)   When the network is determined to be free of traffic, the device sends its message.

c.   Switched Networks

1)   As described on page 313, in a LAN, all the devices and all the transmission media belong to one organization.

a)   This single ownership of infrastructure assets plus the ability to unify all communication on a single protocol make for great efficiency and security.

2)   When communication must cross organizational boundaries or travel beyond a limited geographical range, this single ownership principle no longer applies. A WAN is the applicable model.

a)   A WAN, with its hundreds of users and much greater distances, could never function using the collision-detection-and-retransmission method of Ethernet. To overcome this, the technique called switching is used.

3)   Switching takes two basic forms:

a)   In circuit switching, a single physical pathway is established in the public telephone system, and that pathway is reserved for the full and exclusive use of the two parties for the duration of their communication.

i)   An example is an ordinary landline telephone call or a dial-up connection from a modem. This is obviously a slow and insecure alternative for data transmission.

b)   In packet switching, the data bits making up a message are broken up into "packets" of predefined length. Each packet has a header containing the electronic address of the device for which the message is intended.

4)   Switches are the networking devices that read the address on each packet and send it along the appropriate path to its destination.

a)   A convenient analogy is a group of 18-wheelers loaded with new machinery destined for a remote plant site. The trucks leave the machinery vendor's factory headed to the destination.

i)   As each truck arrives at a traffic light, it stops while vehicles going in other directions pass through the intersection.

ii)   As the trucks arrive at the plant site, they are unloaded and the machinery is installed.

5)   By allowing message flow from many different organizations to pass through common points, switches spread the cost of the WAN infrastructure.

a)   Frame relay and ATM (asynchronous transfer mode) are examples of fast packet switched network protocols.

d.   Routed Networks

1)   Routers have more intelligence than hubs, bridges, or switches.

a)   Routers have tables stored in memory that tell them the most efficient path along which each packet should be sent.

b)   An analogy is the trucks leave the machinery vendor's factory with the same destination.

i)   As the trucks stop at each intersection, traffic cops redirect them down different routes depending on traffic conditions.

ii)   As the trucks arrive in unknown sequence at the plant site, they are held until the machinery can be unloaded in the correct order.

2)   Routing is what makes the Internet possible.

a)   Transmission Control Protocol/Internet Protocol (TCP/IP) is the suite of routing protocols that makes it possible to interconnect many thousands of devices from dozens of manufacturers all over the world through the Internet.

      b)   IP addressing (also called dotted decimal addressing) is the heart of Internet routing. It allows any device anywhere in the world to be recognized on the Internet through the use of a standard-format IP address.

          i)   Each of the four decimal-separated elements of the IP address is a numeral between 0 and 255, for example: 128.67.111.25.

      c)   Dynamic host configuration protocol (DHCP) allows tremendous flexibility on the Internet by enabling the constant reuse of IP addresses.

          i)   Routers generally have their IP addresses hardcoded when they are first installed. However, the individual client devices on most organizational networks are assigned an IP address by DHCP from a pool of available addresses every time they boot up.

  e.   Wireless Networks

    1)   The Wi-Fi family of protocols supports client devices within a radius of about 300 feet around a wireless router. This usable area is called a hotspot.

      a)   Wi-Fi avoids the collisions inherent in Ethernet by constantly searching for the best frequency within its assigned range to use.

      b)   Security was a problem in early incarnations of Wi-Fi. Later versions alleviated some of these concerns with encryption.

    2)   The Bluetooth standard operates over a much smaller radius than Wi-Fi, about 30 feet. This distance permits the creation of what has come to be called the personal area network or PAN (i.e., a network of devices for a single user).

      a)   Bluetooth is considerably slower than Wi-Fi.

    3)   The WiMax standard uses microwaves to turn an entire city into a hotspot, reviving the old MAN model. The radius is about 10 miles, and it is generally faster than traditional Wi-Fi.

    4)   Radio-frequency identification (RFID) technology involves the use of a combined microchip with antenna to store data about a product, pet, vehicle, etc. Common applications include

      a)   Inventory tracking
      b)   Lost pet identification
      c)   Tollbooth collection

5. **Network Topology**

  a.   Network topologies are either physical or logical. Physical topology is the set of physical connection points between devices on a LAN or similar network. Logical topology describes the path data travel through the network.

  b.   The following are the basic topology arrangements:

    1)   A **bus** network has a main line, and each node is connected to the line. It is the simplest and most common method of networking computers. If a bus network is interrupted (e.g., Ethernet cable becomes unplugged or one device malfunctions), the access points on one side of the network cannot access the computers and other devices on the other side of the network.

    2)   A **ring** network is arranged in a circle, so two paths for data are available. Thus, if an interruption occurs at one point, the data can travel in the opposite direction and still be received.

    3)   In a **star** network, cable segments from each computer are connected to centralized components. If one computer becomes unplugged, the remaining computers are still connected to the network.

4) In a **mesh** network, each computer is connected to every other computer by separate cabling. This configuration provides redundant paths throughout the network. If one cable fails, another will take over the traffic.

6. **Voice Communications**

a. Voice communication channels differ from the data channels connecting the CPU and peripheral equipment. They are the communications media for transmitting voice signals and are classified according to their capacity.

1) An example of a voiceband channel is a telephone line.

2) Internet telephony, known as voice-over IP (VoIP), is any transmission of two-way voice communication that uses the Internet for all or part of its path. This can be performed with (a) traditional telephone devices; (b) desktop computers equipped with a sound card, microphone, and speakers; or (c) terminals dedicated to this function.

b. Voice recognition input devices are still another alternative to keyboard input. These systems compare the speaker's voice patterns with prerecorded patterns. Advanced systems now have large vocabularies and shorter training periods. They allow for dictation and are not limited to simple commands.

c. A voice output device converts digital data into speech using prerecorded sounds.

d. A cell phone uses radio waves to transmit voice and data through antennas in a succession of cells or defined geographic areas.

e. Personal communications service(s) (PCS) is a cellular technology based on lower-power, higher-frequency radio waves. The cells (i.e., the geographic areas of signal coverage) must be smaller and more numerous, but the phones should be smaller and less expensive and be able to operate where other such devices cannot.

f. Voicemail converts spoken messages from analog to digital form, transmits them over a network, and stores them on a disk. Messages are then converted back to analog form when the recipient desires to hear them. Afterward, they may be saved, forwarded, or deleted.

g. Conducting an electronic meeting among several parties at remote sites is teleconferencing. It can be accomplished by telephone or electronic mail group communication software.

1) Videoconferencing permits the conferees to see each other on video screens.

2) These practices have grown in recent years as companies have attempted to cut their travel costs.

Stop and review! You have completed the outline for this subunit. Study multiple-choice questions 9 through 12 beginning on page 325.

13.5 SOFTWARE LICENSING

1. **Rights Pertaining to Software**

a. Software is copyrightable, but a substantial amount is in the public domain. Networks of computer users may share such software.

1) Shareware is software made available for a fee (usually with an initial free trial period) by the owners to users through a distributor (or websites or electronic bulletin board services).

b. Software piracy is a problem for vendors. Any duplication of the software beyond what is allowed in the software license agreement is illegal.

1) The best way to detect an illegal copy of application software is to compare the serial number on the screen with the vendor's serial number.

        2) Use of unlicensed software increases the risk of introducing computer viruses into the organization. Such software is less likely to have been carefully tested.

        3) To avoid legal liability, controls also should be implemented to prevent use of unlicensed software that is not in the public domain. A software licensing agreement permits a user to employ either a specified or an unlimited number of copies of a software product at given locations, at particular machines, or throughout the organization. The agreement may restrict reproduction or resale, and it may provide subsequent customer support and product improvements.

        4) Software piracy can expose an organization's people to both civil and criminal penalties. The Business Software Alliance (BSA) is a worldwide trade group that coordinates software vendors' efforts to prosecute the illegal duplication of software.

  c. Diskless workstations increase security by preventing the copying of software to a flash drive from a workstation. This control not only protects the company's interests in its data and proprietary programs but also guards against theft of licensed third-party software.

  d. To shorten the installation time for revised software in a network, an organization may implement electronic software distribution (ESD), which is the computer-to-computer installation of software on workstations. Instead of weeks, software distribution can be accomplished in hours or days and can be controlled centrally. Another advantage of ESD is that it permits the tracking of PC program licenses.

Stop and review! You have completed the outline for this subunit. Study multiple-choice question 13 on page 326.

13.6 CONTINGENCY PLANNING

1. **Overview**

  a. The information security goal of data availability is primarily the responsibility of the IT function.

  b. Contingency planning is the name commonly given to this activity.

        1) **Disaster recovery** is the process of resuming normal information processing operations after the occurrence of a major interruption.

        2) **Business continuity** is the continuation of business by other means during the period in which computer processing is unavailable or less than normal.

  c. Plans must be made for two major types of contingencies: those in which the data center is physically available and those in which it is not.

        1) Examples of the first type of contingency are (a) power failure, (b) random intrusions such as viruses, and (c) deliberate intrusions such as hacking incidents. The organization's physical facilities are sound, but immediate action is required to continue normal processing.

        2) The second type of contingency is much more serious. It is caused by disasters such as floods, fires, hurricanes, or earthquakes. An occurrence of this type requires an alternate processing facility.

2. **Backup and Rotation**

  a. Periodic backup and offsite rotation of computer files is the most basic part of any disaster recovery or business continuity plan.

        1) An organization's data are more valuable than its hardware. Hardware can be replaced for a price, but each organization's data are unique and indispensable to operations. If it is destroyed, it cannot be replaced. For this reason, periodic backup and rotation are essential.

b. A typical backup routine duplicates all data files and application programs once a month. Incremental changes are then backed up and taken to an offsite location once a week. (Application files and data must be backed up because both change.)

1) In case of an interruption of normal processing, the organization's systems can be restored such that, at most, 7 days of business information is lost. This is not ideal, but it is preferable to a complete loss of files that could bankrupt the organization.

c. The offsite location must be temperature- and humidity-controlled and guarded against physical intrusion. Just as important, it must be far enough away from the site of main operations not to be affected by the same natural disaster. Adequate backup is useless if the files are not accessible or have been destroyed.

3. **Risk Assessment Steps**

a. Identify and prioritize the organization's critical applications.

1) Not all of an organization's systems are equally important. The firm must decide which vital applications it simply cannot do business without and in what order they should be brought back into operation.

b. Determine the minimum recovery time frames and minimum hardware requirements.

1) How long will it take to reinstall each critical application, and what platform is required? If the interruption has been caused by an attack, such as a virus or hacker, how long will it take to isolate the problem and eliminate it from the system?

c. Develop a recovery plan.

4. **Disaster Recovery Plan (DRP)**

a. Disaster recovery is the process of regaining access to data (e.g., hardware, software, and records), communications, work areas, and other business processes.

b. Thus, a DRP that is established and tested must be developed in connection with the business continuity plan. It should describe IT recovery strategies, including details about procedures, vendors, and systems.

1) Detailed procedures must be updated when systems and businesses change. The following are examples of items addressed by the DRP:

a) Data center
b) Applications and data needed
c) Servers and other hardware
d) Communications
e) Network connections
f) IT infrastructure (e.g., log-on services and software distribution)
g) Remote access services
h) Process control systems
i) File rooms
j) Document management systems

c. The following are considerations for choosing DRP strategies:

1) The DRP should be based on the business impact analysis.
2) The recovery abilities of critical service providers must be assessed.
3) The recovery of IT components often must be combined to recover a system.
4) Service providers (internal and external) must furnish recovery information, such as their (a) responsibilities, (b) limitations, (c) recovery activities, (d) recovery time and point objectives, and (e) costs.

     5) Strategies for components may be developed independently. The objective is the best, most cost-effective solution that (a) allows user access and (b) permits components to work together, regardless of where systems are recovered.

     6) Security and compliance standards must be considered.

5. **Contingencies with Data Center Available**

   a. The purchase of backup electrical generators protects against power failures. These can be programmed to begin running automatically as soon as a dip in electric current is detected. This practice is widespread in settings such as hospitals where 24-hour availability is crucial.

   b. Attacks such as viruses and denial-of-service require a completely different response. The system must be brought down gracefully to halt the spread of the infection. The IT staff must be well trained in the nature of the latest virus threats to know how to isolate the damage and bring the system back to full operation.

6. **Contingencies with Data Center Unavailable**

   a. The most extreme contingency is a disaster that makes the organization's main facility unusable. To prepare for these cases, organizations contract for alternate processing facilities.

   b. An **alternate processing facility** is a physical location maintained by an outside contractor for the purpose of providing processing facilities for customers in case of disaster.

     1) The recovery center, like the off-site storage location for backup files, must be far enough away from the main facility that it is not affected by the same natural disaster. Usually, organizations contract for backup facilities in another city.

     2) When processing is no longer possible at the principal site, the backup files are retrieved from the secure storage location and taken to the recovery center.

   c. Recovery centers take two basic forms. Organizations determine which facility is best by calculating the trade-off between the cost of the contract and the cost of downtime.

     1) A **hot site** is a fully operational processing facility that is immediately available. The organization generally contracts with a service provider.

       a) For a fee, the service provider agrees to have a hardware platform and communications lines substantially identical to the organization's ready for use 24 hours a day, 365 days a year.

       b) This solution is the least risky and most expensive.

       c) Any contract for a hot site must include a provision for annual testing.

         i) The service provider agrees to a window of time in which the organization can declare a fake disaster, load its backup files onto the equipment at the hot site, and determine how long it takes to resume normal processing.

     2) A **warm site** is a compromise between a cold and hot site, combining features of both.

       a) Resources are available at the site but may need to be configured to support the production system.

       b) Some data may need to be restored.

       c) Typical recovery time ranges from 2 days to 2 weeks.

3) A **cold site** is a shell facility with sufficient electrical power, environmental controls, and communications lines to permit the organization to install its own newly acquired equipment.

    a) On an ongoing basis, this solution is much less expensive.

    b) However, the time to procure replacement equipment can be weeks or months. Also, emergency procurement from equipment vendors can be very expensive.

7. **Fault Tolerance**

    a. A fault-tolerant computer has additional chips and disk storage as well as a backup power supply. This technology is used for mission-critical applications that cannot afford to suffer downtime.

        1) The technology that permits fault-tolerance is the redundant array of inexpensive (or independent) disks, or RAID. It is a group of multiple hard drives with special software that allows for data delivery along multiple paths. If one drive fails, the other disks can compensate for the loss.

    b. High-availability computing is used for less-critical applications because it provides for a short recovery time rather than the elimination of recovery time.

8. **Business Continuity Management (BCM) Overview**

    a. The objective of BCM is to restore critical processes and to minimize financial and other effects of a disaster or business disruption.

    b. BCM is the third component of an emergency management program. Its time frame is measured in hours and days if not weeks. The other components are

        1) Emergency response, the goal of which is lifesaving, safety, and initial efforts to limit the effects of a disaster to asset damage. Its time frame is measured in hours if not minutes.

        2) Crisis management, the focus of which is managing communications and senior management activities. Its time frame is measured in days if not hours.

9. **Elements of BCM**

    a. **Management Support**

        1) Management must assign adequate resources to preparing, maintaining, and practicing a business continuity plan.

    b. **Risk Assessment and Mitigation**

        1) The entity must (a) define credible risk events (threats), (b) assess their effects, and (c) develop risk mitigation strategies.

    c. **Business Impact Analysis**

        1) This analysis identifies business processes necessary to functioning in a disaster and determines how soon they should be recovered.

        2) The organization (a) identifies critical processes, (b) defines the recovery time objective (RTO) and the recovery point objective (RPO) for processes and resources, and (c) identifies the other parties (e.g., vendors and other divisions of the organization) and physical resources (e.g., critical equipment and records) needed for recovery.

            a) A recovery time objective is the duration of time and service level within which a process must be restored. A recovery point objective is the amount of data the organization can afford to lose.

            b) The cost of a recovery solution ordinarily increases as either objective decreases.

d.   **Business Recovery and Continuity Strategy**

   1)   A crucial element of business recovery is the existence of a comprehensive and current disaster recovery plan, which addresses the actual steps, people, and resources required to recover a critical business process. (Disaster recovery plans were discussed in greater detail earlier.)

   2)   The organization plans for

   a)   Alternative staffing (e.g., staff remaining at the site, staff at another site, or staff of another organization),

   b)   Alternative sourcing (e.g., use of nonstandard products and services, use of diverse suppliers, outsourcing to organizations that provide standard services, or reciprocal agreements with competitors),

   c)   Alternative work spaces (e.g., another organization facility, remote access with proper security, or a commercial recovery site), and

   d)   The return to normal operations (e.g., entry of manually processed data, resolution of regulatory and financial exceptions, return of borrowed equipment, and replenishment of products and supplies).

e.   **Education, Awareness, and Maintenance**

   1)   Education and awareness (including training exercises) are vital to BCM and execution of the business continuity plan.

   2)   The BCM capabilities and documentation must be maintained to ensure that they remain effective and aligned with business priorities.

f.   **Business Continuity**

   1)   According to The IIA, large-scale exercises (or testing) of the BCM programs and BC plans should be conducted at least annually.

   2)   The following are different types of exercises:

   a)   A **desk check** is a review of the written plan to ensure accuracy of the documentation. It is the least invasive type of exercise or test.

   b)   The **orientation** or plan walk-through method ensures that all team members understand their new roles and the basic plan content and format. This method allows the employees expected to implement the plan to walk through the document informally. Normally, this type of low-intensity event does not constitute a test.

   c)   A **tabletop exercise** simulates an emergency situation in an informal, stress-free environment. The purpose is to help team members understand the importance of their roles and responsibilities.

   d)   **Communication testing** normally involves actual contact with business partners and employees. The objectives include (1) validating the contact information of key stakeholders, (2) training participants in how to use mass notification and otherwise perform any roles they have in the response, (3) properly configuring mass notification tools, and (4) identifying communication gaps where timely communication could falter during a disaster.

   e)   An **IT environment walk-through** involves conducting an announced or unannounced disaster simulation and executing documented system recovery procedures.

   f)   **End-to-end testing** determines whether an application is performing as designed from start to finish. The test validates connectivity to the organization's production site.

Stop and review! You have completed the outline for this subunit. Study multiple-choice questions 14 through 20 beginning on page 327.

QUESTIONS

13.1 Functional Areas of IT Operations

1. Which of the following terms best describes the type of control practice evidenced by a segregation of duties between computer programmers and computer operators?

- A. Systems development control.
- B. Hardware control.
- C. Applications control.
- D. Organizational control.

Answer (D) is correct.

REQUIRED: The type of control practice evidenced by a segregation of duties between computer programmers and computer operators.

DISCUSSION: Organizational control concerns the proper segregation of duties and responsibilities within the information systems function. For example, programmers should not have access to the equipment, and operators should not have programming ability. Although proper segregation is desirable, functions that would be considered incompatible if performed by a single individual in a manual activity are often performed through the use of an information systems program or series of programs. Therefore, compensating controls may be necessary, such as library controls and effective supervision.

Answer (A) is incorrect. Systems development controls concern systems analysis, design, and implementation. Answer (B) is incorrect. Hardware controls are incorporated into the equipment. Answer (C) is incorrect. Applications controls pertain to specific programs. They include input, processing, and output controls.

2. An organization's computer help-desk function is usually a responsibility of the

- A. Applications development unit.
- B. Systems programming unit.
- C. Computer operations unit.
- D. User departments.

Answer (C) is correct.

REQUIRED: The entity in charge of a computer help desk.

DISCUSSION: Help desks are usually a responsibility of computer operations because of the operational nature of their functions. A help desk logs reported problems, resolves minor problems, and forwards more difficult problems to the appropriate information systems resources, such as a technical support unit or vendor assistance.

Answer (A) is incorrect. Applications development is responsible for developing systems, not providing help to end users. Answer (B) is incorrect. The responsibility of systems programming is to implement and maintain system-level software, such as operating systems, access control software, and database systems software. Answer (D) is incorrect. User departments usually lack the expertise to solve computer problems.

3. For control purposes, which of the following should be organizationally segregated from the computer operations function?

- A. Data conversion.
- B. Surveillance of screen display messages.
- C. Systems development.
- D. Minor maintenance according to a schedule.

Answer (C) is correct.

REQUIRED: The activity that should be segregated from computer operations.

DISCUSSION: Systems development is performed by systems analysts and application programmers.

Answer (A) is incorrect. Data conversion may be assigned to computer operations. Answer (B) is incorrect. Surveillance of screen display messages may be assigned to computer operations. Answer (D) is incorrect. Minor maintenance according to a schedule may be assigned to computer operations.

13.2 Enterprise-Wide Resource Planning (ERP)

4. An enterprise-wide resource planning (ERP) system integrates the organization's computerized subsystems and may also provide links to external parties. An advantage of ERP is that

    A. The reengineering needed for its implementation should improve business processes.

    B. Customizing the software to suit the unique needs of the organization will facilitate upgrades.

    C. It can be installed by organizations of all sizes.

    D. The comprehensiveness of the system reduces resistance to change.

Answer (A) is correct.
    REQUIRED: The advantage of ERP.
    DISCUSSION: The benefits of ERP may significantly derive from the business process reengineering that is needed for its implementation. Using ERP software that reflects the best practices forces the linked subunits in the organization not only to redesign and improve their processes but also to conform to one standard.
    Answer (B) is incorrect. The disadvantages of ERP are its extent and complexity, which make customization of the software difficult and costly. Answer (C) is incorrect. ERP software is costly and complex. It is usually installed only by the largest enterprises. Answer (D) is incorrect. Implementing an ERP system is likely to encounter significant resistance because of its comprehensiveness.

5. A principal advantage of an ERP system is

    A. Program-data dependence.

    B. Data redundancy.

    C. Separate data updating for different functions.

    D. Centralization of data.

Answer (D) is correct.
    REQUIRED: The principal advantage of an ERP system.
    DISCUSSION: An advantage of an ERP system is the elimination of data redundancy through the use of a central database. In principle, information about an item of data is stored once, and all functions have access to it. Thus, when the item (such as a price) is updated, the change is effectively made for all functions. The result is reliability (data integrity).
    Answer (A) is incorrect. An ERP system uses a central database and a database management system. A fundamental characteristic of a database is that applications are independent of the physical structure of the database. Writing programs or designing applications to use the database requires only the names of desired data items, not their locations. Answer (B) is incorrect. An ERP system eliminates data redundancy. Answer (C) is incorrect. An ERP system is characterized by one-time data updating for all organizational functions.

6. A manufacturing resource planning (MRP II) system

    A. Performs the same back-office functions for a manufacturer as an ERP system.

    B. Uses a master production schedule.

    C. Lacks the forecasting and budgeting capabilities typical of an ERP system.

    D. Performs the same front-office functions for a manufacturer as an ERP system.

Answer (B) is correct.
    REQUIRED: The true statement about MRP II.
    DISCUSSION: Manufacturing resource planning (MRP II) continued the evolution begun with MRP. It is a closed-loop manufacturing system that integrates all facets of manufacturing, including production, sales, inventories, schedules, and cash flows. The same system is used for accounting and finance functions, which use the same transactions and numbers. MRP II uses an MPS (master production schedule), a statement of the anticipated manufacturing schedule for selected items for selected periods. MRP also uses the MPS. Thus, MRP is a component of an MRP II system.
    Answer (A) is incorrect. An MRP II system does not integrate all the subsystems internal to the organization (back-office functions), such as human resources and customer service. Answer (C) is incorrect. MRP II includes forecasting and planning capacities for generating cash and other budgets. Answer (D) is incorrect. MRP, MRP II, and traditional ERP do not provide for front-office functions, that is, connections with customers, suppliers, owners, creditors, and strategic allies.

13.3 Web Infrastructure

7. The Internet consists of a series of networks that include

A. Gateways to allow personal computers to connect to mainframe computers.

B. Bridges to direct messages through the optimum data path.

C. Repeaters to physically connect separate local area networks (LANs).

D. Routers to strengthen data signals between distant computers.

Answer (A) is correct.
REQUIRED: The composition of the Internet.
DISCUSSION: The Internet facilitates information transfer among computers. Gateways are hardware or software products that allow translation between two different protocol families. For example, a gateway can be used to exchange messages between different email systems.
Answer (B) is incorrect. Routers are used to determine the best path for data. Answer (C) is incorrect. Bridges connect LANs. Answer (D) is incorrect. Repeaters strengthen signals.

8. In general, mainframe or server production programs and data are adequately protected against unauthorized access. Certain utility software may, however, have privileged access to software and data. To compensate for the risk of unauthorized use of privileged software, IT management can

A. Prevent privileged software from being installed on the mainframe.

B. Restrict privileged access to test versions of applications.

C. Limit the use of privileged software.

D. Keep sensitive programs and data on an isolated machine.

Answer (C) is correct.
REQUIRED: The best alternative information systems management can take to minimize unauthorized use of privileged software.
DISCUSSION: Since certain utility software may have privileged access to software and data stored on the mainframe or server, management must control the use of this utility software. Management should limit the use of this software to only those individuals with appropriate authority.
Answer (A) is incorrect. Privileged software may be needed to modify programs and data. Answer (B) is incorrect. Privileged access may be necessary to modify the final versions of applications. Answer (D) is incorrect. Authorized users must access sensitive programs and data through their workstations that are connected to the mainframe or server.

13.4 IT System Communications

9. A local area network (LAN) is best described as a(n)

A. Computer system that connects computers of all sizes, workstations, terminals, and other devices within a limited proximity.

B. System to allow computer users to meet and share ideas and information.

C. Electronic library containing millions of items of data that can be reviewed, retrieved, and analyzed.

D. Method to offer specialized software, hardware, and data-handling techniques that improve effectiveness and reduce costs.

Answer (A) is correct.
REQUIRED: The best description of a local area network (LAN).
DISCUSSION: A LAN is a local distributed computer system, often housed within a single building. Computers, communication devices, and other equipment are linked by cable. Special software facilitates efficient data communication among the hardware devices.
Answer (B) is incorrect. A LAN is more than a system to allow computer users to share information. In addition, it is an interconnection of a computer system. Answer (C) is incorrect. A LAN is not a library. Answer (D) is incorrect. A LAN does not require specialized hardware.

10. Which of the following represents the greatest exposure to the integrity of electronic funds transfer data transmitted from a remote terminal?

A. Poor physical access controls over the data center.

B. Network viruses.

C. Poor system documentation.

D. Leased telephone circuits.

Answer (D) is correct.
REQUIRED: The greatest exposure to the integrity of EFT data transmitted from a remote terminal.
DISCUSSION: Leased telephone circuits represent a direct exposure to the risk of breached data integrity. They use public lines that can be easily identified and tapped.
Answer (A) is incorrect. Poor physical access controls represent a secondary exposure for compromise of remote data communications lines. Answer (B) is incorrect. Network viruses represent a secondary exposure for compromise of remote data communications lines. Answer (C) is incorrect. Poor system documentation represent a secondary exposure for compromise of remote data communications lines.

11. A type of network that is used to support interconnections within a building is known as a(n)

- A. Local area network.
- B. Wide area network.
- C. Metropolitan area network.
- D. Value-added network.

Answer (A) is correct.
REQUIRED: The type of network that is used to support interconnections within a building.
DISCUSSION: A communication network consists of one or more computers and their peripheral equipment linked together. Local area networks (LANs) link together hardware and other equipment within a limited area such as a building so that users can share data and hardware devices.
Answer (B) is incorrect. Wide area networks consist of a conglomerate of LANs over widely separated locations. Answer (C) is incorrect. A metropolitan area network connects devices across an urban area. Answer (D) is incorrect. A value-added network is a type of privately owned WAN.

12. When two devices in a data communications system are communicating, there must be agreement as to how both data and control information are to be packaged and interpreted. Which of the following terms is commonly used to describe this type of agreement?

- A. Asynchronous communication.
- B. Synchronous communication.
- C. Communication channel.
- D. Communication protocol.

Answer (D) is correct.
REQUIRED: The agreement as to how both data and control information are to be packaged and interpreted.
DISCUSSION: A protocol is a set of formal rules or conventions governing communication between a sending and a receiving device. It prescribes the manner by which data are transmitted between these communications devices. In essence, a protocol is the envelope within which each message is transmitted throughout a data communications network.
Answer (A) is incorrect. Asynchronous communication is a mode of transmission. Communication is in disjointed segments, typically character by character, preceded by a start code and ended by a stop code. Answer (B) is incorrect. Synchronous communication is a mode of transmission in which a continuous stream of blocks of characters result in faster communications. Answer (C) is incorrect. A communication channel is a transmission link between devices in a network. The term is also used for a small processor that controls input-output devices.

13.5 Software Licensing

13. Which of the following would be the most appropriate starting point for a compliance evaluation of software licensing requirements for an organization with more than 15,000 computer workstations?

- A. Determine if software installation is controlled centrally or distributed throughout the organization.
- B. Determine what software packages have been installed on the organization's computers and the number of each package installed.
- C. Determine how many copies of each software package have been purchased by the organization.
- D. Determine what mechanisms have been installed for monitoring software usage.

Answer (A) is correct.
REQUIRED: The most appropriate starting point for a compliance evaluation of software licensing requirements in a large entity.
DISCUSSION: The logical starting point is to determine the point(s) of control. Evidence of license compliance can then be assessed. For example, to shorten the installation time for revised software in a network, an organization may implement electronic software distribution (ESD), which is the computer-to-computer installation of software on workstations. Instead of weeks, software distribution can be accomplished in hours or days and can be controlled centrally. Another advantage of ESD is that it permits tracking or metering of PC program licenses.
Answer (B) is incorrect. Before taking this step, an auditor should first determine whether installation is controlled centrally. This determination affects how the auditor will gather information about the installed software. Answer (C) is incorrect. This procedure helps an auditor determine whether software was legitimately purchased. However, a better starting point is determining where the software is installed. Answer (D) is incorrect. Monitoring usage is not as important as determining installation procedures when evaluating licensing compliance.

13.6 Contingency Planning

14. Contingency plans for information systems should include appropriate backup agreements. Which of the following arrangements would be considered too vendor-dependent when vital operations require almost immediate availability of computer resources?

A. A "hot site" arrangement.

B. A "cold site" arrangement.

C. A "cold and hot site" combination arrangement.

D. Using excess capacity at another data center within the organization.

Answer (B) is correct.
    REQUIRED: The contingency plan that is too vendor-dependent.
    DISCUSSION: Organizations should maintain contingency plans for operations in the case of a disaster. These plans usually include off-site storage of important backup data and an arrangement for the continuation of operations at another location. A cold site has all needed assets in place except the needed computer equipment and is vendor-dependent for timely delivery of equipment.
    Answer (A) is incorrect. A hot site has all needed assets in place and is not vendor-dependent. Answer (C) is incorrect. A cold and hot site combination allows the hot site to be used until the cold site is prepared and is thus not too vendor-dependent. Answer (D) is incorrect. Excess capacity would ensure that needed assets are available and would not be vendor-dependent.

15. A company updates its accounts receivable master file weekly and retains the master files and corresponding update transactions for the most recent 2-week period. The purpose of this practice is to

A. Verify run-to-run control totals for receivables.

B. Match internal labels to avoid writing on the wrong volume.

C. Permit reconstruction of the master file if needed.

D. Validate groups of update transactions for each version.

Answer (C) is correct.
    REQUIRED: The purpose of periodic retention of master files and transaction data.
    DISCUSSION: Periodic backup and retention of both master files and transaction files is an integral part of any business continuity plan. If the data center is unavailable, these can be used to restore the master file and resume processing.
    Answer (A) is incorrect. Comparison of batch totals is a control over the completeness of processing, not a recovery procedure. Answer (B) is incorrect. Internal labels may avoid destruction of data but do not aid in recovery. Answer (D) is incorrect. Validation may avoid destruction of data but does not aid in recovery.

16. If a corporation's disaster recovery plan requires fast recovery with little or no downtime, which of the following backup sites should it choose?

A. Hot site.

B. Warm site.

C. Cold site.

D. Quick site.

Answer (A) is correct.
    REQUIRED: The type of backup facility that has fast recovery and little or no downtime.
    DISCUSSION: A company uses a hot site backup when fast recovery is critical. The hot site includes all software, hardware, and other equipment necessary for a company to carry out operations. Hot sites are expensive to maintain and may be shared with other organizations with similar needs.
    Answer (B) is incorrect. A warm site provides an intermediate level of backup. Its use results in more downtime than a hot site. Answer (C) is incorrect. A cold site is a shell facility suitable for quick installation of computer equipment. Disaster recovery would take more time in a cold site than a hot site. Answer (D) is incorrect. There is no backup site called a quick site.

17. Which of the following series identifies recovery solutions and sites for which a recovery plan exists?

A. Red, yellow, green.

B. High, medium, low.

C. Fast, moderate, slow.

D. Hot, warm, cold.

Answer (D) is correct.
    REQUIRED: The series used to identify recovery solutions and sites for which a recovery plan exists.
    DISCUSSION: The following are recovery solutions and sites for which a recovery plan exists:
    Hot -- Resources are available at the site(s), and data are synchronized in real time to permit recovery immediately or within hours.
    Warm -- Resources are available at the site(s) but may need to be configured to support the production system. Some data may need to be restored. Typical recovery time is 2 days to 2 weeks.
    Cold -- Sites have been identified with space and base infrastructure. Resources are not available at the sites. Data will likely need to be restored. Typical recovery time is 2 weeks to a month.

18. In conducting an audit of an organization's disaster recovery capability, which of the following would an auditor consider to be the most serious weakness?

    A. Tests use recovery scripts.

    B. Hot-site contracts are 2 years old.

    C. Backup media are stored on-site.

    D. Only a few systems are tested annually.

Answer (C) is correct.
    REQUIRED: The most serious weakness in an organization's disaster recovery capability.
    DISCUSSION: A crucial element of business recovery is the existence of a comprehensive and current disaster recovery plan. A comprehensive plan provides for (1) emergency response procedures, (2) alternative communication systems and site facilities, (3) information systems backup, (4) disaster recovery, (5) business impact assessments and resumption plans, (6) procedures for restoring utility services, and (7) maintenance procedures for ensuring the readiness of the organization in the event of an emergency or disaster. Storing backup media on-site is a weakness in the plan. They should not be located where they can be affected by the same event that interrupted the system's activities.
    Answer (A) is incorrect. Use of scripts is a common practice to sequence the activities required for resumption of business. Answer (B) is incorrect. Contracts for off-site facilities are not updated frequently. Answer (D) is incorrect. Generally, the limited test-time window will only permit testing a few systems.

19. Business continuity management provides for all but which of the following?

    A. Segregation of duties.

    B. Alternative work spaces.

    C. Business impact analysis.

    D. Alternative sourcing.

Answer (A) is correct.
    REQUIRED: The item not included in business continuity management.
    DISCUSSION: As part of an entity's business recovery and continuity strategy, it plans for alternative staffing, sourcing, and work spaces as well as for the return to normal operations. Segregation of duties, however, is a category of controls.
    Answer (B) is incorrect. BCM provides for alternative work spaces. Answer (C) is incorrect. BCM provides for business impact analysis. Answer (D) is incorrect. BCM provides for alternative sourcing.

20. Which component of an emergency management program of a business normally has the longest time frame?

    A. Emergency response.

    B. Crisis management.

    C. Continuity management.

    D. Communications management.

Answer (C) is correct.
    REQUIRED: The component of an EMP with the longest time frame.
    DISCUSSION: The objective of business continuity management is to restore critical processes and to minimize the financial effects of a disaster or business disruption. Its time frame is measured in hours and days if not weeks.
    Answer (A) is incorrect. The time frame of emergency response is measured in hours if not minutes. Answer (B) is incorrect. The time frame of crisis management is typically measured in days if not hours. Answer (D) is incorrect. Communicating with stakeholders (including the public) about a crisis and the steps for restoring business processes is the focus of crisis management.

Access the **CIA Review System** from your Gleim Personal Classroom
to continue your studies with exam-emulating multiple-choice questions!

STUDY UNIT FOURTEEN
BASIC AND INTERMEDIATE CONCEPTS
OF FINANCIAL ACCOUNTING

(26 pages of outline)

This study unit is the first of five covering **Section VII: Financial Management** from The IIA's CIA Exam Syllabus. This section makes up 10% to 20% of Part 3 of the CIA exam and is tested at the **awareness level**. The relevant portion of the syllabus is highlighted below. (The complete syllabus is in Appendix A.)

VII. FINANCIAL MANAGEMENT (10%–20%)

> **A. Financial Accounting and Finance**
>
> 1. Basic concepts and underlying principles of financial accounting (e.g., statements, terminology, relationships)
>
> 2. Intermediate concepts of financial accounting (e.g., bonds, leases, pensions, intangible assets, R&D)
>
> 10. Inventory valuation

B. Managerial Accounting

NOTE: Item A. 2. is partially covered in Study Unit 15. Items A. 3.-9. and 11. are covered in Study Units 15 and 16. Item A. 12. is covered in Study Unit 20.

14.1 CONCEPTS OF FINANCIAL ACCOUNTING

1. **The Objective of General-Purpose Financial Reporting**

    a. The objective of general-purpose financial reporting is to report financial information that is **useful in making decisions** about providing resources to the reporting entity.

    b. The primary users of financial information are current or prospective investors and creditors who cannot obtain it directly.

    1) Their decisions depend on expected returns.

    2) Accordingly, users need information that helps them to assess the potential for future net cash inflows.

    c. The information reported relates to the entity's economic resources and claims to them (financial position) and to changes in those resources and claims.

    1) Information about economic resources and claims helps to evaluate liquidity, solvency, financing needs, and the probability of obtaining financing.

d.   Changes in economic resources and claims to them may result from (1) the entity's performance (e.g., the income statement) or (2) other events and transactions, such as issuing debt and equity (balance sheet). Information about financial performance is useful for

1)   Understanding the return on economic resources, its variability, and its components;

2)   Evaluating management; and

3)   Predicting future returns.

e.   Financial statement analysis is described in Study Unit 15, Subunits 6 through 11.

2.   **Accounting Assumptions**

a.   Certain assumptions about the environment in which the reporting entity operates are used in the preparation of the financial statements.

b.   **Going-concern assumption.** It is assumed that the entity (1) will operate indefinitely and (2) will not be liquidated.

c.   **Economic-entity assumption.** The reporting entity is separately identified for the purpose of economic and financial accountability. Thus, the economic affairs of owners and managers are kept separate from those of the reporting entity.

1)   The legal entity and the economic entity are not necessarily the same. For example, consolidated reporting is permitted, if not required, even though the parent and its subsidiaries are legally distinct entities.

d.   **Monetary-unit (unit-of-money) assumption.** Accounting records are kept in terms of money. Using money as the unit of measure is the best way of providing economic information to users of financial statements.

e.   **Periodicity (time period) assumption.** Financial statements are prepared periodically throughout the life of an entity to ensure the timeliness of information.

1)   The periodicity assumption requires reporting estimates in the financial statements. It sacrifices some degree of faithful representation of information for increased relevance and timeliness.

3.   **Qualitative Characteristics of Useful Financial Information**

a.   For financial information to be useful in decision making, it must have the following qualitative characteristics:

1)   **Relevance.** Relevant information is able to make a difference in user decisions. To do so, it must have predictive value, confirmatory value, or both.

a)   Something has predictive value if it can be used as an input in a predictive process.

b)   Something has confirmatory value with respect to prior evaluations if it provides feedback that confirms or changes (corrects) them.

c)   Materiality. Information is material if its omission or misstatement can influence user decisions.

2)   **Faithful representation.** Useful information faithfully represents the economic phenomena that it purports to represent.

a)   A representation is perfectly faithful if it is complete (containing what is needed for user understanding), neutral (unbiased in its selection and presentation), and free from error (but not necessarily perfectly accurate).

3) **Comparability.** Information should be comparable with similar information for (a) other entities and (b) the same entity for another period or date. Thus, comparability allows users to understand similarities and differences.

   a) Consistency is a means of achieving comparability. It is the use of the same methods, for example, accounting principles, for the same items.

4) **Verifiability.** Information is verifiable (directly or indirectly) if knowledgeable and independent observers can reach a consensus (but not necessarily unanimity) that it is faithfully represented.

5) **Timeliness.** Information is timely when it is available in time to influence decisions.

6) **Understandability.** Understandable information is clearly and concisely classified, characterized, and presented.

4. **Constraints**

   a. The **cost constraint** affects all financial reporting. It states that the cost of reporting should be justified by the benefits.

   b. The **conservatism constraint** is a response to uncertainty. When alternative accounting methods are appropriate, generally the one having the less favorable effect on net income and total assets is preferable.

   c. The **industry practices constraint** is that the applicable reporting framework (GAAP) may not be followed in certain industries to avoid reporting misleading or unnecessary information.

5. **Accounting Principles**

   a. The following four principles provide guidelines for recording financial information.

   1) **Historical cost principle.** Transactions are recorded initially at cost because that is the most objective determination of fair value.

   2) **Full-disclosure principle.** Financial statement users should be able to assume that financial information that could influence users' judgment is reported in the financial statements.

   3) **Revenue recognition principle.** Revenues and gains should be recognized **when (a) realized or realizable and (b) earned**.

      a) Revenues and gains are realized when goods or services have been exchanged for cash or claims to cash. Revenues and gains are realizable when goods or services have been exchanged for assets that are readily convertible into cash or claims to cash.

      b) Revenues are earned when the earning process has been substantially completed, and the entity is entitled to the resulting benefits or revenues.

      c) Thus, revenue on sales can be recognized in the statement of income even if the cash from sales is not received yet.

   4) **Matching principle.** Expenses should be recognized in the same period as directly related revenues. Matching is essentially synonymous with associating cause and effect. Such a direct relationship is found when the cost of goods sold is recognized in the same period as the revenue from the sale of the goods.

6.   **Measurement Attributes**

a.   **Measurement** is the determination of the amounts at which the items are to be recognized in the financial statements.

b.   **Historical cost** is the acquisition price of an asset. It is ordinarily adjusted subsequently for amortization (which includes depreciation) or other allocations.

c.   **Current (replacement) cost** is the amount of cash that would have to be paid for a current acquisition of the same or an equivalent asset.

d.   **Net realizable value** is the cash or equivalent expected to be received for an asset in the due course of business, minus the costs of completion and sale.

e.   **Fair value** is the price that would be received to sell an asset or paid to transfer a liability in an orderly transaction between market participants at the measurement date.

f.   **Present value** incorporates the time value of money concept. Determination of the present value of an asset or liability requires discounting, at an appropriate interest rate, the related future cash flows expected to occur in the due course of business.

Stop and review! You have completed the outline for this subunit. Study multiple-choice questions 1 and 2 beginning on page 354.

14.2 FINANCIAL STATEMENTS

1.   **A Full Set of Financial Statements**

a.   Financial statements are the primary means of communicating financial information to external parties. Additional information is provided by financial statement notes, supplementary information, and other disclosures. Information typically disclosed in notes is essential to understanding the financial statements.

b.   A full set of financial statements includes the following statements:

1)   Statement of financial position
2)   Income statement
3)   Statement of comprehensive income
4)   Statement of changes in equity
5)   Statement of cash flows

c.   A full set of financial statements can be found in Appendix D.

2.   **Statement of Financial Position**

a.   The statement of financial position, also called the **balance sheet**, reports the amounts in the accounting equation at a moment in time, such as at the end of the fiscal year. This equation reports resources (assets) on one side and the claims to those resources (liabilities and equity) on the other side.

The Accounting Equation

Assets = Liabilities + Equity (net assets)

1)   **Assets** are resources controlled by the entity as a result of past events. They represent probable future economic benefits to the entity. Examples include inventory; accounts receivable; investments; and property, plant, and equipment.

2)   **Liabilities** are present obligations of the entity arising from past events. Their settlement is expected to result in an outflow of economic benefits from the entity. Examples include loans, bonds issued by the entity, and accounts payable.

3) **Equity** is the residual interest in the assets of the entity after subtracting all its liabilities. Examples include company's common stock, preferred stock, and retained earnings.

   a) Equity is affected not only by operations but also by transactions with owners, such as dividends and contributions.

b. Assets and liabilities are separated in the statement of financial position into **current** and **noncurrent** categories.

   1) Current assets are generally expected to be realized in cash or sold or consumed in 1 year from the balance sheet date.

   2) Current liabilities are generally expected to be settled or liquidated in 1 year from the balance sheet date.

   3) Some variation of the following classifications is used by most entities:

Assets	Liabilities
Current assets:	Current liabilities:
Cash	Accounts payable
Certain investments	Current notes payable
Accounts and notes receivable	Current maturities of noncurrent liabilities
Inventories	Accrued expenses
Prepaid expenses	Noncurrent liabilities:
Noncurrent assets:	Noncurrent notes payable
Certain investments and funds	Bonds payable
Property, plant, and equipment (PPE)	Employee-related obligations
Intangible assets	Deferred income taxes
Other noncurrent assets	
	Equity
	Investments by owners
	Retained earnings (income reinvested)
	Accumulated other comprehensive income
	Noncontrolling interest in a consolidated entity

c. A comprehensive example of a statement of financial position is in Appendix D.

d. The following are the major limitations of the statement of financial position (balance sheet):

   1) Many balance sheet items, such as fixed assets, are measured at historical cost, which may not equal their current market value (fair value).

   2) The preparation of a balance sheet requires estimates and management judgment.

   3) The balance sheet reports an entity's financial position at a single moment in time. Balances may vary significantly a few days before or after the statement date.

3. **Income Statement**

a. The income statement reports the results of an entity's operations over a period of time, such as a year.

The Income Equation

Income (loss) = Revenues + Gains − Expenses − Losses

   1) **Revenues** are inflows or other enhancements of assets or settlements of liabilities (or both) from delivering or producing goods, providing services, or other activities that qualify as ongoing major or central operations.

   2) **Gains** are increases in equity (or net assets) other than from revenues or investments by owners.

   3) **Expenses** are outflows or other usage of assets or incurrences of liabilities (or both) from delivering or producing goods, providing services, or other activities that qualify as ongoing major or central operations.

4)   **Losses** are decreases in equity (or net assets) other than from expenses or distributions to owners.

EXAMPLE

Income Statement

Net sales	US $ 200,000
Cost of goods sold	(150,000)
Gross profit	US $ 50,000
Selling expenses	(6,000)
Administrative expenses	(5,000)
Income from operations	US $ 39,000
Other revenues and gains	3,500
Other expenses and losses	(2,500)
Income before taxes	US $ 40,000
Income taxes	(16,000)
Net income	US $ 24,000

A more detailed example format is in Appendix D.

---

b.   Revenue ordinarily is recognized upon the delivery of goods or services when the earning process is completed. However, in some cases, revenue may be recognized before or after delivery.

1)   Revenue on long-term construction projects can be recognized over the construction period and **prior to delivery** using the **percentage-of-completion** method. This method records (a) all contract costs in an inventory account (construction in progress) and (b) all amounts billed in a contra-inventory account (progress billings). Revenue recognized depends on (a) the total estimated revenue on the project and (b) the percentage of the project completed as of the reporting date. This percentage ordinarily is the ratio of costs incurred to date to estimated total costs.

a)   The revenue recognized for the period equals revenue recognized to date (total expected revenue from the project × the percentage of completion to date), minus revenue recognized in prior periods.

2)   Receivables may be collectible over an extended period, and no reasonable basis may exist for estimating the degree of collectability. Under U.S. GAAP, such revenue may be recognized **after delivery** using the following methods:

a)   Under the **installment method**, the amount of revenues recognized for the period equals the cash collected during that period. A partial gross profit on a sale is recognized as each installment is collected. This amount equals the cash collected on installment sales for the period multiplied by the gross profit percentage on installment sales for the period.

b)   Under the **cost recovery method**, no profit is recognized until collections exceed the cost of the item sold. Subsequent receipts increase gross profit from the sale, and revenue is recognized.

c.   A **discontinued operation**, if one exists, is presented net of tax in a separate section of the income statement after income from continuing operations. It reports (1) income or loss from operations of the component that has been disposed of or is classified as held for sale and (2) gain or loss on the disposal of the component.

d.   The following are major limitations of the income statement:

1)   The financial statements report accrual-basis results for the period. An entity may recognize revenue and report net income before any cash was actually received.

a)   For example, the data from the income statement itself do not suffice for assessing liquidity. This statement must be analyzed along with other financial statements, such as the balance sheet and the statement of cash flows.

2) The income statement does not always show all items of income and expense. Some items are reported on a statement of other comprehensive income and are not included in the calculation of net income.

3) The preparation of the income statement requires estimates and management judgment.

4. **Statement of Comprehensive Income**

   a. All nonowner changes in equity must be presented either in one continuous statement or in two separate but consecutive statements (an income statement and a statement of other comprehensive income).

      1) Comprehensive income for a period consists of (a) net income or loss (the bottom line of the income statement) and (b) **other comprehensive income (OCI)**.

      2) The following are examples of components of OCI:

         a) The effective portion of a gain or loss on a hedging instrument in a cash flow hedge

         b) A gain or loss on remeasurement of certain financial assets

         c) Translation gains and losses for financial statements of foreign operations

         d) Certain amounts associated with accounting for defined benefit postretirement plans

---

EXAMPLE

Statement of Other Comprehensive Income

Net income		US $ 24,000
OCI (net of tax):		
Loss on defined benefit postretirement plans	US $(2,000)	
Gains on foreign currency translation	4,500	
Gains on remeasuring certain financial assets	1,100	
Effective portion of losses on cash flow hedges	(800)	2,800
Total comprehensive income		US $ 26,800

---

5. **Statement of Changes in Equity**

   a. This statement reconciles the beginning balance for each component of equity to the ending balance.

   b. Each change is disclosed separately in the statement. The following are common changes in equity balances during the accounting period:

      1) Net income (loss) for the period increases (decreases) retained earnings.

      2) Distributions to owners (dividends paid) decreases retained earnings.

      3) An issue of common stock increases common stock. If the amount paid is above the par value of the stock, additional paid-in capital also increases.

      4) OCI increases accumulated OCI.

   c. The accounting for equity is described in Study Unit 15, Subunit 5.

   d. A comprehensive example of statement of changes in equity is in Appendix D.

6. **Statement of Cash Flows**

   a. The primary purpose of the statement of cash flows is to provide relevant information about the cash receipts and cash payments of an entity during the period. Thus, it provides information about cash inflows and outflows from the operating, investing, and financing activities of the entity.

b. The statement of cash flows explains the change in cash and cash equivalents during the period. It reconciles the beginning balance with the ending balance.

EXAMPLE

The following is an example of the summarized format of the statement of cash flows (headings only). The amounts of cash and cash equivalents at the beginning and end of the year are taken from the balance sheet.

Entity A's Statement of Cash Flows for the Year Ended December 31, Year 1

Net cash provided by (used in) operating activities	US $XXX
Net cash provided by (used in) investing activities	XXX
Net cash provided by (used in) financing activities	XXX
Net increase (decrease) in cash and cash equivalents during the year	US $XXX
Cash and cash equivalents at beginning of year (January 1, Year 1)	XXX
Cash and cash equivalents at end of year (December 31, Year 1)	US $XXX

A more detailed example format is in Appendix D.

---

c. **Operating activities** are all transactions and other events that are not financing or investing activities. Cash flows from operating activities primarily are derived from the principal revenue-producing activities of the entity. The two acceptable methods of presentation of cash flows from operating activities are the direct and the indirect methods:

1) The **direct method** presents major classes of gross operating cash receipts and payments and their sum (net cash flow from operating activities).

2) The **indirect method** reconciles net income to cash flow from operating activities. Certain adjustments to net income must be made because (a) net income is reported on the accrual basis, not the cash basis; and (b) certain financing and investing cash flows are reported in net income.

    a) The following must be **added to net income**:

        i)   Increases in current operating liabilities (e.g., accounts payable and interest payable).

        ii) Decreases in current operating assets (e.g., inventory and receivables).

        iii) Noncash losses and expenses (e.g., depreciation expense).

        iv) Losses and expenses whose cash effects are related to investing or financing cash flows; e.g., a loss on disposal of equipment is related to investing activities.

    b) The following must be **subtracted from net income**:

        i)   Decreases in current operating liabilities (e.g., accounts payable and interest payable).

        ii) Increases in current operating assets (e.g., inventory and receivables).

        iii) Noncash revenues and gains.

        iv) Revenues and gains whose cash effects are related to investing or financing cash flows; e.g., a gain on extinguishment of debt is related to financing activities.

    NOTE: The net cash flow from operating activities is the same under both methods. The only difference is the presentation.

    d. Cash flows from **investing activities** represent the extent to which expenditures have been made for resources intended to generate future income and cash flows.

        1) The following are examples of **cash flows** from investing activities:

            a) Cash payments to acquire (cash receipts from sale of) (1) property, plant, and equipment; (2) intangible assets; and (3) other long-lived assets.

            b) Cash payments to acquire (cash receipts from sale and maturity of) equity and debt securities of other entities.

    e. Cash flows from **financing activities** generally involve the cash effects of transactions and other events that relate to the issuance, settlement, or reacquisition of the entity's debt and equity instruments.

        1) The following are examples of **cash inflows** from financing activities:

            a) Cash proceeds from issuing shares and other equity instruments (obtaining resources from owners)

            b) Cash proceeds from issuing loans, notes, bonds, and other short-term or long-term borrowings

        2) The following are examples of **cash outflows** from financing activities:

            a) Cash repayments of amounts borrowed

            b) Payments of cash dividends

7. Notes to the Financial Statements

    a. Notes describe the basis of preparation and the significant policies applied, make required disclosures not presented on the face of the statements, and provide additional information needed for a fair presentation. Information typically disclosed in notes is essential to understanding the financial statements.

        1) The first note accompanying any set of complete financial statements generally describes significant accounting policies, such as the use of estimates and rules for revenue recognition.

        2) Notes disclosures and schedules specifically related to the balance sheet include (a) investment securities; (b) maturity patterns of bond issues; (c) significant uncertainties, such as pending litigation; and (d) details of capital stock issues.

        3) Notes disclosures and schedules specifically related to the income statement include (a) earnings per share, (b) depreciation schedules, and (c) components of income tax expense.

8. Financial Statement Relationships

    a. Financial statements complement each other. They describe different aspects of the same transactions, and more than one statement is necessary to provide information for a specific economic decision.

    b. The components of one statement relate to those of other statements. Among the relationships are those listed below and on the next page.

        1) Net income or loss from the statement of income is reported and accumulated in the retained earnings account, a component of the equity section of the statement of financial position.

        2) The components of cash and equivalents from the statement of financial position are reconciled with the corresponding items in the statement of cash flows.

        3) Items of equity from the statement of financial position are reconciled with the beginning balances on the statement of changes in equity.

        4) Ending inventories are reported in current assets on the statement of financial position and are reflected in the calculation of cost of goods sold on the statement of income.

5) Amortization and depreciation reported in the statement of income also are reflected in asset and liability balances in the statement of financial position.

NOTE: Appendix D contains a complete set of financial statements. The complementary relationships among these statements are lettered.

Stop and review! You have completed the outline for this subunit. Study multiple-choice questions 3 through 5 on page 355.

14.3 THE ACCRUAL BASIS OF ACCOUNTING

1. **Accrual Basis**

   a. Financial statements are prepared under the accrual basis of accounting. Accrual accounting records the financial effects of transactions and other events and circumstances when they occur rather than when their associated cash is paid or received.

      1) Revenues are recognized in the period in which they were earned even if the cash will be received in a future period.

      2) Expenses are recognized in the period in which they were incurred even if the cash will be paid in a future period.

      NOTE: Under the cash basis, revenues are recognized when cash is received, and expenses are recognized when cash is paid. Financial statements cannot be prepared under the cash basis of accounting.

2. **Accruals and Deferrals**

   a. **Accruals** anticipate future cash flows. They reflect the amounts of cash that must be paid or received at some later date for goods or services received or provided today.

      1) For example, an entity incurs an expense by having its carpets cleaned, with the price due within 10 days. The entity has incurred a liability (owes money) because it has already received the benefits of the service.

      2) The entity records an accrued expense to acknowledge that it must pay cash to compensate another party for a service already performed and recognizes an expense for the services that were already received.

      (Dr) Maintenance expense   US $800
        (Cr) Accounts payable   US $800

         a) No cash has passed from the entity to the cleaner, but both the income statement and the statement of financial position are affected. The debit to an expense reflects a current consumption of economic benefit, and the credit to accounts payable reflects the future cash outflow.

   b. **Deferrals** arise from past cash flows. They are amounts of cash paid or received today in anticipation of goods or services to be received or provided at some later date.

      1) For example, a magazine publisher has received cash from subscribers entitling them to receive the next 12 issues. The publisher must deliver a product over the next year, but it has already received the benefits of the cash.

      2) The publisher must record deferred revenue (a liability), also called unearned income, to acknowledge its obligation to other parties.

      (Dr) Cash   US $24,000
        (Cr) Deferred subscription income   US $24,000

         a) Cash has passed from the customers to the publisher, and the publisher must now provide a product. The debit to an asset reflects the cash inflow, and the credit to a liability reflects the outstanding obligation.

3) Another common deferral is prepaid expense. It is a cash prepayment for goods or services to be received over a specified period. In this example, an entity paid at the beginning of the year for 3 years of insurance premiums in advance.

(Dr) Prepaid insurance   US $120,000
    (Cr) Cash   US $120,000

a) Cash has passed from the entity to the insurer, who must now provide a service. The debit to an asset reflects the future benefit expected, and the credit to cash reflects the immediate cash payment.

3. **Allocation**

a. Allocation is the accrual-accounting process of distributing an amount according to a plan or formula. Assigning a total cost to the accounting periods expected to be benefited is a common allocation.

1) In the prepaid insurance example, the entity received a third of the benefit during the first year after the prepayment. Thus, it allocates one-third of the prepayment to expense recognized in Year 1 (US $120,000 ÷ 3 = US $40,000).

(Dr) Insurance expense   US $40,000
    (Cr) Prepaid insurance   US $40,000

2) Depreciation of capital assets and amortization of intangible assets (other than goodwill) over their estimated useful lives are also time-based allocations.

4. **Relationship between Cash Amounts and Accrual-Basis Amounts**

a. Financial statement accrual-basis amounts can be calculated based on the relationship between receivables, payables, accruals, and deferrals.

b. The following calculations represent the relationship between the amount of cash paid or received and the amount of revenue or expense as it is recognized in the income statement (prepared under the accrual basis).

Cash collected from customers	US $ XXX	Cash paid to suppliers	US $ XXX
Ending accounts receivable	XXX	Ending accounts payable	XXX
Beginning accounts receivable	(XXX)	Beginning accounts payable	(XXX)
Net Sales (accrual basis)	US $ XXX	Purchases (accrual basis)	US $ XXX
Expenses paid during the period	US $ XXX	Cash received during the period	US $ XXX
Beginning prepaid expenses	XXX	Beginning deferred income	XXX
Ending prepaid expenses	(XXX)	Ending deferred income	(XXX)
Expenses recognized (accrual basis)	US $ XXX	Income recognized (accrual basis)	US $ XXX

EXAMPLE

On January 1 and December 31 of the current year, an entity had the following balances:

	January 1	December 31
Accounts receivable	US $15,000	US $25,000
Prepaid expenses	7,000	5,000

During the year, cash collections totaled US $40,000, and cash expenses paid totaled US $27,000.

The amount of sales revenue recognized for the year is US $50,000 [$40,000 + ($25,000 – $15,000)]. The increase in receivables is an earned amount with no cash inflow. This increase should be added to the amount of cash collected in order to calculate the amount of accrual-basis revenues.

The amount of expenses recognized for the year is US $29,000 [$27,000 + ($7,000 – $5,000)]. The decrease in prepaid expenses is an expense recognized with no cash outflow. This decrease should be added to the amount of cash expenses paid in order to calculate the amount of accrual-basis expenses.

NOTE: The easiest way to solve questions about converting cash-basis amounts into accrual-basis amounts and vice versa is by using the calculations described above.

Stop and review! You have completed the outline for this subunit. Study multiple-choice questions 6 and 7 on page 356.

14.4 THE ACCOUNTING PROCESS

1. **The Accounting System**

   a. An accounting system consists of a set of **accounts**, recorded in a **journal** and posted to a **ledger**. It records the effects of the transactions and other events and circumstances that must be recognized by the entity. The accounting system classifies the items, summarizes their effects, and reports the results in the form of **financial statements**.

   b. The accounting system is based on the **debit-credit** and **double-entry** convention. In accordance with the convention, a debit is an increase (decrease) in a given account, and a credit is a decrease (increase) in the same account. For each account, the balance equals the sum of the amounts debited and credited. Moreover, the monetary amount of the total debits must equal the total credits.

2. **Permanent and Temporary Accounts**

   a. Assets, liabilities, and equity are recorded in **permanent (real) accounts**. Their balances at the end of one accounting period (the balance sheet date) are carried forward as the beginning balances of the next accounting period.

   b. Revenues, expenses, gains, losses, and dividends are recorded in **temporary (nominal) accounts** because they record the transactions, events, and other circumstances during a period of time. These accounts are closed (reduced to zero) at the end of each accounting period, and their balances are transferred to real accounts.

      1) For example, the total of nominal accounts for the period (the net income or loss and the dividends) is transferred to the retained earnings (real) account. Thus, the ending retained earnings account equals the beginning amount, plus net income for the period (or minus net loss), minus dividends.

   c. An entity's **chart of accounts** names the accounts used in that entity's accounting system. The following table summarizes the application of the debit-credit convention:

	Permanent (Real) Accounts			Temporary (Nominal) Accounts	
	Balance Sheet			Income Statement	
	Assets	Liabilities	Equity (Net Assets)	Revenues & Gains	Expenses & Losses
Increase	Debit	Credit	Credit	Credit	Debit
Decrease	Credit	Debit	Debit	Debit	Credit

3. **Journal Entries and the Accounting Cycle**

   a. **Journal entries** record the financial effects of transactions, events, and other circumstances in the accounting system. For every journal entry, the total debited must equal the total credited. Every journal entry therefore must affect at least two accounts, and the effects (debit and credit) must be posted to specific accounts.

   b. The **accounting cycle** is the series of steps taken to maintain financial records in accordance with the accrual basis. After identification and measurement of items to be recorded, the steps in the accounting cycle are as follows:

   Step 1: Journalize transactions
   Step 2: Post journal entries to the ledgers
   Step 3: Prepare an unadjusted trial balance
   Step 4: Record entries to adjust accrued and deferred accounts
   Step 5: Prepare an adjusted trial balance
   Step 6: Prepare financial statements
   Step 7: Record entries to close temporary (nominal) accounts
   Step 8: Prepare a post-closing trial balance (optional)
   Step 9: Record entries to reverse the accrual entries (optional)

1) Journal entries are recorded in books of original entry (journals).

2) Accounts' balances are maintained in the **general ledger**. Journal entries may be posted to the appropriate ledgers either immediately (in real-time automated systems) or overnight (in batch systems).

3) The financial records must be closed at the end of each period before preparation of accrual-basis financial statements. The first step in the closing process is preparing an unadjusted trial balance.

   a) A **trial balance** is a report of the balances of every account in the general ledger, providing proof that total debits equal total credits.

4) **Adjusting entries** are made as of the balance sheet date to record the effects on periodic revenue and expense of deferrals (prepaid expenses and unearned revenues) and accruals (revenues earned but not yet realized in cash and expenses incurred but not yet paid in cash). Other adjustments also may be necessary, e.g., recognition of depreciation and amortization expense.

   a) The exact adjusting journal entry that should be recorded depends on how the original transaction was recorded in the first place.

EXAMPLE

In the prepaid insurance example at the top of page 339, assume that the payment for the 3 years of insurance premium was recognized as insurance expense at the beginning of the year:

(Dr) Insurance expense	US $120,000	
(Cr) Cash		US $120,000

This means that the insurance expense account and prepaid insurance account are reported in the unadjusted trial balance at US $120,000 and US $0, respectively. Since only one-third of the amount paid is for the current-year insurance, the correct accrual-basis balances that should be reported in the financial statements are US $40,000 for insurance expense and US $80,000 for prepaid insurance. Thus, the year-end adjusting entry is to decrease insurance expense by US $80,000 (Cr) and recognize prepaid insurance of US $80,000 (Dr):

(Dr) Prepaid insurance	US $80,000	
(Cr) Insurance expense		US $80,000

After the adjusting entry, the adjusted balance of insurance expense is US $40,000 ($120,000 – $80,000), and the adjusted balance of prepaid insurance is US $80,000.

Now assume that the payment for the 3 years of insurance premium was recognized as prepaid insurance at the beginning of the year:

(Dr) Prepaid insurance	US $120,000	
(Cr) Cash		US $120,000

This means that the insurance expense account and prepaid insurance account are reported in the unadjusted trial balance at US $0 and US $120,000, respectively. Thus, the year-end adjusting entry is to recognize insurance expense of US $40,000 (Dr) and decrease prepaid insurance by US $40,000 (Cr):

(Dr) Insurance expense	US $40,000	
(Cr) Prepaid insurance		US $40,000

After the adjusting entry, the adjusted balance of insurance expense is US $40,000, and the adjusted balance of prepaid insurance is US $80,000 ($120,000 – $40,000).

---

5) An adjusted trial balance is prepared to prove that total debits in the general ledger still equal total credits after the posting of adjusting entries.

6) The adjusted trial balance is used to prepare financial statements.

7) The temporary (nominal) accounts must now be closed (reduced to zero). Closing entries transfer (close) temporary account balances to the income summary account (net income or loss for the period). The income summary account is then transferred to retained earnings.

8) A post-closing trial balance can be prepared to prove that total debits in the general ledger still equal total credits after closing the nominal accounts.

9) Reversing entries reverse the effects of adjusting entries to simplify the future bookkeeping process.

Stop and review! You have completed the outline for this subunit. Study multiple-choice questions 8 and 9 on page 356.

14.5 CASH AND ACCOUNTS RECEIVABLE

1. **Cash**

   a. All cash balances on hand and on deposit that are readily available for current operating purposes are reported as cash. Restricted cash is reported under a separate caption. Because cash is the most liquid asset, it is usually the first asset listed on the balance sheet.

2. **Bank Reconciliation**

   a. A bank reconciliation is a schedule comparing the cash balance per books with the balance per bank statement (usually received monthly). The common approach is to reconcile both the bank balance and the book balance to reach the true balance. The bank and book balances usually vary. Thus, the reconciliation permits the entity to determine whether the difference is attributable to normal conditions, errors, or fraud. It is also a basis for entries to adjust the books to reflect unrecorded items.

      1) **Items known to the entity but not to the bank** are (a) outstanding checks, (b) deposits in transit, and (c) errors made by the bank.

      2) **Items known to the bank but not to the entity** are amounts added (collections and interest) or subtracted (or not added) by the bank (insufficient funds checks and service charges).

Common Reconciliation Items

	To Book Balance	To Bank Balance
Additions	Interest earned Deposits collected Errors	Deposits in transit Errors
Subtractions	Service charges NSF checks Errors	Outstanding checks Errors

3. **Accounts Receivable**

   a. Accounts receivable, often called trade receivables, are the amounts owed to an entity by its customers.

   b. Because collection in full of all accounts receivable is unlikely, they are reported at **net realizable value (NRV)**.

      1) NRV of accounts receivable equals gross accounts receivable minus allowance for uncollectible accounts.

      2) Thus, an allowance contra to accounts receivable is established. This method attempts to match bad debt expense with the related revenue.

      3) The bad debt expense recognized for the period increases the allowance for uncollectible accounts. The allowance for uncollectible accounts is a contra account to accounts receivable. Thus, the recognition of bad debt expense decreases the balance of accounts receivable.

   c. The two common methods of measuring bad debt expense and the allowance for uncollectible accounts are the percentage-of-sales method (an income statement approach) and the percentage-of-receivables method (a balance sheet approach).

    d.   The **allowance method** systematically records bad debt expense as a percentage of either sales or the level of accounts receivable on an annual basis.

        1)   Some customers are unwilling or unable to satisfy their debts. As specific accounts receivable are written off, they are charged to the allowance account.

Allowance for uncollectible accounts	US $XXX	
Accounts receivable		US $XXX

        2)   Thus, the write-off of a particular bad debt has no effect on bad debt expense. Write-offs do not affect the carrying amount of net accounts receivable because the reductions of gross accounts receivable and the allowance are the same.

    e.   The **income statement approach** calculates bad debt expense as a percentage of credit sales reported on the income statement.

EXAMPLE

A company's year-end unadjusted trial balance reports the following amounts:

Gross accounts receivable	US $100,000 Dr
Allowance for uncollectible accounts (year-beginning balance)	1,000 Cr
Sales on credit	250,000 Cr

According to past experience, 1% of the company's credit sales have been uncollectible. The company uses the income statement approach to calculate bad debt expense.

The bad debt expense recognized for the year is US $2,500 ($250,000 × 1%). The company records the following adjusting journal entry:

Bad debt expense	US $2,500	
Allowance for uncollectible accounts		US $2,500

The total adjusted balances of allowance for uncollectible accounts and bad debt expense are US $3,500 ($1,000 + $2,500) and US $2,500, respectively. The company reports net accounts receivable of US $96,500 ($100,000 − $3,500) in its balance sheet and bad debt expense of US $2,500 in its statement of income.

---

    f.   The **balance sheet approach** estimates the balance that should be recorded in the allowance based on the collectibility of ending gross accounts receivable. Bad debt expense is the amount necessary to adjust the allowance.

        1)   An entity rarely has a single rate of uncollectibility for all accounts. Thus, an entity using the balance sheet approach generally prepares an **aging schedule** for accounts receivable.

EXAMPLE of an Aging Schedule

	Balance		Percentage Historically Uncollectible		Balance Needed in Allowance
31 - 60 days old	US $440,000	×	2%	=	US $ 8,800
61 - 90 days old	120,000	×	8%	=	9,600
91 - 120 days old	75,000	×	11%	=	8,250
Over 120 days old	13,000	×	16%	=	2,080
Totals	US $648,000				US $28,730

---

        2)   If the beginning balance of the allowance was a credit of US $9,010, the entry is as follows:

Bad debt expense (US $28,730 − $9,010)	US $19,720	
Allowance for uncollectible accounts		US $19,720

g.   Occasionally, a customer will pay on an account previously written off.

1)   The first entry is to **reestablish the account** for the amount the customer has agreed to pay (any remainder remains written off).

Accounts receivable	US $XXX	
Allowance for uncollectible accounts		US $XXX

2)   The second entry records the receipt of cash.

Cash	US $XXX	
Accounts receivable		US $XXX

h.   Bad debt expense is not affected when (1) an account receivable is written off or (2) an account previously written off becomes collectible.

The following equation illustrates the reconciliation of the beginning and ending balances of the allowance for uncollectible accounts:

Beginning allowance for uncollectible accounts	US $XXX
Bad debt expense recognized for the period	XXX
Accounts receivable written off	(XXX)
Collection of accounts receivable previously written off	XXX
Ending allowance for uncollectible accounts	US $XXX

Under the income statement approach, bad debt expense is a percentage of sales on credit, and the ending balance of the allowance is calculated using the equation above.

Under the balance sheet approach, the ending balance of the allowance is a percentage of the ending balance of accounts receivable, and bad debt expense is calculated using the equation above.

Stop and review! You have completed the outline for this subunit. Study multiple-choice question 10 on page 357.

14.6 INVENTORY

1.   **Costs Included in Inventory**

a.   The cost of inventory includes the purchase price (net of allowances and returns), shipping charges, and any other costs necessary to bring the inventory to a location and condition ready for use.

1)   Goods shipped FOB shipping point are included in the buyer's inventory after they are shipped (while in transit).

2)   Goods shipped FOB destination are included in the seller's inventory until they are delivered at their destination.

3)   Goods on consignment are included in the seller's inventory.

a)   Under a consignment arrangement, the consignor ships goods to the consignee, who acts as a sales agent for the consignor. The goods are in the physical possession of the consignee but remain the property of the consignor and are included in its inventory.

b)   Revenue and the related cost of goods sold (including freight costs) for consigned goods are recognized by the consignor only upon sale and delivery to a customer. Accordingly, revenue recognition occurs when notification is received that the consignee has sold the goods.

2. **Inventory Systems**

   a. A **perpetual inventory** system tracks every item purchased and sold. This system is generally more suitable for entities that sell relatively expensive and heterogeneous items and require continuous monitoring of inventory and cost of goods sold accounts; automobile dealers are an example. Under this system,

      1) Purchases and other items related to inventory costing are charged directly to inventory.

      2) Inventory and cost of goods sold are adjusted as sales occur. Thus, the amount of inventory on hand and the cost of goods sold can be determined at any point of time.

      3) The bookkeeping is more complex and expensive. This is one disadvantage of the perpetual inventory system.

   b. In the **periodic inventory** system, inventory and cost of goods sold are updated at specific intervals, such as quarterly or annually, based on the results of a physical count. Bookkeeping is simpler under this system. Thus, entities with relatively inexpensive and homogeneous items, such as wheat dealers, that have no need to continuously monitor their inventory and cost of goods sold will generally use this system. Under the periodic system,

      1) Goods bought from suppliers and other items related to inventory costing usually are tracked during the period in a separate temporary account (purchases).

      2) The beginning inventory balance remains unchanged until the end of the period when the purchases account is closed.

      3) Changes in inventory and cost of goods sold are recorded only at the end of the period, based on the physical count.

3. **Ending Inventory and Cost of Goods Sold**

   a. Ending inventory affects both the statement of financial position (balance sheet) and the income statement.

      1) For a retailer, cost of goods sold is calculated based on changes in inventory:

<table>
<tr><td colspan="2" align="center"><u>Retailer</u></td></tr>
<tr><td>Beginning inventory</td><td>US $ XXX</td></tr>
<tr><td>Plus: net purchases</td><td>XXX</td></tr>
<tr><td>Plus: freight-in</td><td>XXX</td></tr>
<tr><td>Goods available for sale</td><td>US $ XXX</td></tr>
<tr><td>Minus: ending inventory</td><td>(XXX)</td></tr>
<tr><td>Cost of goods sold</td><td>US $ XXX</td></tr>
</table>

      2) For a manufacturer, cost of goods sold is calculated as follows:

<table>
<tr><td colspan="3" align="center"><u>Manufacturer</u></td></tr>
<tr><td>Beginning raw materials inventory</td><td>US $ XXX</td><td></td></tr>
<tr><td>Purchases during the period</td><td>XXX</td><td></td></tr>
<tr><td>Ending raw materials inventory</td><td>(XXX)</td><td></td></tr>
<tr><td>Direct materials used in production</td><td></td><td>US $XXX</td></tr>
<tr><td>Direct labor costs</td><td></td><td>XXX</td></tr>
<tr><td>Manufacturing overhead costs (fixed + variable)</td><td></td><td>XXX</td></tr>
<tr><td>Total manufacturing costs</td><td></td><td>US $ XXX</td></tr>
<tr><td>Beginning work-in-process inventory</td><td></td><td>XXX</td></tr>
<tr><td>Ending work-in-process inventory</td><td></td><td>(XXX)</td></tr>
<tr><td>Cost of goods manufactured</td><td></td><td>US $ XXX</td></tr>
<tr><td>Beginning finished goods inventory</td><td></td><td>XXX</td></tr>
<tr><td>Ending finished goods inventory</td><td></td><td>(XXX)</td></tr>
<tr><td>Cost of goods sold</td><td></td><td>US $ XXX</td></tr>
</table>

4.   **Inventory Cost Valuation Methods**

a.   **Specific Identification Method**

1)   The specific identification method requires determining which specific items are sold and thus reflects the actual physical flow of goods. Specific costs are attributed to identified items of inventory.

2)   This system is appropriate for items that are not ordinarily interchangeable and for items that are segregated for a specific project.

3)   Specific identification is the most accurate method since it identifies each item of inventory separately. However, it is also the most expensive since it requires detailed records.

b.   When the inventory items purchased/produced are identical and ordinarily interchangeable, the use of specific identification is inappropriate. In such circumstances, the acceptance of several assumptions with respect to the flow of cost factors such as **average**, **FIFO**, or **LIFO** may be appropriate for the measurement of periodic income. The selected method should be the one that, under the circumstances, most clearly reflects periodic income.

c.   **Average Method**

1)   The average method assumes that goods are indistinguishable and are therefore measured at an average of the costs incurred. The average may be calculated on the periodic basis or as each additional purchase occurs.

2)   The **moving-average method** is used under the **perpetual** inventory accounting system. It requires determination of a new weighted-average inventory cost after each purchase. This cost is used for every sale until the next purchase.

EXAMPLE

The following data relate to a company's Year 1 activities:

Date	Transaction	Number of units	Purchase price per unit (US $)	Sale price per unit (US $)
January 1	Beginning balance	100	20	
March 1	Purchase	20	32	
April 1	Sale	70		40
June 1	Purchase	30	14	
October 1	Sale	40		24

Under the **moving-average method**, the year-end inventory and Year 1 cost of goods sold are calculated as follows:

Date	Activity	Units	Price (US $)	Cost of inventory purchased (sold)	Inventory total balance	On-hand units	Cost per unit
January 1	Beg. bal.	100	20		US $2,000 (100 × 20)	100	**US $20**
March 1	Purchase	20	32	US $640 = 20 × US $32	US $2,640 (2,000 + 640)	120	**US $22** ($2,640 ÷ 120)
April 1	Sale	70	22	US $(1,540) = 70 × US $22	US $1,100 (2,640 − 1,540)	50	**US $22** ($1,100 ÷ 50)
June 1	Purchase	30	14	US $420 = 30 × US $14	US $1,520 (1,100 + 420)	80	**US $19** ($1,520 ÷ 80)
October 1	Sale	40	19	US $(760) = 40 × US $19	**US $760** (1,520 − 760)	40	**US $19** ($760 ÷ 40)

The cost of **inventory** on December 31, Year 1, is **US $760**. The Year 1 **cost of goods sold** is **US $2,300**.

Beginning inventory	US $2,000
Purchases (US $640 + $420)	1,060
Ending inventory	(760)
Cost of goods sold (US $1,540 + $760)	**US $2,300**

3) The **weighted-average method** is used under the **periodic** inventory accounting system. The average cost is determined only once, at the end of the period. The weighted-average cost per unit is used to calculate the amounts of period-end inventory and the cost of goods sold for the period.

a) The weighted-average cost per unit is calculated as follows:

$$\frac{\text{Cost of period-beginning inventory (\$) + Cost of purchases during the period (\$)}}{\text{Number of period-beginning inventory + Number of units purchased during the period}}$$

EXAMPLE

Under the **weighted-average method**, the year-end inventory and Year 1 cost of goods sold are calculated as follows:

First, the weighted-average cost per unit should be calculated.

$$\frac{\text{Cost of year-beginning inventory + Cost of purchases during the period}}{\text{Number of year-beginning inventory + Number of units purchased}} = \frac{\text{US \$2,000 + \$1,060}}{100 + 20 + 30} = \text{US \$20.4}$$

Then, by using the weighted-average cost per unit (WACPU), the year-end inventory and Year 1 cost of goods sold can be calculated:

Beginning inventory	US $2,000	
Purchases	1,060	
Ending inventory	(816)	(40 × $20.4) = (WACPU × Year end, number of inventory units)
Cost of goods sold	**US $2,244**	(110 × $20.4) = (WACPU × Number of units sold during the period)

---

d. **FIFO (First-In, First-Out) Method**

1) The FIFO method assumes that the first items of inventory purchased or produced are the first sold.

2) Ending inventory consists of the latest purchases or production output.

3) Under the FIFO method, year-end inventory and cost of goods sold for the period will be the same regardless of whether the perpetual or the periodic inventory accounting system is used.

EXAMPLE

Using the data from the example on the previous page, the year-end cost of inventory is calculated as follows:

Under the FIFO method, the cost of these 40 units consists of the **latest purchases** and is equal to **US $740**.

Date of purchase	Units	Price per unit	Total cost
June 1, Year 1	30	US $14	US $420
March 1, Year 1	10	32	320
Year-end inventory	**40**		**US $740**

The Year 1 cost of goods sold is equal to **US $2,320**.

Beginning inventory	US $2,000
Purchases (US $640 + $420)	1,060
Ending inventory	(740)
Cost of goods sold	**US $2,320**

---

e. **LIFO (Last-In, First-Out) Method**

1) The LIFO method assumes the newest items of inventory are sold first. Thus, the items remaining in inventory are recognized as if they were the oldest.

2) Under the LIFO method, the perpetual and the periodic inventory accounting systems may result in different amounts for the cost of year-end inventory and cost of goods sold.

3) LIFO is permissible under U.S. GAAP (U.S. generally accepted accounting principles) but not under IFRS (international financial reporting standards).

4) Under the **periodic** inventory accounting system, the calculation of inventory and cost of goods sold is made at the end of the period.

EXAMPLE

In the previous example, we determined that the number of units at year end is 40. The year-end cost of inventory is therefore calculated as follows:

Under the LIFO method, the cost of these 40 units consists of the **earliest purchases** (beginning inventory) equal to **US $800** ($20 × 40).

The Year 1 cost of goods sold is equal to **US $2,260**.

Beginning inventory	US $2,000
Purchases (US $640 + $420)	1,060
Year-end inventory	(800)
Cost of goods sold (US $1,540 + $760)	**US $2,260**

---

5) Under the **perpetual** inventory accounting system, the cost of goods sold is calculated every time the sale occurs and consists of the most recent (latest) purchases.

5. **Inventory Estimation**

   a. An estimate of inventory may be needed when an exact count is not feasible, e.g., for interim reporting purposes or when inventory records have been destroyed. The gross profit method may be used for inventory estimation.

      1) Gross profit margin (gross profit percentage) equals gross profit divided by sales.

      2) The following calculation is used to estimate the ending inventory and cost of goods sold:

Gross Profit Method

Beginning inventory		US $ XXX
Purchases		XXX
Goods available for sale		US $ XXX
Sales	US $ XXX	
Gross profit (Sales × Gross profit margin)	(XXX)	
Costs of goods sold [Sales × (1 – gross profit margin)]		(XXX)
Ending inventory		US $ XXX

EXAMPLE

A retailer needs to estimate ending inventory for quarterly reporting purposes. The firm's best estimate of the gross percentage is its historical rate of 25%. The following additional information is available:

Net sales	US $1,000,000
Purchases	300,000
Beginning inventory	800,000

Estimated cost of goods sold for the quarter is US $750,000 [$1,000,000 × (1 – 25%)]. Estimated ending inventory is therefore US $350,000 ($800,000 + $300,000 – $750,000).

Stop and review! You have completed the outline for this subunit. Study multiple-choice questions 11 through 15 beginning on page 357.

14.7 PROPERTY, PLANT, AND EQUIPMENT AND INTANGIBLE ASSETS

1. **Overview**

   a. Property, plant, and equipment (PPE), also called fixed assets, consists of tangible property expected to benefit the entity for more than 1 year that is held for the production or supply of goods or services, rental to others, or administrative purposes.

2. **PPE -- Initial Measurement**

    a. The historical/initial cost of PPE includes

        1) The net purchase price (minus trade discounts and rebates, plus purchase taxes and import duties) and

        2) The directly attributable costs of bringing the asset to the location and condition needed for its intended operation, such as architects' and engineers' fees, site preparation, delivery and handling, installation, assembly, and testing.

    b. Interest (borrowing costs) attributable to the acquisition, construction, or production of a PPE asset constructed for internal use is included in its initial cost.

3. **PPE -- Subsequent Expenditures**

    a. **Capital expenditures** provide additional benefits by improving the quality of services rendered by the asset, extending its useful life, or increasing its output. These expenditures are capitalized to the asset's cost.

    b. **Revenue expenditures** (expenses) maintain an asset's normal service capacity. These costs are recurring, are not expected to benefit future periods, and are expensed as incurred.

        1) Routine, minor expenditures made to maintain the operating efficiency of PPE are ordinarily expensed as incurred.

4. **PPE -- Measurement Subsequent to Initial Recognition**

    a. An item of PPE is reported in the financial statements at its carrying amount. This amount is equal to the historical cost minus accumulated depreciation and impairment losses.

Historical/initial cost	US $ XXX
Accumulated depreciation	(XXX)
Impairment losses	(XXX)
Asset's carrying amount	US $ XXX

5. **PPE -- Depreciation**

    a. **Depreciation** is the process of systematically and rationally allocating the depreciable base of a tangible capital asset over its expected useful life. The periodic depreciation expense is recognized in the income statement. Accumulated depreciation is a contra-asset account.

        1) The debit is to depreciable expense, and the credit is to accumulated depreciation.

    b. The asset's **depreciable base** (i.e., the amount to be allocated) is calculated as follows:

Depreciable base = Historical cost – Estimated salvage value (residual value)

    c. **Estimated useful life** is the period over which the entity expects to receive services/ economic benefits from the asset.

    d. **Salvage value** is the amount that the entity expects to obtain from disposal of the asset at the end of the asset's useful life.

    e. Land has an indefinite useful life and therefore must not be depreciated. Thus, the depreciable base of property that consists of land and/or a building is the depreciable base of the building.

EXAMPLE of Depreciable Base Calculation

At the beginning of Year 1, a manufacturer paid US $270,000 for a new machine.

Depreciable base = US $270,000 – $20,000 = US $250,000

The entity estimates that, at the end of the machine's 5-year useful life, it will be able to sell the machine for US $20,000.

6. **Depreciation Methods**

    a. **Straight-line** (S-L) depreciation allocates the depreciable base evenly over the estimated useful life of the asset. This is the simplest method because an equal amount of depreciation is charged to each period of the asset's useful life.

$$Periodic\ depreciation\ expense = \frac{Depreciable\ base}{Estimated\ useful\ life}$$

EXAMPLE of Straight-Line Depreciation

A manufacturer applies straight-line depreciation:

Year	Depreciable Base	Estimated Useful Life	Depreciation Expense	Accumulated Depreciation	Carrying Amount at Year End
1	US $250,000	5	US $50,000	US $ 50,000	US $220,000
2	250,000	5	50,000	100,000	170,000
3	250,000	5	50,000	150,000	120,000
4	250,000	5	50,000	200,000	70,000
5	250,000	5	50,000	250,000	20,000

---

    b. **The units-of-production** method allocates a proportional amount of the asset's cost based on its level of output.

$$Periodic\ depreciation\ expense = Depreciable\ base \times \frac{Units\ produced\ during\ current\ period}{Estimated\ total\ lifetime\ units}$$

    c. Accelerated depreciation methods, such as the declining balance and sum-of-the-years'-digits methods, result in decreasing depreciation charges over the life of the asset.

7. **PPE -- Disposal**

    a. When an item of PPE is sold, the gain or loss on disposal is the difference between the net proceeds and the carrying amount of the asset. Depreciation (if any) is recognized to the date of sale, the carrying amount is removed from the books, the proceeds are recorded, and any gain or loss is recognized.

        1) A gain on disposal is recognized if the proceeds are greater than the carrying amount.

        2) A loss on disposal is recognized if the proceeds are lower than the carrying amount.

8. **PPE -- Reconciliation Equation**

    a. The following calculation illustrates the changes in the carrying amount of the PPE account during the period:

Beginning PPE	US $ XXX
Purchases during the period	XXX
Depreciation expense	(XXX)
Disposals during the period	(XXX)
Ending PPE	US $ XXX

9. **Intangible Assets -- Definition**

    a. An intangible asset is an identifiable, nonmonetary asset that lacks physical substance. Examples of intangible assets include licenses, patents, copyrights, franchises, and trademarks.

    b. Internally generated goodwill must not be recognized as an asset, but goodwill acquired in a business combination is recognized as an intangible asset.

10. Intangible Assets -- Amortization

a. An intangible asset is carried at cost minus any accumulated amortization and impairment losses.

b. Amortization of an intangible asset with a **finite useful life** begins when it is available for use. Its amortizable amount is systematically allocated over its useful life (much like depreciation for PPE items).

c. An intangible asset with an **indefinite useful life** is not amortized. Instead, it is tested for impairment at least annually.

11. Internally Developed Intangible Assets

a. Under U.S. GAAP, **research and development** (R&D) costs must be **expensed as incurred** and are never capitalized. Thus, **internally developed** intangible assets are not recognized on the balance sheet. For example, R&D cost incurred in developing a patent must be expensed, and no intangible asset is recognized. However, an acquired patent must be recognized as an intangible asset at cost.

     1) **Research** is planned search or critical investigation aimed at discovery of new knowledge.

     2) **Development** is translation of research findings or other knowledge into a plan or design for a new or improved product or process.

b. Under IFRS, research costs must be expensed as incurred. But development costs may result in recognition of intangible assets if certain criteria are met.

Stop and review! You have completed the outline for this subunit. Study multiple-choice questions 16 through 18 on page 359.

14.8 THE TIME VALUE OF MONEY

1. Time Value and Interest

a. A quantity of money to be received or paid in the future ordinarily is worth less than the same amount now. The difference is measured in terms of interest calculated using the appropriate discount rate.

     1) Interest is paid by a borrower or investee to a lender or investor for the use of money. It is a percentage of the amount (the principal) borrowed or invested.

b. Time value of money concepts have many applications. For example, they affect the accounting for noncurrent receivables and payables (bonds and notes), leases, and certain employee benefits.

2. The Present Value of a Single Amount

a. The present value (PV) of an amount is the value today of some future payment. It equals the future payment times the present value of 1 (a factor found in a standard table) for the given number of periods and interest rate.

EXAMPLE of Factors for PV of an Amount

No. of Periods	Present Value		
	6%	8%	10%
1	0.943	0.926	0.909
2	0.890	0.857	0.826
3	0.840	0.794	0.751
4	0.792	0.735	0.683
5	0.747	0.681	0.621

The present value of US $1,000, to be received in 3 years and discounted at 8%, is US $794 ($1,000 × 0.794).

3. **Present Value of Annuities**

   a. An annuity is a series of equal payments at equal intervals of time, e.g., US $1,000 at the end of every year for 10 years.

      1) An **ordinary annuity** (annuity in arrears) is a series of payments occurring at the end of each period.

      2) An **annuity due** (annuity in advance) is a series of payments occurring at the beginning of each period.

   b. The PV of an annuity is the value today of a series of future equal payments at equal intervals discounted at a given rate.

EXAMPLE of PV of an Ordinary Annuity

The present value factor of an ordinary annuity of 1 at 11% for 7 periods is 4.712. The present value of seven payments of US $5,000 made at the end of each period and discounted at 11% equals US $23,560 ($5,000 × 4.712).

---

4. **The Future Value (FV) of an Amount**

   a. The FV of an amount is the amount available at a specified time in the future based on a single investment (deposit) today.

   b. The interest factor for the FV of a present amount equals the reciprocal of the interest factor for the PV of a future amount, assuming the same interest rate and number of periods.

      1) For example, the factor for the FV of an amount is 1.191 for three periods at 6%. Thus, the factor for the PV of an amount for three periods at 6% is 0.840 (1 ÷ 1.191).

EXAMPLE

Future Value Factor of a Single Amount

No. of Periods	6%	8%	**10%**
1	1.060	1.080	1.100
2	1.124	1.166	1.210
3	1.191	1.260	1.331
4	1.262	1.360	**1.464**
5	1.338	1.469	1.610

The future value of US $1,000 invested today for 4 years at 10% interest will be US $1,464 ($1,000 present value of a single amount × 1.464 future value factor).

Stop and review! You have completed the outline for this subunit. Study multiple-choice question 19 on page 360.

14.9 BONDS

1. **Nature of Bonds**

   a. A bond is a formal contract to pay an amount of money (face amount) at the maturity date plus interest at the stated rate at specific intervals.

EXAMPLE

At the beginning of the year, a company issues 200 8%, 5-year, US $5,000 bonds. Annual cash interest payments will be made at the end of each year. The total face amount of bonds issued is US $1,000,000 (200 bonds × $5,000 face amount), and the annual interest payment is US $80,000 ($1,000,000 face amount × 8% stated rate).

---

b. The proceeds received from the investors on the day the bonds are sold equal the present value of the sum of the future cash flows expected to be received from the bonds. These proceeds equal

1) The present value of the face amount plus
2) The present value of the annuity of interest payments.

c. The bonds are recognized in the financial statements as the amount of proceeds paid for them, i.e., the face amount of the bonds plus any premium or minus any discount,

1) As a debt in the issuer's financial statements
2) As an investment in the investors' financial statements

2. **Bond Issuance**

a. The cash proceeds from the sale of bonds can be equal to, less than, or greater than the face amount of the bonds depending on the relationship of the bonds' stated rate of interest to the market rate of interest on the date the bonds are sold.

1) If the stated rate is equal to the market rate, the cash proceeds equal the face amount of the bonds.
2) If the stated rate is greater than the current market rate, the cash proceeds are greater than the face amount, and the bonds are sold at **premium**.
3) If the stated rate is lower than the current market rate, the cash proceeds are lower than the face amount, and the bonds are sold at **discount**.

b. The current market rate of interest is used to discount the cash flows expected to be received by the investor (paid by the issuer) from the bonds.

EXAMPLE

The following calculation uses the data from the previous example and the following present value factors:

	At 6%	At 10%
Present value of 1 for 5 periods	0.747	0.621
Present value of ordinary annuity of 1 for 5 periods	4.212	3.791

(1) Assume that the market interest rate was 6% on the date the bonds were issued.

Present value of face amount (US $1,000,000 × 0.747)	US $ 747,000
Present value of cash interest (US $80,000 × 4.212)	336,960
Cash proceeds from bonds issue	US $1,083,960

The amount of premium is US $83,960 ($1,083,960 proceeds – $1,000,000 face amount).

(2) Assume that the market interest rate was 10% on the date the bonds were issued.

Present value of face amount (US $1,000,000 × 0.621)	US $621,000
Present value of cash interest (US $80,000 × 3.791)	303,280
Cash proceeds from bonds issue	US $924,280

The amount of discount is US $75,720 ($1,000,000 face amount – $924,280 proceeds).

---

3. **Amortization of Premium or Discount**

a. Bond premium or discount must be amortized over the life of the bonds using the **effective-interest method** (the market interest rate on the date the bond was sold). Under this method, interest expense changes every period and equals the following:

> *Annual interest expense = Carrying amount of the bond*
> *at the beginning of the period × Effective interest rate*

    b.   The annual interest expense consists of the cash interest paid plus the effect of amortization of premium or discount.

        1)   When the bond is issued at premium, annual interest expense equals cash interest paid minus the amount of premium amortized.

        2)   When the bond is issued at discount, annual interest expense equals cash interest paid plus the amount of discount amortized.

        3)   The carrying amount of bonds as they are presented in the financial statements equals the face amount plus the premium (or minus the discount).

EXAMPLE of Amortization of a Premium and Discount

Using the data from the previous example, the following interest expense will be recognized by the company in the first 2 years of the bonds:

(1) When market interest rate was 6% and bonds were issued at premium:

	A					B		A – B
Year	Beginning Carrying Amount of Bonds	Market Interest Rate	Interest Expense	Cash Interest Paid		Premium Amortized	Remaining Premium	Ending Carrying Amount of Bonds
1	US $1,083,960	× 6%	= US $65,038	– US $80,000	=	US $14,962	US $68,998	US $1,068,998
2	1,068,998	× 6%	= 64,140	– 80,000	=	15,860	53,138	1,053,138

(2) When market interest rate was 10% and bonds were issued at discount:

	A					B		A + B
Year	Beginning Carrying Amount of Bonds	Market Interest Rate	Interest Expense	Cash Interest Paid		Discount Amortized	Remaining Discount	Ending Carrying Amount of Bonds
1	US $924,280	× 10%	= US $92,428	– US $80,000	=	US $12,428	US $63,292	US $936,708
2	936,708	× 10%	= 93,671	– 80,000	=	13,671	49,621	950,379

---

        4)   At the maturity date, the discount or premium is fully amortized, and the carrying amount of the bonds equals the face amount.

Stop and review! You have completed the outline for this subunit. Study multiple-choice question 20 on page 360.

QUESTIONS

14.1 Concepts of Financial Accounting

1. A newly acquired plant asset is to be depreciated over its useful life. The rationale for this process is the

    A.   Economic entity assumption.

    B.   Monetary unit assumption.

    C.   Materiality assumption.

    D.   Going concern assumption.

Answer (D) is correct.
    REQUIRED: The rationale for depreciation.
    DISCUSSION: A basic feature of financial accounting is that the entity is assumed to be a going concern in the absence of evidence to the contrary. The going concern concept is based on the empirical observation that many entities have an indefinite life. The reporting entity is assumed to have a life long enough to fulfill its objectives and commitments and therefore to depreciate wasting assets over their useful lives.
    Answer (A) is incorrect. The economic entity assumption provides that economic activity can be identified with a particular unit of accountability. Answer (B) is incorrect. The monetary unit assumption provides that all transactions and events can be measured in terms of a common denominator, for instance, the euro. Answer (C) is incorrect. Materiality is an entity-specific aspect of relevance, a fundamental qualitative characteristic. Information is material if it can influence a user's decision. Thus, in the case of plant assets, certain items may be expensed rather than capitalized and depreciated because they are not material. The difference in treatment is not large enough to influence users if the item is not material.

2. An objective of financial reporting is

   A. Providing information useful to investors, creditors, donors, and other users for decision making.

   B. Assessing the adequacy of internal control.

   C. Evaluating management results compared with standards.

   D. Providing information on compliance with established procedures.

Answer (A) is correct.

   REQUIRED: The objective of financial reporting.

   DISCUSSION: The objective is to report financial information that is useful in making decisions about providing resources to the reporting entity. Primary users of financial information are current or prospective investors and creditors who cannot obtain it directly. Their decisions depend on expected returns.

   Answer (B) is incorrect. Assessing the adequacy of internal control is a function of internal auditing, not financial reporting. Answer (C) is incorrect. Evaluating management results compared with standards is a function of internal auditing, not financial reporting. Answer (D) is incorrect. Providing information on compliance with established procedures is a function of internal auditing, not financial reporting.

14.2 Financial Statements

3. The management of ABC Corporation is analyzing the financial statements of XYZ Corporation because ABC is strongly considering purchasing a block of XYZ ordinary shares that would give ABC significant influence over XYZ. Which financial statement should ABC primarily use to assess the amounts, timing, and certainty of future cash flows of XYZ Company?

   A. Income statement.

   B. Statement of changes in equity.

   C. Statement of cash flows.

   D. Statement of financial position.

Answer (C) is correct.

   REQUIRED: The financial statement used to assess the amounts, timing, and uncertainty of future cash flows.

   DISCUSSION: A statement of cash flows provides information about the cash receipts and cash payments of an entity during a period. This information helps investors, creditors, and other users to assess the entity's ability to generate cash and cash equivalents and the needs of the entity to use those cash flows. Historical cash flow data indicate the amount, timing, and certainty of future cash flows. It is also a means of verifying past cash flow assessments and of determining the relationship between profits and net cash flows and the effects of changing prices.

   Answer (A) is incorrect. The statement of income is prepared on an accrual basis and is not meant to report cash flows. Answer (B) is incorrect. The statement of changes in equity is prepared on the accrual basis. Answer (D) is incorrect. The statement of financial position reports on financial position at a moment in time.

4. Suppose that an entity has paid one of its liabilities twice during the year, in error. The effects of this mistake would be

   A. Assets, liabilities, and equity are understated.

   B. Assets, net income, and equity are unaffected.

   C. Assets and liabilities are understated.

   D. Assets and net income and equity are understated, and liabilities are overstated.

Answer (C) is correct.

   REQUIRED: The effects of paying a liability twice.

   DISCUSSION: When a liability is paid, an entry debiting accounts payable and crediting cash is made. If an entity erroneously pays a liability twice, the accounts payable and cash accounts will be understated by the amount of the liability. Hence, assets and liabilities will be understated.

   Answer (A) is incorrect. The double payment of a liability does not affect expenses of the period so it does not affect net income and equity. Answer (B) is incorrect. Assets will be reduced. Answer (D) is incorrect. Both assets and liabilities will be understated, and net income and equity will be unaffected.

5. In a statement of cash flows (indirect method), depreciation expense should be presented as

   A. An inflow of cash.

   B. An outflow of cash.

   C. An addition to net income in converting net income or loss to net cash flows from operating activities.

   D. A deduction from net income in converting net income or loss to net cash flows from operating activities.

Answer (C) is correct.

   REQUIRED: The presentation of depreciation expense in a statement of cash flows (indirect method).

   DISCUSSION: Under the indirect method, net income is reconciled to cash flow from operating activities. The net income for the period was calculated using the accrual method of accounting. Depreciation expense is a noncash expense included in net income. Thus, it must be added to net income to determine the net cash flow from operating activities.

   Answer (A) is incorrect. Depreciation does not involve an inflow or outflow of cash. Depreciation is a noncash operating expense. Answer (B) is incorrect. Depreciation is a noncash operating expense. Answer (D) is incorrect. Depreciation expense should be added.

14.3　The Accrual Basis of Accounting

6. To calculate net sales, an increase in <List A> must be <List B> cash receipts from customers.

	List A	List B
A.	Accounts receivable	Added to
B.	Accounts receivable	Subtracted from
C.	Accounts payable	Added to
D.	Accounts payable	Subtracted from

Answer (A) is correct.
REQUIRED: The calculation of net sales.
DISCUSSION: To convert from the cash basis (cash receipts) to the accrual basis (net sales), the increase in net accounts receivable must be added to cash receipts from customers.

7. The publisher of a popular magazine offers a special discounted price for a 3-year subscription. At the end of the reporting period, the amount that has already been collected but pertains to future periods is best referred to as

A. Accrued subscriptions revenue (an asset account).

B. Deferred subscriptions revenue (a liability account).

C. Earned subscriptions revenue (a revenue account).

D. Precollected subscriptions receivable (a deferred asset account).

Answer (B) is correct.
REQUIRED: The best description of revenue that has already been collected but pertains to future periods.
DISCUSSION: Revenue is recognized in the period in which the recognition criteria are met. Thus, when it is received in advance, the amount applicable to future periods is deferred. This deferral arises because the entity still must satisfy an obligation to perform in the future before it is entitled to the future economic benefits. The amount received in advance is considered a liability because it represents a present obligation arising from a past event. Accordingly, deferred or unearned revenue is an amount that has been received but that has not met the recognition criteria for revenue.
Answer (A) is incorrect. An accrued revenue is revenue that has met the recognition criteria but has not been received. Answer (C) is incorrect. The revenue will be recognized in future periods when forthcoming issues of the magazine are published and distributed to the subscribers. Answer (D) is incorrect. "Precollected receivable" is not a standard accounting term.

14.4　The Accounting Process

8. The correct order of the following steps of the accounting cycle is

A. Posting, closing, adjusting, reversing.

B. Posting, adjusting, closing, reversing.

C. Posting, reversing, adjusting, closing.

D. Adjusting, posting, closing, reversing.

Answer (B) is correct.
REQUIRED: The proper sequence of steps in the accounting cycle.
DISCUSSION: After identification and measurement of items to be recorded, the steps in the accounting cycle are, in order, (1) journalizing transactions, (2) posting journal entries to the ledgers, (3) preparing an unadjusted trial balance, (4) recording adjusting entries, (5) preparing an adjusted trial balance, (6) preparing financial statements, (7) closing temporary (nominal) accounts, (8) preparing a post-closing trial balance (optional), and (9) reversing the accrual entries (optional).
Answer (A) is incorrect. Adjusting entries are made prior to closing. Answer (C) is incorrect. Reversing entries are made after adjustments and closing entries. Answer (D) is incorrect. Posting is done prior to adjusting.

9. In performing an audit, you encounter an adjusting journal entry recorded at year end that contains a debit to rental revenue and a credit to unearned rental revenue. The purpose of this journal entry is to record

A. Accrued revenue.

B. Unexpired cost.

C. Expired cost.

D. Deferred revenues.

Answer (D) is correct.
REQUIRED: The purpose of an adjusting entry debiting rental revenue and crediting deferred revenue rental.
DISCUSSION: A deferred revenue is a revenue item that has been received but has not met the recognition criteria. The journal entry described in the question is an adjusting entry to transfer an amount from the revenue account to a liability (deferred revenue) account. The initial collection of cash in advance from the tenant was apparently recorded by a credit to revenue. An adjusting entry is therefore required at year end to transfer any remaining amount that does not qualify for revenue recognition.
Answer (A) is incorrect. An accrued revenue has met the recognition criteria but has not yet been received. The journal entry described indicates that collection has been made. Answer (B) is incorrect. The entry concerns a revenue rather than an expense transaction. Answer (C) is incorrect. The entry concerns a revenue rather than an expense transaction.

14.5 Cash and Accounts Receivable

10. On January 1, a new landscaping firm, Bandit27 Co., acquired a fleet of vehicles, all the necessary tools and equipment, and a parking and storage facility. It began operations immediately. It is now the end of the first year of operations, and the first set of year-end financial statements is being prepared.

During the first year of operations, the company experienced a 5% bad debt rate on credit sales. None of the bad debts are expected to be recovered, given that 5% is the industry average level of bad debts. Total credit sales for the year were US $400,000. The year-end balance of accounts receivable includes uncollected overdue accounts of US $100,000. Half of the uncollected overdue amounts are estimated to be uncollectible. If Bandit27 Co. uses the <List A> approach to estimate bad debt expense, the estimated bad debt expense will be <List B>.

	List A	List B
A.	Statement of financial position	US $20,000
B.	Statement of financial position	US $100,000
C.	Income statement	US $20,000
D.	Income statement	US $50,000

Answer (C) is correct.
 REQUIRED: The estimated bad debts.
 DISCUSSION: Using the income statement approach, the bad debt expense is determined using a percentage of total credit sales. Thus, bad debt expense is US $20,000 ($400,000 credit sales × 5% estimated bad debt rate).
 Answer (A) is incorrect. US $20,000 is the bad debt expense calculated using the income statement approach. Answer (B) is incorrect. Under the statement of financial position approach, the amount estimated to be uncollectible is US $50,000 ($100,000 × 50%). Answer (D) is incorrect. The estimated bad debt expense using the statement of financial position approach is US $50,000.

14.6 Inventory

11. The cost of materials has risen steadily over the year. Which of the following methods of estimating the ending balance of the materials inventory account will result in the highest profit, assuming all other variables remain constant?

 A. Last-in, first-out (LIFO).

 B. First-in, first-out (FIFO).

 C. Weighted average.

 D. Specific identification.

Answer (B) is correct.
 REQUIRED: The inventory flow assumption yielding the highest profit given rising prices.
 DISCUSSION: Profit will be higher when cost of goods sold is lower, other factors held constant. Cost of goods sold equals beginning inventory, plus purchases, minus ending inventory. Accordingly, cost of goods sold will be lowest when the ending inventory is highest. In an inflationary environment, ending inventory is highest under FIFO because the older, less expensive items are deemed to have been sold, leaving the more expensive items in the ending inventory.
 Answer (A) is incorrect. LIFO yields the lowest profit. Answer (C) is incorrect. In an inflationary environment, weighted average results in a lower profit than FIFO. Answer (D) is incorrect. Under specific identification, the newest (most expensive) items are not necessarily in the ending inventory. The result is a higher cost of goods sold and lower profit than under FIFO.

12. A retail entity maintains a markup of 25% based on cost. The entity has the following information for the current year:

Purchases of merchandise	US $690,000
Freight-in on purchases	25,000
Sales	900,000
Ending inventory	80,000

Beginning inventory was

 A. US $40,000

 B. US $85,000

 C. US $110,000

 D. US $265,000

Answer (B) is correct.
 REQUIRED: The beginning inventory.
 DISCUSSION: Cost of goods sold for a period equals beginning inventory, plus purchases, plus freight-in, minus ending inventory. Given that sales reflect 125% of cost, cost of goods sold must equal US $720,000 ($900,000 sales ÷ 1.25). Consequently, the beginning inventory must have been US $85,000 ($720,000 COGS + $80,000 EI – $690,000 purchases – $25,000 freight-in).
 Answer (A) is incorrect. US $40,000 is based on a 25% markup on sales. Answer (C) is incorrect. US $110,000 results from omitting freight-in from the computation of cost of goods available for sale. Answer (D) is incorrect. US $265,000 results from using the sales figure for cost of goods sold.

13. An entity had the following account balances in the pre-closing trial balance:

Opening inventory	US $100,000
Closing inventory	150,000
Purchases	400,000
Transportation-in	6,000
Purchase discounts	40,000
Purchase allowances	15,000
Returned purchases	5,000

The entity had net purchases for the period of

A. US $340,000

B. US $346,000

C. US $370,000

D. US $376,000

Answer (B) is correct.

REQUIRED: The net purchases.

DISCUSSION: Purchase discounts, allowances, and returns are subtractions from purchases because they are reductions of cost. Transportation-in is an addition because it increases cost. Thus, net purchases equals US $346,000 ($400,000 + $6,000 – $40,000 – $15,000 – $5,000).

Answer (A) is incorrect. Failing to include transportation-in in the calculation results in US $340,000. Answer (C) is incorrect. Improperly omitting transportation-in and adding, rather than subtracting, purchase allowances results in US $370,000. Answer (D) is incorrect. Improperly adding, rather than subtracting, purchase allowances results in US $376,000.

14. The following selected data from statements of financial position on December 31, Year 1, and December 31, Year 2, are presented below:

	12/31/Year 1	12/31/Year 2
Inventory	US $120,000	US $140,000
Trade accounts payable	62,000	49,000

Additional information for Year 2:

1. Cash payments to suppliers of merchandise were US $180,000.

Cost of goods sold in Year 2 was

A. US $147,000

B. US $160,000

C. US $167,000

D. US $180,000

Answer (A) is correct.

REQUIRED: The cost of goods sold.

DISCUSSION: Cost of goods sold equals beginning inventory, plus purchases, minus ending inventory. To determine cost of goods sold, purchases must be calculated. Purchases equal US $167,000 ($49,000 ending accounts payable + $180,000 payments to suppliers – $62,000 beginning accounts payable). Thus, cost of goods sold equals US $147,000 ($120,000 beginning inventory + $167,000 purchases – $140,000 ending inventory).

Answer (B) is incorrect. US $160,000 results from assuming that US $180,000 of cash payments to suppliers equaled purchases. Answer (C) is incorrect. US $167,000 equals purchases. Answer (D) is incorrect. US $180,000 is the amount of cash payments to suppliers.

15. The following information is available for an entity for the quarter ended March 31 of the current year:

Merchandise inventory, as of January 1 of the current year	US $ 30,000
Sales	200,000
Purchases	190,000

The gross profit margin is normally 20% of sales. What is the estimated cost of the merchandise inventory at March 31 of the current year?

A. US $20,000

B. US $40,000

C. US $60,000

D. US $180,000

Answer (C) is correct.

REQUIRED: The estimated cost of merchandise inventory.

DISCUSSION: Using the gross profit method, cost of goods sold for the quarter is estimated to be US $160,000 [$200,000 sales × (1.0 – 0.2)]. Goods available for sale was US $220,000 ($30,000 beginning inventory + $190,000 purchases). Estimated ending inventory is therefore US $60,000 ($220,000 goods available for sale – $160,000 estimated cost of goods sold).

Answer (A) is incorrect. The difference between sales for the period and cost of goods available for sale is US $20,000. Answer (B) is incorrect. The amount of gross profit is US $40,000. Answer (D) is incorrect. Improperly subtracting the gross profit from cost of goods available for sale results in US $180,000.

14.7 Property, Plant, and Equipment and Intangible Assets

16. A theme park purchased a new, exciting ride and financed it through the manufacturer. The following facts pertain:

Purchase price	US $800,000
Delivery cost	50,000
Installation cost	70,000
Cost of trial runs	40,000
Interest charges for first year	60,000

The straight-line method is to be used. Compute the depreciation on the equipment for the first year assuming an estimated service life of 5 years.

    A. US $160,000

    B. US $184,000

    C. US $192,000

    D. US $204,000

Answer (C) is correct.
    REQUIRED: The depreciation expense.
    DISCUSSION: Under the straight-line method, the annual depreciation expense for an asset equals the asset's amount (cost – residual value) divided by the asset's estimated useful life. The cost of the asset includes its price and the directly attributable costs of bringing it to working condition for intended use. Thus, the depreciation expense is US $192,000 [($800,000 purchase price + $50,000 delivery cost + $70,000 installation cost + $40,000 trial-run cost) ÷ 5-year estimated service life]. Borrowing costs incurred after the asset is prepared for its intended use are expensed even if the allowed alternative treatment of such costs is followed, and the asset otherwise satisfies the criteria for capitalization of such expenses.
    Answer (A) is incorrect. US $160,000 excludes the delivery, installation, and trial-run costs. Answer (B) is incorrect. US $184,000 excludes the trial-run cost. Answer (D) is incorrect. US $204,000 includes the borrowing costs.

17. An entity sells a piece of machinery, for cash, prior to the end of its estimated useful life. The sale price is less than the carrying amount of the asset on the date of sale. The entry that the entity uses to record the sale is

    A. Cash
        Accumulated depreciation -- machinery
        Loss on disposal of machinery
            Machinery

    B. Cash
        Accumulated depreciation -- machinery
            Gain on disposal of machinery
            Machinery

    C. Cash
        Expense -- disposal of machinery
            Accumulated depreciation -- machinery
            Machinery

    D. Cash
        Machinery
            Accumulated depreciation -- machinery
            Gain on disposal of machinery

Answer (A) is correct.
    REQUIRED: The entry to record sale of machinery at less than its carrying amount.
    DISCUSSION: Cash is debited for the amount of the sale proceeds. Machinery and the related accumulated depreciation are eliminated by a credit and a debit, respectively. Because the sale price was less than the carrying amount of the asset on the date of sale, a loss on disposal should be recognized in net income or loss.
    Answer (B) is incorrect. A loss on disposal should be recognized in net income. Answer (C) is incorrect. Accumulated depreciation should be debited. Answer (D) is incorrect. A loss and accumulated depreciation should be debited.

18. An entity purchases office equipment for US $525,000 on account. Select the appropriate journal entry to record this transaction.

    A. Office expense   US $525,000
        Accounts payable   US $525,000

    B. Office equipment   US $525,000
        Accounts payable   US $525,000

    C. Accounts payable   US $525,000
        Office expense   US $525,000

    D. Accounts payable   US $525,000
        Office equipment   US $525,000

Answer (B) is correct.
    REQUIRED: The appropriate journal entry to record a purchase of equipment on account.
    DISCUSSION: The purchase of office equipment represents the acquisition of an asset. An increase in an asset is recorded by a debit. The purchase on account increases liabilities. An increase in a liability is recorded by a credit.
    Answer (A) is incorrect. The charge would be to an expense account only if the amount were immaterial. Answer (C) is incorrect. An increase in accounts payable is recorded by a credit. The purchase of equipment results in an asset that is recorded by a debit to an asset account. Also, the charge would be to an expense account only if the amount were immaterial. Answer (D) is incorrect. An increase in a liability is recorded by a credit. An increase in an asset is recorded by a debit.

14.8   The Time Value of Money

19. If the amount to be received in 4 years is US $137,350, and given the correct factor from the 10% time-value-of-money table below, what is the current investment?

Interest Factors for 10%

Periods	FV	PV	FV of Ordinary Annuity	PV of Ordinary Annuity
1	1.1000	.9091	1.0000	.9091
2	1.2100	.8264	2.1000	1.7355
3	1.3310	.7513	3.3100	2.4869
4	1.4641	.6830	4.6410	3.1699
5	1.6105	.6029	6.1051	3.7908

- A.   US $30,034.33
- B.   US $43,329.44
- C.   US $93,810.05
- D.   US $201,094.14

Answer (C) is correct.

REQUIRED: The current investment required to receive a future amount of money at a given interest rate.

DISCUSSION: The current investment is the present value of the given future amount. It equals the future amount multiplied by the factor for the present value of US $1 for four periods at 10%. Accordingly, the current investment is US $93,810.05 ($137,350 × .6830).

Answer (A) is incorrect. US $30,034.33 cannot be derived from any of the time value factors given. Answer (B) is incorrect. US $43,329.44 results from incorrectly dividing by the factor for the present value of an ordinary annuity for four periods. Answer (D) is incorrect. US $201,094.14 results from incorrectly using the factor for the future value of US $1 for four periods.

14.9   Bonds

20. If bonds are initially sold at a discount and the effective-interest method of amortization is used, interest expense

- A.   In the earlier periods will be less than interest expense in the later periods.
- B.   In the earlier periods will be greater than interest expense in the later periods.
- C.   Will equal the cash interest payment each period.
- D.   Will be less than the cash interest payment each period.

Answer (A) is correct.

REQUIRED: The effect on interest expense if bonds are initially sold at a discount and the effective-interest method of amortization is used.

DISCUSSION: Interest expense equals the carrying amount of the liability at the beginning of the period times the effective interest rate. The carrying amount of the liability equals the face amount of the bond minus the discount. As the discount is amortized over the life of the bond, the carrying amount increases. Consequently, the interest expense increases over the term of the bond.

Answer (B) is incorrect. Interest expense will increase over the term of the bonds. Answer (C) is incorrect. Interest expense exceeds the cash interest payment when bonds are issued at a discount. The reason is that the effective rate is higher than the nominal rate. The excess of interest expense over the cash payment is the amount of discount amortized each period. Answer (D) is incorrect. Interest expense exceeds the cash interest payment when bonds are issued at a discount. The reason is that the effective rate is higher than the nominal rate. The excess of interest expense over the cash payment is the amount of discount amortized each period.

Access the **CIA Review System** from your Gleim Personal Classroom to continue your studies with exam-emulating multiple-choice questions!

STUDY UNIT FIFTEEN
ADVANCED CONCEPTS OF FINANCIAL ACCOUNTING AND FINANCIAL STATEMENT ANALYSIS

(18 pages of outline)

This study unit is the second of five covering **Section VII: Financial Management** from The IIA's CIA Exam Syllabus. This section makes up 10% to 20% of Part 3 of the CIA exam and is tested at the **awareness level**. The relevant portion of the syllabus is highlighted below. (The complete syllabus is in Appendix A.)

VII. FINANCIAL MANAGEMENT (10%–20%)

    A. Financial Accounting and Finance

> 2. Intermediate concepts of financial accounting (e.g., bonds, leases, pensions, intangible assets, R & D)
> 3. Advanced concepts of financial accounting (e.g., consolidation, partnerships, foreign currency transactions)
> 4. Financial statement analysis (e.g., ratios)

    B. Managerial Accounting

NOTE: Items A. 1. and A. 10. are covered in Study Unit 14. Item A. 2. is partially covered in Study Unit 14. Items A. 5.-9. and 11. are covered in Study Unit 16. Item A. 12. is covered in Study Unit 20.

15.1 PENSIONS

1. **Definition**

   a. A pension plan is a type of retirement plan to which an employer makes periodic contributions of assets to be set aside for employees' future benefit. The two main types of pension plans are the defined contribution plan and the defined benefit plan.

2. **Defined Contribution Plan**

   a. A defined contribution plan provides an individual account for each participating employee. Benefits that the employees will receive during retirement depend on

      1) The amount contributed to the plan by the employer and the employee and
      2) The returns earned on investments of those contributions.

   b. The employer's only obligation is to make periodic deposits of the amounts defined by the plan's formula in return for the services rendered by employees.

      1) Thus, the employer does not guarantee the amount of benefits that the employees will receive during retirement.
      2) The employees bear the investment risk (the benefit of gain or risk of loss from assets contributed to the plan).

c.   The employer's **annual pension expense** is the amount of the contribution required by the pension plan's formula.

1)   The employer reports an **asset** only if the contribution made is greater than the amount required by the pension plan's formula.

2)   The employer reports a **liability** only if the contribution made is less than the amount required by the pension plan's formula.

3.   **Defined Benefit Plan**

a.   A defined benefit plan defines an amount of pension benefit to be provided to each employee. The employer is responsible for providing the agreed benefits and, therefore, bears actuarial risk and investment risk.

b.   The benefits that the employer is required to pay depend on future events, such as how long an employee lives, how many years of service the employee renders, and the employee's compensation before retirement. Many of these events cannot be controlled by the employer. Thus, the total benefit is not precisely determinable and can only be estimated by using actuarial assumptions.

c.   The projected benefit obligation (PBO) is the actuarial present value of all benefits attributed by the pension benefit formula to employee service rendered prior to that date.

d.   Plan assets are contributions to the pension plan made by the employer to at least partially cover the PBO. These plan assets are usually stocks, bonds, and other investments. They are segregated and restricted, generally in a trust, to provide for pension benefits.

e.   Statement of financial position (balance sheet). The employer recognizes a noncurrent liability or asset depending on whether the projected benefit obligation is underfunded or overfunded.

1)   A pension liability is recognized in the employer's year-end balance sheet if the PBO exceeds the fair value of plan assets.

   Pension liability = Underfunded PBO

2)   A pension asset is recognized if the fair value of plan assets exceeds the PBO.

   Pension asset = Overfunded PBO

f.   Income statement. The employer recognizes periodic pension expense based on many factors. These include employee service performed in the current period, interest on the benefit obligation, the return on the investments of the pension fund, etc.

Stop and review! You have completed the outline for this subunit. Study multiple-choice questions 1 and 2 on page 379.

15.2 LEASES AND CONTINGENCIES

1.   **Definition of a Lease**

a.   A lease is a long-term contract in which the owner of property (the lessor) allows another party (the lessee) to use the property for a stated period in exchange for a stated payment.

b.   The primary issue is whether the lease agreement transfers substantially all the benefits and risks of ownership of the asset to the lessee.

1)   If it does, the lease is classified as a **capital lease** (also called a **finance lease**).

2)   If it does not, the lease is classified as an **operating lease** and is accounted for as a long-term rental contract.

2. **Lease Classification Test**

   a. A lease agreement transfers substantially all the benefits and risk of ownership of the asset to the lessee if at least **one of the following criteria** is met:

      1) The lease provides for the transfer of ownership of the leased property.

      2) The lease contains a bargain purchase option (BPO).

         a) A bargain purchase option gives the lessee the right to purchase the leased property for a price lower than its expected fair value at the date the BPO becomes exercisable.

      3) The lease term is 75% or more of the estimated economic life of the leased property.

      4) The present value of the minimum lease payments is at least 90% of the fair value of the leased property.

         a) Minimum lease payments equal minimum rental payments plus the amount of residual value (or the minimum rental payments plus the amount of BPO).

3. **Capital (Finance) Lease**

   a. In a **capital lease**, the lessor transfers substantially all of the benefits and risks of ownership to the lessee. Such a lease is a purchase-and-financing agreement.

   b. The **lessee** recognizes in its financial statements the **leased asset** (e.g., debit tangible asset) and a **lease liability** (e.g., credit lease obligation) at an amount equal to the present value of the minimum lease payments.

      1) Since the leased asset is recognized in the lessee's balance sheet, the lessee depreciates it.

      2) The lease liability is decreased as cash payments are made by the lessee. Interest expense also is recognized.

   c. The **lessor** removes the leased asset from its financial statements (e.g., credit lease asset) and recognizes a receivable from lease (e.g., debit receivable) for the present value of cash to be received from the lease.

      1) The receivable is decreased as cash payments are received by the lessor. Interest revenue also is recognized.

4. **Operating Lease**

   a. In an **operating lease**, the lessor retains substantially all of the benefits and risks of ownership. Such a lease is a regular rental agreement.

   b. The **lessor** reports periodic rental revenue for the amount of rents received but continues to recognize and depreciate an asset.

   c. The **lessee** reports periodic rental expense for the amount of rents paid, but no leased asset or liability is recognized.

5. **Contingencies**

   a. A contingency involves **uncertainty** as to possible loss (a loss contingency) or gain (a gain contingency). It ultimately will be resolved when one or more future events occur or do not occur.

   b. A **contingent liability** and a **loss contingency** are recognized when a loss contingency is probable and can be reasonably estimated. The following are examples of loss contingencies:

      1) Pending or threatened litigation
      2) **Warranties** and obligations for product defects
      3) Uncollectibility of receivables
      4) Guarantees, e.g., of the residual value of a leased asset or of the debt of another
      5) Coupons (premiums) offered to customers

   c. A gain contingency is recognized in the financial statements only when it is **realized**.

Stop and review! You have completed the outline for this subunit. Study multiple-choice questions 3 and 4 beginning on page 379.

15.3 FOREIGN CURRENCY TRANSACTIONS

1. **Definition**

    a. The terms of a foreign currency transaction are stated in a currency different from the entity's functional currency. For example, if an entity whose functional currency is the U.S. dollar purchases inventory on credit from a German entity, payment is to be in euros.

2. **Initial Recognition of the Transaction**

    a. The initial measurement of the transaction must be in the reporting entity's functional currency.

        1) The exchange rate used is the rate in effect on the date the transaction was initially recognized.

<u>EXAMPLE</u> of Foreign Currency Transaction

On November 15, Year 1, JRF Corporation, a U.S. entity, purchases and receives inventory from Paris Corporation, a French entity. The transaction is fixed in euros and calls for JRF to pay Paris €500,000 on January 15, Year 2. On November 15, Year 1, the euro-dollar exchange rate is US $1.2 to €1.

November 15, Year 1:		
Inventory	US $600,000	
Accounts payable (€500,000 × 1.2 exchange rate)		US $600,000

---

3. **Gain or Loss on Exchange Rate Difference**

    a. A foreign currency transaction gain or loss results from a change in the exchange rate between the date the transaction was recognized, the financial statements date, and the date the transaction is settled.

    b. This gain or loss is included in the income statement in the period the exchange rate changes. If the monetary aspect of the transaction has not yet occurred at the end of the period, monetary items (accounts payable and accounts receivable) are translated and presented at the year-end exchange rate.

<u>EXAMPLE</u> of Foreign Currency Transaction

In continuation of the previous example, the euro-dollar exchange rate was US $1.4 to €1 on December 31, Year 1, and US $1.55 for €1 on January 15, Year 2.

December 31, Year 1 (financial statements day):		
Loss on foreign currency transactions	US $100,000	
Accounts payable [US $600,000 – (€500,000 × 1.4 year-end exchange rate)]		US $100,000

For the period between the initial recognition of the transaction (November 15, Year 1) and the financial statements date (December 31, Year 1), the dollar has depreciated against the euro. Now the €500,000 euros cost US $700,000 (500,000 × 1.4). In December 31, Year 1, financial statements accounts payable are reported at US $700,000, and loss on foreign currency transaction is reported at US $100,000.

January 15, Year 2 (transaction settlement day):		
Accounts payable	US $700,000	
Loss on foreign currency transactions [500,000 × (1.55 − 1.4)]	75,000	
Cash (€500,000 × 1.55 settlement date exchange rate)		US $775,000

The loss of US $75,000 on foreign currency transactions is included in the Year 2 income statement.

NOTE: The total loss recognized on the exchange rate difference is US $175,000 [500,000 × (1.2 − 1.55)].

Stop and review! You have completed the outline for this subunit. Study multiple-choice question 5 on page 380.

15.4 BUSINESS COMBINATIONS AND CONSOLIDATED FINANCIAL STATEMENTS

1. **Investment in Equity Securities**

    a. The accounting for an investment in common stock of an investee depends on the influence that the investor has over the investee.

Voting Interest	Presumed Influence	Accounting Method
100%		
	Control	Consolidation
50%		
	Significant	Equity Method
20%		
	Little or None	Fair Value or Other Method
0%		

    b. When the investor has little or no influence over the investee (holds less than 20% of the voting interests), the investment may be classified as follows:

        1) **Trading or fair value option.** Under either method, the investment is measured at fair value in the balance sheet, and the changes in its fair value (unrealized holding gains and losses) are recognized in the income statement.

        2) **Available-for-sale.** The investment is measured at fair value in the balance sheet, and the changes in its fair value (unrealized holding gains and losses) are recognized as an item of other comprehensive income.

    c. When the investor has significant influence over the investee (holds between 20% and 50% of the voting interests), the investment in equity securities is accounted for using the **equity method**.

        1) The investment is initially recognized at cost.

        2) The investor recognizes in income its share of the investee's net income or loss for the period.

        3) Dividends from the investee are treated as a return of an investment and decrease the investment balance.

2. **Business Combination**

    a. A business combination is a transaction or event in which an acquirer obtains control of one or more businesses.

        1) **Control** (controlling financial interest) is the direct or indirect ability to determine the direction of management and policies of the investee. An entity is presumed to have control when it acquires **more than 50%** of the voting interests (e.g., shares of common stock) of a second entity.

        2) A **parent** is an entity that controls one or more subsidiaries.

        3) A **subsidiary** is an entity in which another entity, known as its parent, holds a controlling financial interest.

3. **Acquisition Method**

    a. A business combination must be accounted for using the acquisition method. This method involves

        1) Identifying the acquirer and

        2) Identifying the acquisition date, i.e., the date on which the acquirer obtains control of the acquiree.

b. At the acquisition date, the acquirer (parent) must recognize and measure

1) Identifiable assets acquired,
2) Liabilities assumed,
3) Any noncontrolling interest, and
4) Goodwill or a gain from bargain purchase.

c. **Measurement principle** -- The identifiable assets acquired, liabilities assumed, and any noncontrolling interest in the subsidiary are recognized separately from goodwill and must be measured at **acquisition-date fair value**.

d. **Noncontrolling interest** (NCI) is the portion of equity (net assets) in a subsidiary not attributable, directly or indirectly, to the parent.

1) At the acquisition date, NCI is measured at fair value.
2) A NCI is reported in the equity section of the consolidated balance sheet separately from the parent's shareholders' equity.
3) If the parent holds all the outstanding common stock of the subsidiary, no NCI is recognized.

e. Goodwill recognized on a business combination is an intangible asset reflecting the future economic benefits arising from those assets acquired in the combination that are not individually identified and separately recognized.

1) Goodwill has an indefinite useful life. Thus, it must not be amortized subsequent to its initial recognition and is instead periodically tested for impairment.
2) The parent presents any goodwill recognized in its consolidated balance sheet as one amount under noncurrent assets.
3) Remember, goodwill can be recognized only on a business combination. Internally generated goodwill must not be recognized in the financial statements.
4) Goodwill recognized equals the excess of a) over b) below:

   a) The sum of the acquisition-date **fair value** of the consideration transferred, any NCI recognized, and any previously held equity interest in the acquiree
   b) The acquisition-date fair value of identifiable assets acquired and liabilities assumed (fair value of net assets acquired)

EXAMPLE

Entity C acquired 80% of the outstanding common stock of Entity D for US $192,000. Entity D's acquisition-date fair values of identifiable assets and liabilities were US $350,000 and US $140,000, respectively. The acquisition-date fair value of NCI was US $48,000. The goodwill is calculated as follows:

Consideration transferred		US $192,000
Noncontrolling interest		48,000
Acquisition-date fair value of identifiable net assets (assets – liabilities) acquired:		
Assets	US $350,000	
Liabilities	(140,000)	(210,000)
Goodwill		US $ 30,000

---

5) If b) exceeds a) above, an ordinary **gain from bargain purchase** must be recognized in the parent's consolidated statement of income.

4. **Consolidated Financial Statements**

a. When one entity (parent) controls another (subsidiary), consolidated financial statements must be issued by the parent regardless of the percentages of ownership.

1) Consolidated reporting is required even when majority ownership is indirect, i.e., when a subsidiary holds a majority interest in another subsidiary.

b. **Consolidated financial statements** are the general-purpose financial statements of a parent with one or more subsidiaries. They present amounts for the parent and all its subsidiaries as if they were a **single economic entity**.

c. Required consolidated reporting is an example of substance over form. Even if the two entities remain legally separate, the financial statements are more meaningful to users if they see the effects of control by one over the other.

d. **Consolidated procedures**. The starting point of the consolidation process is the parent-only and subsidiary-only adjusted trial balances (parent's and subsidiary's separate financial statements). The following steps must be performed when preparing consolidated financial statements:

   1) All line items of assets, liabilities, revenues, expenses, gains, losses, and OCI items of a subsidiary are added item by item to those of the parent. These items are reported at the consolidated amounts.

   2) The periodic net income or loss of a consolidated subsidiary attributable to NCI are presented separately from the periodic net income or loss attributable to the shareholders of the parent.

   3) All the equity amounts of the subsidiary are eliminated (not presented in the consolidated financial statements).

   4) The carrying amount of the parent's investment in the subsidiary as it is presented in the parent-only financial statements is eliminated (not presented in the consolidated financial statements).

   5) Goodwill recognized at the acquisition date is presented separately as an intangible asset.

   6) NCI is reported separately in one line item in the equity section. The NCI must be adjusted for its proportionate share of (a) the subsidiary's net income (increase) or net loss (decrease) for the period, (b) dividends declared by the subsidiary (decrease), and (c) items of OCI recognized by the subsidiary.

   7) Intraentity balances, transactions, income, and expenses must be eliminated in full.

      a) Consolidating entities routinely conduct business with each other. The effect of these intraentity transactions must be eliminated in full during the preparation of the consolidated financial statements.

      b) Consolidated financial statements report the financial position, results of operations, and cash flows as if the consolidated entities were a single economic entity. Thus, all line items in the consolidated financial statements must be presented at the amounts that would have been reported if the intraentity transactions had never occurred.

      c) After adding together all the assets, liabilities, and income statement items of a parent and a subsidiary, eliminating journal entries for intraentity transactions must be recorded for proper presentation of the consolidated financial statements.

e. An example of a full set of consolidated financial statements can be found in Appendix D.

Stop and review! You have completed the outline for this subunit. Study multiple-choice questions 6 and 7 beginning on page 380.

15.5 CORPORATE EQUITY ACCOUNTS AND PARTNERSHIPS

1. **Corporate Equity**

   a. The equity accounts of a corporation include contributed capital, treasury stock, retained earnings, and items included in accumulated other comprehensive income.

2. **Corporate Equity -- Contributed Capital**

   a. Contributed capital represents amounts invested by owners in exchange for stock (common or preferred).

      1) **Common stock** -- The common shareholders are the owners of the entity. They have voting rights and may receive dividends at the discretion of the board of directors.

      2) **Preferred stock** -- Preferred shareholders have the right to receive (a) dividends at a specified rate (before common shareholders may receive any) and (b) distributions before common shareholders (but after creditors) upon liquidation. Preferred stock can be cumulative, callable, or redeemable.

         a) The dividends on preferred stock equal the par value of the stock times its stated rate.

   b. **Issuance of shares** -- Cash received is debited, the appropriate class of capital stock is recognized (credited) for the total **par value**, and **additional paid-in capital** is recognized (credited) for the difference.

EXAMPLE of Stock Issuance

A company issued 50,000 shares of its US $1 par value common stock. The market price was US $17 per share on the day of issue.

Cash (50,000 shares × US $17 market price)	US $850,000	
Common stock (50,000 shares × US $1 par value per share)		US $ 50,000
Additional paid-in capital (difference)		800,000

A company also issued 10,000 $50 par value, 6% preference shares. The market price was $62 per share on the day of issue.

Cash (10,000 shares × US $62 market price)	US $620,000	
Common stock (10,000 shares × US $50 par value per share)		US $500,000
Additional paid-in capital (difference)		120,000

---

   c. When an entity reacquires its previously issued and outstanding shares, these shares are held as **treasury stock**. The acquisition of treasury shares results in a direct decrease in equity. This acquisition reduces the shares outstanding but not the shares authorized.

      1) Treasury shares are not assets, and dividends are not paid on them.

      2) The most common method for recording shares held as treasury stock is the cost method. Under this method, reacquired shares are recorded at their acquisition cost.

3. **Corporate Equity -- Retained Earnings and Dividends**

   a. Retained earnings is accumulated net income or loss. It is increased by net income and decreased by net loss and dividends.

   b. The following entries are recorded when the dividend is declared and paid:

Declaration		Payment	
Retained earnings US $XXX		Dividends payable US $XXX	
Dividends payable	US $XXX	Cash	US $XXX

c.   The amount of retained earnings (ending balance) as it is reported in the balance sheet can be calculated as follows:

Beginning retained earnings	US $XXX
Plus net income for the period (or minus net loss)	XXX
Minus dividends declared this period	(XXX)
Ending retained earnings	US $XXX

d.   The beginning balance of retained earnings is adjusted for the cumulative effect on the income statement of (1) changes in accounting principle and (2) corrections of errors in prior-period financial statements. Accordingly, these items must not be included in the calculation of current-period net income.

4.   **Corporate Equity -- Stock Dividends and Splits**

a.   A **stock dividend** involves no distribution of cash or other property. Stock dividends are accounted for as a reclassification of equity (transfer from retained earnings to common stock), not as liabilities.

1)   The recipient does not recognize income. It has the same proportionate interest in the entity and the same total carrying amount as before the stock dividend.

b.   **Stock splits** are issuance of shares that do not affect any aggregate par or stated value of shares issued and outstanding or total equity.

1)   No entry is made, and no transfer from retained earnings occurs.

5.   **Partnership Formation**

a.   A partnership is an association of two or more persons to carry on, as co-owners, a business for profit.

b.   Partners **contribute cash and other property** as the basis of their equity in a partnership. Cash is recorded at its nominal amount and property at its **fair value**.

c.   Partnership equity includes only the partners' capital accounts.

6.   **Partnership Income or Loss**

a.   Profit and loss are distributed equally among partners unless the partnership agreement provides otherwise.

1)   If the partnership agreement specifies how profits are to be shared but is silent with respect to losses, then losses are divided in the same manner as profits.

7.   **Liquidation of a Partnership -- Process**

a.   When the partners dissolve their partnership, the process of liquidating noncash assets and settling liabilities begins. The liquidation process has four steps:

1)   First, any gain or loss realized from the actual sale of assets is allocated to the partners' capital accounts in accordance with the profit-and-loss ratio.

2)   Second, remaining noncash assets are assumed to have a fair value of zero, resulting in an assumed loss equal to their carrying amounts. This amount is allocated to the partners' accounts in accordance with the profit-and-loss ratio.

3)   Third, if at least one of the partners' capital accounts has a deficit balance, the deficit is allocated to the remaining partners' accounts.

4)   Fourth, the final balances in the partnership accounts equal the amounts of cash, if any, that may be distributed to the partners.

Stop and review! You have completed the outline for this subunit. Study multiple-choice questions 8 and 9 on page 381.

15.6 FINANCIAL STATEMENT ANALYSIS -- LIQUIDITY RATIOS

1. **Use**

   a. Liquidity is an entity's ability to pay its current obligations as they come due and remain in business in the short run.

   b. Liquidity depends on the ease with which current assets can be converted to cash. Liquidity ratios measure this ability by relating an entity's liquid assets to its current liabilities at a moment in time.

EXAMPLE -- Statement of Financial Position

RESOURCES			FINANCING		
	Current Year End	Prior Year End		Current Year End	Prior Year End
CURRENT ASSETS:			**CURRENT LIABILITIES:**		
Cash and equivalents	US $ 325,000	US $ 275,000	Accounts payable	US $ 200,000	US $ 125,000
Available-for-sale securities	165,000	145,000	Accrued interest on note	5,000	5,000
Accounts receivable (net)	120,000	115,000	Current maturities of L.T. debt	100,000	100,000
Notes receivable	55,000	40,000	Accrued salaries and wages	15,000	10,000
Inventories	85,000	55,000	Income taxes payable	70,000	35,000
Prepaid expenses	10,000	5,000			
Total current assets	**US $ 760,000**	**US $ 635,000**	**Total current liabilities**	**US $ 390,000**	**US $ 275,000**
NONCURRENT ASSETS:			**NONCURRENT LIABILITIES:**		
Equity-method investments	US $ 120,000	US $ 115,000	Bonds payable	US $ 500,000	US $ 600,000
Property, plant, and equipment	1,000,000	900,000	Long-term notes payable	90,000	60,000
Minus: accum. depreciation	(85,000)	(55,000)	Employee-related obligations	15,000	10,000
Goodwill	5,000	5,000	Deferred income taxes	5,000	5,000
Total noncurrent assets	**US $1,040,000**	**US $ 965,000**	**Total noncurrent liabilities**	**US $ 610,000**	**US $ 675,000**
			Total liabilities	**US $1,000,000**	**US $ 950,000**
			EQUITY:		
			Ordinary shares, US $1 par	US $ 500,000	US $ 500,000
			Share premium on O.S.	230,000	100,000
			Retained earnings	70,000	50,000
			Total equity	**US $ 800,000**	**US $ 650,000**
Total assets	**US $1,800,000**	**US $1,600,000**	**Total liabilities and equity**	**US $1,800,000**	**US $1,600,000**

2. **Working Capital**

   a. Net working capital consists of the resources the company would have to continue operating in the short run if it had to settle all of its current liabilities at once.

$$Current\ assets - Current\ liabilities$$

EXAMPLE

Current year: US $760,000 – $390,000 = US $370,000
Prior year: US $635,000 – $275,000 = US $360,000

Although the company's current liabilities increased, its current assets increased by US $10,000 more. The company has more working capital.

3. **Current Ratio**

   a. The current ratio, also called the working capital ratio, is the most common measure of liquidity.

$$\frac{Current\ assets}{Current\ liabilities}$$

EXAMPLE

Current year: US $760,000 ÷ $390,000 = 1.95
Prior year: US $635,000 ÷ $275,000 = 2.31

Although working capital increased in absolute terms (US $10,000), current assets now provide less proportional coverage of current liabilities than in the prior year.

           1)   A low current ratio indicates a possible liquidity problem. An overly high ratio indicates that management may not be investing idle assets productively.

4.   **Quick (Acid-Test) Ratio**

    a.   The quick (acid-test) ratio excludes inventories and prepaid expenses from the numerator because they are difficult to liquidate at their stated amounts. The quick ratio is therefore a more conservative measure than the basic current ratio.

$$\frac{\textit{Cash and equivalents + Marketable securities + Net receivables}}{\textit{Current liabilities}}$$

EXAMPLE

Current year: (US $325,000 + $165,000 + $120,000 + $55,000) ÷ $390,000 = 1.71
Prior year: (US $275,000 + $145,000 + $115,000 + $40,000) ÷ $275,000 = 2.09

Despite its increase in total working capital, the company's position in its most liquid assets declined.

---

           1)   This ratio measures the firm's ability to easily pay its short-term debts while avoiding the problem of inventory valuation.

Stop and review! You have completed the outline for this subunit. Study multiple-choice questions 10 through 12 beginning on page 382.

15.7 FINANCIAL STATEMENT ANALYSIS -- ACTIVITY RATIOS

1.   **Use**

    a.   Activity ratios reflect how quickly major noncash assets are converted to cash.

           1)   These ratios measure results for an accounting period. Thus, they relate information from the statement of financial position to information from the income statement.

EXAMPLE of an Income Statement

	Current Year	Prior Year
Net sales	US $ 1,800,000	US $ 1,400,000
Cost of goods sold	(1,450,000)	(1,170,000)
Gross profit	US $ 350,000	US $ 230,000
SG&A expenses	(200,000)	(160,000)
Operating income	US $ 150,000	US $ 70,000
Other income and expenses	(65,000)	(25,000)
Income before interest and taxes	US $ 85,000	US $ 45,000
Interest expense	(15,000)	(10,000)
Income before taxes	US $ 70,000	US $ 35,000
Income taxes (40%)	(28,000)	(14,000)
Net income	US $ 42,000	US $ 21,000

2.   **Receivables Activity Formulas**

    a.   The **accounts receivable turnover ratio** is the number of times in a year the total balance of receivables is converted to cash.

$$\textit{Accounts receivable turnover} = \frac{\textit{Net credit sales}}{\textit{Average accounts receivable}}$$

           1)   Average accounts receivable equals beginning accounts receivable plus ending accounts receivable, divided by two.

EXAMPLE

All of the company's sales are on credit. Net trade receivables at the reporting date of the second prior year were US $105,000.

Current year: US $1,800,000 ÷ [($120,000 + $115,000) ÷ 2] = 15.3 times
Prior year: US $1,400,000 ÷ [($115,000 + $105,000) ÷ 2] = 12.7 times

The company turned over its trade receivables balance 2.6 more times during the current year, even as receivables were growing in absolute terms. Thus, the company's effectiveness at collecting accounts receivable has improved.

---

    b.   The **average collection period**, also called the **days' sales in receivables**, measures the average number of days between the time of sale and receipt of the invoice amount.

$$Days'\ sales\ in\ receivables = \frac{Days\ in\ year}{Accounts\ receivable\ turnover\ ratio}$$

EXAMPLE

Current year: 365 days ÷ 15.3 times = 23.9 days
Prior year: 365 days ÷ 12.7 times = 28.7 days

The denominator (calculated in the example above) increased, and the numerator is a constant. Accordingly, days' sales must decrease. In addition to improving its collection practices, the company also may have become better at assessing the creditworthiness of its customers.

---

    3.   **Inventory Activity Ratios**

        a.   Two ratios measure the efficiency of inventory management.

        b.   **Inventory turnover** measures the number of times in a year the total balance of inventory is converted to cash or receivables.

$$Inventory\ turnover = \frac{Cost\ of\ goods\ sold}{Average\ inventory}$$

            1)   Average inventory equals beginning inventory plus ending inventory, divided by two.

            2)   Generally, the higher the inventory turnover rate, the more efficient the inventory management of the entity. A high rate may imply that the entity is not carrying excess levels of inventory or inventory that is obsolete.

EXAMPLE

The balance in inventories at the balance sheet date of the second prior year was US $45,000.

Current year: US $1,450,000 ÷ [($85,000 + $55,000) ÷ 2] = 20.7 times
Prior year: US $1,170,000 ÷ [($55,000 + $45,000) ÷ 2] = 23.4 times

The company did not turn over its inventory as often during the current year as in the prior year. A lower turnover is expected during a period of growing sales (and increasing inventory). It is not necessarily a sign of poor inventory management.

---

        c.   **Days' sales in inventory** measures the average number of days that pass between the acquisition of inventory and its sale.

$$Days'\ sales\ in\ inventory = \frac{Days\ in\ year}{Inventory\ turnover\ ratio}$$

EXAMPLE

Current year: 365 days ÷ 20.7 times = 17.6 days
Prior year: 365 days ÷ 23.4 times = 15.6 days

Because the numerator is a constant, the decreased turnover means that days' sales in inventory increased. This is a common phenomenon during a period of increasing sales.

---

4. **Operating Cycle**

    a. A firm's **operating cycle** is the amount of time that passes between the acquisition of inventory and the collection of cash on the sale of that inventory.

    Operating cycle = Days' sales in inventory + Days' sales in receivables

EXAMPLE

    Current year: 17.6 days + 23.9 days = 41.5 days
    Prior year: 15.6 days + 28.7 days = 44.3 days

    The entity has slightly reduced its operating cycle while increasing sales and inventory.

5. **Cash Conversion Cycle**

    a. A firm's cash conversion cycle is the amount of time that passes between the actual outlay of cash for inventory purchases and the collection of cash from the sale of that inventory.

    *Cash conversion cycle = Average collection period +
    Days' sales in inventory − Average payables period*

    1) The accounts payable turnover ratio is the number of times during a period that the firm pays its accounts payable.

    $$Accounts\ payable\ turnover = \frac{Total\ purchases}{Average\ accounts\ payable}$$

    a) Average accounts payable equals beginning accounts payable plus ending accounts payable, divided by two.

    2) The average payables period (also called payables turnover in days, or payables deferral period) is the average time between the purchase of inventories and the payment of cash.

    $$Average\ payable\ period = \frac{Days\ in\ year}{Accounts\ payable\ turnover}$$

    b. The difference between the operating cycle and the cash conversion cycle arises from the fact that the firm's purchases of inventory are made on credit. Thus, the cash conversion cycle is equal to the operating cycle minus the average payables period.

6. **Other Turnover Ratios**

    a. The total assets turnover and fixed assets turnover are broader-based ratios that measure the efficiency with which assets are used to generate revenue.

    1) Both cash and credit sales are included in the numerator.

    $$Total\ assets\ turnover = \frac{Net\ total\ sales}{Average\ total\ assets}$$

    $$Fixed\ assets\ turnover = \frac{Net\ total\ sales}{Average\ net\ fixed\ assets}$$

    a) Average total net fixed assets equal beginning total net fixed assets plus ending total net fixed assets, divided by two.

EXAMPLE

    Current year total assets turnover: US $1,800,000 ÷ [($1,800,000 + $1,600,000) ÷ 2] = 1.06 times
    Current year fixed assets turnover: US $1,800,000 ÷ [($915,000 + $845,000) ÷ 2]   = 2.04 times

    NOTE: The current- and prior-year net carrying amounts of fixed assets are US $915,000 ($1,000,000 − $85,000) and US $845,000 ($900,000 − $55,000), respectively.

Stop and review! You have completed the outline for this subunit. Study multiple-choice questions 13 and 14 on page 383.

15.8 FINANCIAL STATEMENT ANALYSIS -- SOLVENCY RATIOS AND LEVERAGE

1. **Use**

    a.   Solvency is an entity's ability to pay its noncurrent obligations as they come due and remain in business in the long run. The key ingredients of solvency are the entity's capital structure and degree of leverage.

        1)   By contrast, liquidity relates to the ability to remain in business for the short run.

2. **Debt to Total Assets and Debt to Total Equity**

    a.   The debt to total assets ratio (also called the debt ratio) reports the entity's debt per monetary unit of assets.

$$Debt\ ratio = \frac{Total\ liabilities}{Total\ assets}$$

EXAMPLE

Current year: US $1,000,000 ÷ $1,800,000 = 0.556
Prior year: US $ 950,000 ÷ $1,600,000 = 0.594

The company became slightly less reliant on debt in its capital structure during the current year. The company is thus less leveraged than before.

---

    b.   The debt-to-equity ratio is a direct comparison of the firm's debt to its equity.

$$Debt\ to\ equity = \frac{Total\ debt}{Stockholders'\ equity}$$

EXAMPLE

Current year: US $1,000,000 ÷ $800,000 = 1.25
Prior year: US $ 950,000 ÷ $650,000 = 1.46

The amount by which the company's debts exceed its equity stake declined in the current year.

---

        1)   Like the previous ratio, the debt-to-equity ratio reflects long-term debt-payment ability. Again, a low ratio means lower relative debt and better debt repayment ability.

3. **Earnings Coverage**

    a.   Earnings coverage is a creditor's best measure of an entity's ongoing ability to generate the earnings that will allow it to satisfy its debts and remain solvent.

    b.   The times-interest-earned ratio is an income statement approach to evaluating the ongoing ability to meet interest payments on debt obligations.

$$Times\text{-}interest\text{-}earned = \frac{Earnings\ before\ interest\ and\ taxes\ (EBIT)}{Interest\ expense}$$

        1)   When debt is paid (i.e., the debt level is reduced), annual interest payments are reduced.

        2)   An increased times-interest-earned ratio signifies that more profit is available to pay interest on debt and solvency has improved.

EXAMPLE

Current year: US $85,000 ÷ $15,000 = 5.67
Prior year: US $45,000 ÷ $10,000 = 4.50

The entity has improved its ability to pay interest expense. In the prior year, EBIT was only four-and-a-half times interest expense, but in the current year, it is more than five-and-a-half times.

---

4. **Leverage**

   a. Leverage is the relative amount of fixed cost in a firm's overall cost structure. Leverage creates solvency risk because fixed costs must be covered regardless of the level of sales.

      1) Total costs (TC) equals fixed costs (FC) plus variable costs (VC).
      2) A firm's total leverage consists of an operating leverage component and a financial leverage component.

   b. **Operating leverage** is the extent to which a firm's costs of operating are fixed as opposed to variable. The following ratio is one of the ways to measure operating leverage.

   $$Operating\ leverage = Fixed\ costs\ (FC) \div Total\ costs\ (FC + VC)$$

      1) High operating leverage means that a high percentage of a firm's total costs is fixed.
      2) A firm with a high percentage of fixed costs is more risky than a firm in the same industry that relies more on variable costs, but by the same token, it will generate more earnings by increasing sales.

   c. **Financial leverage** is the degree of debt (fixed financial costs) in the firm's financial structure. The following ratio is one of the ways to measure financial leverage.

   $$Financial\ leverage = Total\ assets \div Total\ equity$$

   EXAMPLE

   Current-year financial leverage ratio: US $1,800,000 ÷ $800,000 = 2.25

   ---

      1) High financial leverage means that a high percentage of a firm's total assets is financed by debt.
      2) When a firm has a high percentage of fixed financial costs, the firm takes more risk to increase its earnings per share. (Earnings per share is explained in item 6. on page 377.)

Stop and review! You have completed the outline for this subunit. Study multiple-choice questions 15 and 16 beginning on page 383.

15.9 FINANCIAL STATEMENT ANALYSIS -- ROI AND PROFITABILITY

1. **Return on Invested Capital**

   a. Return on investment, or ROI (also called return on invested capital), is a broad concept for measures that reflect how efficiently an entity is using the resources contributed by its shareholders to generate a profit.

   $$Return\ on\ investment\ (ROI) = \frac{Measure\ of\ profit}{Measure\ of\ capital} = \frac{Operating\ income}{Average\ invested\ capital}$$

   NOTE: The examples below and on the next page use the Statement of Financial Position on page 370 and the Income Statement on page 371.

2. **Return on Assets**

   a. Return on assets, or ROA (also called return on total assets, or ROTA), is the most basic form of the ROI ratio.

   $$Return\ on\ assets\ (ROA) = \frac{Net\ income}{Average\ total\ assets}$$

   EXAMPLE

   Current year: US $42,000 ÷ [($1,800,000 + $1,600,000) ÷ 2] = 0.025

   During the current year, the company generated US $0.025 in net income for each dollar invested in the company's assets.

   ---

3.   **DuPont Model**

a.   The original DuPont model treats ROA as the product of a two-component ratio.

ROA		**Profit Margin**		**Total Assets Turnover**
$\dfrac{Net\ income}{Average\ total\ assets}$	$=$	$\dfrac{Net\ income}{Net\ sales}$	$\times$	$\dfrac{Net\ sales}{Average\ total\ assets}$

1)   The advantage of this analysis is that it examines both the results of operations and the efficiency of asset usage in generating sales.

EXAMPLE

Current-year profit margin: US $42,000 net income ÷ $1,800,000 total sales = 0.0233

1.   Profit margin of 0.0233 means that the company generates US $0.0233 of net income from each US $1 of sales.
2.   The total assets turnover is 1.06 (as calculated on page 373).
3.   The ROA is 0.025 = 0.0233 × 1.06

---

4.   **Return on Equity**

a.   Return on equity (ROE) is the second version of the ROI ratio.

$$Return\ on\ equity\ (ROE) = \frac{Net\ income}{Average\ total\ equity}$$

1)   Average total equity equals beginning total equity plus ending total equity, divided by two.

2)   This ratio measures the return available to all shareholders.

EXAMPLE

Current-year ROE: US $42,000 net income ÷ [($800,000 + $650,000) ÷ 2] = 0.058

---

b.   The DuPont model has been adapted and expanded. One widely used variation treats ROE as the product of three components.

$$ROE = Profitability \times Turnover \times Equity\ multiplier$$

$$ROE = \frac{Net\ income}{Net\ sales} \times \frac{Net\ sales}{Average\ total\ assets} = \frac{Average\ total\ assets}{Average\ total\ equity}$$

5.   **Other Profitability Ratios**

a.   Three common percentages measure profitability directly from the income statement:

$$Gross\ profit\ margin = \frac{Gross\ profit}{Net\ sales}$$

$$Operating\ income\ margin = \frac{Operating\ income}{Net\ sales}$$

$$Net\ income\ margin = \frac{Net\ income}{Net\ sales}$$

EXAMPLE

Current-year gross profit margin: US $350,000 ÷ $1,800,000 = 19.4%
Current-year operating income margin: US $150,000 ÷ $1,800,000 = 8.3%
Current-year net income margin: US $ 42,000 ÷ $1,800,000 = 2.3%

---

b.   A vertical common-size analysis can be useful in measurement of these ratios.

6. **Earnings per Share**

   a. Basic earnings per share (EPS) is a ratio of particular interest to the corporation's common shareholders. It is a profitability ratio that measures the amount of current-period earnings that can be associated with a single share of a corporation's common stock.

$$EPS = \frac{Net\ income\ -\ Preferred\ dividends}{Weighted\text{-}average\ number\ of\ common\ shares\ outstanding}$$

   1) The numerator often is called income available to common shareholders.
   2) EPS is calculated only for common stock because common shareholders are the residual owners of a corporation.
   3) The weighted-average number of common shares outstanding is determined by relating the portion of the period that the shares were outstanding to the total time in the period.

   b. An entity that has **potential common shares** (e.g., convertible bonds, convertible preferred stock, and share options) must report diluted EPS in addition to basic EPS. The calculation includes the effects of dilutive potential common shares. Dilution is a reduction in basic EPS resulting from the assumption that potential common shares were converted to common stock.

Stop and review! You have completed the outline for this subunit. Study multiple-choice questions 17 and 18 on page 384.

15.10 FINANCIAL STATEMENT ANALYSIS -- CORPORATE VALUATION

1. **Book Value per Common Share**

   a. Book value per common share equals the amount of net assets available to shareholders divided by the number of shares outstanding.

$$Book\ value\ per\ common\ share = \frac{Total\ equity\ -\ Liquidation\ value\ of\ preferred\ stock}{Common\ stock\ outstanding}$$

   1) Book value per common share is the amount per share of the company's net assets at their book value (carrying amounts) that will be received by the common shareholders upon the liquidation of the company.
   2) This amount may be misleading because the book value of net assets may differ materially from their market or liquidation value.

2. **Price-Earnings (P-E) Ratio**

   a. The price-earnings ratio measures the amount that investors are willing to pay for US $1 of the company's earnings.

$$Price\text{-}Earnings = \frac{Market\ price\ of\ share}{Earnings\ per\ share\ (EPS)}$$

   1) Generally, the higher the ratio, the more confidence the market has in the company's ability to grow and produce higher returns for the investors.

3. **Dividend Payout Ratio**

   a. Increasing shareholder wealth is the fundamental goal of any business. The dividend payout ratio measures the portion of available earnings the entity actually distributed to shareholders.

$$Dividend\ payout\ ratio = \frac{Dividend\ paid\ per\ share}{Earnings\ per\ share} = \frac{Total\ dividends}{Net\ income}$$

   1) Growing entities tend to have a low payout. They prefer to use earnings for expansion.

4.   **Dividend Yield Ratio**

a.   The dividend yield measures the percentage of a share's market price that was returned as dividends. This ratio can be applied to both common and preferred stock.

$$\text{Dividend yield ratio} = \frac{\text{Dividends per share}}{\text{Market price per share}}$$

Stop and review! You have completed the outline for this subunit. Study multiple-choice question 19 on page 385.

15.11 FINANCIAL STATEMENT ANALYSIS -- COMMON-SIZE FINANCIAL STATEMENTS AND MULTIPLE RATIOS

1.   **Common-Size Financial Statements and Multiple Ratios**

a.   **Common-size financial statements** are expressed in percentages.

1)   **Horizontal common-size analysis** focuses on changes in operating results and financial position during two or more accounting periods. The changes are expressed in terms of percentages of corresponding amounts in a base period.

2)   **Vertical common-size analysis** concerns the relationships among financial statement items of a single accounting period expressed in terms of a percentage relationship to a base item (the base is 100%). For example, income statement items may be expressed as percentages of sales, and balance sheet items may be expressed as a percentage of total assets.

EXAMPLE		
	Current Year	**Prior Year**
Net sales	100.0%	100.0%
Cost of goods sold	(80.6%)	(83.6%)
Gross profit	**19.4%**	**16.4%**
SG&A expenses	(11.1%)	(11.4%)
Operating income	**8.3%**	**5.0%**
Other income and expenses	(3.6%)	(1.8%)
Income before interest and taxes	4.7%	3.2%
Interest expense	(0.8%)	(0.7%)
Income before taxes	3.9%	2.5%
Income taxes (40%)	(1.6%)	(1.0%)
Net income	**2.3%**	**1.5%**

b.   The income statements above are presented in the **common-size** format. Line items on common-size statements are expressed as percentages of net sales (on the income statement) or total assets (on the statement of financial position).

1)   Thus, on a common-size income statement, net sales is 100%, and all other amounts are a percentage of net sales. On the statement of financial position, total assets and the total of liabilities and equity are each 100%.

2)   Each line item can be interpreted in terms of its proportion of the baseline amount. This process is **vertical analysis**.

Stop and review! You have completed the outline for this subunit. Study multiple-choice question 20 on page 385.

QUESTIONS

15.1 Pensions

1. On December 31, Year 1, Entity A determines the following information in relation to its defined benefit pension plan:

Fair value of plan assets	US $210,000
Projected benefit obligation (PBO)	US $260,000

In its Year 1 financial statements, Entity A reports a pension <List A> of <List B> for the <List C> PBO.

	List A	List B	List C
A.	Liability	US $50,000	Unfunded
B.	Asset	US $210,000	Overfunded
C.	Liability	US $260,000	Unfunded
D.	Liability	US $50,000	Overfunded

Answer (A) is correct.
REQUIRED: The proper reporting of the pension-related balance.
DISCUSSION: Entity A recognizes a pension liability to the extent its PBO is unfunded. This excess of the PBO over the fair value of the plan assets is US $50,000 ($260,000 – $210,000).
Answer (B) is incorrect. A pension asset is recognized if the fair value of plan assets is greater than the PBO. Answer (C) is incorrect. The amount of US $260,000 is the PBO, not the unfunded amount of the PBO. Answer (D) is incorrect. An overfunded PBO results in recognition of a pension asset.

2. Which of the following statements is true for a defined contribution pension plan?

A. The employer is required to contribute a certain amount each period based on the plan's formula.

B. The employer bears the risk of the plan's investment performance.

C. Retirement benefits received by employees are defined by the plan's formula.

D. The employer and employees are required to contribute equal amounts to the pension fund.

Answer (A) is correct.
REQUIRED: The true statement about a defined contribution plan.
DISCUSSION: Under a defined contribution plan, the employer's only obligation is to periodically deposit a certain amount in the pension fund.
Answer (B) is incorrect. The employees bear the risk of the plan's investment performance. Answer (C) is incorrect. The benefits received by employees are defined by the plan's formula under a defined benefit plan, not a defined contribution plan. Answer (D) is incorrect. Equal contributions are not required for a defined contribution plan.

15.2 Leases and Contingencies

3. Capital and operating leases differ in that the lessor

A. Obtains use of the asset only under a capital lease.

B. Is using the lease as a source of financing only under an operating lease.

C. Makes rent payments that are actually installment payments constituting a payment of both principal and interest only under a capital lease.

D. Finances the transaction through the leased asset only under a capital lease.

Answer (D) is correct.
REQUIRED: The difference between capital and operating leases.
DISCUSSION: A lease is either a rental or an installment purchase arrangement between a lessor (the owner or seller of the property) and a lessee (the renter or purchaser). The issue in all leases is whether substantially all of the benefits and risks of ownership have been transferred from the lessor to the lessee. If so, the lease should be capitalized because it is a purchase-and-financing arrangement. If they have not transferred, the lease is a rental arrangement (an operating lease).
Answer (A) is incorrect. The lessor transfers use of the asset under both types of leases to the lessee. The lessor does not obtain use of the asset. Answer (B) is incorrect. The lessee uses the lease as a source of financing under a capital lease, not an operating lease. The lessor is the source of financing because it extends credit to the lessee. Answer (C) is incorrect. The lessee makes payments to the lessor under both types of leases. The lessor does not make payments.

4. Which of the following is an example of a contingent liability?

A. A retail store in a shopping mall pays the lessor a minimum monthly rent plus an agreed-upon percentage of sales.

B. An entity is refusing to pay the invoice for the annual audit because it seems higher than the amount agreed upon with the public accounting entity's partner.

C. An entity accrues income tax payable in its interim financial statements.

D. A lessee agrees to reimburse a lessor for a shortfall in the residual value of an asset under lease.

Answer (D) is correct.
REQUIRED: The example of a contingent liability.
DISCUSSION: The liability resulting from a guarantee is contingent on the lessor's not receiving the full residual value from a third party. A liability is recognized for a guarantee even if the probability of loss is remote.
Answer (A) is incorrect. The amount of rent is not uncertain. Rent expense can be accrued as sales occur. Answer (B) is incorrect. A service was received, and the entity owes an amount. The amount is not contingent on a future event. The entity can accrue the amount that it expected the invoice to show. Answer (C) is incorrect. As of the date of the interim financial statements, the income tax is payable because earnings have occurred. The amount or the timing of the payment as of the date of the statements is not uncertain.

15.3 Foreign Currency Transactions

5. On September 22, Year 1, a corporation purchased merchandise from an unaffiliated foreign entity for 10,000 units of the foreign entity's local currency. On that date, the spot rate was US $.55. The corporation paid the bill in full on March 20, Year 2, when the spot rate was US $.65. The closing rate was US $.70 on December 31, Year 1. What amount should the corporation report as a foreign currency transaction loss in its income statement for the year ended December 31, Year 1?

A. US $0

B. US $500

C. US $1,000

D. US $1,500

Answer (D) is correct.
REQUIRED: The amount of foreign currency transaction loss to be reported in the income statement.
DISCUSSION: A receivable or payable fixed in a foreign currency is adjusted to its current exchange rate at the end of the reporting period. The resulting gain or loss should be reported in the income statement. It is the difference between the spot rate (dollar amount to buy one unit of the foreign currency) on the date the transaction originates (the rate applied in the prior year) and the closing rate. Thus, the entity recognizes a transaction loss at the end of Year 1 because the U.S. dollar weakened against the foreign currency (more U.S. dollars are needed to buy 10,000 units of that currency). The loss is US $1,500 [10,000 units × ($0.55 – $0.70)].
Answer (A) is incorrect. A loss resulted when the spot rate (dollar amount to buy one unit of the foreign currency) increased. Answer (B) is incorrect. US $500 results from using the rates at 12/31/Yr 1 and 3/20/Yr 2. Answer (C) is incorrect. US $1,000 results from using the rates at 9/22/Yr 1 and 3/20/Yr 2.

15.4 Business Combinations and Consolidated Financial Statements

6. Entity X owns 90% of Entity Y. Early in the year, X lent Y US $1,000,000. No payments have been made on the debt by year end. Proper accounting at year-end in the consolidated financial statements would

A. Eliminate 100% of the receivable, the payable, and the related interest.

B. Eliminate 100% of the receivable and the payable but not any related interest.

C. Eliminate 90% of the receivable, the payable, and the related interest.

D. Eliminate 90% of the receivable and the payable but not any related interest.

Answer (A) is correct.
REQUIRED: The accounting treatment of a loan made by a parent to a subsidiary.
DISCUSSION: In a consolidated statement of financial position, reciprocal balances, such as receivables and payables, between a parent and a consolidated subsidiary should be eliminated in their entirety regardless of the portion of the subsidiary's shares held by the parent. Thus, all effects of the US $1,000,000 loan should be eliminated in the preparation of the year-end consolidated statement of financial position.

7. Entity A acquires all of the voting shares of Entity B for US $1,000,000. At the time of the acquisition, the net fair value of the identifiable assets acquired and liabilities assumed had a carrying amount of US $900,000 and a fair value of US $800,000. The amount of goodwill Entity A will record on the acquisition date is

A. US $0

B. US $100,000

C. US $200,000

D. US $300,000

Answer (C) is correct.
> **REQUIRED:** The goodwill recorded.
> **DISCUSSION:** Given no prior equity interest or noncontrolling interest, goodwill equals the excess of the fair value of the consideration transferred over the fair value of the net of the identifiable assets acquired and liabilities assumed. Consequently, goodwill is US $200,000 ($1,000,000 – $800,000).
> Answer (A) is incorrect. Goodwill must be recorded. Answer (B) is incorrect. The amount of US $100,000 is the excess of the acquisition cost over the carrying amount. Answer (D) is incorrect. The amount of US $300,000 equals goodwill plus the excess of the carrying amount over fair value.

15.5 Corporate Equity Accounts and Partnerships

8. During the year, an entity's balance sheet accounts increased by the following amounts:

Assets	US $180,000
Liabilities	50,000
Ordinary shares	90,000
Share premium	15,000

Profit for the year was US $42,000. The only other change in retained earnings was for the declaration of cash dividends. The amount of dividends declared was

A. US $2,000

B. US $17,000

C. US $33,000

D. US $67,000

Answer (B) is correct.
> **REQUIRED:** The amount of dividends declared.
> **DISCUSSION:** Assets equals liabilities plus equity. Given an increase of US $180,000 in assets, the sum of liabilities and equity must also have increased by US $180,000. Because liabilities, share capital, and share premium increased by US $155,000 ($50,000 + $90,000 + $15,000), retained earnings must have increased by US $25,000 ($180,000 – $155,000). Given profit of US $42,000, dividends declared must have been US $17,000 ($42,000 – $25,000).
> Answer (A) is incorrect. US $2,000 ignores the 15,000 increase in share premium. Answer (C) is incorrect. US $33,000 equals the increase in assets minus the sum of the increases in share capital accounts and profit. Answer (D) is incorrect. US $67,000 equals profit plus the increase in net assets other than from owner contributions.

9. When property other than cash is invested in a partnership, at what amount should the noncash property be credited to the contributing partner's capital account?

A. Fair value at the date of contribution.

B. Contributing partner's original cost.

C. Assessed valuation for property tax purposes.

D. Contributing partner's tax basis.

Answer (A) is correct.
> **REQUIRED:** The credit to the contributing partner's capital account when noncash assets are invested.
> **DISCUSSION:** The capital account should be credited for the current fair value of the assets at the date of the contribution.
> Answer (B) is incorrect. Cost does not reflect depreciation or appreciation of the property. Answer (C) is incorrect. Fair value best reflects the economic substance of the transaction. Answer (D) is incorrect. Tax basis is determined differently than the true economic value of the property.

15.6 Financial Statement Analysis -- Liquidity Ratios

Questions 10 through 12 are based on the following information.

RST Corporation's Statements of Financial Position End of Year 5 and Year 6

Assets	Year 6	Year 5
Current assets:		
Cash	US $ 5,000	US $ 4,000
Marketable securities	3,000	2,000
Accounts receivable (net)	16,000	14,000
Inventory	30,000	20,000
Total current assets	$ 54,000	$ 40,000
Noncurrent assets:		
Long-term investments	11,000	11,000
PP&E	80,000	70,000
Intangibles	3,000	4,000
Total assets	US $148,000	US $125,000
Liabilities and Equity		
Current liabilities:		
Accounts payable	US $ 11,000	US $ 7,000
Accrued payables	1,000	1,000
Total current liabilities	$ 12,000	$ 8,000
Bonds payable, 10%, due Year 12	30,000	30,000
Total liabilities	US $ 42,000	US $ 38,000
Equity:		
Common stock,		
2,400 shares, US $10 par	US $ 24,000	US $ 24,000
Retained earnings	82,000	63,000
Total equity	$106,000	$ 87,000
Total liabilities and equity	US $148,000	US $125,000

The market value of RST's ordinary shares at the end of Year 6 was US $100 per share.

10. What is RST's current ratio at the end of Year 6?

A. 4.5 to 1.

B. 2.4 to 1.

C. 2.0 to 1.

D. 1.5 to 1.

Answer (A) is correct.
REQUIRED: The current ratio at the end of Year 6.
DISCUSSION: The current ratio equals current assets divided by current liabilities. At the end of Year 6, it was 4.5 to 1 (US $54,000 ÷ $12,000).
Answer (B) is incorrect. A ratio of 2.4 to 1 results from dividing current liabilities by the amount of cash, which is not a meaningful ratio. Answer (C) is incorrect. A ratio of 2.0 to 1 is the quick (acid-test) ratio (cash, marketable securities, and net receivables divided by total current liabilities). Answer (D) is incorrect. A ratio of 1.5 to 1 results from dividing total current liabilities by the sum of cash and marketable securities, which is not a meaningful ratio.

11. What is RST's acid-test (or quick) ratio at the end of Year 6?

A. 2.40 to 1.

B. 2.18 to 1.

C. 2.00 to 1.

D. 1.50 to 1.

Answer (C) is correct.
REQUIRED: The acid-test ratio at the end of Year 6.
DISCUSSION: The acid-test or quick ratio equals the sum of the quick assets (net accounts receivable, marketable securities, and cash) divided by current liabilities. This ratio at the end of Year 6 is 2.0 to 1 [(US $5,000 + $3,000 + $16,000) ÷ $12,000].
Answer (A) is incorrect. A ratio of 2.4 to 1 results from dividing total current liabilities (US $12,000) by the amount of cash (US $5,000), which is not a meaningful ratio. Answer (B) is incorrect. A ratio of 2.18 to 1 results from dividing quick assets (US $5,000 + $3,000 + $16,000) by accounts payable (US $11,000) results in 2.18. The denominator should include all current liabilities other than accounts payable. Answer (D) is incorrect. A ratio of 1.5 to 1 results from dividing total current liabilities (US $12,000) by the sum of cash (US $5,000) and marketable securities (US $3,000), which is not a meaningful ratio.

12. Based on a comparison of RST's quick ratios in Year 5 and Year 6, what is a likely conclusion?

    A.   RST has improved its management of long-term investments in Year 6.

    B.   RST has written off obsolete inventory in Year 6.

    C.   RST's ability to meet short-term financing needs has declined since Year 5.

    D.   RST's ability to meet short-term financing needs has improved since Year 5.

Answer (C) is correct.
    REQUIRED: The likely conclusion based on a comparison of consecutive-year quick ratios.
    DISCUSSION: RST's quick ratio decreased from 2.5 in Year 5 [(US $4,000 cash + $2,000 marketable securities + $14,000 net A/R) ÷ $8,000] to 2.0 in Year 6 [(US $5,000 + $3,000 + $16,000) ÷ $12,000]. RST has fewer assets that are easily convertible to cash available to meet current liabilities. Thus, its ability to meet short-term financing needs (i.e., liquidity) has declined.
    Answer (A) is incorrect. The quick ratio compares the quick assets (current assets minus inventory) with current liabilities; it does not provide a basis for conclusions about long-term investments. Answer (B) is incorrect. The quick ratio does not consider inventory. Answer (D) is incorrect. RST is less liquid in Year 6.

15.7 Financial Statement Analysis -- Activity Ratios

13. An analysis of inventory turnover in a store's clothing department indicated extremely low turnover. Which of the following would most likely increase the turnover rate?

    A.   Increase inventories.

    B.   Increase sales incentives.

    C.   Increase selling prices.

    D.   Decrease the frequency of purchases but maintain the same level of inventory.

Answer (B) is correct.
    REQUIRED: The action that would most likely increase the turnover rate.
    DISCUSSION: Inventory turnover equals cost of sales divided by average inventory. Reducing inventory therefore increases turnover. Sales incentives to improve sales should lower inventory levels.
    Answer (A) is incorrect. Increasing the denominator of the ratio would only further decrease turnover. Answer (C) is incorrect. Increasing price would probably decrease sales, thereby further decreasing turnover. Answer (D) is incorrect. A constant inventory level would not affect the turnover rate.

14. An entity has a high fixed assets turnover ratio. What conclusion can a financial analyst draw from this?

    A.   The entity may be overcapitalized.

    B.   The entity may have a problem with employees converting inventory to personal use.

    C.   The entity may be undercapitalized.

    D.   The entity has favorable profitability.

Answer (C) is correct.
    REQUIRED: The implication of a high fixed-assets turnover ratio.
    DISCUSSION: The fixed assets turnover ratio equals net sales divided by net fixed assets. A high ratio indicates either that the entity is undercapitalized, that is, it cannot afford to buy enough fixed assets, or that it uses fixed assets efficiently.
    Answer (A) is incorrect. The ratio may indicate undercapitalization. Answer (B) is incorrect. Fluctuations in inventory do not affect fixed-assets turnover. Answer (D) is incorrect. The fixed assets turnover ratio is not a profitability indicator. It measures the efficiency of asset management.

15.8 Financial Statement Analysis -- Solvency Ratios and Leverage

15. An entity purchased a new machine for US $500,000 by borrowing the required funds from a bank for 180 days. What will be the direct impact of this transaction?

    A.   Decrease the current ratio and increase the debt ratio.

    B.   Increase the current ratio and decrease the debt ratio.

    C.   Increase the current ratio and increase the debt ratio.

    D.   Decrease the current ratio and decrease the debt ratio.

Answer (A) is correct.
    REQUIRED: The direct effect of purchasing a new machine on the current and the debt ratios.
    DISCUSSION: The borrowing of funds for 180 days constitutes short-term borrowing. The new machine is a fixed asset. Current liabilities have increased, and current assets have remained constant. Consequently, the current ratio (current assets ÷ current liabilities) has decreased. Total debt and total assets increased by the same absolute amount, and the debt ratio (total debt ÷ total assets) should have increased, assuming total debt is less than total assets.

16. The times-interest-earned ratio is primarily an indication of

A. Solvency.

B. Liquidity.

C. Asset management.

D. Profitability.

Answer (A) is correct.
   REQUIRED: The purpose of the times-interest-earned ratio.
   DISCUSSION: The times-interest-earned ratio equals profit or loss before taxes and interest divided by interest. It measures the extent to which operating profit can decline before the entity is unable to meet its annual interest cost. Thus, it is a measure of debt-paying capacity (solvency).
   Answer (B) is incorrect. Liquidity ratios, e.g., the current ratio, indicate the relationship of current assets to current liabilities. Answer (C) is incorrect. Asset management ratios indicate how effectively the entity is using its assets. Answer (D) is incorrect. Profitability ratios measure operating results.

15.9 Financial Statement Analysis -- ROI and Profitability

17. Return on investment (ROI) is a very popular measure employed to evaluate the performance of corporate segments because it incorporates all of the major ingredients of profitability (revenue, cost, investment) into a single measure. Under which one of the following combination of actions regarding a segment's revenues, costs, and investment would a segment's ROI always increase?

	Revenues	Costs	Investment
A.	Increase	Decrease	Increase
B.	Decrease	Decrease	Decrease
C.	Increase	Increase	Increase
D.	Increase	Decrease	Decrease

Answer (D) is correct.
   REQUIRED: The circumstances in which ROI always increases.
   DISCUSSION: An increase in revenue and a decrease in costs will increase the ROI numerator. A decrease in investment will decrease the denominator. The ROI must increase in this situation.

18. The following ratios relate to an entity's financial situation compared with that of its industry:

	The Entity	Industry Average
Return on assets (ROA)	7.9%	9.2%
Return on equity (ROE)	15.2%	12.9%

What conclusion could a financial analyst validly draw from these ratios?

A. The entity's product has a high market share, leading to higher profitability.

B. The entity uses more debt than does the average entity in the industry.

C. The entity's profits are increasing over time.

D. The entity's shares have a higher market value to carrying amount than does the rest of the industry.

Answer (B) is correct.
   REQUIRED: The conclusion from comparing ROA and ROE with industry averages.
   DISCUSSION: The use of financial leverage has a multiplier effect on the return on assets. The extended DuPont formula illustrates this point by showing that the return on equity equals the return on assets times the equity multiplier (total assets ÷ ordinary equity). Thus, greater use of debt increases the equity multiplier and the return on equity. In this example, the equity multiplier is 1.92 (15.2% ROE ÷ 7.9% ROA), and the industry average is 1.40 (12.9% ROE ÷ 9.2% ROA). The higher equity multiplier indicates that the entity uses more debt than the industry average.
   Answer (A) is incorrect. The question gave no information about market share. Answer (C) is incorrect. This comparison is with an industry average, not over time. Answer (D) is incorrect. Share valuation is a response to many factors. The higher-than-average return on equity does not mean that the entity has a more favorable market-to-carrying-amount ratio.

15.10 Financial Statement Analysis -- Corporate Valuation

19. An entity has 100,000 outstanding common shares with a market value of US $20 per share. Dividends of US $2 per share were paid in the current year, and the entity has a dividend-payout ratio of 40%. The price-to-earnings (P-E) ratio of the entity is

   A. 2.5

   B. 4

   C. 10

   D. 50

Answer (B) is correct.
   REQUIRED: The P-E ratio.
   DISCUSSION: The P-E ratio equals the share price divided by EPS. If the dividends per share equaled US $2 and the dividend-payout ratio was 40%, EPS must have been US $5 ($2 ÷ .4). Accordingly, the P-E ratio is 4 (US $20 share price ÷ $5 EPS).
   Answer (A) is incorrect. EPS divided by dividends per share equals 2.5. Answer (C) is incorrect. Share price divided by dividends per share equals 10. Answer (D) is incorrect. Price per share divided by the dividend-payout percentage equals 50.

15.11 Financial Statement Analysis -- Common-Size Financial Statements and Multiple Ratios

20. Which of the following financial statement analyses is most useful in determining whether the various expenses of a given entity are higher or lower than industry averages?

   A. Horizontal.

   B. Vertical.

   C. Activity ratio.

   D. Defensive-interval ratio.

Answer (B) is correct.
   REQUIRED: The analysis most useful in determining whether various expenses of an entity are higher or lower than industry averages.
   DISCUSSION: Vertical analysis is the expression of each item on a financial statement in a given period in relation to a base figure. On the income statement, each item is stated as a percentage of sales. Thus, the percentages for the entity in question can be compared with industry norms.
   Answer (A) is incorrect. A horizontal analysis indicates the proportionate change over a period of time and is useful in trend analysis of an individual entity. Answer (C) is incorrect. Activity ratio analysis includes the preparation of turnover ratios such as those for receivables, inventory, and total assets. Answer (D) is incorrect. The defensive-interval ratio is part of a liquidity analysis.

> Access the **CIA Review System** from your Gleim Personal Classroom to continue your studies with exam-emulating multiple-choice questions!

STUDY UNIT SIXTEEN
FINANCE

(25 pages of outline)

This study unit is the third of five covering **Section VII: Financial Management** from The IIA's CIA Exam Syllabus. This section makes up 10% to 20% of Part 3 of the CIA exam and is tested at the **awareness level**. The relevant portion of the syllabus is highlighted below. (The complete syllabus is in Appendix A.)

VII. FINANCIAL MANAGEMENT (10%–20%)

    A. Financial Accounting and Finance

        5. Types of debt and equity
        6. Financial instruments (e.g., derivatives)
        7. Cash management (e.g., treasury functions)
        8. Valuation models
        9. Business valuation
      11. Capital budgeting (e.g., cost of capital evaluation)

    B. Managerial Accounting

NOTE: Items A. 1.-4. and 10. are covered in Study Units 14 and 15. Item A. 12. is covered in Study Unit 20.

16.1 RISK AND RETURN

1. **Rate of Return**

    a. A return is the amount received by an investor as compensation for taking on the risk of the investment.

$$Return\ on\ investment\ =\ Amount\ received\ -\ Amount\ invested$$

EXAMPLE

An investor paid US $100,000 for an investment that returned US $112,000. The investor's return is US $12,000 ($112,000 – $100,000).

    b. The rate of return is the return stated as a percentage of the amount invested.

$$Rate\ of\ return\ =\ \frac{Return\ on\ investment}{Amount\ invested}$$

EXAMPLE

The investor's rate of return is 12% (US $12,000 ÷ $100,000).

2. **Residual Income**

a. Residual income is calculated as follows:

Residual income = Operating income - Target return on invested capital

1) The target return amount is derived by weighting average invested capital with an imputed interest rate. This rate is ordinarily the weighted-average cost of capital, but it may be an arbitrary hurdle rate.

b. Projects with a positive residual income should be accepted, and projects with a negative residual income should be rejected.

c. Residual income is often considered to be superior to ROI (discussed in Study Unit 15). ROI is a percentage measure, and residual income is a monetary measure. Thus, residual income may be more consistent with maximizing profits.

3. **Investment Securities**

a. Financial managers may select from many financial instruments in which to invest and with which to raise money.

b. An inverse relationship exists between the safety of an investment and its potential return. The following is a short list of widely available investment securities:

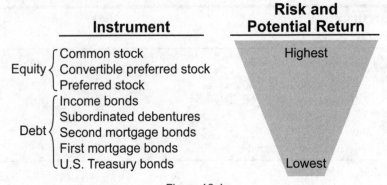

Figure 16-1

c. The reasons for the varying risk and potential return of these securities can be summarized as follows:

1) Equity securities are necessarily more risky than debt because an entity's owners are not legally guaranteed a return.

2) Issuers of debt securities are legally obligated to redeem them. Because these returns are guaranteed, they are lower than those for equity investments.

4. **Asset Valuation -- CAPM**

a. The capital asset pricing model (CAPM) quantifies the expected return on an equity security by relating the security's level of risk to the average return available in the market.

b. The CAPM formula is based on the idea that the investor must be compensated for his or her investment in two ways: time value of money and risk.

1) The time value component is the **risk-free rate** (denoted R_F in the formula). It is the return provided by the safest investments, e.g., U.S. Treasury securities.

2) The risk component consists of

a) The **market risk premium** (denoted $R_M - R_F$) is the return provided by the market over and above the risk-free rate.

        b)   Market risk premium is weighted by a measure of the security's risk, called **beta** (β).

           i)   The effect of an individual security on the volatility of a portfolio is measured by its sensitivity to movements by the overall market. This sensitivity is stated in terms of a stock's beta coefficient (β).

           ii)   Thus, the beta of the market portfolio equals 1, and the beta of U.S. Treasury securities is 0.

CAPM Formula

$$Required\ rate\ of\ return = R_F + \beta(R_M - R_F)$$

Where: R_F = Risk-free return
        R_M = Market return
        β = Measure of the systematic risk or volatility of the individual security in comparison to the market (diversified portfolio)

EXAMPLE

An investor is considering the purchase of a stock with a beta value of 1.2. Treasury bills are currently paying 8.6%, and the average return on the market is 10.1%. (Remember, U.S. Treasuries are considered as close to a risk-free investment as there can be.) To be induced to buy this stock, the return that the investor must receive is calculated as follows:

$$
\begin{aligned}
\text{Required rate of return} &= R_F + \beta(R_M - R_F) \\
&= 8.6\% + 1.2(10.1\% - 8.6\%) \\
&= 8.6\% + 1.8\% \\
&= 10.4\%
\end{aligned}
$$

---

5.   **Two Basic Types of Investment Risk**

    a.   **Systematic risk**, also called **market risk**, is the risk faced by all firms. Changes in the economy as a whole, such as inflation or the business cycle, affect all players in the market.

       1)   For this reason, systematic risk is sometimes referred to as **undiversifiable risk**. Since all investments are affected, this risk cannot be offset through diversification.

    b.   **Unsystematic risk**, also called **unique risk**, is the risk inherent in a particular investment. This type of risk is determined by the firm's industry, products, customer loyalty, degree of leverage, management competence, etc.

       1)   For this reason, unsystematic risk is sometimes referred to as **diversifiable risk**. Since individual investments are affected by the particular strengths and weaknesses of the firm, this risk can be offset through diversification.

6.   **Types of Investment Risk**

    a.   **Credit default risk** is the risk that the borrower will default and will not be able to repay the principal or interest that it is obligated to pay. This risk can be gauged by the use of credit-rating agencies.

    b.   **Liquidity risk** is the risk that a security cannot be sold on short notice for its market value.

    c.   **Maturity risk**, also called **interest rate risk**, is the risk that an investment security will fluctuate in value between the time it was issued and its maturity date. The longer the time until maturity, the greater the degree of maturity risk.

    d.   **Inflation risk** is the risk that purchasing power will be lost while the loan is at the borrower's disposal.

    e.   **Political risk** is the probability of loss from actions of governments, such as from changes in tax laws or environmental regulations or from expropriation of assets.

    f.   **Exchange rate risk** is the risk of loss because of fluctuation in the relative value of foreign currency.

g. **Business risk** (or **operations risk**) is the risk of fluctuations in earnings before interest and taxes or in operating income when the firm uses no debt. It is the risk inherent in its operations that excludes **financial risk**, which is the risk to the shareholders from the use of financial leverage. Business risk depends on factors such as demand variability, sales price variability, input price variability, and amount of operating leverage.

7. **Portfolio Management**

a. The goal of portfolio management is to construct a basket of securities that generates a return without the risks associated with holding a single security. An investor wants to maximize return and minimize risk when choosing a portfolio of investments.

1) Portfolio **return** is simply the weighted average of the returns on the individual securities in the portfolio.

2) Portfolio **risk** is usually less than a simple average of the risks of the securities in the portfolio. One of the goals of diversification is to offset the unsystematic risk.

b. The **coefficient of correlation** can measure the degree to which the prices of two stocks, are related. It has a range from 1.0 to –1.0.

1) Perfect positive correlation (1.0) means that the prices of two securities always move together.

2) Perfect negative correlation (–1.0) means that the prices of two securities always move in the opposite direction.

3) If a pair of securities has a coefficient of correlation of 1.0, the risk of the two together is the same as the risk of each security by itself. If a pair of securities has a coefficient of correlation of –1.0, all specific (unsystematic) risk has been eliminated.

c. The ideal portfolio consists of securities with a wide enough variety of coefficients of correlation so that only market risk remains.

Stop and review! You have completed the outline for this subunit. Study multiple-choice questions 1 and 2 on page 412.

16.2 DERIVATIVES

1. **Overview**

a. A **derivative instrument** is an investment transaction in which the parties' gain or loss is derived from some other economic event, for example, the price of a given stock, a foreign currency exchange rate, or the price of a certain commodity.

1) One party enters into the transaction to speculate (incur risk), and the other enters into it to hedge (avoid risk).

b. Derivatives are a type of financial instrument, along with cash, accounts receivable, notes receivable, bonds, preferred shares, etc.

2. **Options**

a. A party who buys an option has bought the right to demand that the counterparty (the seller or "writer" of the option) buy or sell an underlying asset on or before a specified future date. The buyer holds all of the rights, and the seller has all of the obligations. The buyer pays a fee to be able to dictate – in the future – whether the seller buys or sells the underlying asset from or to the buyer.

1) A **call option** gives the buyer (holder) the right to purchase (i.e., the right to "call" for) the underlying asset (stock, currency, commodity, etc.) at a fixed price.

2) A **put option** gives the buyer (holder) the right to sell (i.e., the right to "put" onto the market) the underlying asset (stock, currency, commodity, etc.) at a fixed price.

3) The asset that is subject to being bought or sold under the terms of the option is referred to as the **underlying**.

4) The party buying an option is referred to as the **holder**. The seller is referred to as the **writer**.

5) The exercise of an option is always at the discretion of the option holder (the buyer) who has, in effect, bought the right to exercise the option or not. The seller of an option has no choice; (s)he must perform if the holder chooses to exercise.

6) An option has an expiration date after which it can no longer be exercised.

3. **Components of Option Price**

a. The price of an option (the option premium) consists of two components: intrinsic value and the time premium, also called extrinsic value.

$$Option\ premium\ =\ Intrinsic\ value\ +\ Time\ premium$$

b. The **exercise price** is the price at which the holder can purchase (in the case of a call option) or sell (in the case of a put option) the asset underlying the option contract.

c. The **intrinsic value of a call option** is the amount by which the exercise price is less than the current price of the underlying.

1) If an option has a positive intrinsic value, it is said to be in-the-money.

EXAMPLE

An investor holds call options for 200 shares of Locksley Corporation with an exercise price of US $48 per share. Locksley stock is currently trading at US $50 per share. The investor's options have an intrinsic value of US $2 each ($50 – $48).

---

2) If an option has an intrinsic value of US $0, it is said to be out-of-the-money.

EXAMPLE

An investor holds call options for 200 shares of Locksley Corporation with an exercise price of US $48 per share. Locksley stock is currently trading at US $45 per share. The investor's options are out-of-the-money (they have no intrinsic value).

---

d. The **intrinsic value of a put option** is the amount by which the exercise price is greater than the current price of the underlying.

1) If an option has a positive intrinsic value, it is said to be in-the-money.

EXAMPLE

An investor holds put options for 200 shares of Locksley Corporation with an exercise price of US $48 per share. Locksley stock is currently trading at US $45 per share. The investor's options have an intrinsic value of US $3 each ($48 – $45).

---

2) If an option has an intrinsic value of US $0, it is said to be out-of-the-money.

EXAMPLE

An investor holds put options for 200 shares of Locksley Corporation with an exercise price of US $48 per share. Locksley stock is currently trading at US $50 per share. The investor's options are out-of-the-money (they have no intrinsic value).

---

e. Time Premium

1) The more time that exists between the writing of an option and its expiration, the riskier any investment is. Since the buyer's loss of an option is limited to the option premium, an increase in the term of an option (both calls and puts) will result in an increase in the time premium.

4. **Forward Contracts**

   a. One method of mitigating risk is the simple forward contract. The two parties agree that, at a set future date, one of them will perform and the other will pay a specified amount for the performance.

      1) A common example is that of a retailer and a wholesaler who agree in September on the prices and quantities of merchandise that will be shipped to the retailer's stores in time for the winter holiday season. The retailer has locked in a price and a source of supply, and the wholesaler has locked in a price and a customer.

   b. In a forward contract, each party has an obligation, i.e., to deliver merchandise or to pay. Neither has the option of nonperformance.

      1) Forward contracts are heavily used in foreign currency exchange.

5. **Futures Contracts**

   a. A futures contract is a commitment to buy or sell an asset at a fixed price during a specific future period; unlike with a forward contract, the counterparty is unknown.

   b. Futures contracts are actively traded on futures exchanges.

      1) The clearinghouse randomly matches sellers who will deliver during a given period with buyers who are seeking delivery during the same period.

   c. Because futures contracts are actively traded, the result is a **liquid market** in futures that permits buyers and sellers to net out their positions.

   d. Another distinguishing feature of futures contracts is that the market price is posted and netted to each person's account at the close of every business day. This practice is called **mark-to-market**.

      1) A mark-to-market provision minimizes a futures contract's chance of default because profits and losses on the contracts must be received or paid each day through a clearinghouse (and because the clearinghouse guarantees the transactions).

6. **Swap Contracts**

   a. A **swap** transaction is an exchange of one party's stream of payments for another party's stream of payments with a different pattern.

      1) For example, an **interest rate swap** is an exchange of one party's interest payments based on a **fixed rate** for another party's interest payments based on a **variable rate**.

      2) An interest rate swap is appropriate when one counterparty prefers the payment pattern of the other. For example, a firm with fixed-rate debt may have revenues that vary with interest rates. It may prefer variable-rate debt so that its debt service will correlate directly with its revenues.

7. **Hedging**

   a. Hedging is the process of using offsetting commitments to minimize or avoid the effects of adverse price movements. Hedging transactions often are used to protect positions in commodity buying, foreign currency, and future cash flows.

      1) Thus, the purchase or sale of a derivative or other instrument is a hedge if it is expected to neutralize the risk of a recognized asset or liability, an unrecognized firm commitment, a forecasted transaction, etc.

      2) An example of the hedging approach is financing an asset with a financial instrument of the same approximate maturity as the life of the asset. The basic concept is that the entity has the entire life of the asset to recover the amount invested before having to pay the lender.

b. **Long position** hedges are futures contracts that are purchased to protect against price increases.

    1) For example, if a flour company buys and uses 1 million bushels of wheat each month, it may wish to guard against increases in wheat costs. If so, it will purchase futures contracts to buy 1 million bushels of wheat at the current price one month from today. This long position hedge will result in gains if the price of wheat increases (offsetting the actual increased costs).

c. **Short position** hedges are futures contracts that are sold to protect against price declines.

Stop and review! You have completed the outline for this subunit. Study multiple-choice questions 3 through 5 beginning on page 412.

16.3 CORPORATE CAPITAL STRUCTURE -- DEBT FINANCING

1. **Debt vs. Equity**

    a. The balance sheet of an entity can be depicted as the perfect balance between the firm's resources and its capital structure. The resources consist of the assets the firm deploys in its attempts to earn a return. The capital structure consists of the amounts contributed by outsiders (debt) and insiders (equity) to make the use of these assets possible.

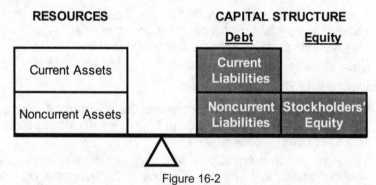

Figure 16-2

    1) Arriving at the appropriate mix of debt and equity in the capital structure is a challenge all corporations face. Each component of the capital structure bears a cost that changes as economic conditions change and as more or less of that component is deployed.

2. **Aspects of Bonds**

    a. Bonds are the principal form of long-term debt financing for corporations and governmental entities.

        1) A bond is a formal contractual obligation to pay an amount of money (called the par value, maturity amount, or face amount) to the holder at a certain date, plus, in most cases, a series of cash interest payments based on a specified percentage (called the stated rate or coupon rate) of the face amount at specified intervals.

        2) All of the terms of the agreement are stated in a document called an indenture.

b. In general, the longer the term of a bond is, the higher the return (yield) demanded by investors to compensate for increased risk will be. This relationship is depicted graphically by the yield curve.

Positive (Normal) Yield Curve

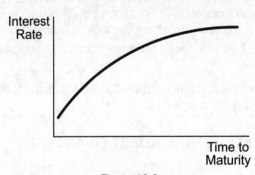

Figure 16-3

c. A bond indenture may require the issuer to establish and maintain a **bond sinking fund**. The objective of making payments into the fund is to segregate and accumulate sufficient assets to pay the bond principal at maturity.

d. Advantages of Bonds to the Issuer

1) Interest paid on debt is tax deductible. This is by far the most significant advantage of debt. For a corporation facing a 40%-50% marginal tax rate, the tax savings produced by the deduction of interest can be substantial.

2) Basic control of the firm is not shared with debtholders.

e. Disadvantages of Bonds to the Issuer

1) Unlike returns on equity investments, the payment of interest and principal on debt is a legal obligation. If cash flow is insufficient to service debt, the firm could become insolvent.

2) The legal requirement to pay debt service raises a firm's risk level. Shareholders will consequently demand higher capitalization rates on retained earnings, which may result in a decline in the market price of the stock.

3) Bonds may require some collateral that restricts the entity's assets.

4) The amount of debt financing available to the individual firm is limited. Generally accepted standards of the investment community will usually dictate a certain debt-equity ratio for an individual firm. Beyond this limit, the cost of debt may rise rapidly, or debt may not be available.

3. **Types of Bonds**

a. Maturity Pattern

1) A **term bond** has a single maturity date at the end of its term.
2) A **serial bond** matures in stated amounts at regular intervals.

b. Valuation

1) **Variable (or floating) rate bonds** pay interest that is dependent on market conditions.

2) **Zero-coupon or deep-discount bonds** bear no stated rate of interest and thus involve no periodic cash payments; the interest component consists entirely of the bond's discount.

3) **Commodity-backed bonds** are payable at prices related to a commodity such as gold.

   c. Redemption Provisions

      1) **Callable bonds** may be repurchased by the issuer at a specified price before maturity. During a period of falling interest rates, this allows the issuer to replace old high-interest debt with new low-interest debt.

      2) **Convertible bonds** may be converted into equity securities of the issuer at the option of the holder under certain conditions. The ability to become equity holders is an inducement to potential investors, allowing the issuer to offer a lower coupon rate.

   d. Securitization

      1) **Mortgage bonds** are backed by specific assets, usually real estate.

      2) **Debentures** are backed by the borrower's general credit but not by specific collateral.

   e. Ownership

      1) **Registered bonds** are issued in the name of the holder. Only the registered holder may receive interest and principal payments.

      2) **Bearer bonds** are not individually registered. Interest and principal are paid to whoever presents the bond.

   f. Priority

      1) **Subordinated debentures** and second mortgage bonds are junior securities with claims inferior to those of senior bonds.

   g. Repayment Provisions

      1) **Income bonds** pay interest contingent on the issuer's profitability.

      2) **Revenue bonds** are issued by governmental units and are payable from specific revenue sources.

4. **Bond Ratings**

   a. Investors can judge the creditworthiness of a bond issue by consulting the rating assigned by a credit-rating agency. The higher the rating, the more likely the firm is to make good its commitment to pay the interest and principal.

   b. This field is dominated by the three largest firms: Moody's, Standard & Poor's, and Fitch.

      1) **Investment-grade bonds** are considered safe investments and thus have the lowest yields. The highest rating assigned is "triple-A." Some fiduciary organizations (such as banks and insurance companies) are only allowed to invest in investment-grade bonds.

      2) **Non-investment grade bonds**, also called speculative-grade bonds, high-yield bonds, or junk bonds, carry high risk.

Stop and review! You have completed the outline for this subunit. Study multiple-choice questions 6 though 8 beginning on page 413.

16.4 CORPORATE CAPITAL STRUCTURE -- EQUITY FINANCING

1. **Relevant Terminology**

   a. The most widely used classes of stock are common and preferred. The following basic terminology is related to stock.

      1) Stock **authorized** is the maximum amount of stock that a corporation is legally allowed to issue.

      2) Stock **issued** is the amount of stock authorized that has actually been issued by the corporation.

      3) Stock **outstanding** is the amount of stock issued that has been purchased and is held by shareholders.

2. **Common Stock**

    a. The **common shareholders** are the owners of a corporation, and their rights as owners, although reasonably uniform, depend on the laws where it is incorporated.

        1) Equity ownership involves risk because holders of shares are not guaranteed a return and are last in priority in a liquidation.

    b. Advantages to the Issuer

        1) Dividends are not fixed. They are paid from profits when available.
        2) They have no fixed maturity date for repayment of the capital.
        3) The sale of common shares increases the creditworthiness of the entity by providing more equity.

    c. Disadvantages to the Issuer

        1) New common shares dilute earnings per share available to existing shareholders because of the greater number of shares outstanding.
        2) Underwriting costs (i.e., costs of issuing common shares) are typically higher for shares than other forms of financing.
        3) Too much equity may raise the average cost of capital of the entity above its optimal level.
        4) Cash dividends on common shares are not tax-deductible; they must be paid out of after-tax profits.

    d. Common shareholders may have preemptive rights

        1) Preemptive rights give common shareholders the right to purchase any additional issuances in proportion to their current ownership. Thus, they can maintain their ownership percentages.

    e. **Common stock valuation** based on dividend yield models

        1) When the dividend per share of common stock is constant and expected to be paid continuously, the price per share is calculated as follows:

            $$P_0 = D \div r$$

            P_0 = Price per share now
            D = Dividend per share (constant)
            r = Required rate of return (cost of common stock)

        2) The **constant growth model** (dividend discount model) assumes that dividend per share and price per share grow at the same constant rate. The price per share can be calculated as follows:

            $$P_0 = \frac{D_0(1 + g)}{r - g} = \frac{D_1}{r - g}$$

            P_0 = Price per share now
            D_0 = Dividend per share now
            D_1 = Dividend per share expected next year
            r = Required rate of return (cost of common stock)
            g = Growth rate (constant)

            a) According to this model, the market value of an entity's outstanding stock will be higher if investors have a lower required return on equity.

EXAMPLE

Today a company paid dividends of US $10 per share. The dividends are expected to grow at a constant rate of 5% per year. If the investors' required rate of return is 8%, the current market value of the company's share will be US $350.

$$P_0 = \frac{D_0(1 + g)}{r - g} = \frac{US \$10(1 + 5\%)}{8\% - 5\%} = US \$350$$

---

3) The required rate of return (the cost of common stock) can be derived from the dividend growth model.

$$r = \frac{D_1}{P_0} + g$$

4) The price per share (P_0) upon issuance equals the net proceeds from the issuance (gross proceeds – flotation costs). Flotation costs are also called issuance costs.

3. **Preferred Stock**

a. Preferred stock has features of debt and equity. It has a fixed charge, but payment of dividends is not an obligation.

1) Debt holders have priority over preferred shareholders in liquidation.

b. Advantages to the Issuer

1) Preferred stock is a form of equity and therefore increases the creditworthiness of the entity.

2) Control is still held by common shareholders.

3) Since preferred stock does not require periodic payments, failure to pay dividends will not lead to bankruptcy.

c. Disadvantages to the Issuer

1) Cash dividends paid are not tax deductible as a tax expense and are paid with taxable income.

2) In periods of economic difficulty, cumulative (past) dividends may create major managerial and financial problems for the firm.

d. Typical Provisions of Preferred Stock Issues

1) Par value. Par value is the liquidation value, and a percentage of par equals the preferred dividend.

2) Priority in assets and earnings. If the entity goes bankrupt, the preferred shareholders have priority over common shareholders.

3) Accumulation of dividends. If preferred dividends are cumulative, dividends in arrears must be paid before any common dividends can be paid.

4) Convertibility. Preferred share issues may be convertible into common shares at the option of the shareholder.

5) Participation. Preferred shares may receive the entity's earnings beyond the stated dividend level. For example, 8% participating preferred shares might pay a dividend each year greater than 8% when the entity is extremely profitable. But nonparticipating preferred shares will receive no more than is stated on the face of the share.

e.   **Preferred stock valuation**

1)   The future cash flows from the preferred stock are assumed to consist only of the estimated future annual dividends (D_p).

$$D_p = \textit{Par value of preferred stock} \times \textit{Preferred dividend rate}$$

2)   The discount rate used is the investor's required rate of return (r).

3)   Unlike a bond, which has a specific maturity date, preferred stock is assumed to be outstanding in perpetuity.

$$\textit{Preferred stock price}(P_p) = \frac{D_p}{r}$$

EXAMPLE

The value of a share of preferred stock with a par value of US $100 and a dividend rate of 5% to an investor with a required rate of return of 10% is US $50 [($100 × 5%) ÷ 10%].

---

4.   **Debt vs. Equity Financing**

a.   The main differences between debt financing (involving the payment of interest) and equity financing (involving the payment of dividends) can be summarized as follows:

	Equity Financing	Debt Financing
Effect on company's control	Yes	No
Cost of issuing	Higher	Lower
Effect on net income	No	Yes
Dilution of EPS	Yes	No
Effect on solvency risk	No	Yes
Tax deductibility of payments	No	Yes

Stop and review! You have completed the outline for this subunit. Study multiple-choice questions 9 and 10 on page 414.

16.5 CORPORATE CAPITAL STRUCTURE -- COST OF CAPITAL

1.   **Overview**

a.   Investors provide funds to corporations with the understanding that management will deploy those funds in such a way that the investor will ultimately receive a return.

1)   If management does not generate the investors' required rate of return, the investors will sell their stock on the secondary market, causing the value of the stock to drop. Creditors will then demand higher rates on the firm's debt.

2)   For this reason, the investors' required rate of return (also called their opportunity cost of capital) becomes the firm's cost of capital.

b.   A firm's cost of capital is typically used to discount the future cash flows of long-term projects. Investments with a rate of return higher than the cost of capital will increase the value of the firm, i.e., shareholders' wealth. (The cost of capital is not used in connection with working capital since short-term needs are met with short-term funds.)

1)   Providers of equity capital are exposed to more risk than are lenders because

a)   The firm is not legally obligated to pay them a return and

b)   Creditors have priority in case of liquidation.

2)   To compensate for this higher risk, equity investors demand a higher return, making equity financing more expensive than debt.

2. **Component Costs of Capital**

    a.   A firm's financing structure consists of three components: long-term debt, preferred equity, and common equity (retained earnings are treated as part of common equity in this analysis for reasons given below).

        1)   The rate of return demanded by holders of each is the component cost for that form of capital.

    b.   The component cost of **long-term debt** is the after-tax interest rate on the debt (interest payments are tax-deductible by the firm).

$$\textit{Effective rate} \times (1.0 - \textit{Marginal tax rate})$$

    c.   The component cost of **preferred stock** is computed using the dividend yield ratio.

$$\textit{Cash dividend on preferred stock} \div \textit{Market price of preferred stock}$$

        1)   The market price of preferred stock upon issuance equals the net proceeds from the issuance (gross proceeds – flotation costs). Flotation costs, also called issuance costs, reduce the net proceeds received, thereby raising the cost of capital.

    d.   The component cost of **retained earnings** is considered to be the same as that for common stock (if the firm cannot find a profitable use for retained earnings, it should be distributed to the common shareholders in the form of dividends so that they can find their own alternative investments).

EXAMPLE

A company has outstanding bonds with a coupon rate of 7% and an effective rate of 5%. The company's 9%, US $60 par-value preferred stock is currently trading at US $67.50 per share, while its US $1 par-value common stock trades at US $1.40 per share and pays a 14% dividend. The applicable tax rate is 35%.

The company's component costs of capital are calculated as follows:

Long-Term Debt	Preferred Equity	Common Equity
Cost = Effective rate × (1.0 – Tax rate)	Cost = Cash dividend ÷ Market price	Cost = Cash dividend ÷ Market price
= 5% × (1.0 – .35)	= (US $60 × 9%) ÷ $67.50	= (US $1 × 14%) ÷ $1.40
= 5% × .65	= US $5.40 ÷ $67.50	= US $.14 ÷ $1.40
= 3.25%	= 8%	= 10%

---

3. **Weighted-Average Cost of Capital (WACC)**

    a.   Corporate management usually designates a target capital structure for the firm, i.e., the proportions that each component of capital should comprise in the overall combination.

        1)   An example might be 10% debt, 20% preferred stock, and 70% common stock.

    b.   A firm's WACC is a single, composite rate of return on its combined components of capital. The weights are based on the firm's target capital structure.

EXAMPLE

The company has set a target capital structure of 20% long-term debt, 30% preferred equity, and 50% common equity. The weighted-average cost of capital can thus be calculated as follows:

	Target Weight		Cost of Capital		Weighted Cost
Long-term debt	20%	×	3.25%	=	0.65%
Preferred equity	30%	×	8%	=	2.40%
Common equity	50%	×	10%	=	5.00%
					8.05%

4.   **Optimal Capital Structure**

a.   Standard financial theory provides a model for the optimal capital structure of every firm. This model holds that shareholder wealth-maximization results from **minimizing the weighted-average cost of capital**. Thus, the focus of management should not be only on maximizing earnings per share (EPS can be increased by taking on more debt, but debt increases risk).

1)   The relevant relationships are depicted below:

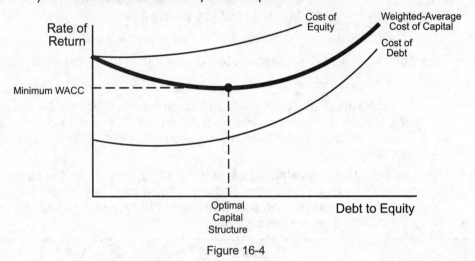

Figure 16-4

a)   Ordinarily, firms cannot identify this optimal point precisely. Thus, they should attempt to find an optimal range for the capital structure.

5.   **Marginal Cost of Capital**

a.   The marginal cost of capital is the cost to the entity of the next monetary unit of new capital raised after existing internal sources are exhausted. Each additional monetary unit raised becomes increasingly expensive as investors demand higher returns to compensate for increased risk.

EXAMPLE

A company has determined that it requires US $4,000,000 of new funding to fulfill its plans. Retained earnings are insufficient, and the entity wants to maintain its capital structure of 30% long-term debt and 70% equity. The cost of raising the US $2,800,000 shortfall between retained earnings and funding needs will be at some rate above the current WACC.

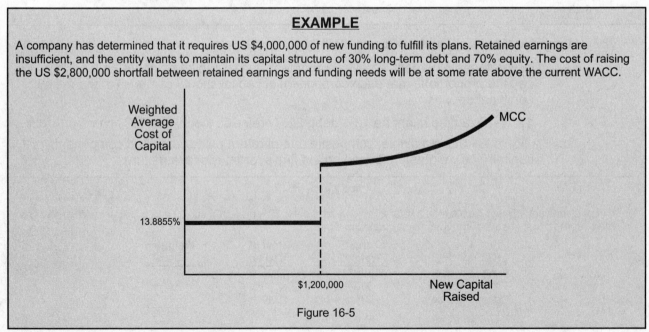

Figure 16-5

Stop and review! You have completed the outline for this subunit. Study multiple-choice questions 11 and 12 on page 415.

16.6 CAPITAL BUDGETING

1. **Capital Budgeting -- Basics**

   a. Capital budgeting is the process of planning and controlling investments for long-term projects.

   b. A capital project usually involves substantial expenditures. Planning is crucial because of uncertainties about capital markets, inflation, interest rates, and the money supply.

   c. Capital budgeting applications include

      1) Buying equipment
      2) Building facilities
      3) Acquiring a business
      4) Developing a product or product line
      5) Expanding into new markets
      6) Replacement of equipment

2. **Relevant Cash Flows**

   a. The first step in assessing the desirability of a potential capital project is to identify the relevant cash flows.

      1) Relevant cash flows do not include sunk costs, i.e., those that have already been paid or are irrevocably committed to be paid. No matter which alternative is selected, sunk costs are already spent and are thus irrelevant to a decision.

   b. The relevant cash flows for capital budgeting are

      1) Cost of new equipment
      2) Annual after-tax cash savings or inflows
      3) Proceeds from disposal of old equipment/residual (salvage) value

         a) The gain or loss on disposal of old equipment is **not** a relevant cash flow.

      4) Adjustment for depreciation expense on new equipment (called the depreciation tax shield) since it reduces taxable income and thereby reduces cash outflow for tax expense

---

EXAMPLE

A company's annual recurring operating cash income from a new machine is US $100,000. The annual depreciation expense on this machine is US $20,000. The effective tax rate is 40%. To calculate the company's after-tax annual cash flows from the new machine, the annual depreciation expense must be taken into account.

Operating cash inflow	US $100,000	Taxable income	US $80,000
Depreciation expense	(20,000)	Effective tax rate	× 40%
Annual taxable income	US $ 80,000	Income tax payment	US $32,000

Operating cash inflow	US $100,000
Income tax payment	(32,000)
After-tax cash flow	US $ 68,000

After-tax cash flow can also be calculated as follows:

Operating cash flow net of taxes [US $100,000 × (1.0 – .40)]	US $60,000
Depreciation tax shield [US $20,000 × 40%]	8,000
Annual after-tax cash flow	US $68,000

NOTE: Depreciation expense affects cash inflow only through income tax considerations.

---

3. **Net Present Value (NPV)**

   a. Net present value (NPV) involves discounting the relevant cash flows using the required rate of return as the discount rate. This rate is also called the hurdle rate or opportunity cost of capital.

b.   A capital project's net present value is the difference between the present value of the net cash savings or inflows expected over the life of the project and the required dollar investment.

1)   If the difference is positive, the project should be undertaken. If the difference is negative, it should be rejected.

EXAMPLE

The Juan Fangio Co. is considering the purchase of a machine for US $250,000 that will have a useful life of 10 years with no residual (salvage) value. The machine is expected to generate an annual operating cash savings of US $60,000 over its useful life and would be depreciated on the straight-line basis, resulting in annual depreciation expense of US $25,000 ($250,000 ÷ 10 years). Fangio's internal rate of return is 12%, and its effective tax rate is 40%.

The present value of US $1 for 10 periods at 12% is 0.322, and the present value of an ordinary annuity of US $1 for 10 periods at 12% is 5.650. Fangio calculates the net present value of this potential investment as follows:

Present value of cash savings		
Annual operating cash savings/inflows		US $ 60,000
Annual tax expense:		
Tax expense on annual cash savings		
(60,000 × 40%)	US $(24,000)	
Depreciation tax shield (25,000 × 40%)	10,000	(14,000)
After-tax net annual cash savings		US $ 46,000
Times: PV factor for an ordinary annuity		× 5.650
Present value of net cash savings		US $259,900
Required investment		
Cost of new equipment		US $250,000
Net present value of investment		
Present value of net cash savings		US $259,900
Less: required investment		(250,000)
Net present value of investment		US $ 9,900

The positive net present value indicates that the project should be undertaken.

---

c.   Use of the net present value method involves the implicit assumption that cash flows are reinvested at the entity's minimum required rate of return.

4.   **Internal Rate of Return (IRR)**

a.   The internal rate of return of a project is the discount rate at which the investment's net present value equals zero. In other words, it is the rate that equates the present value of the expected cash inflows with the present value of the expected cash outflows.

1)   If the internal rate of return is higher than the company's hurdle rate, the investment is desirable. If the internal rate of return is lower, the project should be rejected.

IRR > Hurdle rate: Accept project

IRR < Hurdle rate: Reject project

EXAMPLE

John Lauda, Inc., has a hurdle rate of 12% for all capital projects. The firm is considering a project that calls for a cash outlay of US $200,000 that will create savings in after-tax cash costs of US $52,000 for each of the next 5 years. The applicable present value factor is 3.846 (US $200,000 ÷ $52,000). Consulting a table of present value factors for an ordinary annuity for 5 periods places this factor somewhere between 9% and 10%. Since this is less than Lauda's hurdle rate, the project will be rejected.

5. **Comparing Net Present Value (NPV) and Internal Rate of Return (IRR)**

    a. The reinvestment rate becomes critical when choosing between the NPV and IRR methods.

        1) NPV assumes the cash flows from the investment can be reinvested at the particular project's discount rate, that is, the desired rate of return.

    b. The NPV and IRR methods give the same accept/reject decision if projects are independent. Independent projects have unrelated cash flows. Hence, all acceptable independent projects can be undertaken.

        1) However, if projects are **mutually exclusive**, only one project can be accepted. The others must be rejected.

        2) The NPV and IRR methods may rank projects differently if

            a) The cost of one project is greater than the cost of another.

            b) The timing, amounts, and directions of cash flows differ among projects.

            c) The projects have different useful lives.

            d) The cost of capital or desired rate of return varies over the life of a project. The NPV can easily be determined using different desired rates of return for different periods. The IRR determines one rate for the project.

            e) Multiple investments are involved in a project. NPV amounts are addable, but IRR rates are not. The IRR for the whole is not the sum of the IRRs for the parts.

        3) The IRR method assumes that the cash flows will be reinvested at the internal rate of return.

            a) If the project's funds are not reinvested at the IRR, the ranking calculations obtained may be in error.

            b) The NPV method gives a better grasp of the problem in many decision situations because the reinvestment is assumed to be in the desired rate of return.

6. **Payback Period**

    a. The payback period is the number of years required for the net cash savings or inflows to equal the original investment, i.e., the time necessary for an investment to pay for itself.

        1) Companies using the payback method set a maximum length of time within which projects must pay for themselves to be considered acceptable.

    b. If the cash flows are constant, the formula is

$$Payback\ period = \frac{Initial\ investment}{Annual\ after\text{-}tax\ cash\ savings/inflows}$$

        1) Note that no consideration is made for the time value of money under this method.

EXAMPLE with Constant Cash Flows

John Lauda also applies a 4-year payback period test on all capital projects.

Payback period = US $200,000 ÷ $52,000 = 3.846 years

Judged by this criterion, the project is acceptable because its payback period is less than the company's maximum.

c.   If the cash flows are not constant, the calculation must be in cumulative form.

EXAMPLE with Varying Cash Flows

Assume that John Lauda's initial investment is US $160,000 and that, instead of the smooth inflows predicted on page 402, the project's cash stream is expected to vary. The payback period is calculated as follows:

End of Year	Cash Savings	Remaining Initial Investment
Initial investment	US $ --	US $160,000
Year 1	48,000	112,000
Year 2	54,000	58,000
Year 3	54,000	4,000
Year 4	60,000	--

The project is acceptable because its payback period is over 3 years and under 4 years and is less than the company's maximum.

---

d.   The strength of the payback method is its simplicity.

  1)   To some extent, the payback period measures risk. The longer the period, the more risky the investment.

e.   The payback method has the following two significant weaknesses:

  1)   It does not recognize the time value of money. Weighting all cash inflows equally ignores the benefits of early receipts and delayed payments.

  2)   It neglects total project profitability by disregarding all cash inflows after the payback cutoff date. Applying a single cutoff date to every project results in accepting many marginal projects and rejecting good ones.

7.   **Accounting Rate of Return**

a.   The accounting rate of return is a measure used to assess potential capital projects that ignores the time value of money.

$$\text{Accounting rate of return} = \frac{\text{Annual increase in GAAP net income}}{\text{Required investment}} = \frac{\text{Annual cash inflow} - \text{Depreciation}}{\text{Initial investment}}$$

EXAMPLE

A manufacturer is considering the purchase of a new piece of machinery that would cost US $250,000 and would decrease annual after-tax cash costs by US $40,000. The machine is expected to have a 10-year useful life, no salvage value, and would be depreciated on the straight-line basis. The firm calculates the accounting rate of return on this machine as follows:

Annual cash savings	US $ 40,000
Less: annual depreciation expense (US $250,000 ÷ 10 years)	(25,000)
Annual increase in accounting net income	US $ 15,000
Divided by: purchase price of new equipment	÷ 250,000
Accounting rate of return	6%

---

  1)   The advantage of this method is that the financial statement numbers are readily available.

  2)   The disadvantages of this method are that financial statement numbers (a) are affected by the company's choices of accounting methods and (b) do not represent cash flows.

8. **Economic Value Added**

     a. Economic value added (EVA) is the formula for residual income adjusted for the opportunity cost of capital.

     b. The basic formula can be stated as follows:

After-tax operating income	US $XXX,XXX
Investment (capital used) × Cost of capital (WACC)	(XX,XXX)
Economic value added	US $ XX,XXX

EXAMPLE

A company invested US $200,000 in a new operating segment. The current-year net income of the segment was US $21,000. The company's cost of capital is 9%.

Net income	US $21,000
Investment × Cost of capital (US $200,000 × 9%)	(18,000)
Economic value added	US $ 3,000

The economic value is positive. Thus, the investment in a new operating segment increased shareholder value.

---

     c. EVA represents a business unit's true economic profit primarily because a charge for the cost of equity capital is implicit in the cost of capital.

         1) The cost of equity is an opportunity cost, that is, the return that could have been obtained on the best alternative investment of similar risk.

         2) Hence, EVA measures the marginal benefit obtained by using resources in a particular way. It is useful for determining whether a segment of a business is increasing shareholder value.

Stop and review! You have completed the outline for this subunit. Study multiple-choice questions 13 and 14 beginning on page 415.

16.7 CASH MANAGEMENT AND WORKING CAPITAL

1. **Managing the Level of Cash**

     a. As part of his theory of money demand, English economist John Maynard Keynes outlined three motives for holding cash:

         1) The transactional motive, i.e., to use as a medium of exchange

         2) The precautionary motive, i.e., to provide a cushion for unexpected contingencies

         3) The speculative motive, i.e., to take advantage of unexpected opportunities

     b. The goal of cash management is to determine and maintain the firm's optimal cash balance.

         1) This is not the same as "maximizing cash." Since ready cash does not earn a return, only the amount needed to satisfy current obligations as they come due should be kept. Striking this balance is the essence of cash management.

     c. The firm's optimal level of cash should be determined by a cost-benefit analysis.

         1) The need to satisfy the three motives listed above must be balanced against the opportunity cost of missed investments in marketable securities.

     d. A **compensating balance** is a minimum amount that the bank requires the firm to keep in its demand (checking) account. Compensating balances are noninterest-bearing and are meant to compensate the bank for various services rendered, such as unlimited check writing. These funds are obviously unavailable for short-term investment and thus incur an opportunity cost.

2. **Speeding Up Cash Collections**

    a. The period of time from when a payor puts a check in the mail until the funds are available in the payee's bank is called float. Companies use various strategies to reduce the float time on receipts (and to stretch the float time on payments, discussed in item 3. below).

    b. A **lockbox** system is the single most important strategy for expediting the receipt of funds.

        1) Customers submit their payments to a post office box rather than to the company's offices. Bank personnel remove the envelopes from the mailbox and deposit the checks to the company's account immediately. The remittance advices must then be transported to the company for entry into the accounts receivable system. The bank generally charges a flat monthly fee for this service.

        2) For firms doing business nationwide, a lockbox network is appropriate. The country is divided into regions according to customer population patterns. A lockbox arrangement is then established with a bank in each region.

    c. A firm employing a lockbox network will usually engage in concentration banking. The regional banks that provide lockbox services automatically transfer their daily collections to the firm's principal bank, where they can be used for disbursement and short-term investment.

3. **Slowing Cash Disbursements**

    a. A **draft** is a three-party instrument in which one person (the drawer) orders a second person (the drawee) to pay money to a third person (the payee).

        1) A check is the most common form of draft. A check is an instrument payable on demand in which the drawee is a bank. Consequently, a draft can be used to delay the outflow of cash.

        2) A draft can be dated on the due date of an invoice and will not be processed by the drawee until that date, thereby eliminating the necessity of writing a check earlier than the due date or using an electronic funds transfer (EFT). Thus, the outflow is delayed until the check clears the drawee bank.

    b. A **payable through draft** (PTD) differs from a check in that (1) it is not payable on demand and (2) the drawee is the payor, not a bank. After the payee presents the PTD to a bank, the bank in turn presents it to the issuer. The issuer then must deposit sufficient funds to cover the PTD. Use of PTDs thus allows a firm to maintain lower cash balances.

        1) Drawbacks are that vendors obviously prefer to receive an instrument that will be paid on demand, and banks generally impose higher processing charges for PTDs.

    c. A **zero-balance account** (ZBA) carries, as the name implies, a balance of $0. At the end of each processing day, the bank transfers just enough from the firm's master account to cover all checks presented against the ZBA that day.

        1) This practice allows the firm to maintain higher balances in the master account from which short-term investments can be made. The bank generally charges a fee for this service.

    d. **Disbursement float** is the period of time from when the payor puts a check in the mail until the funds are deducted from the payor's account. In an effort to stretch disbursement float, a firm may mail checks to its vendors while being unsure that sufficient funds will be available to cover them all.

        1) For these situations, some banks offer overdraft protection, in which the bank guarantees (for a fee) to cover any shortfall with a transfer from the firm's master account.

4. **Idle Cash and Its Uses**

   a. Idle cash incurs an opportunity cost. To offset this cost, firms invest their idle cash balances in marketable securities.

   b. Beyond earning a modest return, the most important aspects of marketable securities management are liquidity and safety. Marketable securities management thus concerns low-yield, low-risk instruments that are traded on highly active markets, commonly referred to as money market instruments.

   c. The money market is the market for short-term investments where companies invest their temporary surpluses of cash. The money market is not formally organized but consists of many financial institutions, companies, and government agencies offering a wide array of instruments of various risk levels and short- to medium-range maturities.

5. **Permanent and Temporary Working Capital**

   a. **Working capital**, as used by accountants, is calculated as follows:

   $$Working\ capital\ =\ Current\ assets\ -\ Current\ liabilities$$

   b. Trying to apply a simple rule such as "current assets should be financed with current liabilities" is not appropriate to the practice of working capital management.

      1) Some level of liquid current assets must be maintained to meet the firm's long-term minimum needs regardless of the firm's level of activity or profitability. This is termed permanent working capital.

      2) As the firm's needs for current assets change on a seasonal basis, temporary working capital is increased and decreased.

6. **Spontaneous Financing**

   a. Spontaneous financing is the amount of current liabilities, such as trade payables and accruals, that arises naturally in the ordinary course of business without the firm's financial managers needing to take deliberate action.

   b. Trade credit arises when a company is offered credit terms by its suppliers.

EXAMPLE

A vendor has delivered goods and invoiced the company for US $160,000 on terms of net 30. The company has effectively received a 30-day interest-free US $160,000 loan.

---

   c. Accrued expenses, such as salaries, wages, interest, dividends, and taxes payable, are another source of (interest-free) spontaneous financing.

7. **Short-Term vs. Long-Term Financing**

   a. The firm's temporary working capital usually cannot be financed only by spontaneous financing. Therefore, the firm must decide whether to finance it with short-term or long-term financing.

      1) The interest rate on long-term debt is higher than on the short-term. Therefore, long-term financing is more expensive than short-term.

      2) On the other hand, the shorter the maturity schedule of a firm's debt obligation, the greater the risk that the firm will be unable to meet principal and interest payments. This can lead to insolvency.

   b. In general, short-term financing is more risky and less expensive than long-term financing.

8. **Maturity Matching**

   a. Ideally, a firm would be able to offset each element of its temporary working capital with a short-term liability of similar maturity. For example, a short-term loan could be taken out as the winter season approached and repaid with the collections made from holiday sales.

9. **Conservative Policy**

   a.   A firm that adopts a conservative financing policy seeks to minimize liquidity risk by financing its temporary working capital mostly with long-term debt.

   b.   This approach takes advantage of the certainty inherent in long-term debt.

      1)   The locked-in interest rate mitigates interest rate risk (the risk that rates will rise in the short run), and the distant maturity date mitigates liquidity risk (the inability to repay a current obligation when due).

   c.   The drawbacks are

      1)   That working capital sits idle during periods when it is not needed
      2)   That long-term debt is more expensive

10. **Aggressive Policy**

   a.   An aggressive financing policy involves reducing liquidity and accepting a higher risk of short-term cash flow problems in an effort to increase profitability.

      1)   The riskiest working capital financing policy is financing permanent current assets with short-term debt.

   b.   This approach avoids the incurrence of the opportunity cost of funds tied up by the conservative policy, but it runs the risk of either unexpectedly high interest rates or even the total unavailability of financing in the short run.

11. **Summary**

Risk and Profitability in Relation to Financing

Working Capital Component	Financed with	
	Short-Term Debt	Long-Term Debt
Temporary	Medium	Low
Permanent	High	Medium

Stop and review! You have completed the outline for this subunit. Study multiple-choice questions 15 through 17 on page 416.

16.8 SHORT-TERM FINANCING

1. **Spontaneous Financing -- Trade Credit**

   a.   All entities require financing from outside sources to carry on day-to-day operations. These usually take the form of either spontaneous financing, in the form of trade credit offered by vendors, or bank loans.

   b.   If a supplier offers an early payment discount (e.g., terms of 2/10, n/30, meaning a 2% discount is given if the invoice is paid within 10 days or the entire balance is due in 30 days), it is usually to the entity's advantage to avail itself of the discount. The annualized cost of not taking a discount can be calculated with the following formula:

Cost of Not Taking a Discount

$$\frac{Discount\ \%}{100\%\ -\ Discount\ \%} \times \frac{Days\ in\ year}{Total\ payment\ period\ -\ Discount\ period}$$

EXAMPLE

A vendor has delivered goods and invoiced the company on terms of 2/10, net 30. The company has chosen to pay on day 30. The effective annual rate the company paid by forgoing the discount is calculated as follows (using a 360-day year):

Cost of not taking discount = [2% ÷ (100% − 2%)] × [360 days ÷ (30 days − 10 days)]
= (2% ÷ 98%) × (360 days ÷ 20 days)
= 2.0408% × 18
= 36.73%

Only entities in dire cash flow situations would incur a 36.73% cost of funds.

---

2. **Formal Financing Arrangements**

    a. Commercial banks offer short-term financing in the form of term loans and lines of credit.

        1) A **term loan**, such as a note, must be repaid by a definite time.

        2) A **line of credit** allows the company to continuously reborrow amounts up to a certain ceiling as long as certain minimum payments are made each month (similar to a consumer's credit card).

3. **Simple Interest Short-Term Loans**

    a. A simple interest loan is one in which the interest is paid at the end of the loan term. The amount of interest to be paid is based on the nominal (stated) rate and the principal of the loan (amount needed).

$$Interest\ expense = Principal\ of\ loan \times Stated\ rate$$

EXAMPLE

A company obtained a short-term bank loan of US $15,000 at an annual interest rate of 8%. The interest expense on the loan is US $1,200 ($150,000 × 8%).

The stated rate of 8% is also the effective rate.

---

    b. The **effective rate** on any financing arrangement is the ratio of the amount the company must pay to the amount the company gets use of.

$$Effective\ interest\ rate = \frac{Interest\ expense\ (interest\ to\ be\ paid)}{Usable\ funds\ (net\ proceeds)}$$

EXAMPLE

A company obtained a short-term bank loan of US $15,000 at an annual interest rate of 8%. The bank charges a loan origination fee of US $500.

$$\begin{aligned}
Effective\ rate &= Interest\ paid \div Net\ proceeds \\
&= (US\ \$15,000 \times 8\%) \div (\$15,000 - \$500) \\
&= US\ \$1,200 \div \$14,500 \\
&= 8.27\%
\end{aligned}$$

The effective interest rate (8.27%) is higher than the stated interest rate (8%) because the net proceeds are lower than the principal.

---

4. **Discounted Loans**

    a. A discounted loan is one in which the interest and finance charges are paid at the beginning of the loan term.

$$Total\ borrowings = \frac{Amount\ needed}{(1.0 - Stated\ rate)}$$

EXAMPLE

A company needs to pay a US $90,000 invoice. Its bank has offered to extend this amount at an 8% nominal rate on a discounted basis.

$$\begin{aligned}
Total\ borrowings &= Amount\ needed \div (1.0 - Stated\ rate) \\
&= US\ \$90,000 \div (100\% - 8\%) \\
&= US\ \$90,000 \div 92\% \\
&= US\ \$97,826
\end{aligned}$$

---

b.   Because the borrower gets the use of a smaller amount, the effective rate on a discounted loan is higher than its nominal rate.

EXAMPLE

Effective rate = Net interest expense (annualized) ÷ Usable funds
= (US $97,826 × 8%) ÷ $90,000
= US $7,826 ÷ $90,000
= 8.696%

---

c.   As with all financing arrangements, the effective rate can be calculated without reference to dollar amounts.

$$\text{Effective rate on discounted loan} = \frac{\text{Stated rate}}{(1.0 - \text{Stated rate})}$$

EXAMPLE

The entity calculates the effective rate on this loan without using dollar amounts.

Effective rate = Stated rate ÷ (1.0 − Stated rate)
= 8% ÷ (100% − 8%)
= 8% ÷ 92%
= 8.696%

---

5.   **Loans with Compensating Balances**

a.   To reduce risk, banks sometimes require borrowers to maintain a compensating balance during the term of a financing arrangement.

$$\text{Total borrowings} = \frac{\text{Amount needed}}{(1.0 - \text{Compensating balance \%})}$$

EXAMPLE

A company has received an invoice for US $120,000 with terms of 2/10, net 30. The entity's bank will lend it the necessary amount for 20 days so the discount can be taken on the 10th day at a nominal annual rate of 6% with a compensating balance of 10%.

Total borrowings = Amount needed ÷ (1.0 − Compensated balance %)
= (US $120,000 × 98%) ÷ (100% − 10%)
= US $117,600 ÷ 90%
= US $130,667

---

b.   As with a discounted loan, the borrower has access to a smaller amount than the face amount of the loan and so pays an effective rate higher than the nominal rate.

EXAMPLE

Effective rate = Net interest expense (annualized) ÷ Usable funds
= (US $130,667 × 6%) ÷ $117,600
= US $7,840 ÷ $117,600
= 6.667%

---

c.   Once again, the dollar amounts involved are not needed to determine the effective rate.

$$\text{Effective rate with comp. balance} = \frac{\text{Stated rate}}{(1.0 - \text{Compensating balance \%})}$$

EXAMPLE

Effective rate = Stated rate ÷ (1.0 − Compensating balance %)
= 6% ÷ (100% − 10%)
= 6% ÷ 90%
= 6.667%

---

6. **Money Market Instruments**

    a. Bankers' acceptances are drafts drawn by a nonfinancial entity on deposits at a bank.

        1) The acceptance by the bank is a guarantee of payment at maturity. The payee can thus rely on the creditworthiness of the bank rather than on that of the (presumably riskier) drawer.

        2) Because they are backed by the prestige of a large bank, these instruments are highly marketable once they have been accepted.

    b. Commercial paper consists of short-term, unsecured notes payable issued in large denominations (US $100,000 or more) by large corporations with high credit ratings to other corporations and institutional investors, such as pension funds, banks, and insurance companies.

        1) Maturities of commercial paper are at most 270 days. No general secondary market exists for commercial paper. Commercial paper is a lower-cost source of funds than bank loans. It is usually issued at below the prime rate.

7. **Treasury Securities**

    a. U.S. Treasury securities are considered to be the safest investment because they are backed by the U.S. government.

        1) **Treasury bills** (T-bills) have maturities of 1 year or less. They do not pay interest but are sold on a discount basis.

            a) They can be traded in international money markets.

        2) **Treasury notes** (T-notes) and **treasury bonds** (T-bonds) have maturities of 1 to 10 years and 10 years or longer, respectively. They provide the lender with a coupon (interest) payment every 6 months.

8. **Secured Financing**

    a. Loans can be secured by pledging receivables, i.e., committing the proceeds of the receivables to paying off the loan. A bank will often lend up to 80% of outstanding receivables, depending upon the average age of the accounts and the assessed likelihood of their collectibility.

    b. A **warehouse receipt** is a form of secured short-term financing using inventory as security for the loan.

        1) A third party, such as a public warehouse, holds the collateral and serves as the creditor's agent, and the creditor receives the terminal warehouse receipts as evidence of its rights in the collateral.

        2) A field warehouse is established when the warehouser takes possession of the inventory on the debtor's property. The inventory is released (often from a fenced-in area) as needed for sale. Warehouse receipts may be negotiable or nonnegotiable.

9. **Factoring Receivables and Securitization**

    a. When an entity pledges receivables, the entity retains ownership of the accounts and simply commits to sending the proceeds to a creditor. Under a **factoring arrangement**, the entity sells the accounts receivable outright. The financing cost is usually high.

        1) However, an entity that uses a factor can eliminate its credit department and accounts receivable staff. Also, bad debts are eliminated from the statement of financial position. These reductions in costs can more than offset the fee charged by the factor. The factor can often operate more efficiently than its clients because of the specialized nature of its service.

    b. **Securitization** is the transfer of a portfolio of financial assets to a trust, mutual fund, or other entity and the sale of beneficial interests in that entity to investors.

Stop and review! You have completed the outline for this subunit. Study multiple-choice questions 18 through 20 on page 417.

QUESTIONS

16.1 Risk and Return

1. The risk that securities cannot be sold at a reasonable price on short notice is called

    A. Default risk.

    B. Interest-rate risk.

    C. Purchasing-power risk.

    D. Liquidity risk.

Answer (D) is correct.
    REQUIRED: The term for the risk that securities cannot be sold at a reasonable price on short notice.
    DISCUSSION: An asset is liquid if it can be converted to cash on short notice. Liquidity (marketability) risk is the risk that assets cannot be sold at a reasonable price on short notice. If an asset is not liquid, investors will require a higher return than for a liquid asset. The difference is the liquidity premium.
    Answer (A) is incorrect. Default risk is the risk that a borrower will not pay the interest or principal on a loan. Answer (B) is incorrect. Interest-rate risk is the risk to which investors are exposed because of changing interest rates. Answer (C) is incorrect. Purchasing-power risk is the risk that inflation will reduce the purchasing power of a given sum of money.

2. The difference between the required rate of return on a given risky investment and that of a risk-free investment with the same expected return is the

    A. Risk premium.

    B. Coefficient of variation.

    C. Standard error of measurement.

    D. Beta coefficient.

Answer (A) is correct.
    REQUIRED: The amount above the risk-free rate that represents the difference between the required rate of return on a risky investment and that of a risk-free investment with the same expected return.
    DISCUSSION: The market risk premium is the amount above the risk-free rate required to include average investors to enter the market. The risk premium is the portion of expected return attributed to the increased risk.
    Answer (B) is incorrect. The coefficient of variation represents the standard deviation of an investment's returns divided by the mean returns. Answer (C) is incorrect. The standard error represents a measure of variability in the investment's returns. Answer (D) is incorrect. The beta coefficient represents the sensitivity of the investment's returns to the market returns.

16.2 Derivatives

3. An entity has recently purchased some shares of a competitor as part of a long-term plan to acquire the competitor. However, it is somewhat concerned that the market price of these shares could decrease over the short run. The entity could hedge against the possible decline in the shares' market price by

    A. Purchasing a call option on those shares.

    B. Purchasing a put option on those shares.

    C. Selling a put option on those shares.

    D. Obtaining a warrant option on those shares.

Answer (B) is correct.
    REQUIRED: The means of hedging against the possible decline in the shares' market price.
    DISCUSSION: A put option is the right to sell shares at a given price within a certain period. If the market price falls, the put option may allow the sale of shares at a price above market, and the profit of the option holder will be the difference between the price stated in the put option and the market price, minus the cost of the option, commissions, and taxes. The entity that issues the shares has nothing to do with put (and call) options.
    Answer (A) is incorrect. A call option is the right to purchase shares at a given price within a specified period. Answer (C) is incorrect. Selling a put option could force the entity to purchase additional shares if the option is exercised. Answer (D) is incorrect. A warrant gives the holder a right to purchase shares from the issuer at a given price (it is usually distributed along with debt).

4. The activity of trading futures with the objective of reducing or controlling risk is called

   A. Insuring.

   B. Hedging.

   C. Short-selling.

   D. Factoring.

Answer (B) is correct.
   REQUIRED: The name for the activity of trading futures with the objective of reducing or controlling risk.
   DISCUSSION: Hedging is the use of offsetting commitments to minimize the effect of adverse future price movements. Thus, a financial manager may limit many risk exposures by trading in futures markets.
   Answer (A) is incorrect. Insurance is a contract in which the insurer undertakes to guarantee the insured against loss from specified contingencies or perils up to a specified amount. Answer (C) is incorrect. Short-selling is the sale of commodities or shares that are not owned in anticipation of a price decline. Answer (D) is incorrect. Factoring is the sale of accounts receivable.

5. A call option on an ordinary share is more valuable when there is a lower

   A. Market value of the underlying share.

   B. Exercise price on the option.

   C. Time to maturity on the option.

   D. Variability of market price on the underlying share.

Answer (B) is correct.
   REQUIRED: The circumstance under which a call option is more valuable.
   DISCUSSION: The lower the exercise price, the more valuable the call option. The exercise price is the price at which the call holder has the right to purchase the underlying share.
   Answer (A) is incorrect. A call option is the right to purchase an ordinary share at a set price for a set time period. If the underlying share has a lower market value, the call option is less, not more, valuable. Answer (C) is incorrect. A call option is less, not more, valuable given less time to maturity. When the option has less time to maturity, the chance that the share price will rise is smaller. Answer (D) is incorrect. A call option is less, not more, valuable if the price of the underlying share is less variable. Less variability means a lower probability of a price increase.

16.3 Corporate Capital Structure -- Debt Financing

6. Capital structure decisions involve determining the proportions of financing from

   A. Short-term or long-term debt.

   B. Debt or equity.

   C. Short-term or long-term assets.

   D. Retained earnings or common equity.

Answer (B) is correct.
   REQUIRED: Capital structure decisions.
   DISCUSSION: Debt and equity are the two elements of an entity's capital structure.
   Answer (A) is incorrect. The capital structure also includes equity. Answer (C) is incorrect. Assets are not part of the capital structure. Answer (D) is incorrect. The capital structure also includes debt and preferred equity.

7. Which of the following scenarios would encourage a company to use short-term loans to retire its 10-year bonds that have 5 years until maturity?

   A. The company expects interest rates to increase over the next 5 years.

   B. Interest rates have increased over the last 5 years.

   C. Interest rates have declined over the last 5 years.

   D. The company is experiencing cash flow problems.

Answer (C) is correct.
   REQUIRED: The scenario that would encourage a company to use short-term debt to retire long-term debt.
   DISCUSSION: If interest rates have declined, refunding with short-term debt may be appropriate. The bonds pay a higher interest rate than the new short-term debt. Assuming that rates continue to fall, the short-term debt can itself be refunded with debt having a still lower interest charge. The obvious risk is that interest rates may rise, thereby compelling the company to choose between paying off the debt or refunding it at higher rates.
   Answer (A) is incorrect. The company will not benefit from short-term loans if interest rates rise. Answer (B) is incorrect. The company should maintain the existing debt if prevailing interest rates are higher. Answer (D) is incorrect. The company increases the cash flow problem by shifting to short-term loans.

8.

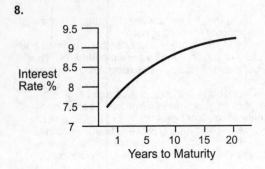

Years to Maturity

The yield curve shown implies that the

- A. Credit risk premium of corporate bonds has increased.

- B. Credit risk premium of municipal bonds has increased.

- C. Long-term interest rates have a higher annualized yield than short-term rates.

- D. Short-term interest rates have a higher annualized yield than long-term rates.

Answer (C) is correct.

REQUIRED: The implication of the yield curve.

DISCUSSION: The term structure of interest rates is the relationship between yield to maturity and time to maturity. This relationship is depicted by a yield curve. Assuming the long-term interest rate is an average of expected future short-term rates, the curve will be upward sloping when future short-term interest rates are expected to rise. Furthermore, the normal expectation is for long-term investments to pay higher rates because of their higher risk. Thus, long-term interest rates have a higher annualized yield than short-term rates.

Answer (A) is incorrect. The yield curve does not reflect the credit risk premium of bonds. Answer (B) is incorrect. The yield curve does not reflect the credit risk premium of bonds. Answer (D) is incorrect. Long-term interest rates should be higher than short-term rates.

16.4 Corporate Capital Structure -- Equity Financing

9. An entity must select from among several methods of financing arrangements when meeting its capital requirements. To acquire additional growth capital while attempting to maximize earnings per share, an entity should normally

- A. Attempt to increase both debt and equity in equal proportions, which preserves a stable capital structure and maintains investor confidence.

- B. Select debt over equity initially, even though increased debt is accompanied by interest costs and a degree of risk.

- C. Select equity over debt initially, which minimizes risk and avoids interest costs.

- D. Discontinue dividends and use current cash flow, which avoids the cost and risk of increased debt and the dilution of EPS through increased equity.

Answer (B) is correct.

REQUIRED: The financing arrangement that should be selected to acquire additional growth capital while attempting to maximize earnings per share.

DISCUSSION: Earnings per share will ordinarily be higher if debt is used to raise capital instead of equity, provided that the entity is not over-leveraged. The reason is that the cost of debt is lower than the cost of equity because interest is tax deductible. However, the prospect of higher EPS is accompanied by greater risk to the entity resulting from required interest costs, creditors' liens on the entity's assets, and the possibility of a proportionately lower EPS if sales volume fails to meet projections.

Answer (A) is incorrect. EPS is not a function of investor confidence and is not maximized by concurrent proportional increases in both debt and equity. EPS are usually higher if debt is used instead of equity to raise capital, at least initially. Answer (C) is incorrect. Equity capital is initially more costly than debt. Answer (D) is incorrect. Using only current cash flow to raise capital is usually too conservative an approach for a growth-oriented entity. Management is expected to be willing to take acceptable risks to be competitive and attain an acceptable rate of growth.

10. Common shareholders with preemptive rights are entitled to

- A. Vote first at annual meetings.

- B. Purchase any additional bonds sold by the entity.

- C. Purchase any additional shares sold by the entity.

- D. Gain control of the entity in a proxy fight.

Answer (C) is correct.

REQUIRED: The privilege enjoyed by common shareholders with preemptive rights.

DISCUSSION: Preemptive rights protect common shareholders' proportional ownership interests from dilution in value. A secondary purpose is to maintain the shareholders' control of the entity. Accordingly, the preemptive right, whether granted by statute or by the corporate charter, grants common shareholders the power to acquire on a pro rata basis any additional common shares sold by the entity. Preemptive rights also apply to debt convertible into common shares.

Answer (A) is incorrect. There is no prescribed order of shareholder voting. Answer (B) is incorrect. Preemptive rights concern only equity ownership. Thus, they do not apply to nonconvertible debt. Answer (D) is incorrect. A proxy fight is an attempt to gain control of an entity by persuading shareholders to grant their voting rights to others.

16.5 Corporate Capital Structure -- Cost of Capital

11. An entity has made the decision to finance next year's capital projects through debt rather than additional equity. The benchmark cost of capital for these projects should be the

   A. Before-tax cost of new-debt financing.

   B. After-tax cost of new-debt financing.

   C. Cost of equity financing.

   D. Weighted-average cost of capital.

Answer (D) is correct.
   REQUIRED: The benchmark cost of capital.
   DISCUSSION: A weighted average of the costs of all financing sources should be used, with the weights determined by the usual financing proportions. The terms of any financing raised at the time of initiating a particular project do not represent the cost of capital for the entity. When an entity achieves its optimal capital structure, the weighted-average cost of capital is minimized. The cost of capital is a composite, or weighted average, of all financing sources in their usual proportions. The cost of capital should also be calculated on an after-tax basis.
   Answer (A) is incorrect. The weighted-average cost of capital is calculated on an after-tax basis. Answer (B) is incorrect. The weighted-average cost of capital consists of both debt and equity components calculated on an after-tax basis. Answer (C) is incorrect. The cost of capital is an after-tax composite, or weighted average, of all financing sources in their usual proportions.

12. The marginal cost of capital (MCC) curve for an entity rises twice, first when the entity has raised US $75 million and again when US $175 million of new funds has been raised. These increases in the MCC are caused by

   A. Increases in the returns on the additional investments undertaken.

   B. Decreases in the returns on the additional investments undertaken.

   C. Decreases in the cost of at least one of the financing sources.

   D. Increases in the cost of at least one of the financing sources.

Answer (D) is correct.
   REQUIRED: The reason for the increases in the MCC.
   DISCUSSION: The MCC is a weighted average of the costs of various new financing sources. If the cost of any source of new financing increases, the MCC curve will rise. The curve shifts upward with each incremental increase in financing cost because the lowest-cost sources are assumed to be used first.
   Answer (A) is incorrect. Financing costs do not directly depend on rates of return on investment. Answer (B) is incorrect. Financing costs do not directly depend on rates of return on investment. Answer (C) is incorrect. As additional funds are raised, an increase in the cost of a source of financing, not a decrease, will result in an increase in the MCC.

16.6 Capital Budgeting

13. A project has an initial outlay of US $1,000. The projected cash inflows are

Year 1	US $200
Year 2	200
Year 3	400
Year 4	400

What is the investment's payback period?

   A. 4.0 years.

   B. 3.5 years.

   C. 3.4 years.

   D. 3.0 years.

Answer (B) is correct.
   REQUIRED: The payback period.
   DISCUSSION: Cash inflows are assumed to occur equally throughout the Years 1 through 4. At the end of Year 3, US $800 ($200 + $200 + $400) will have been received. The remaining $200 will be received in one half of Year 4 (US $200 ÷ $400).
   Answer (A) is incorrect. The total cash inflow over 4.0 years is US $1,200 ($200 + $200 + $400 + $400)]. Answer (C) is incorrect. Cash inflows over 3.5 years will total US $960 [($200 + $200 + $400) + ($400 × 0.4)]. Answer (D) is incorrect. The 3-year total is US $800 ($200 + $200 + $400).

14. Which of the following phrases defines the internal rate of return on a project?

A. The number of years it takes to recover the investment.

B. The discount rate at which the net present value of the project equals zero.

C. The discount rate at which the net present value of the project equals one.

D. The weighted-average cost of capital used to finance the project.

Answer (B) is correct.
REQUIRED: The definition of the IRR.
DISCUSSION: The IRR is the discount rate at which the investment's NPV equals zero. Accordingly, it is the rate that equates the present value of the expected cash inflows with the present value of the expected cash outflows.
Answer (A) is incorrect. The payback period is the number of years it takes to recover the investment. Answer (C) is incorrect. The IRR is the discount rate at which the NPV is zero. Answer (D) is incorrect. The weighted-average cost of capital is the single, composite rate of return on the components of capital used to finance the project.

16.7 Cash Management and Working Capital

15. Why would an entity maintain a compensating cash balance?

A. To make routine payments and collections.

B. To pay for banking services.

C. To provide a reserve in case of unforeseen fluctuations in cash flows.

D. To take advantage of bargain purchase opportunities that may arise.

Answer (B) is correct.
REQUIRED: The use of a compensating cash balance.
DISCUSSION: The compensating cash balance is the money left in a checking account in the bank in order to compensate the bank for services it provides.
Answer (A) is incorrect. The cash balance maintained for making routine payments and collections is called the transactions balance. Answer (C) is incorrect. The cash balance maintained as a reserve for unforeseen cash flow fluctuations is called the precautionary balance. Answer (D) is incorrect. It is the speculative cash balance that is maintained in order to enable the entity to take advantage of any bargain purchase opportunities that may arise.

16. A lockbox system

A. Reduces the need for compensating balances.

B. Provides security for late night deposits.

C. Reduces the risk of having checks lost in the mail.

D. Accelerates the inflow of funds.

Answer (D) is correct.
REQUIRED: The true statement about a lockbox system.
DISCUSSION: A lockbox system is one strategy for expediting the receipt of funds. Customers submit their payments to a mailbox controlled by the bank rather than to the company's offices. Bank personnel remove the envelopes from the mailbox and deposit the checks to the company's account immediately. The remittance advices must then be transported to the company for entry into the accounts receivable system. The bank generally charges a flat monthly fee for this service.
Answer (A) is incorrect. A lockbox system is not related to compensating balances; a compensating balance may be required by a covenant in a loan agreement that requires a company to maintain a specified balance during the term of the loan. Answer (B) is incorrect. A lockbox system is a process by which payments are sent to a bank's mailbox, which is checked during normal post office hours. Answer (C) is incorrect. The use of a lockbox system entails sending checks through the mail to a post office box. Thus, it does not reduce the risk of losing checks in the mail.

17. Which one of the following provides a spontaneous source of financing for a firm?

A. Accounts payable.

B. Mortgage bonds.

C. Accounts receivable.

D. Debentures.

Answer (A) is correct.
REQUIRED: The item that provides a spontaneous source of financing.
DISCUSSION: Trade credit is a spontaneous source of financing because it arises automatically as part of a purchase transaction. Because of its ease in use, trade credit is the largest source of short-term financing for many firms, both large and small.
Answer (B) is incorrect. Mortgage bonds and debentures do not arise automatically as a result of a purchase transaction. Answer (C) is incorrect. The use of receivables as a financing source requires an extensive factoring arrangement and often involves the creditor's evaluation of the credit ratings of the borrower's customers. Answer (D) is incorrect. Mortgage bonds and debentures do not arise automatically as a result of a purchase transaction.

16.8 Short-Term Financing

18. The correct equation for calculating the approximate percentage cost, on an annual basis, of not taking trade discounts is

A. $\dfrac{Discount\ \%}{100\ -\ Discount\ \%} \times \dfrac{360}{[Days\ credit\ is\ outstanding\ -\ Discount\ period]}$

B. $\dfrac{Discount\ \%}{100} \times \dfrac{360}{[Days\ credit\ is\ outstanding\ -\ Discount\ period]}$

C. $\dfrac{100\ -\ Discount\ \%}{Discount\ \%} \times \dfrac{360}{[Days\ credit\ is\ outstanding\ -\ Discount\ period]}$

D. $\dfrac{Discount\ \%}{100\ -\ Discount\ \%} \times \dfrac{[Days\ credit\ is\ outstanding\ -\ Discount\ period]}{360}$

Answer (A) is correct.
REQUIRED: The equation for calculating the percentage cost of not taking trade discounts.
DISCUSSION: The first term of the formula is the periodic cost of the trade discount, calculated as the cost per unit of trade credit (discount %) divided by the funds made available by not taking the discount (100% – discount %). The second term represents the number of times per year this cost is incurred. The product of these terms is the approximate annual percentage cost of not taking the trade discount. A precise formula would incorporate the effects of compounding when calculating the annual cost.
Answer (B) is incorrect. The denominator of the first term should represent the funds made available by not taking the discount (100% – discount %). Answer (C) is incorrect. The first term is the reciprocal of the correct term. Answer (D) is incorrect. The second term is the reciprocal of the correct term.

19. An entity has accounts payable of US $5 million with terms of 2% discount within 15 days, net 30 days (2/15, net 30). It can borrow funds from a bank at an annual rate of 12%, or it can wait until the 30th day when it will receive revenues to cover the payment. If it borrows funds on the last day of the discount period in order to obtain the discount, its total cost will be

A. US $51,000 less.

B. US $75,500 less.

C. US $100,000 less.

D. US $24,500 more.

Answer (B) is correct.
REQUIRED: The effect on total cost of taking a cash discount.
DISCUSSION: To take advantage of the 2% discount, the entity will need to borrow US $4,900,000 ($5,000,000 × 98%). The interest on this amount for the 15 days until revenues are received to repay it amounts to US $24,500 [$4,900,000 principal × 12% annual interest rate × (15 ÷ 360) duration of loan], and the total cost will be US $4,924,500. The total cost if the discount is not taken will be US $5,000,000, resulting in a savings of US $75,500 by taking out the loan.
Answer (A) is incorrect. The amount of US $51,000 less is based on a 30-day borrowing period. Answer (C) is incorrect. The amount of US $100,000 less does not consider the interest paid. Answer (D) is incorrect. The amount of US $24,500 more reflects interest paid but ignores the discounted price.

20. Factoring is the

A. Selling of accounts receivable by one entity to another.

B. Selling of inventory by one entity to another.

C. Conversion of accounts receivable to bad debt on financial statements for accounts that are long overdue.

D. Adjustment of inventories on financial statements for supplies that have become obsolete.

Answer (A) is correct.
REQUIRED: The definition of factoring.
DISCUSSION: A factor purchases an entity's accounts receivable and assumes the risk of collection. The seller receives money immediately to reinvest in new inventories. The financing cost is usually high: about 2 points or more above prime, plus a fee for collection. Factoring has been traditional in the textile industry for years, and companies in many industries have recently found it an efficient means of operation. An entity that uses a factor can eliminate its credit department, accounts receivable staff, and bad debts. These reductions in costs can more than offset the fee charged by the factor, which can often operate more efficiently than its clients because of the specialized nature of its service.

Access the **CIA Review System** from your Gleim Personal Classroom to continue your studies with exam-emulating multiple-choice questions!

STUDY UNIT SEVENTEEN
MANAGERIAL ACCOUNTING I

(23 pages of outline)

This study unit is the fourth of five covering **Section VII: Financial Management** from The IIA's CIA Exam Syllabus. This section makes up 10% to 20% of Part 3 of the CIA exam and is tested at the **awareness level**. The relevant portion of the syllabus is highlighted below. (The complete syllabus is in Appendix A.)

VII. FINANCIAL MANAGEMENT (10%–20%)

A. **Financial Accounting and Finance**
B. **Managerial Accounting**

1. General concepts
2. Costing systems (e.g., activity-based, standard)
3. Cost concepts (e.g., absorption, variable, fixed)

NOTE: Items B. 4., 5., 6., 7., and 8. are covered in Study Unit 18.

17.1 COST MANAGEMENT TERMINOLOGY

1. **Basic Definitions**

   a. A **cost** is the measure of a resource used up for some purpose.

      1) For financial reporting, a cost can be either capitalized as an asset or expensed.

   b. A **cost object** is any entity to which costs can be attached.

      1) Examples are products, processes, employees, departments, and facilities.

   c. A **cost driver** is the basis used to assign costs to a cost object.

      1) A cost driver is an activity measure, such as direct labor hours or machine hours, that is a factor in causing the incurrence of cost.

2. **Manufacturing vs. Nonmanufacturing**

   a. The costs of manufacturing a product can be classified as follows:

      1) **Direct materials** are tangible inputs to the manufacturing process that feasibly can be traced to the product, e.g., sheet metal welded together for a piece of heavy equipment.

         a) All costs of bringing materials to the production line, e.g., transportation-in, are included in the cost of direct materials.

      2) **Direct labor** is the cost of human labor that feasibly can be traced to the product, e.g., the wages of the welder.

      3) **Manufacturing overhead** consists of all costs of manufacturing that are not direct materials or direct labor.

         a) Indirect materials are tangible inputs to the manufacturing process that feasibly cannot be traced to the product, e.g., the welding compound used to put together a piece of heavy equipment.

        b)   Indirect labor is the cost of human labor connected with the manufacturing process that feasibly cannot be traced to the product, e.g., the wages of assembly line supervisors and janitorial staff.

        c)   Factory operating costs include utilities, real estate taxes, insurance, depreciation on factory equipment, etc.

  b.   Manufacturing costs are often grouped into the following classifications:

      1)   **Prime cost** equals **direct materials plus direct labor**, i.e., those costs directly attributable to a product.

      2)   **Conversion cost** equals **direct labor plus manufacturing overhead**, i.e., the costs of converting materials into the finished product.

  c.   The following are nonmanufacturing costs:

      1)   Selling (marketing) costs are incurred in getting the product from the factory to the consumer, e.g., sales personnel salaries and product transportation.

      2)   Administrative expenses are incurred for activities not directly related to producing or marketing the product, e.g., executive salaries and depreciation on the headquarters building.

3.   **Product vs. Period**

  a.   An important issue in managerial accounting is whether to capitalize a cost as part of finished goods inventory or to expense it as incurred.

      1)   **Product costs** (inventoriable costs) are capitalized as part of finished goods inventory. They eventually become a component of cost of goods sold.

      2)   **Period costs** are expensed as incurred. They are not capitalized in finished goods inventory and are thus excluded from cost of goods sold.

  b.   This distinction is crucial because of the required treatment of manufacturing costs for external financial reporting purposes.

4.   **Direct vs. Indirect**

  a.   **Direct costs** are associated with a particular cost object in an economically feasible way. They can be traced to that object.

      1)   Examples are the direct materials and direct labor inputs to a manufacturing process discussed in items 2.a.1) and 2).

  b.   **Indirect costs** cannot be associated with a particular cost object in an economically feasible way and must be allocated to that object.

      1)   Examples are the indirect materials and indirect labor inputs to a manufacturing process discussed in item 2.a.3).

      2)   To simplify the allocation process, indirect costs often are collected in cost pools.

          a)   A cost pool is an account into which similar cost elements with a common cause are accumulated.

          b)   Manufacturing overhead is a commonly used cost pool into which various untraceable costs of the manufacturing process are accumulated.

  c.   **Common costs** are indirect costs shared by two or more users.

      1)   Because common costs cannot be directly traced to the users that generate the costs, they must be allocated on a systematic and rational basis.

      2)   An example is depreciation on a headquarters building. It is a direct cost when accounting for the building as a whole. However, it is a common cost of the departments located in the building and must be allocated to them.

Stop and review! You have completed the outline for this subunit. Study multiple-choice questions 1 through 4 beginning on page 441.

17.2 COST BEHAVIOR AND RELEVANT RANGE

1. **Variable Costs**

   a. Variable costs vary directly with the volume of production, such as direct materials.

   b. Variable cost per unit is constant in the short run regardless of the level of production.

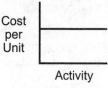

Figure 17-1

   c. However, variable costs in total vary directly and proportionally with changes in volume.

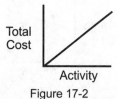

Figure 17-2

EXAMPLE of a Variable Cost

An entity requires one unit of direct material to be used in each finished good it produces.

Number of Outputs Produced	Input Cost per Unit	Total Cost of Inputs
0	US $10	US $ 0
100	10	1,000
1,000	10	10,000
5,000	10	50,000
10,000	10	100,000

---

2. **Fixed Costs**

   a. Fixed costs in total remain unchanged in the short run regardless of production level. For example, the amount paid for an assembly line is the same even if it is not used.

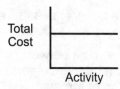

Figure 17-3

   b. However, fixed cost per unit varies indirectly with the activity level.

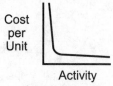

Figure 17-4

EXAMPLE of a Fixed Cost

The historical cost of the assembly line is fixed, but its cost per unit decreases as production increases.

Number of Outputs Produced	Cost of Assembly Line	Per-Unit Cost of Assembly Line
100	US $1,000,000	US $10,000
1,000	1,000,000	1,000
5,000	1,000,000	200
10,000	1,000,000	100

---

3. **Other Cost Behaviors**

   a. Mixed (semivariable) costs combine fixed and variable elements. For example, rental expense on a car may consist of a flat fee per month plus an additional fee for each mile driven.

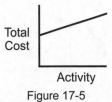

Total
Cost

Activity

Figure 17-5

EXAMPLE of a Mixed Cost

The entity rents a piece of machinery to make its production line more efficient. The rental is US $150,000 per year plus US $1 for every unit produced.

Number of Outputs Produced	Fixed Cost of Extra Machine	Variable Cost of Extra Machine	Total Cost of Extra Machine
0	US $150,000	US $ 0	US $150,000
100	150,000	100	150,100
1,000	150,000	1,000	151,000
5,000	150,000	5,000	155,000
10,000	150,000	10,000	160,000

---

   b. The fixed and variable portions of a mixed cost may not be set by contract as in the previous example and must be estimated. Two methods of estimating mixed costs are in general use:

   1) The high-low method generates a regression line by basing the equation on only the highest and lowest values in the series of observations.

   a) The difference in cost between the highest and lowest levels of activity (not output) is divided by the difference in the activity level to determine the variable portion of the cost.

EXAMPLE of the High-Low Method

An entity has the following cost data:

Month	Machine Hours	Maintenance Costs
April	1,000	US $2,275
May	1,600	3,400
June	1,200	2,650
July	800	1,900
August	1,200	2,650
September	1,000	2,275

The numerator can be derived by subtracting the cost at the lowest level, July, from the cost at the highest level, May, (US $3,400 − $1,900 = US $1,500).

– Continued on next page –

EXAMPLE – Continued

The denominator can be derived by subtracting the lowest level of activity, July, from the highest level, May, (1,600 – 800 = 800).

The variable portion of the cost is therefore US $1.875 per machine hour (US $1,500 ÷ 800).

The fixed portion can be calculated by inserting the appropriate values for either the high or low month in the range:

$$
\begin{aligned}
\text{Fixed portion} &= \text{Total cost} - \text{Variable portion} \\
&= \text{US } \$1,900 - (\$1.875 \times 800 \text{ hours}) \\
&= \text{US } \$1,900 - \$1,500 \\
&= \text{US } \$400
\end{aligned}
$$

The regression equation is y = 400 + 1.875x

y = Total cost
x = Machine hours

---

  b) The major criticism of the high-low method is that the high and low points may be abnormalities not representative of normal events.

   2) The regression (scattergraph) method is more complex. It determines the average rate of variability of a mixed cost rather than the variability between the high and low points in the range.

4. **Relevant Range and Marginal Cost**

  a. The **relevant range** defines the normal limits within which per-unit variable costs remain constant and fixed costs do not change. It is valid for a specified time span.

   1) The relevant range is established by such factors as the efficiency of an entity's current manufacturing plant and its agreements with labor unions and suppliers.

  b. Relevant range and marginal cost are related concepts.

   1) **Marginal cost** is the additional (also called incremental) cost incurred by generating one additional unit of output. Accordingly, marginal cost remains constant across the relevant range.

    a) However, the relevant range exists only for a specified time span. Thus, all costs are variable in the long run.

   2) Investment in new, more productive equipment results in higher total fixed costs but also may result in lower total and per-unit variable costs.

Stop and review! You have completed the outline for this subunit. Study multiple-choice question 5 on page 442.

17.3 ACTIVITY-BASED COSTING

1. **Drawbacks of Volume-Based Systems**

  a. ABC is a response to the significant increase in the incurrence of indirect costs resulting from the rapid advance of technology. ABC is a refinement of an existing costing system (job-order or process).

   1) Under a traditional (volume-based) costing system, overhead is simply dumped into a single cost pool and spread evenly across all end products.

   2) Under ABC, indirect costs are attached to activities that are then rationally allocated to end products.

   3) ABC may be used by manufacturing, service, or retailing entities.

   4) ABC may be used in a job-order system or a process-cost system.

b. The inaccurate averaging or spreading of indirect costs over products or service units that use different amounts of resources is called **peanut-butter costing**. Peanut-butter costing results in product-cost cross-subsidization, the condition in which the miscosting of one product causes the miscosting of other products.

c. The peanut-butter effect of using a traditional (i.e., volume-based) costing system can be summarized as follows:

1) Direct labor and direct materials are traced to products or service units.

2) A single pool of indirect costs (overhead) is accumulated for a given organizational unit.

3) Indirect costs from the pool are assigned using an allocative (rather than a tracing) procedure, such as using a single overhead rate for an entire department, e.g., US $3 of overhead for every direct labor hour.

   a) The effect is an averaging of costs that may result in significant inaccuracy when products or service units do not use similar amounts of resources.

EXAMPLE

The effect of product-cost cross-subsidization can be illustrated as follows:

1. A company produces two products. Both products require 1 unit of direct material and 1 hour of direct labor. Raw materials costs are US $14 per unit, and direct labor is US $70 per hour.

2. During the month just ended, the company produced 1,000 units of Product A and 100 units of Product B. Manufacturing overhead for the month totaled US $20,000.

3. Using direct labor hours as the overhead allocation base, per-unit costs and profits are calculated as follows:

	Product A	Product B	Total
Direct materials	US $ 14,000	US $ 1,400	
Direct labor	70,000	7,000	
Overhead {US $20,000 × [$70,000 ÷ ($70,000 + $7,000)]}	18,182		
Overhead {US $20,000 × [$7,000 ÷ ($70,000 + $7,000)]}		1,818	
Total costs	US $102,182	US $ 10,218	US $112,400
Selling price	US $ 119.99	US $ 139.99	
Cost per unit	(102.18)	(102.18)	
Profit per unit	US $ 17.81	US $ 37.81	

4. The company's management accountants have determined that overhead consists almost entirely of production line setup costs and that the two products require equal setup times. Allocating overhead on this basis yields vastly different results.

	Product A	Product B	Total
Direct materials	US $14,000	US $ 1,400	
Direct labor	70,000	7,000	
Overhead (US $20,000 × 50%)	10,000		
Overhead (US $20,000 × 50%)		10,000	
Total costs	US $94,000	US $18,400	US $112,400
Selling price	US $119.99	US $139.99	
Cost per unit	(94.00)	(184.00)	
Profit (loss) per unit	US $ 25.99	US $ (44.01)	

5. Rather than the profit the company believed it was making on both products using peanut-butter costing, it is losing money on every unit of Product B that it sells. The high-volume Product A has been heavily subsidizing the setup costs for the low-volume Product B.

d. The example on the previous page assumes a single component of overhead for clarity. In reality, overhead is typically made up of many components. The peanut-butter effect of traditional overhead allocation is illustrated in the following diagram:

Overhead Allocation in a Traditional (Volume-Based) Cost Accumulation System

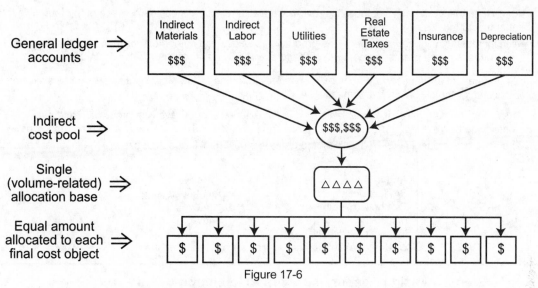

Figure 17-6

2. **Volume-Based vs. Activity-Based**

   a. Volume-based systems were appropriate when most manufacturing costs were direct. However, overhead costs do not always fluctuate with volume. ABC addresses the increasing complexity and variety of overhead costs.

   b. Activity-based systems involve

      1) Identifying organizational activities that result in overhead

      2) Assigning the costs of resources consumed by the activities

      3) Assigning the costs of the activities by appropriate cost drivers to final cost objects

3. **Steps in Activity-Based Costing**

   a. **Step 1 – Activity Analysis**

      1) An activity is a set of work actions undertaken within the entity, and a cost pool is established for each activity.

      2) Activities are classified in a hierarchy according to the level of the production process at which they take place.

         a) **Unit-level activities** are performed for each unit of output produced. Examples are using direct materials and using direct labor.

         b) **Batch-level activities** occur for each group of outputs produced. Examples are materials ordering, materials handling, and production line setup.

         c) **Product-sustaining** (or service-sustaining) **activities** support the production of a particular product (or service), irrespective of the level of production. Examples are product design, engineering changes, and testing.

         d) **Facility-sustaining activities** concern overall operations and therefore cannot be traced to products at any point in the production process. Examples are accounting, human resources, maintenance of physical plant, and safety/security arrangements.

EXAMPLE

Fabulous Foundry uses a job-order system to accumulate costs for the custom pipe fittings of all sizes that it produces. Since the 1950s, Fabulous has accumulated overhead costs in six general ledger accounts (indirect materials, indirect labor, utilities, real estate taxes, insurance, and depreciation), combined them into a single indirect cost pool, and allocated the total to its products based on machine hours.

- At the time this system was established, overhead was a relatively small percentage of the foundry's total manufacturing costs.
- With increasing reliance on robots in the production process and computers for monitoring and control, overhead is now a greater percentage of the total while direct labor costs have shrunk.

To obtain better data about product costs, Fabulous has decided to refine its job-order costing system by switching to activity-based costing for the allocation of overhead.

- The foundry's management accountants conducted extensive interviews with production and sales personnel to determine how the incurrence of indirect costs can be viewed as activities that consume resources.
- The accountants identified five activities and created a cost pool for each to capture the incurrence of indirect costs:

Activity	Hierarchy
Product design	Product-sustaining
Production setup	Batch-level
Machining	Unit-level
Inspection & testing	Unit-level
Customer maintenance	Facility-sustaining

---

b.　**Step 2 – Assign Resource Drivers to Resource Costs**

　　1)　Identifying resource costs is not the simple matter it is in volume-based overhead allocation.

　　　　a)　A separate accounting system may be necessary to track resource costs separately from the general ledger.

　　2)　Once the resources have been identified, resource drivers are designated to allocate resource costs to the activity cost pools.

　　　　a)　Resource drivers (causes) are measures of the resources consumed by an activity.

EXAMPLE

Fabulous Foundry's management accountants identified the following resources used by its indirect cost processes:

Resource	Driver
Computer processing	CPU cycles
Production line	Machine hours
Materials management	Hours worked
Accounting	Hours worked
Sales & marketing	Number of orders

---

c.　**Step 3 – Allocate Resource Costs to Activity Cost Pools**

　　1)　Once the resource drivers are determined, the dollar amount of resources per resource driver can be determined.

　　　　a)　One method of doing this could be dividing the total dollar amount of a resource cost by the total amount of the resource driver used by the entire entity.

　　2)　Costs of resources are then allocated to activity cost pools based on the amount of resource drivers used by each activity cost pool.

EXAMPLE

Fabulous Foundry's management accountants have determined that a total amount of US $1,000,000 of Materials Management was used over a total of 100,000 hours worked. Fabulous's management accountants will therefore allocate US $10 ($1,000,000 ÷ 100,000 hours) to each activity pool for each hour of Materials Management worked for each cost pool.

Activity	Amount Allocated
Product Design	US $250,000 for 25,000 hours
Production Setup	US $270,000 for 27,000 hours
Machining	US $450,000 for 45,000 hours
Inspection & Testing	US $30,000 for 3,000 hours
Customer Maintenance	US $0 for 0 hours

---

      3)   This allocation is done for each resource. This is termed first-stage allocation.

          a)   Some cost activities may not be allocated resources if that cost activity did not use those resources.

  d.   **Step 4 – Allocate Activity Cost Pools to Final Cost Objects**

      1)   The final step in enacting an ABC system is allocating the activity cost pools to final cost objects. This is termed second-stage allocation.

      2)   Once the cost drivers are determined, the dollar amount of activity pool per activity driver can be determined.

          a)   One method of doing this could be dividing the total dollar amount assigned to an activity cost pool by the total amount the activity driver used by the entire entity.

      3)   Costs are reassigned to final-stage (or, if intermediate cost objects are used, next-stage) cost objects on the basis of activity drivers.

          a)   Activity drivers are measures of the demands made on an activity by next-stage cost objects, such as the number of parts in a product used to measure an assembly activity.

EXAMPLE

Fabulous Foundry's management accountants have designated these drivers to associate with their corresponding activities:

Activity	Driver
Product design	Number of products
Production setup	Number of setups
Machining	Number of units produced
Inspection & testing	Number of units produced
Customer maintenance	Number of orders

EXAMPLE

Knight Company is a manufacturer of pants and coats. The following information pertains to the company's current-month activities:

Manufacturing overhead costs		Cost driver
Plant utilities and real estate taxes	US $150,000	Square footage
Materials handling	40,000	Pounds of direct material used
Inspection and testing	10,000	Number of units produced
	US $200,000	

Current-month activity level

	Pants	Coats	Total
Direct labor hours	20,000	5,000	25,000
Plant square footage	400	600	1,000
Pounds of direct material used	10,000	6,000	16,000
Number of units produced	15,000	3,000	18,000

Using direct labor hours as the overhead allocation base (traditional volume-based system), the manufacturing overhead costs are allocated as follows:

$$\text{Pants: US } \$200,000 \times (20,000 \div 25,000) = \text{US } \$160,000$$
$$\text{Coats: US } \$200,000 \times (5,000 \div 25,000) = \text{US } \$40,000$$

$$\text{Manufacturing overhead costs per pant: US } \$160,000 \div 15,000 = \text{US } \$10.67$$
$$\text{Manufacturing overhead costs per coat: US } \$40,000 \div 3,000 = \text{US } \$13.33$$

Under an activity-based costing system, the manufacturing overhead costs are allocated as follows:

	Pants		Coats	
Plant utilities and real estate taxes	US $150,000 × (400 ÷ 1,000) =	US $60,000	US $150,000 × (600 ÷ 1,000) =	US $ 90,000
Material handling	US $40,000 × (10,000 ÷ 16,000) =	25,000	US $40,000 × (6,000 ÷ 16,000) =	15,000
Inspection and testing	US $10,000 × (15,000 ÷ 18,000) =	8,333	US $10,000 × (3,000 ÷ 18,000) =	1,667
		US $93,333		US $106,667

$$\text{Manufacturing overhead costs per pant = US } \$93,333 \div 15,000 = \text{US } \$6.22$$
$$\text{Manufacturing overhead costs per coat = US } \$106,667 \div 3,000 = \text{US } \$35.56$$

Stop and review! You have completed the outline for this subunit. Study multiple-choice questions 6 through 9 beginning on page 442.

17.4 PROCESS COSTING

1. **Uses of Process Costing**

    a.   Process cost accounting assigns costs to inventoriable goods or services. It applies to relatively homogeneous products that are mass produced on a continuous basis (e.g., petroleum products, thread, and computer monitors).

    b.   Instead of using subsidiary ledgers to track specific jobs, process costing typically uses a work-in-process account for each department through which the production of output passes.

    c.   Process costing calculates the average cost of all units as follows:

        1)   Costs are accumulated for a cost object that consists of a large number of similar units of goods or services,

        2)   Work-in-process is stated in terms of equivalent units, and

        3)   Unit costs are established.

2. **Accumulation of Costs**

    a.   The accumulation of costs under a process-costing system is by department rather than by project to reflect its continuous, homogeneous nature.

    b.   The physical inputs required for the production process are obtained from suppliers.

    c.   Direct materials are added by the first department in the process.

d. Conversion costs, which include direct labor and manufacturing overhead, incurred by the first department are added.

e. The products may move from one department to the next.

f. If necessary, the second department adds more direct materials and more conversion costs.

g. When processing is finished in the last department, all costs are transferred to finished goods.

h. As products are sold, sales are recorded and the costs are transferred to cost of goods sold.

i. The changes to these accounts during the period can be summarized as follows:

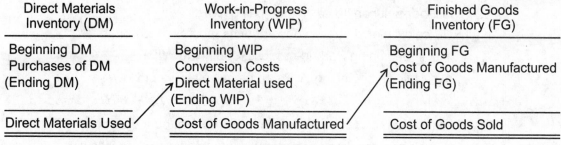

Direct Materials Inventory (DM)	Work-in-Progress Inventory (WIP)	Finished Goods Inventory (FG)
Beginning DM Purchases of DM (Ending DM)	Beginning WIP Conversion Costs Direct Material used (Ending WIP)	Beginning FG Cost of Goods Manufactured (Ending FG)
Direct Materials Used	Cost of Goods Manufactured	Cost of Goods Sold

Figure 17-7

3. Process Costing Flow Diagram

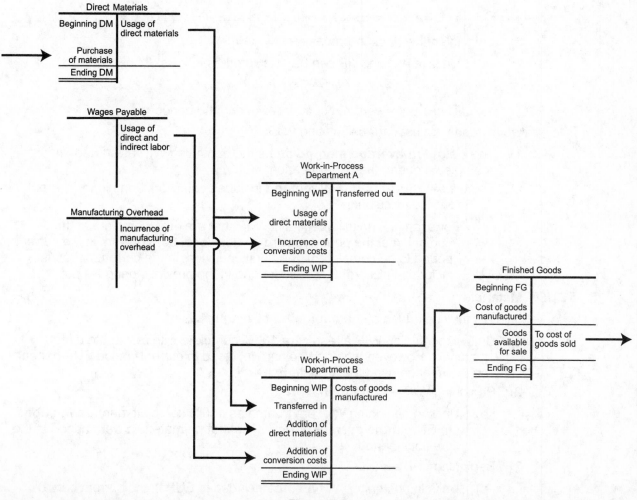

Figure 17-8

4. **Equivalent Units of Production (EUP)**

    a. Some units are unfinished at the end of the period. For each department to account adequately for costs attached to its unfinished units, the units must be restated in terms of equivalent units of production (EUP).

        1) EUP are the complete units that could have been produced using the inputs consumed during the period.

EXAMPLE

One thousand work-in-process units completed 80% for direct materials and 60% for conversion costs represent 800 EUP of direct materials (1,000 × 80%) and 600 EUP of conversion costs (1,000 × 60%).

---

        2) Cost-per-unit can be calculated using EUP.

    b. In all EUP calculations, three groups of units must be accounted for:

        1) Units in beginning work-in-process (beginning WIP)

            a) Units in beginning WIP can be calculated as follows:

Beginning WIP = Units transferred out + Ending WIP − Units started

        2) Units started and completed during the current period

            a) Units started and completed can be calculated as follows:

Units started and completed = Units transferred out − Beginning WIP

Or

Units started and completed = Units started − Ending WIP

        3) Units in ending work-in-process (ending WIP)

            a) Units in ending WIP can be calculated as follows:

Ending WIP = Beginning WIP + Units started − Units transferred out

            b) These units were not completed during the period.

    c. Two methods are used for calculating EUP:

        1) The **weighted-average method** treats the beginning WIP as started and completed during the current period.

        2) The **first-in, first-out (FIFO) method** includes only work done in the current period in the calculation.

            a) For example, units in beginning WIP that are 40% complete at the beginning of the period require an additional 60% of work in the current period to be completed. The additional work in the current period is included in EUP, but the work done in the previous period is not.

5. **EUP – Materials**

    a. Materials may be added at the **beginning of the process**.

        1) Units in beginning WIP already are 100% complete with respect to direct materials. However, whether they are included in current-period EUP depends on the method used to calculate EUP.

        2) Beginning WIP -- **Weighted-average**

            a) Units in beginning WIP are treated as 100% complete and **are included in EUP in the current period** even though materials were added in the previous period.

        3) Beginning WIP -- **FIFO**

            a) Units in beginning WIP are **not** included in EUP in the current period because all materials were added in the previous period.

4) Units started and completed always are 100% complete with respect to direct materials.

5) Units in ending WIP are 100% complete with respect to direct materials when all materials are added at the beginning of the production process.

a) All materials are treated as added in the current period.

b. Materials may be added **evenly** throughout the process.

1) The method used and the completion percentage should be determined.

2) Beginning WIP -- **Weighted-average**

a) Units in beginning WIP are treated as 100% complete and **will produce EUP in the current period** even though materials were added in the previous period.

3) Beginning WIP -- **FIFO**

a) The completion percentage for the current period equals 100% minus the completion percentage for the beginning WIP. The result is the percentage completed in the current period.

b) For example, if 1,000 units in beginning WIP are 30% complete with respect to materials, 70% (100% − 30%) will be completed in the current period.

i) EUP from beginning WIP equal 700 (1,000 units × 70%).

4) Units started and completed always are 100% complete with respect to direct materials.

5) The EUP in ending WIP depend on the completion percentage.

a) For example, if 1,000 units in ending WIP are 60% complete with respect to materials, 60% were completed in the current period.

i) EUP in ending WIP equal 600 (1,000 units × 60%).

c. Materials may be added at a **specific time** during production.

1) Whether materials are included in the current period's calculation of EUP depends on (a) when materials are added, (b) whether that point was reached, and (c) the method used.

2) Beginning WIP -- **Weighted-average**

a) Units in beginning WIP are treated as started and completed in the current period regardless of when materials were added.

3) Beginning WIP -- **FIFO**

a) If the point at which materials are added is reached during the current period, beginning WIP will include EUP.

b) If the point at which materials are added was reached during the previous period, beginning WIP will not include EUP for the current period.

c) For example, assume that materials are added when physical units are 50% complete. If beginning WIP is 20% complete, materials have not been added. All materials will be added in the current period, and the units will count 100% toward EUP.

i) If beginning WIP is 60% complete, materials were added in the prior period, and no materials will be added in the current period. Thus, no EUP for these materials are included in the current period.

4) Units started and completed always are 100% complete with respect to direct materials.

5) Ending WIP

    a) If the point at which materials are added is reached during the current period, ending WIP will include EUP for the current period.

    b) If the point at which materials are added is reached during the next period, ending WIP will not include EUP for the current period.

    c) For example, assume that materials are added when units are 50% complete. If ending WIP is 20% complete, materials have not been added. Thus, no EUP from ending WIP will be included in the current period.

6. **EUP – Conversion Costs**

    a. Because conversion costs generally are added throughout the process, these calculations are similar to those in item 5.b.

    b. The method used and the completion percentage should be determined.

        1) Beginning WIP -- **Weighted-average**

            a) Beginning WIP is treated as 100% complete and will include **EUP in the current period** even though conversion costs were added in the previous period.

        2) Beginning WIP -- **FIFO**

            a) The completion percentage for the current period equals 100% minus the completion percentage for the beginning WIP. The result is the percentage completed in the current period.

            b) For example, if 1,000 units in beginning WIP are 20% complete with respect to conversion costs, 80% (100% – 20%) will be completed in the current period.

                i) EUP from beginning WIP equal 800 (1,000 units × 80%).

        3) Units started and completed always are 100% complete with respect to conversion costs.

        4) The completion percentage determines the EUP included in ending WIP.

            a) For example, if 1,000 units in ending WIP are 10% complete with respect to conversion costs, 10% were completed in the current period.

                i) EUP included in ending WIP equal 100 (1,000 units × 10%).

EXTENDED EXAMPLE

Quantity Schedule

	Units	Completed for Direct Materials	Completed for Conversion Costs
Beginning work-in-process	2,000	80%	40%
Units started during period	8,000		
Units to account for	10,000		
Units transferred to next department	9,000		
Ending work-in-process	1,000	90%	70%
Units accounted for	10,000		

In all EUP calculations, three kinds of units must be accounted for:

- Beginning WIP: 2,000 (given)
- Units started and completed in the current period

    9,000 Units transferred out   8,000 Units started
 – 2,000 Beginning WIP   – 1,000 Ending WIP
    7,000 Units started and completed   7,000 Units started and completed

- Ending WIP: 1,000 (given)

– Continued on next page –

EXTENDED EXAMPLE – Continued

Section A.

EUP for direct materials – added at beginning of process:

When direct materials are added at the beginning of the process

- Under weighted-average, prior period and current period costs are considered. Thus, direct materials costs included in beginning WIP and those added during the period are used in the calculation.
- Under FIFO, only current period activity is considered. Because all DM were added in the previous period, no DM costs are added in the current period.
- Under both methods, ending WIP is by definition 100% complete with respect to materials. However, the ending inventory is only 70% complete with respect to conversion costs.

	Weighted Average					FIFO				
Beginning WIP	2,000 units	×	100% (a)	=	2,000	2,000 units	×	0% (c)	=	0
Started and completed	7,000 units	×	100%	=	7,000	7,000 units	×	100%	=	7,000
Ending WIP	1,000 units	×	100% (b)	=	1,000	1,000 units	×	100% (d)	=	1,000
Totals	10,000				**10,000**	10,000				**8,000**

(a) Always 100% (c) Needed to complete
(b) Degree of completion (d) Degree of completion

One way to remember the difference between weighted average and FIFO is to consider the calculation for beginning inventory. Under weighted average, costs are averaged for two periods. Thus, work for two periods (2,000 units) is considered. Under FIFO, layers are considered. Because the current period layer is zero, the EUP equal zero.

When direct materials are added evenly throughout the process

- Under weighted-average, the treatment of beginning WIP is the same as that when materials are added at the beginning (i.e., all units treated as started and completed in the current period).
- Under FIFO, the costs incurred in the current period for beginning WIP are only those needed to complete them.
- Under both methods, the EUP in ending WIP equal the percentage of completion.

Section B.

EUP for direct materials – added throughout process:

When direct materials are added evenly throughout the process

- Under weighted-average, the treatment of beginning WIP is the same as that when materials are added at the beginning (i.e., all physical units are treated as 100% complete and included in EUP for the current period).
- Under FIFO, the costs incurred in the current period for beginning WIP are only those needed for completion.
- Under both methods, the EUP in ending WIP equal the percentage of completion times the number of physical units.

Ending inventory is 90% complete, and beginning inventory is 80% complete.

	Weighted Average					FIFO				
Beginning WIP	2,000 units	×	100% (a)	=	2,000	2,000 units	×	20% (c)	=	400
Started and completed	7,000 units	×	100%	=	7,000	7,000 units	×	100%	=	7,000
Ending WIP	1,000 units	×	90% (b)	=	900	1,000 units	×	90% (d)	=	900
Totals	10,000				**9,900**	10,000				**8,300**

(a) Always 100% (c) Needed to complete
(b) Degree of completion (d) Degree of completion

Conversion costs by their nature are added evenly throughout the process. Based on the quantity schedule, ending inventory is 70% complete with respect to conversion costs.

– Continued on next page –

EXTENDED EXAMPLE – Continued

Section C.

EUP for conversion costs:

	Weighted Average				FIFO			
Beginning WIP	2,000 units	×	100% (a)	= 2,000	2,000 units	×	60% (c)	= 1,200
Started and completed	7,000 units	×	100%	= 7,000	7,000 units	×	100%	= 7,000
Ending WIP	1,000 units	×	70% (b)	= 700	1,000 units	×	70% (d)	= 700
Totals	10,000			**9,700**	10,000			**8,900**

(a) Always 100%   (c) Needed to complete
(b) Degree of completion   (d) Degree of completion

The costs to be allocated are as follows:

	Direct Materials	Conversion Costs		Total
Beginning work-in-process	US $25,000	US $10,000	=	US $ 35,000
Added during the month	55,000	50,000	=	105,000
				US $140,000

The per-unit costs under each of the two methods can now be derived.

- Under the weighted-average method, all costs for the current period and in beginning work-in-process are included in the calculation.
- Under the FIFO method, only the costs incurred in the current period are included in the calculation because only the work performed in the current period is included in EUP.

Per-unit costs – direct materials added at beginning of process:

Ending WIP is 70% complete as to conversion costs.

	Weighted-average		FIFO	
Direct materials:	$\dfrac{US \$25,000 + \$55,000}{10,000\ EUP}$ =	US $ 8.000	$\dfrac{US \$55,000}{8,000\ EUP}$ =	US $ 6.875
Conversion costs:	$\dfrac{US \$10,000 + \$50,000}{9,700\ EUP}$ =	US $ 6.186	$\dfrac{US \$50,000}{8,900\ EUP}$ =	US $ 5.618
Total per-unit cost		**US $14.186**		**US $12.493**

Per-unit costs – direct materials added throughout process:

	Weighted-average		FIFO	
Direct materials:	$\dfrac{US \$25,000 + \$55,000}{9,900\ EUP}$ =	US $ 8.081	$\dfrac{US \$55,000}{8,300\ EUP}$ =	US $6.627
Conversion costs:	$\dfrac{US \$10,000 + \$50,000}{9,700\ EUP}$ =	US $ 6.186	$\dfrac{US \$50,000}{8,900\ EUP}$ =	US $5.618
Total per-unit cost		**US $14.267**		**US $1.245**

7. **Other Cost Accumulation Systems**

   a. Job-order costing is appropriate when producing products with individual characteristics or when identifiable groupings are possible.

      1) Costs are attached to specific jobs. Each job will result in a single, identifiable end product.

      2) Examples are any industries that generate custom-built products, such as shipbuilding.

b. Backflush costing delays the assignment of costs until the goods are finished.

   1) After production is finished for the period, standard costs are flushed backward through the system to assign costs to products. The result is that detailed tracking of costs is eliminated.

   2) Backflush costing is best suited to companies that maintain low inventories because costs can flow directly to cost of goods sold. It is often used with just-in-time (JIT) inventory, one of the goals of which is the maintenance of low inventory levels.

     a) Backflush costing complements JIT because it simplifies costing.

c. Activity-based costing (ABC) attaches costs to activities rather than to physical goods.

   1) Subunit 17.3 provides a thorough explanation.

8. **Spoilage and Scrap**

a. **Normal spoilage** occurs under normal operating conditions. It is essentially uncontrollable in the short run. Because it is expected under efficient operations, it is treated as a product (inventoriable) cost, that is, absorbed into the cost of the good output.

b. **Abnormal spoilage** is not expected to occur under normal, efficient operating conditions. It is typically treated as a period cost (a loss). Recognizing the loss resulting from abnormal spoilage under process costing is a multi-step process.

   1) The manufacturer establishes inspection points, that is, the places in the production process where goods not meeting specifications are pulled from the process. This is in contrast to job-order costing, in which a unit can be judged to be spoiled at any time.

     a) The typical arrangement is to inspect units as they are being transferred from one department to the next. This way, each department has its own amount of spoilage, calculated using its own equivalent-unit costs.

   2) The loss is equal to the number of units of abnormal spoilage multiplied by the department's equivalent-units costs, whether weighted-average or FIFO.

Loss on abnormal spoilage	US $XXX
Work-in-process – Department A	US $XXX

c. Scrap consists of materials left over from the production process. If scrap is sold, it reduces factory overhead. If it is discarded, it is absorbed into the cost of the good output.

Stop and review! You have completed the outline for this subunit. Study multiple-choice questions 10 through 15 beginning on page 444.

17.5 ABSORPTION (FULL) VS. VARIABLE (DIRECT) COSTING

1. **Overview**

a. One crucial distinction between cost accounting for external financial reporting and internal reporting is the difference between absorption (or full) costing and variable (or direct) costing.

2. **Absorption Costing**

a. Under **absorption costing** (sometimes called full or full absorption costing), the fixed portion of manufacturing overhead is included in the cost of each product.

   1) Product cost includes all manufacturing costs, both fixed and variable.

   2) Sales minus absorption-basis cost of goods sold equals **gross margin**.

   3) Total selling and administrative (S&A) expenses (i.e., both fixed and variable) are then subtracted from gross margin to determine operating income.

3. Variable Costing

a. This method (sometimes called direct costing) is more appropriate for internal reporting.

 1) Product cost includes only the variable portion of manufacturing costs.

 2) Variable-basis cost of goods sold and the variable portion of S&A expenses are subtracted from sales to arrive at contribution margin.

   a) This figure (Sales – Total variable costs) is an important element of the variable costing income statement because it is the amount available for covering fixed costs (both manufacturing and S&A).

   b) For this reason, some accountants call the method contribution margin reporting.

 3) The term "direct costing" is somewhat misleading because it suggests traceability, which is not what is meant in this context. "Variable costing" is more suitable.

 4) Contribution margin is an important metric internally but is generally considered irrelevant to outside financial statement users.

4. Justification for Variable Costing

a. Under variable costing, fixed overhead cost is considered a cost of maintaining capacity, not a cost of production.

 1) To illustrate, a company has a fixed rental expense of US $10,000 per month on its factory building. That cost will be US $10,000 regardless of whether there is any production.

   a) If the company produces zero units, the cost will be US $10,000; if the company produces 10,000 units, the cost will be US $10,000.

 2) Therefore, the US $10,000 is not viewed as a cost of production and is not added to the cost of the inventories produced. That US $10,000 was a cost of maintaining a certain level of production capacity.

b. To emphasize, variable costing is used only for internal decision-making purposes; it is not permitted for external financial reporting or for tax calculation.

 1) The main advantage of the variable costing method is that income cannot be manipulated by management action, whereas management can manipulate income when using the absorption method (explained in item 7. on page 439).

c. EXAMPLE: During its first month in business, a firm produced 100 units and sold 80 while incurring the following costs:

Direct materials	US $1,000
Direct labor	2,000
Variable overhead	1,500
Manufacturing costs used in variable costing	**US $4,500**
Fixed overhead	3,000
Manufacturing costs used in absorption costing	**US $7,500**

 1) The impact on the financial statements from using one method over the other can be seen in these calculations:

	Absorption Basis	Variable Basis
Manufacturing costs	US $7,500	US $4,500
Divided by: units produced	÷ 100	÷ 100
Per-unit cost	US $ 75	US $ 45
Times: ending inventory	× 20	× 20
Value of ending inventory	**US $1,500**	**US $ 900**

2) The per-unit selling price of the finished goods was US $100, and the company incurred US $200 of variable selling and administrative expenses and US $600 of fixed selling and administrative expenses.

d. The following are partial income statements prepared using the two methods:

	Absorption Costing (Required under GAAP)		Variable Costing (For Internal Reporting Only)	
Sales		**US $ 8,000**		**US $ 8,000**
Beginning finished goods inventory	US $ 0		US $ 0	
Product Costs — Plus: variable production costs	4,500 (a)		4,500 (a)	
Plus: fixed production costs	3,000 (b)			
Goods available for sale	US $7,500		US $4,500	
Less: ending finished goods inventory	(1,500)		(900)	
Cost of goods sold		**US $(6,000)**		**US $(3,600)**
Less: variable S&A expenses				(200) (c)
Gross margin (abs.) / Contribution margin (var.)		**US $ 2,000**		**US $ 4,200**
Period Costs — Less: fixed production costs				(3,000) (b)
Less: variable S&A expenses		(200) (c)		
Less: fixed S&A expenses		(600) (d)		(600) (d)
Operating income		**US $ 1,200**		**US $ 600**

1) The US $600 difference in operating income (US $1,200 – $600) is the difference between the two ending inventory values (US $1,500 – $900).

a) In essence, the absorption method carries 20% of the fixed overhead costs (US $3,000 × 20% = $600) on the balance sheet as an asset because 20% of the month's production (100 available – 80 sold = 20 on hand) is still in inventory.

2) This calculation is for illustrative purposes only. The difference in operating income is exactly the difference in ending inventory only when beginning inventory is US $0.

5. **Effects on Operating Income**

a. As production and sales levels change, the two methods have varying impacts on operating income.

1) When everything produced during a period is sold that period, the two methods report the same operating income.

a) Total fixed costs budgeted for the period are charged to sales revenue in the period under both methods.

2) When production and sales are not equal for a period, the two methods report different operating income.

b. When production exceeds sales, ending inventory expands.

1) Under absorption costing, some fixed costs are included in ending inventory. Under variable costing, all costs are expensed.

2) **When production exceeds sales, operating income is higher under absorption costing than it would be under variable costing.**

c. When production is less than sales, ending inventory contracts.

1) Under absorption costing, fixed costs included in beginning inventory are expensed. Under variable costing, only the current period's fixed costs are expensed.

2) **When production is less than sales, operating income is higher under variable costing than it would be under absorption costing.**

d.   Many companies prefer variable costing for internal reporting because of the perverse incentive inherent in absorption costing.

1)   Whenever production exceeds sales, less fixed cost is expensed under the absorption basis, and operating income always increases.

2)   A production manager can thus **increase absorption-basis operating income merely by increasing production**, regardless of customer demand.

a)   The company must also deal with the increased carrying costs resulting from increased inventory.

3)   This practice, called producing for inventory, can be effectively discouraged by using variable costing for performance reporting and consequent bonus calculation.

EXTENDED EXAMPLE of Absorption and Variable Operating Income

A company has the following sales and cost data:

	Year 1	Year 2	Year 3
Production in units	40,000	50,000	0
Sales in units	30,000	30,000	30,000
Ending inventory in units (FIFO)	10,000	30,000	0

Unit sales price	US $1.00
Unit variable cost	US $0.50
Fixed manufacturing costs	US $4,000 per year
Variable S&A expenses	US $0.03 per unit
Fixed S&A expenses	US $1,000 per year

Compare the 3-year income statements prepared under the two methods:

Absorption Costing (Required for external reporting)				Variable Costing (For internal reporting only)			
	Year 1	Year 2	Year 3		Year 1	Year 2	Year 3
Sales	**US $30,000**	**US $30,000**	**US $30,000**	**Sales**	**US $30,000**	**US $30,000**	**US $30,000**
Beginning inventory	US $ 0	US $ 6,000	US $17,500	Beginning inventory	US $ 0	US $ 5,000	US $15,000
Variable mfg. costs	20,000	25,000	0	Variable mfg. costs	20,000	25,000	0
Fixed mfg. costs	4,000	4,000	4,000				
Goods available for sale	US $24,000	US $35,000	US $21,500	Goods avail. for sale	US $20,000	US $30,000	US $15,000
Less: ending inventory*	(6,000)	(17,500)	0	Less: ending inventory	(5,000)	(15,000)	0
Absorption COGS	**US $18,000**	**US $17,500**	**US $21,500**	**Variable COGS**	**US $15,000**	**US $15,000**	**US $15,000**
				Variable S&A exps.	(900)	(900)	(900)
Gross margin	**US $12,000**	**US $12,500**	**US $ 8,500**	**Contribution margin**	**US $14,100**	**US $14,100**	**US $14,100**
				Fixed mfg. costs	(4,000)	(4,000)	(4,000)
Variable S&A expenses	(900)	(900)	(900)				
Fixed S&A expenses	(1,000)	(1,000)	(1,000)	Fixed S&A expenses	(1,000)	(1,000)	(1,000)
Operating income	**US $10,100**	**US $10,600**	**US $ 6,600**	**Operating income**	**US $ 9,100**	**US $ 9,100**	**US $ 9,100**

Note that, assuming zero inventory at the beginning of Year 1 and at the end of Year 3, the total operating income for the 3-year period is the same under either costing method.

	Absorption Costing	Variable Costing
Year 1	US $10,100	US $ 9,100
Year 2	10,600	9,100
Year 3	6,600	9,100
3-Year Total	**US $27,300**	**US $27,300**

-- Continued on the next page --

EXTENDED EXAMPLE -- Continued

Absorption costing shows a higher operating income than variable costing in Years 1 and 2 because fixed overhead has been capitalized and does not get expensed until Year 3. Variable costing, on the other hand, treats fixed overhead as an expense of the period in which the cost is incurred. In Year 2, despite the same cash flow, there is a US $1,500 difference between the final operating income figures. There is an even greater difference in Year 3.

If fixed costs increase relative to variable costs, the differences become more dramatic (here, 50% of the selling price is variable manufacturing cost, and fixed overhead is no more than 20% of the variable manufacturing cost).

From an internal point of view, a manager can manipulate absorption income by changing production levels. But, with variable costing, a manager cannot manipulate simply by changing production levels.

Note that, under the absorption method, management was able to show higher incomes in Years 1 and 2 by overproducing. If the manager was offered a bonus for a higher level of income, (s)he could obtain the bonus by producing more units than could be sold. As a result, some fixed costs would be added to the balance sheet as inventories. Thus, the income statement and balance sheet both look good, despite the fact that the production manager has done a bad thing: (S)he has produced excessive inventories that require the company to incur storage and financing costs. Spoilage may also be a result.

*Ending inventory is calculated on the weighted-average basis. The use of FIFO would result in slightly different numbers in Year 2 under the absorption method, but the impact would be the same.

---

6. **Summary of Effects on Income and Ending Inventory**

    a. The value of ending inventory is **never** higher under variable costing than it is under absorption costing because fixed manufacturing costs are not included in inventory under variable costing.

    b. Income and inventory levels will differ whenever sales and production differ.

        1) Income will be higher or lower under variable costing depending upon whether inventories are increased during the period or liquidated.

        2) If inventories increase during a period, the variable costing method will show a lower income because all fixed costs are being subtracted on the income statement, while under the absorption method, some fixed costs are being capitalized as inventories.

        3) Variable costing will show a higher income in periods when inventories decline because the absorption method forces the subtraction of current period fixed costs included in inventory sold, plus some fixed costs incurred (and capitalized) in prior periods.

    c. Under variable costing, profits always move in the same direction as sales volume. Profits reported under absorption costing behave erratically and sometimes move in the opposite direction from sales trends.

    d. In the long run, the two methods will report the same total profits if sales equal production. The inequalities between production and sales are usually minor over an extended period.

7. **Benefits of Variable Costing**

    a. Although the use of variable costing for financial statements is prohibited, most agree about its superiority for internal reporting. It is far better suited than absorption costing to the needs of management.

        1) Management requires a knowledge of cost behavior under various operating conditions. For planning and control, management is more concerned with treating fixed and variable costs separately than with calculating full costs.

        2) Full costs are usually of dubious value because they contain arbitrary allocations of fixed cost.

    b. Under the variable costing method, a production manager cannot manipulate income levels by overproducing. Given the same cost structure every year, the income levels will be based on sales, not the level of production.

c.   Under variable costing, the cost data for profit planning and decision making are readily available from accounting records and statements. Reference to auxiliary records and supplementary analyses is not necessary.

1)   For example, cost-volume-profit relationships and the effects of changes in sales volume on net income can easily be computed from the income statement prepared under the variable costing concept, but not from the conventional absorption cost income statement based on the same data.

d.   Profits and losses reported under variable costing have a relationship to sales revenue and are not affected by inventory or production variations.

e.   Absorption cost income statements may show decreases in profits when sales are rising and increases in profits when sales are decreasing, which may be confusing to management. Attempts at explanation by means of volume variances often compound rather than clarify the confusion.

f.   When variable costing is used, the favorable margin between selling prices and variable cost should provide a constant reminder of profits forgone because of lack of sales volume. A favorable margin justifies a higher production level.

g.   The full impact of fixed costs on net income, partially hidden in inventory values under absorption costing, is emphasized by the presentation of costs on an income statement prepared under variable costing.

h.   Proponents of variable costing maintain that fixed factory overhead is more closely correlated to capacity to produce than to the production of individual units.

8.   **Further Aspects of Variable Costing**

a.   Variable costing is also preferred over absorption costing for studies of relative profitability of products, territories, and other segments of a business. It concentrates on the contribution that each segment makes to the recovery of fixed costs that will not be altered by decisions to make and sell. Under variable costing procedures,

1)   The marginal income concept leads to better pricing decisions, which are the principal advantage of variable costing.

2)   The impact of fixed costs on net income is emphasized by showing the total amount of such costs separately in financial reports.

3)   Out-of-pocket expenditures required to manufacture products conform closely with the valuation of inventory.

4)   The relationship between profit and the major factors of selling price, sales mix, sales volume, and variable manufacturing and nonmanufacturing costs is measured in terms of a single index of profitability.

a)   This profitability index, expressed as a positive amount or as a ratio, facilitates the analysis of cost-volume-profit relationships, compares the effects of two or more contemplated courses of action, and aids in answering many questions that arise in profit planning.

5)   Inventory changes have no effect on the breakeven computations.

6)   Marginal income figures facilitate appraisal of products, territories, and other business segments without having the results hidden or obscured by allocated joint fixed costs.

7)   Questions regarding whether a particular part should be made or bought can be more effectively answered if only variable costs are used.

a)   Management must consider whether to charge the product being made with variable costs only or to charge a percentage of fixed costs as well.

b)   Management must also consider whether the making of the part will require additional fixed costs and a decrease in normal production.

8) Disinvestment decisions are facilitated because whether a product or department is recouping its variable costs can be determined.

   a) If the variable costs are being covered, operating a department at an apparent loss may be profitable.

9) Management is better able to judge the differences between departments if certain fixed costs are omitted from the statements instead of being allocated arbitrarily.

10) Costs are guided by sales.

   a) Under variable costing, cost of goods sold will vary directly with sales volume, and the influence of production on gross profit is avoided.

   b) Variable costing also eliminates the possible difficulties of having to explain over- or underapplied manufacturing overhead to higher management.

Stop and review! You have completed the outline for this subunit. Study multiple-choice questions 16 through 20 beginning on page 446.

QUESTIONS

17.1 Cost Management Terminology

1. A company experienced a machinery breakdown on one of its production lines. As a consequence of the breakdown, manufacturing fell behind schedule, and a decision was made to schedule overtime to return manufacturing to schedule. Which one of the following methods is the proper way to account for the overtime paid to the direct laborers?

A. The overtime hours times the sum of the straight-time wages and overtime premium would be charged entirely to manufacturing overhead.

B. The overtime hours times the sum of the straight-time wages and overtime premium would be treated as direct labor.

C. The overtime hours times the overtime premium would be charged to repair and maintenance expense, and the overtime hours times the straight-time wages would be treated as direct labor.

D. The overtime hours times the overtime premium would be charged to manufacturing overhead, and the overtime hours times the straight-time wages would be treated as direct labor.

Answer (D) is correct.
REQUIRED: The proper way to account for the overtime paid to the direct laborers.
DISCUSSION: Direct labor costs are wages paid to labor that can feasibly be specifically identified with the production of finished goods. Factory overhead consists of all costs, other than direct materials and direct labor, that are associated with the manufacturing process. Thus, straight-time wages would be treated as direct labor; however, because the overtime premium cost is a cost that should be borne by all production, the overtime hours times the overtime premium should be charged to manufacturing overhead.
Answer (A) is incorrect. The straight-time wages times the overtime hours should still be treated as direct labor. Answer (B) is incorrect. Only the straight-time wages times the overtime hours is charged to direct labor. Answer (C) is incorrect. Labor costs are not related to repairs and maintenance expense.

2. An example of a direct labor cost is wages paid to a

	Factory Machine Operator	Supervisor in a Factory
A.	No	No
B.	No	Yes
C.	Yes	Yes
D.	Yes	No

Answer (D) is correct.
REQUIRED: An example of a direct labor cost.
DISCUSSION: Direct labor costs are wages paid to labor that can be specifically identified with the production of finished goods. Because the wages of a factory machine operator are identifiable with a finished product, those wages are considered a direct labor cost. Because the supervisor's salary is not identifiable with the production of finished goods, it is a part of factory overhead and thus not a direct labor cost.
Answer (A) is incorrect. The machine operator's wages are directly identifiable with the production of finished goods. Answer (B) is incorrect. The machine operator's wages are directly identifiable with the production of finished goods, while the salary of a factory supervisor is not. Answer (C) is incorrect. The salary of a factory supervisor is not directly identifiable with the production of finished goods.

3. In cost terminology, conversion costs consist of

    A.   Direct and indirect labor.

    B.   Direct labor and direct materials.

    C.   Direct labor and factory overhead.

    D.   Indirect labor and variable factory overhead.

Answer (C) is correct.
    REQUIRED: The components of conversion costs.
    DISCUSSION: Conversion costs consist of direct labor and manufacturing overhead. These are the costs of converting raw materials into a finished product.
    Answer (A) is incorrect. All manufacturing overhead is included in conversion costs, not just indirect labor. Answer (B) is incorrect. Direct materials are not an element of conversion costs; they are a prime cost. Answer (D) is incorrect. Direct labor is also an element of conversion costs.

4. Direct materials cost is a

	Conversion Cost	Prime Cost
A.	No	No
B.	No	Yes
C.	Yes	Yes
D.	Yes	No

Answer (B) is correct.
    REQUIRED: The classification of direct materials cost.
    DISCUSSION: Direct materials and direct labor are a manufacturer's prime costs. Conversion cost consists of direct labor and factory overhead.
    Answer (A) is incorrect. Direct materials cost is a prime cost. Answer (C) is incorrect. Direct materials cost is not a conversion cost. Answer (D) is incorrect. Direct materials cost is a prime cost but not a conversion cost.

17.2 Cost Behavior and Relevant Range

5. An assembly plant accumulates its variable and fixed manufacturing overhead costs in a single cost pool, which is then applied to work in process using a single application base. The assembly plant management wants to estimate the magnitude of the total manufacturing overhead costs for different volume levels of the application activity base using a flexible budget formula. If there is an increase in the application activity base that is within the relevant range of activity for the assembly plant, which one of the following relationships regarding variable and fixed costs is true?

    A.   The variable cost per unit is constant, and the total fixed costs decrease.

    B.   The variable cost per unit is constant, and the total fixed costs increase.

    C.   The variable cost per unit and the total fixed costs remain constant.

    D.   The variable cost per unit increases, and the total fixed costs remain constant.

Answer (C) is correct.
    REQUIRED: The effect on variable and fixed costs of a change in activity within the relevant range.
    DISCUSSION: Total variable cost changes when changes in the activity level occur within the relevant range. The cost per unit for a variable cost is constant for all activity levels within the relevant range. Thus, if the activity volume increases within the relevant range, total variable costs will increase. A fixed cost does not change when volume changes occur in the activity level within the relevant range. If the activity volume increases within the relevant range, total fixed costs will remain unchanged.
    Answer (A) is incorrect. The variable cost per unit and the total fixed costs will remain constant if the activity level increases within the relevant range. Answer (B) is incorrect. The variable cost per unit and the total fixed costs will remain constant if the activity level increases within the relevant range. Answer (D) is incorrect. The variable cost per unit and the total fixed costs will remain constant if the activity level increases within the relevant range.

17.3 Activity-Based Costing

6. Which of the following is true about activity-based costing?

    A.   It should not be used with process or job costing.

    B.   It can be used only with process costing.

    C.   It can be used only with job costing.

    D.   It can be used with either process or job costing.

Answer (D) is correct.
    REQUIRED: The true statement about ABC.
    DISCUSSION: Activity-based costing may be used by manufacturing, service, or retailing entities and in job-order or process costing systems.
    Answer (A) is incorrect. Activity-based costing may be used with either process or job costing. Answer (B) is incorrect. Activity-based costing may be used with either process or job costing. Answer (C) is incorrect. Activity-based costing may be used with either process or job costing.

7. A company with three products classifies its costs as belonging to five functions: design, production, marketing, distribution, and customer services. For pricing purposes, all company costs are assigned to the three products. The direct costs of each of the five functions are traced directly to the three products. The indirect costs of each of the five business functions are collected into five separate cost pools and then assigned to the three products using appropriate allocation bases. The allocation base that will most likely be the best for allocating the indirect costs of the distribution function is

A. Number of customer phone calls.

B. Number of shipments.

C. Number of sales persons.

D. Dollar sales volume.

Answer (B) is correct.
  REQUIRED: The allocation base that will most likely be the best for allocating the indirect costs of the distribution function.
  DISCUSSION: The number of shipments is an appropriate cost driver. A cause-and-effect relationship may exist between the number of shipments and distribution costs.
  Answer (A) is incorrect. The number of customer phone calls has little relation to distribution. It is probably more closely related to customer service. Answer (C) is incorrect. The number of sales persons is not related to distribution. It is more closely related to marketing. Answer (D) is incorrect. The dollar sales volume is not necessarily related to distribution. It is more likely related to marketing.

8. Cost allocation is the process of assigning indirect costs to a cost object. The indirect costs are grouped in cost pools and then allocated by a common allocation base to the cost object. The base that is employed to allocate a homogeneous cost pool should

A. Have a cause-and-effect relationship with the cost items in the cost pool.

B. Assign the costs in the pool uniformly to cost objects even if the cost objects use resources in a nonuniform way.

C. Be a nonfinancial measure (e.g., number of setups) because a nonfinancial measure is more objective.

D. Have a high correlation with the cost items in the cost pool as the sole criterion for selection.

Answer (A) is correct.
  REQUIRED: The characteristic of a base used to allocate a homogeneous cost pool.
  DISCUSSION: A cost allocation base is the common denominator for systematically correlating indirect costs and a cost object. The cost driver of the indirect costs is ordinarily the allocation base. In a homogeneous cost pool, all costs should have the same or a similar cause-and-effect relationship with the cost allocation base.
  Answer (B) is incorrect. If an allocation base uniformly assigns costs to cost objects when the cost objects use resources in a nonuniform way, the base is smoothing or spreading the costs. Smoothing can result in undercosting or overcosting of products, with adverse effects on product pricing, cost management and control, and decision making. Answer (C) is incorrect. Financial measures (e.g., sales dollars and direct labor costs) and nonfinancial measures (e.g., setups and units shipped) can be used as allocation bases. Answer (D) is incorrect. High correlation between the cost items in a pool and the allocation base does not necessarily mean that a cause-and-effect relationship exists. Two variables may move together without such a relationship. The perceived relationship between the cost driver (allocation base) and the indirect costs should have economic plausibility and high correlation.

9. Which of the following statements about activity-based costing (ABC) is **false**?

A. Activity-based costing is useful for allocating marketing and distribution costs.

B. Activity-based costing is more likely to result in major differences from traditional costing systems if the firm manufactures only one product rather than multiple products.

C. In activity-based costing, cost drivers are what cause costs to be incurred.

D. Activity-based costing differs from traditional costing systems in that products are not cross-subsidized.

Answer (B) is correct.
  REQUIRED: The false statement about activity-based costing (ABC).
  DISCUSSION: ABC determines the activities that will serve as cost objects and then accumulates a cost pool for each activity using the appropriate activity base (cost driver). It is a system that may be employed with job order or process costing methods. Thus, when there is only one product, the allocation of costs to the product is trivial. All of the cost is assigned to the one product; the particular method used to allocate the costs does not matter.
  Answer (A) is incorrect. Marketing and distribution costs should be allocated to specific products. Answer (C) is incorrect. ABC determines the activities that will serve as cost objects and then accumulates a cost pool for each activity using the appropriate activity base (cost driver). Answer (D) is incorrect. Under ABC, a product is allocated only those costs that pertain to its production; that is, products are not cross-subsidized.

17.4 Process Costing

10. A company employs a process cost system using the first-in, first-out (FIFO) method. The product passes through both Department 1 and Department 2 in order to be completed. Units enter Department 2 upon completion in Department 1. Additional direct materials are added in Department 2 when the units have reached the 25% stage of completion with respect to conversion costs. Conversion costs are added proportionally in Department 2. The production activity in Department 2 for the current month was as follows:

Beginning work-in-process inventory (40% complete with respect to conversion costs)	15,000
Units transferred in from Department 1	80,000
Units to account for	95,000
Units completed and transferred to finished goods	85,000
Ending work-in-process inventory (20% complete with respect to conversion costs)	10,000
Units accounted for	95,000

How many equivalent units for direct materials were added in Department 2 for the current month?

- A. 70,000 units.
- B. 80,000 units.
- C. 85,000 units.
- D. 95,000 units.

Answer (A) is correct.
REQUIRED: The equivalent units for direct materials added in Department 2 for the current month.
DISCUSSION: Beginning inventory is 40% complete. Thus, direct materials have already been added. Ending inventory has not reached the 25% stage of completion, so direct materials have not yet been added to these units. Thus, the equivalent units for direct materials calculated on a FIFO basis are equal to the units started and completed in the current period (85,000 units completed – 15,000 units in BWIP = 70,000 units started and completed).
Answer (B) is incorrect. The number of units transferred in from Department 1 was 80,000. Answer (C) is incorrect. Improperly using the weighted-average method to calculate equivalent units results in 85,000. Answer (D) is incorrect. The total of the units to be accounted for is 95,000.

11. A new advertising agency serves a wide range of clients including manufacturers, restaurants, service businesses, department stores, and other retail establishments. The accounting system the advertising agency has most likely adopted for its recordkeeping in accumulating costs is

- A. Job-order costing.
- B. Operation costing.
- C. Relevant costing.
- D. Process costing.

Answer (A) is correct.
REQUIRED: The most likely accounting system adopted by a company with a wide range of clients.
DISCUSSION: Job-order costing is used by organizations whose products or services are readily identified by individual units or batches. The advertising agency accumulates its costs by client. Job-order costing is the most appropriate system for this type of nonmanufacturing firm.
Answer (B) is incorrect. Operation costing would most likely be employed by a manufacturer producing goods that have common characteristics plus some individual characteristics. This would not be an appropriate system for an advertising agency with such a diverse client base. Answer (C) is incorrect. Relevant costing refers to expected future costs that are considered in decision making. Answer (D) is incorrect. Process costing is employed when a company mass produces a homogeneous product in a continuous fashion through a series of production steps.

12. The units transferred in from the first department to the second department should be included in the computation of the equivalent units for the second department under which of the following methods of process costing?

	FIFO	Weighted-Average
A.	Yes	Yes
B.	Yes	No
C.	No	Yes
D.	No	No

Answer (A) is correct.
REQUIRED: The cost flow method(s) that include(s) transferred-in costs in EUP calculations.
DISCUSSION: The units transferred from the first to the second department should be included in the computation of equivalent units for the second department regardless of the cost flow assumption used. The transferred-in units are considered raw materials added at the beginning of the period.
Answer (B) is incorrect. Units transferred in also should be included in the EUP computation under the weighted-average method. Answer (C) is incorrect. Units transferred in also should be included in the EUP computation under the FIFO method. Answer (D) is incorrect. Units transferred in should be included in the EUP computation under both methods.

13. In a process-costing system, the cost of abnormal spoilage should be

A. Prorated between units transferred out and ending inventory.

B. Included in the cost of units transferred out.

C. Treated as a loss in the period incurred.

D. Ignored.

Answer (C) is correct.
REQUIRED: The best accounting treatment for abnormal spoilage.
DISCUSSION: Abnormal spoilage is spoilage that is not expected to occur under normal, efficient operating conditions. Because of its unusual nature, abnormal spoilage is typically treated as a loss in the period in which it is incurred.
Answer (A) is incorrect. Abnormal spoilage costs are not considered a component of the cost of good units produced. Answer (B) is incorrect. Abnormal spoilage costs are not considered a component of the cost of good units produced. Answer (D) is incorrect. Abnormal spoilage costs must be taken out of the manufacturing account.

14. Three commonly employed systems for product costing are termed job-order costing, operations costing, and process costing. Match the type of production environment with the costing method used.

	Job-Order Costing	Operations Costing	Process Costing
A.	Auto repair	Clothing manufacturer	Oil refining
B.	Loan processing	Drug manufacturing	Custom printing
C.	Custom printing	Paint manufacturing	Paper manufacturing
D.	Engineering design	Auto assembly	Motion picture production

Answer (A) is correct.
REQUIRED: The match of the types of production environments with the costing methods.
DISCUSSION: Job-order costing is appropriate when producing products with individual characteristics and/or when identifiable groupings are possible. Process costing should be used to assign costs to similar products that are mass produced on a continuous basis. Operations costing is a hybrid of job order and process costing systems. It is used by companies that manufacture goods that undergo some similar and some dissimilar processes. Thus, job-order costing would be appropriate for auto repair, operations costing for clothing manufacturing, and process costing for oil refining.
Answer (B) is incorrect. Custom printing would use job-order costing. Answer (C) is incorrect. Paint manufacturing would use process costing. Answer (D) is incorrect. Motion picture production would use job-order costing.

15. Companies characterized by the production of basically homogeneous products will most likely use which of the following methods for the purpose of averaging costs and providing management with unit-cost data?

A. Job-order costing.

B. Direct costing.

C. Absorption costing.

D. Process costing.

Answer (D) is correct.
REQUIRED: The method of averaging costs and providing management with unit cost data used by companies with homogeneous products.
DISCUSSION: Like products that are mass produced should be accounted for using process costing techniques to assign costs to products. Costs are accumulated by departments or cost centers rather than by jobs, work-in-process is stated in terms of equivalent units, and unit costs are established on a departmental basis. Process costing is an averaging process that calculates the average cost of all units.
Answer (A) is incorrect. Job-order costing is employed when manufacturing involves different (heterogeneous) products. Answer (B) is incorrect. Direct costing includes only variable manufacturing costs in unit cost. It may be used whether products are homogeneous or heterogeneous and with either process or job-order costing. Answer (C) is incorrect. Absorption costing includes all manufacturing costs as part of the cost of a finished product. It may be used whether products are homogeneous or heterogeneous and with either process or job-order costing.

17.5 Absorption (Full) vs. Variable (Direct) Costing

16. Using the variable costing method, which of the following costs are assigned to inventory?

	Variable Selling and Administrative Costs	Variable Factory Overhead Costs
A.	Yes	Yes
B.	Yes	No
C.	No	No
D.	No	Yes

Answer (D) is correct.
REQUIRED: The costs assigned to inventory.
DISCUSSION: Under variable costing, only variable manufacturing costs (not variable selling, general, and administrative costs) are assigned to inventory. Variable factory overhead is a variable manufacturing cost. Thus, it is assigned to inventory.

17. During its first year of operations, a company produced 275,000 units and sold 250,000 units. The following costs were incurred during the year:

Variable costs per unit:
Direct materials	US $15.00
Direct labor	10.00
Manufacturing overhead	12.50
Selling and administrative	2.50

Total fixed costs:
Manufacturing overhead	US $2,200,000
Selling and administrative	US $1,375,000

The difference between operating profit calculated on the absorption-costing basis and on the variable-costing basis is that absorption-costing operating profit is

A. US $200,000 greater.

B. US $220,000 greater.

C. US $325,000 greater.

D. US $62,500 less.

Answer (A) is correct.
REQUIRED: The difference between absorption-costing and variable-costing operating profit.
DISCUSSION: Absorption-costing operating profit will exceed variable-costing operating income because production exceeds sales, resulting in a deferral of fixed manufacturing overhead in the inventory calculated using the absorption method. The difference of US $200,000 is equal to the fixed manufacturing overhead per unit (US $2,200,000 ÷ 275,000 = US $8.00) times the difference between production and sales (275,000 − 250,000 = 25,000, which is the inventory change in units).
Answer (B) is incorrect. Units produced, not units sold, should be used as the denominator to calculate the fixed manufacturing cost per unit. Answer (C) is incorrect. Fixed selling and administrative costs are not properly inventoriable under absorption costing. Answer (D) is incorrect. Variable selling and administrative costs are period costs under both variable- and absorption-cost systems in the determination of operating profit.

18. In a company, products pass through some or all of the production departments during manufacturing, depending upon the product being manufactured. Direct material and direct labor costs are traced directly to the products as they flow through each production department. Manufacturing overhead is assigned in each department using separate departmental manufacturing overhead rates. The inventory costing method that the manufacturing company is using in this situation is

A. Absorption costing.

B. Activity-based costing.

C. Backflush costing.

D. Variable costing.

Answer (A) is correct.
REQUIRED: The appropriate inventory costing method.
DISCUSSION: Under absorption costing, inventories include all direct manufacturing costs and both variable and fixed manufacturing overhead (indirect) costs.
Answer (B) is incorrect. Activity-based costing develops cost pools for activities and then allocates those costs to cost objects based on the drivers of the activities. Answer (C) is incorrect. A backflush costing system applies costs based on output. Answer (D) is incorrect. Variable costing excludes fixed manufacturing overhead costs from inventoriable costs and treats them as period costs.

19. When comparing absorption costing with variable costing, which of the following statements is **not** true?

- A. Absorption costing enables managers to increase operating profits in the short run by increasing inventories.
- B. When sales volume is more than production volume, variable costing will result in higher operating profit.
- C. A manager who is evaluated based on variable costing operating profit would be tempted to increase production at the end of a period in order to get a more favorable review.
- D. Under absorption costing, operating profit is a function of both sales volume and production volume.

Answer (C) is correct.
REQUIRED: The false statement comparing absorption costing and variable costing.
DISCUSSION: Absorption (full) costing is the accounting method that considers all manufacturing costs as product costs. These costs include variable and fixed manufacturing costs whether direct or indirect. Variable (direct) costing considers only variable manufacturing costs to be product costs, i.e., inventoriable. Fixed manufacturing costs are considered period costs and are expensed as incurred. If production is increased without increasing sales, inventories will rise. However, all fixed costs associated with production will be an expense of the period under variable costing. Thus, this action will not artificially increase profits and improve the manager's review.
Answer (A) is incorrect. Increasing inventories increases absorption costing profit as a result of capitalizing fixed factory overhead. Answer (B) is incorrect. When sales volume exceeds production, inventories decline. Thus, fixed factory overhead expensed will be greater under absorption costing. Answer (D) is incorrect. Under variable costing, operating profit is a function of sales. Under absorption costing, it is a function of sales and production.

20. In an income statement prepared using the variable-costing method, fixed factory overhead would

- A. Not be used.
- B. Be used in the computation of operating income but not in the computation of the contribution margin.
- C. Be used in the computation of the contribution margin.
- D. Be treated the same as variable factory overhead.

Answer (B) is correct.
REQUIRED: The treatment of fixed factory overhead in an income statement based on variable costing.
DISCUSSION: Under the variable-costing method, the contribution margin equals sales minus variable expenses. Fixed selling and administrative costs and fixed factory overhead are deducted from the contribution margin to arrive at operating income. Thus, fixed costs are included only in the computation of operating income.
Answer (A) is incorrect. Fixed factory overhead is deducted from the contribution margin to determine operating income. Answer (C) is incorrect. Only variable expenses are used in the computation of the contribution margin. Answer (D) is incorrect. Variable factory overhead is included in the computation of contribution margin and fixed factory overhead is not.

Access the **CIA Review System** from your Gleim Personal Classroom to continue your studies with exam-emulating multiple-choice questions!

STUDY UNIT EIGHTEEN
MANAGERIAL ACCOUNTING II

(24 pages of outline)

This study unit is the fifth of five covering **Section VII: Financial Management** from The IIA's CIA Exam Syllabus. This section makes up 10% to 20% of Part 3 of the CIA exam and is tested at the **awareness level**. The relevant portion of the syllabus is highlighted below. (The complete syllabus is in Appendix A.)

VII. FINANCIAL MANAGEMENT (10%–20%)

   A. **Financial Accounting and Finance**

   B. **Managerial Accounting**

   4. Relevant cost
   5. Cost-volume-profit analysis
   6. Transfer pricing
   7. Responsibility accounting
   8. Operating budget

NOTE: Items B. 1., 2., and 3. are covered in Study Unit 17.

18.1 BUDGET SYSTEMS

1. **Purposes of a Budget**

   a. The budget is a planning tool.

      1) A budget forces management to evaluate the assumptions used and the objectives identified in the budgetary process.

   b. The budget is a control tool.

      1) A budget helps control costs by setting guidelines and provides a framework for manager performance evaluations.

   c. The budget is a motivational tool.

      1) A budget helps to motivate employees. Employees are particularly motivated if they help prepare the budget.

   d. The budget is a means of communication and coordination.

      1) A budget states the entity's objectives in numerical terms. It thus requires segments of the entity to communicate and cooperate.

2. **Participation in the Budget Process**

   a. Participation in the budget preparation process is up and down the organization.

      1) The budget process begins with the mission statement formulated by the **board of directors**.

      2) **Senior management** translates the mission statement into a strategic plan with measurable, realizable goals.

3) A **budget committee/department** composed of top management is formed to draft the budget calendar and budget manual. The budget committee/department also reviews and approves the departmental budgets submitted by operating managers.

    a) A budget director's primary responsibility is to compile the budget and manage the budget process.

4) **Middle and lower management** receive their budget instructions, draw up their departmental budgets in conformity with the guidelines, and submit them to the budget committee.

b. **Top-down (authoritative) budgeting** is imposed by upper management and therefore has less of a chance of acceptance by those on whom the budget is imposed.

    1) This approach has the advantage of ensuring consistency across functional areas. It is also far less complex and time-consuming than coordinating input from middle and lower levels.

c. **Bottom-up (participative) budgeting** is characterized by general guidance from the highest levels of management, followed by extensive input from middle and lower management. Because of this level of participation within the company, there is usually a greater chance of acceptance.

    1) Disadvantages of participative standards setting include its time and money costs. In addition, the quality of participation is affected by the goals, values, beliefs, and expectations of those involved.

	Advantages	Disadvantages
Top-down budgeting	• Ensures consistency across all functional areas • Is far less complex and time-consuming than coordinating input from the middle and lower levels	• An imposed budget is much less likely to promote a sense of commitment
Bottom-up budgeting	• Encourages employees to have a sense of ownership of the output of the process, resulting in acceptance of, and commitment to, objectives expressed in the budget • Enables employees to relate performance to rewards or penalties • Provides a broader information base (middle- and lower-level managers often are far better informed about operational realities than senior managers)	• Higher costs in time and money • Quality of participation is affected by the objectives, values, beliefs, and expectations of those involved • Creation of budgetary slack

d. Participation in developing a budget may result in a **padding** of the budget, also known as budgetary slack.

    1) **Budgetary slack** is the excess of resources budgeted over the resources necessary to achieve organizational goals. This must be avoided if a budget is to have its desired effects.

        a) The natural tendency of a manager is to negotiate for a less stringent measure of performance so as to avoid unfavorable variances from expectations.

    2) Management may create slack by overestimating costs and underestimating revenues.

        a) A firm may decrease slack by emphasizing the consideration of all variables, holding in-depth reviews during budget development, and allowing for flexibility in making additional budget changes.

        b) A manager who expects his or her request to be reduced may inflate the amount.

      c)   If a budget is to be used as a performance evaluator, a manager asked for an estimate may provide one that is easily attained.

   3)   The existence of slack can have both positive and negative effects on the budgeting process. The existence of slack can reduce the planning benefits of a budget, since the budget may not be entirely accurate.

      a)   For example, a cash budget might show that US $500,000 needs to be borrowed this month, whereas that amount is not really needed because managers were just being cautious.

      b)   Alternatively, the lack of slack may discourage managers from implementing new programs or might cause managers to avoid routine maintenance when the budget does not show funds available in a particular period.

3.   **The Use of Cost Standards**

   a.   Standard costs are **predetermined expectations** about how much a unit of input, a unit of output, or a given activity should cost.

      1)   The use of standard costs in budgeting allows the standard-cost system to alert management when the actual costs of production differ significantly from the standard.

   b.   A standard cost is not just an average of past costs but an objectively determined estimate of what a cost should be. Standards may be based on accounting, engineering, or statistical quality control studies.

      1)   Because of the impact of fixed costs in most businesses, a standard costing system is usually not effective unless the company also has a flexible budgeting system.

4.   **Developing Standards**

   a.   **Activity analysis** identifies, describes, and evaluates the activities that go into producing a particular output. Determining the resources and steps that go into the production process aids in the development of standard costs.

      1)   Each operation requires its own unique set of inputs and preparations. Activity analysis describes what these inputs are and who performs these preparations.

         a)   Inputs include the amounts and kinds of equipment, facilities, materials, and labor. Engineering analysis, cost accounting, time-and-motion study, and other approaches may be useful.

      2)   **Historical data** may be used to set standards by firms that lack the resources to engage in the complex task of activity analysis.

   b.   For **direct materials**, there is often a direct relationship between unit price and quality. In establishing its cost standards, a manufacturer must decide whether it will use an input that is

      1)   Cheaper per unit but will ultimately result in using more because of low quality or

      2)   More expensive per unit but will ultimately result in using less because of lower waste and spoilage.

   c.   For **direct labor**, the complexity of the production process and the restrictions on pay scales imposed by union agreements have the most impact on formulating cost standards. Human resources also must be consulted to help project the costs of benefits.

   d.   Standards can be set using the top-down (authoritative) approach or the bottom-up (participative) approach.

      1)   A form of the bottom-up approach that involves line managers and their supervisors, accountants, engineers, and other interested employees before standards are accepted by top management is also called the team development approach.

5.   **Theoretical vs. Practical Standards**

    a.   **Ideal (theoretical) standards** are standard costs that are set for production under optimal conditions. For this reason, they are also called perfection or maximum efficiency standards.

        1)   They are based on the work of the most skilled workers with no allowance for waste, spoilage, machine breakdowns, or other downtime.

        2)   Often called "tight" standards, they can have positive behavioral implications if workers are motivated to strive for excellence. However, they are not widely used because they can have negative behavioral effects if the standards are perceived as impossible to attain.

        3)   Ideal standards have been adopted by some companies that apply continuous improvement and other total quality management principles.

        4)   Ideal standards are ordinarily replaced by currently attainable standards for cash budgeting, product costing, and budgeting departmental performance. Otherwise, accurate financial planning will be impossible.

    b.   **Currently attainable (practical) standards** are defined as the performance that is expected to be achieved by reasonably well-trained workers with an allowance for normal spoilage, waste, and downtime.

        1)   An alternative interpretation is that practical standards represent possible but difficult-to-attain results.

6.   **The Master Budget**

    a.   The master budget, also called the comprehensive budget or the annual profit plan, consists of the organization's operating and financial plans for a specified period (ordinarily a year or single operating cycle).

        1)   Carefully drafting the budget calendar is important. Lower-level budgets are inputs to higher-level budgets.

        2)   The master budget consists of the operating budget and the financial budget. Both consist of interrelated sub-budgets.

    b.   In the **operating budget**, the emphasis is on obtaining and using current resources. It contains the following components:

        1)   Sales budget
        2)   Production budget
        3)   Direct materials budget
        4)   Direct labor budget
        5)   Manufacturing overhead budget
        6)   Cost of goods sold budget
        7)   Nonmanufacturing budget

            a)   R&D budget
            b)   Selling and administrative budget

                i)   Design budget
                ii)   Marketing budget
                iii)   Distribution budget
                iv)   Customer service budget
                v)   Administrative budget

        8)   Pro forma income statement

    c.   In the **financial budget**, the emphasis is on obtaining the funds needed to purchase operating assets. It contains the following:

        1)   Capital budget (completed before the operating budget is begun)

        2)   Cash budget

            a)   Projected cash payment schedule
            b)   Projected cash collection schedule

        3)   Pro forma statement of financial position

        4)   Pro forma statement of cash flows

7.   **Sales Budget**

    a.   The sales budget is the first budget prepared because sales volume affects production and purchasing levels, operating expenses, and cash flows.

        1)   Thus, expectations about sales drive the entire budget process.

    b.   Once a firm can estimate sales, the next step is to decide how much to produce or purchase.

        1)   Sales are usually budgeted by product or department. The sales budget also establishes targets for sales personnel.

        2)   Sales credit policies can have a large effect on the sales budget.

EXAMPLE of a Sales Budget

	April	Ref.
Projected sales in units	1,000	SB1
Selling price	× US $ 400	
Projected total sales	US $400,000	SB2

---

8.   **Production Budgets**

    a.   Production budgets (for manufacturing firms) are based on sales in units (not dollars) plus or minus desired inventory buildup or reduction.

        1)   They are prepared for each department and each item. Production budgets are usually stated in units instead of dollars.

    b.   When the production budget has been completed, it is used to prepare three additional budgets:

        1)   Materials purchases, which is similar to the purchases budget of a merchandising firm

        2)   Direct labor budget, which includes hours, wage rates, and total dollars

        3)   Manufacturing overhead budget, which is similar to a departmental expenses budget

---

EXAMPLE of a Production Budget

The company's finished goods beginning inventory is 100 units at US $125 cost per unit, for a total of US $12,500, and the desired finished goods ending inventory is 120 units.

	Source	April	Ref.
Projected sales in units	SB1	1,000	
Plus: desired ending inventory		120	
Minus: beginning inventory		(100)	
Units to be produced		1,020	PB

---

9. **Purchases Budget**

    a.   The purchases budget for a retailer is prepared after projected sales are estimated.

        1)   It is prepared on a monthly or even a weekly basis.

        2)   Purchases can be planned so that stockouts are avoided.

        3)   Inventory should be at an appropriate level to avoid unnecessary carrying costs.

        4)   It is similar to the production budget example on the previous page. However, the units are purchased rather than produced.

10. **Direct Materials Budget**

    a.   The direct materials budget includes units and input prices.

        1)   Two dollar amounts are calculated in the direct materials budget: the cost of materials actually used in production and the total cost of materials purchased.

EXAMPLE of a Direct Materials Budget

The company's materials beginning inventory is 1,000 units at US $18 cost per unit, and the desired raw material ending inventory is 980 units.

Materials Used (Quantity)	Source	April	Ref.
Finished units to be produced	PB	1,020	
Times: materials per finished product		× 4	
Total units needed for production		4,080	DMB1

Materials Purchased	Source	April	Ref.
Units needed for production	DMB1	4,080	
Plus: desired units in ending inventory		980	
Minus: beginning inventory		(1,000)	
Raw materials to be purchased		4,060	
Times: materials cost per unit		× US $ 20	
Cost of materials to be purchased		US $81,200	DMB2

Materials Used (US $)	Source	April	Ref.
Beginning inventory (1,000 × US $18)		US $18,000	
Plus: purchases of materials	DMB2	81,200	
Minus: desired ending inventory (980 × US $20)		(19,600)	
Cost of materials used in production		US $79,600	DMB3

---

11. **Direct Labor Budget**

    a.   The direct labor budget depends on wage rates, amounts and types of production, numbers and skill levels of employees to be hired, etc.

    b.   In addition to the regular wage rate, the total direct labor cost per hour may also include employer FICA taxes, health insurance, life insurance, and pension contributions.

EXAMPLE of a Direct Labor Budget

The company's human resources department has determined that the total cost per direct labor hour is US $18.

	Source	April	Ref.
Units to be produced	PB	1,020	
Times: direct labor hours per unit		× 2	
Projected total direct labor hours		2,040	DLB1
Times: direct labor cost per hour		× US $ 18	
Total projected direct labor cost		US $36,720	DLB2

12. **Manufacturing Overhead Budget**

    a.   The manufacturing overhead budget reflects the nature of overhead as a mixed cost, i.e., one that has a variable component and a fixed component (mixed costs are defined in Study Unit 17, Subunit 2).

    b.   **Variable overhead** contains those elements that vary with the level of production, such as the following:

        1)   Indirect materials
        2)   Some indirect labor
        3)   Variable factory operating costs (e.g., electricity)

EXAMPLE of a Variable Overhead Budget

The company applies variable overhead to production on the basis of direct labor hours.

	Source	April	Ref.
Projected total direct labor hours	DLB1	2,040	
Variable OH rate per direct labor hour		× US $ 3	
Projected variable overhead		US $6,120	MOB1

---

    c.   **Fixed overhead** contains those elements that remain the same regardless of the level of production, such as the following:

        1)   Real estate taxes
        2)   Insurance
        3)   Depreciation

EXAMPLE of a Fixed Overhead Budget

	April	Ref.
Projected fixed overhead	US $9,000	MOB2

---

13. **Cost of Goods Sold Budget**

    a.   The cost of goods sold budget combines the projections for the three major inputs (materials, labor, and overhead). The result directly affects the pro forma income statement. Cost of goods sold is the largest cost for a manufacturer.

EXAMPLE of a Cost of Goods Sold Budget

	Source	April		Ref.
Beginning finished goods inventory			US $ 12,500	
Manufacturing costs:				
Direct materials used	DMB3	US $79,600		
Direct labor employed	DLB2	36,720		
Variable overhead	MOB1	6,120		
Fixed overhead	MOB2	9,000		
Cost of goods manufactured			131,440	
Cost of goods available for sale			US $143,940	
Ending finished goods inventory				
(120 units × US $130)			(15,600)	
Cost of goods sold			US $128,340	CGSB

---

14. **Nonmanufacturing Budget**

    a.   The nonmanufacturing budget consists of the individual budgets for R&D, design, marketing, distribution, customer service, and administrative costs. The development of separate budgets for these functions reflects a value chain approach.

        1)   An alternative is to prepare a single budget for selling and administrative (S&A) costs of nonproduction functions.

b.   The variable and fixed portions of selling and administrative costs must be treated separately.

1)   Some S&A costs vary directly and proportionately with the level of sales. As more product is sold, sales representatives must travel more miles and serve more customers.

2)   Other S&A expenses, such as sales support staff, are fixed. They must be paid at any level of sales.

15. **Pro Forma Income Statement**

a.   The pro forma income statement is the end of the operating budget process.

1)   Financial statements are pro forma when they reflect projected results rather than actual ones.

b.   The pro forma income statement is used to decide whether the budgeted activities will result in an acceptable level of income. If the initial projection is a loss or an unacceptable level of income, adjustments can be made to the components of the master budget.

EXAMPLE of a Pro Forma Income Statement

Manufacturing Company
Pro Forma Statement of Income
Month of April

Sales		US $400,000
Beginning finished goods inventory	US $ 12,500	
Plus: cost of goods manufactured	131,440	
Goods available for sale	US $143,940	
Minus: ending finished goods inventory	(15,600)	
Cost of goods sold		(128,340)
Gross margin		US $271,660
Minus: selling and administrative expenses		(82,000)
Operating income		US $189,660
Minus: other revenues/expenses/gains/losses		(15,000)
Earnings before interest and taxes		US $174,660
Minus: interest expense		(45,000)
Earnings before income taxes		US $129,660
Minus: income taxes (40%)		(49,200)
Net income		US $ 80,460

Stop and review! You have completed the outline for this subunit. Study multiple-choice questions 1 through 4 beginning on page 473.

18.2 BUDGET METHODOLOGIES

1.   **Project Budgets**

a.   A project budget consists of all the costs expected to attach to a particular project, such as the design of a new airliner or the building of a single ship.

1)   The costs and profits associated with it are significant enough to be tracked separately.

b.   A project will typically use resources from many parts of the organization, e.g., design, engineering, production, marketing, accounting, and human resources.

1)   All of these aspects of the project budget must align with those of the entity's master budget.

EXAMPLE of a Project Budget

Function	1st Quarter	2nd Quarter	3rd Quarter	4th Quarter	Totals
Design	US $ 800,000	US $ 200,000	US $ --	US $ --	US $1,000,000
Engineering	500,000	1,200,000	400,000	--	2,100,000
Production	--	2,100,000	1,500,000	1,500,000	5,100,000
Marketing	--	100,000	200,000	200,000	500,000
Accounting	100,000	100,000	100,000	100,000	400,000
Human Resources	20,000	20,000	20,000	20,000	80,000
Totals	**US $1,420,000**	**US $3,720,000**	**US $2,220,000**	**US $1,820,000**	**US $9,180,000**

2. **Activity-Based Budgeting (ABB)**

    a. ABB applies activity-based costing principles (this is discussed further in Study Unit 17, Subunit 3) to budgeting. It focuses on the numerous activities necessary to produce and market goods and services and requires analysis of cost drivers.

        1) Budget line items are related to activities performed.

        2) This approach contrasts with the traditional emphasis on functions or spending categories. The costs of non-value-added activities are quantified.

    b. Activity-based budgeting provides greater detail than traditional budgeting, especially regarding indirect costs, because it permits the isolation of numerous cost drivers.

        1) A cost pool is established for each activity, and a cost driver is identified for each pool.

        2) The budgeted cost for each pool is determined by multiplying the demand for the activity by the estimated cost of a unit of the activity.

3. **Zero-Based Budgeting (ZBB)**

    a. ZBB is a budget and planning process in which each manager must justify his or her department's entire budget every budget cycle.

        1) ZBB differs from the traditional concept of incremental budgeting, in which the current year's budget is simply adjusted to allow for changes planned for the coming year.

        2) The managerial advantage of incremental budgeting is that the manager has to make less effort to justify changes in the budget.

    b. Under ZBB, a manager must begin the budget process every year from a base of zero. All expenditures must be justified regardless of variance from previous years.

        1) The objective is to encourage periodic reexamination of all costs in the hope that some can be reduced or eliminated.

    c. The major limitation of ZBB is that it requires more time and effort to prepare than a traditional budget.

4. **Continuous (Rolling) Budgeting**

    a. A continuous (rolling) budget is revised on a regular (continuous) basis. Typically, such a budget is continuously extended for an additional month or quarter in accordance with new data as the current month or quarter ends.

        1) For example, if the budget cycle is 1 year, a budget for the next 12 months will be available continuously as each month ends.

    b. The principal advantage of a rolling budget is that it requires managers to always be thinking ahead.

        1) The disadvantage is the amount of time managers must constantly spend on budget preparation.

5.   **Kaizen Budgeting**

a.   The Japanese term "kaizen" means continuous improvement, and kaizen budgeting assumes the continuous improvement of products and processes. It requires estimates of the effects of improvements and the costs of their implementation.

1)   Accordingly, kaizen budgeting is based not on the existing system but on changes yet to be made.

2)   Budget targets, for example, target costs, cannot be reached unless those improvements occur.

6.   **Static and Flexible Budgeting**

a.   The static (master) budget is **prepared before the period begins and is left unchanged**. The static budget is based on only one level of expected activity (output that was planned at the beginning of the period).

1)   **Standard costs** are predetermined expectations about how much a unit of input, a unit of output, or a given activity should cost.

a)   The use of standard costs in budgeting allows the standard-cost system to alert management when the actual costs of production differ significantly from the standard.

Standard cost of input = Units of input per single unit of output × Price per unit of input

2)   A standard cost is not just an average of past costs but an objectively determined estimate of what a cost should be. Standards may be based on accounting, engineering, or statistical quality control studies.

EXAMPLE of a Static Budget

A company has the following static budget for the upcoming month based on production and sales of 1,000 units:

Sales revenue (US $400 per unit)	US $400,000
Minus: variable costs (US $160 per unit)	(160,000)
Contribution margin	US $240,000
Minus: fixed costs	(200,000)
Operating income	US $ 40,000

---

b.   A flexible budget based on standard costs is prepared for the actual level of output achieved for the period.

EXAMPLE of a Flexible Budget

A company has the following flexible budget for the upcoming month based on production and sales of 800 units, 1,000 units, and 1,200 units.

	Flexible Budget Based on 800 Units	Static Budget Based on 1,000 Units	Flexible Budget Based on 1,200 Units
Sales revenue (US $400 per unit)	US $320,000	US $400,000	US $480,000
Minus: variable costs (US $160 per unit)	(128,000)	(160,000)	(192,000)
Contribution margin	US $192,000	US $240,000	US $288,000
Minus: fixed costs	(200,000)	(200,000)	(200,000)
Operating income	US $ (8,000)	US $ 40,000	US $ 88,000

It is clear that operating income is highly sensitive to the activity level.

Stop and review! You have completed the outline for this subunit. Study multiple-choice questions 5 through 7 on page 474.

18.3 COST-VOLUME-PROFIT (CVP) ANALYSIS

1. **Purpose**

   a. Also called **breakeven analysis**, CVP analysis is a tool for understanding the interaction of revenues with fixed and variable costs.

      1) It explains how changes in assumptions about cost behavior and the relevant ranges in which those assumptions are valid may affect the relationships among revenues, variable costs, and fixed costs at various production levels.

      2) Thus, CVP analysis allows management to determine the probable effects of changes in sales volume, sales price, product mix, etc.

   b. The **breakeven point** is the level of output at which total revenues equal total expenses.

      1) It is the point at which all fixed costs have been covered and operating income is zero.

2. **Assumptions of CVP**

   a. Cost and revenue relationships are predictable and linear. These relationships are true over the relevant range of activity and specified time span.

   b. Unit selling prices do not change.

   c. Inventory levels do not change; i.e., production equals sales.

   d. Total variable costs change proportionally with volume, but unit variable costs do not change.

   e. Fixed costs remain constant over the relevant range of volume, but unit fixed costs vary indirectly with volume.

   f. The revenue (sales) mix does not change.

   g. The time value of money is ignored.

3. **Breakeven Point for a Single Product**

   a. The breakeven point can be calculated in units and in sales dollars.

      1) The simplest calculation for breakeven in units is to divide fixed costs by the unit contribution margin (UCM).

$$UCM = Unit\ sales\ price - Unit\ variable\ cost$$

$$Breakeven\ point\ in\ units = \frac{Fixed\ costs}{UCM}$$

      2) The breakeven point in sales dollars equals fixed costs divided by the contribution margin ratio (CMR).

$$CMR = \frac{UCM}{Unit\ selling\ price}$$

$$Breakeven\ point\ in\ dollars = \frac{Fixed\ costs}{CMR}$$

EXAMPLE

A manufacturer's product has a unit sales price of US $0.60 and a unit variable cost of US $0.20. Fixed costs are US $10,000.

Unit selling price	US $0.60
Minus: unit variable costs	(0.20)
Unit contribution margin (UCM)	US $0.40

Breakeven point in units	= Fixed costs ÷ UCM
	= US $10,000 ÷ $0.40
	= 25,000 units

The manufacturer's contribution margin ratio is 66.667% (US $0.40 ÷ $0.60).

Breakeven point in dollars	= Fixed costs ÷ CMR
	= US $10,000 ÷ .66667
	= US $15,000

---

4. **Margin of Safety**

    a. The margin of safety is the excess of budgeted sales over breakeven sales.

        1) It is the amount by which sales can decline before losses occur.

        Margin of safety = Planned sales – Breakeven sales

        2) The margin of safety ratio is the percentage by which sales exceed the breakeven point.

        $$Margin\ of\ safety\ ratio = \frac{Margin\ of\ safety}{Planned\ sales}$$

EXAMPLE

In units:

Margin of safety = Planned sales – Breakeven sales
= 35,000 – 25,000
= 10,000 units

Margin of safety ratio $= \dfrac{Margin\ of\ safety}{Planned\ sales}$

$= \dfrac{US\ \$10,000}{US\ \$35,000}$

= 28.6%

In dollars:

Margin of safety = Planned sales – Breakeven sales
= (35,000 units × US $0.60) – $15,000
= US $21,000 – $15,000
= US $6,000

Margin of safety ratio $= \dfrac{Margin\ of\ safety}{Planned\ sales}$

$= \dfrac{US\ \$6,000}{US\ \$21,000}$

= 28.6%

---

5. **Target Operating Income**

    a. An amount of operating income, either in dollars or as a percentage of sales, is frequently required.

        1) By treating target income as an additional fixed cost, CVP analysis can be applied.

        $$Target\ income\ in\ units = \frac{Fixed\ costs + Target\ operating\ income}{UCM}$$

EXAMPLE

The manufacturer from the previous example with the US $0.40 contribution margin per unit wants to find out how many units must be sold to generate US $25,000 of operating income.

Target unit volume = (Fixed costs + Target operating income) ÷ UCM
= (US $10,000 + $25,000) ÷ $0.40
= US $35,000 ÷ $0.40
= 87,500 units

---

6. **Target Net Income**

    a. A variation of this problem asks for net income (an after-tax amount) instead of operating income (a pretax amount).

    $$Target\ income\ in\ units = \frac{Fixed\ costs + [Target\ net\ income \div (1.0 - tax\ rate)]}{UCM}$$

        1) EXAMPLE: The manufacturer wants to generate US $30,000 of net income. The effective tax rate is 40%.

        Target unit volume = {Fixed costs + [Target net income ÷ (1.0 – .40)]} ÷ UCM
        = [US $10,000 + ($30,000 ÷ .60)] ÷ $.40
        = 150,000 units

7. **Other Target Income Applications**

   a. Analysis of other target income applications use the standard formula for operating income.

   Operating income = Sales – Variable costs – Fixed costs

EXAMPLE

If units are sold at US $6.00 and variable costs are US $2.00, how many units must be sold to realize operating income of 15% (US $6.00 × .15 = $.90 per unit) before taxes, given fixed costs of US $37,500?

$$\text{Operating income} = \text{Sales} - \text{Variable costs} - \text{Fixed costs}$$
$$\text{US } \$0.90 \times Q = (\$6.00 \times Q) - (\$2.00 \times Q) - \$37,500$$
$$\text{US } \$3.10 \times Q = \$37,500$$
$$Q = 12,097 \text{ units}$$

Selling 12,097 units results in US $72,582 of revenues. Variable costs are US $24,194, and operating income is US $10,888 ($72,582 × 15%). The proof is that variable costs of US $24,194, plus fixed costs of US $37,500, plus operating income of US $10,888, equals US $72,582 of sales.

---

   b. The operating income formula can also be used in this situation.

EXAMPLE

If variable costs are US $1.20, fixed costs are US $10,000, and selling price is US $2, and the company targets a US $5,000 after-tax profit when the tax rate is 30%, the calculation is as follows:

$$\text{US } \$ 2Q = [\$5,000 \div (1.0 - 0.3)] + \$1.20Q + \$10,000$$
$$\text{US } \$.8Q = \$7,142.86 + \$10,000$$
$$\text{US } \$.8Q = \$17,142.86$$
$$Q = \text{US } \$17,142.86 \div \$.8$$
$$Q = 21,428.575 \text{ units}$$

If the company plans to sell 21,429 units at US $2 each, revenue will be US $42,858. The following is the pro forma income statement for the target net income:

Sales (21,429 × US $2)	US $ 42,858
Minus: variable costs (21,429 × US $1.20)	(25,715)
Contribution margin	US $ 17,143
Minus: fixed costs	(10,000)
Operating income	US $ 7,143
Income taxes (30%)	(2,143)
Net income	US $ 5,000

Stop and review! You have completed the outline for this subunit. Study multiple-choice questions 8 through 10 on page 475.

18.4 RELEVANT COSTS AND DECISION MAKING

1. **Relevant vs. Irrelevant Factors**

   a. In decision making, an organization must focus only on relevant revenues and costs. To be relevant, the revenues and costs must

      1) Be received or incurred in the future.

         a) Costs that have already been incurred or to which the organization is committed, called sunk costs, have no bearing on any future decisions.

         b) EXAMPLE: A manufacturer is considering upgrading its production equipment owing to the obsolescence of its current machinery. The amounts paid for the existing equipment are sunk costs. They make no difference in the decision to modernize.

2) Differ among the possible courses of action.

    a) EXAMPLE: A union contract may require 6 months of wage continuance in case of a plant shutdown. Thus, 6 months of wages must be disbursed regardless of whether the plant remains open.

b. Only avoidable costs are relevant.

    1) An avoidable cost may be saved by not adopting a particular option. Avoidable costs might include variable materials costs and direct labor costs.

    2) An unavoidable cost is one that cannot be avoided if a particular action is taken.

        a) For example, if a company has a long-term lease on a building, closing the business in that building will not eliminate the need to pay rent. Thus, the rent is an unavoidable cost.

c. Incremental (marginal or differential) costs are inherent in the concept of relevance.

    1) Throughout the relevant range, the incremental cost of an additional unit of output is the same. Once a certain level of output is reached, however, the current production capacity is insufficient, and another increment of fixed costs must be incurred.

EXAMPLE

A firm produces a product for which it incurs the following unit costs:

Direct materials	US $2.00
Direct labor	3.00
Variable overhead	.50
Fixed overhead	.50
Total cost	US $6.00

The product normally sells for US $10 per unit. An application of marginal analysis is necessary if a foreign buyer, who has never before been a customer, offers to pay US $5.60 per unit for a special order of the firm's product. The immediate reaction might be to refuse the offer because the selling price is less than the average cost of production.

However, marginal analysis results in a different decision. Assuming that the firm has idle capacity, only the additional costs should be considered. In this example, the only marginal costs are for direct materials, direct labor, and variable overhead. No additional fixed overhead costs would be incurred. Because marginal revenue (the US $5.60 selling price) exceeds marginal costs (US $2 materials + $3 labor + $.50 variable OH = US $5.50 per unit), accepting the special order will be profitable.

If a competitor bids US $5.80 per unit, the firm can still profitably accept the special order while underbidding the competitor by setting a price below US $5.80 per unit but above US $5.50 per unit.

---

2. **Submitting Bids for the Lowest Selling Price**

a. Bids should be made at prices that meet or exceed incremental cost depending on how competitive the bid needs to be.

    1) A bid lower than incremental cost can result in lower profit for the company.

        a) However, lower bids are more competitive and are therefore closer to incremental cost.

    2) The company must weigh quantitative and qualitative factors when deciding on a final bid.

        a) Whether available capacity exists affects whether fixed costs will be included in the lowest possible bid price.

3. **Special Orders When Available Capacity Exists**

a. When a manufacturer has available production capacity, there is no opportunity cost involved when accepting a special order. This occurs because fixed costs are already committed and there is still available capacity.

    1) When capacity is available, fixed costs are **irrelevant**.

2) The company should accept the order if the minimum price for the product is equal to the variable costs.

EXAMPLE

Normal unit pricing for a manufacturer's product is as follows:

Direct materials and labor	US $15.00
Variable overhead	3.00
Fixed overhead	5.00
Variable selling	1.50
Fixed selling and administrative	12.00
Total cost	US $36.50

If the manufacturer receives a special order for which capacity exists, the lowest bid the company could offer is US $19.50 ($15.00 + $3.00 + $1.50).

---

4. **Special Orders in the Absence of Available Capacity**

   a. When a manufacturer lacks available production capacity, the differential (marginal or incremental) costs of accepting the order must be considered.

      1) Although fixed costs are committed, since there is no available capacity, the manufacturer will have to reduce production of existing product lines to fill the special order.

      2) This means that the revenue, variable costs, and fixed costs related to reduced production of existing product lines are **relevant**.

EXAMPLE

Using the information from the example above, if the manufacturer receives a special order for which capacity does not exist, the lowest bid the company could offer is US $36.50.

In addition to fixed costs, any revenue lost from reducing or stopping production on other product lines would be relevant when determining the lowest acceptable bid price.

---

5. **Make-or-Buy Decisions (Insourcing vs. Outsourcing)**

   a. The firm should use available resources as efficiently as possible before outsourcing.

      1) If the total relevant costs of production are **less** than the cost to buy the item, it should be made in-house.

      2) If the total relevant costs of production are **more** than the costs to buy the item, it should be bought (outsourced).

   b. As with a special order, the manager considers only the costs relevant to the investment decision. The key variable is total relevant costs, not all total costs.

      1) Sunk costs are irrelevant.

      2) Costs that do not differ between two alternatives should be ignored because they are not relevant to the decision being made.

      3) Opportunity costs must be considered when idle capacity is not available. They are of primary importance because they represent the forgone opportunities of the firm.

         a) In some situations, a firm may decide to stop processing one product in order to free up capacity for another product, reducing relevant costs, affecting the decision to make or buy.

   c. The firm also should consider the qualitative aspects of the decision.

      1) Will the product quality be as high if a component is outsourced rather than produced internally?

      2) How reliable are the suppliers?

6. **Make-or-Buy Decisions When Available Capacity Exists**

   a.   When capacity is available, fixed costs are **irrelevant** in deciding whether to make or buy the product.

EXAMPLE

Lawton must determine whether to make or buy an order of 1,000 frames. Lawton can purchase the frames for US $13 or choose to make them in-house. Lawton currently has adequate available capacity. Cost information for the frames is as follows:

Total variable costs	US $10
Allocable fixed costs	5
Total unit costs	US $15

Because capacity is available, the allocable fixed costs are not relevant. The total relevant costs of US $10 are less than the US $13 cost to purchase. Lawton should make the frames.

---

7. **Make-or-Buy Decisions in the Absence of Available Capacity**

   a.   When capacity is not available, the differential (marginal or incremental) costs of accepting the order must be considered.

   1)   The revenue, variable costs, and fixed costs related to reduced production of existing product lines are **relevant** in deciding whether to make or buy the product.

EXAMPLE

Lawton has received another special order for 1,000 frames, but this month there is no available capacity.

Since there is no available capacity, the allocable fixed costs are relevant. The total relevant costs of US $15 are more than the US $13 cost to purchase, therefore, Lawton should purchase the frames.

---

8. **Sell-or-Process-Further Decisions**

   a.   In determining whether to sell a product at the split-off point or process the item further at additional cost, the joint cost of the product is irrelevant because it is a sunk cost.

   1)   **Joint (common) costs** are those costs incurred up to the point where the products become separately identifiable, called the split-off point.

   a)   Joint costs include direct materials, direct labor, and manufacturing overhead. Because they are not separately identifiable, they must be allocated to the individual joint products.

   b.   At the split-off point, the joint products acquire separate identities and costs incurred after the split-off point are separable costs.

   1)   Separable costs can be identified with a particular joint product and are allocated to a specific unit of output.

   2)   Separable costs are relevant when determining whether to sell or process further.

   c.   Because joint costs cannot be traced to individual products, they must be allocated. The methods available for this allocation include the following:

   1)   The physical-measure-based approach employs a physical measure, such as volume, weight, or a linear measure.

   2)   Market-based approaches assign a proportionate amount of the total cost to each product on a monetary basis.

   a)   Sales-value at split-off method
   b)   Estimated net realizable value (NRV) method
   c)   Constant-gross-margin percentage NRV method

d. The **physical-unit method** allocates joint production costs to each product based on their relative proportions of the measure selected.

 1) EXAMPLE: A refinery processes 1,000 barrels of crude oil and incurs US $100,000 of processing costs. The process results in the following outputs. Under the physical unit method, the joint costs up to split-off are allocated as follows:

Asphalt	US $100,000 × (300 barrels ÷ 1,000 barrels) =	US $ 30,000
Fuel oil	US $100,000 × (300 barrels ÷ 1,000 barrels) =	30,000
Diesel fuel	US $100,000 × (200 barrels ÷ 1,000 barrels) =	20,000
Kerosene	US $100,000 × (100 barrels ÷ 1,000 barrels) =	10,000
Gasoline	US $100,000 × (100 barrels ÷ 1,000 barrels) =	10,000
Joint costs allocated		US $100,000

 2) The physical-unit method's simplicity makes it appealing, but it does not match costs with the individual products' revenue-generating potential.

 3) However, its limitations are that it treats low-value products that are large in size as if they were valuable. As a result, a large, low-value product might always show a loss, but small, high-value products will always show a profit.

e. The **sales-value at split-off method** is based on the relative sales values of the separate products at split-off.

 1) EXAMPLE: The refinery estimates that the five outputs can sell for the following prices at split-off:

Asphalt	300 barrels @ US $ 60/barrel =	US $ 18,000
Fuel oil	300 barrels @ US $180/barrel =	54,000
Diesel fuel	200 barrels @ US $160/barrel =	32,000
Kerosene	100 barrels @ US $ 80/barrel =	8,000
Gasoline	100 barrels @ US $180/barrel =	18,000
Total sales value at split-off		US $130,000

The total expected sales value for the entire production run at split-off is thus US $130,000. Multiply the total joint costs to be allocated by the proportion of the total expected sales of each product:

Asphalt	US $100,000 × ($18,000 ÷ $130,000) =	US $ 13,846
Fuel oil	US $100,000 × ($54,000 ÷ $130,000) =	41,539
Diesel fuel	US $100,000 × ($32,000 ÷ $130,000) =	24,615
Kerosene	US $100,000 × ($ 8,000 ÷ $130,000) =	6,154
Gasoline	US $100,000 × ($18,000 ÷ $130,000) =	13,846
Joint costs allocated		US $100,000

f. The **estimated net realizable value (NRV)** method also allocates joint costs based on the relative market values of the products.

 1) The significant difference is that, under the estimated NRV method, all separable costs necessary to make the product salable are subtracted before the allocation is made.

 2) EXAMPLE: The refinery estimates final sales prices as follows:

Asphalt	300 barrels @ US $ 70/barrel =	US $ 21,000
Fuel oil	300 barrels @ US $200/barrel =	60,000
Diesel fuel	200 barrels @ US $180/barrel =	36,000
Kerosene	100 barrels @ US $ 90/barrel =	9,000
Gasoline	100 barrels @ US $190/barrel =	19,000

From these amounts, separable costs are subtracted (these costs are given):

Asphalt	US $21,000 – $1,000 =	US $ 20,000
Fuel oil	US $60,000 – $1,000 =	59,000
Diesel fuel	US $36,000 – $1,000 =	35,000
Kerosene	US $ 9,000 – $2,000 =	7,000
Gasoline	US $19,000 – $2,000 =	17,000
Total net realizable value		US $138,000

Multiply the total joint costs to be allocated by the proportion of the final expected sales of each product:

Asphalt	US $100,000 × ($20,000 ÷ $138,000) =	US $ 14,493
Fuel oil	US $100,000 × ($59,000 ÷ $138,000) =	42,754
Diesel fuel	US $100,000 × ($35,000 ÷ $138,000) =	25,362
Kerosene	US $100,000 × ($ 7,000 ÷ $138,000) =	5,072
Gasoline	US $100,000 × ($17,000 ÷ $138,000) =	12,319
Joint costs allocated		US $100,000

g. The **constant-gross-margin percentage NRV** method is based on allocating joint costs so that the gross-margin percentage is the same for every product.

1) The three steps under this method are

a) Determine the overall gross-margin percentage.

b) Subtract the appropriate gross margin from the final sales value of each product to calculate total costs for that product.

c) Subtract the separable costs to arrive at the joint cost amount.

2) EXAMPLE: The refinery uses the same calculation of expected final sales price as under the estimated NRV method:

Asphalt	300 barrels @ US $ 70/barrel =	US $ 21,000
Fuel oil	300 barrels @ US $200/barrel =	60,000
Diesel fuel	200 barrels @ US $180/barrel =	36,000
Kerosene	100 barrels @ US $ 90/barrel =	9,000
Gasoline	100 barrels @ US $190/barrel =	19,000
Total of final sales prices		US $145,000

The final sales value for the entire production run is thus US $145,000. From this total, the joint costs and total separable costs are deducted to arrive at a total gross margin for all products:

US $145,000 – $100,000 – $7,000 = US $38,000

The gross margin percentage can then be derived:

US $38,000 ÷ $145,000 = 26.21%

Deduct gross margin from each product to arrive at a cost of goods sold:

Asphalt	US $21,000 – ($21,000 × 26.21%) =	US $15,497
Fuel oil	US $60,000 – ($60,000 × 26.21%) =	44,276
Diesel fuel	US $36,000 – ($36,000 × 26.21%) =	26,565
Kerosene	US $ 9,000 – ($ 9,000 × 26.21%) =	6,641
Gasoline	US $19,000 – ($19,000 × 26.21%) =	14,021

Deduct the separable costs from each product to arrive at the allocated joint costs:

Asphalt	US $15,497 – $1,000 =	US $ 14,497
Fuel oil	US $44,276 – $1,000 =	43,276
Diesel fuel	US $26,565 – $1,000 =	25,565
Kerosene	US $ 6,641 – $2,000 =	4,641
Gasoline	US $14,021 – $2,000 =	12,021
Joint costs allocated		US $100,000

EXAMPLE

Chief uses a joint process that yields two products, X and Y. Each product can be sold at its split-off point or processed further. All the additional processing costs are variable and can be traced to each product. Joint production costs are US $25,000. Other sales and cost data are as follows:

	Product X	Product Y
Sales value at split-off point	US $55,000	US $30,000
Final sales value if processed further	75,000	45,000
Additional costs beyond split-off	12,000	17,000

Chief must evaluate whether the profit would be higher to sell at the split-off point or to process further:

	Product X	Product Y
Sales value	US $ 75,000	US $ 45,000
Allocated joint costs	(16,176)*	(8,824)**
Further processing costs	(12,000)	(17,000)
Profit	US $ 46,824	US $ 19,176

	Split Off X	Split Off Y
Sales value	US $ 55,000	US $ 30,000
Allocated joint costs	16,176*	(8,824)**
Profit	US $ 38,824	US $ 21,176

$$* \left[\left(\frac{US \$55,000}{\$55,000 + \$30,000}\right) \times \$25,000\right]$$

$$** \left[\left(\frac{US \$30,000}{\$55,000 + \$30,000}\right) \times \$25,000\right]$$

The profit is higher for Product X after further processing and higher for Y at the split-off point. Accordingly, Chief should process Product X further and sell Product Y at the split-off point.

---

9. Add-or-Drop-a-Segment Decisions

a. Disinvestment decisions are the opposite of capital budgeting decisions, i.e., to terminate an operation, product or product line, business segment, branch, or major customer rather than start one.

   1) In general, if the marginal cost of a project exceeds the marginal revenue, the firm should disinvest.

b. Four steps should be taken in making a disinvestment decision:

   1) Identify fixed costs that will be eliminated by the disinvestment decision, e.g., insurance on equipment used.

   2) Determine the revenue needed to justify continuing operations. In the short run, this amount should at least equal the variable cost of production or continued service.

   3) Establish the opportunity cost of funds that will be received upon disinvestment (e.g., salvage value).

   4) Determine whether the carrying amount of the assets is equal to their economic value. If not, reevaluate the decision using current fair value rather than the carrying amount.

c. When a firm disinvests, excess capacity exists unless another project uses this capacity immediately. The cost of idle capacity should be treated as a relevant cost.

EXAMPLE

A company needs to decide whether to discontinue unprofitable segments. Abbreviated income statements of the two possible unprofitable segments are shown below. The other segments, not shown, are profitable with income over US $200,000.

	Department A	Department B
Sales	US $275,000	US $115,000
Cost of goods sold	160,000	55,000
Other variable costs	130,000	50,000
Allocated corporate costs	70,000	30,000
Income (loss)	(90,000)	(20,000)

Only relevant costs should be considered in making this decision. Since the allocated corporate costs are still going to be incurred if the segment is discontinued, these costs should be ignored. Therefore, the income (loss) for each segment is calculated as follows:

	Department A	Department B
Sales	US $ 275,000	US $115,000
Cost of goods sold	(160,000)	(55,000)
Other variable costs	(130,000)	(50,000)
Income (loss)	US $ (15,000)	US $ 10,000

Since US $15,000 will be saved if Department A discontinued, it should be discontinued. However, discontinuing Department B will negate US $10,000 of profit, so it should continue.

Stop and review! You have completed the outline for this subunit. Study multiple-choice questions 11 through 15 beginning on page 476.

18.5 RESPONSIBILITY ACCOUNTING

1. **Overview**

   a. The primary distinction between centralized and decentralized organizations is the degree of freedom of decision making by managers at many levels. Centralization assumes decision making must be consolidated so that activities throughout the organization may be more effectively coordinated.

   1) In decentralization, decision making occurs at as low a level as possible. The premise is that a local manager can make better decisions than a centralized manager.

   2) Decentralization typically reflects larger companies that are divided into multiple segments.

   3) In most organizations, a mixture of these approaches is used.

2. **Types of Responsibility Centers**

   a. A well-designed responsibility accounting system establishes responsibility centers (also called strategic business units). Their purposes are to (1) encourage managerial effort to attain organizational objectives, (2) motivate managers to make decisions consistent with those objectives, and (3) provide a basis for managerial compensation.

   b. A **cost center**, e.g., a maintenance department, is responsible for costs only.

   1) Cost drivers are the relevant performance measures.

   2) A disadvantage of a cost center is the potential for cost shifting. For example, variable costs for which a manager is responsible might be replaced with fixed costs for which (s)he is not.

      a) Another disadvantage is that long-term issues may be disregarded when the emphasis is on, for example, annual cost amounts.

      b) Another issue is allocation of service department costs to cost centers.

3) Service centers exist primarily (and sometimes solely) to provide specialized support to other organizational subunits. They are usually operated as cost centers.

c. A **revenue center**, e.g., a sales department, is responsible for revenues only.

1) Revenue drivers are the relevant performance measures. They are factors that influence unit sales, such as changes in prices and products, customer service, marketing efforts, and delivery terms.

d. A **profit center**, e.g., an appliance department in a retail store, is responsible for revenues and expenses.

e. An **investment center**, e.g., a branch office, is responsible for revenues, expenses, and invested capital.

1) The performance of investment centers can be evaluated on a return on investment basis, i.e., on the effectiveness of asset use.

3. **Performance Measures and Manager Motivation**

a. Each responsibility center is structured such that a logical group of operations is under the direction of a single manager.

1) Measures are designed for every responsibility center to monitor performance.

b. **Controllability.** The performance measures on which the manager's incentive package are based must be, as far as practicable, under the manager's direct influence.

1) Controllable factors can be thought of as those factors that a manager can influence in a given time period.

a) Inevitably, some costs (especially common costs, such as the costs of central administrative functions) cannot be traced to particular activities or responsibility centers.

2) Controllable cost is not synonymous with variable cost. Often, this classification is particular to the level of the organization.

a) For instance, the fixed cost of depreciation may not be a controllable cost of the manager of a revenue center but may be controllable by the division vice president to which that manager reports.

c. **Goal congruence.** These performance measures must be designed such that the manager's pursuit of them ties directly to accomplishment of the organization's overall goals.

1) Suboptimization results when segments of the organization pursue goals that are in that segment's own best interests rather than those of the organization as a whole.

d. Along with the responsibility, a manager must be granted sufficient authority to control those factors on which his or her incentive package is based.

4. **Common Costs**

a. Common costs are the costs of products, activities, facilities, services, or operations shared by two or more cost objects. The term "joint costs" is frequently used to describe the common costs of a single process that yields two or more joint products.

1) The costs of service centers and headquarters are common examples.

b. Because common costs are indirect costs, identification of a direct cause-and-effect relationship between a common cost and the actions of the cost object to which it is allocated can be difficult.

1) Such a relationship promotes acceptance of common-cost allocation by managers who perceive the fairness of the procedure.

5. **Financial vs. Nonfinancial Measures**

a. Each type of responsibility center described has its own appropriate financial performance measures.

1) Cost centers -- Variable costs, total costs
2) Revenue centers -- Gross sales, net sales
3) Profit centers -- Sales, gross margin, operating income
4) Investment centers

    a) Return on investment, residual income (discussed in Study Units 15 and 16)

    b) Return on assets, return on common equity, economic rate of return on common stock, economic value added (also discussed in Study Units 15 and 16)

b. Nonfinancial performance measures are not standardized and thus can take any form appropriate to the SBU under review.

Stop and review! You have completed the outline for this subunit. Study multiple-choice questions 16 and 17 beginning on page 478.

18.6 TRANSFER PRICING

1. **Overview**

a. Transfer prices are charged by one segment of an organization for goods and services it provides to another segment of the same organization.

1) Transfer pricing is used by profit and investment centers (a cost center's costs are allocated to producing departments).

b. Upper management's challenge is to set transfer-pricing policy such that segment managers achieve overall entity goals by pursuing their segment goals.

c. Thus, transfer pricing should motivate managers by encouraging goal congruence and managerial effort.

1) Goal congruence is alignment of a manager's individual goals with those of the organization.

2) Managerial effort is the extent to which a manager attempts to accomplish a goal.

2. **Three Basic Methods for Determining Transfer Prices**

a. Cost plus pricing sets price at the selling segment's full cost of production plus a reasonable markup.

b. Market pricing uses the price the selling segment could obtain on the open market.

c. Negotiated pricing gives the segments the freedom to bargain among themselves to agree on a price.

EXAMPLE of Transfer Price Calculation

A conglomerate refines nitrogen and manufactures fertilizer. Upper management is considering the factors involved in setting transfer-pricing policy. External markets exist for both products. The Fertilizer Division would like to pay only the Nitrogen Division's cost plus 10%. The Nitrogen Division wants to sell at the market price. When forced to compromise, management of the two divisions settled on an average of the two prices. The Nitrogen Division's results under the three alternatives are calculated as follows:

Nitrogen Division	Full Cost Plus 10%	Market Price	Negotiated Price
Revenues:			
Revenue per cubic-foot	US $ 3.30	US $ 4.00	US $ 3.65
Times: cubic feet	× 10,000	× 10,000	× 10,000
Total division revenue	**US $ 33,000**	**US $ 40,000**	**US $ 36,500**
Costs (for all three prices):			
Purchase cost per cubic foot	US $ 2.00		
Division variable costs	0.25		
Division fixed costs	0.75		
Per-cubic-foot division costs	US $ 3.00		
Times: cubic feet	× 10,000		
Total division costs	**US $ 30,000**		
Operating income:			
Total division revenue	US $ 33,000	US $ 40,000	US $ 36,500
Total division costs	(30,000)	(30,000)	(30,000)
Division operating income	**US $ 3,000**	**US $ 10,000**	**US $ 6,500**

The Fertilizer Division's results under the three alternatives are calculated as follows:

Fertilizer Division	
Revenues:	
Revenue per pound	US $ 14.00
Times: pounds	× 5,000
Total division revenue	**US $ 70,000**
Costs:	
Division variable costs	US $ 4.00
Division fixed costs	0.50
Per-pound division costs	US $ 4.50
Times: pounds	× 5,000
Total division costs	**US $ 22,500**

	Full Cost Plus 10%	Market Price	Negotiated Price
Operating income:			
Total division revenue	US $ 70,000	US $ 70,000	US $ 70,000
Transferred-in costs	(33,000)	(40,000)	(36,500)
Total division costs	(22,500)	(22,500)	(22,500)
Division operating income	**US $ 14,500**	**US $ 7,500**	**US $ 11,000**

The motive of each manager to set a different price is clear. However, the following calculation shows that the choice among the three methods is irrelevant to the organization as a whole. Motivating management is the main concern of transfer pricing.

	Full Cost Plus 10%	Market Price	Negotiated Price
Nitrogen Division operating income	US $ 3,000	US $10,000	US $ 6,500
Fertilizer Division operating income	14,500	7,500	11,000
Combined operating incomes	**US $17,500**	**US $17,500**	**US $17,500**

3.   **Minimum Transfer Price**

a.   The minimum price that a seller is willing to accept is calculated as follows:

$$\text{Minimum transfer price} = \text{Incremental cost to date} + \text{Opportunity cost of selling internally}$$

1)   The opportunity cost of selling internally varies depending on two factors: the existence of an external market for the product and whether the seller has excess capacity.

4.   **Choice of Transfer Price**

a.   Scenario 1 -- External market exists and seller has no excess capacity

1)   The opportunity cost to sell internally is the contribution margin the seller would have received selling on the external market.

2)   The seller can sell everything it produces on the open market, so this margin must be included in the transfer price to make selling internally worthwhile.

b.   Scenario 2 -- External market exists and seller has excess capacity

1)   Both segments benefit from any price between the floor of the incremental cost to date and a ceiling of the market price.

2)   The seller cannot demand the full contribution margin because the open market may not purchase its full output.

c.   Scenario 3 -- No external market exists

1)   The seller cannot demand anything above its incremental cost to date.

5.   **Multinational Considerations**

a.   When segments are located in different countries, taxes and tariffs may override any other considerations when setting transfer prices.

EXAMPLE of Multinational Pricing

The Nitrogen Division is located in Canada, which imposes a combined tax and tariff burden of 45%, while the Fertilizer Division located in the U.S. is subject only to a 20% income tax.

	Full Cost Plus 10%	Market Price	Negotiated Price
Nitrogen Division operating income	US $ 3,000	US $10,000	US $ 6,500
Fertilizer Division operating income	14,500	7,500	11,000
Combined operating incomes	**US $17,500**	**US $17,500**	**US $17,500**
Canadian taxes and tariffs (45%)	US $ 1,350	US $ 4,500	US $ 2,925
U.S. income tax (20%)	2,900	1,500	2,200
Combined tax liability	**US $ 4,250**	**US $ 6,000**	**US $ 5,125**

If tax minimization is the entity's overall goal, upper management is no longer unconcerned about which transfer-pricing policy to select.

---

b.   Exchange rate fluctuations, threats of expropriation, and limits on transfers of profits outside the host country are additional concerns.

1)   Thus, because the best transfer price may be a low one because of the existence of tariffs or a high one because of the existence of foreign exchange controls, the effect may be to skew the performance statistics of management.

2)   The high transfer price may result in foreign management appearing to show a lower return on investment than domestic management, but the ratio differences may be negated because a different transfer-pricing formula is used.

Stop and review! You have completed the outline for this subunit. Study multiple-choice questions 18 through 20 on page 479.

QUESTIONS

18.1 Budget Systems

1. The major objectives of any budget system are to

A. Define responsibility centers, provide a framework for performance evaluation, and promote communication and coordination among organization segments.

B. Define responsibility centers, facilitate the fixing of blame for missed budget predictions, and ensure goal congruence between superiors and subordinates.

C. Foster the planning of operations, provide a framework for performance evaluation, and promote communication and coordination among organization segments.

D. Foster the planning of operations, facilitate the fixing of blame for missed budget predictions, and ensure goal congruence between superiors and subordinates.

Answer (C) is correct.
   REQUIRED: The major objectives of any budget system.
   DISCUSSION: A budget is a realistic plan for the future expressed in quantitative terms. The process of budgeting forces a company to establish goals, determine the resources necessary to achieve those goals, and anticipate future difficulties in their achievement. A budget is also a control tool because it establishes standards and facilitates comparison of actual and budgeted performance. Because a budget establishes standards and accountability, it motivates good performance by highlighting the work of effective managers. Moreover, the nature of the budgeting process fosters communication of goals to company subunits and coordination of their efforts. Budgeting activities by entities within the company must be coordinated because they are interdependent. Thus, the sales budget is a necessary input to the formulation of the production budget. In turn, production requirements must be known before purchases and expense budgets can be developed, and all other budgets must be completed before preparation of the cash budget.
   Answer (A) is incorrect. Responsibility centers are determined prior to budgeting. Answer (B) is incorrect. Responsibility centers are determined prior to budgeting, budgets do not fix blame but rather measure performance, and goal congruence is promoted but not ensured by budgets. Answer (D) is incorrect. Budgets do not fix blame but rather measure performance, and goal congruence is promoted but not ensured by budgets.

2. One of the primary advantages of budgeting is that it

A. Does not take the place of management and administration.

B. Bases the profit plan on estimates.

C. Is continually adapted to fit changing circumstances.

D. Requires departmental managers to make plans in conjunction with the plans of other interdependent departments.

Answer (D) is correct.
   REQUIRED: The primary advantage of budgeting.
   DISCUSSION: A budget is a quantitative model of a plan of action developed by management. A budget functions as an aid to planning, coordination, and control. Thus, a budget helps management to allocate resources efficiently and to ensure that subunit goals are congruent with those of other subunits and of the organization.
   Answer (A) is incorrect. Budgeting, far from taking the place of management and administration, makes them even more important. Answer (B) is incorrect. Basing the profit plan on estimates is a necessity, not an advantage. Answer (C) is incorrect. Adaption to changing circumstances is a commitment that upper management must make; it is not inherent in a budget.

3. The master budget

A. Shows forecasted and actual results.

B. Reflects controllable costs only.

C. Can be used to determine manufacturing cost variances.

D. Contains the operating budget.

Answer (D) is correct.
   REQUIRED: The purpose of the master budget.
   DISCUSSION: The operating and financial budgets are subsets of the master budget. Thus, quantified estimates by management from all functional areas are contained in the master budget. These results are then combined in a formal quantitative model recognizing the organization's objectives, inputs, and outputs.
   Answer (A) is incorrect. The master budget does not contain actual results. Answer (B) is incorrect. The master budget reflects all applicable expected costs, whether or not controllable by individual managers. Answer (C) is incorrect. The master budget is not structured to allow determination of manufacturing cost variances, which requires using the flexible budget and actual results.

4. Budgets are a necessary component of financial decision making because they help provide a(n)

    A. Efficient allocation of resources.

    B. Means to use all the firm's resources.

    C. Automatic corrective mechanism for errors.

    D. Means to check managerial discretion.

Answer (A) is correct.
    REQUIRED: The major benefit of budgets.
    DISCUSSION: A budget is a quantitative model of a plan of action developed by management. A budget functions as an aid to planning, coordination, and control. Thus, a budget helps management to allocate resources efficiently.
    Answer (B) is incorrect. Budgets are designed to use resources efficiently, not just use them. Answer (C) is incorrect. Budgets per se provide for no automatic corrections. Answer (D) is incorrect. Budgets are a management tool and are not designed to thwart managerial discretion.

18.2 Budget Methodologies

5. Individual budget schedules are prepared to develop an annual comprehensive or master budget. The budget schedule that provides the necessary input data for the direct labor budget is the

    A. Sales forecast.

    B. Materials purchases budget.

    C. Schedule of cash receipts and disbursements.

    D. Production budget.

Answer (D) is correct.
    REQUIRED: The budget schedule that provides the input data for the direct labor budget.
    DISCUSSION: A master budget typically begins with the preparation of a sales budget. The next step is to prepare a production budget. Once the production budget has been completed, the next step is to prepare the direct labor, materials, and overhead budgets. Thus, the production budget provides the input necessary for the completion of the direct labor budget.
    Answer (A) is incorrect. The sales forecast is insufficient for completion of the direct labor budget. Answer (B) is incorrect. The materials purchases budget is not needed to prepare a direct labor budget. Answer (C) is incorrect. The schedule of cash receipts and disbursements cannot be prepared until after the direct labor budget has been completed.

6. The major feature of zero-based budgeting (ZBB) is that it

    A. Takes the previous year's budgets and adjusts them for inflation.

    B. Questions each activity and determines whether it should be maintained as it is, reduced, or eliminated.

    C. Assumes all activities are legitimate and worthy of receiving budget increases to cover any increased costs.

    D. Focuses on planned capital outlays for property, plant, and equipment.

Answer (B) is correct.
    REQUIRED: The major feature of ZBB.
    DISCUSSION: ZBB is a planning process in which each manager must justify his or her department's full budget for each period. The purpose is to encourage periodic reexamination of all costs in the hope that some can be reduced or eliminated.
    Answer (A) is incorrect. Traditional or incremental budgeting takes the previous year's budgets and adjusts them for inflation. Answer (C) is incorrect. ZBB is a planning process in which each manager must justify his or her department's full budget for each period. The purpose is to encourage periodic reexamination of all costs in the hope that some can be reduced or eliminated. Answer (D) is incorrect. It is a definition of a capital budget.

7. A company has budgeted sales of 24,000 finished units for the forthcoming 6-month period. It takes 4 pounds of direct materials to make one finished unit. Given the following:

	Finished units	Direct materials (pounds)
Beginning inventory	14,000	44,000
Target ending inventory	12,000	48,000

How many pounds of direct materials should be budgeted for purchase during the 6-month period?

    A. 48,000

    B. 88,000

    C. 92,000

    D. 96,000

Answer (C) is correct.
    REQUIRED: The pounds of direct materials budgeted for purchase during the period.
    DISCUSSION: Required production of finished units is 22,000 units (target ending inventory of 12,000 + sales of 24,000 − beginning inventory of 14,000). Thus, 88,000 pounds of direct materials (22,000 × 4 lb. per unit) must be available. Required purchases of direct materials equal 92,000 pounds (target ending inventory of 48,000 + usage of 88,000 − beginning inventory of 44,000).
    Answer (A) is incorrect. The target ending inventory is 48,000. Answer (B) is incorrect. The amount that must be available for production is 88,000 pounds of direct material. The desired 4,000-lb. increase in direct materials inventory must also be added. Answer (D) is incorrect. The changes in finished goods and direct materials inventories were not considered.

18.3 Cost-Volume-Profit (CVP) Analysis

8. A company manufactures a single product. Estimated cost data regarding this product and other information for the product and the company are as follows:

Sales price per unit	US $40
Total variable production cost per unit	US $22
Sales commission (on sales)	5%
Fixed costs and expenses:	
Manufacturing overhead	US $5,598,720
General and administrative	US $3,732,480
Effective income tax rate	40%

The number of units the company must sell in the coming year in order to reach its breakeven point is

A. 388,800 units.

B. 518,400 units.

C. 583,200 units.

D. 972,000 units.

Answer (C) is correct.
    REQUIRED: The number of units to reach the breakeven point.
    DISCUSSION: The breakeven point is determined by dividing total fixed costs by the unit contribution margin (UCM). The total fixed costs are US $9,331,200 ($5,598,720 manufacturing overhead + $3,732,480 general and administrative). The UCM is US $16 ($40 sales price – $22 variable production cost – $2 commission). Thus, the breakeven point is 583,200 units (US $9,331,200 fixed costs ÷ $16 UCM).
    Answer (A) is incorrect. Failing to subtract the variable costs per unit from the sales price results in 388,800 units. Answer (B) is incorrect. Failing to include sales commissions in total variable costs results in 518,400 units. Answer (D) is incorrect. Improperly including taxes in total variable costs causes an understatement of unit contribution margin, resulting in 972,000 units.

9. The most likely strategy to reduce the breakeven point would be to

A. Increase both the fixed costs and the contribution margin.

B. Decrease both the fixed costs and the contribution margin.

C. Decrease the fixed costs and increase the contribution margin.

D. Increase the fixed costs and decrease the contribution margin.

Answer (C) is correct.
    REQUIRED: The strategy to reduce the breakeven point.
    DISCUSSION: A ratio can be reduced either by decreasing the numerator or increasing the denominator. The breakeven point in units equals fixed costs divided by the unit contribution margin. The breakeven point in sales dollars is the fixed costs divided by the contribution margin ratio. Because fixed costs are in the numerator and the contribution margin is in the denominator, decreasing the fixed costs and increasing the contribution margin reduces the breakeven point.
    Answer (A) is incorrect. Increasing the fixed costs increases the breakeven point. Answer (B) is incorrect. Decreasing the contribution margin increases the breakeven point. Answer (D) is incorrect. Increasing fixed costs and decreasing the contribution margin increases the breakeven point.

10. A retail company determines its selling price by marking up variable costs 60%. In addition, the company uses frequent selling price markdowns to stimulate sales. If the markdowns average 10%, what is the company's contribution margin ratio?

A. 27.5%

B. 30.6%

C. 37.5%

D. 41.7%

Answer (B) is correct.
    REQUIRED: The contribution margin ratio.
    DISCUSSION: The company's selling price can be stated in terms of the unit variable cost (UVC):

$$\text{Selling price} = \text{UVC} \times 1.6 \text{ markup} \times .90 \text{ markdown}$$
$$= \text{UVC} \times 1.44$$

This can be substituted in the formula for contribution margin ratio (CMR) and solved as follows:

$$\begin{aligned}
\text{CMR} &= \text{UCM} \div \text{Selling price} \\
&= (\text{Selling price} - \text{UVC}) \div \text{Selling price} \\
&= [(\text{UVC} \times 1.44) - \text{UVC}] \div (\text{UVC} \times 1.44) \\
&= (\text{UVC} \times .44) \div (\text{UVC} \times 1.44) \\
&= 30.56\%
\end{aligned}$$

    Answer (A) is incorrect. Improperly omitting markdowns from the denominator results in 27.5%. Answer (C) is incorrect. Improperly omitting markdowns results in 37.5%. Answer (D) is incorrect. Improperly omitting markdowns from the numerator results in 41.7%.

18.4 Relevant Costs and Decision Making

Questions 11 through 13 are based on the following information. The segmented income statement for a retail company with three product lines is presented below:

	Total Company	Product Line 1	Product Line 2	Product Line 3
Volume (in units)		20,000	28,000	50,000
Sales revenue	US $2,000,000	US $800,000	US $700,000	US $500,000
Costs & expenses:				
Administrative	US $ 180,000	US $ 60,000	US $ 60,000	US $ 60,000
Advertising	240,000	96,000	84,000	60,000
Commissions	40,000	16,000	14,000	10,000
Cost of sales	980,000	360,000	420,000	200,000
Rent	280,000	84,000	140,000	56,000
Salaries	110,000	54,000	32,000	24,000
Total costs & expenses	US $1,830,000	US $670,000	US $750,000	US $410,000
Operating income (loss)	US $ 170,000	US $130,000	US $ (50,000)	US $ 90,000

The company buys the goods in the three product lines directly from manufacturers' representatives. Each product line is directed by a manager whose salary is included in the administrative expenses. Administrative expenses are allocated to the three product lines equally because the administration is spread evenly among the three product lines. Salaries represent payments to the workers in each product line and therefore are traceable costs of each product line. Advertising promotes the entire company rather than the individual product lines. As a result, the advertising is allocated to the three product lines in proportion to the sales revenue. Commissions are paid to the salespersons in each product line based on 2% of gross sales. Rent represents the cost of the retail store and warehouse under a lease agreement with 5 years remaining. The product lines share the retail and warehouse space, and the rent is allocated to the three product lines based on the square footage occupied by each of the product lines.

11. The company has an opportunity to promote one of its product lines by making a one-time US $7,000 expenditure. The company can choose only one of the three product lines to promote. The incremental sales revenue that would be realized from this US $7,000 promotion expenditure in each of the product lines is estimated as follows:

	Increase in Sales Revenue
Product Line 1	US $15,000
Product Line 2	20,000
Product Line 3	14,000

In order to maximize profits, the promotion expenditure should be spent on <List A>, resulting in an increase in operating income of <List B>.

	List A	List B
A.	Product Line 2	US $13,000
B.	Product Line 2	US $5,000
C.	Product Line 3	US $1,400
D.	Product Line 3	US $1,120

Answer (D) is correct.

REQUIRED: The product line to be promoted by a one-time advertising expenditure and the resulting income increase.

DISCUSSION: Fixed costs, being irrelevant, are ignored. The first step is to determine the contribution margin ratio for each product line.

	Product Line 1	Product Line 2	Product Line 3
Sales revenue	US $800,000	US $700,000	US $500,000
Commissions	US $ 16,000	US $ 14,000	US $ 10,000
Cost of sales	360,000	420,000	200,000
Total variable costs	US $376,000	US $434,000	US $210,000
Contribution margin	US $424,000	US $266,000	US $290,000
Divided by sales:	÷ 800,000	÷ 700,000	÷ 500,000
CM ratio	53%	38%	58%

The incremental promotion cost (US $7,000) is subtracted from the incremental revenue to determine the marginal benefit of promoting each product line.

Incremental revenue	US $ 15,000	US $ 20,000	US $ 14,000
Times: CM ratio	× .53	× .38	× .58
Incremental contribution margin	$ 7,950	$ 7,600	$ 8,120
Minus: promotion cost	(7,000)	(7,000)	(7,000)
Incremental profits	US $ 950	US $ 600	US $ 1,120

The promotion expense should be spent on Product Line 3, resulting in an increase in operating income of US $1,120.

Answer (A) is incorrect. Product Line 2 has an increased profit of US $600. Answer (B) is incorrect. Product Line 2 has an increased profit of US $600. Answer (C) is incorrect. US $1,400 omits the commissions from the calculation.

12. One company executive has expressed concern about the operating loss that has occurred in Product Line 2 and has suggested that Product Line 2 be discontinued. If Product Line 2 is dropped, the manager of the line would be retained and assigned other duties with the company, but the other employees would not be retained. Management has indicated that the nature of the company's advertising might change with the elimination of Product Line 2, but the total dollar amount would not change. If Product Line 2 were to be dropped, the operating income of the company would

A. Increase by US $50,000.

B. Decrease by US $94,000.

C. Decrease by US $234,000.

D. Increase by US $416,000.

Answer (C) is correct.

REQUIRED: The operating income effect of dropping a product line.

DISCUSSION: The operating income will decrease. Product Line 2 income will be lost, but only the traceable costs of commissions, cost of sales, and salaries will be avoided. Accordingly, the decrease will be US $234,000 [$–700,000 + ($14,000 + $420,000 + $32,000)]. The other shared costs will have to be absorbed by the two remaining product lines.

Answer (A) is incorrect. An increase of US $50,000 assumes the revenue will be lost and all of its costs will be avoided. Answer (B) is incorrect. A decrease of US $94,000 results from treating rent as an avoidable cost. Answer (D) is incorrect. An increase of US $416,000 subtracts the costs that will not be avoided if Product Line 2 is dropped from the lost sales revenue.

13. A customer, operating in an isolated foreign market, has approached the head salesperson for Product Line 1 and offered to purchase 4,000 units of a special-order product over the next 12 months. This product would be sold in the same manner as Product Line 1's other products except that the customer is hoping for a price break. Product Line 1's cost to purchase this product (cost of sales) would be US $14.70. Product Line 1 has excess capacity, meaning that the rate or amount of the remaining operating costs would not change as a consequence of the purchase and sale of this special-order product. The minimum selling price for this special-order product would be

A. US $15.00

B. US $17.30

C. US $27.50

D. US $30.20

Answer (A) is correct.

REQUIRED: The minimum selling price for a special-order product.

DISCUSSION: Product Line 1 needs to cover its variable out-of-pocket costs as a minimum on this special-order product; therefore, any selling price greater than the variable cost will contribute towards profits. Thus, the minimum selling price of the special-order product is the variable cost divided by 1 minus the commission rate, or US $15 [$14.70 ÷ (1.0 – .02)].

Answer (B) is incorrect. US $17.30 includes the average cost of salaries (at the new volume level of 24,000 units) as a cost that needs to be covered when determining the minimum selling price. Answer (C) is incorrect. US $27.50 is calculated based on a full cost approach. Answer (D) is incorrect. US $30.20 adds all costs and expenses (except cost of sales) and divides them by the original volume level of 20,000 units to determine the average operating costs. The new cost of sales is added to the average operating costs to determine the minimum selling price.

Questions 14 and 15 are based on the following information. A company manufactures and sells a single product. It takes 2 machine hours to produce one unit. Annual sales are expected to be 75,000 units. Annual production capacity is 200,000 machine hours. Expected selling price is US $10 per unit. Cost data for manufacturing and selling the product are as follows:

Variable costs (per unit)
Direct materials	US $3.00
Direct labor	1.00
Variable manufacturing overhead	0.80
Variable selling	2.00

Fixed costs (per year)
Fixed manufacturing overhead	US $90,000
Fixed selling	60,000

14. The company receives a special order for 10,000 units at US $7.60. Variable selling cost for each of these 10,000 units will be US $1.20 instead of the normal US $2.00. This special order will not affect regular sales of 75,000 units. If the company accepts this special order, its profit will

A. Increase by US $8,000.

B. Increase by US $16,000.

C. Decrease by US $4,000.

D. Decrease by US $12,000.

Answer (B) is correct.
REQUIRED: The change in profit resulting from a special order.
DISCUSSION: If the company accepts the special order, its revenue will increase by US $76,000 (10,000 units × $7.60). However, its incremental cost will include only the variable costs because fixed manufacturing and selling costs will be unchanged. The increase in cost from accepting the special order is US $60,000 [10,000 units × ($3.00 + $1.00 + $0.80 + $1.20)]. Thus, acceptance of the special order will increase profits by US $16,000 ($76,000 − $60,000).

15. The company estimates that by reducing its selling price to US $9.30 per unit, it can increase sales to 90,000 units annually. Fixed costs per year and unit variable costs will remain unchanged. If the company reduces its selling price to US $9.30 per unit, its profit will

A. Decrease by US $5,000.

B. Decrease by US $15,000.

C. Decrease by US $45,000.

D. Increase by US $15,000.

Answer (B) is correct.
REQUIRED: The effect on profit if selling price is reduced.
DISCUSSION: Because total fixed costs are unaffected, the change in profit is the change in the contribution margin. The contribution margin at the current selling price is US $240,000 [75,000 units × ($10 − $3 − $1 − $0.80 − $2)]. The contribution margin at the US $9.30 selling price is US $225,000 [90,000 units × ($9.30 − $3 − $1 − $0.80 − $2)]. Hence, profit will be reduced by US $15,000 ($240,000 − $225,000) if the selling price is lowered to US $9.30.

18.5 Responsibility Accounting

16. Which of the following is **not** true of responsibility accounting?

A. Managers should only be held accountable for factors over which they have significant influence.

B. The focus of cost center managers will normally be more narrow than that of profit center managers.

C. Every factor that affects a firm's financial performance ultimately is controllable by someone, even if that someone is the person at the top of the firm.

D. When a responsibility account system exists, operations of the business are organized into separate areas controlled by individual managers.

Answer (C) is correct.
REQUIRED: The false statement about responsibility accounting.
DISCUSSION: Responsibility accounting stresses that managers are responsible only for factors under their control. For this purpose, the operations of the business are organized into responsibility centers. Costs are classified as controllable and uncontrollable. This implies that some revenues and costs can be changed through effective management. Management may then focus on deviations for either reinforcement or correction. Thus, the statement that every factor is ultimately controllable by someone is not a premise of responsibility accounting.
Answer (A) is incorrect. Responsibility accounting holds managers responsible only for what they can control. Answer (B) is incorrect. A cost center manager is concerned with costs only, whereas a profit center manager is concerned with costs and revenues. Answer (D) is incorrect. This is the essence of responsibility accounting. Each manager is held accountable for factors under their control.

17. In a responsibility accounting system, managers are accountable for

   A. Variable costs but not for fixed costs.

   B. Product costs but not for period costs.

   C. Incremental costs.

   D. Costs over which they have significant influence.

Answer (D) is correct.
   REQUIRED: The accountability of managers in a responsibility accounting system.
   DISCUSSION: The most desirable measure for evaluating a departmental manager is one that holds the manager responsible for the revenues and expenses (s)he can control. Controllability is the basic concept of responsibility accounting.
   Answer (A) is incorrect. All variable costs may not be controllable, but some, if not all, fixed costs might be controllable. Answer (B) is incorrect. Not all budgeted costs are controllable by managers. Answer (C) is incorrect. All product costs may not be controllable, but some, if not all, period costs might be controllable.

18.6 Transfer Pricing

18. The price that one division of a company charges another division for goods or services provided is called the

   A. Market price.

   B. Transfer price.

   C. Outlay price.

   D. Distress price.

Answer (B) is correct.
   REQUIRED: The price that one division of a company charges another for goods or services provided.
   DISCUSSION: A transfer price is the price charged by one segment of an organization for a product or service supplied to another segment of the same organization.
   Answer (A) is incorrect. Market price is an approach to determine a transfer price. Answer (C) is incorrect. Outlay price is an approach to determine a transfer price. Answer (D) is incorrect. Distress price is an approach to determine a transfer price.

19. A carpet manufacturer maintains a retail division consisting of stores stocking its brand and other brands, and a manufacturing division that makes carpets and pads. An outside market exists for carpet padding material in which all padding produced can be sold. The proper transfer price for padding transferred from the manufacturing division to the retail division is

   A. Variable manufacturing division production cost.

   B. Variable manufacturing division production cost plus allocated fixed factory overhead.

   C. Variable manufacturing division production cost plus variable selling and administrative cost.

   D. The market price at which the retail division could purchase padding.

Answer (D) is correct.
   REQUIRED: The proper transfer price for padding transferred from the manufacturing division to the retail division.
   DISCUSSION: The three basic criteria that the transfer pricing system in a decentralized company should satisfy are to (1) provide information allowing central management to evaluate divisions with respect to total company profit and each division's contribution to profit, (2) stimulate each manager's efficiency without losing each division's autonomy, and (3) motivate each divisional manager to achieve his or her own profit goal in a manner contributing to the company's success. The market price should be used as the transfer price to avoid waste and maximize efficiency in a competitive economy (an outside market in which all padding produced can be sold). This price also measures the product's profitability and the division managers' performance in a competitive environment.

20. An entity produces a good in country A and sells some of its output in country B. Selling prices are identical in the two countries. The corporate tax rates are 40% in country A and 20% in country B. Assuming that the entity does not increase or decrease production, it should <List A> sales in country B and set as <List B> a transfer price as possible, in order to minimize global taxes.

	List A	List B
A.	Maximize	High
B.	Maximize	Low
C.	Minimize	High
D.	Minimize	Low

Answer (B) is correct.
   REQUIRED: The strategy for minimizing global taxes.
   DISCUSSION: The tax-minimizing strategy is to minimize taxable income where tax rates are high and to maximize taxable income where tax rates are low. Consequently, the entity should sell more in country B but set a low transfer price. This dual strategy minimizes sales and profits in country A, minimizes cost of sales in country B, and maximizes sales and profits in country B.
   Answer (A) is incorrect. If selling prices are identical, the tax-minimizing strategy involves maximizing sales in country B. However, to report the highest possible profits in the lower tax country, input costs must be minimized. The transfer price paid to the production facility in country A must therefore be set as low as possible. Answer (C) is incorrect. A strategy of minimizing sales in country B and maximizing reported cost of goods sold in country B would result in the lowest reported profit in the lower tax country, thereby maximizing taxes paid. Answer (D) is incorrect. The tax-minimizing strategy involves maximizing sales revenue in the lower tax country, not minimizing it.

STUDY UNIT NINETEEN
GLOBAL BUSINESS ENVIRONMENT

(13 pages of outline)

This study unit is the first of two covering **Section VIII: Global Business Environment** from The IIA's CIA Exam Syllabus. This section makes up 0% to 10% of Part 3 of the CIA exam and is tested at the **awareness level**. The relevant portion of the syllabus is highlighted below. (The complete syllabus is in Appendix A.)

VIII. GLOBAL BUSINESS ENVIRONMENT (0%–10%)

A. Economic/Financial Environments
1. Global, multinational, international, and multi-local compared and contrasted
2. Requirements for entering the global marketplace
3. Creating organizational adaptability
4. Managing training and development

B. Cultural/Political Environments
1. Balancing global requirements and local imperatives
2. Global mindsets (personal characteristics/competencies)
3. Sources and methods for managing complexities and contradictions
4. Managing multicultural teams

C. Legal and Economics — General Concepts (e.g., contracts)

D. Impact of Government Legislation and Regulation on Business (e.g., trade legislation)

19.1 ASPECTS OF GLOBAL BUSINESS DEVELOPMENT

In the 2000s, globalization of the world's economic system accelerated. Thus, besides such technical issues as exchange rates and tax differences, internal auditors also must be aware of the cultural aspects of global business. They affect marketing, human resource management, and many other aspects of commercial activity.

1. **Overview**

   a. Globalization is driven by the digital revolution that facilitates international commerce by providing capabilities that did not exist relatively few years ago. It is also driven by such political events as the fall of the Soviet Union in the 1990s, the growth of China as an economic power, the emergence of other economic powers (e.g., India and Brazil), the expansion of the European Union, and the creation of other regional free trade zones.

      1) These technological and political factors are intertwined with social changes. They include (a) greater concern for the rights of women and minorities; (b) the advance of multilingualism; and (c) the convergence of tastes in fashion, music, and certain other cultural factors.

      2) Accordingly, these factors favor globalization by reducing trade barriers, reducing costs of coordination, increasing economies of scale, and encouraging standardization and global branding.

2.   **Entering The Global Marketplace**

   a.   Foreign Markets

      1) Attractiveness of a foreign market is a function of such factors as geography, income, climate, population, the product, and the unmet needs of the market.

         a) Entry into a market abroad may be based on many factors, for example, psychic proximity. Thus, a first-time venture abroad might be in a market with a related culture, language, or laws.

      2) The internationalization process is of crucial interest to nations that wish to encourage local firms to grow and to operate globally. It involves the following steps:

         a) Lack of regular exports;

         b) Export via independent agents to a few markets, with later expansion to more countries;

         c) Creation of sales subsidiaries in larger markets; and

         d) Establishment of plants in foreign countries.

   b.   Methods of expanding into international markets include the following:

      1) **Licensing** gives firms in foreign countries the right to produce or market products or services within a geographical area for a fee.

         a) Licensing a process, patent, trade secret, etc., is a way to enter a foreign market with little immediate risk. However,

            i)   The licensor may have insufficient control over the licensee's operations,

            ii) The licensor loses profits if the arrangement succeeds, and

            iii) The licensee ultimately may become a competitor.

      2) **Exporting** is the sale of goods manufactured in one country and then sold in other countries.

         a) Indirect export requires lower investment than direct export and is less risky because of the intermediaries' expertise.

      3) An **indirect export strategy** operates through intermediaries, such as

         a) Home-country merchants who buy and resell the product,

         b) Home-country agents who negotiate transactions with foreign buyers for a commission,

         c) Cooperatives that represent groups of sellers, and

         d) Export-management firms that receive fees for administering the firm's export efforts.

      4) **Direct investment** has many advantages and risks.

         a) The advantages include

            i)   Cheaper materials or labor,

            ii) Receipt of investment incentives from the host government,

            iii) A strong relationship with interested parties in the host country,

            iv) Control of the investment,

            v) A better image in the host country, and

            vi) Market access when domestic content rules are in effect.

         b) Direct investment is risky because of

            i)   Exposure to currency fluctuations,

            ii) Expropriation,

            iii) Potentially high exit barriers, and

            iv) Restraints on sending profits out of the country.

5) In a **local storage and sale arrangement**, products manufactured in one country are then shipped to a marketing facility located in another country.

6) **Local component assembly** involves shipping individual parts from one country to an assembly facility in a second country. They are then turned into a salable product and sold in the second country or exported to other countries.

7) In **multiple or joint ventures**, several firms, even competitors, work together to create products that are sold under one or more brand names in different countries. They share responsibility, ownership, costs, and profits.

3. **Limited Entry**

a. The following are factors indicating that few national markets should be entered:

1) Entry costs are high;
2) Market control costs are high;
3) Product adaptation costs are high;
4) Communication adaptation costs are high;
5) The first countries selected have large populations, high income, and a high rate of growth; and
6) A dominant firm can erect high entry barriers.

4. **Progression of International Marketing**

a. International marketing has three broad stages:

1) **Export division.** This is the first step for an organization when it begins selling products beyond its own borders. Generally, a firm's initial entry is in other markets that share a common language or similar cultural norms.

2) **International division.** Large corporations make this step before becoming true global organizations. They generally focus their efforts in certain geographical regions that are led either from a central structure or are locally run and managed.

   a) Moreover, operating units report to the head of the division, not to a CEO or executive committee. Operating units may be geographical units, world product groups, or subsidiaries.

3) **Global organization.** All elements of the organization are directed toward creating and selling products to a worldwide market. Thus, all elements of the firm can be made to be more efficient in the global arena.

   a) These elements include management, production facilities, and the procurement of raw materials and components.

   b) Glocalization of a global organization localizes some of its elements but standardizes other elements.

5. **Factors of National Advantage**

a. A country has a **comparative advantage** in the global marketplace when it can achieve a lower cost of production due to a focus on, and a cooperative specialization in, a particular product.

b. A firm has a **competitive advantage** when it can achieve a lower cost of production on particular items compared with firms in another country because of local factors. Sources of competitive advantage include

1) A lower cost of production through natural resources or geography,
2) Quality or market factor differences, and
3) Supplementary supply patterns that enhance production advantages.

    c.   The factors of national advantage can be used by firms to identify their home-country advantages. It also can be used by governments to develop policies to create national advantages industries can exploit.

        1)   Factor conditions are specific production factors that include skilled labor, infrastructure, etc. Firms in each country naturally select those industries that give them an advantage due to their unique factor conditions.

        2)   Home demand conditions determine the inherent demand for goods or services that originate within the home country. Home markets exert a much higher influence on a firm's ability to recognize consumer trends than those in a foreign market.

        3)   Related and supporting industries determine whether industries within the home country provide support for a given industry. Firms in countries that have a close-knit group of industries that support each other have an advantage over firms in other nations that do not.

        4)   Firm strategy, structure, and rivalry. How much firms work together or compete with each other can determine the advantage firms in a particular nation may have over others. Also, organizational structure, how firms are established, and how they are managed contribute to effectiveness in the global business environment.

6.   **Strategies for Global Marketing Organization**

    a.   Four broad strategies are generally recognized:

        1)   A **multinational (transnational) strategy** adopts a portfolio approach. Its emphasis is on national markets because the need for global integration is not strong, and the driving forces of localization (cultural, commercial, and technical) predominate.

            a)   The product is customized for each market and therefore incurs higher production costs.

            b)   This strategy is most effective given large differences between countries.

            c)   Also, exchange rate risk is reduced when conducting business in this manner.

            d)   Transnational firms lack a national identity, but they rely on a decentralized structure for management and decision making.

                i)   They tend to be more aware of local customs and market forces because they take much more of their input from a local or regional management team.

        2)   A **global strategy** regards the world as one market. Among its determinants are ambition, positioning, and organization.

            a)   The product is essentially the same in all countries with some adaptions.

            b)   Faster product development and lower production costs are typical.

            c)   The disadvantage of this strategy is the complexity of integration and coordination needed to keep operations running smoothly.

            d)   Global firms are primarily managed from one central country. Even though their products may be sold throughout the world, their headquarters and most of their policy decisions are set from a central base of operations.

                i)   Global firms plan, operate, and coordinate their activities worldwide. Thus, a global firm secures cost or product differentiation advantages not available to domestic firms.

3) In an **international strategy,** the value chain is controlled and marketed from the organization's home country, but products are sold globally.

    a) The product is essentially the same in all countries.

    b) Decision making is centralized with the home country.

    c) This strategy allows for strong control of operations with less coordination from host countries.

    d) The disadvantage of this strategy is that the value chain in a host country is not developed.

4) A **multilocal** or **multidomestic strategy** uses subsidiaries in the host countries to control operations.

    a) The product is adapted for each country.

    b) Decision making is usually left to the subsidiaries.

    c) This strategy allows for customization for local markets and the use of local resources. Also, less coordination is required by decision makers in the home country.

    d) The disadvantage of this strategy is higher costs and lower economies of scale.

b. Two compromise strategies adopt elements of the broad strategies.

1) A **glocal strategy** seeks the benefits of localization (flexibility, proximity, and adaptability) and global integration.

    a) Successful telecommunications firms are examples of balancing these elements of localization and global integration.

    b) Local responsiveness is indicated when local product tastes and preferences, regulations, and barriers are significant.

    c) Global integration is indicated when demand is homogeneous and economies of productive scale are large.

2) A **regional strategy** combines elements of multinational, international, and multilocal strategies. The goal of this strategy is to create regional products and a regional value chain.

7. **International Trade**

a. The following are three important considerations for firms that engage in international trade:

1) Regional Free Trade Zones

    a) The European Union (EU) is a group of 28 European nations that have lowered trade barriers among member states, 18 of which share a common currency and trade policy.

    b) The nations bound by the North American Free Trade Agreement (NAFTA) are the U.S., Mexico, and Canada. NAFTA may be expanded into South American countries.

    c) Mercosul is a free trade agreement among South American nations. They include Argentina, Brazil, Uruguay, and Paraguay. Chile and Bolivia are associate members.

    d) APEC (the Asian Pacific Economic Cooperation forum) is a collection of Pacific-rim nations, including the NAFTA countries, China, and Japan, dedicated to promoting increased trade with each other and the rest of the world.

2) A cartel is an organization of sellers (e.g., the oil cartel OPEC) who undertake joint action to maximize members' profits by controlling the supply, and therefore the price, of their product.

    a) In many nations, such conduct is illegal. The reason is that the monopolistic and anticompetitive practices of cartels reduce supply, raise prices, and limit competition. Also, the relevant industry tends to be less efficient.

3) Dumping violates international agreements.

    a) It occurs when a firm charges a price (1) lower than that in its home market or (2) lower than the cost to make the product.

    b) Dumping may be done to penetrate a market or as a result of export subsidies.

Stop and review! You have completed the outline for this subunit. Study multiple-choice questions 1 through 7 beginning on page 493.

19.2 GLOBAL ADAPTABILITY

1. **International Marketing Programs**

    a. Firms that operate globally must choose a marketing program after considering the need for adaptation to local circumstances. The possibilities lie on a continuum from a purely standardized marketing mix to a purely adapted marketing mix.

        1) The first chooses to standardize products, promotion, and distribution. The second adapts the elements of the mix to each local market.

            a) Worldwide standardization of all elements should be the lowest cost marketing strategy. However, even well-established global brands ordinarily undergo some adaptation to local markets.

        2) The following are strategies for product and promotion adaptation:

            a) Using a straight extension strategy, a higher profit potential exists because virtually no changes are made in the product or its promotion.

                i) But the risk is that foreign consumers may not be familiar with this type of product or readily accept it.

            b) Using a product adaptation strategy, a firm makes changes in the product for each market but not in its promotion. This strategy may reduce potential profit but also may provide a marketing advantage by considering local wants and needs.

            c) Using a product invention strategy, a new product is created specifically for a certain country or regional market. A product may either include advancements for developed countries or have certain elements removed in places where a lower cost is important.

                i) Backward invention is the reintroduction of an earlier version of the product to meet local needs. This variation of the invention strategy reflects the possibility that different countries may be in different stages of the international product life cycle.

                ii) Forward invention requires developing a new product for the unique needs of a foreign market.

            d) Communication adaptation is a strategy that does not change the product, but advertising and marketing campaigns are changed to reflect the local culture and beliefs.

            e) A dual adaptation strategy changes both the product and the promotion to provide the best chance of acceptance in a foreign market.

2. **Global Pricing**

  a. The gray market is a problem for a firm that sells products at different prices in different countries.

    1) In a gray market, products imported from one country to another are sold in a third country or even in the original exporter's country. The purpose is to make a profit from differences in retail prices.

      a) These activities clearly lower the profits in some markets of the firm that was the initial seller.

  b. One response is to monitor the practices of distributors and retaliate if necessary.

  c. A second response is to charge higher prices to the low-cost distributors to reduce their incentives to participate in a gray market.

  d. A third response is to differentiate products sold in different countries, e.g., by adapting the product or offering distinct service features.

  e. The price escalation problem requires setting different prices in different countries.

    1) Price escalation is caused by an accumulation of additional costs, for example,

      a) Changes in currency exchange rates;
      b) Transportation expenses;
      c) Profits earned by importers, wholesalers, and retailers; and
      d) Import duties.

    2) Three strategies address price escalation:

      a) A firm may set a standard (uniform) price globally. However, this strategy may result in overpricing of the product in some markets and underpricing of the product in others.

      b) A firm may set a market-based price in each market. The weakness of this strategy is that it ignores cost differences. It also may create a gray market between certain regions.

      c) A firm may set a cost-based price in each market with a standard markup. In a region or country where costs are high, this strategy may result in prices that are too high to be competitive within the local market.

    3) A transfer price is the price charged by one subunit of a firm to another. When the subsidiary-buyer is in a foreign country, the higher the transfer price, the higher the potential tariffs.

      a) However, the tax levied on a subsequent sale by the subsidiary will be lower because of its higher acquisition cost.

    4) Distribution channels are a necessity to ensure goods are successfully transferred from the production facility to end users. These channels include three distinct links that must work well together.

      a) The international marketing headquarters (export department or international division) is where decisions are made about the subsequent channels and other aspects of the marketing mix.

      b) Channels between nations carry goods to foreign borders. They include air, land, sea, or rail transportation channels.

        i) At this stage, in addition to transportation methods, intermediaries are selected (e.g., agents or trading companies), and financing and risk management decisions are reached.

      c) Channels within nations take the goods from the border or entry point to the ultimate users of the products.

        i) Among nations, the number of the levels of distribution, the types of channels, and the size of retailers vary substantially.

3.   **Steps to Brand Globally**

    a.   The following steps should be taken to minimize the risks of expanding into foreign markets and to maximize growth potential:

        1)   A firm must understand how diverse markets connect to form a global branding landscape. Individual countries vary in their historical acceptance of products and services.

            a)   However, firms also may capitalize on similarities that are found in certain areas and regions.

        2)   Branding and brand building must be a process. New markets must be developed where none previously existed.

            a)   Thus, global firms must build awareness of the product and then create sources of brand equity.

        3)   Establishing a marketing infrastructure is crucial. To create a successful marketing structure, the firm either must merge with the local marketing channels or create a completely new method of distribution.

        4)   Integrated marketing communications should be developed. Markets must be approached with a broad range of messages, and sole reliance on advertising should be avoided.

            a)   Other marketing communications include merchandising, promotions, and sponsorship.

        5)   The firm may create branding partnerships. Global firms often form alliances with local distribution channels to increase their profitability while decreasing their marketing costs.

        6)   The firm should determine the ratio of standardization and customization. Products that can be sold virtually unchanged throughout several markets provide a greater profit opportunity for a global firm.

            a)   However, cultural differences may require extensive customization to appeal to markets in different countries.

        7)   The firm should determine the balance of local and global control. Local managers may understand the wants and needs of their market, but the global firm still must retain control of certain elements of the marketing process and strategy.

        8)   The firm should establish local guidelines so that local sales and profit goals are met.

        9)   The firm should create a global brand equity tracking system. This equity system is a set of research processes that provide the marketers with pertinent information.

            a)   The marketers can use this tracking system to create both long- and short-term strategies for expanding product sales and reach.

        10)   The firm should maximize brand elements. Large global firms can achieve much greater expansion rates when the brand elements are successfully employed at the launch of a product or service.

Stop and review! You have completed the outline for this subunit. Study multiple-choice questions 8 through 12 beginning on page 495.

19.3 LEADERSHIP IN GLOBAL OPERATIONS

1. **Characteristics of Successful Leaders**

   a. The most important characteristic of a successful leader has been determined to be the ability to develop additional leaders within his or her own team. The following are other common characteristics of successful leaders in global organizations:

      1) Extensive international travel during childhood prior to entering the working world.

      2) Influence and encouragement by family.

      3) A series of events that shaped their belief systems to include a foundation of honesty and trustworthiness.

      4) Key learning experiences that instilled the ability to be flexible and adaptable in a variety of situations.

      5) Strong role models who emphasized the importance of being fair, consistent, and true to inner principles and beliefs.

      6) Effective interpersonal skills and the ability to communicate successfully with a variety of individuals.

      7) Ability to speak one or more additional languages and extensive exposure to nonnative cultures.

      8) Effective problem-solving skills that draw from a multidisciplinary approach. The best candidates have varied backgrounds and can draw on a multitude of life experiences.

2. **Leadership Styles**

   a. Research has been conducted on different leadership styles in various countries.

      1) Based on the path-goal approach, a style should be adopted that (a) complements (but does not duplicate) the factors in the environment and (b) is consistent with employees' traits. The following are the four basic styles of leadership:

         a) A **directive style** establishes specific expectations, guidelines, schedules, rules, and standards.

         b) A **supportive style** regards employees as equals and attempts to improve their circumstances.

         c) A **participative style** involves consultation with employees and serious attention to their ideas.

         d) An **achievement-oriented style** sets high goals, emphasizes continuous improvement, and maintains confidence that employees will perform.

      2) The participative style, although not always the best, is the most widely accepted internationally.

      3) The directive style is the least accepted internationally. It was not deemed appropriate in the U.S., the U.K., Canada, Australia, Germany, and Sweden.

      4) The achievement-oriented style was found unacceptable in such countries as Brazil, France, Italy, and Japan.

      5) The supportive style was not accepted in such countries as Brazil, France, India, and Sweden.

3. **Managerial Attitudes**

   a. The importance of managerial attitudes toward global operations should be stressed. The following are the three basic types:

      1) An **ethnocentric attitude** assumes that the home country's people, practices, and ideas are superior to all others. Thus, the firm's identification is with the owner's nationality.

         a) Authority and decision making are centralized, so communication is likely to involve a high volume of information flow in the form of orders and advice to subsidiaries.

    b)   Home-country standards are likely to be used for performance evaluation of entities and individuals.

    c)   The ethnocentric attitude is perpetuated by recruiting and developing home-country individuals for key posts throughout the firm.

    d)   The advantages of an ethnocentric attitude are simplicity and close control. The disadvantages are

        i)   Social and political problems in foreign countries,
        ii)   Poor feedback,
        iii) Ineffective planning,
        iv) Lack of flexibility and innovative thinking, and
        v)   High turnover of managers in foreign subsidiaries.

2)   A **polycentric attitude** assumes that cultural differences require local managers to make most decisions because they are more knowledgeable about local conditions than are central administrators.

    a)   Thus, development of local managerial talent is crucial, and operating performance is primarily evaluated based on results.

        i)   Consequently, methods, training, and incentives vary significantly among subsidiaries.

    b)   Furthermore,

        i)   Control is predominantly local,
        ii)   The firm is identified with the nationality of the host nation, and
        iii) Relatively little communication occurs with central administration or among subsidiaries.

    c)   One disadvantage is that local operations may have inefficiencies because of duplication of activities.

        i)   Another disadvantage is that the goals of local entities may not be consistent with those of the firm as a whole.

    d)   Advantages are

        i)   More capable and motivated local managers,
        ii)   Better results in local markets,
        iii) Local development of new product ideas, and
        iv) Stronger support by host governments.

3)   A **geocentric attitude** is truly internationally oriented while absorbing the best that various cultures offer.

    a)   It is a completely balanced approach with the following qualities:

        i)   Full collaboration between central administrators and subsidiaries,
        ii)   Control and evaluation methods that harmonize local and overall firm standards, and
        iii) Frequent communication in all directions (i.e., between central administrators and subsidiaries and among subsidiaries).

    b)   Moreover, talent, not nationality, determines personnel decisions throughout the firm.

Stop and review! You have completed the outline for this subunit. Study multiple-choice questions 13 through 17 beginning on page 496.

19.4 HUMAN RESOURCES ISSUES IN GLOBAL OPERATIONS

1. **Overview**

    a. Cross-cultural differences are important for global firms. Culture is the distinct set of values, beliefs, and symbols that guide patterns of behavior in a group.

    1) In international business, misunderstanding and conflict arise because people from different cultures have fundamentally different assumptions, values, etc.

    b. A distinction is made between high-context and low-context cultures.

    1) In high-context cultures (e.g., Japanese, Chinese, Arabic, and Korean), much meaning is transmitted by nonverbal cues and situational circumstances.

    a) Thus, a person's status in a firm, rank in society, and reputation convey the primary message.

    2) In low-context cultures (e.g., northern European and North American), primary messages are transmitted verbally.

    a) Accordingly, precise written contractual agreements are highly valued in a low-context culture.

    i) In contrast, social events are more valued in a high-context culture.

2. **Other Causes of Cultural Diversity**

    a. Cultures are different in many ways.

    1) Individualistic cultures are societies that place a higher value on the rights and accomplishments of individual persons within the society. Examples are the U.S., the U.K., Canada, and Australia.

    a) Collectivist cultures focus much more on the goals of family, friends, country, and the organization. Examples are China, India, Mexico, Japan, and Egypt.

    2) The perception of time as it relates to business and social life varies with the culture.

    a) Polychronic time is based on a perception that time is nonlinear, flexible, and multidimensional. This perception is typical of Mediterranean, Latin American, and Arabic cultures.

    b) Monochronic time is based on a perception that time is the same for everyone and is measurable in standard units. This perception is common in northern Europe and the U.S.

    i) These western cultures believe in punctuality and that time should not be wasted.

    3) Interpersonal space varies from only a few inches to several feet. Managers must be aware of these distances because they may be dramatically different from culture to culture.

    a) For example, northern Europeans and North Americans tend to prefer holding conversations at arm's length.

    b) In Arabic and Asian cultures, however, the preferred conversational distance may be only 6 inches.

    4) Because of the differences in language even within the same country, special care must be taken not to make mistakes or offend others in a foreign land.

    a) It is nearly impossible for someone who has studied a foreign language only briefly to understand its subtleties.

    5) Global firms must respect local religious beliefs and customs to be successful. For example, local religious holidays, days off from work, and food restrictions should be understood.

3. **Global Mindset**

    a.   The development of a global perspective and cultural awareness is a global mindset. This mindset embraces the global environment and understands international business management.

    b.   Characteristics and competencies of a global mindset include the following:

        1)   Valuing and promoting multiculturalism.
        2)   Fostering global learning.
        3)   Understanding cultural differences.
        4)   Global business savvy.
        5)   Ability to foster effective diversity policies.

4. **How American Management Theories Work in Other Countries**

    a.   Psychologist Geert Hofstede identified the following five distinct culture dimensions that distinguish one culture from another:

        1)   Power distance is the degree of acceptance of unequal distribution of power in an organization.

        2)   The individualism-collectivism dimension addresses whether (a) the organization protects its members in return for their loyalty or (b) the individual must meet his or her own security needs.

        3)   The masculinity versus femininity dimension is the balance of (a) masculine traits (aggressiveness, acquisitiveness, and performance) and (b) the traditionally female traits (concern for others and the quality of life).

        4)   Uncertainty avoidance relates to the extent of the threat posed by (a) ambiguous circumstances, (b) the significance of rules, and (c) the pressure for conformity.

        5)   Long-term orientation is how much society values long-standing traditions and values. It includes (a) perseverance, (b) thrift, (c) ordering relationships by status, and (d) having a sense of shame. Short-term orientation includes (a) reciprocating social obligations, (b) respect for tradition, (c) protecting one's "face," and (d) personal steadiness and stability. Most East Asian countries, followed by Eastern and Central Europe, are long-term oriented.

    b.   The U.S. has (1) a low ranking on uncertainty avoidance and long-term orientation, (2) a less low ranking on power distance, (3) a high ranking on masculinity, and (4) the highest ranking on individualism.

        1)   The conclusion, given the wide variance of these results with those for many other countries, is that American management theories need to be altered when applied in other countries.

    c.   Americans experience a high rate of failure when living and working abroad primarily as a result of not being adequately prepared to succeed within the new culture. Failure does not usually result from technical incompetence.

        1)   American firms will probably enjoy greater success if they better prepare their executives for cultural differences.

5. **Training for Work in a Foreign Culture**

    a.   Any training program for those working internationally should contain the following:

        1)   Documentary programs provide text-based or videotape preview of the history, culture, institutions, beliefs, and economy of the foreign country.

        2)   Cultural assimilation practice is similar to role-play techniques that are frequently used to train salespeople. Problem scenarios are presented to managers and workers, and they are coached on how to respond to them.

3) Language instruction is provided by various means to senior executives and mid-level managers who are now expected to learn the language of the country where they will be working.

   a) Some languages take years, not months, to master, but multilingual ability is a necessity.

4) Sensitivity training is focused mainly on educating workers about the beliefs and mores of the foreign country. Special care is given to topics that might bring embarrassment to a manager or offend his or her hosts.

5) Experience in the field involves actually traveling to the foreign country and interacting with its people. Usually, one or more guides are available to answer questions and provide feedback.

6) A firm's management training for work in a foreign country should be part of a planned career path that includes selection, orientation and training, and repatriation (professional and cultural readjustment).

   a) The last step includes a commitment from the firm that the manager will not be at a professional disadvantage because of his or her work abroad.

      i) The process also should address the needs of families.

6. **Managing Multicultural Teams**

   a. Successful global managers are able to read individual behavior, group dynamics, and situations as well as the locals do.

   b. This ability is known as cultural intelligence. It involves seeing the world as someone else does and being able to adapt appropriately.

Stop and review! You have completed the outline for this subunit. Study multiple-choice questions 18 through 20 on page 498.

QUESTIONS

19.1 Aspects of Global Business Development

1. A firm expands into international markets to

A. Be in foreign markets.

B. Eliminate foreign competition

C. Pursue new, higher-profit opportunities.

D. Preclude piracy of the firm's products.

Answer (C) is correct.
   REQUIRED: The reason to expand globally.
   DISCUSSION: A firm may decide to go abroad for many reasons, for example, to respond to a competitive challenge in its home country by another global firm, to pursue opportunities yielding greater profits, to achieve economies of scale, to diversify, or to follow customers who need international service.
   Answer (A) is incorrect. A firm should enter international markets for well-defined purposes, not for some vague reason such as establishing a presence. Answer (B) is incorrect. A firm's counterattack in a foreign market is not likely to eliminate the competitor. However, it may serve as a market signal that will influence the foreign competitor's behavior in a way favorable to the firm. Answer (D) is incorrect. Expansion does not prevent piracy.

2. A firm wishing to become global must consider how many national markets to enter. A firm should enter fewer national markets when

A. Communication adaptation costs are low.

B. The product need not be adapted.

C. Entry costs are low.

D. The first countries chosen are heavily populated and have high incomes.

Answer (D) is correct.
   REQUIRED: The reason for a global firm to enter fewer national markets.
   DISCUSSION: The following are factors indicating that few national markets should be entered: (1) Entry costs are high; (2) market control costs are high; (3) product adaptation costs are high; (4) communication adaptation costs are high; (5) the first countries selected have large populations, high incomes, and high income growth; and (6) a dominant firm can erect high entry barriers.
   Answer (A) is incorrect. Low communication adaptation costs argue for operations in many countries. Answer (B) is incorrect. Low product adaptation costs argue for operations in many countries. Answer (C) is incorrect. Low entry costs argue for operations in many countries.

3. When a multinational firm decides to sell its products abroad, one of the risks the firm faces is that the government of the foreign market charges the firm with dumping. Dumping occurs when

    A. The same product sells at different prices in different countries.

    B. A firm charges less than the cost to make the product so as to enter or win a market.

    C. Lower quality versions of the product are sold abroad so as to be affordable.

    D. Transfer prices are set artificially high so as to minimize tax payments.

Answer (B) is correct.
    REQUIRED: The nature of dumping.
    DISCUSSION: Dumping is an unfair trade practice that violates international agreements. It occurs when a firm charges a price (1) lower than that in its home market or (2) lower than the cost to make the product. Dumping may be done to penetrate a market or as a result of export subsidies.
    Answer (A) is incorrect. In a gray market, the same product sells at different prices in different countries. The effect differs from that of dumping. A seller in a low-price market tries to sell the goods in a higher-price market. Unlike the dumping case, the objective is not to penetrate a market. Instead, a dealer seeks to resell at a favorable price. Answer (C) is incorrect. Selling a lower quality product at a fair price is a perfectly acceptable strategy. Answer (D) is incorrect. A transfer price is a price charged to a subunit of an enterprise. Setting a high price to avoid an unfavorable tax rate has the opposite effect of dumping, assuming the subunit passes the cost on to its customers.

4. An advantage of a direct investment strategy when entering a foreign market is

    A. Reduction in the capital at risk.

    B. Shared control and responsibility.

    C. Assurance of access when the foreign country imposes domestic content rules.

    D. Avoidance of interaction with the local bureaucracy.

Answer (C) is correct.
    REQUIRED: The advantage of direct investment.
    DISCUSSION: Direct investment has many advantages: (1) cheaper materials or labor, (2) receipt of investment incentives from the host government, (3) a strong relationship with interested parties in the host country, (4) control of the investment, (5) a better image in the host country, and (6) market access when domestic content rules are in effect. However, direct investment is risky because of exposure to currency fluctuations, expropriation, potentially high exit barriers, and restraints on sending profits out of the country.
    Answer (A) is incorrect. Direct investment maximizes capital at risk. Answer (B) is incorrect. Direct investment avoids shared control and responsibility. Answer (D) is incorrect. Direct investment means a closer relationship with governmental entities in the host country.

5. The inherent attractiveness of a national market is most likely increased by which factor?

    A. The firm's strategic position.

    B. The market's exclusion from a regional free trade zone.

    C. Unmet needs of a developing nation.

    D. Product adaptation is costly.

Answer (C) is correct.
    REQUIRED: The factor most likely increasing market attractiveness.
    DISCUSSION: Attractiveness is a function of such factors as geography, income, climate, population, and the product. Another major factor is the unmet needs of a developing nation, for example, China or India.
    Answer (A) is incorrect. The inherent attractiveness of a national market is primarily determined by its characteristics. Answer (B) is incorrect. Given the emergence of regional free trade blocs (e.g., the European Union, APEC, or Mercosul), a firm is more likely to enter a regional rather than a purely national market. Answer (D) is incorrect. Low adaptation costs are attractive.

6. A U.S. firm most likely may decide to enter the Australian market because of

    A. Geography.

    B. The unmet needs of an undeveloped country.

    C. Psychic proximity.

    D. Population.

Answer (C) is correct.
    REQUIRED: The most likely reason for a U.S. firm to enter the Australian market.
    DISCUSSION: Attractiveness of a foreign market is a function of such factors as geography, income, climate, population, and the product. Another major factor is the unmet needs of a developing nation, for example, China or India. Entry into a market abroad may be based on many factors, for example, psychic proximity. Thus, a first-time venture abroad might be in a market with a related culture, language, or laws.
    Answer (A) is incorrect. Australia is far from the U.S. Answer (B) is incorrect. Australia is a developed country. Answer (D) is incorrect. Australia is not heavily populated.

7. A country has the greatest comparative advantage in international trade when

    A. Firms in the country have a lower cost of production because of natural resources.

    B. It has an absolute advantage with respect to at least one input to production.

    C. Firms in the country have a lower cost of production because of transportation and other geographic factors.

    D. It produces whatever it can produce most efficiently.

Answer (D) is correct.
    REQUIRED: The nature of comparative advantage.
    DISCUSSION: A country has a comparative advantage when it can achieve a lower cost of production due to a focus on and a cooperative specialization in a particular product. The greatest advantage from trade is obtained when each nation specializes in producing what it can produce most efficiently. If nations specialize and then exchange with others, more is produced and consumed than if each nation tries to be self-sufficient. Specialization of labor is beneficial for individuals; the same principle applies to nations.
    Answer (A) is incorrect. A firm has a competitive advantage when it can achieve a lower cost of production on particular items compared with firms in another country because of factors that are indigenous to its country. Answer (B) is incorrect. Comparative advantage compares costs within a single country. Absolute advantage compares the costs of inputs between countries. Answer (C) is incorrect. A firm has a competitive advantage when it can achieve a lower cost of production on particular items compared with firms in another country because of factors that are indigenous to its country.

19.2 Global Adaptability

8. A firm wishing to sell its well-known brand of men's clothing in a certain foreign country redesigned the products because of the greater average size of consumers in that country. However, the firm retained the same basic advertising campaign. This firm has adopted which adaptation strategy?

    A. Straight extension.

    B. Product adaptation.

    C. Forward invention.

    D. Backward invention.

Answer (B) is correct.
    REQUIRED: The adaptation strategy followed.
    DISCUSSION: Using a product adaptation strategy, a firm makes changes to the product for each market but not its promotion. This strategy may reduce profit potential but also may provide a marketing advantage by considering local wants and needs.
    Answer (A) is incorrect. The product was adapted. Answer (C) is incorrect. No new product was created. Answer (D) is incorrect. No older product was reintroduced.

9. A firm that manufactures refrigerators sold ice boxes in urban areas of less developed countries. Many residents lacked electricity to power refrigerators but could purchase blocks of ice from local vendors for use in ice boxes. According to Keegan's model of adaptation strategies, this firm adopted a strategy of

    A. Product adaptation.

    B. Dual adaptation.

    C. Backward invention.

    D. Forward invention.

Answer (C) is correct.
    REQUIRED: The adaptation strategy followed.
    DISCUSSION: Using a product invention strategy, a new product is created specifically for a certain country or regional market. A product may either include advancements for developed countries or have certain elements removed in places where a lower cost is important. Thus, an ice box, a precursor of the modern refrigerator, is a backward invention.
    Answer (A) is incorrect. The refrigerator was not adapted. An older precursor product was reintroduced. Answer (B) is incorrect. Dual adaptation involves product adaptation, not invention. Answer (D) is incorrect. Forward invention is the development of a new product.

10. A firm sold the same product in many foreign countries but changed the ad copy to allow for language and cultural differences. The firm adopted which adaptation strategy?

    A. Product adaptation.

    B. Communication adaptation.

    C. Dual adaptation.

    D. Straight extension.

Answer (B) is correct.
    REQUIRED: The adaptation strategy followed.
    DISCUSSION: Communication adaptation is a strategy that does not change the product, but advertising and marketing campaigns are changed to reflect the local culture and beliefs. For example, a firm may use one message but with changes in language, name, and colors. It may use a consistent theme but change the ad copy in each market. Another option is for a firm to devise a group of ads from which each market may choose the most effective. Still another option is to develop promotion campaigns locally.
    Answer (A) is incorrect. The firm did not change the product. Answer (C) is incorrect. A dual adaptation strategy changes both the product and promotion to provide the best chance of acceptance in a foreign market. Answer (D) is incorrect. The firm changed the product's promotion.

11. A firm buys new computer equipment from bankrupt companies and resells it in foreign markets at prices significantly below those charged by competitors. The firm is

    A. Engaged in dumping.

    B. Engaged in price discrimination.

    C. Operating in a gray market.

    D. Operating in a black market.

Answer (C) is correct.
    REQUIRED: The term for sale in a higher-price market of goods acquired cheaply in another market.
    DISCUSSION: In a gray market, products imported from one country to another are sold in a third country or even in the original exporter's country. The purpose is to make a profit from the differences in retail prices. These activities clearly lower the profits in some markets of the firm that was the initial seller.
    Answer (A) is incorrect. Dumping is sale below cost or at less than the price charged in the home market. Answer (B) is incorrect. Price discrimination involves illegally selling the same products at different prices to different customers. Answer (D) is incorrect. Black market operations are illegal.

12. A firm that decides to operate globally by changing its product and its promotion methods has chosen

    A. A dual adaptation strategy.

    B. The backward variant of a product invention strategy.

    C. The forward variant of a product invention strategy.

    D. A straight extension strategy.

Answer (A) is correct.
    REQUIRED: The adaptation strategy followed.
    DISCUSSION: Communication adaptation is a strategy that does not change the products, but advertising and marketing campaigns are changed to reflect the local culture and beliefs. In contrast, a dual adaptation strategy changes both the product and the promotion to provide the best chance of acceptance in a foreign market.
    Answer (B) is incorrect. The backward variant of a product invention strategy reintroduces an earlier version to meet local needs. Answer (C) is incorrect. The forward variant of a product invention strategy develops a new product. Answer (D) is incorrect. Using a straight extension strategy, a higher profit potential exists because virtually no changes are made in the product or its promotion. There is a downside potential if foreign consumers are not familiar with this type of product or do not readily accept it.

19.3 Leadership in Global Operations

13. According to research on the international contingency model of leadership, which path-goal leadership style is most likely to be accepted around the world as culturally appropriate?

    A. Directive.

    B. Participative.

    C. Supportive.

    D. Achievement-oriented.

Answer (B) is correct.
    REQUIRED: The path-goal leadership style most likely to be accepted around the world.
    DISCUSSION: A participative style involves consultation with employees and serious attention to their ideas. The participative style, although not always the best, is the most widely accepted internationally. Every country surveyed found it to be culturally acceptable.
    Answer (A) is incorrect. The directive style is the least accepted internationally. It was not deemed appropriate in the U.S., U.K., Canada, Australia, Germany, and Sweden. Answer (C) is incorrect. The supportive style was not accepted in such countries as Brazil, France, India, and Sweden. Answer (D) is incorrect. The achievement-oriented style was found unacceptable in such countries as Brazil, France, Italy, and Japan.

14. Managerial attitudes toward global operations are viewed by researcher Howard Perlmutter as a key to understanding multinational firms. A geocentric attitude is indicated by

    A. An identification with national perspectives even though the firm is genuinely international.

    B. Control and evaluation methods that are locally determined.

    C. Decision making concentrated in the central administrative authority.

    D. Little communication among subsidiaries.

Answer (A) is correct.
    REQUIRED: The indicator of a geocentric attitude.
    DISCUSSION: A geocentric attitude is truly internationally oriented while absorbing the best that various cultures offer. It is a completely balanced approach with full collaboration between central administrators and subsidiaries, control and evaluation methods that harmonize local and overall firm standards, and frequent communication in all directions (i.e., between central administrators and subsidiaries and among subsidiaries). Moreover, talent, not nationality, determines personnel decisions throughout the firm.
    Answer (B) is incorrect. Having control and evaluation methods that are locally determined is an indicator of a polycentric attitude. Answer (C) is incorrect. Decision making concentrated in the central administrative authority is an indicator of an ethnocentric attitude. Answer (D) is incorrect. Little communication among subsidiaries is an indicator of an ethnocentric attitude.

15. For a multinational firm, which of the following is a disadvantage of an ethnocentric staffing policy in which all key management positions are filled by parent-company nationals?

- A. An ethnocentric staffing policy significantly raises compensation, training, and staffing costs.

- B. An ethnocentric staffing policy produces resentment among the firm's employees in host countries.

- C. An ethnocentric staffing policy limits career mobility for parent-country nationals.

- D. An ethnocentric staffing policy isolates headquarters from foreign subsidiaries.

Answer (B) is correct.
  REQUIRED: The disadvantage of ethnocentric staffing of key positions.
  DISCUSSION: An ethnocentric staffing policy assumes that the home country's people, practices, and ideas are superior to all others. Thus, the firm's identification is with the owner's nationality. Authority and decision making are centralized, so communication is likely to involve a high volume of information flow in the form of orders and advice to subsidiaries. Home-country standards are likely to be used for performance evaluation of entities and individuals.
  Answer (A) is incorrect. The key disadvantages of a geocentric staffing policy are that it significantly raises compensation, training, and staffing costs. Although an ethnocentric strategy involves relocation costs and higher compensation for expatriate managers, it allows the overall compensation structure to follow national levels in each country. Answer (C) is incorrect. This strategy limits career mobility of host country employees, not parent company employees. Answer (D) is incorrect. A polycentric staffing policy isolates headquarters from foreign subsidiaries.

16. According to research on path-goal leadership styles done in many countries, which styles are neither the most nor the **least** accepted internationally?

1. Directive
2. Supportive
3. Participative
4. Achievement-oriented

- A. 1 and 2.

- B. 1 and 3.

- C. 2 and 4.

- D. 3 and 4.

Answer (C) is correct.
  REQUIRED: The path-goal leadership styles that are neither the most nor the least accepted internationally.
  DISCUSSION: The participative style, although not always the best, is the most widely accepted internationally. The directive style is the least accepted internationally. It was not deemed appropriate in the U.S., U.K., Canada, Australia, Germany, and Sweden. The achievement-oriented style was found unacceptable in such countries as Brazil, France, Italy, and Japan. The supportive style was not accepted in such countries as Brazil, France, India, and Sweden.
  Answer (A) is incorrect. The directive style is least accepted. Answer (B) is incorrect. The directive style is least accepted, and the participative style is most accepted. Answer (D) is incorrect. The participative style is most accepted.

17. With the globalization of economies, many organizations have expanded their operations to international locations. As an advisor to management, an internal auditor will most likely recommend that a geocentric, or worldwide, attitude be adopted. Select the reason the geocentric attitude is preferred.

- A. It promotes a simpler organizational structure.

- B. It provides greater autonomy for host country managers.

- C. It provides the best balance of local and worldwide objectives.

- D. It promotes tighter organizational control.

Answer (C) is correct.
  REQUIRED: The reason for a geocentric attitude.
  DISCUSSION: The geocentric attitude is truly internationally oriented while absorbing the best that various cultures offer. It is a completely balanced approach with the following qualities: (1) full collaboration between central administrators and subsidiaries, (2) control and evaluation methods that harmonize local and overall firm standards, and (3) frequent communication in all directions (i.e., between central administrators and subsidiaries and among subsidiaries). Moreover, talent, not nationality, determines personnel decisions throughout the firm.
  Answer (A) is incorrect. The ethnocentric attitude provides the simplest organizational structure. Answer (B) is incorrect. The polycentric attitude provides greatest autonomy for host-country managers. Answer (D) is incorrect. The ethnocentric attitude promotes tightest organizational control.

19.4 Human Resources Issues in Global Operations

18. The cultural dimensions of organizational behavior in 40 countries have been studied. The United States ranked the highest in which dimension?

A. Power distance.

B. Uncertainty avoidance.

C. Individualism.

D. Masculinity.

Answer (C) is correct.

REQUIRED: The cultural dimension in which the United States ranked the highest.

DISCUSSION: The individualism-collectivism dimension addresses whether the organization or individual must meet his or her own security needs.

Answer (A) is incorrect. The U.S. had a moderately low ranking on power distance. Answer (B) is incorrect. The U.S. had a low ranking on uncertainty avoidance. Answer (D) is incorrect. The U.S. had a high, but not the highest, ranking on masculinity.

19. In some regions of the world, business is conducted more often through personal relationship building than through legal contracts. This is an example of a

A. Cultural factor.

B. Commercial factor.

C. Technical factor.

D. Legal factor.

Answer (A) is correct.

REQUIRED: The factor exemplified by conducting business more often through personal relationship building than through legal contracts.

DISCUSSION: In high-context cultures (e.g., Japanese, Chinese, Arabic, and Korean), much meaning is transmitted by nonverbal cues and situational circumstances. Thus, a person's status in a firm, rank in society, and reputation convey the primary message. In low-context cultures (e.g., northern Europe and North America), primary messages are transmitted verbally. Hence, precise written contractual agreements are highly valued. In contrast, social events are more highly valued in a high-context culture. Attitudes, tastes, behavior, and social codes are cultural factors. Accordingly, a preference for personal relationships rather than precise written contracts is a cultural factor.

Answer (B) is incorrect. Distribution, customization, and responsiveness are the commercial factors. Answer (C) is incorrect. Standards, spatial presence, transportation, and languages are technical factors. Answer (D) is incorrect. Regulation and national security issues are legal factors.

20. Zing Consulting recently hosted a workshop to educate international managers about the beliefs and morals of the foreign country where they will be conducting business. This workshop is an example of

A. Hands-on experience.

B. Awareness training.

C. Documentary programs.

D. Sensitivity training.

Answer (D) is correct.

REQUIRED: The type of workshop described.

DISCUSSION: Sensitivity training is focused mainly on educating workers about the beliefs and mores of the foreign country. Special care is given to topics that might embarrass a manager or offend his or her hosts.

Answer (A) is incorrect. Experience in the field involves actually traveling to the foreign country and interacting with its people. Usually, one or more guides are available to answer questions and provide feedback. Answer (B) is incorrect. "Awareness training" is not a meaningful term in this context. Answer (C) is incorrect. Documentary programs provide a text-based or video preview of the history, culture, institutions, beliefs, and economy of the foreign culture.

Access the **CIA Review System** from your Gleim Personal Classroom to continue your studies with exam-emulating multiple-choice questions!

STUDY UNIT TWENTY
LEGAL, ECONOMIC, AND REGULATORY ISSUES

(20 pages of outline)

This study unit is the second of two covering **Section VIII: Global Business Environment** from The IIA's CIA Exam Syllabus. This section makes up 0% to 10% of Part 3 of the CIA exam and is tested at the **awareness level**. Also covered in this study unit is Taxation schemes from **Section VII: Financial Management**. The relevant portions of the syllabus are highlighted below. (The complete syllabus is in Appendix A.)

VII. **FINANCIAL MANAGEMENT (10%–20%)**

    A. **Financial Accounting and Finance**

        12. Taxation schemes (e.g., tax shelters, VAT)

NOTE: The rest of item VII.A. is covered in Study Units 14-16.

VIII. **GLOBAL BUSINESS ENVIRONMENT (0%–10%)**

    A. **Economic/Financial Environments**

    B. **Cultural/Political Environments**

    C. **Legal and Economics — General Concepts (e.g., contracts)**

    D. **Impact of Government Legislation and Regulation on Business (e.g., trade legislation)**

20.1 CONTRACTS

1. **Contract Law**

    a. No part of commercial law is more important than contract law. Billions of contract-based agreements to transfer property and services are negotiated daily by individuals, businesses, and governments.

    b. Promise keeping is essential for planning in a modern complex society. Without a legal system committed to enforcement of private contracts, everyday transactions in a free-enterprise economy would be impossible.

        1) Contract law allows parties to enter into private agreements with assurance that they are enforceable against a party that fails to perform.

    c. A contract is a promise or an agreement that the law recognizes as establishing a duty of performance. It is enforceable by applying a remedy for its breach.

2. **Agreement**

    a. The most basic element of a contract is a voluntary agreement by the parties. Agreement requires the mutual assent of the contracting parties reached through an offer by the offeror and acceptance by the offeree.

b.   An offer is a statement or other communication that, if not terminated, confers upon the offeree the power of acceptance. An offer need not be in any particular form to be valid. It must

1)   Be communicated to an offeree,
2)   Indicate an intent to enter into a contract, and
3)   Be sufficiently definite and certain.

c.   Communication of an offer may be done in various ways and may occur over time. However, at some moment in the formation of a contract, each party expresses an intent to enter into a legally binding and enforceable agreement.

1)   Whether an offer has been made is determined by an objective standard that uses the following test: Would a reasonable person assume that the power of acceptance had been conferred upon him or her, i.e., that an offer has been made?

a)   An offer must be made with serious intent, not in anger, great excitement, or jest.

2)   Language constituting an offer should be distinguished from that merely soliciting or inviting offers. Communications between parties may simply be preliminary negotiations concerning a possible contract. A party may initiate negotiations by suggesting the general nature of a possible contract.

d.   An offer also must be definite and certain. If an offer is indefinite or vague or lacking an essential provision, no agreement arises from an attempt to accept it because the courts cannot tell what the parties are bound to do.

1)   However, minor details left for future determination do not make an agreement too vague to be an offer.

e.   An offer does not remain effective forever. The offer will terminate under any of the following circumstances:

1)   Revocation by the offeror,
2)   Rejection or counteroffer by the offeree,
3)   Death or incompetency of either the offeror or offeree,
4)   Destruction of the specific subject matter to which the offer relates,
5)   Subsequent illegality of the offer, or
6)   Lapse of a specified or reasonable time.

f.   Acceptance of an offer is essential to the formation of a contract. An agreement consists of an offer and an acceptance.

1)   To be effective, an acceptance must relate to the terms of the offer. The acceptance must be positive, unequivocal, and unconditional. It may not change, subtract from, add to, or qualify in any way the terms of the offer.

3.   **Consideration**

a.   Consideration is what is given to make a promise enforceable. It is the primary basis for the enforcement of agreements in contract law. Ordinarily, if a promise is not supported by consideration, it is not enforceable.

b.   One requirement of consideration is mutuality of obligation. Both parties must give consideration. Consequently, something of legal value must be given in a bargained-for exchange when the parties intend an exchange.

c.   The second required element of consideration is legal sufficiency (something of legal value). Consideration is legally sufficient to render a promise enforceable if the promisor receives a legal benefit or the promisee incurs a legal detriment.

   1)   To incur a legal detriment, the promisee must do (or promise to do) something that (s)he is not legally obligated to do. A legal detriment also consists of not doing (or promising not to do) something (s)he is legally entitled to do.

      a)   A cause-and-effect relationship must exist between the promise made by one party and the detriment incurred by the other.

4.   **Capacity**

   a.   Parties to a contract must possess legal capacity. Capacity is the mental ability to make a rational decision, which includes the ability to perceive and appreciate all relevant facts. Three classes of parties are legally limited in their capacity to contract: minors (also known as infants), mentally incompetent persons, and intoxicated parties.

      1)   For public policy reasons, parties in these three groups are protected from the enforcement of most contracts against them.

5.   **Legality**

   a.   Legality is an essential requirement for an agreement to be valid and enforceable. Formation or performance of an agreement may violate a criminal law, constitute a civil wrong upon which a suit may be filed, or be determined by a court to be contrary to public policy. In these instances, the agreement is illegal and unenforceable.

   b.   An agreement that is contrary to public policy has a negative effect on society that outweighs the interests of the parties. This principle reflects a balancing by the courts of freedom of contract and the public interest. Examples of agreements that may violate public policy are

      1)   Agreements to unduly restrain competition;
      2)   Clauses that excuse one of the parties from any liability;
      3)   Contracts calling for immoral or illegal acts; and
      4)   Agreements found to be unfair, oppressive, or unconscionable.

6.   **Written Contracts**

   a.   An oral contract is as enforceable as a written contract. However, the statute of frauds may require that some contracts be in writing to be enforceable. For example, the following are required to be in writing to be enforceable:

      1)   Contracts for the sale of an interest in land

      2)   Contracts that by their terms cannot possibly be performed within 1 year (e.g., some employment contracts)

      3)   Contracts to answer for the debt or duty of another (e.g., a guarantee or a suretyship)

      4)   Contracts for the sale of goods for US $500 or more

Stop and review! You have completed the outline for this subunit. Study multiple-choice questions 1 and 2 beginning on page 518.

20.2 ECONOMIC MEASURES

1. **Measuring the Gross Domestic Product**

   a. The **gross domestic product (GDP)** is the principal measure of national economic performance. It is the total market value of all final goods and services produced within the boundaries of a country, whether by domestic of foreign-owned sources, during a specified period of time (usually a year).

      1) To avoid double counting, the value added to each good or service at each stage of production incrementally over the period must be summed. Alternatively, the total market value of all final goods and services may be added.

   b. GDP is calculated without regard to the ownership of productive resources. Thus, the value of the output of a factory abroad is excluded regardless of the ownership, but the output of a foreign-owned factory is included in the host country's GDP.

   c. Three approaches to the measurement of GDP are available: the expenditures approach, the income approach, and the production approach.

      1) The expenditures approach calculates GDP as the sum of all expenditures in the economy.

	Personal consumption expenditures
+	Investment expenditures by business
+	Governmental expenditures for goods and services
+	Net exports (Total exports – Total imports)
	Gross domestic product (GDP)

      2) The income approach arrives at the same total GDP as the expenditures approach through a different calculation.

	Salaries and wages
+	Rental income
+	Interest income
+	Profits of corporations, proprietors, and partnerships
	National income
+	Indirect business taxes
+	Net income of foreigners
	Net domestic product (NDP)
+	Depreciation (consumption of fixed capital)
	Gross domestic product (GDP)

         a) The income approach produces two intermediate figures that macroeconomists find useful: national income and net domestic product.

      3) The production approach calculates GDP by estimating the gross value of domestic sales and subtracting the costs of materials, supplies, and services used to produce final goods and services.

   d. GDP is a monetary measure; therefore, comparing GDP over time requires adjustment (of nominal GDP) for changes in the price level.

      1) **Nominal GDP** (the basic GDP) involves adding the total market value of all final goods and services in current dollars.

      2) **Real GDP.** To facilitate year-to-year comparisons, nominal GDP is adjusted for changes in the general price level so it can be reported in constant currency (the consumer price index is discussed on page 504).

$$Real\ GDP\ =\ \frac{Nominal\ GDP}{Price\ index\ (in\ hundredths)}$$

2. **Business Cycles**

    a. Economic growth can be measured as an increase in real GDP or in real per capita GDP over a period of time.

    b. Economic growth is not always steady. The overall trend of growth is periodically interrupted by periods of instability. This tendency toward instability within the context of overall growth is termed the business cycle and can be depicted by the following graph:

    The Business Cycle

    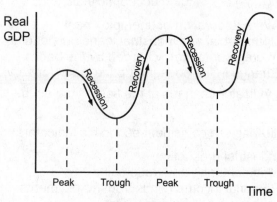

    Figure 20-1

    1) At a **peak**, the economy is at full employment and produces maximum output for the current level of resources and technology.

    2) A **recession** is defined as a period during which real GDP falls and unemployment rises.

        a) A severe recession with a decrease in prices is called depression.

    3) In a **trough**, economic activity reaches its lowest ebb.

    4) During a **recovery**, output and employment rise.

3. **Economic Indicators**

    a. Economists use economic indicators to forecast changes in economic activity. Economic indicators are variables that in the past have had a high correlation with the change in GDP.

        1) The best-known sets of economic indicators are those prepared by The Conference Board, a private research group.

        2) Indicators may lead, lag, or coincide with economic activity.

    b. A leading economic indicator is a forecast of future economic trends.

        1) A change in any of the following leading economic indicators suggests a future change in real GDP in the same direction:

            a) The average workweek for production workers
            b) New orders for consumer goods and materials
            c) Stock prices
            d) New orders for nondefense capital goods
            e) Building permits for houses
            f) The money supply
            g) Index of consumer indications
            h) The spread between short-term and long-term interest rates

2) A change in either of the following leading economic indicators suggests a future change in real GDP in the opposite direction:

   a) Initial claims for unemployment insurance (because more people out of work indicates slowing business activity)

   b) Vendor performance (because vendors have slack time and are carrying high levels of inventory)

c. A lagging indicator changes after the change in the economic activity has occurred.

   1) The following are lagging economic indicators:

      a) Average duration of unemployment
      b) Commercial and industrial loans outstanding
      c) Average prime rate charged by the banks
      d) Change in the consumer price index for services

d. A coincident indicator changes at the same time as the change in the economic activity.

   1) The following are coincident economic indicators:

      a) Industrial production
      b) Manufacturing and trade sales
      c) Personal income minus transfer payments

4. **Inflation and Consumer Price Index**

   a. **Inflation** is an increase in the general level of prices in the economy. The value of any unit of money (e.g., the U.S. dollar) is measured by how many goods and services can be acquired in exchange for it. This is referred to as a currency's purchasing power.

      1) Thus, an inflation in currency is a decrease in the purchasing power of that currency.

   b. A **consumer price index (CPI)** is a measure of the price of a market basket of goods and services in 1 year compared with the price in a designated base year. By definition, the index for the base year is 100.

$$CPI = \frac{Cost\ of\ market\ basket\ in\ current\ year}{Cost\ of\ market\ basket\ in\ base\ year} \times 100$$

   c. The rate of inflation is calculated by comparing the change in the 2 years' consumer price indexes.

$$\frac{Current\text{-}year\ price\ index\ -\ Prior\text{-}year\ price\ index}{Prior\text{-}year\ price\ index}$$

EXAMPLE

If the price index of the market basket was 10% higher than the base year in Year 3 and was 15% higher in Year 4, the inflation rate for Year 4 is

$$\frac{115 - 110}{110} = 4.55\%$$

---

d. The distinction between nominal income and real income is important for understanding the effect of inflation.

   1) **Nominal income** is the amount of money received by a consumer as wages, interest, rent, and profits.

   2) **Real income** is the purchasing power of the income received, regardless of how it is denominated. Purchasing power relates directly to the consumer's standard of living.

   3) Real income shrinks when nominal income does not keep pace with inflation.

    e.   The efficiency of business relationships and growth rely on relatively stable pricing (low inflation). When inflation is unexpected and high, it can cause economic chaos and reduce the efficiency of business relationships.

        1)   There are two types of inflation:

            a)   **Demand-pull inflation** is generated by demand outpacing the supply of goods to satisfy it. Since the economy cannot produce enough to keep up with demand, the prices of existing goods are bid up.

            b)   **Cost-push inflation** is generated by increased per-unit production costs, which are passed on to consumers in the form of higher prices. Increases in raw materials costs are the principal cause.

5.   **Unemployment**

    a.   Unemployment is the failure of the economy to fully employ its labor force.

    b.   **Frictional unemployment** is the amount of unemployment caused by the normal operation of the labor market.

        1)   Frictionally unemployed people include those moving to another place, those ceasing work temporarily to pursue further education and training, and those who are simply between jobs.

        2)   This definition acknowledges that a certain amount of unemployment exists at any given time.

    c.   **Structural unemployment** results when the composition of the workforce does not match the need. It is the result of changes in consumer demand, technology, and geographical location.

        1)   As consumers' desires shift, certain skills become obsolete.

        2)   For example, the computer revolution has drastically changed the skills required for many jobs and completely eliminated others.

    d.   **Cyclical unemployment** is directly related to the level of an economy's output. For this reason, it is sometimes called deficient-demand unemployment.

        1)   As consumers slow their spending, entities cut back production and lay off workers.

    e.   **Full Employment**

        1)   The natural rate of unemployment consists of the sum of frictional and structural unemployment.

            a)   Economists consider the economy to be at full employment when all unemployed workers are in these categories.

            b)   The rate varies over time because of demographic and institutional changes in the economy.

        2)   The economy's potential output is the real (inflation-adjusted) domestic output that could be achieved if the economy sustained full employment.

            a)   This concept illustrates the importance of providing all interested workers with productive jobs.

    f.   **Macroeconomic Effects of Unemployment**

        1)   Lost value to the economy is the primary economic cost of unemployment. The goods not produced and services not provided by idle workers can never be regained.

        2)   Unemployment has social costs, including loss of skills, personal and family stress, violence and other crime, and social upheaval.

6.   **Monetary Policy**

a.   Money is created by a country's banking system. The level of economic activity in an economy is closely related to its supply of money. Any policy designed to affect the money supply, and thus the economy, is considered monetary policy.

   1)   The central bank controls the money supply. A change in the money supply has an inverse effect on interest rates in the economy.

      a)   The Federal Reserve Board, also known as the Fed, is the body responsible for managing the supply of money in the United States.

      b)   The European Central Bank (ECB) is the main body responsible for managing the supply of money in the European Union.

b.   The purpose of monetary policy is to balance the goals of gradual, steady economic growth and price stability (manageable inflation). A change in the money supply affects the economy by changing the interest rate.

   1)   An increase in the money supply (expansionary monetary policy) decreases the interest rate in the economy, which stimulates investment spending by businesses and increases GDP.

   2)   A decrease in the money supply (tight monetary policy) increases the interest rate in the economy, which in turn depresses investment spending by businesses. A fall in investment spending reduces GDP, which decreases the price level and reduces inflation.

c.   A nation's central bank has the following three main tools of monetary policy at its disposal to achieve its goals.

   1)   **Open-market operations** are the most valuable tool. The central bank can either purchase government securities from, or sell them to, commercial banks. For example:

      a)   United States experiences high inflation. The Fed wishes to tighten the money supply. The Fed sells government securities on the open market; i.e., it takes money out of the economy and gives securities in exchange.

      b)   United States experiences a recession. The Fed wishes to loosen the money supply. The Fed purchases governmental securities on the open market; i.e., it takes securities off the market and injects money.

   2)   Changes in the **required reserve ratio** are used less frequently. A commercial bank must have a certain percentage of its total deposits on reserve. The required reserve ratio is the percentage of deposits that must be kept on hand.

      a)   Lowering the percentage is expansionary monetary policy. It allows the banks to put more of their excess reserves into issuing loans, increasing the money supply.

      b)   Raising the percentage has the opposite effect.

   3)   Changing the **discount rate** at which banks can borrow money from the central bank.

      a)   Lowering the discount rate encourages borrowing. As more banks borrow, the money supply will increase.

      b)   Raising the discount rate discourages borrowing. As fewer banks borrow, the money supply will decrease.

Stop and review! You have completed the outline for this subunit. Study multiple-choice questions 3 through 7 beginning on page 519.

20.3 INTERNATIONAL TRADE

1.   **Comparative Advantage**

   a.   The laws of supply and demand affect imports and exports in the same way that they affect domestic goods. For example, a decrease in oil production in a single country can raise the world price of oil.

      1)   Net exports is the amount of a country's exports minus its imports. A nation has net imports if its imports exceed its exports.

   b.   The exchange ratio (terms of trade) is the ratio of a country's exports relative to its imports.

$$Terms\ of\ trade\ =\ \frac{Price\ of\ exportable\ goods}{Price\ of\ importable\ goods}\ \times\ 100$$

EXAMPLE

Country A's entire exports for the year consist of US $800,000 worth of coffee to Country B. Country B's entire exports consist of US $1,000,000 worth of concrete to Country A.

Country A's terms of trade is thus 80 [(US $800,000 ÷ $1,000,000) × 100]. Country B's terms of trade is 125 [(US $1,000,000 ÷ $800,000) × 100].

---

      1)   When the ratio falls, a country is said to have deteriorating terms of trade. When the ratio is less than 100, the country is an overall loser in terms of world trade.

   c.   Countries vary greatly in their efficiency in producing certain goods because of differences in such factors as the following:

      1)   Climatic and geographical conditions
      2)   Human capacities
      3)   Supply and type of capital accumulation
      4)   Proportions of resources
      5)   Political and social climates

   d.   Given these differences, countries can mutually benefit from trade.

      1)   The greatest advantage from trade is obtained when each nation specializes in producing what it can produce most efficiently or, more precisely, least inefficiently.

         a)   If nations specialize and then exchange with others, more is produced and consumed than if each nation tries to be self-sufficient.

      2)   Specialization of labor is beneficial for individuals. The same principle applies to nations.

      3)   The reason for this phenomenon is **comparative advantage**.

         a)   Comparative advantage is based on the principle of relative opportunity costs.

         b)   A country has a comparative advantage in the production of a good when it has a lower opportunity cost than another producer. That is, it has to sacrifice fewer units of another good to generate an additional unit of the first good.

         c)   A nation theoretically exports goods in which it has a comparative advantage and imports goods in which it has a comparative disadvantage.

2.   **Trade Barriers**

a.   According to classical economics, individuals (as a whole) are best off under free trade. However, governments often establish policies designed to interfere in the workings of the marketplace.

b.   **Protectionism** is any measure taken by a government to protect domestic producers. Protectionism takes many forms.

1)   **Tariffs** are consumption taxes designed to restrict imports, e.g., a tax on German beer. Governments raise tariffs to discourage consumption of imported products. Domestic producers are not subject to the tariff and will therefore have a price advantage over their foreign competitors. However, absent such competition, the domestic price of the item will be higher. Domestic producers will sell more at a higher price, and domestic consumers will consume less following the price increase.

a)   Revenue tariffs are usually applied to products that are not produced domestically. Their purpose is to provide the government with tax revenue.

2)   **Trade quotas** set fixed limits on different products, e.g., French wine.

a)   In the short run, trade quotas will help a country's balance of payments position by increasing domestic employment, but the prices of the products produced also will increase.

b)   Trade quotas can save domestic jobs. Thus, unemployment will decline. Because jobs will be saved in industries that are less efficient than foreign competitors, productivity will decline.

c)   An **embargo** is a total ban on some kinds of imports. It is an extreme form of the trade quota.

3)   **Domestic content rules** require that at least a portion of any imported product be constructed from parts manufactured in the importing nation.

a)   This rule is sometimes used by capital-intensive nations. Parts can be produced using idle capacity and then sent to a labor-intensive country for final assembly.

4)   **Voluntary export restrictions** are agreements entered into by exporters to reduce the number of products made available in a foreign country in an attempt to avoid official sanctions.

a)   These restrictions can harm consumers. Because the supply of the product desired by consumers in the importing country is held artificially low, the exporter sometimes can charge a price high enough to earn abnormal profits.

5)   A **trigger price mechanism** automatically imposes a tariff barrier against unfairly cheap imports by levying a duty (tariff) on all imports below a particular price (the price that activates the tariff).

6)   **Antidumping rules** prevent foreign producers from selling excess goods on the domestic market at less than cost to eliminate competitors and gain control of the market.

7)   **Exchange controls** limit foreign currency transactions and set exchange rates. The purpose is to limit the ability of a seller to remove (repatriate) its earnings from the country.

    8)   **Export subsidies** are payments by the government to producers in certain industries in an attempt to increase exports.

        a)   A government may impose countervailing duties on imported goods if those goods were produced in a foreign country with the aid of a governmental subsidy.

    9)   **Special tax benefits** to exporters are an indirect form of export subsidy. However, the WTO has ruled some of these tax benefits to be illegal.

    10)   Certain exports may require licenses. For example, sales of technology with military applications are limited by western nations that are members of the Coordinating Committee for Multilateral Export Controls.

    11)   An extreme form of protectionism is the expropriation of the assets of a foreign entity. It is also the greatest political risk of doing business abroad.

  c.   The economic effects of tariffs and quotas can be summarized as follows:

    1)   Workers are shifted from relatively efficient export industries into less efficient, protected industries. Real wages decline as a result, as does total world output.

    2)   Under a tariff, the excess paid by the customer for an imported good goes into the government treasury where it can be spent for any purpose.

        a)   Under a quota, prices are also driven up (by the induced shortage), but the excess goes to the exporter in the foreign country.

    3)   A tariff is imposed on all importers equally. Thus, the more efficient ones will still be able to set their prices lower than the less efficient ones.

        a)   An import quota, on the other hand, does not affect foreign importers equally. Import licenses may be assigned as much for political favoritism as on any other grounds.

  d.   Advocates of trade barriers advance three basic arguments in favor of protectionism:

    1)   Reducing imports protects domestic jobs.
    2)   Certain industries are essential to national security.
    3)   Industries need protection in the early stages of development.

  e.   Some special-interest groups are strong and well-organized. They lobby effectively to pass legislation that restricts free trade.

Stop and review! You have completed the outline for this subunit. Study multiple-choice questions 8 through 11 beginning on page 520.

20.4 CURRENCY EXCHANGE RATES AND MARKETS

1.   **Buying in a Foreign Market**

  a.   Sellers who engage in international trade generally require that they be paid in their own currency.

    1)   For international exchanges to occur, the seller's currency and the buyer's currency must be easily converted at some prevailing exchange rate. (An exchange rate is the price of one country's currency in terms of another country's currency.)

2.   **Fixed Exchange Rates**

  a.   One unit of a currency is set equal to a given number of units of another currency by law.

EXAMPLE

In July 1986, the Saudi riyal was fixed at a ratio of 3.75 riyals to 1 U.S. dollar. Because the U.S. buys a large quantity of oil from Saudi Arabia, this fixed rate has the advantage of adding stability to the U.S. oil market.

3.   **Floating (Flexible) Exchange Rates**

a.   The market is allowed to determine the exchange rate of two currencies.

1)   Thus, supply and demand functions exist for currencies.

2)   The rate at which the supply and demand for a currency in terms of another currency are equal is the equilibrium exchange rate.

EXAMPLE

Given the supply and demand curves below, domestic parties can exchange 20 local currency units (LCUs) for 1 foreign currency unit (FCU).

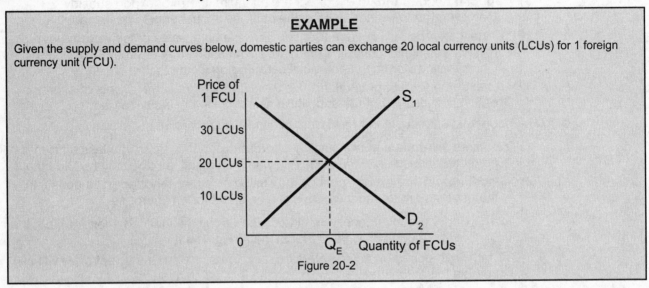

Figure 20-2

---

b.   A seller normally wants to be paid in its own currency. Thus, when the demand for a foreign country's products rises, demand for its currency also rises.

EXAMPLE

Assuming a fixed supply of FCUs, the equilibrium price of FCUs increases. This relationship is depicted by the rightward shift of the demand curve below:

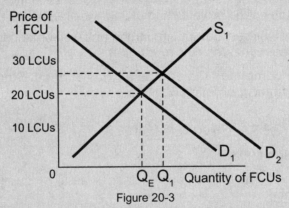

Figure 20-3

If a domestic buyer wants 1 FCU, it must pay 27.5 LCUs. Thus, LCUs have lost purchasing power (depreciated), and FCUs have gained purchasing power (appreciated).

---

1)   In general, the purchasing power of a currency moves in the same direction as demand for that country's output.

c.   When one currency can be exchanged for more units of another currency, the first currency is said to have **appreciated (strengthened)** with respect to the second currency. By the same token, the second currency is said to have **depreciated (weakened)** against the first.

EXAMPLE

A U.S. company buys merchandise from an EU company for €1,000,000, due in 60 days. On the day of the sale, US $0.795 is required to buy a single euro. By the 60th day, US $0.812 is required to buy a euro. The dollar has thus weakened against the euro, and the euro has strengthened against the dollar; i.e., the dollar has lost purchasing power with respect to the euro. The U.S. firm only needed US $795,000 to pay off a €1,000,000 debt on the date of sale but must now use US $812,000 to pay off the €1,000,000 debt.

---

    d.   The following factors affect currency exchange rates:

       1)   **Relative income levels** – Citizens with higher incomes look for new consumption opportunities in other countries, driving up the demand for those currencies.

           a)   Thus, as incomes rise in one country, the prices of foreign currencies rise as well, and the local currency will depreciate.

       2)   **Relative interest rates** – When the interest rates in a given country rise relative to those of other countries, more investors purchase the high-interest country's currency to make investments, driving up the demand for this currency.

           a)   Thus, as interest rates increase in one country, the prices of the local currency rise as well, and the local currency will appreciate.

       3)   **Relative inflation rates** – When the rate of inflation in a given country rises relative to the rates of other countries, the products of that country become relatively expensive and the demand for that country's currency falls.

           a)   Thus, as a result of inflation in a foreign country, the domestic currency has appreciated with respect to the currency of the foreign country with higher inflation.

           b)   The difference between the countries' inflation rates is approximately equal to the change in the currency exchange rate between the two countries.

  4. **Spot and Forward Exchange Rates**

    a.   Exchange rates are set in the spot market and the forward market. The relevant market depends on when the transaction will be settled.

       1)   The **spot rate** is the number of units of a foreign currency that can be received today in exchange for a single unit of the domestic currency.

EXAMPLE

A currency trader is willing to give 1.6 Swiss francs today in exchange for a single British pound. Today's spot rate for the pound is therefore 1.6 Swiss francs, and today's spot rate for the franc is £0.625 (1 ÷ F1.6).

---

       2)   The **forward rate** is the number of units of a foreign currency that can be received in exchange for a single unit of the domestic currency at some definite date in the future.

EXAMPLE

The currency trader contracts to provide 1.8 Swiss francs in exchange for a single British pound 30 days from now. Today's 30-day forward rate for the pound is therefore 1.8 Swiss francs, and the 30-day forward rate for the franc is £0.555 (1 ÷ F1.8).

---

    b.   If the domestic currency fetches more units of a foreign currency in the forward market than in the spot market, the domestic currency is said to be trading at a **forward premium** with respect to the foreign currency.

EXAMPLE

Since the pound is fetching more francs in the forward market than in the spot market (F1.8 > F1.6), the pound is currently trading at a forward premium with respect to the franc. This reflects the market's belief that the pound is going to increase in value in relation to the franc.

---

    c.   If the domestic currency fetches fewer units of a foreign currency in the forward market than in the spot market, the domestic currency is said to be trading at a **forward discount** with respect to the foreign currency.

EXAMPLE

Since the franc is fetching fewer pounds in the forward market than in the spot market (£0.555 < £0.625), the franc is currently trading at a forward discount with respect to the pound. This reflects the market's belief that the franc is going to lose value in relation to the pound.

---

    d.   The implications of these relationships can be generalized as follows:

If the domestic currency is trading at a	Then it is expected to
Forward premium	Gain purchasing power
Forward discount	Lose purchasing power

5. **Mitigating Exchange Rate Risk**

    a.   Fluctuations in currency exchange rates can have a significant impact on a firm's profitability.

    b.   Transaction exposure is the exposure to fluctuations in exchange rates between the date a transaction is entered into and the settlement date.

        1)   To address transaction exposure, a firm must

            a)   Estimate its net cash flows in each currency for impacted transactions.
            b)   Measure the potential effect of exposure in each currency.
            c)   Use hedging tools to mitigate exposure to exchange rate fluctuations.

    c.   Basic Hedging Principles

        1)   When a debtor is to pay a foreign currency at some point in the future, the risk is that the foreign currency will appreciate in the meantime, making it more expensive in terms of the debtor's domestic currency. The hedge is to purchase the foreign currency forward to lock in a definite price.

EXAMPLE

A U.S. company knows that it will need 100,000 Canadian dollars in 60 days to pay an invoice. The firm thus hedges by purchasing 100,000 Canadian dollars 60 days forward. The company is essentially buying a guarantee that it will have C $100,000 available for use in 60 days. The 60-day forward rate for a Canadian dollar is US $0.99. Thus, for the privilege of having a guaranteed receipt of 100,000 Canadian dollars, the company will commit now to paying US $99,000 in 60 days.

---

        2)   When a creditor is to receive a foreign currency at some point in the future, the risk is that the foreign currency will depreciate in the meantime, making it worth less in terms of the creditor's domestic currency. The hedge is to sell the foreign currency forward to lock in a definite price.

EXAMPLE

A U.S. company knows that it will be receiving 5,000,000 pesos in 30 days from the sale of some equipment at one of its facilities in Mexico. The spot rate for a peso is US $0.77, and the 30-day forward rate is US $0.80. The firm wants to be sure that it will be able sell the pesos it will be receiving in 30 days for US $0.80 each. The firm thus hedges by selling 5,000,000 pesos 30 days forward. The company is buying a guarantee that it will be able to sell 5,000,000 pesos in 30 days and receive US $4,000,000 (5,000,000 × US $0.80) in return.

Stop and review! You have completed the outline for this subunit. Study multiple-choice questions 12 through 15 beginning on page 521.

20.5 METHODS OF TAXATION

1. **Tax Uses**

   a. Government, at all levels, finances its expenditures by taxation. Thus, taxes generate government revenues. National governments also use taxation as a means of implementing fiscal policy regarding inflation, full employment, economic growth, etc.

   b. One reason for taxation is that individuals should pay tax based on the benefits received from the services (e.g., paying for the use of a public park or swimming pool). Another view is that consumers should pay taxes based on their ability to pay (e.g., taxes on income and wealth).

2. **Tax Rate Structures**

   a. **Progressive.** Higher income persons pay a higher percentage of their income in taxes.

      1) Indexing is a means of avoiding the unfairness that results when inflation increases nominal but not real taxable income, subjecting it to higher tax rates. Adjusting tax bracket, deduction, and exemption amounts by reference to some index of inflation avoids this problem.

   b. **Proportional.** At all levels of income, the percentage paid in taxes is constant.

   c. **Regressive.** As income increases, the percentage paid in taxes decreases (e.g., sales, payroll, property, or excise taxes). For example, an excise tax is regressive because its burden falls disproportionately on lower-income persons. As personal income increases, the percentage of income paid declines because an excise tax is a flat amount per quantity of the good or service purchased.

      1) An **excise tax** increases the selling price of the product. This price increase will have a less negative effect on sales volume for products with less elastic demand. Examples of products with low elasticity of demand include gasoline, tobacco, and alcohol. The tax revenue generated by an increase in excise taxes is therefore higher if the tax is levied on products with less elastic demand.

         a) Demand is price elastic if a given percentage change in price results in a greater percentage change in revenues in the opposite direction.

3. **Tax Rates**

   a. The marginal tax rate is the rate applied to the last unit of taxable income.

      1) The **average tax rate** is the total tax liability divided by the amount of taxable income.

      2) The **effective tax rate** is the total tax liability divided by total economic income (includes amounts that do not have tax consequences).

4. **Direct vs. Indirect**

   a. Direct taxes are imposed upon the taxpayer and paid directly to the government, e.g., the personal income tax.

      1) Indirect taxes are levied against others and therefore only indirectly on the individual taxpayer, e.g., corporate income taxes.

5. **Tax Credits**

   a. Tax credits, e.g., the Investment Tax Credit, are deductions on the income tax return that lower investment cost and increase a project's net present value.

6. **Incidence of Taxation**

    a.   Who actually bears a particular tax is not always obvious. Accordingly, the person who actually bears an indirect tax may not be the one who pays the tax to the government.

    b.   The incidence of taxation is important when a government wants to change the tax structure. Because taxation is a form of fiscal policy, the government needs to know who will actually bear the burden of a tax, not just who will statutorily pay it.

    c.   Taxes such as the corporate income tax and corporate property and excise taxes are often shifted to customers in the form of higher prices.

          1)   However, sellers ordinarily must bear part of the burden. Passing on the entire tax might reduce unit sales unacceptably by raising the price too high. Thus, the effect of the tax is to reduce supply (because suppliers' costs increase) and quantity demanded by buyers (because the price increases). The combined loss of sellers and buyers is called the deadweight loss or excess burden of taxation.

    d.   Taxes such as windfall profits taxes are not shifted to customers via higher prices. This type of one-time-only tax levied on part of the output produced does not increase the equilibrium price of the taxed good.

    e.   Supply-side economists use the Laffer Curve to attempt to explain how people react to varying rates of income taxation. For example, if the income tax rate is 0%, zero revenue will be raised by government. Similarly, if the tax rate is 100%, income tax revenue will probably be zero because an earner who faces a tax rate of 100% will not work.

          1)   The optimal income tax rate will bring in the most revenue possible. A rate that is either too high or too low will generate less than optimal tax revenues.

          2)   Supply-side economists do not state that lowering income tax rates will produce more revenue. Instead, they claim that, if the rates are too high, lowering rates will produce more revenue because output and national income will increase. This result, in theory, should follow because of increased incentives to work, invest, and save.

          3)   However, economic policy should not be confused with political considerations. There are obvious political reasons for having higher or lower tax rates on certain income levels. Thus, the theory underlying the Laffer Curve does not address questions of redistributionist politics.

          4)   A criticism of the Laffer Curve is that it does not prescribe the optimal tax rate. The only way to know whether the current tax rates are too high or too low is to change them and see whether revenues increase.

              a)   Critics also have observed that the incentives provided by tax cuts may have relatively small supply-side effects and that those effects may be felt only in the very long run.

              b)   Still another potential problem is that cutting taxes in an expanding economy may overstimulate demand, thereby increasing inflation.

7. **International Tax Considerations**

    a.   Multinational corporations frequently derive income from several countries. The government of each country in which a corporation does business may enact statutes imposing one or more types of tax on the corporation.

    b.   Treaties. To avoid double taxation, two or more countries may adopt treaties to coordinate or synchronize the effects of their taxing statutes.

          1)   Treaties also are used to integrate other governmental goals, e.g., providing incentives for desired investment.

          2)   A treaty might modify the rules in a country's statutes that designate the source country of income or the domicile of an entity.

    c.   Multinational Corporations

        1)   Most countries tax only the income sourced to that country.

        2)   But some countries tax worldwide income (from whatever source derived) of a domestic corporation. Double taxation is avoided by allowing a credit for income tax paid to foreign countries or by treaty provisions.

        3)   In the case of foreign corporations, a country may tax only income sourced to it. Ordinarily, such income is effectively connected with engaging in a trade or business of the country. Certain source income, e.g., gain on the sale of most shares, may not be taxed.

8.   **Value-Added Tax (VAT)**

    a.   Many major industrial nations have adopted a value-added tax (VAT).

        1)   The tax is levied on the value added to goods by each business unit in the production and distribution chain. The amount of value added is the difference between sales and purchases. Each entity in the chain collects the tax on its sales, takes a credit for taxes paid on purchases, and remits the difference to the government.

        2)   The consumer ultimately bears the tax through higher prices.

        3)   A VAT encourages consumer savings because taxes are paid only on consumption, not on savings. Because the VAT is based on consumption, people in the lower income groups spend a greater proportion of their income on this type of tax. Thus, the VAT is regressive.

        4)   Only those businesses that make a profit have to pay income taxes. The VAT, however, requires all businesses to pay taxes, regardless of income.

        5)   The VAT tax is not a useful tool for fiscal policy purposes.

Stop and review! You have completed the outline for this subunit. Study multiple-choice questions 16 through 18 beginning on page 522.

20.6 REGULATION OF BUSINESS

1.   **Agencies and Commissions**

    a.   An administrative agency is any public officer or body that makes rules and renders decisions.

        1)   An agency or commission may regulate a specific industry or one area affecting all industries.

        2)   Agencies and commissions may have the functions of investigation, enforcement, rule making, and adjudication. They do not impose criminal sanctions.

        3)   They must act within the authority granted by the enabling statutes.

        4)   Administrative agency rules and regulations

            a)   Should not go beyond the scope of the delegated authority of its enabling statutes

            b)   May be issued under a general grant of authority to an agency to regulate an industry

            c)   May be issued under a specific grant of authority to an agency to make detailed rules carrying out objectives of a statute

        5)   Courts interpret statutes, regulations, and the actions of agencies when a dispute develops and one or both parties wish a judicial determination.

        6)   Some rules and regulations, agencies, and legislation have sunset provisions that require periodic review and reenactment. Otherwise, they terminate.

2. **Economic Regulation**

   a. Such regulation usually affects prices and service to the public and is ordinarily industry-specific.

3. **Social Regulation**

   a. This type of regulation has broader objectives and more extensive effects. It addresses quality of life issues that are difficult for market forces to remedy, such as workplace and product safety, pollution, and fair employment practices. It applies to most industries.

      1) Social regulation has been criticized on the grounds that it (a) is costly; (b) contributes to overregulation; (c) may inhibit innovation; (d) increases inflation; and (e) may place a disproportionate burden on small entities, thereby having an anticompetitive effect.

      2) Another criticism is that regulators are perceived to have little concern for the relation of marginal benefits and marginal costs.

4. **Securities Law**

   a. One purpose is to provide complete and fair disclosure to potential investors in an initial issuance of securities.

      1) Disclosure is through a filing with a government agency. Potential investors may be required to receive a disclosure document, the contents of which may be highly regulated.

      2) Exemptions. Certain securities and transactions may be exempt, for example, transactions by a person not an issuer, underwriter, or dealer. Other exemptions also may be available.

      3) Civil liability may be imposed on parties associated with a filing that contains a misstatement or omission of a material fact.

         a) Liability also may be imposed for (1) failing to make a required filing or to deliver a required disclosure document to investors or (2) making a sale prior to a required filing.

      4) Antifraud liability may be imposed on sellers in an initial issuance of securities. Liability also may result from selling a security using a communication containing an untrue statement, or an omission, of a material fact.

   b. Other purposes are to regulate trading of securities after initial issuance, provide adequate information to investors, and prevent insiders from unfairly using nonpublic information.

      1) Registration may be necessary for (a) securities exchanges, (b) brokers and dealers, (c) securities traded on exchanges, and (d) high-volume securities traded over the counter. Moreover, issuers may be required to file reports.

      2) Insiders (officers, directors, and certain shareholders) may be required to surrender to the entity any short-swing profits earned on purchases and sales. They also may be prohibited from buying or selling shares based on inside information not available to the public.

         a) Insider trading is buying or selling securities of an entity by any individuals who are aware of material nonpublic information not available to the general public. These individuals have a fiduciary obligation to shareholders or potential shareholders.

         b) Civil and criminal penalties for insider trading may be imposed.

3) Antifraud provisions related to subsequent trading may make unlawful any fraudulent scheme.

4) In some countries, legislation prohibits secret payments to persons in foreign countries for purposes contrary to public policy. Examples are corrupt payments to foreign officials, political parties, or candidates for office for the purpose of obtaining or retaining business.

5. **Antitrust Law**

    a. Competition controls private economic power, increases output, and lowers prices. It promotes the following:

    1) Efficient allocation of resources (resulting in lower prices)
    2) Greater choice by consumers
    3) Greater business opportunities
    4) Fairness in economic behavior
    5) Avoidance of concentrated political power resulting from economic power

    b. Restraints of trade in domestic or foreign commerce may be prohibited.

    1) But only unreasonable restraints may be illegal.
    2) Some restraints may be automatically treated as violations.

        a) Price fixing is usually the most prosecuted violation.

    c. Other antitrust laws may prohibit the acquisition of shares or assets of another entity if the effect may be to substantially lessen competition or to create a monopoly.

    1) The following are other actions that may be prohibited by antitrust laws:

        a) Tying or tie-in sales (sales in which a buyer must take other products to buy the first product)

        b) Exclusive dealing (a requirement by the seller that a buyer not deal with the seller's competitors)

        c) Price discrimination

            i) Sellers may not be allowed to grant, and buyers may not induce, unfair discounts and other preferences. However, price discrimination may be justified by cost savings or the need to meet competition.

    2) Interlocking directorates also could be prohibited even if the entities ceased to be competitors.

    d. Unfair methods of competition and unfair or deceptive acts in commerce, including false or misleading advertising, are antitrust violations in some countries.

6. **Consumer Protection**

    a. A government agency may help to maintain the safety of drugs, food, cosmetics, etc., and also may enforce laws requiring the labeling of hazardous substances.

    1) New drugs may be required to be thoroughly tested before they are marketed. But the premarket review is usually based upon research supplied by the manufacturers.

    b. Other consumer protection laws may

    1) Prohibit deceptive packaging and labeling.
    2) Give consumers the right to obtain the information reported by credit agencies.
    3) Protect the public from unreasonable risk of injury from consumer products. They may emphasize safety standards for new products.

      4) Prohibit discrimination in providing credit and

        a) Provide consumers with rights in contesting billing errors,

        b) Prohibit mailing of unsolicited credit cards, or

        c) Limit a consumer's liability for unauthorized use of lost or stolen credit cards.

      5) Regulate written warranties on consumer products.

      6) Prohibit abuses of consumers' rights by collection agencies.

      7) Require disclosure of the terms and conditions of consumer credit.

7. **Environmental Protection**

    a. An agency may be created to centralize environmental control functions of the national government.

    b. A national environmental policy may be established, and the consideration of environmental issues by government agencies may be promoted.

      1) Thus, agencies may be required to consider the adverse environmental effects of their actions, proposals, legislation, and regulations.

    c. Air quality standards may be established for listed pollutants. The law may determine emission standards for stationary and mobile sources of pollution.

    d. The law also may establish national water quality standards and pollution standards for each industry.

      1) It also may provide for a discharge permit program and grants and loans for publicly owned treatment plants.

      2) Additional provisions may apply to oil spills and toxic chemicals.

    e. Still other laws may be designed to control hazardous waste.

      1) Management requirements may be imposed on generators, transporters, and owners of hazardous waste and on operators of treatment, storage, and disposal facilities.

Stop and review! You have completed the outline for this subunit. Study multiple-choice questions 19 and 20 on page 523.

QUESTIONS

20.1 Contracts

1. Lamar became homeless at a very young age and was taken in by Aunt and Uncle. Many years later, Lamar became a detective in the city police department. When Aunt disappeared and was not heard from for a month, the case was assigned to Lamar. Uncle also came to Lamar and asked him to promise to find Aunt in return for the years of support. Lamar agreed to Uncle's request. Which of the following is true?

A. Lamar's contractual duty to find Aunt is based on past consideration.

B. Lamar has no contractual duty to find Aunt.

C. If Uncle had also promised Lamar US $1,000 for finding Aunt, he would be liable when Lamar found her.

D. Lamar will be liable for breach of contract if he does not find Aunt.

Answer (B) is correct.

    REQUIRED: The true statement regarding contractual duty.

    DISCUSSION: Lamar has a pre-existing legal duty to find Aunt. Consideration does not exist if an existing duty was imposed by law or a person is already under a contractual agreement to render a specified performance. Lamar will suffer no new legal detriment by promising to find Aunt. Thus, no contractual obligation exists.

    Answer (A) is incorrect. Past consideration does not satisfy the consideration requirement for the formation of a contract. Answer (C) is incorrect. Lamar has a pre-existing legal duty to find Aunt. Answer (D) is incorrect. Lamar has not made a valid contract with Uncle.

2. The necessary elements of a contract include

A. Some form of writing, equal consideration, and legal capacity.

B. Formal execution, definite terms, and a valid offer and acceptance.

C. Offer and acceptance, consideration, legal capacity, and mutual assent.

D. Bilateral promises, legal capacity, and legality of purpose.

Answer (C) is correct.
   REQUIRED: Elements of a contract that are necessary.
   DISCUSSION: Contracts require each of the following:

1. Offer and acceptance
2. Mutual assent (meeting of the minds)
3. Consideration (bargained-for exchange)
4. Legality (legal purpose)
5. Capacity of parties (legal ability)

   Answer (A) is incorrect. An oral contract is usually enforceable. Consideration must be legally sufficient and must be bargained for but need not have equal market value. Answer (B) is incorrect. Most contracts are informal (simple), and if a term is missing, it can be implied by the court, with the exception of a quantity term. Answer (D) is incorrect. Promises can be unilateral or divisible.

20.2 Economic Measures

3. Which of the following may provide a leading indicator of a future increase in gross domestic product?

A. A reduction in the money supply.

B. A decrease in the issuance of building permits.

C. An increase in the timeliness of delivery by vendors.

D. An increase in the average hours worked per week of production workers.

Answer (D) is correct.
   REQUIRED: The leading indicator.
   DISCUSSION: An economic indicator is highly correlated with changes in aggregate economic activity. A leading indicator changes prior to a change in the direction of the business cycle. The leading indicators included in the Conference Board's index are (1) average weekly hours worked by manufacturing workers, (2) unemployment claims, (3) consumer goods orders, (4) share prices, (5) orders for fixed assets, (6) building permits, (7) timeliness of deliveries, (8) money supply, (9) consumer confidence, and (10) the spread between the yield on 10-year Treasury bonds and the federal funds rate. An increase in weekly hours worked by production workers is favorable for economic growth.
   Answer (A) is incorrect. A falling money supply is associated with falling GDP. Answer (B) is incorrect. A decline in the issuance of building permits signals lower expected building activity and a falling GDP. Answer (C) is incorrect. An increase in the timeliness of delivery by vendors indicates reduced demand and potentially falling GDP.

4. If the government of a country uses its foreign currency reserves to <List A> its own currency in the foreign currency market, the effect is to <List B> domestic aggregate demand.

	List A	List B
A.	Purchase	Not affect
B.	Purchase	Decrease
C.	Sell	Not affect
D.	Sell	Decrease

Answer (B) is correct.
   REQUIRED: The effect on domestic aggregate demand of a government's purchase or sale of its own currency.
   DISCUSSION: Aggregate demand is the amount of real domestic output that domestic consumers, foreign buyers, governments, and businesses want to purchase at each price level. One factor that changes aggregate demand is net export spending. Exchange rates are among the determinants of net export spending. When a government intervenes in the foreign currency market to purchase its own currency, that currency appreciates. One result is that the trade balance is affected. Exports fall as domestic goods become more costly from the perspective of foreign consumers. Imports rise as foreign goods become less costly for domestic consumers. Consequently, net exports and domestic aggregate demand also decline.
   Answer (A) is incorrect. If a government increases the demand for its own currency, the currency will appreciate. This action will alter the trade balance and the level of aggregate demand. Answer (C) is incorrect. A sale of the currency by the domestic government will cause the currency to depreciate. This action will alter the trade balance and the level of aggregate demand. Answer (D) is incorrect. If the government intervenes and causes a depreciation of the domestic currency, exports will rise and imports will fall. Net exports will therefore rise if the currency depreciates, so aggregate demand will increase.

5. Some economic indicators lead the economy into a recovery or recession, and some lag it. An example of a lag variable is

    A. Chronic unemployment.

    B. Orders for consumer and producer goods.

    C. Housing starts.

    D. Consumer expectations.

Answer (A) is correct.
    REQUIRED: The example of a lag variable.
    DISCUSSION: Economists use a variety of economic indicators to forecast turns in the business cycle. Economic indicators are variables that in the past have had a high correlation with aggregate economic activity. The best known are the composite indexes calculated by The Conference Board, a private research group with more than 2,700 corporate and other members worldwide. Indicators may lead, lag, or coincide with economic activity. The Conference Board's lagging indicators include average duration of unemployment in weeks, the change in the index of labor cost per unit of output, the average prime rate charged by banks, the ratio of manufacturing and trade inventories to sales, the commercial and industrial loans outstanding, the ratio of consumer installment credit outstanding to personal income, and the change in the CPI for services.

6. Net domestic product is composed of the total market value of all

    A. Final goods and services produced in the economy in 1 year.

    B. Goods and services produced in the economy in 1 year.

    C. Final goods and services produced in the economy in 1 year minus the capital consumption allowance.

    D. Goods and services produced in the economy in 1 year minus the capital consumption allowance.

Answer (C) is correct.
    REQUIRED: The composition of net domestic product.
    DISCUSSION: Net domestic product is the market value of all final goods and services produced within the boundaries of a country within 1 year minus the capital consumption allowance.
    Answer (A) is incorrect. Net domestic product is calculated net of the capital consumption allowance. Answer (B) is incorrect. Net domestic product includes only final goods. The inclusion of intermediate goods would involve double counting. Also, net domestic product is calculated net of the capital consumption allowance. Answer (D) is incorrect. Net domestic product does not include intermediate goods. The inclusion of intermediate goods would involve double counting.

7. In the output or "expenditures" approach to measuring a country's gross domestic product, which of the following calculations is used?

    A. Consumption + Investment + Government purchases + Expenditures by foreigners.

    B. Consumption + Investment + Government purchases – Expenditures by foreigners.

    C. Consumption + Investment – Government purchases – Expenditures by foreigners.

    D. Consumption – Investment – Government purchases – Expenditures by foreigners.

Answer (A) is correct.
    REQUIRED: The calculation used in the output or expenditures approach to measuring GDP.
    DISCUSSION: GDP can be calculated using an income approach or an expenditures approach because what is spent on a product or service is income to those who contributed resources to its production and marketing. Thus, the amount spent to purchase the GDP is identical with the income derived from its production and sale. Under the output or expenditures approach, GDP equals the sum of consumption expenditures by households, investment by business, government purchases of goods and services, and expenditures by foreigners (net exports).

20.3 International Trade

8. The economic reasoning dictating that each nation specialize in the production of goods that it produces relatively more efficiently than other nations and import those goods that are produced relatively more efficiently by other nations is called the doctrine of

    A. Efficient trade.

    B. Diminishing returns.

    C. Relative competition.

    D. Comparative advantage.

Answer (D) is correct.
    REQUIRED: The reason each nation should specialize in those goods it produces relatively more efficiently than other nations.
    DISCUSSION: The doctrine of comparative advantage relates to comparative costs within one country. It holds that a country should produce those products in which it has a comparative advantage, not necessarily those products in which it has an absolute advantage. The doctrine suggests that a country should produce those products for which the greatest efficiencies are attainable even if it could also produce other goods more efficiently than another nation. In the long run, importing a product in which a country has an absolute advantage but not a comparative advantage will result in an overall increase in global production.

9. Which of the following is a tariff?

A. Licensing requirements.

B. Consumption taxes on imported goods.

C. Unreasonable standards pertaining to product quality and safety.

D. Domestic content rules.

Answer (B) is correct.
REQUIRED: The example of a tariff.
DISCUSSION: Tariffs are excise taxes on imported goods imposed either to generate revenue or protect domestic producers. Thus, consumption taxes on imported goods are tariffs.
Answer (A) is incorrect. Licensing requirements limit exports, e.g., of militarily sensitive technology. Answer (C) is incorrect. Unreasonable standards pertaining to product quality and safety are nontariff trade barriers. Answer (D) is incorrect. Domestic content rules require that a portion of an imported good be made in the importing country.

10. Which one of the following groups would be the primary beneficiary of a tariff?

A. Domestic producers of export goods.

B. Domestic producers of goods protected by the tariff.

C. Domestic consumers of goods protected by the tariff.

D. Foreign producers of goods protected by the tariff.

Answer (B) is correct.
REQUIRED: The primary beneficiaries of a tariff.
DISCUSSION: Despite the advantages of free trade, nations often levy tariffs to discourage the importation of certain products. A tariff is a tax on imports intended to protect a domestic producer from foreign competition. For instance, a tariff on imported autos benefits domestic auto manufacturers because it is an additional cost imposed on domestic consumers of such products. The disadvantages of the tariff are that it may protect an inefficient domestic producer and increase prices paid by domestic consumers.
Answer (A) is incorrect. Domestic producers of export goods are not benefited. Indeed, they may be harmed by retaliatory tariffs. Answer (C) is incorrect. Domestic consumers must pay higher prices for imported goods. Answer (D) is incorrect. The foreign producers will be forced to bear an additional cost.

11. The United States imports shoes from Thailand. When Thailand drops the prices on its shoes, the U.S. reacts by imposing a tariff on Thai shoes. The U.S. has invoked a(n)

A. Exchange control.

B. Harmonized tariff schedule.

C. Voluntary import restriction.

D. Trigger price mechanism.

Answer (D) is correct.
REQUIRED: The term referring to a newly imposed tariff.
DISCUSSION: A trigger price mechanism automatically imposes a tariff barrier against unfairly cheap imports by levying a duty (tariff) on all imports below a particular reference price (the price that "triggers" the tariff).
Answer (A) is incorrect. Exchange controls limit foreign currency transactions and set exchange rates; they do not impose tariffs. Answer (B) is incorrect. A harmonized tariff schedule is simply a listing of applicable tariff rates. It has nothing to do with dumping rules. Answer (C) is incorrect. Voluntary import restriction is not a meaningful term in this context.

20.4 Currency Exchange Rates and Markets

12. An entity has a foreign-currency-denominated trade payable, due in 60 days. To eliminate the foreign currency exchange-rate risk associated with the payable, the entity could

A. Sell foreign currency forward today.

B. Wait 60 days and pay the invoice by purchasing foreign currency in the spot market at that time.

C. Buy foreign currency forward today.

D. Borrow foreign currency today, convert it to domestic currency on the spot market, and invest the funds in a domestic bank deposit until the invoice payment date.

Answer (C) is correct.
REQUIRED: The means of eliminating exchange-rate risk.
DISCUSSION: The entity can arrange to purchase the foreign currency today rather than in 60 days by buying the currency in the forward market. This hedging transaction will eliminate the exchange-rate risk associated with the trade payable.
Answer (A) is incorrect. A forward market sale of foreign currency is appropriate to hedge a receivable denominated in a foreign currency. Answer (B) is incorrect. Waiting to buy the currency in 60 days does not eliminate the risk of an adverse exchange-rate movement. Answer (D) is incorrect. This strategy would be comparable to a future sale of the foreign currency at a rate known today, which would not provide the currency needed to pay the invoice. However, the opposite strategy would be an effective money market hedge. If the entity converted domestic currency to foreign currency in the spot market today and invested in a foreign bank deposit or treasury bill, it could then use the proceeds from the foreign investment to pay the invoice in 60 days.

13. If the central bank of a country raises interest rates sharply, the country's currency will likely

    A. Increase in relative value.

    B. Remain unchanged in value.

    C. Decrease in relative value.

    D. Decrease sharply in value at first and then return to its initial value.

Answer (A) is correct.
    REQUIRED: The effect on a country's currency if its central bank raises interest rates sharply.
    DISCUSSION: Exchange rates fluctuate depending upon the demand for each country's currency. If a country raises its interest rates, its currency will appreciate. The demand for investment at the higher interest rates will shift the demand curve for the currency to the right. The reverse holds true for a decrease in interest rates.
    Answer (B) is incorrect. The currency should increase in relative value when interest rates in the country rise sharply. More investors will want to earn the higher rates of interest. Answer (C) is incorrect. The currency should increase in relative value when interest rates in the country rise sharply. More investors will want to earn the higher rates of interest. Answer (D) is incorrect. The currency should increase in relative value when interest rates in the country rise sharply. More investors will want to earn the higher rates of interest.

14. Exchange rates are determined by

    A. Each industrial country's government.

    B. The International Monetary Fund.

    C. Supply and demand in the foreign currency market.

    D. Exporters and importers of manufactured goods.

Answer (C) is correct.
    REQUIRED: The factor that determines foreign exchange rates.
    DISCUSSION: Although currencies can be supported by various means for short periods, the primary determinant of exchange rates is the supply of and demand for the various currencies. Under current international agreements, exchange rates are allowed to float. During periods of extreme fluctuations, however, governments and central banks may intervene to maintain stability in the market.
    Answer (A) is incorrect. Governments have only temporary influence, if any, on the setting of exchange rates. Answer (B) is incorrect. The International Monetary Fund has only temporary influence, if any, on the setting of exchange rates. Answer (D) is incorrect. Exporters and importers have only temporary influence, if any, on the setting of exchange rates.

15. Two countries have flexible exchange rate systems and an active trading relationship. If incomes <List A> in country 1, everything else being equal, then the currency of country 1 will tend to <List B> relative to the currency of country 2.

	List A	List B
A.	Rise	Remain constant
B.	Fall	Depreciate
C.	Rise	Depreciate
D.	Remain constant	Appreciate

Answer (C) is correct.
    REQUIRED: The effect of a change in incomes in one nation on its currency.
    DISCUSSION: If incomes in country 1 rise, consumers in country 1 will increase their imports from country 2. The resulting increase in the supply of country 1's currency will result in a tendency for it to depreciate relative to the currency of country 2.
    Answer (A) is incorrect. If incomes in country 1 rise, the result will be a tendency for it to devalue relative to the currency of country 2. Answer (B) is incorrect. If incomes in country 1 fall, consumers in country 1 will reduce their imports. The resulting decrease in the supply of country 1's currency will result in a tendency for it to appreciate relative to the currency of country 2. Answer (D) is incorrect. If incomes in country 1 remain constant, the currency of country 1 will not tend to appreciate or depreciate relative to the currency of country 2.

20.5 Methods of Taxation

16. A taxpayer who earns US $50,000 during the year and pays a 15% tax rate on the first US $30,000 of income and a 30% tax rate on all earnings over US $30,000 has a(n)

    A. Marginal tax rate of 15%.

    B. Marginal tax rate of 21%.

    C. Average tax rate of 21%.

    D. Average tax rate of 22.5%.

Answer (C) is correct.
    REQUIRED: The nature and amount of the tax rate.
    DISCUSSION: The average tax rate is calculated using the weighted-average method. The weight assigned to each rate is determined by the proportion of taxable income subject to it. The average tax rate is 21% [(US $30,000 ÷ $50,000) × .15 + ($20,000 ÷ $50,000) × .30].
    Answer (A) is incorrect. The marginal tax rate is 30%. The marginal tax rate equals the highest rate paid. Answer (B) is incorrect. The marginal tax rate is 30%. The marginal tax rate equals the highest rate paid. Answer (D) is incorrect. A rate of 22.5% is a simple numerical average.

17. General sales taxes tend to be regressive with respect to income because

    A. A larger portion of a lower income person's income is subject to the tax.

    B. A smaller portion of a lower income person's income is subject to the tax.

    C. The tax rate is higher for person with lower income.

    D. The tax claims an increasing amount of income as income rises.

Answer (A) is correct.
    REQUIRED: The reason general sales taxes tend to be regressive with respect to income.
    DISCUSSION: A sales tax is regressive with respect to income even though the rate is the same regardless of the buyer's income. The reason is that a greater percentage of a low-income individual's income is exposed to the tax. A higher-income individual should be able to save more and therefore shield a greater percentage of his or her income from the tax.
    Answer (B) is incorrect. A larger portion of a lower-income person's income is subject to the tax. Answer (C) is incorrect. The general sales tax rate is uniform for all taxpayers. Answer (D) is incorrect. If the tax claims an increasing amount of income as income rises, it is progressive, not regressive.

18. On what basis is value-added tax collected?

    A. The difference between the value of an entity's sales and the value of its purchases from other domestic entities.

    B. The difference between the selling price of a real estate property and the amount the entity originally paid for the property.

    C. The value of an entity's sales to related companies.

    D. The profit earned on an entity's sales.

Answer (A) is correct.
    REQUIRED: The basis for collecting a value-added tax.
    DISCUSSION: A value-added tax (VAT) is collected on the basis of the value created by the entity. This tax is measured by the difference between the value of the entity's sales and the value of its purchases. A VAT is, in effect, a retail sales tax. Because a consumer can avoid the tax by not purchasing, a VAT encourages saving and discourages consumption.
    Answer (B) is incorrect. The difference between the selling price of a real estate property and the amount the entity originally paid for the property is a capital gain. Answer (C) is incorrect. The value of an entity's sales to related companies is the internal transfer price. Answer (D) is incorrect. The profit earned on an entity's sales is subject to the income tax.

20.6 Regulation of Business

19. Which one of the following examples of corporate behavior would most clearly represent a violation of antitrust law?

    A. A retailer offers quantity discounts to large institutional buyers.

    B. The members of a labor union meet and agree not to work for a specific entity unless the starting wage is at least a specified amount per hour.

    C. Two entities that are in different, unrelated industries merge.

    D. Two entities in the same industry agree in a telephone conversation to submit identical bids on a government contract.

Answer (D) is correct.
    REQUIRED: The item that would most clearly represent a violation of antitrust law.
    DISCUSSION: Antitrust law addresses restraints of trade. Some types of arrangements are considered automatic violations. These violations may include price fixing, division of markets, group boycotts, and resale price maintenance. Agreeing to submit identical bids on a government contract is a form of price fixing.
    Answer (A) is incorrect. Quantity discounts are not prohibited. Answer (B) is incorrect. Antitrust laws usually do not apply to labor unions. Answer (C) is incorrect. Only mergers that could lead to restraint of trade are outlawed.

20. The primary reason for social regulation is that

    A. The free market provides minimal safety and environmental protection.

    B. Consumer and environmental groups are politically powerful.

    C. Social benefits from such regulations always exceed the costs.

    D. Social regulation is more desirable.

Answer (A) is correct.
    REQUIRED: The primary reason for social regulation.
    DISCUSSION: Social regulation concerns quality of life issues, e.g., workplace and product safety, environmental degradation, and fair employment practices. The abuses addressed are those that are difficult for market forces to remedy. For example, consumers may purchase products on the basis of price and quality but without regard to the environmental impact of their production, and unsafe working conditions may be tolerated by individuals who have few opportunities for other employment.
    Answer (B) is incorrect. Although consumer and environmental groups may occasionally exercise some lobbying power, they are typically underfunded and would have little impact on legislatures in the absence of an obvious need for social regulation. Answer (C) is incorrect. There is great difficulty in measuring both the benefits and costs of most social regulation. Answer (D) is incorrect. No regulation is desirable, but some regulation is necessary when market forces are ineffective.

APPENDIX A
THE IIA CIA EXAM SYLLABUS AND CROSS-REFERENCES

For your convenience, we have reproduced verbatim The IIA's CIA Exam Syllabus for this CIA exam part (global.theiia.org/certification/cia-certification/Pages/Exam-Syllabus.aspx). Note that "proficiency level" means the candidate should have a thorough understanding and the ability to apply concepts in the topics listed. Those levels labeled "awareness level" mean the candidate must have a grasp of the terminology and fundamentals of the concepts listed. We also have provided cross-references to the study units and subunits in this book that correspond to The IIA's more detailed coverage. If one entry appears above a list, it applies to all items. Please visit The IIA's website for updates and more information about the exam. Rely on the Gleim materials to help you pass each part of the exam. We have researched and studied The IIA's CIA Exam Syllabus as well as questions from prior exams to provide you with an excellent review program.

NOTE: All items in this section of the syllabus will be tested at the Awareness knowledge level unless otherwise indicated below.

PART 3 – INTERNAL AUDIT KNOWLEDGE ELEMENTS

I. **Governance/Business Ethics (5-15%)**

    A. Corporate/Organizational Governance Principles – **Proficiency Level (P)** (1.1-1.3)
    B. Environmental and Social Safeguards (1.4)
    C. Corporate Social Responsibility (1.5)

II. **Risk Management (10-20%) – Proficiency Level (P)**

    A. Risk Management Techniques (2.1)
    B. Organizational Use of Risk Frameworks (2.2)

III. **Organizational Structure/Business Processes and Risks (15-25%)**

    A. Risk/Control Implications of Different Organizational Structures (3.1)

    B. Structure (e.g., centralized/decentralized) (3.2-3.3)

    C. Typical Schemes in Various Business Cycles (e.g., procurement, sales, knowledge, supply-chain management) (3.4)

    D. Business Process Analysis (e.g., workflow analysis and bottleneck management, theory of constraints) (3.5)

    E. Inventory Management Techniques and Concepts (4.1-4.2)

    F. Electronic Funds Transfer (EFT)/Electronic Data Interchange (EDI)/E-commerce (4.3)

    G. Business Development Life Cycles (4.4)

    H. The International Organization for Standardization (ISO) Framework (4.5)

    I. Outsourcing Business Processes (4.6)

IV. **Communication (5-10%)**

    A. Communication (e.g., the process, organizational dynamics, impact of computerization) (5.1-5.3)

    B. Stakeholder Relationships (5.4)

V.   **Management/Leadership Principles (10-20%)**

   A.   Strategic Management

      1.   Global analytical techniques (6.1)

         a.   Structural analysis of industries (6.2)
         b.   Competitive strategies (e.g., Porter's model) (6.3)
         c.   Competitive analysis (6.4)
         d.   Market signals (6.5)
         e.   Industry evolution (7.1)

      2.   Industry environments (7.2-7.5)

         a.   Competitive strategies related to:

            1.   Fragmented industries
            2.   Emerging industries
            3.   Declining industries

         b.   Competition in global industries

            1.   Sources/impediments
            2.   Evolution of global markets
            3.   Strategic alternatives
            4.   Trends affecting competition

      3.   Strategic decisions

         a.   Analysis of integration strategies (8.1)
         b.   Capacity expansion (8.2)
         c.   Entry into new businesses (8.3)

      4.   Forecasting (8.4-8.6)

      5.   Quality management (e.g., TQM, Six Sigma) (8.7-8.10)

      6.   Decision analysis (8.1)

   B.   Organizational Behavior

      1.   Organizational theory (structures and configurations) (9.1)

      2.   Organizational behavior (e.g., motivation, impact of job design, rewards, schedules) (9.2)

      3.   Group dynamics (e.g., traits, development stages, organizational politics, effectiveness) (9.3-9.5)

      4.   Knowledge of human resource processes (e.g., individual performance management, supervision, personnel sourcing/staffing, staff development) (9.6)

      5.   Risk/control implications of different leadership styles (10.1)

      6.   Performance (productivity, effectiveness, etc.) (9.6)

   C.   Management Skills/Leadership Styles

      1.   Lead, inspire, mentor, and guide people, building organizational commitment and entrepreneurial orientation (10.1)

      2.   Create group synergy in pursuing collective goals (10.2)

      3.   Team-building and assessing team performance (10.2)

D. Conflict Management (10.3-10.4)

    1. Conflict resolution (e.g., competitive, cooperative, and compromise) (10.3)
    2. Negotiation skills (10.4)
    3. Conflict management (10.3)
    4. Added-value negotiating (10.4)

E. Project Management/Change Management

    1. Change management (10.5)
    2. Project management techniques (10.6)

VI. IT/Business Continuity (15-25%)

A. Security

    1. Physical/system security (e.g., firewalls, access control) (11.1)
    2. Information protection (e.g., viruses, privacy) (11.2)
    3. Application authentication (11.3)
    4. Encryption (11.3)

B. Application Development

    1. End-user computing (11.4)
    2. Change control – **Proficiency Level (P)** (11.5)
    3. Systems development methodology – **Proficiency Level (P)** (11.6)
    4. Application development – **Proficiency Level (P)** (11.6)
    5. Information systems development (11.6)

C. System Infrastructure

    1. Workstations (12.1)

    2. Databases (12.1)

    3. IT control frameworks (e.g., eSAC, COBIT) (12.2-12.4)

    4. Functional areas of IT operations (e.g., data center operations) (13.1)

    5. Enterprise-wide resource planning (ERP) software (e.g., SAP R/3) (13.2)

    6. Data, voice, and network communications/connections (e.g., LAN, VAN, and WAN) (13.4)

    7. Server (13.3)

    8. Software licensing (13.5)

    9. Mainframe (13.3)

    10. Operating systems (13.4)

    11. Web infrastructure (13.3)

D. Business Continuity

    1. IT contingency planning (13.6)

VII. **Financial Management (10-20%)**

    A.   Financial Accounting and Finance

        1.   Basic concepts and underlying principles of financial accounting (e.g., statements, terminology, relationships) (14.1-14.8)

        2.   Intermediate concepts of financial accounting (e.g., bonds, leases, pensions, intangible assets, R&D) (14.9, 15.1-15.2)

        3.   Advanced concepts of financial accounting (e.g., consolidation, partnerships, foreign currency transactions) (15.3-15.5)

        4.   Financial statement analysis (e.g., ratios) (15.6-15.11)

        5.   Types of debt and equity (16.3-16.4)

        6.   Financial instruments (e.g., derivatives) (16.2)

        7.   Cash management (e.g., treasury functions) (16.7)

        8.   Valuation models (14.6)

        9.   Business valuation (15.10)

      10. Inventory valuation (14.6)

      11. Capital budgeting (e.g., cost of capital evaluation) (16.5-16.6)

      12. Taxation schemes (e.g., tax shelters, VAT) (20.5)

    B.   Managerial Accounting

        1.   General concepts (17.1)
        2.   Costing systems (e.g., activity-based, standard) (17.3-17.4)
        3.   Cost concepts (e.g., absorption, variable, fixed) (17.2, 17.5)
        4.   Relevant cost (18.4)
        5.   Cost-volume-profit analysis (18.3)
        6.   Transfer pricing (18.6)
        7.   Responsibility accounting (18.5)
        8.   Operating budget (18.1-18.2)

VIII. **Global Business Environment (0-10%)**

    A.   Economic/Financial Environments

        1.   Global, multinational, international, and multi-local compared and contrasted (19.1)
        2.   Requirements for entering the global marketplace (19.1-19.2)
        3.   Creating organizational adaptability (19.2)
        4.   Managing training and development (19.4)

    B.   Cultural/Political Environments

        1.   Balancing global requirements and local imperatives (19.2)
        2.   Global mindsets (personal characteristics/competencies) (19.3-19.4)
        3.   Sources and methods for managing complexities and contradictions (19.3-19.4)
        4.   Managing multicultural teams (19.3-19.4)

    C.   Legal and Economics — General Concepts (e.g., contracts) (20.1-20.5)

    D.   Impact of Government Legislation and Regulation on Business (e.g., trade legislation) (20.6)

APPENDIX B
THE IIA STANDARDS AND PRACTICE
ADVISORIES DISCUSSED IN PART 3

Gleim Subunit	Performance Standard
1.2	2110 - Governance
2.1	2120 - Risk Management

Gleim Subunit	Practice Advisory
1.2	2110-1: Governance: Definition
1.2	2110-2: Governance: Relationship with Risk and Control
1.2	2110-3: Governance: Assessments
2.1	2120-1: Assessing the Adequacy of Risk Management Processes
1.3, 11.2	2130.A1-1: Information Reliability and Integrity
11.2	2130.A1-2: Evaluating an Organization's Privacy Framework

APPENDIX C
THE IIA EXAMINATION BIBLIOGRAPHY

The Institute has prepared a listing of references for the CIA exam as of September 2015, reproduced below. These publications have been chosen by the Professional Certifications Department as reasonably representative of the common body of knowledge for internal auditors. However, all of the information in these texts will not be tested. When possible, questions will be written based on the information contained in the suggested reference list. This bibliography is provided to give you an overview of the scope of the exam.

The IIA bibliography is reproduced for your information only. The texts you need to prepare for the CIA exam depend on many factors, including

1. Innate ability
2. Length of time out of school
3. Thoroughness of your undergraduate education
4. Familiarity with internal auditing due to relevant experience

CIA EXAM REFERENCES

Title/URL	Author	Year Published	Publisher
Accounting Principles, with CD, 10th Edition URL: http://amzn.to/1F4AnWQ	Jerry J. Weygandt, Donald E. Kieso, Paul D. Kimmel	2011	Wiley Text Books
Competitive Strategy: Techniques for Analyzing Industries and Competitors URL: http://amzn.to/1MsP9ZJ	Michael E. Porter	1998	The Free Press
COSO - Internal Control — Integrated Framework: 2013 (Framework) URL: http://bit.ly/1OhgSNi	The American Institute of Certified Public Accountants	2013	American Institute of Certified Public Accountants (AICPA)
Enterprise Risk Management — Integrated Framework URL: http://bit.ly/1Qkots0	Committee of Sponsoring Organizations of the Treadway Commission (COSO)	2004	COSO
Internal Auditing: Assurance & Advisory Services, 2nd and 3rd Editions URL: http://bit.ly/1KjAavF	Kurt F. Reding, Paul J. Sobel, Urton L. Anderson, Michael J. Head, Sridhar Ramamoorti, Mark Salamasick, Cris Riddle	2013	The Institute of Internal Auditors Research Foundation
International Professional Practices Framework (IPPF), including*: ● Definition ● Standards ● Code of Ethics ● Practice Advisories/Implementation Guides ● Practice Guides ● Global Technology Audit Guides (GTAGs) ● Guide to Assessment of IT Risk (GAIT) *Mission and Core Principles are **NOT** included at this time. URL: http://bit.ly/1AilTOC	The Institute of Internal Auditors, Inc.	Updated continually	The Institute of Internal Auditors, Inc.
Management, 10th, 11th, and 12th Editions URL: http://amzn.to/1KsDXdp	Robert Kreitner and Charlene Cassidy	2012	South-Western College Pub

-- Continued on next page --

CIA EXAM REFERENCES – *Continued*

Title/URL	Author	Year Published	Publisher
Position Papers: ● The Three Lines of Defense in Effective Risk Management and Control ● The Role of Internal Auditing in Enterprise-wide Risk Management ● The Role of Internal Auditing in Resourcing the Internal Audit Activity *URL: http://bit.ly/1LjrGZG*	The Institute of Internal Auditors, Inc.	2009, 2013	The Institute of Internal Auditors, Inc.
Sawyer's Guide for Internal Auditors, 5th and 6th Editions *URL: http://bit.ly/1OzgBEL*	L.B. Sawyer	2012	The Institute of Internal Auditors Research Foundation

AVAILABILITY OF PUBLICATIONS

The listing on the previous page and above presents only some of the current technical literature available, and The IIA does not carry all of the reference books. Quantity discounts are provided by The IIA. Visit global.theiia.org/knowledge/pages/bookstore.aspx, or request a current catalog by phone or mail.

The IIARF Bookstore
1650 Bluegrass Lakes Pkwy
Alpharetta, GA 30004-7714
iiapubs@pbd.com
(877) 867-4957 (toll-free in U.S.) or (770) 280-4183 (outside U.S.)

Contact the publisher directly if you cannot obtain the desired texts from The IIA or your local bookstore. Begin your study program with the Gleim CIA Review, which most candidates find sufficient. If you need additional reference material, borrow books mentioned in The IIA's bibliography from colleagues, professors, or a library.

APPENDIX D
SAMPLE FINANCIAL STATEMENTS

We have annotated these audited financial statements to show how the various elements interrelate. For instance, (a) is the year-end balance of cash and equivalents; this annotation is found on both the balance sheet and the statement of cash flows.

FORD MOTOR COMPANY AND SUBSIDIARIES
CONSOLIDATED INCOME STATEMENT
(in millions, except per share amounts)

	For the years ended December 31,		
	2012	2011	2010
Revenues			
Automotive	US $126,567	US $128,168	US $119,280
Financial Services	7,685	8,096	9,674
Total revenues	134,252	136,264	128,954
Costs and expenses			
Automotive cost of sales	112,578	113,345	104,451
Selling, administrative and other expenses	12,182	11,578	11,909
Financial Services interest expense	3,115	3,614	4,345
Financial Services provision for credit and insurance losses	86	(33)	(216)
Total costs and expenses	127,961	128,504	120,489
Automotive interest expense	713	817	1,807
Automotive interest income and other non-operating income/(expense), net	1,185	825	(362)
Financial Services other income/(loss), net	369	413	315
Equity in net income/(loss) of affiliated companies	588	500	538
Income before income taxes	7,720	8,681	7,149
Provision for/(Benefit from) income taxes	2,056	(11,541)	592
Net income	5,664 (a)	20,222 (b)	6,557 (c)
Less: Income/(Loss) attributable to noncontrolling interests	(1)	9	(4)
Net income/(loss) attributable to Ford Motor Company	US $ 5,665	US $ 20,213	US $ 6,561

AMOUNTS PER SHARE ATTRIBUTABLE TO FORD MOTOR COMPANY COMMON AND CLASS B STOCK

Basic income	US $ 1.48	US $ 5.33	US $ 1.90
Diluted income	US $ 1.42	US $ 4.94	US $ 1.66
Cash dividends declared	US $ 0.15	US $ 0.05	US $ –

CONSOLIDATED STATEMENT OF COMPREHENSIVE INCOME
(in millions)

	For the years ended December 31,		
	2012	2011	2010
Net income	US $ 5,664	US $ 20,222	US $ 6,557
Other comprehensive income/(loss), net of tax			
Foreign currency translation	142	(720)	(2,234)
Derivative instruments	6	(152)	(24)
Pension and other postretirement benefits	(4,268)	(3,553)	(1,190)
Net holding gain/(loss)	–	2	(2)
Total other comprehensive income/(loss), net of tax	(4,120) (d)	(4,423) (e)	(3,450) (f)
Comprehensive income	1,544	15,799	3,107
Less: Comprehensive income/(loss) attributable to noncontrolling interests	(1)	7	(5)
Comprehensive income attributable to Ford Motor Company	US $ 1,545	US $ 15,792	US $ 3,112

FORD MOTOR COMPANY AND SUBSIDIARIES
CONSOLIDATED BALANCE SHEET
(in millions)

	December 31, 2012	December 31, 2011
ASSETS		
Cash and cash equivalents	US $ 15,659 (g)	US $ 17,148 (h)
Marketable securities	20,284	18,618
Finance receivables, net	71,510	69,976
Other receivables, net	10,828	8,565
Net investment in operating leases	16,451	12,838
Inventories	7,362	5,901
Equity in net assets of affiliated companies	3,246	2,936
Net property	24,942	22,371
Deferred income taxes	15,185	15,125
Net intangible assets	87	100
Other assets	5,000	4,770
Total assets	US $190,554	US $178,348
LIABILITIES		
Payables	US $ 19,308	US $ 17,724
Accrued liabilities and deferred revenue	49,407	45,369
Debt	105,058	99,488
Deferred income taxes	470	696
Total liabilities	US $174,243	US $163,277
Redeemable noncontrolling interest	322	–
EQUITY		
Capital stock		
Common Stock, par value US $0.01 per share (3,745 million shares issued)	US $ 39 (i)	US $ 37 (j)
Class B Stock, par value US $0.01 per share (71 million shares issued)	1 (i)	1 (j)
Capital in excess of par value of stock	20,976 (k)	20,905 (l)
Retained earnings	18,077 (m)	12,985 (n)
Accumulated other comprehensive income/(loss)	(22,854) (o)	(18,734) (p)
Treasury stock	(292) (q)	(166) (r)
Total equity attributable to Ford Motor Company	US $ 15,947 (s)	US $ 15,028 (t)
Equity attributable to noncontrolling interests	42	43
Total equity	US $ 15,989	US $ 15,071
Total liabilities and equity	US $190,554	US $178,348

FORD MOTOR COMPANY AND SUBSIDIARIES
CONDENSED CONSOLIDATED STATEMENT OF CASH FLOWS
(in millions)

	For the years ended December 31,		
	2012	2011	2010
Cash flows from operating activities of continuing operations			
Net cash provided by/(used in) operating activities	US $ 9,045	US $ 9,784	US $ 11,477
Cash flows from investing activities of continuing operations			
Capital expenditures	(5,488)	(4,293)	(4,092)
Acquisitions of retail and other finance receivables and operating leases	(39,208)	(35,866)	(28,873)
Collections of retail and other finance receivables and operating leases	32,333	33,964	37,757
Purchases of securities	(95,135)	(68,723)	(100,150)
Sales and maturities of securities	93,749	70,795	101,077
Cash change due to initial consolidation of businesses	191	–	94
Proceeds from sale of business	66	333	1,318
Settlements of derivatives	(737)	353	(37)
Elimination of cash balances upon disposition of discontinued/held-for-sale operations	–	(69)	(456)
Other	(61)	465	270
Net cash provided by/(used in)investing activities	(14,290)	(3,041)	6,908
Cash flows from financing activities of continuing operations			
Cash dividends	(763)	–	–
Purchases of Common Stock	(125)	–	
Sales of Common Stock	–	–	1,339
Changes in short-term debt	1,208	2,841	(1,754)
Proceeds from issuance of other debt	32,436	35,921	30,821
Principle payments on other debt	(29,210)	(43,095)	(47,625)
Payments on notes/transfer of cash equivalents to the UAW Voluntary Employee Benefit Association ("VEBA") Trust	–	–	(7,302)
Other	159	92	100
Net cash provided by/(used in) financing activities	3,705	(4,241)	(24,421)
Effect of exchange rate changes on cash and cash equivalents	51	(159)	(53)
Net increase/(decrease) in cash and cash equivalents	US $ (1,489)	US $ 2,343	US $ (6,089)
Cash and cash equivalents at January 1	US $ 17,148	US $ 14,805	US $ 20,894
Net increase/(decrease) in cash and cash equivalents	(1,489)	2,343	(6,089)
Cash and cash equivalents at December 31	US $ 15,659 (g)	US $ 17,148 (h)	US $ 14,805

FORD MOTOR COMPANY AND SUBSIDIARIES
CONSOLIDATED STATEMENT OF EQUITY
(in millions)

Equity/(Deficit) Attributable to Ford Motor Company

	Capital Stock	Cap. in Excess of Par Value of Stock	Retained Earnings/ (Accumulated Deficit)	Accumulated Other Comprehensive Income/(Loss)	Treasury Stock	Total	Equity/ (Deficit) Attributable to Non-controlling Interests	Total Equity/ (Deficit)
Balance at December 31, 2009	US $34	US $10,786	US $(13,599)	US $(10,864)	US $(177)	US $ (7,820)	US $ 38	US $(7,782)
Net income	–	–	6,561	–	–	6,561	(4)	6,557 (c)
Other comprehensive income/(loss), net of tax	–	–	–	(3,449)	–	(3,449)	(1)	(3,450) (f)
Common stock issued (including share-based compensation impacts)	4	4,017	–	–	–	4,021	–	4,021
Treasury stock/other	–	–	–	–	14	14	–	14
Cash dividends declared	–	–	–	–	–	–	(2)	(2)
Balance at December 31, 2010	US $38	US $20,803	US $ (7,038)	US $(14,313)	US $(163)	US $ (673)	US $ 31	US $ (642)
Balance at December 31, 2010	US $38	US $20,803	US $ (7,038)	US $(14,313)	US $(163)	US $ (673)	US $ 31	US $ (642)
Net income	–	–	20,213	–	–	20,213	4	20,222 (b)
Other comprehensive income/(loss), net of tax	–	–	–	(4,421)	–	(4,421)	(2)	(4,423) (e)
Common stock issued (including share-based compensation impacts)	–	102	–	–	–	102	–	102
Treasury stock/other	–	–	–	–	(3)	(3)	5	2
Cash dividends declared	–	–	(190)	–	–	(190)	–	(190)
Balance at December 31, 2011	US $38 (j)	US $20,905 (l)	US $ 12,985 (n)	US $(18,734) (p)	US $(166) (r)	US $15,028 (t)	US $ 43	US $15,071
Balance at December 31, 2011	US $38	US $20,905	US $12,985	US $(18,734)	US $(166)	US $15,028	US $ 43	US $15,071
Net income	–	–	5,665	–	–	5,665	(1)	5,664 (a)
Other compensation income/(loss), net of tax	–	–	–	(4,120)	–	(4,120)	–	(4,120) (d)
Common stock issued (including share-based compensation impacts)	2	71	–	–	–	73	–	73
Treasury stock/other	–	–	–	–	(126)	(126)	–	(126)
Cash dividends declared	–	–	(573)	–	–	(573)	–	(573)
Balance at December 31, 2012	US $40 (i)	US $20,976 (k)	US $ 18,077 (m)	US $(22,854) (o)	US $(292) (q)	US $ 15,947 (s)	US $ 42	US $15,989

APPENDIX E
GLOSSARY OF ACCOUNTING TERMS
U.S. TO BRITISH VS. BRITISH TO U.S.

U.S. TO BRITISH

Accounts payable	Trade creditors
Accounts receivable	Trade debtors
Accrual	Provision (for liability or charge)
Accumulated depreciation	Aggregate depreciation
Additional paid-in capital	Share premium account
Allowance	Provision (for diminution in value)
Allowance for doubtful accounts	Provision for bad debt
Annual Stockholders' Meeting	Annual General Meeting
Authorized capital stock	Authorized share capital
Bellweather stock	Barometer stock
Bylaws	Articles of Association
Bond	Loan finance
Capital lease	Finance lease
Certificate of Incorporation	Memorandum of Association
Checking account	Current account
Common stock	Ordinary shares
Consumer price index	Retail price index
Corporation	Company
Cost of goods sold	Cost of sales
Credit Memorandum	Credit note
Equity	Reserves
Equity interest	Ownership interest
Financial statements	Accounts
Income statement	Profit and loss account
Income taxes	Taxation
Inventories	Stocks
Investment bank	Merchant bank
Labor union	Trade union
Land	Freehold
Lease with bargain purchase option	Hire purchase contract
Liabilities	Creditors
Listed company	Quoted company
Long-term investments	Fixed asset investments
Long-term lease	Long leasehold
Merchandise trade	Visible trade
Mutual funds	Unit trusts
Net income	Net profit
Note payable	Bill payable
Note receivable	Bill receivable
Paid-in surplus	Share premium
Par value	Nominal value
Pooling of interests method	Merger accounting
Preferred stock	Preference share
Prime rate	Base rate
Property, plant, and equipment	Tangible fixed assets
Provision for bad debts	Charge
Purchase method	Acquisition accounting
Purchase on account	Purchase on credit
Retained earnings	Profit and loss account
Real estate	Property
Revenue	Income
Reversal of accrual	Release of provision
Sales on account	Sales on credit
Sales/revenue	Turnover
Savings and loan association	Building society
Shareholders' equity	Shareholders' funds
Stock	Inventory
Stockholder	Shareholder
Stock dividend	Bonus share
Stockholders' equity	Share capital and reserves or Shareholders' funds
Taxable income	Taxable profit
Treasury bonds	Gilt-edged stock (gilts)

BRITISH TO U.S.

Accounts .... Financial statements
Acquisition accounting .... Purchase method
Aggregate depreciation .... Accumulated depreciation
Annual General Meeting .... Annual Stockholders' Meeting
Articles of Association .... Bylaws
Authorized share capital .... Authorized capital stock
Barometer stock .... Bellweather stock
Base rate .... Prime rate
Bill payable .... Note payable
Bill receivable .... Note receivable
Bonus share .... Stock dividend
Building society... Savings and loan association
Charge .... Provision for bad debts
Company .... Corporation
Cost of sales .... Cost of goods sold
Credit note .... Credit Memorandum
Creditors .... Liabilities
Current account .... Checking account
Finance lease .... Capital lease
Fixed asset investments .... Long-term investments
Freehold .... Land
Gilt-edged stock (gilts) .... Treasury bonds
Hire purchase contract .... Lease with bargain purchase option
Income .... Revenue
Inventory .... Stock
Loan finance .... Bond
Long leasehold .... Long-term lease
Memorandum of Association .... Certificate of Incorporation
Merchant bank .... Investment bank
Merger accounting .... Pooling of interests method
Net profit .... Net income
Nominal value .... Par value
Ordinary shares .... Common stock
Ownership interest .... Equity interest
Preference share .... Preferred stock
Profit and loss account .... Income statement
Profit and loss account .... Retained earnings
Property .... Real estate
Provision for bad debt .... Allowance for doubtful accounts
Provision (for diminution in value) .... Allowance
Provision (for liability or charge) .... Accrual
Purchase on credit .... Purchase on account
Quoted company .... Listed company
Release of provision .... Reversal of accrual
Reserves .... Equity
Retail price index .... Consumer price index
Sales on credit .... Sales on account
Share capital and reserves or Shareholders' funds .... Stockholders' equity
Shareholder .... Stockholder
Shareholders' funds .... Shareholders' equity
Share premium .... Paid-in surplus
Share premium account .... Additional paid-in capital
Stocks .... Inventories
Tangible fixed assets .... Property, plant, and equipment
Taxable profit .... Taxable income
Taxation .... Income taxes
Trade creditors .... Accounts payable
Trade debtors .... Accounts receivable
Trade union .... Labor union
Turnover .... Sales/revenue
Unit trusts .... Mutual funds
Visible trade .... Merchandise trade

INDEX

More CIA Exam Medal Winners Passed Using Gleim

The best opportunity for success

❝ When I decided to sit for the CIA Examination, I considered a number of review providers because I wanted to invest in a product that would provide me with the best opportunity for success. While there are a number of review programs out there, I previously had great success with Gleim's Exam Questions & Explanations (EQE) products that I used for supplementing my textbooks and learning materials in college. That being the case, I decided on Gleim's CIA Review, and I am thankful that I did. The Gleim Review books were comprehensive and provided me with a thorough understanding of the materials. I also found the practice questions to be very representative of the types of questions that are seen on the actual exam. Furthermore, beyond simply providing me with the information necessary to excel on the CIA Exam, the review materials also delivered knowledge that I could immediately apply on the job, and I continue to use the book series as a reference. Given that Gleim's materials helped me to achieve the William S. Smith Certificate of Excellence, I would recommend anyone interested in sitting for the CIA exam consider Gleim Review, and I will certainly choose Gleim products for my future certification review needs. ❞

Stephen D. Jones

A valuable support for preparing for the CIA exams

❝ I found in Gleim books a valuable support for preparing for the CIA exams: they are written in a very clear way, the method suggested for studying the content is very effective, and the information is organized in a rational way.

The tests are also an excellent support for being successful with the exams, and they contain additional "practical" examples. After understanding their content, the actual exams are not a surprise. The test software is user friendly and very effective, enabling you to focus on those areas deserving more attention or additional insight. To recap, Gleim material is an authoritative source for passing CIA exams at the first attempt and, even more important, is a reference for a "real life" auditor. ❞

Alessandro Segalini

An integral part of my test preparation

❝ The Gleim CIA Review System was an integral part of my test preparation. The review material was presented in a logical way that made it easy to create a structured study plan. It also focused on the most critical information necessary to successfully pass the exam. The question bank included with the system was an essential part of my preparation. The questions helped reinforce the concepts discussed in each section of the material and a clear explanation of the correct answer was provided for each question. In addition, the review sessions are timed, which allowed for feedback on question pace and helped simulate a real testing environment. This allowed me to walk into each part of the exam feeling well prepared. The preparation the Gleim CIA Review System provided, not only helped me pass each part on the first attempt, but it was also an important factor in allowing me to win an IIA Certificate of Excellence. ❞

Jeffrey Haniff